Lecture Notes in Computer Science 2720

Edited by G. Goos, J. Hartmanis, and J. van Leeuwen

T0141981

Springer
Berlin
Heidelberg
New York
Hong Kong
London
Milan
Paris
Tokyo

Mário Marques Freire   Pascal Lorenz
Mike Myung-Ok Lee (Eds.)

High-Speed Networks
and Multimedia
Communications

6th IEEE International Conference, HSNMC 2003
Estoril, Portugal, July 23-25, 2003
Proceedings

 Springer

Series Editors

Gerhard Goos, Karlsruhe University, Germany
Juris Hartmanis, Cornell University, NY, USA
Jan van Leeuwen, Utrecht University, The Netherlands

Volume Editors

Mário Marques Freire
University of Beira Interior, Department of Informatics
Rua Marques d'Ávila e Bolama, 6201-001 Covilhã, Portugal
E-mail: mario@di.ubi.pt

Pascal Lorenz
Université de Haute Alsace
IUT, 34 rue du Grillenbreit, 68008 Colmar, France
E-mail: lorenz@ieee.org

Mike Myung-Ok Lee
Dongshin University
Faculty of Information and Communication Engineering
252 Daeho-Dong, Naju, Chonnam 520-714, Republic of Korea
E-mail: mikelee@dsu.ac.kr

Cataloging-in-Publication Data applied for

Bibliographic information published by Die Deutsche Bibliothek
Die Deutsche Bibliothek lists this publication in the Deutsche Nationalbibliografie;
detailed bibliographic data is available in the Internet at <http://dnb.ddb.de>.

CR Subject Classification (1998): C.2, H.5.1, H.3, K.4, K.6, D.2

ISSN 0302-9743
ISBN 3-540-40542-9 Springer-Verlag Berlin Heidelberg New York

Springer-Verlag Berlin Heidelberg New York
a member of BertelsmannSpringer Science+Business Media GmbH

http://www.springer.de

© Springer-Verlag Berlin Heidelberg 2003
Printed in Germany

Typesetting: Camera-ready by author, data conversion by Boller Mediendesign
Printed on acid-free paper   SPIN: 10928943   06/3142   5 4 3 2 1 0

Preface

On behalf of the Organizing and Program Committees of the 6th IEEE International Conference on High-Speed Networks and Multimedia Communications (HSNMC 2003), it was our great pleasure to welcome the participants to the HSNMC 2003, held from July 23 to July 25, 2003, in Estoril, Portugal. In recent years, significant advances in high-speed networks and multimedia communications have been made throughout the world. The objective of the conference was to promote high-speed networks and multimedia communications related research and development activities and to encourage communication between researchers and engineers throughout the world in this area.

In response to the call for papers, a total of 105 papers were submitted from 28 countries, from which 60 were accepted for presentation in 15 technical sessions. Each paper was peer reviewed by several members of the Program Committee or additional reviewers. The conference program covered a variety of research topics which are of current interest, such as quality of service, integrated and differentiated services, multicasting, peer-to-peer networking, real-time issues and protocols for IP networks, IP-over-WDM, multimedia streaming, video, TCP performance, network and information management issues, WDM networks, optical switching and performance monitoring, CDMA, mobile and wireless networks, and traffic models. Together with four tutorials and three plenary sessions, these technical presentations addressed the latest research results from international industry and academia and reported on findings on high-speed networks and multimedia communications.

We would like to thank the members of the International Program Committee and the additional reviewers. Without their support, the program organization of this conference would not have been possible. We also thank all authors of the papers submitted to the conference. We are also indebted to many organizations that made this conference possible, namely IEEE, IEE, the Institute of Telecommunications (Portugal), and Springer-Verlag. In particular, we thank the members of the Organizing Committee for their help in all aspects of the organization of this conference. We hope that you enjoyed this International Conference on High-Speed Networks and Multimedia Communications at Estoril, Portugal, if you attended, and that you found it a useful forum for the exchange of ideas, results and recent findings. We also hope that you spent some time visiting some of the several points of interest on the Estoril coast and in Lisbon.

July 2003   Mário Freire, Pascal Lorenz and Mike Myung-Ok Lee

HSNMC 2003 Conference Committees

General Chair

Mário Freire (Portugal) - University of Beira Interior/IT Coimbra

General Co-chairs

Pascal Lorenz (France) - University of Haute Alsace
Mike Myung-Ok Lee (Korea) - Dongshin University

International Program Committee

R. Addie (Australia) - University of Southern Queensland
A.P. Alves (Portugal) - University of Oporto/INESC
K. Al-Begain (UK) - University of Bradford
C. Belo (Portugal) - IST/IT Lisbon
A. Benslimane (France) - University of Belfort
B. Bing (USA) - Georgia Institute of Technology
F. Boavida (Portugal) - University of Coimbra
D. Bonjour (France) - CNET
A. Brandwajn (USA) - University of California, Santa Cruz
A. Casaca (Portugal) - IST/INESC
J.P. Coudreuse (France) - Mitsubishi
J. Craveirinha (Portugal) - University of Coimbra/INESC Coimbra
J. Crowcroft (UK) - University College London
K. Eshraghian (Australia) - Edith Cowan University
M. Figueiredo (Portugal) - IST/IT Lisbon
F. Fontes (Portugal) - PT Inovação/IT Aveiro
M. Freire (Portugal) - University of Beira Interior/IT Coimbra
B. Gavish (USA) - Vanderbilt University
J. Halpern (USA) - Newbridge Networks, Inc.
Z. Hulicki (Poland) - University of Cracow
R. Israel (France) - IEEE
S. Komandur (USA) - Ascend Communications
D. Kouvatsos (UK) - University of Bradford
S. Kumar (USA) - Ericsson
G.S. Kuo (Taiwan) - National Central University
F. Le Faucheur (France) - Cisco
M. Lee (Korea) - Dongshin University
P. Lorenz (France) - University of Haute Alsace
Z. Mammeri (France) - University of Toulouse

A. Martins (Portugal) - University of Aveiro
N. Mastorakis (Greece) - Military Institutions of University Education
S. Moyer (USA) - Bellcore
E. Monteiro (Portugal) - University of Coimbra
R. Muraine (France) - Newbridge
M.S. Nunes (Portugal) - IST/INESC
G. Omidyar (USA) - Computer Sciences Corp.
J.J. Pansiot (France) - University of Strasbourg
F. Pereira (Portugal) - IST/IT Lisbon
M. Potts (Switzerland) - Martel
G. Pujolle (France) - University of Versailles/Saint-Quentin
P. Queluz (Portugal) - IST/IT Lisbon
S. Rao (Switzerland) - Ascom
A. Reid (UK) - British Telecom
S. Ritzenthaler (France) - Alcatel
R. Rocha (Portugal) - IST/IT Lisbon
P. Rolin (France) - ENST Bretagne
H. Silva (Portugal) - University of Coimbra/IT Coimbra
A. Sousa (Portugal) - University of Aveiro/IT Aveiro
G. Swallow (USA) - Cisco
H. Tobiet (France) - Clemessy
R. Valadas (Portugal) - University of Aveiro/IT Aveiro
P. Veiga (Portugal) - University of Lisbon
E. Vazquez Gallo (Spain) - University of Madrid
V.A. Villagra (Spain) - University of Madrid

Organizing Committee

C. Salema (Portugal) - IST/IT Lisbon
L. Sá (Portugal) - University of Coimbra/IT Coimbra
H. Silva (Portugal) - University of Coimbra/IT Coimbra
F. Perdigão (Portugal) - University of Coimbra/IT Coimbra
J. Rodrigues (Portugal) - University of Beira Interior/IT Coimbra
C. Belo (Portugal) - IST/IT Lisbon
R. Rocha (Portugal) - IST/IT Lisbon
A. Rodrigues (Portugal) - IST/IT Lisbon

List of Additional Reviewers

R.L. Aguiar (Portugal) - University of Aveiro
L. Bernardo (Portugal) - New University of Lisbon
F. Caldeira (Portugal) - Polytechnic Institute of Viseu
P. Carvalho (Portugal) - University of Coimbra
I. Chaves (Portugal) - Instituto Pedro Nunes

Table of Contents

Quality of Service

Network and Information Management Issues

WDM Networks

Mobile and Wireless Networks

Video

CDMA

Real Time Issues and Protocols for IP Networks

Multimedia Streaming

Optical Switching and Performance Monitoring

TCP Performance

Voice over IP

Traffic Models

Author Index

Dynamic Mapping between the Controlled-Load IntServ Service and the Assured Forward DiffServ PHB

António Pereira[1, 2] and Edmundo Monteiro[2]

[1] Polytechnic Institute of Leiria
Department of Informatics Engineering, ESTG
Morro do Lena – Alto do Vieiro 2411-901 Leiria – Portugal
apereira@estg.ipleiria.pt
http://www.estg.ipleiria.pt
[2] University of Coimbra
Laboratory of Communications and Telematics
CISUC / DEI, Pólo II, Pinhal de Marrocos 3030-290 Coimbra – Portugal
edmundo@dei.uc.pt
http://lct.dei.uc.pt

Abstract. This work addresses the interconnection of the IntServ and DiffServ models. In particular, new mapping mechanisms between the Controlled-Load service (CL) of the IntServ model and the Assured Forward (AF) Per-Hop-Behaviours group of the DiffServ model, are proposed and analysed by simulation. The proposed mechanisms have a dynamic nature and they are associated to an admission control such that the state of the network is reflected in the new admission decisions of the new IntServ flows into the DiffServ network. For the same IntServ destination network, the behaviour of the previous flows is taken into account. The results show that the functionality of IntServ networks can be extended through DiffServ regions without perceptible degradation of QoS. Moreover the dynamic mapping mechanisms take into account the state of the network, improve the use of the available resources for each AF class and guarantee the AF class QoS even when congestion rises.

1   The Problem

The research effort in the area of the quality of service (QoS) provision on the Internet has been carried out by the IETF (Internet Engineering Task Force) according to two main models: the Differentiated Services (DiffServ) model [1] and the Integrated Services (IntServ) model [2, 3]. These two models have been developed by two work groups of the IETF [4, 5].

The IntServ model provides individually QoS guarantees to each flow. For such, it needs to make resource reservation in network elements intervening in the communication. For resources reservation the Resource Reservation Protocol is used (RSVP) [6, 7]. The IntServ model supports two distinct services: Guaranteed service (GS) [8] for applications with strict needs of throughput, limited delay and null losses; Controlled-Load service (CL) [9] that emulates the behaviour of the best-effort service in

M.M. Freire, P. Lorenz, M.M.-O. Lee (Eds.): HSNMC 2003, LNCS 2720, pp. 1-10, 2003.

an unloaded network. The need of maintenance of state information on the individual flows is usually pointed as the origin of the scalability problems of the IntServ model.

The DiffServ model embodies the second approach where the flows are aggregated in service classes (CoS) according to specific characteristics. The packets belonging to specific classes are forwarded according to their Per Hop Behaviour (PHB) associated with the DiffServ Code point (DSCP) [10], which is included in the field Type of Service (ToS) of the IP header. Currently the DiffServ model supports Expedited Forwarding (EF) PHB destined to offer a service of type "virtual leased line" with throughput guarantees and limited delays [11]. Also, the Assured Forwarding (AF) PHBs group that exhibits a similar behaviour to the low loaded network for traffic that is in accordance with the service contract [12].

In order to combine the superior scalability of the DiffServ model with IntServ superior QoS support capabilities, the ISSL (Integrated Services to over Specific Link Layers) working group of the IETF [13] proposed the interoperation between these two models [14]. The defined approach combines the IntServ model features – capability to establish and maintain resources reservations trough the network elements – with the scalability provided by the DiffServ model. The IntServ model is applicable at the network edge, where the number of flows is small, while the DiffServ model is applicable in the network core to take advantage of its scalability. The boundary routers between these two networks are responsible for mapping the IntServ flows into the DiffServ classes. These functions include the choice of the most appropriate PHB to support the flow and the use of admission control (AC) and policing functions on the flows at the entrance of the DiffServ region.

In DiffServ networks admission control is based in Bandwidth Brokers (BBs) and in pricing schemes associated with Service Level Agreements (SLAs) at the entrance of the DiffServ Domains. This solution does not intrinsically solve the problem of congestion control. Upon overload in a given service class, all flows in that class suffer a potential QoS degradation. To solve this and to integrate the DiffServ and IntServ models in a end-to-end service delivery model with the associated task of reservation, a new admission control function, which can determine whether to admit a service differentiated flow along the nominated network is needed [15]. There are several proposals of admission control mechanisms that can be used to address this problem. One approach of admission control developed at LCT-UC [16] uses a metric to evaluate a congestion index (CI) at each network element to admit or not a new flow [17, 18]. Other approaches use packet probing [19, 20, 21], aggregation of RSVP messages [22, 23] between an ingress egress routers or Bandwidth Brokers (BBs) [24]. The issue of the choice of the admission control mechanisms was left open by the ISSL IETF group [25].

In this work a mapping mechanism between the Controlled-Load service of the IntServ model and the Assured Forwarding PHB group of the DiffServ model is proposed. This option was due to the less difficulty of the problem when compared with the mapping between service GS and PHB EF and to the wider acceptance of IntServ CL service among network equipment manufacturers. This mapping mechanism includes a dynamic admission control module that takes into account the state of the DiffServ network. In this approach, the decision of mapping and admitting a new IntServ flow in the DiffServ network is based on the behaviour of previous flows to the same IntServ destination network.

Besides this section the article has the following structure. Section 2 describes the proposed dynamic mapping mechanisms. It includes the architecture, the mapping algorithm and the admission control module developed. In Section 3 the simulation scenario is presented as well as an evaluation of the proposed mechanisms. Finally, in Section 4, some conclusions and directions for future work are presented.

2   Proposed Solution

In the border between the IntServ and DiffServ regions, the network elements must perform the mapping of the requested IntServ service into a DiffServ class of service. The DiffServ class must be selected in a way to support the type of IntServ service requested for the application. Taking into account the already defined IntServ services (CL and GS), the PHBs currently available in DiffServ (AF and EF) and, considering the characteristics of each service and PHB respectively, the choice of mapping between service CL and PHB AF and between service GS and PHB EF is evident.

The mapping of the CL service into the AF PHBs must be based on the burst time of the CL flow [25]. This way, the flows are grouped in the AF class which provides the better guarantee that the packet average queue delay does not exceed the burst time of the flow. The mapping can be static or dynamic: static mapping is defined by the administrator of the network; dynamic mapping is driven according to the characteristics of the existing traffic in the network.

The mapping mechanism proposed in this work, intends to complement the control traffic of the DiffServ network by using a dynamic Admission Control mechanism that reflects the network state. In the adopted strategy, the decision of mapping and admitting a new flow at the ingress of the DiffServ region is based on the behaviour of previous flows with going to the same IntServ network. This behaviour is a consequence of the delays and losses suffered by the flow in the DiffServ region. The underlying idea is inspired in the congestion control mechanism used in TCP/IP, applied to the admission control and mapping of IntServ flows in DiffServ classes.

The strategy adopted is based in the observation of flows at the ingress and the egress of DiffServ domains to evaluate if the QoS of the mapping flow was degraded or not. In the case where no degradation occurs new flows can be admitted and mapped. On the other hand, if the QoS characteristics have been degraded, no more flows can be admitted into the DiffServ network ingress and the number of active flows must be reduced. By monitoring the flows at the egress of the DiffServ domain, the QoS characteristics are evaluated on the basis of the packet loss, since the queuing delay is less representative [19] and more difficult to treat with passive measurements due to its wide variability and to the difficulty of clock synchronization.

2.1   Mapping System Architecture

The proposed strategy for mapping IntServ flows into DiffServ classes is based on two mechanisms located in the network elements at the boundary of the DiffServ region: the mapping and the meter. In the edge router at the ingress of DiffServ domain, the mapping mechanism makes the mapping of CL flows into the AF class which better supports the type of service defined by the IntServ message. This mechanism acts on the basis of the information supplied by the meter mechanism located in edge router at the egress of the DiffServ domain.

In Figure 1 the integration of the mapping mechanism with the IntServ and Diff-Serv modules is illustrated. The meter module shown in Figure 2 belongs to the Diff-Serv model and should not be misunderstood with the meter mechanism. Besides doing the necessary measurement to the operation of the DiffServ network, this module also counts, for each flow, the packets marked with determined DSCP. This information together with the one sent by the meter mechanism at the egress edge router allows the evaluation of the behaviour of the flows in the DiffServ region.

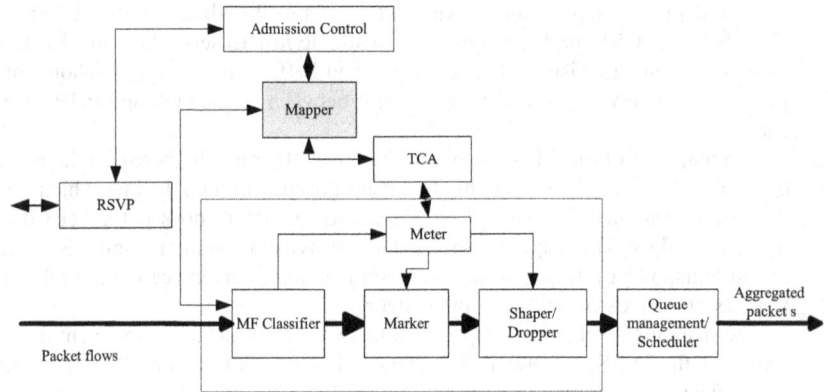

Fig. 1. The mapping mechanism

The meter mechanism, illustrated in Figure 2, interacts with the modules of the Int-Serv model, and with the meter module of the DiffServ model (which is responsible for accounting, for each flow, the packets in agreement with the attributed DSCP). Whenever a RSVP message of reserve removal occurs, the collected information is inserted in a new object called DIFFSERV_STATUS and is sent to the ingress edge router of the DiffServ domain such that it can be taken into account for the next flow mapping.

2.2   Mapping Algorithm

The algorithm used for the mapping mechanism is activated in the ingress edge router by the RSVP_RESV messages. These messages include a *filterspec* and a *flowspec* fields. The filterspec field specifies the flow used in the configuration of the Multi-Field classifier. The flowspec field specifies the intended QoS characteristics for the flow and is used for updating the available resources. In the case of dynamic mapping, the flowspec is also used to determine the flow burst time.

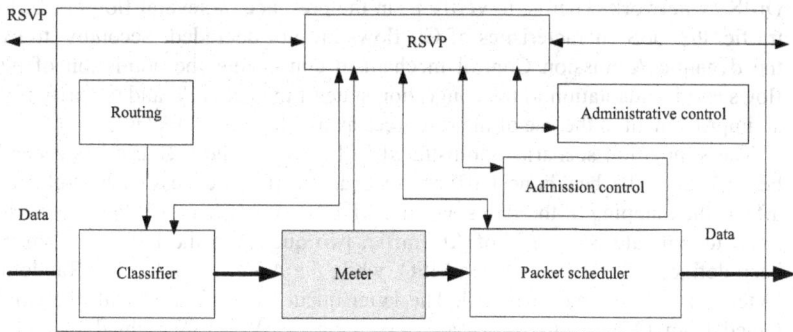

Fig. 2. The meter mechanism

After the identification of the flow and the intended QoS characteristics, the mapping mechanism of edge router verifies the existence of a static mapping table entry defined for that flow. If this entry exists, the available resources in the TCA are updated, the packet classifier is configured and a RSVP_RESV message is sent upstream to the router in IntServ network. When the entry corresponding to the TCA does not exist, or the resources in this TCA are not available, a RSVP_ERR message is sent downstream to the IntServ routers in order to remove the reservation.

In the case where a static mapping is not defined, the edge router uses the dynamic mapping. The mapping module evaluates the burst time of the flow and identifies, if any, the AF class that better guarantees that this burst time is not exceeded. Then, it verifies if the flow can be mapped based on the previous behaviour of the flows mapped for the same destination network identified by the NHOP field of the message. If the mapping is made, the available resources are refreshed, the packet classifier is configured and a RSVP_RESV message is sent to the upstream router. If either the AF class is not defined or the network is congested, then a RSVP_ERR message will be sent.

In the meter mechanism at the egress edge router, the information about the flow (number of packets received for each DSCP) is generated after receiving a reserve removal message (RSVP_ResvTear, for example). This information is inserted in a new RSVP object – DIFFSERV_STATUS – and added to the RSVP message, which will be sent later to the mapping mechanism of the ingress edge router. This router is identified by the field PHOP, when the RSVP_PATH message is received.

3   Evaluation of the Proposed Mechanisms

In this section the evaluation of the proposed mechanism for dynamic mapping of CL flows into AF classes is made. The evaluation was supported by the implementation of the mapping mechanisms in the Network Simulator v.2 environment (NS2) [26] integrated with the available NS2 IntServ and DiffServ modules [27].

The evaluation has two distinct objectives. Firstly, to verify if the proposed mechanisms are able to extend the functionality of the IntServ network through the

DiffServ network. That is, to verify if, in the presence of several flows of best-effort traffic, the QoS characteristics of CL flows are not degraded. Secondly, to evaluate the dynamic Admission Control mechanism concerning the admission of new CL flows and its adaptation to the congestion state of the network, and to verify if there is an improvement in the use of the resources available in the AF classes.

The simulation scenario is illustrated in Figure 3. The scenario has a bandwidth bottleneck in the backbone DiffServ to evaluate if the excess of best-effort traffic affects the mapping of the flows. For the AF class a profile of 1 Mbps was defined. In order to separate BE traffic of AF traffic, two queues in the DiffServ domain have been defined. The BE queue is a FIFO, while the AF queue is a RIO (Random Early Detection with in and Out) [28]. The latter queue is configured with the values obtained from [27]. Both queues are served by the WFQ (Weighted Fair Queuing) scheduler [29], which is configured such that the profile defined for the AF class is assured.

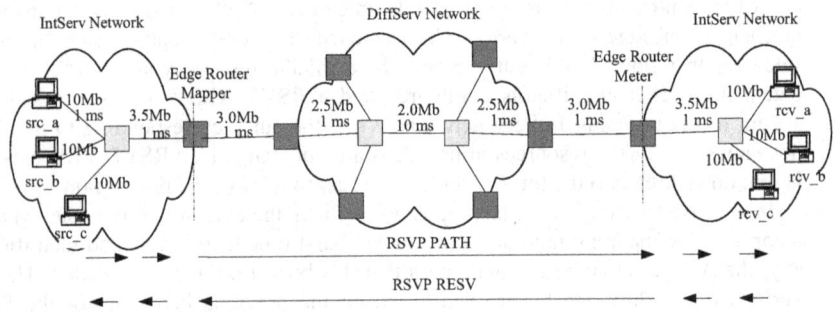

Fig. 3. Simulation scenario

In the tests made, the dynamic mapping of CL flows into the AF PHB with a dynamic admission control mechanism that takes into account the state of the DiffServ network was evaluated, in the presence best-effort flows of 100 Kbps. The delays, the losses and the throughput of CL flows have been measured as for different network loads. The number of existent mapped flows (N_Flows) in the class AF as well as the maximum number allowed (N_MaxFlows) in the DiffServ network was recorded. These values are obtained from the dynamic admission control mechanism whenever a reserve removal of a CL flow previously mapped occurs.

In the scenario presented, 15 best-effort flows of 100 Kbps each were generated to the network to congest the bandwidth bottleneck. Reserve requests of CL flows of 100Kbps are generated every 15 seconds. The flow is mapped and transmitted if resources are available in the IntServ network and if the dynamic admission control at the DiffServ domain entrance accepts the request.

After 250 seconds of simulation time, and every 50 seconds thereafter, the existent flow reserves are removed in the same order they were created. In this way more reserve requests and mappings are allowed than reserve releases. This allows the evaluation de dynamic Admission Control mechanism.

Figure 4 shows the results obtained by using the dynamic Admission Control mechanism in the mapping of the CL flows into an AF class. The analysis of the figure shows that the flows were admitted until the number of flows of the predefined profile is attained. Afterwards, new flows were admitted only if the reserve of a previous mapped flow is released and if these flows did not suffer any QoS degradation. In such case one flow is added to N_MaxFlows.

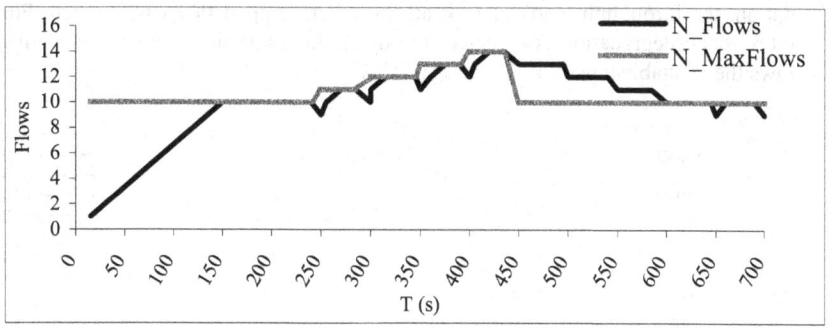

Fig. 4. CL Flows CL admitted in DiffServ Network by Dynamic Admission Control

When QoS degradation occurs, the maximum number of flows allowed drops to the value supported by the profile defined initially. In this way, the AF class can recover from the degradation. The variable N_MaxFlows is updated only when the state of the network is verified after the degradation. The state of the network is known when a new mapped flow probes the network. If this new flow does not suffer QoS degradation, one flow is added to N_MaxFlows and the process of mapping new flows repeats. Otherwise one flow is subtracted to N_MaxFlows and will be updated only when a new mapped flow probes the network.

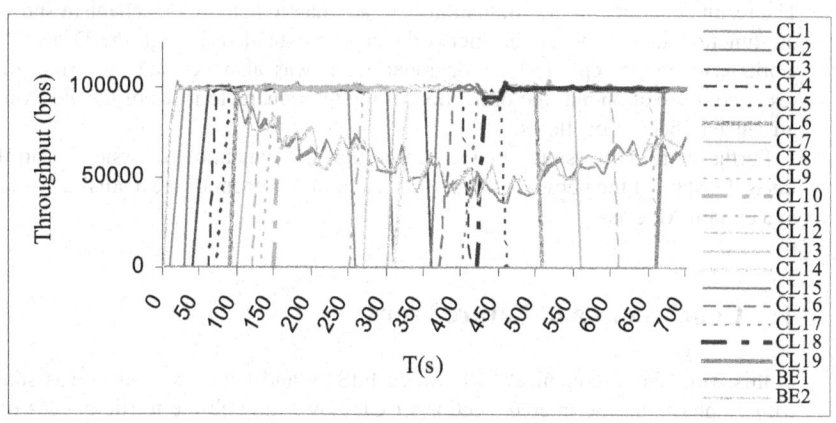

Fig. 5. Throughput of CL and BE flows

The simulation results regarding throughput are presented in Figure 5. The results regarding delays are presented in Figure 6.

Both figures show that when the CL flows are mapped/admitted all the BE flows suffer the same throughput and delay degradation whereas the CL flows maintain a reserved throughput which increases slightly the delay when the mapped flows increase. It can also be seen from the figures that the dynamic Admission Control takes advantage of the available resources and that whenever a mapped flow causes degradation, the throughput and delay of all the other mapped flows is affected. Furthermore, once degradation is detected, the dynamic Admission Control mechanism allows the reestablishment of the AF class QoS.

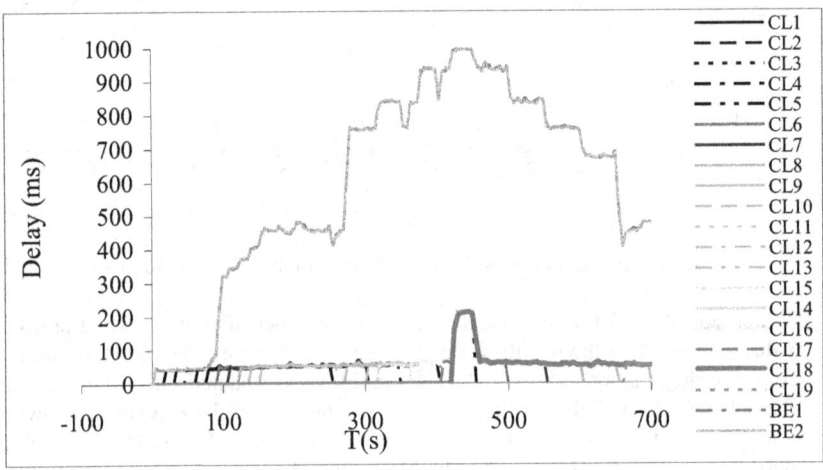

Fig. 6. Delays of CL and BE flows

The results obtained in the simulation with a dynamic mapping mechanism show that the functionality of the IntServ networks can be extended through the DiffServ networks without perceptible QoS degradation. It was also verified the effect of the resource reservation and the protection of the QoS characteristics of CL flows in the presence of best-effort flows.

Furthermore, the results obtained show that the dynamic Admission Control reflects the state of the network and provides an improvement of the available resources of a certain AF class.

4   Conclusions and Future Work

In this work the interconnection between IntServ and DiffServ models was studied, with emphasis on the interconnection of CL flows through the traffic classes of the AF PHBs group.

A mapping mechanism is proposed to act between the two models. The mechanism is based on dynamic Admission Control in which the active flows serves as probing to the following ones, reflecting the state of congestion of the DiffServ network in the admission decision and mapping of new IntServ flows.

The evaluation results of the proposed dynamic mapping mechanism show that the functionality of the IntServ networks can be extended through the DiffServ networks.

The positive effect of the resources reservation in the IntServ model and the protection of the QoS characteristics of CL flows in the presence of best-effort flows were also verified. Furthermore the results shown that the dynamic mapping takes into account the state of the network to map new CL flows into AF classes and to re-establish AF class QoS once degradation is detected.

The future work (already in course) will address the validation of a dynamic mapping mechanism in more demanding scenarios with more AF classes and with different types of traffic to be generated in the IntServ network. Also other scenarios will be studied including more IntServ networks in the boundary and more DiffServ networks in the core.

In a second phase, the behaviour of the dynamic mapping mechanisms will be evaluated in DiffServ networks badly dimensioned, in the presence of non conformant traffic in situations of forced congestion.

Acknowledgments

This work was partially financed by the Ministry of Science and High Level Education (Project QoSII) and by PRODEPIII, Measure 5, Action 5.3.

References

1. D. Black et al., An Architecture for Differentiated Services, RFC 2475, IETF, Dec. 1998.
2. R. Braden et al., Integrated Services in the Internet Architecture: an Overview, RFC 1633, IETF, June, 1994.
3. S. Shenker et al., General Characterization Parameters for Integrated Service Network Elements, RFC 2215, IETF, September 1997.
4 IntServ workgroup charters, http://www.ietf.org/html.charters/IntServ-charter.html.
5. DiffServ workgroup charters, http://www.ietf.org/html.charters/DiffServ-charter.html.
6. J. Wroclawski, The Use of RSVP with IETF Integrated Services, RFC 2210, IETF, September 1997.
7. R. Braden et al., Resource Reservation Protocol (RSVP) – Version 1 Functional Specification, RFC 2205, IETF, September 1997.
8. S. Shenker et al., Specification of Guaranteed Quality of Service, RFC 2212, IETF, Sep. 1997.
9. J. Wroclawski, Specification of the Controlled-load Network Element Service, RFC 2211, IETF, September 1997.
10. K. Nichols et al., Definition of the Differentiated Services Field (DS Field) in the IPv4 and IPv6 Headers, RFC 2474, IETF, December 1998.
11. B. Davie et al., An Expedited Forwarding PHB, RFC 3246, IETF, March 2002.

12. J. Heinanen et al., Assured Forwarding PHB Group, RFC 2597, IETF, June 1999.
13. ISSLL workgroup charters, http://www.ietf.org/html.charters/issll-charter.html.
14. Y. Bernetwork et al., A Framework for Integrated Services Operation over DiffServ Networks, RFC 2998, IETF, November 2000.
15. G. Houston, Next Steps for the IP QoS Architecture, RFC 2990, IETF, November 2000.
16. D. Lourenço et al., "Definição do Mecanismo de Controlo de Admissão para o Modelo de serviços do LCT-UC", in Proc. of CRC2000, FCCN, Viseu, Portugal, Nov. 16-17, 2000.
17. E. Monteiro et al., "A Scheme for the Quantification of Congestion in Communication Services and Systems", in Proc. of SDNE'96, IEEE Computer Society, Macau, June 3-4, 1996.
18. G. Quadros, et al., "An Approach to Support Traffic Classes in IP Networks", in Proceedings of QofIS2000, Berlin, Germany, September 25-26, 2000.
19. L. Breslau et al., "Endpoint Admission Control: Architectural Issues and Performance", in Proceedings of ACM SIGCOM 2000, Stockholm, Sweden, August 2000.
20. V. Eleck et al., "Admission Control Based on End-to-End Measurements", in Proceedings of IEEE INFOCOM 2000, Tel Aviv, Israel, March 2000.
21. G. Bianchi et al., A migration Path to provide End-to-End QoS over Stateless networks by Means of a probing-driven Admission Control, Internet Draft, IETF, July 2001.
22. F. Baker et al., Aggregation of RSVP for IPv4 and IPv6 Reservations, RFC3175, IETF, September 2001.
23. Y. Bernet, Format of the RSVP DCLASS Object, RFC2996, IETF, November 2000.
24. Z. Zhang et al.. "Decoupling QoS Control from Core Routers: A Novel Bandwidth Broker Architecture for Scalable Support of Guaranteed Services", in Proceedings of ACM SIGCOM 2000, Stockholm, Sweden, August 2000.
25. J. Wroclawski et al., Integrated Services Mappings for Differentiated Services Networks, Internet Draft, IETF, February 2001.
26. Network Simulator – NS (version 2), http://www.isi.edu/nsnam/ns/
27. J. F. Rezende, "Assured Service Evaluation", IEEE Global Telecommunications Conference - Globecom'99, Rio de Janeiro, Brazil, December 1999.
28. D. Clark et al., "Explicit Allocation of Best Effort Packet Delivery Service", IEEE/ACM Transactions on Networking, vol. 6, no 4, August de 1998.
29. H. Zhang, "Service Disciplines for Guaranteed Performance Service in Packet-Switching Networks," Proc. IEEE, vol. 83, no 10, October 1995.

Analytical Approach and Verification of a DiffServ-Based Priority Service

Christos Bouras and Afrodite Sevasti

Research Academic Computer Technology Institute-CTI, 61 Riga Feraiou Str., 26221 Patras,
Greece
Department of Computer Engineering and Informatics, University of Patras, 26500 Rion,
Patras, Greece
{bouras, sevastia}@cti.gr

Abstract. The provision of Quality of Service (QoS) in a seamless way over the dominating internetworking protocol of our times (IP), has been a challenge for many researchers in the past years. Strict qualitative guarantees have proven difficult to provide in a way that has discouraged efforts in the area. The lack of a coherent provisioning methodology has been identified as the main reason for this. In this work, we are attempting an analytical yet straightforward approach to the provisioning methodology proposed for premium service of high-quality demanding traffic in the wide-area. Our approach is based on a series of well-known results of queuing theory but is proven to provide good approximations to experimental results as well as worthwhile qualitative guarantees.

1.   Introduction

The DiffServ framework has been designed for the provision of QoS services in large-scale environments, where the extensive aggregation of flows does not allow solutions for QoS provisioning on a per-flow scale. At the same time, DiffServ is a framework and as such, it provides guidelines rather than strictly defined service models. Network designers have, thus, at their disposal multiple different individual mechanisms and alternatives for QoS services' implementation. This results in a variety of solutions, the compatibility and relevant importance of which can rarely be pinpointed. Our work attempts to approach analytically and evaluate a set of guidelines for the provision of a high-priority service to quality-demanding traffic in wide-area networks, while at the same time ensuring deterministic upper bounds to critical metrics, such as one-way delay.

Dimensioning and provisioning QoS on the DiffServ framework basis has been the topic of many research initiatives in the last years. Some of them focus in DiffServ-based QoS service models and definitions ([4],[6],[9]) while others perform experimental studies on individual mechanisms and modules of DiffServ-based QoS services ([5],[7],[8]).

Also a number of analytical approaches have been presented in the latest years, some of which are briefly presented here. In [13], the authors are proposing the use of a statistical rather than deterministic analysis for the estimation of loss rate and delay

M.M. Freire, P. Lorenz, M.M.-O. Lee (Eds.): HSNMC 2003, LNCS 2720, pp. 11-20, 2003.
© Springer-Verlag Berlin Heidelberg 2003

guarantees along a multistage network for packets served in aggregates by a non-preemptive priority service. The main reason for this is that deterministic analysis seems to be too pessimistic while statistical analysis allows for better approximation of quality metrics in the expense of statistical guarantees. The results of this work that are relevant to the analysis made here is the validity of the M/D/1 queuing model in the analysis of queues serving aggregates of flows with non-pre-emptive priority. Delays and buffer saturation probabilities are estimated using a Poisson stream of MTU-sized packets for each such flow aggregate and end-to-end delay guarantees are estimated with respect to the waiting time in queues of packets along a multistage network.

In [14], the authors are proposing a closed loop edge-based framework for flow control having as an ultimate goal, that of providing QoS. Their approach is also focused on the accumulation of packets at each router attributed to each flow for a sequence of routers. However, this is in the framework of devising a flow control mechanism based on the operation of TCP and aiming at preserving queue occupancy (and thus queuing delays) to desired levels for a certain level of quality.

In this work, we are aiming at the analytical modeling of the situation imposed when a high-priority service is introduced to a best-effort IP network. We are also combining a service definition with a set of mechanisms, towards an integrated solution for QoS provisioning to quality-demanding traffic, with bounded quality guarantees. With respect to the related work done so far, the contribution of this work is two-fold: we initially provide an analytical model for dimensioning and provisioning a high-priority service to IP multimedia traffic over a backbone topology. In the sequel, we use simulation in order to verify our analytically supported provisioning model.

In section 2 of this paper, the model used for both the analytical and simulation work is provided. In section 3, the analytical approach of DiffServ-based QoS service is provided. In section 4, a set of scenarios verifying the analysis of section 3 and demonstrating the performance of the service are provided. This paper concludes with our intended future work on this topic and conclusions drawn from the work carried out so far.

1.1.   The Model

The case that will be further investigated in this work is that of dimensioning and providing a high-priority, low latency QoS service for aggregated traffic in a wide-area network. This service, referred to as 'Gold' service from now on, is built according to the Expedited Forwarding Per-Hop-Behavior ([1]) of the DiffServ framework. The Gold service aims at offering the equivalent of an end-to-end virtual leased line (VLL) service at the IP layer across multiple domains. In general, traffic requesting for such a service is sensitive to delay, jitter and packet losses, so the proposed service and provisioning method will be evaluated against these metrics.

For each of the customers (C_i) an appropriate SLA that specifies the characteristics (traffic envelope) of the marked as Gold traffic injected by C_i into the network is required. The Gold service then guarantees a specific rate of service for each aggregate, a specific bounded end-to-end delay (D), bounded jitter and minimal packet losses to all the legitimate aggregates served by it. Legitimate aggregates are those the

traffic envelope of which is examined (and enforced if necessary) by the use of a poli-
cer for each one of them, as depicted in Figure 1.

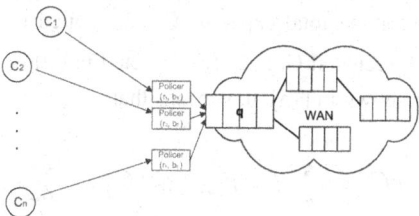

Fig. 1. Enforcing token bucket profiles to Gold service customers

One of the most common policers used and supported by commercial network
equipment is that of a token bucket (r, b), that imposes conformance to an average
rate and maximum burst size to the incoming traffic. Gold traffic aggregates are
served by priority queues (like q of Figure 1) along the wide area network. The aim
of the analytical and experimental study that follows is to investigate rules and principles for the Gold service provisioning and the quality achieved for Gold traffic.

2. Analytical Study

For the Gold service provisioning, it is proposed to use appropriate configuration of
all the routers comprising the network in order to ensure the existence of proper buffering space and for the Gold traffic to be served with the required quality.
  The basic principles on which the service dimensioning is based are:
- The configuration of routers so that Gold traffic will receive at least a strictly
  bounded minimum service rate at each router, regardless of the load imposed on
  the router
- The policing of the total of Gold traffic entering each Point-of-Presence (PoP) is
  such that the arrival rate of the aggregated Gold traffic entering the PoP router,
  created by the merging of all Gold aggregates of customers attached to a specific
  PoP does not exceed the minimum rate of service that Gold traffic receives at each
  egress interface of the router (according to [1]).
- Based on these principles, the goal of Gold service provisioning would be:
- To assure that each flow participating in a Gold traffic aggregate originating from a
  customer attached to a PoP demonstrates a throughput equal to or larger than that
  of entering the network as it exits the network.
- Delay and jitter for the packets of this flow are both bounded between the points
  where the packets enter and exit the network, while the flow perceives negligible
  or zero packet losses

2.1. Gold Service Dimensioning

As explained extensively in [15], Gold service provisioning is based on resources' over-provisioning and therefore the provision of capacity guarantees can be obtained by ensuring that for the total capacity C_q appointed to each router queue serving Gold traffic the aggregated Gold traffic injected into this queue is only a percentage of C_q. As it was shown in [15], this means that

$$\sum_i r_i \le kC_q \Rightarrow \sum_i l_i \times r_{access} \le kC_q \Rightarrow \sum_i l_i \le \frac{kC_q}{r_{access}}. \tag{1}$$

Factor k determines the over-provisioning factor for the implementation of the Gold service on an outbound interface of an ingress router while r_{access} determines the capacity of the interface through which each customer is attached to the WAN for each customer C_i (assumed to be constant for all customers for simplicity), r_i the token bucket profile rate with which the Gold aggregate injected by customer i to the WAN is policed and l_i the percentage of r_{access} that can be used for Gold traffic for each customer C_i. It is important to stress out at this point that the value of l_i or r_i is one upon which the customer can be charged for receiving the service.

If S_q is the set of customers that are able to inject a Gold traffic aggregate through ingress router queue q, there is also a limitation to the value of C_q, which should not exceed a percentage of the capacity of the WAN backbone links. This means that

$$C_q \le m \times C, \text{ with } m \in (0,1). \tag{2}$$

so that under heavy load, best effort traffic will not face denial of service. From (1) and (2) it follows that

$$\sum_{S_q} l \times r_{access} \le k \times C_q \le k \times m \times C \Rightarrow l \le \frac{m \times C}{|S_q| \times r_{access}} \times k. \tag{3}$$

where l_i has again been considered equal to l for all customers for simplicity. Thus, the percentage of Gold capacity on customers' access links to the WAN is limited for each customer according to k, the over-provisioning factor of Gold traffic on the backbone. In the experimental analysis to follow it will be demonstrated how k affects perceived quality by the traffic served with the Gold service and will provide relevant guidelines. Recommendations from related work ([10]) and other experimental evidence ([11]) lead to the selection of small values for k, in the range of $(0.05, 0.2)$. After selecting the over provisioning factor, the analysis above can be used to determine the values of l_i's in a Gold service provisioning scenario.

Apart from transmission rate guarantees, bounded end-to-end delay can be ensured for the whole of Gold traffic by selecting the token bucket policing profile for each aggregate i served by a ingress router so that the worst-case delay that Gold traffic packets will face during their stay in each router j will not exceed a maximum value $D_{\max j}$. Again here the over-provisioning factor seems to play a crucial role. As outlined again in [15], the guaranteed bounded delay that a packet can face from the moment it enters until it exits the WAN is denoted by:

$$D_{tot} \leq \sum_j D_{\max j} + \sum_n D_{prop_n} + \sum_n D_{trans_n} . \qquad (4)$$

where D_{trans_k} is the transmission delay and D_{prop_k} is the propagation delay of the packet on transmission line n. Equation (4) adds up all delays that a packet faces on each router j and every transmission line it crosses. The following analysis deals with the value of $D_{\max j}$, since the values of D_{trans_k} and D_{prop_k} cannot be affected by the implementation of a service over existent equipment/transmission lines. Also for clarity purposes, the analysis that will follow deals only with the metric of end-to-end delay. However, the experimental approach that will follow anticipates for jitter as well. Under the assumption of Poisson traffic (exponential inter-arrival times) for both Gold and best-effort (BE) aggregates, assuming a general service time distribution and a non-preemptive priority scheduler providing Gold traffic with the highest priority, $D_{\max j}$ on router j for Gold packets can be expressed as:

$$D_{\max j} = \frac{R}{1 - k_j}. \qquad (5)$$

where k_j is the service rate for Gold traffic in j (arrival rate to service rate ratio, see also (1)) and R is the mean residual time in the router, given by:

$$R = \frac{1}{2} \lambda_{Gold} \overline{X^2_{Gold}} + \frac{1}{2} \lambda_{BE} \overline{X^2_{BE}} . \qquad (6)$$

where λ_{Gold} is the arrival rate of Gold traffic to the Gold traffic queue ($\sum_i r_i$ for an ingress router in (1)) and $\overline{X^2_{Gold}}$ is the second moment of service time for traffic entering the router (corresponding values for best-effort traffic are denoted similarly, but for simplicity without losing generality one can assume that $\overline{X^2_{Gold}} = \overline{X^2_{BE}} = \overline{X^2}$).

One immediate observation from (6) is that arrival to service ratio (k_j) for the Gold queue has to be sufficiently limited (a strong indication for over-provisioning requirements) so as to make $D_{\max j}$ limited on the end-to-end path and thus achieve the quality required in terms of end-to-end delay. Actually, arrival to service ratio (k_j) and the arrival rate ($\sum_i r_i$) are the only parameters in the disposal of the Gold service designer in order to achieve bounded queuing delay. Based on a known service time distribution (e.g. deterministic distribution for VoIP traffic comprising of constant size IP packets), the value of $\overline{X^2}$ to be used in (6) can be determined. The Gold service designer can proceed in determining R from (6) and $D_{\max j}$ in (5) and finally providing an end-to-end guarantee via (4).

From the analysis made above it has become apparent that the selection of the policing profile (especially the value of r_i) of each Gold aggregate injected by a customer to a WAN PoP and the provisioning factor or utilization at each router queue serving Gold traffic can affect the delay guarantees provided by the WAN to its Gold service customers. In Figure 2, an indicative comparison of the queuing delay perceived by an experimental set-up and the corresponding theoretical bound for a single router queue is provided.

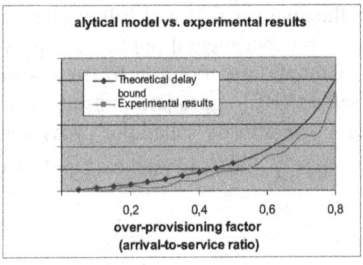

Fig. 2. Comparative presentation of theoretical and experimental queuing delays

Inversely, provided that specific need for bounded delay exists, e.g. 40ms for VoIP traffic crossing the network one can determine the token bucket profiles that can be offered to SLAs with customers.

3.   Experimental Study

In this section, a series of experiments that validate the service provisioning principles already outlined and investigate the different alternatives for Gold service provision are described. These experiments aim at:
- Demonstrating how appropriate provisioning of the Gold service affects the quality guarantees provided to eligible traffic and providing useful guidelines wrt the overprovisioning required
- Studying how well the theoretical bounds are approximated by experimental environments set up in a variety of topologies and scenarios. Guaranteed delay has been our main concern here

The components of the simulation environment that have been used are analytically presented in [12]. The experiments carried out aim at investigating the Gold service provisioning on the backbone of a WAN, comprised by a number of PoPs, to which a number of customers with different access capacities are attached. Gold traffic on the backbone links co-exist with background traffic served as best effort and inserted to the topology as cross-traffic ([2],[3]). An introductory work of the experiments presented here are provided in [15]. For all experiments the value of MTU has 1500 bytes. The scheduling mechanism simulated at the routers has been that of Modified Deficit Round Robin of Cisco GSRs.

3.1. Determining the Over-Provisioning Factor for Gold Service

In this section a series of experiments that investigate the efficient over-provisioning factor (parameter k in (1)) values through different scenarios are conducted. This work aims at adding to related existent work, by considering k as an input parameter to the Gold service provisioning methodology and examining how well the experimental results approach the theoretical ones for different values of k. For the experiments presented, Poisson modeling of traffic has been used. The experimental setup was this of Figure 3.

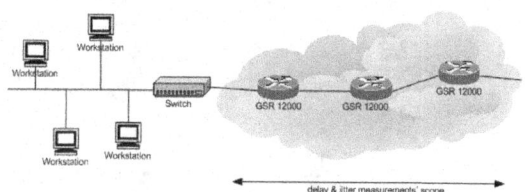

Fig. 3. Over-provisioning factor monitoring testbed

The workstations were configured to transmit VBR traffic over an Ethernet LAN and the aggregated traffic was then injected to a backbone of Cisco GSRs, using MDRR-ALT scheduling. The configuration imposed on each GSR was such that the over-provisioning factor k in $\sum_i r_i \leq kC_q$, where r_i are the token bucket rate policers configured in the ingress interface of the entering backbone GSR for each one of the workstations ranged from 97% to 30%, for the different cases tested. In all of the three cases, it holds that $\sum_i r_i < C_q$, so that Gold traffic is always over-provisioned with a varying over-provisioning grade. In Figure 4, the throughput measured between the measurement points of the simulated topology is presented. It is obvious how over-provisioning factors above the level of 80% affect the throughput perceived by Gold traffic.

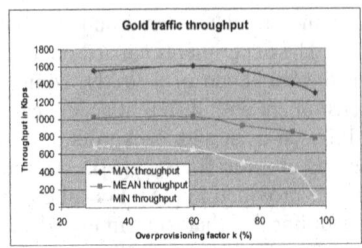

Fig. 4. Throughput measurements for the topology of Figure 3

A second experiment with different levels of aggregation has also been conducted according to the topology of Figure 5. Here, the same traffic is inserted to the backbone cloud, however, not a single point of entry is used. All of the routers are configured so that $\sum_i r_i \leq kC_q$ at each router, however in this experiment, $\sum_i r_i$ is different for each router and therefore the capacity reserved for the Gold traffic C_q has been adjusted accordingly.

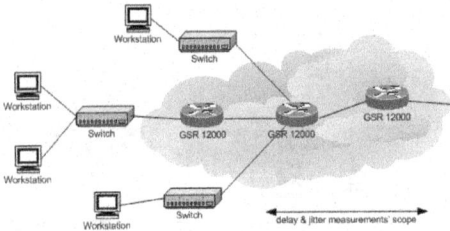

Fig. 5. Over-provisioning factor monitoring testbed with different aggregation levels

In this experimental setup, the points of throughput measurement are shifted to a scope where all of the Gold traffic flows are aggregated (i.e. the last hop of the packets' route in the backbone network). As can be seen from Figure 6, the throughput

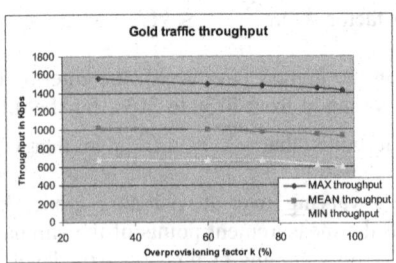

Fig. 6. Throughput measurements for the topology of Figure 5

achieved is now more smoothed wrt the different over-provisioning factors used and this is explained by the fact that traffic is injected gradually to the network and the router policing mechanisms provide a better statistical spreading of Gold traffic.

3.2. Verification of Theoretical Delay Guarantees

In this section, a comparison of the theoretical model with experimental results is presented for the case of delay guarantees. The results of the previous two section, as far as the over-provisioning factor k is concerned are taken into consideration. However, the focus here is on how well delay guarantees are achieved, always in comparison with the theoretical expected values, for more realistic scenarios than that indicatively presented in Figure 2 of section 3.1.

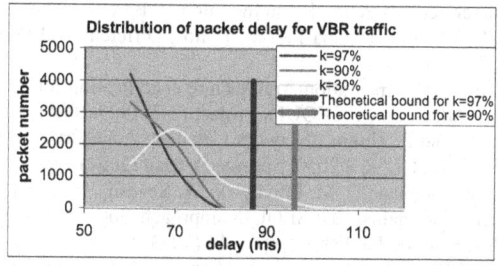

Fig. 7. The effects of MDRR-ALT scheduling in the delay perceived by VBR traffic

The measurements presented here have been performed over the topology of Figure 3. As can be seen from Figure 7, the experimental results for the case of high over-provisioning are confirmed by the theoretical bounds calculated by (4),(5),(6).

4.   Future Work and Conclusions

Most of the work presented here has been based on Poisson traffic modeling. Part of our future work will consist of applying the methodology proposed to different traffic mixes, taking into more recent findings, such as that of self-similar traffic. Our future work on the Gold service will also concentrate on an analytical approach for the jitter guarantees that can be provided for a service such as that of Gold. We also intend to further deploy and evaluate the proposed algorithm for the dimensioning of the Gold service that, according to the analysis made here, will be useful for network administrators in order to introduce the service to their networks.

The work presented in this paper aims at providing an analytical estimation of the qualitative guarantees that can be provided by a high-quality service to IP traffic over a wide area network. We also provide guidelines for dimensioning the service by estimating worst-case bounds on quality metrics. A brief presentation of a simulation set-up used to simulate Gold service provisioning to quality demanding traffic together with how that verified the preceding analysis has been provided.

References

[1] V. Jacobson et al., An Expedited Forwarding PHB, IETF RFC 2598 (1999)

[2] C. Dovrolis, D. Stiliadis and P. Ramanathan, Proportional Differentiated Services: Delay Differentiation and packet Scheduling, IEEE/ACM Transactions in Networking (2002)

[3] M. Yuksel, B. Sikdar, K.S. Vastola, B. Szymanski, Workload generation for ns Simulations of WANs and the Internet, Proceedings of Communication Networks and Distributed Systems Modelling and Simulation Conference, San Diego, CA (2000)

[4] M. Goyal, A. Durresi, C. Liu and R. Jain, Performance Analysis of Assured Forwarding, Internet Draft (draft-goyal-diffserv-afstdy-00) (2000)

[5] I. Yeom, N. Reddy, Impact of marking strategy on aggregated flows in a differentiated services network, proceedings of IWQoS workshop (1999)

[6] S. Shalunov, B. Teitelbaum, Qbone Scavenger Service (QBSS) Definition, Internet2 Technical report, Proposed Service Definition, (2001)

[7] M. May, J-C. Bolot, A. Jean-Marie and C. Diot, Simple performance models of tagging schemes for service differentiation in the Internet, Proc. Infocom '99, New York (1999)

[8] TF-TANT Task Force, Tiziana Ferrari, Editor, Differentiated Services: Experiment report, Phase 2 (2000)

[9] M. Campanella, Implementation Architecture specification for the Premium IP service, Delivrable D2.1-Addendum 1, SEQUIN Project (IST-1999-20841) (2001)

[10] Y. Le Boudec and P. Thiran, 'Network Calculus: A Theory of Deterministic Queuing Systems for the Internet, LNCS 2050, Springer Verlag (2001)

[11] C. Bouras, M. Campanella, M. Przybylski, A. Sevasti, 'QoS and SLA aspects across multiple management domains: The SEQUIN approach, Journal of Future Generation Computer Systems, 939, Elsevier Publishing, pp. 1-14 (2003)

[12] C. Bouras, D. Primpas, A. Sevasti, A. Varnavas, Enhancing the DiffServ architecture of a simulation environment, Sixth IEEE International Workshop on Distributed Simulation and Real Time Applications ((DS-RT 2002), Texas, USA, (2002)

[13] T. Bonald, A. Proutiere, J. Roberts, Statistical Performance Guarantees for Streaming Flows using Expedited Forwarding, Proc. Infocom 2001, pp. 1104-1112 (2001)

[14] D. Harrison, Y. Xia, S. Kalyanaraman, K. Ramachandran, An edge-based Framework for Flow-Control, submitted for publication

[15] C. Bouras, A. Sevasti, Deployment of a DiffServ-based priority service in a MAN/WAN environment, The International Conference on Advanced Information Networking and Applications (AINA), Xi'an, China, (2003)

Evaluation of Integrated Services Support on Linux

Elisabete Reis[1,2] and Edmundo Monteiro[2]

[1]Polytechnic Institute of Coimbra
ISCAC, Quinta Agrícola, Bencanta
2040-316 Coimbra – Portugal
http://www.iscac.pt
elreis@dei.uc.pt
[2]University of Coimbra
Laboratory of Communications and Telematics
CISUC / DEI, Pólo II, Pinhal de Marrocos
3030-290 Coimbra – Portugal
http://lct.dei.uc.pt
edmundo@dei.uc.pt

Abstract. Linux operating system kernel offers a wide variety of traffic control functions, including the mechanisms required to support the Integrated Services architecture developed in the IETF. The main objective of this work is the evaluation of the Linux Traffic Control IntServ implementation. The evaluation is focused in the Guaranteed Service due to the more stringent needs of this service. The evaluation assessed performance behaviour under different traffic loads, scalability and stability. The results shown that the Linux IntServ implementation has some limitations in the support of the Guaranteed Service loss and delay requirements, especially for a high number of flows with small packet sizes.

1   Introduction

The increasing use of applications with stringent requirements on transit delay, bandwidth and losses, raised the need for the development of communication systems with Quality of Service (QoS) capabilities. The Integrated Services Model (IntServ) was developed by the Internet Engineering Task Force to answer to some of these needs in the Internet.

Currently the IntServ model supports two kinds of services: the Guaranteed Service (GS) [1] and the Controlled-Load Service (CL) [2]. The CL service emulates the Best-effort service over an unloaded network and is useful to support elastic applications. GS offers stringent loss and delay guarantees and was designed to support real-time traffic.

Although some negative impact in the performance of the routers in backbone networks, the IntServ model has interesting characteristics either for Internet Service Providers (ISPs) or for end users.

This is due to the possibility of the differentiated treatment of application flows provided by this model that enable the support elastic and real-time traffic. This capability allows ISPs to offer new services, with QoS guarantees, to the end users.

M.M. Freire, P. Lorenz, M.M.-O. Lee (Eds.): HSNMC 2003, LNCS 2720, pp. 21-30, 2003.

Nevertheless this described advantages, IntServ is usually associated with performance and scalability problems due to the need of per flow treatment inside the network.

The main objective of this work is the experimental study and evaluation of the IntServ model, aiming at the assessment of its performance, stability and scalability. The study was focused in GS because it is the most exigent service regarding resources consumption. The Linux IntServ implementation was chosen to build the test platform because of its openness and wide dissemination.

Linux kernel supports a number of advanced networking features, including QoS. The QoS support provides a framework for the implementation of various IP QoS models like Integrated Services and Differentiated Services, in a module generically denominated Traffic Control (TC).

The Linux Traffic Control module consists of four building blocks: queuing disciplines, classes, filters and policing. Currently there are many queuing disciplines supported in Linux [3], including Class Based Queuing (CBQ), Clark-Shenker-Zhang (CSZ), Priority, Token Bucket Flow (TBF), Stochastic Fair Queuing (SFQ), Random Early Detection (RED) and First In First Out (FIFO).

In the Linux implementation tested, CBQ is the only discipline that is able to handle RSVP and Integrated Services, and thus it is the discipline used in this work.

The CBQ discipline assumes that a flow that has been accepted by the admission control module for GS will be assigned its own class with the highest priority [4]. Since all flows belong to classes that have the same priority, they will be served in weighted round robin scheduling (WRR).

The rest of the paper is organized as follows. Section 2 describes the experimental testbed; Section 3 performance experiments, Section 4 scalability evaluation and Section 5 stability evaluation. Conclusions and future work topics are presented in Section 6.

2   Experimental Testbed

In order to evaluate the Linux Traffic Control modules in the support of the Integrated Services model a Ethernet testbed was built with two end-hosts (Sender and Receiver) interconnected through three serially interconnected routers (Router A, B and C). All routers run the Linux operating system, Red-Hat 5.2, kernel 2.2.8, with RSVP installed. The Linux Traffic Control modules were installed and configured in the kernel of the routers to support RSVP operation.

The link between the Router A (the router next to the sender) and Router B was configured to operate at 10 Mbps to create a congestion bottleneck. All the other links were configured at 100 Mbps.

The Class-Based Queuing service discipline was activated and configured on the output interfaces of all routers. The link-sharing structure configured such the total capacity of the link was distributed as follows: 45% of bandwidth was allocated to best-effort traffic, 5% to RSVP control messages and 50% to IntServ GS flows. With this setup several combinations of data flows of GS and best-effort flows where generated. Best-effort traffic was generated with the *mgen* tool. For GS traffic flow generation the Chariot tool was used.

During the experiments, a number of parameters were measured and analysed to achieve insight on the service provided by routers. These parameters included: queuing delay, loss rate and bandwidth (parameters that reflect the characteristics of GS) and also queue lengths, number of queued packets and number of reclassified packets. To capture these parameters, a number of tools were used including *ttt* (Tele Traffic Taper) and an improved version of *tc* (Linux Traffic Control configuration tool). The Linux kernel was modified to enable the measurement of maximum and average packet queuing delays. The measures were taken in the router where the bottleneck was created (Router A), since the other routers of the testbed are connected at 100 Mbps and all traffic, including best-effort traffic, is forwarded without significant delays or losses.

After the preliminary validation tests, three different set of experiments were done. The first set aimed at the evaluation of the performance of the service provided to flows under different traffic loads. The second set was dedicated to scalability evaluation. The capability of routers to provide the required level of service for a variable and large number of flows was evaluated. Finally, the third group of testes had the objective of stability evaluation.

In the next sections the results of the experimental evaluation done are described. Some previous results of this study are included in references [5, 6].

3   Performance Evaluation

The main objective of this test set is the performance evaluation of the Linux Traffic Control provision of GS. This evaluation was done for different traffic loads, when all guaranteed flows were conforming with traffic specification and also when some guaranteed flows were non-conforming to this specification. The performance of network resources usage was also evaluated.

In all tests 4 GS flows were generated with a reserved bandwidth of 0,5 Mbps each. In the tests with non-conforming flows, the last three flows where the non-conforming. A reclassified traffic class was created to accommodate non-conformant reclassified GS traffic. The total load generated in each test was a combination of GS flow traffic and best-effort traffic to induce congestion.

A total load in the range from a small to a large percentage of the capacity of the output interface of Router A (bottleneck capacity) was generated (20% to 200%). Since the load of GS flows remained constant, the best-effort traffic was responsible for the increasing in the network load.

The analysis of the results shows that GS flows didn't suffer losses, even under high loads (Fig 1). However, best-effort traffic has a considerably different behaviour since they don't suffer losses until congestion occurs, around 90% of bottleneck capacity. After this value, the percentage of best-effort dropped packets raises significantly and increasingly, with the level of congestion in the router.

The analysis of Fig. 1 also shows that conforming and non-conforming GS have a different behaviour. Even though, non-conforming flows violate the established agreement, these flows don't suffer losses until congestion occurs. This is due to the fact that non-conformant traffic is not immediately dropped but is reclassified to a lower priority class (Reclassified Class). When congestion starts, the amount of dropped packets from non-conforming flows rises significantly until best-effort traffic begins to loose packets. It can be concluded that best-effort traffic is warmed with the presence of non-conforming GS flows.

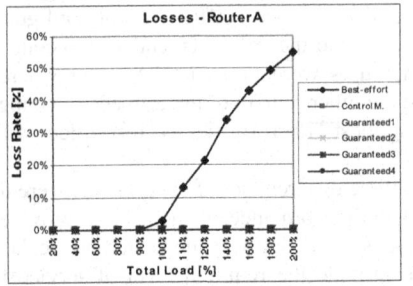 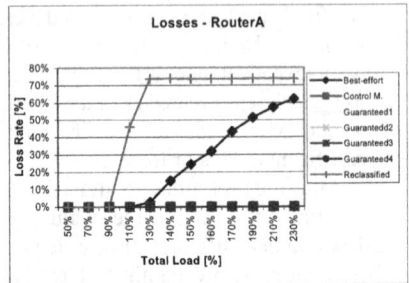

Fig. 1. Loss rate with conforming (left) and non-conforming (right) flows

The analysis of delay behaviour in Fig. 2 shows that when the router becomes congested, GS flows also suffer a noticeable increase in the maximum queuing delay. After the congestion point is reached and as the load in the router increases, the queuing delay experienced by conforming GS flows remains approximately constant, while the maximum delay experienced by non-conforming GS flows and by best-effort traffic increases significantly.

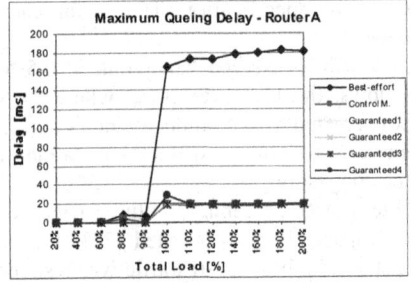 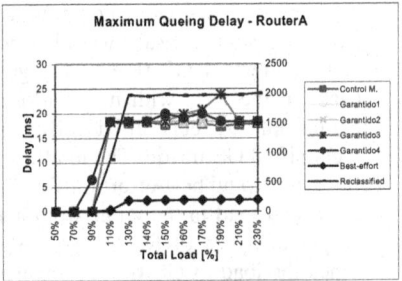

Fig. 2. Maximum queuing delay with conforming (left) and non-conforming (right) flows

From Fig. 2 it can also be concluded that best-effort traffic is warmed by the existence of non-conforming GS flows. The maximum queuing delay and loss rate, experienced by the best-effort traffic is higher when non-conforming flows are present.

The analysis of the tests in this section showed that, under all traffic loads generated, the bandwidth guarantees of GS flows were respected (0,5 Mbps). This commitment was verified even in the presence of non-conforming GS flows.

4 Scalability Evaluation

The deployment of Quality of Service in the Internet requires scalable solutions. In the present section the scalability characteristics of the Linux Traffic Control were evaluated for the support of the IntServ Guarantee Service.

For this purpose, three groups of tests were done with three different packet lengths: 1500 bytes (maximum length supported by Ethernet networks), 256 bytes (intermediate length) and 64 bytes (small length). In each test group a constant load of 10 Mbps was generated into the network while the number of active flows was changed. The maximum number of GS flows used in the experimentation was 15. This limit is imposed by the Linux Traffic Control implementation. Tests were carried out with 4, 6, 8, 10, 12 and 14 GS flows. All the flows (best-effort and GS) were generated with UDP traffic. The total reservation didn't exceed 50% of total link bandwidth (5 Mbps). The evaluation was based on the behaviour of GS flows in the presence of best-effort traffic.

Different bandwidth reservations have made to each GS flow to make the analysis of results easier: the reservations were made from 0,11 Mbps to 0,52 Mbps, with 0,03 Mbps intervals (with the exception of the last flow that was limited by the admission control functions).

4.1 Tests with 1500 Bytes Packets

The results of the tests with 1500 byte packets (Fig. 3) show that GS flows didn't experience losses, even for a large number flows. The Linux implementation of GS satisfies the commitment of providing a service without losses for these test specifications.

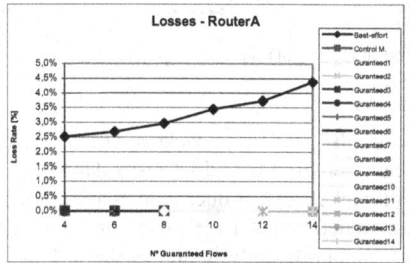 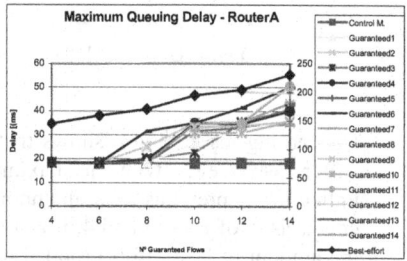

Fig. 3. Loss rate (left) and queuing delay (right) with 1500 byte packets

Concerning loss, the left side of Fig. 3 shows that, as the number of GS flows increased the percentage of dropped best-effort packets rose significantly. This was due to the fact that the lower priority flows are only served after the higher priority ones. In this case, the scheduler will spend more time processing high priority flows, degrading the performance of best-effort traffic.

The right side of Fig. 3 shows that the maximum queuing delay experienced by the guaranteed flows increases with the number of GS flows (left axis), causing service degradation. Best-effort traffic (right axis) performance was also damaged with the presence of a higher number of GS flows. This fact is even more significant because the degradation occurs for small loads of best-effort traffic. This behaviour is due to the fact that with more high priority flows the scheduler spends less time processing packets from the best-effort queue, and this traffic is delayed even for lower loads.

The bandwidth guarantees provided were also evaluated according to the test conditions described. It was verified that with a larger number of GS flows some of these didn't received the bandwidth that was previously reserved. Although the bandwidth commitment wasn't satisfied, the difference was not relevant and loses didn't occur.

4.2   Tests with 256 Bytes Packets

Since the applications with GS requirements normally generate small packets (e.g. audio and real time video), the impact of packet length in the behaviour of GS and best-effort flows was evaluated. The tests in the previous section were repeated using 256 bytes packets for GS flows and keeping 1500 bytes packets to best-effort flows. The results are shown in Fig. 4.

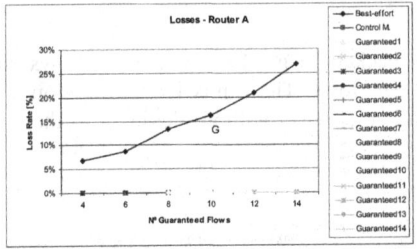 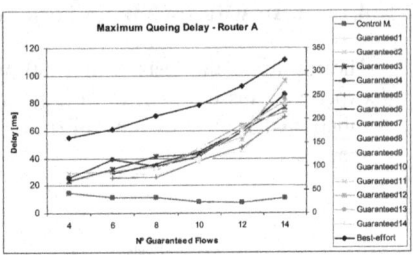

Fig. 4. Loss rate (left) and queuing delay (right) with 256 byte packets

Concerning losses, Fig 4 shows that, like with 1500 bytes packets, GS flows didn't suffer losses, even with the maximum number of flows (14 flows). However, and unlike in the previous tests, the number of packets in GS queues increased. Form the comparison of Figs. 3 and 4, it can be concluded that, for the same number of flows, the amount of best-effort dropped packets is significantly higher in the test with GS flows 256 bytes packets.

Regarding the maximum queuing delay, the right side of Fig. 4 shows an increase in delay experienced by all guaranteed flows and also by best-effort traffic. This fact is more evident with a larger number of GS flows.

Concerning throughput, once more it was verified, that with a high number of GS flows some of theses flows didn't received the bandwidth that was previously reserved. A higher number of GS packets, even while the load was kept constant, imposed a larger computational processing overhead on the real time scheduler.

4.3   Tests with 64 Bytes Packets

In the previous tests, GS QoS requirements were globally satisfied, although it was already noticeable that the degradation increased with the number of flows and with the reduction in the packet size. So, it is somewhat predictable that, for small packet sizes, GS flows requirements can no longer be satisfied by the Linux Traffic Control implementation. To verify this assumption, the tests were repeated once more with 64 bytes packets GS flows. The results are shown in Figs. 5 and 6.

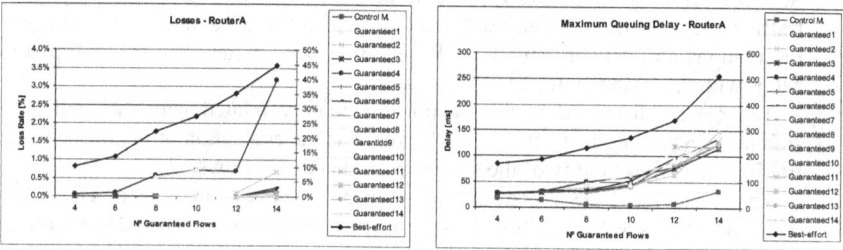

Fig. 5. Loss rate (left) and queuing delay (right) with 64 byte packets

The analysis of the results (Fig. 5) confirms the failure of the Linux Traffic Control implementation to support the requirements of a high number of GS flows with small packet sizes.

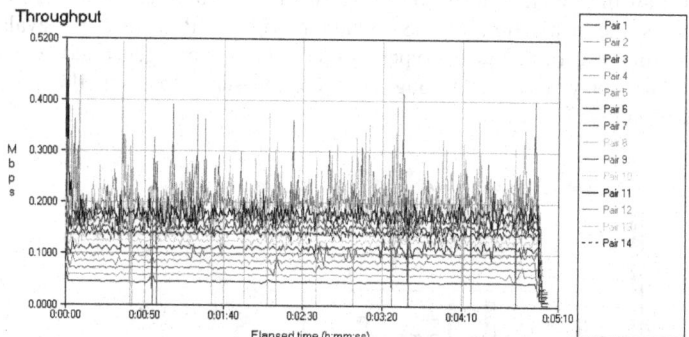

Fig. 6. Throughput of GS flows of 64 bytes packets

Like in the tests with larger packets (1500 and 256 bytes), the maximum queuing delay experienced by GS and best-effort flows increased significantly with the number of active GS flows, even when the total load was kept constant. However, and unlike the tests discussed before, some GS flows experienced losses in the tests with a high number of flows. It is also interesting to notice that GS flows with more losses were the flows with larger reservations.

The guarantees concerning bandwidth were also evaluated in this test (Fig. 6) and it was verified that flows didn't receive the bandwidth that was reserved.

To conclude the results of the tests in this section shown that the Linux Traffic Control IntServ implementation doesn't support GS loss and bandwidth requirements and doesn't scale with the number of flows for small packet sizes.

5   Stability Evaluation

The stability evaluation of the Linux IntServ implementation support of Guaranteed Service was done considering the parameters that can induce instability, namely: traffic mix, presence of Controlled Load traffic, bandwidth assignment to classes with reservations and network structure. Reservation were made from 0,11 Mbps to 0,52 Mbps with 0,03 Mbps intervals.

The results discussed in this section are mainly related with the evaluation of stability concerning the traffic mix. The aim was the evaluation of the influence of the traffic type in the stability of the service provided to GS flows.

The behaviour of GS was evaluated under different combinations of TCP-TCP and TCP-UDP flows in competition for the same router resources. The configuration with 14 GS flows of 64 bytes packets was chosen because previous tests showed that this was the most demanding configuration.

5.1   Tests with TCP Traffic Only

Since all the previous tests were done with UDP, the main objective of the present tests is the evaluation of GS behavior with TCP traffic. To evaluate stability behaviour regarding traffic types, 14 GS flows were generated with TCP traffic. Queuing delay, loss and throughput were measured for each flow. The results are shown in Fig. 7.

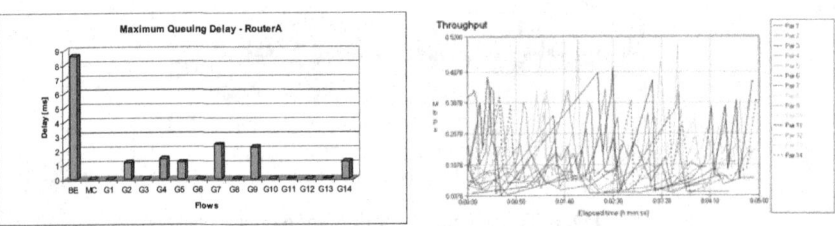

Fig. 7. Maximum queuing delays (left) and throughput (right) with TCP traffic

The analysis of queue sizes revealed that, due to the effect of TCP flow control, queues were empty most of the times and the scheduler didn't use it's ability to differentiate between different flows. These results show that TCP flow control mechanisms hinder IntServ Traffic Control modules to operate correctly. The results also show that the bandwidth provided to GS flows was protected from best-effort flows. Nevertheless this protection, the differences among GS flows were significant due to the TCP congestion control mechanisms.

5.2   Tests with TCP and UDP Traffic

The behaviour of Guaranteed Service flows with UDP and TCP traffic was also evaluated with TCP traffic on odd flows and UDP traffic on even flows. The results are shown in Figs. 8 and 9.

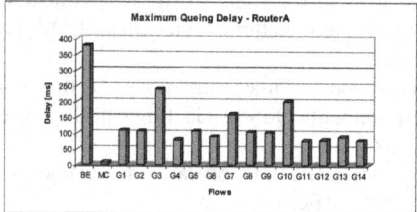 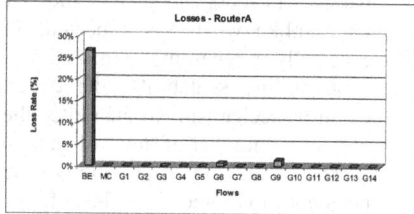

Fig. 8. Queuing delay (left) and loss (right) of TCP (odd) and UDP (even) flows

The analysis of Fig. 8 shows that queuing delays experienced by TCP and UDP flows were not significantly different. As stated before, and also in this case, the implementation was unable to provide service differentiation, independently of the traffic type. Regarding losses the difference between UDP and TCP flows was not noticeable.

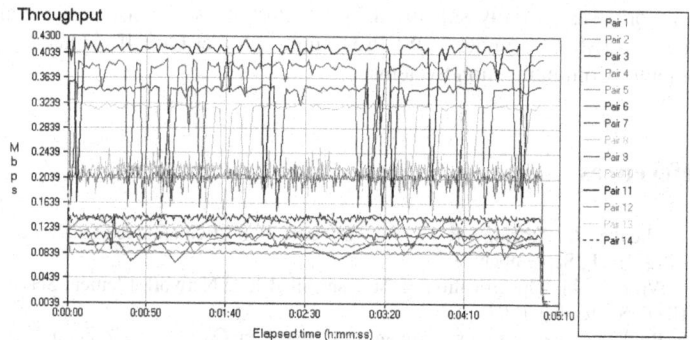

Fig. 9. Throughput of TCP (odd) and UDP (even) flows

Given the different characteristic of TCP and UDP traffic it seamed obvious that the UDP flows should get the major part of system resources. That is, due to the adaptive characteristics of TCP flows, the resources not used by TCP traffic should be used by UDP flows. However, the results shown that TCP flows got better service regarding bandwidth (Fig. 9). This behaviour was unexpected and can be attributed to the Linux Traffic Control IntServ scheduler configuration to protect TCP flows when in the presence of UDP traffic.

6   Conclusions and Future Work

In this paper an evaluation of the Linux Traffic Control implementation of the IntServ Guaranteed Service support was made. The evaluation addressed performance, scalability and stability issues.

Concerning performance, the implementation was able to control of GS QoS parameters independently of the state of load in the routers. The results also show that, unlike what was expected, TCP flows got better service than UDP flows, especially in regarding to throughput.

Regarding scalability, the experiments show some limitations of the Traffic Control mechanisms to guarantee the requirements QoS of GS flows in the presence of a larger number of flows of small packets.

The evaluation of stability regarding the traffic mix revealed some unexpected behaviour to protect TCP flows from of UDP traffic.

The experiments reported in this paper were conducted on a relatively small testbed and at low line speeds. From the identified limitations it can be induced that the implementation under study suffers from scalability problems when used in wider scenarios at high speed. Future work will address the evaluation of Guaranteed Service in WAN scenarios and the integration of IntServ with a DiffServ networks.

Acknowledgements

This work was partially supported by the Portuguese Ministry of Science and High Education (MCES), under POSI Programme project QoS II – Quality of Service in Computer Communication Systems.

References

1. S. Shenker, C. Partridge, R. Guérin, "Specification of Guaranteed Quality of Service", RFC 2212, IETF, September 1997.
2. J. Wroclawski, "Specification of the Controlled-load Network Element Service", RFC 2211, IETF, September 1997.
3. S. Radhakrishnan , "Linux – Advanced Networking Overview – Version1", August 1999.
4. S. Floyd, M. Speer, "Experimental Results for Class-Based Queueing", September 1998, not published.
5. E. Reis, F. Melo, M. Oliveira, G. Quadros, E. Monteiro, "Quality of Service on the Internet: Evaluation of the IntServ Architecture on the Linux Operating System", Proceedings of the 3rd Conference on Telecommunications (ConfTele2001), Figueira da Foz, 22-23 de Abril, 2001.
6. E. Reis, E. Monteiro, "Estudo da Escalabilidade da Implementação do Modelo IntServ em Linux", Proceedings of the 5th Conferência sobre Redes de Computadores - Tecnologias e Aplicações (CRC'2002), FCCN, Universidade do Algarve, Faro, Portugal, 26-27 Setembro, 2002.

End-to-End QoS Mapping in IntServ-over-DiffServ Architectures

Zoubir Mammeri

IRIT – Paul Sabatier University
118 route de Narbonne
31062 Toulouse, France
mammeri@irit.fr

Abstract. With numerous emerging real-time and multimedia applications, there has been much interest for developing mechanisms which enable real-time services over the Internet with guaranteed QoS. One of the promising configurations to support real-time traffics is by combining capabilities of IntServ and DiffServ architectures. However, guaranteeing end-to-end QoS over such architectures -generally composed of chains of multiple independently administered IntServ and DiffServ domains- requires the deployment of several mechanisms and many untaken steps remain on the road to achieving this. In particular, multiple domains may consider different QoS parameters and/or manage them differently. In this paper, we deal with the problem of mapping QoS parameters -particularly the bandwidth and delay requirements- to support hard real-time communications.

1 Introduction

The Internet has traditionally provided support for best effort traffic only. However, with numerous emerging real-time and multimedia applications such as video conferencing, there has been much interest for developing mechanisms which enable real-time services over the Internet. In addition, real-time and multimedia applications require more sophisticated management of those system components, which affect the Quality of Service (QoS) delivered to the users, than for data-only systems. The underlying concepts of bandwidth, throughput, delay, jitter, reliability, perceived quality and cost are the foundations of what is known as QoS [1].

Management of QoS includes various aspects, relating to the nature of perceived quality. To meet QoS requirements, all components of a service must work correctly. Currently, there are many solutions for network management to manage network elements and for systems management to manage hardware and software elements on which a service depends. These solutions are adept at offering views into the network or system, but do not offer a common view of the end-to-end application. From a technical perspective, the central QoS issue is the provision of predictable and coordinated access to system resources, encompassing the endsystems and the network. Work related to the provision of QoS guarantees has dealt with various types of networks, particularly with ATM, IP and local area networks. This paper focuses on IP (Internet). Work on QoS-enabled IP networks has led to two distinct approaches: the Integrated Services architecture (IntServ) [2] and its accompanying

M.M. Freire, P. Lorenz, M.M.-O. Lee (Eds.): HSNMC 2003, LNCS 2720, pp. 31–40, 2003.

signaling protocol, RSVP [3], and the Differentiated Services architecture (DiffServ) [4]. One potential picture for next generation Internet is that end-users (hosts) are connected to IntServ networks and IntServ networks are interconnected by DiffServ networks. A DiffServ region is a set of contiguous DiffServ domains which can offer differentiated services. Service Level Agreements (SLAs) are fixed between IntServ and DiffServ networks and between DiffServ networks in a same region.

From the end-user's point of view, QoS should be supported end-to-end between any pair of hosts. However, this goal is not immediately attainable in the context of IntServ over DiffServ. It will require interdomain QoS support, and many untaken steps remain on the road to achieving this. At least, there are two essential steps, the interoperation between IntServ and DiffServ architectures [5], and the cooperation between independent DiffServ networks to provide QoS guarantees. The problem of providing QoS in an efficient manner is a complex one, involving multiple inter-related aspects, including QoS specification, QoS mapping, resource provisioning, call admission control, traffic policing, routing, scheduling, and pricing. Great strides have been made in the past few years and in recent progress in defining QoS-enabled architectures for the Internet by the IETF. In this paper, we focus on QoS mapping.

Distributed multimedia and real-time applications require end-to-end QoS guarantees for their flows. However, the expression of QoS is different from level to level. Therefore, mapping which translates the QoS parameters from level to level is required. In this paper we focus on QoS mapping related to ways in which DiffServ networks can be used in the context of the IntServ architecture to support the delivery of end-to-end QoS. When QoS mapping is considered many (yet unanswered) questions arise for end-users and for the Internet service providers [6]:
- How to map application specific service agreements to specify differentiated services based on QoS requirements?
- Given a QoS specification, how to monitor QoS at different levels: end-user level, application level, system level, network level?
- Given an end-user SLA, how to map that SLA to parameter values at different levels (e.g., how would a particular response time map to network level congestions)?
- Internet is composed of multiple independently administered domains (autonomous systems). How to map QoS requirements of a domain onto those of another one?
- One domain may guarantee some type of QoS (e.g., bandwidth) and another one guarantees another QoS type (e.g., delay). In this context, how to map QoS requirements to guarantee end-to-end QoS?
- How to map QoS requirements on DiffServ codepoints?

Our aim in this paper is to bring some answers to the previous questions. The stress is mainly laid on the mappings between user QoS requirements, SLAs and DiffServ codepoints. We focus on two QoS parameters, bandwidth and delay, in the context of hard real-time applications (i.e., applications that require strict guarantees of QoS). The rest of the paper is structured as follows. In section 2, we review the main work related to QoS in the Internet. In section 3, we present a generic model to characterize, from a QoS point of view, the components of QoS-aware communication paths over IntServ and DiffServ domains. In section 4, mapping of QoS parameters is developed. Section 5 gives some conclusions and perspectives.

2   Background and Related Work

2.1   Integrated Services Architecture and RSVP

The Integrated services (IntServ) architecture [2] defined the models for expressing service types, quantifying resource requirements and for determining the availability of the requested resources at relevant network elements. The IntServ architecture assumes that some explicit setup mechanism is used to convey information to routers so that they can provide requested services to individual flows that require them. While RSVP (ReSerVation Protocol) [3] is the most widely known example of such a setup mechanism, the IntServ architecture is designed to accommodate other mechanisms. IntServ/RSVP model has the advantage that it can guarantee QoS based on a quantitative specification of resource requirements. In this model, RSVP signals per-flow resource requirements to network elements, using IntServ parameters. These network elements apply IntServ admission control to signaled requests. In addition, traffic control mechanisms on the network elements are configured to ensure that each admitted flow receives the service requested in strict isolation from other traffic. Every intermediate router being aware of the RSVP has to maintain traffic handling state for each traffic flow reserved, which results in overload to the routers. These requirements cause scalability problem for deploying IntServ/RSVP model. IntServ model can support controlled-load service [7] and guaranteed service [8] as well as the best effort service. Guaranteed service provides delay-bounded service agreements for real-time applications requiring severe delay constraints. Controlled load service provides a form of statistical delay service agreement.

2.2   DiffServ Architecture and Service Level Agreements

In contrast to the per-flow orientation of IntServ, DiffServ networks classify packets into one or a small number of aggregated flows or classes, based on the DiffServ codepoint (DSCP) in the packet's IP header [4]. At each DiffServ router, packets are subjected to a per-hop behavior (PHB) treatment, which is invoked by the DSCP. Packets with the same DSCP get the same per-hop forwarding treatment (or PHB) everywhere inside a single DiffServ domain. DiffServ eliminates the need for per-flow state and per-flow processing and therefore scales well to large networks. However, DiffServ provides QoS not based on a quantitative specification of resource requirements. In DiffServ, traffic flows having similar QoS requirements are marked with the same DSCP value, thus aggregated into a flow having a common PHB that provides the same level of QoS. Therefore, the QoS enjoyed by each flow is dependent on the behavior of the other aggregated flows. At present, two PHB groups have been defined by IETF: Assured Forwarding (AF) PHB group and Expedited Forwarding (EF) PHB group. The AF PHB group is a means for a provider DiffServ domain to offer different levels of forwarding assurances for IP packets [9]. The EF PHB group can be used to build a low loss, low latency, low jitter, assured bandwidth, end-to-end service through DiffServ domains [10].

Two types of routers are distinguished in a DiffServ domain: boundary (or edge) and core (or interior) routers. Boundary routers in a DiffServ network classify each transmitted packet and mark with an appropriate DSCP value the IP header of the packet based on the results of the classification. Core routers process and forward the packet based on the DSCP value and the predetermined SLA. The IETF [11] introduced the term "per-domain behavior" (PDB) to describe the behavior experienced by a particular set of packets as they cross a DiffServ domain. A PDB is characterized by specific metrics that quantify the treatment a set of packets with a particular DSCP will receive as it crosses a DiffServ domain. This abstraction level makes it easier to compose cross-domain services.

A *Service level agreements* (SLA) is defined as a contract between the service provider and the customer that specifies the QoS level that can be expected. It includes the expected behavior of the service and the parameters for QoS [12]. At present, SLA based services are static, manually set up, have medium to long-term lead-times and are usually provided over a single network domain. There are a number of parameters used today in SLAs. These parameters include: timeliness (delay, jitter, round-trip delay), bandwidth, service availability/reliability, customer support, and legal issues (penalties, contract cancellation,...). Given the SLAs, ISPs must decide how to configure their boundary routers so that they know how to handle the incoming traffics. This process is called resource allocation. The efficient management of SLAs is a new challenge and very important issue in Internet service management. Research issues on SLA are mainly related to SLA parameter definition, SLA measurement, SLA compliance report, and QoS management [13, 14].

IntServ and DiffServ architectures are independent each other. However, these architectures may be combined. The goal is to combine their respective benefits such as supporting end-to-end QoS in IntServ/RSVP and good scalability in DiffServ. Therefore, a framework for interoperation between IntServ/RSVP and DiffServ has been proposed by IETF [5]. RSVP messages in the framework can be transmitted from a host to another via a DiffServ network. There are edge routers (ER) and boundary routers (BR) located at the border between the IntServ/RSVP network and the DiffServ network, and their functions are determined based on whether the DiffServ network are aware of RSVP or not. One picture of the future Internet is that hosts (end-users) will be connected to IntServ networks which are connected via DiffServ networks. In this case, IntServ network is considered as an access network.

2.3   QoS Mapping

Many components (such as hosts, protocol stacks of intermediates routers, operating systems) cooperate to provide end-to-end QoS guarantees to end-users. End-users specify their QoS requirements at application level. In the networks, each layer in the protocol stacks may offer its own version of QoS guarantees. Furthermore, different QoS guarantees may be provided at each intermediate sub-network or domain. It is therefore important to map QoS parameters from one level to another. The role of QoS mapping can be looked at from many distinct, but related, viewpoints [15]: between two QoS-enabled protocol layers, between two domains, between two regions, between aggregated flows, etc. There are some papers that deal with mapping from application performance to network parameters. [6] provided a statistical analysis on mapping application level response time to network related parameters by using some queuing models. [16] presented a methodology to graphically characterize the response time. [15] presented a framework to be used to predict end-to-end QoS at the application layer based on mapping of QoS guarantees across layers in the protocol stack and concatenation of guarantees across multiple sub-networks. [17] proposed a translator that maps QoS parameters between IntServ/RSVP and DiffServ. [18] proposed a framework for studying the end-to-end packet loss mapping between the various layers of the transport protocol stack in ATM networks. [19] considered the transmission path of video-on-demand traffic behavior aggregate through the DiffServ domain, and proposed a (stochastic) method to compute the parameters of EF PHB. [20] described mappings of Integrated services over LANs built from IEEE 802 network segments. [21] proposed a framework for supporting Integrated services on shared and switched LAN infrastructure. [22] described an architecture for providing integrated services over low-bitrate links. [23] proposed a framework for mapping end-to-end RSVP reservations onto aggregate reservations.

3   Generic Network Model for QoS Analysis

3.1   Internetworking Model and SLA Specification

In the internetworking model we consider in this paper, the end-users (hosts) are connected to IntServ routers, and there may be one or many DiffServ domains on the path between the sender and the receiver of a flow. We believe that these path configurations may be the case in the next generation Internet. For any data flow, the access network of the flow sender is called *sender IntServ domain* and the access network of the flow receiver is called *receiver IntServ domain*.

To be able to manage and guarantee end-to-end QoS on paths (possibly) crossing several DiffServ domains, some information related to the global structure of interconnection of the domains and the SLAs between these domains is necessary to be known at different points of the communication paths. Not all the communication components (routers) need to know all the SLAs. Only partial views of service level specifications are required to select paths between senders and receivers. Each SLA s between a couple of boundary routers is specified by a $QoS(s)$ 3-tuple which contains three components: the guaranteed bandwidth, the guaranteed deadline, and the guarantee quality, which is equal to "firm guarantee" without any other rule, because we only deal with hard real-time communications. Notice that other QoS parameters (such as jitter and loss rate) may be added to extend our model.

Let f be a flow whose sender is connected to IntServ domain ISD_s and receiver to another IntServ domain ISD_r. The domains ISD_s and ISD_r are interconnected via a DiffServ region. Some routing protocols are used to determine the path for each flow. It should be noticed that routing is an important issue for QoS-aware architectures, but it is out of the scope of this paper. In this context, each flow f may be specified by [24-26]: traffic specification parameters (maximum transmission unit, token bucket rate, token bucket size, maximum transmission rate), and QoS requirements denoted by a QoS vector $E2E\_QoS_f$ (bandwidth, end-to-end transfer delay).

3.2   Characterization of Path Components

● **IntServ domain characterization**. Each of the two correspondents, the sender and receiver of a flow, is connected to an IntServ domain. The first step of communication is the connection establishment during which a QoS-aware routing protocol is used to select a path. Such a protocol uses information associated with topologies and SLAs of (probably) many domains. The QoS requirements of the sender are propagated hop by hop inside the two IntServ domains. To support hard real-time communications, the implementations of routers inside an IntServ domain must be compliant with the Guaranteed service specification [8]. The sender and receiver IntServ domains take part in providing QoS guarantees for individual flows. We denote by $QoS(ISD_s^f)$, $QoS(ISD_r^f)$ and $QoS(DSR^f)$ the QoS participation of sender IntServ domain, receiver IntServ domain and DiffServ region respectively in providing QoS guarantees for a flow f. The 'sum' (or concatenation) of QoS parts must meet the end-to-end QoS requirements of the flow f. This condition may be formalized by:

$$E2E\_QoS^f \langle\ Concatenation(QoS(ISD_s^f),\ QoS(DSR^f),\ QoS(ISD_r^f))$$

where '$\langle$' means '$\leq$' when bandwidth is considered and '$\geq$' for delay, and *Concatenation* means combining parts of QoS provided by a set of components.

● **DiffServ domain characterization**. With DiffServ architecture, QoS management is realized using supervision and control functions necessary to ensure that the desired QoS properties are attained and sustained. These functions may have different implementations according to QoS requirements to guarantee and according to network policy. Details of these functions are given in [27] who proposed a generic model of DiffServ routers for use in their management and configuration. Composing function implementations yields various types of PHBs. A router may be seen as a 'black box' which provides a given PHB to a DiffServ codepoint or to a group of DiffServ codepoints. As stated in [11], the combination of PHBs of different routers inside a DiffServ domain provides some Per Domain Behavior (PDB) to each DiffServ codepoint (or to each group of DiffServ codepoints).

To carry an analysis of end-to-end QoS guaranteeing, two different levels of abstraction may be used: PHB-based analysis and PDB-based analysis. In the PHB-based analysis, the guarantees provided by each router on path are combined and analyzed to check if end-to-end QoS guarantees may be provided. This type of analysis is fine, but it requires that the PHBs provided by all routers must be known. However, this knowledge requirement is either undesirable (because it limits the actions undertaken by IPSs to configure and accommodate their networks) or impossible (for security considerations or others). Generally, the interior structure and behavior of a DiffServ domain are hidden for its customers. In consequence, the analysis of end-to-end QoS guarantees should be PDB-based. Thereafter, we consider a DiffServ domain as a 'black box' which provides PDBs capable of supporting some SLAs. Each PDB p is defined by a $QoS(p)$ which has two components, the bandwidth and the delay it provides.

For each DiffServ domain, a management and configuration function, denoted by *BDPtoDSCP*, associates each PDB with DiffServ codepoint group. To provide the QoS guarantees required by its clients, a DiffServ domain should determine which

DSCP should be used for which SLA. Another function, denoted by *DSCPtoSLA*, must be used by DiffServ domains to assign the DSCPs to SLAs. Mapping PDB onto DSCPs and DSCPs onto SLAs is policy-dependent.

● **DiffServ region characterization**. When DiffServ domains form a DiffServ region they cooperate to provide QoS guarantees along the region. The egress routers of IntServ domains do not know the structure of the region they use. Each IntServ egress router knows only the DiffServ domains with which it has SLAs. The current IETF's definition of SLA and QoS guarantees apply only to individual DiffServ domains, i.e., that the SLA contracted with a DiffServ domain means that the client will be provided QoS guarantees when its packets traverse the domain, but nothing is said on the QoS guarantees when the packets leave the considered DiffServ domain and enter another one. Recall that the IETF introduced two levels of behavior: Per Hop Behavior and Per Domain Behavior. We introduce a third level of behavior: Per Region Behavior (PRB) that specifies the treatment packets receive along a whole DiffServ region. Multiple DiffServ domains cooperate to provide PRBs. Each DiffServ domain must (partially) know the information related to SLAs in its region in order to be able to select DiffServ domains to support packets that have been marked with some codepoint at the entrance of the DiffServ region. Packets marked with a DSCP equal to c at the entrance of the DiffServ region travel over a chain of DiffServ domains. The intermediate DiffServ domains may eventually remark the packets c-marked at the region entrance under the condition that the treatment associated with the new DSCP must be at least equal to the one 'promised' or contracted at the entrance of the region. As previously mentioned, the concept of QoS and SLA refers to separate DiffServ domains. To provide clients with capabilities providing them with QoS guarantees beyond the DiffServ domain to which their IntServ domain is connected, and thus to reach host destinations everywhere, we propose to define two levels of SLAs: D-SLAs providing QoS guarantees by individual DiffServ domains, and R-SLA providing QoS guarantees over a DiffServ region as a whole. These two levels of SLAs resemble the services known in the traditional telephone network that enables subscribers to have local access, national access and international access.

4   Mapping QoS Parameters

Mappings are made at the border between IntServ and DiffServ domains and between DiffServ domains. In the packet forwarding path, differentiated services are realized by mapping the DSCP contained in the IP packet header to a particular forwarding treatment (PHB), at each network node along its path. Generally, the DSCP may be chosen from a set of mandatory values from a set of recommended values defined in standards, or may have purely local meaning. The first level of mapping is from IntServ classes to DiffServ classes. One of the most accepted mappings is as follows:
- IntServ Guaranteed Service is mapped onto DiffServ Assured Forwarding.
- IntServ Controlled load is mapped onto Expedited Forwarding.
- IntServ Best effort is mapped onto DiffServ best effort.

In our context, only hard real-time flows are considered, so flows receive Guaranteed service in IntServ domains and Assured Forwarding service in DiffServ domains. Assured Forwarding (AF) PHB group [9] defined four AF classes. Within each AF class, packets are marked with one of three possible drop precedence values. In case of congestion, the drop precedence determines the relative importance of the packet within the AF class. The recommended values of the AF codepoints are given in [9].

4.1   DSCP Assignment at the Border IntServ-DiffServ

In general, a newly arriving flow might be assigned to a number of classes. For example, if 100 ms of delay is acceptable, the flow could potentially be assigned to either a 100 ms delay class or a 50 ms delay class. One important question is: of the appropriate traffic classes, which if any have enough capacity available to accept the new flow? In this paper we deal only with hard real-time communications. In consequence, among the existing classes only the ones which provide Assured Forwarding with low drop precedence may be considered. As mentioned previously, DSCPs may be assigned by the DiffServ boundary routers or by the customers. We assume here that DiffServ domains allocate (reserve) sets of DiffServ codepoints (according to the contracted SLAs) to their customers. Thus IntServ egress routers are in charge of assigning DSCPs to flows according to their QoS requirements. The DSCP assignment to flow is policy-dependent and takes into account several aspects and optimization criteria: existing SLAs and their parameters, available DiffServ codepoints, flows currently associated with each codepoint, addresses of flow receivers, available QoS-aware paths, and policy criteria. Many approaches may be used to map flow's QoS requirements onto les DiffServ codepoints:

1) One-to-one assignment: one DSCP is assigned to each individual flow. It is the simplest approach. Unfortunately, this approach cannot be used when the number of flows managed by the egress router is high because the number of codepoints that can be used to obtain assured service is (very) limited.

2) One-to-many assignment: one DSCP is assigned to a group of flows taking into account various considerations: only flows with the same QoS requirements and traffic parameters are aggregated, only flows with the same QoS parameters are aggregated, only flows with similar QoS requirements are aggregated, optimize the number of flows related to each DSCP,... It should be noticed that flow aggregation is an important aspect to consider when using DiffServ domains, because the DiffServ architecture is not really effective for supporting only individual flows.

3) Many-to-one assignment: when multiple SLAs are fixed between an IntServ egress router and a DiffServ domain, the egress router may use several DSCPs for the same flow. For example, if the bandwidth required by a flow is 10 Mb/s, and there two 5 Mb/s SLAs. In this case (which should be rare in practice), the egress router has in charge the dispatching (marking) of the packets from the same flow on 'virtual channels' associated with the chosen DSCPs.

4) Many-to-many assignment: when multiple SLAs are fixed, the ingress router may aggregate a set of flows and it uses two or many DSCPs to mark the packets of these flows. As in the previous technique, the egress router is in charge of dispatching and marking the packets.

It is worth noticing that the QoS mapping problem is quite difficult to solve if the target parameters of the traffics are allowed to change dynamically as flows arrive and depart. It is quite simple if the target parameters of each flow are held fixed.

4.2 DSCP Mapping in DiffServ Domains and DiffServ Region

• **DSCP mapping inside each DiffServ domain**. The SLA may specify packet classification and re-marking rules and may also specify traffic profiles and actions to traffic flows which are in-profile or out-of-profile. The most important points for mapping packets are the boundary routers. Generally, conforming packets are not remarked by interior routers. If a conforming packet is remarked by an interior router, the new (chosen) DSCP must be such that the packet will receive a treatment at least with QoS equivalent to one received by using the previous DSCP. Non-conforming packets are remarked to receive 'lower' QoS or to be discarded. When a real-time is well-behaving, its packets are conforming (except in exceptional cases).

• **Mapping inside a DiffServ region**. Neighbour DiffServ domains must share common knowledge on the assignment of DSCPs. If a DSCP C_i leaving DiffServ domain i is mapped onto DSCP C_j of domain j, the common knowledge must satisfy the condition "QoS provided by domain j to packets marked with DSCP C_j must be at least equal to one provided by domain i to packets marked with DSCP C_i". DiffServ domains belonging to the same region have various manners to manage DSCPs and to share the common information related to the QoS associated with these DSCPs.

5   Conclusions

One of the promising networking architectures to deliver QoS guarantees in the next future Internet is the one based on combining the capabilities of IntServ and DiffServ architectures. However, providing end-to-end QoS guarantees over the Internet is a complex task which requires the deployment of many activities and cooperation between independently administered domains. One important activity is the mapping between user QoS parameters and Internet parameters. In this paper, we studied the problem of mapping between user QoS requirements, SLAs and DiffServ codepoints. We proposed a general framework for the analysis of QoS mapping based on three levels: per hop behavior, per domain behavior and per region behavior. Our work must be continued and extended according to multiple directions: 1) integration of QoS parameters such as jitter and loss rate, 2) our mapping is static and some dynamic aspects should be considered to enforce the reactions to network changes, 3) extend the model to deal with soft real-time communications, 4) handling multicast flows, 5) proposal of a methodology to guide QoS mapping, and finally 6) validate the mapping model with real experimentation is demanded.

References

1. Aurrecoechea, C., Campbell, A.T., Hauw, L.: A Survey of QoS Architectures. ACM Multimedia Systems Journal, Special Issue on QoS Architecture. **6** (1998) 138-151.
2. Braden, R., et al.: Integrated Services in the Internet Architecture: an overview. RFC 1633 (1994).
3. Braden, R., et al.: Resource ReSerVation Protocol (RSVP). RFC 2205 (1997).
4. Blake, S., et al.: An Architecture for Differentiated Services. RFC 2475 (1998).
5. Bernet, Y., et al.: A Framework for Integrated Services Operation over Diffserv Networks. RFC 2998 (2000).
6. Liu, B.H., Ray, P., Jha, S.: Mapping Distributed Applications SLA to Network QoS Parameters. in Proceed. of Int. Conference on Telecommunication (2003). pp. 1230-1235.
7. Wroclawski, J.: Specification of the Controlled-Load Network Element Service. RFC 2211 (1997).
8. Shenker, S., et al.: Specification of Guaranteed Quality of Service. RFC 2212 (1997).
9. Heinanen, J., et al. : Assured Forwarding PHB Group. RFC 2597 (1999).
10. Jacobson, V., et al.: An Expedited Forwarding PHB. RFC 2598 (1999).
11. Nichols, K., Carpenter, B.: Definition of Differentiated Services Per Domain Behaviors and Rules for their Specification. RFC 3086 (2001).
12. Park, L.T., et al.: Management of Service Level Agreements for Multimedia Internet Service using a Utility Model. IEEE Communications Magazine, **39**-5 (2001) 100-106.
13. Lewis, L., Ray, P.: Service Level Management Definition, Architecture, and Research Challenges. in Proceed. of GlobeCom'99. pp. 174-178.
14. Bouillet, E., Mitra, D., Ramakrishnan, K.G.: The Structure and Management of Service Level Agreements in Networks. IEEE J.S.A.C., **20**-4 (2002) 691-699.
15. DaSilva, L.A.: QoS Mapping along the Protocol Stack: Discussion and Preliminary Results. in Proceed. of IEEE Int. Conference on Communications (2000). pp. 713-717.
16. Tse-Au, E.S.H., Morreale, P.A.: End-to-end QoS Measurement: Analytic Methodology of Application Response Time vs. Tunable Latency in IP Networks. in Proceedings of IEEE/IFIP Network Operations and Management Symposium (2000). pp. 129-142.
17. Lee, E., et al.: A Translator between Integrated Service/RSVP and Differentiated Service for End-to-End QoS. in Proceed. of Int. Conf. on Telecommunication (2003). pp. 1394-01.
18. Huard, J.F., Lazar, A.A.: On End-to-End QoS Mapping. in Proceedings of 5th IFIP International Workshop on Quality of Service (1997). pp. 303-314.
19. Koucheryavy, Y., Moltchanov, D., Harju, J.: An Analytical Evaluation of VoD Traffic Treatment within the EF-enabled DiffServ Ingress and Interior Nodes. in Proceedings of International Conference on Telecommunication (2003). pp. 1458-1464.
20. Seaman, M., et al.: Integrated Service Mappings on IEEE 802 Networks. RFC 2815 (2000).
21. Ghanwani, A., et al.: A Framework for Providing Integrated Services over Shared and Switched LAN Technologies. RFC 2816 (2000).
22. Jackowski, S., et al.: Integrated Services Mappings for Low Speed Networks. RFC 2688 (1999).
23. Baker, F., et al.: Aggregation of RSVP for IPv4 and IPv6 Reservations. RFC 3175 (2001).
24. Partridge, C.: A Proposed Flow Specification. RFC 1363 (1992).
25. Shenker, S., Wroclawski, J.: General Characterization Parameters for Integrated Service Network Elements. RFC 2215 (1997).
26. Shenker, S., et al.: Network Element Service Specification Template. RFC 2216 (1997).
27. Bernet, Y., et al.: An informal management model for DiffServ routers. RFC 3290 (2002).

A RTT-based Partitioning Algorithm for a Multi-rate Reliable Multicast Protocol

Moufida Maimour and Cong-Duc Pham

RESO-INRIA, LIP-ENS
ENS, 46 allée d'Italie 69364 Lyon Cedex 07 - France
{mmaimour,cpham}@ens-lyon.fr

Summary. Various Internet applications involve multiple parties and usually adopt a one-to-many communication paradigm (multicast). The presence of multiple receivers in a multicast session rises the problem of *inter-receiver fairness*. Transmitting with a rate which matches the slowest receiver will limit the throughput of other receivers and thus their *satisfaction*. A multi-rate mechanism where the receivers are distributed into subgroups with similar capacities, can improve the inter-receiver fairness for multicast sessions. In this paper, we deal with the problem of receivers partitioning and propose a simple algorithm based on the receivers RTT variations where an explicit estimation of the receivers capacities is avoided. Our partitioning algorithm, although simple, performs an on-the-fly partitioning depending on the receivers' feedback. We show that our partitioning algorithm approximates and in many cases, achieves the optimal solution with a minimum computation effort.

1 Introduction

Various Internet applications involve multiple parties and usually adopt a one-to-many communication paradigm (multicast). The presence of multiple receivers in a multicast session rises the problem of *inter-receiver fairness*. Transmitting with a rate which matches the slowest receiver will limit the throughput of other receivers and thus their *satisfaction*. A multi-rate mechanism can improve the inter-receiver fairness for multicast sessions. The main advantage of a multi-rate scheme is that receivers with different needs can be served at a rate closer to their needs rather than having to match the speed of the slowest receiver. In a multi-rate session, the multicast source can transmit at different rates to different receivers either through a hierarchical scheme (layering) [1, 6, 7] or a replicated scheme (destination set grouping, DSG) [5]. In layered multicast, each receiver controls the rate at which it receives the data, usually by using multiple multicast groups. The receivers join and leave groups depending on their path congestion state so the amount of data being received is always appropriate. Layering schemes provide more economical bandwidth usage than DSG schemes, however layering is more complicated and requires efficient hierarchical encoding/decoding algorithms and synchronization among different layers.

In both layered and replicated schemes, an explicit or an implicit partitioning of the receivers among subgroups is required. This partitioning is performed so that the receivers satisfaction is maximized. Receivers satisfaction can be quantified using a

M.M. Freire, P. Lorenz, M.M.-O. Lee (Eds.): HSNMC 2003, LNCS 2720, pp. 41–51, 2003.
© Springer-Verlag Berlin Heidelberg 2003

utility function as the ones proposed in [3, 8]. Determining the optimal grouping for a multicast session is a difficult problem. In [5], the authors propose a number of grouping heuristics that are guidelines for a multicast source to make its splitting decisions. The authors in [8] consider the optimal partitioning of receivers into groups for multi-rate schemes. They formulated, for a general class of utility function, the partitioning problem as an optimization problem to maximize the sum of receiver utilities. They present a dynamic programming algorithm to solve the partitioning problem, and proved that the solution it finds is optimal. Both of the previous partitioning algorithms require the knowledge of the isolated[1] rates of the different receivers which are not easily obtained in the current Internet. Jiang et al. proposed in [4] a special (two-group) DSG protocol to be deployed in the Internet. They proposed a mechanism based on the experienced losses by a receiver to estimate its isolated rate. This mechanism can be used in loss tolerant applications; however the aim of our work is to be able to perform a partitioning in the context of fully reliable multicast applications where we privilege a conservative approach where losses are to be avoided as much as possible.

In this paper we propose a new partitioning algorithm based on the receivers RTT variations instead of their isolated rates. In this context we propose an other formulation of the utility function using the RTT variations instead of the isolated rates. Our partitioning algorithm, although simple, performs an on-the-fly partitioning depending on the receivers' feedback. Our algorithm approximates and in many cases, achieves the optimal solution without using complex computations. For instance, in [2], a computation is performed on every candidate solution before choosing the one that maximizes the receivers satisfaction. The dynamic programming algorithm proposed in [8] requires less computation effort but still be complex. The remainder of this paper is organized as follows. Our new formulation for the utility function is proposed in section 2. The description of our partitioning algorithm with a study of some of its properties are provided in section 3. Some simulation results are presented in section 4 and section 5 concludes.

2   Utility Function

In a multicast session, the satisfaction of a receiver R_i can be quantified using a utility function (or a receiver fairness measure) that maps the reception rate of the receiver to a fairness value normalized to the range $[0.0, 1.0]$. Authors in [3, 4] proposed $U_i(r) = \min(r_i, r)/\max(r_i, r)$ as a fairness function, where r_i and r are respectively the isolated rate and the R_i receiver's reception rate. This utility function has a value of 1 if the reception rate equals the receiver isolated rate, non-decreasing in the range $[0, r_i]$ and non-increasing in the range $[r_i, \infty]$. This utility function assumes that the isolated rates of the different receivers are known. We propose an other expression of the utility function using the RTT variation experienced by the receiver as a response to a given transmission rate. The RTT variation is a measure which can be easily obtained in the Internet using a ping-like mechanism.

---

[1] The isolated rate [3] is the rate that a receiver would obtain if unconstrained by the other receivers in the group, assuming max-min link sharing.

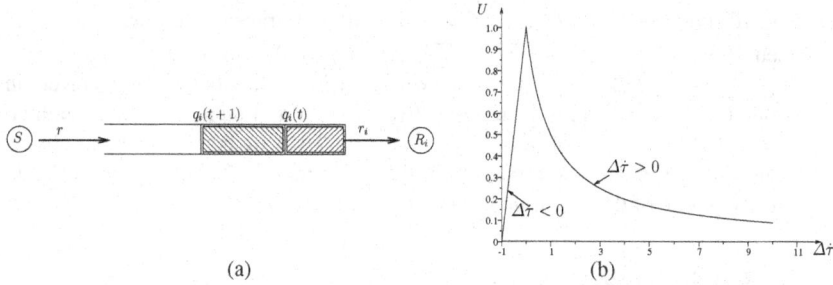

Fig.1. (a) Queue length variation. (b) The inter-receiver fairness as a function of the relative RTT variation.

For the purpose of defining the utility function, we consider the case of one receiver with r_i as the isolated rate. Let r be the transmission rate of the sender in bits/s. When the transmission rate exceeds the bottleneck rate, a queue of packets will build up within the connection. We suppose that the receiver sends periodically (every T seconds) a probing packet toward the source in order to estimate its RTT to the source. Let $q_i(t)$ be this queue size in packets at time t and $\Delta q_i = q_i(t+1) - q_i(t)$ be the positive or negative variation in the queue length during a given time period T upon the reception of the subsequent probing packet (figure 1a). Noting by S the packet size, the queue builds up when $r > r_i$ during T with $\Delta q_i = (r - r_i) T/S$. The RTT variation experienced by the connection during the last T period, $\Delta \tau_i = \Delta q_i S/r_i = (r - r_i) T/r_i$ giving $\Delta \dot{\tau}_i = (r - r_i)/r_i$ where $\Delta \dot{\tau}_i = \Delta \tau_i/T$ can be seen as the *relative* RTT variation experienced by receiver R_i. We can write $r/r_i = 1 + \Delta \dot{\tau}_i$ and the individual receiver utility can be expressed as a function of the relative RTT variation as follows (figure 1b):

$$U_i(r) = \begin{cases} \frac{1}{1+\Delta \dot{\tau}_i} & \text{if } \Delta \dot{\tau}_i \geq 0 \\ 1 + \Delta \dot{\tau}_i & \text{if } \Delta \dot{\tau}_i \in [-1, 0[\end{cases} \qquad (1)$$

We note that the utility function is not defined[2] for $\Delta \dot{\tau}_i < -1$ which corresponds to a negative reception rate ($r < 0$). The receiver that experiences a positive RTT variation could experience losses since its reception rate is greater than its isolated rate. In the case of a negative RTT variation, the receiver will be unsatisfied since it has more bandwidth resources. In a similar way to [3], we define the utility function of a single-rate multicast session as the weighted sum of the individual utility values of receivers in the session: $U(r) = \sum_{i=1}^{n} \alpha_i U_i(r)$ subject to $\sum \alpha_i = 1$ and $\alpha_i \in [0, 1], i = 1, \ldots, n$ where n is the number of the receivers in the multicast session. A multi-rate multicast session consists of one or more subgroups split from an original multicast session. The session utility function in this case is defined as the summation of the utility values obtained by all multicast subgroups, using the single-rate utility measure in each subgroup. More specifically, if a multicast session of receivers $\{R_1, R_2, \ldots, R_N\}$ is split

---

[2] The interested reader can refer to [10] for more details.

into K subgroups $\{G_1, G_2, \ldots, G_K\}$ with different transmission rates $g_1, g_2, \ldots, g_K$, then $U(g_1, g_2, \ldots, g_K) = \sum_{j=1}^{K} \sum_{i=1}^{n_j} \alpha_{i,j} U_{i,j}(g_j)$, subject to $\sum_{i,j} \alpha_{i,j} = 1$ and $\alpha_{i,j} \in [0, 1]$. We have $\sum_j n_j = N$ where n_j is the number of the receivers in subgroup G_j. $U_{i,j}(g_j)$ and $\alpha_{i,j}$ are respectively the utility function and the weight associated to the ith receiver of the jth subgroup. Since we are concerned by a fully reliable multicast, the transmission rate g_j for the receivers in subgroup G_j has to match the minimum rate of the subgroup isolated rates, i.e. $\forall j$, $g_j = \min_{i \in G_j} r_i$

3   Partitioning Algorithm

Given a set of receivers $\{R_1, R_2, \ldots, R_N\}$ with isolated rates $r_1 < r_2 < \ldots < r_N$, the problem consists in splitting this set of receivers into K subgroups (K is less than a maximum number G) to make a partition $P = \{P_0, P_1, \ldots, P_{K-1}\}$ of the receivers so that the overall session utility is maximized. We aim to determine the optimal solution or at least an approximated one (without prior knowledge of the number of subgroups) such that the global receivers utility is greater than a given threshold. Our partitioning algorithm is based on the RTT variation experienced by every receiver and is executed on-the-fly while the source is increasing its rate. The source begins sending packets at a specific minimum rate and increases its rate as long as it does not receive a feedback indicating a relative RTT variation greater than a given threshold $\acute{e}$ (algorithm 1). The aim of algorithm 1 is to partition the receivers among subgroups of "similar" capacities. Initially, P_0 is the set of all the receivers. The source periodically checks if any receiver from P_0 experienced a $\Delta \dot{\tau}$ greater than a given threshold b; if so P_0 is split up into two subgroups $P_1 = \{R_j \in P_0, \Delta \dot{\tau}_j > a\}$ and $P_0 = P_0 - P_1$. Only feedbacks from P_0 are considered by the source for the purpose of next splittings. The source will continue increasing its rate and would if necessary, split P_0 again into two groups P_0 and P_2. The splitting process will continue until G subgroups have already been built or the P_0 is no more "split-able" (with only one element or members of P_0 have similar capacities).

3.1   The Convergence Criteria

One of the most important convergence criterion of the algorithm is the fact that P_0 is no more split-able. Here we demonstrate that the sufficient condition for P_0 to be no longer split-able is (as stated in algorithm 1):

$$\forall j < N, R_j \in P_0, \qquad \frac{1 + \Delta \dot{\tau}_{j+1}}{1 + \Delta \dot{\tau}_j} \geq \rho \,. \qquad (2)$$

For this purpose, we first consider two consecutive[3] receivers R_j and R_{j+1} with isolated rates $r_j < r_{j+1}$. Let γ be the multiplicative factor by which the source rate could be multiplied at every period. Suppose that at a given time the two receivers belong to the same group, this means that none of their RTT variations is greater than

---

[3] we consider two receivers R_i and R_j as *consecutive* (in this order) if their corresponding isolated rates r_i and r_j satisfies $r_i < r_j$ and $\forall k, r_k < r_i < r_j$ or $r_i < r_j < r_k$.

Algorithm 1 Partitioning Algorithm. Input: P_0, a set of receivers. Output: a partition $\{P_0, PK - 1, \ldots, P_2, P_1\}$ where $K \leq G$

Require: $N > 1$ and $a < b < \dot{\epsilon}$

$\rho \leftarrow \frac{a+1}{b+1}$

the source rate $r \leftarrow r_{min}$

$P_0 \leftarrow \{R_j, j = 1, \ldots, N\}$, the set of all the receivers

$i \leftarrow 1$

Periodically,

if $\exists j, R_j \in P_0$ such that $\Delta \dot{\tau}_j > b$ **then**

    $P_i \leftarrow \{R_j \in P_0, \Delta \dot{\tau}_j > a\}$

    $P_0 \leftarrow P_0 - P_i$

    $i \leftarrow i + 1$

    if $\exists j, R_j \in P_0$ such that $\Delta \dot{\tau}_j > \dot{\epsilon}$ **then**

        decrease r

    else

        increase r

    end if

end if

until $i = G$ or $|P_0| = 1$ or $\forall j < N, R_j \in P_0, \frac{1 + \Delta \dot{\tau}_{j+1}}{1 + \Delta \dot{\tau}_j} \geq \rho$

---

the b threshold: $\Delta \dot{\tau}_j = (r - r_j)/r_j < b$ and $\Delta \dot{\tau}_{j+1} = (r - r_{j+1})/r_{j+1} < b$. At the next period the source rate becomes γr rather than r. Receivers R_j and R_{j+1} will no longer continue to be in the same subgroup if their new relative RTT variations $\dot{\tau}_j^+$ and $\dot{\tau}_{j+1}^+$, satisfy: $\Delta \dot{\tau}_j^+ = (r - r_j)/r_j > b$ and $\Delta \dot{\tau}_{j+1}^+ = (r - r_{j+1})/r_{j+1} < a$. Hence $(b+1)r_j < \gamma r < (a+1)r_{j+1}$ and $r_j/r_{j+1} < (a+1)/(b+1) = \rho$ which is the necessary condition so that the two receivers do not belong to the same group according to our partitioning algorithm. Consequently, the sufficient condition for the two receivers to belong to the same group is that the ratio of their isolated rates is greater or equals ρ, i.e. $r_j/r_{j+1} \geq \rho$. Since the isolated rates are not available, using the relative RTT variation instead, the sufficient condition becomes:

$$\forall j \in 1..N - 1, \frac{r_j}{r_{j+1}} = \frac{1 + \Delta \dot{\tau}_{j+1}}{1 + \Delta \dot{\tau}_j} \geq \rho \,. \tag{3}$$

Algorithm 1 converges if G groups are already constructed or when the remaining receivers (i.e. those in P_0) have so similar capacities such that a split is no more possible. This depends on the a and b parameters as stated by condition (2), which is a generalization of (3) for every two consecutive receivers in P_0 (assuming of course that $|P_0| > 1$).

3.2   Lower Bound Guarantee on the Utility Function

We present here an interesting feature of our partitioning algorithm which consists in assuring a lower bound on the resulting utility value depending on the algorithm parameters. We consider one subgroup $G_j, j = 1, \ldots, K$ containing the receivers

$R_{j1}, R_{j2}, \ldots R_{jn_j}$ with isolated rates $r_{j1} < r_{j2} < \ldots < r_{jn_j}$. The reception rate of the G_j's receivers is $g_j = \min_{i \in G_j} r_i = r_{j1}$. Without loss of generality, we put $\alpha_{i,j} = 1/N, \forall i,j$, where N is the number of receivers in the whole multi-rate multicast session. The overall session utility satisfies[4]:

$$U(g_1, g_2, \ldots, g_K) \geq \frac{1}{N} \sum_{j=1}^{K} \frac{1 - \rho^{n_j}}{1 - \rho} . \tag{4}$$

This last relation (4) is very interesting since it provides a lower bound on the session utility function independently of the isolated rates distribution. It is quite obvious that if we want to have a higher utility value, we have to choose a higher ρ. It is worth noting that the number of subgroups is proportional to this parameter.

3.3   Numerical Results

For numerical results about the lower bound guarantees on the utility function, we consider the particular case when the number of receivers in each subgroup is the same i.e. $\forall j, n_j = N/K$. In this case, inequation (4) becomes:

$$U(g_1, g_2, \ldots, g_K) \geq \frac{K}{N} \frac{1 - \rho^{N/K}}{1 - \rho} = U_{min} . \tag{5}$$

Figures 2a,b,c plot the minimum utility value (U_{min}) as a function of the number of the built subgroups for 12 and 48 receivers and for different values of the ρ parameter (0.8, 0.85, 0.9, and 0.95). Figure 2a shows for $\rho = 0.9$, a minimum utility of 0.8 with just 2 subgroups which corresponds to 80% of the maximum utility achieved with a partition of one receiver per subgroup. For 48 receivers with $\rho = 0.9$, only 4 subgroups are sufficient to achieve a minimum utility of 80%. Figure 2c shows the minimum utility as a function of the number of subgroups for different numbers of the receivers ($\rho = 0.9$). We can see that for 6 receivers the minimum utility is at least 80% which increases with the number of subgroups. For 48 receivers, we need approximately 3 and 10 subgroups to assure a minimum utility of 50% and 80% respectively. Increasing the number of receivers increases the required number of subgroups to achieve a minimum receivers satisfaction. An other observation is that increasing the number of subgroups improves the utility value. Figures 2d,e plot the utility gain as a function of the number of subgroups for 12 and 48 receivers respectively. We can see that for 12 receivers and $\rho = 0.8$, with two subgroups we already have a gain of 160% and with 4 subgroups, the gain is about 210%. We can note that independently of ρ, the gain does not increase significantly when increasing the number of subgroups. For instance (figure 2e), with 5 subgroups we can achieve a gain of 2 for $\rho = 0.8$. If we double the number of subgroups from 5 to 10, the gain is only improved by 0.1.

---

[4] For the demonstration, refer to [10]

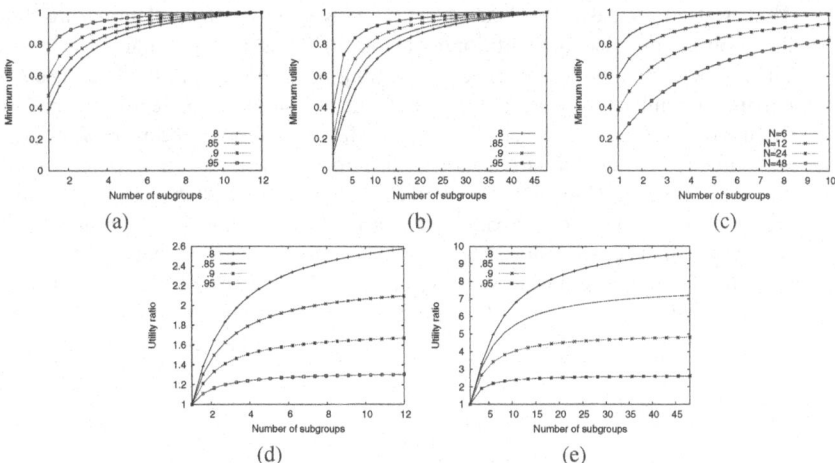

Fig.2. Lower bound on the session utility (a) 12 receivers, (b) 48 receivers, (c) $\rho = 0.9$, varying the number of the receivers. Utility gain (d) 12 receivers, (e) 48 receivers

4   Simulation Results

In order to get an insight into the proposed partitioning algorithm, simulations are performed and for a given number of receivers, the isolated rates are randomly generated following a uniform distribution with different parameters. Our partitioning algorithm is then applied on the resulting set of generated rates and this process is repeated for different values of ρ. A large number of simulations are performed for every set of parameters in order to get stable results. For every simulation, the number of subgroups built is recorded with the corresponding utility value.

4.1   Comparing with the Optimal Solution

In this section, we are comparing the performances of our partitioning algorithm to those of an algorithm that produces the optimal solution. The optimal algorithm consists in computing for each possible partition the corresponding utility value. Then the minimum utility value is saved in order to be compared with the utility achieved by our partitioning algorithm. A large number (about 1500) of simulations have been performed on two sets of rates. The first set consist in rates generated following a uniform distribution between 5 and 10. The second set presents a higher degree of heterogeneity with a uniform distribution between 5 and 55. We have limited ourselves to a partition of only two subgroups.

Figure 3a shows that for the first set of trials, 35% of the trials achieved the optimal solution (this corresponds to the box centered in 0). The three other boxes correspond to the percentage of trials for which the obtained utility is 95%, 90% and 85% of the optimal solution. An interesting remark is that all the obtained utility values are at least 85%.

The results of increasing the heterogeneity (the second set of simulations) are shown in figure 3b. In this case, the partitioning algorithm gives a larger range of utility values. The reason is mainly the fact that our splitting is performed on-the-fly and setting the maximum number of subgroups to 2 limits the performance of the algorithm. Actually the algorithm could take the decision to split the original set of receivers without having an accurate estimation of the capacity of the remaining receivers. This behavior depends on the ρ parameter which has to be well chosen to reflect the heterogeneity degree. Figure 3c is an other way to compare the two sets of simulations for which the cumulative percentage of success is plotted as a function of the decreasing degree of approximability to the optimal solution. We have at least 35% and 9% of trials with the optimal solution for the first and second sets respectively. All of the trials achieve at least 80% and 55% of the optimal utility value for the first and second set of simulations.

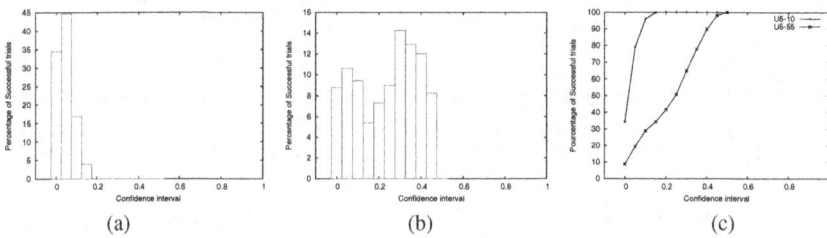

Fig.3. Solution optimality. Uniform distribution between (a) 5 and 10, (b) 5 and 55. (c) comparison of the two sets of results.

4.2   Varying the Number of Subgroups

All the figures of this section show the different points that correspond to the resulting pairs of utility value (or the utility gain) and the number of subgroups. The utility gain is computed using the case where there is only one subgroup as a reference. The curves of figure 4a1 and figure 4a2 show the results of the execution of our algorithm with 12 receivers for which the isolated rates are uniformly distributed between 5 and 10. Figure 4a1 confirms the numerical results. The minimum utility according to figure 2a is 0.4 and 4a1 shows a minimum utility value of approximately 0.6. We can also see that with only 2 subgroups we can achieve a mean utility of 0.9. In figure 4a2, we can see the influence of increasing the number of subgroups. We note that with 2 subgroups, we can increase the receivers' satisfaction by 25%. Increasing the number of subgroups beyond 3 does not increase significantly the receivers' satisfaction (a maximum gain of 1.4 instead of 1.3 with 10 subgroups!). We have similar results for 48 receivers (figure 4b1-b2).

Figure 5 presents the results of having more heterogeneous receivers whose isolated rates are uniformly distributed between 5 and 55. Compared to the first set, with the same number of subgroups, we note that the utility value decreases due to the higher

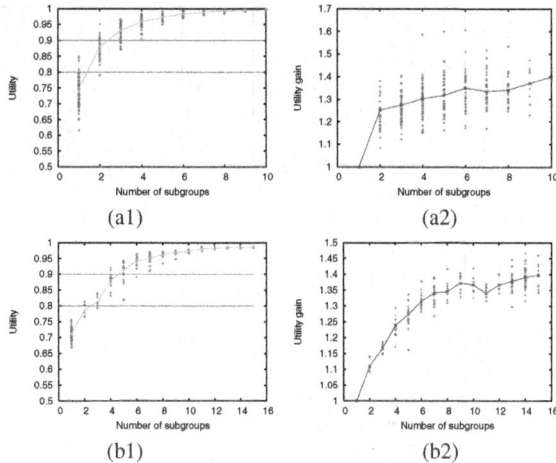

Fig.4. Utility and utility gain for receivers' isolated rates distributed uniformly between 5 and 10. (a) 12 receivers, (b) 48 receivers.

heterogeneity degree. However, we still achieve 0.8 with only 3 subgroups for 12 receivers and with 8 subgroups for 48 receivers. Once again, increasing the number of subgroups beyond a given threshold does not provide significant improvements. We can conclude that independently of the receivers heterogeneity degree, we do not need to increase the number of subgroups beyond a given threshold which is proportional to the receivers heterogeneity degree.

5   Conclusion

In this paper, we proposed a simple partitioning algorithm which does not require the knowledge of the receivers' isolated rates. Our algorithm performs an on-the-fly partitioning algorithm as soon as it receives feedback from the receivers. The knowledge of the RTT variation experienced by every receiver is required but there is no assumption on how the RTT variations are measured (therefore a simple ping method is suitable). The partitioning algorithm can be used by a multi-rate protocol (with a layered or replicated scheme) in order to adapt its number of layers or rates so that the global receivers' satisfaction is improved. One of the nice features of our algorithm is that it assured a minimum utility value depending on the value of ρ. We have shown that our algorithm converges, or at least approximates the optimal solution with a minimum computation effort. A future direction will consist in a deeper study of our algorithm in order to know how its parameters can be chosen according to the receiver's heterogeneity degree.

In this paper, we did not consider the partitioning dynamics due to space limitation. We suppose that the algorithm converges rapidly so that the initial partitioning is not disturbed by receivers changing their isolated rates. After the initial partitioning was performed, if any receiver experienced a RTT variation such that $|\Delta\dot{\tau}| > \dot{\epsilon}$ for a suffi-

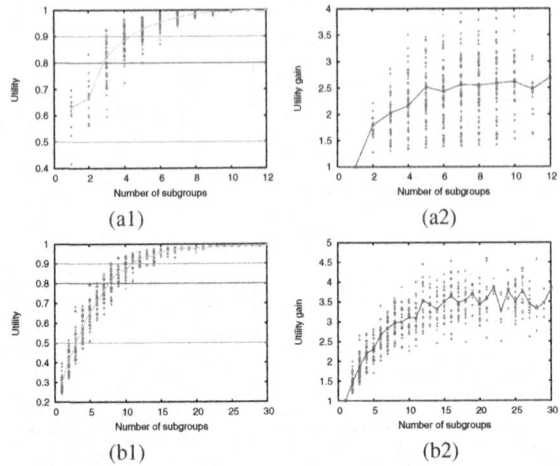

Fig.5. Utility and utility gain for receivers' isolated rates distributed uniformly between 5 and 55. (a) 12 receivers, (b) 48 receivers.

ciently long period, then a decision to move this receiver to a lower or a higher subgroup could be taken. Moreover, we have considered that the source executes the partitioning algorithm. In order to be more scalable, solutions with routers contribution seem to be very promising. We studied the possibility of executing the partitioning algorithm by the routers instead of the source. In this case if we choose a replicated scheme, for the implementation of our approach, we can distribute the data replication burden among some receivers instead of overwhelming the source [9].

References

[1] L. Vicisano at al. Tcp-like congestion control for layered multicast data transfer. In *INFO-COM*, pages 1–8, San Fransisco, USA, 1998.
[2] M. D. Amorim et al. Improving user satisfaction in adaptive multicast video. *IEEE/KICS Journal on Communications and Networks*, 4(3), Sep. 2002.
[3] T. Jiang et al. Inter-receiver fairness: A novel performance measure for multicast ABR sessions. In *SIGMETRICS*, pages 202–211, June 1998.
[4] T. Jiang et al. Inter-receiver fair multicast communication over the internet. In *NOSSDAV*, pages 103–114, June 1999.
[5] T. Jiang et al. On the use of destination set grouping to improve inter-receiver fairness for multicast abr sessions. In *IEEE INFOCOM'00*, March 2000.
[6] V. Jacobson et al. Receiver-driven layered multicast. In *ACM SIGCOMM'96, Stanford, CA*, pages 117–130, August 1996.
[7] X. Li et al. Layered video multicast with retransmission (lvrm): Evaluation of hierarchical rate control. In *INFOCOM'97*, 1997.
[8] Y. Yang et al. Optimal partitioning of multicast receivers. Technical Report TR-2000-10, Univ. of Texas at Austin, May 2000.

[9] M. Maimour and C. Pham. Amca : an active-based multicast congestion avoidance algorithm. Technical Report RR-4689, INRIA, January 2003. Also available as a LIP/ENS Research Report under 2003-07.

[10] M. Maimour and C. Pham. A rtt-based partitioning algorithm for a multi-rate reliable multicast protocol. Technical Report RR-4779, INRIA, March 2003.

Towards Multi-class Based Multicast Routing

Maria João Nicolau[1], António Costa[2], Alexandre Santos[2], and Vasco Freitas[2]

[1] Departamento de Sistemas de Informação,
Universidade do Minho, Campus de Azurém,
4800 Guimarães, Portugal
joao@uminho.pt
[2] Departamento de Informática,
Universidade do Minho, Campus de Gualtar,
4710 Braga, Portugal
{costa,alex,vf}@uminho.pt

Abstract. While Differentiated Services reach maturity, and a few per hop aggregate behaviors are being standardized, little efforts are being carried out to enforce class differentiation by selecting alternative routes. Within a differentiated services multicast scenario, multiple multicast forwarding trees must be found, one per Class of Service (CoS), in order to comply with different per-class Quality of Service (QoS) requirements. This paper presents a new multicast routing protocol enabling per class multicast tree computation. The proposed heuristics enable directed trees establishment, instead of reverse path ones, due to the importance of link asymmetry within an environment which is, essentially, unidirectional. The main assumption supporting this work is that a per class path computation may well complement, at routing level, node level differentiation techniques, thus providing per class differentiated handling. The strategy presented is also useful for network traffic engineering as it potentially enables traffic distribution along different network links.

1 Introduction

Routing multicast traffic requires the construction of a distribution tree (or set of trees). Data packets are delivered using that tree, thus the major goal of the routing protocol is to build a tree with minimum cost. The problem of finding such a tree is NP-complete and is known as *Steiner Tree Problem*[1]. Plenty of heuristics have been proposed to efficiently find multicast trees [2]. The one mostly used by multicast routing protocols consists of building a spanning tree by adding each participant at a time, by means of finding the shortest path from the new participant into the nearest node of the spanning tree. Such a tree is called *Reverse Path Tree*. This heuristic assumes that links connecting any two nodes are symmetric, in other words, assuming that link costs in each direction are equal. However, links can be asymmetric due to different reasons, thus links costs are likely to be different in each direction. Therefore reverse-path routing in asymmetric networks may lead to poor routes. Finding a minimal multicast

M.M. Freire, P. Lorenz, M.M.-O. Lee (Eds.): HSNMC 2003, LNCS 2720, pp. 52–61, 2003.

tree in asymmetric networks, called the *Direct Steiner Tree Problem*, is also NP-complete. There are some theoretical studies [3], focusing on directed graphs, aiming to present approaches to this problem. However, most of the deployed multicast routing protocols, like CBT[4] and PIM-SM[5] are based upon reverse path routing.

In addition, most of the multicast applications are QoS sensitive in nature, thus will benefit from the QoS, or even CoS, support from the underlying network, if available. As well as for unicast routing, there are two different approaches in order to provide QoS to multicast routing: per flow and per class routing. The first one performs routing at flow level. Several strategies have been proposed [6] [7], most of them relying on flooding in order to find a feasible tree branch to connect a new member. The underlying idea is to obtain multiple paths where a new member may connect to the tree. Among candidate paths the new member selects the one that is able to satisfy its QoS requirements. This strategy is suited within the Integrated Services model (IntServ)[8] that aims to provide QoS service guarantees for each individual flow crossing the network, by means of resource allocation.

The main strength of the IntServ model is its ability to provide service guarantees by means of (state-full) resource reservation. However it has several weaknesses too. Each router is required to maintain state information for each flow, thus, scalability problems do arise in operational environments. In addition a significant amount of processing overhead is required within each router, and the connection setup time may even sometimes be greater than the time required for the transmission of all the packets belonging to a specific flow.

The goal of Differentiated Service Architecture (DiffServ) [9] is to provide the benefits of different CoS levels while avoiding the limitations of the IntServ model. This is accomplished by aggregating traffic into specific classes, thus changing the scope from QoS (and per flow) to CoS (per class) guarantees. As DiffServ does not maintain any per flow information, connection setup costs are also eliminated. Most differentiated services implementation proposals make use of control algorithms for aggregating service levels, packet marking and policing, and preferential treatment of marked packets within the network. The issue of routing as a means to enhance aggregate QoS has not yet received the necessary attention. In presence of DiffServ networks, per flow path computation is not adequate. Instead, per class path calculation must be made, and so multiple multicast trees must be computed in order to satisfy different QoS requirements of different traffic classes.

In this paper a new multicast routing protocol is proposed enabling per class multicast routing implementation. The proposed protocol takes link asymmetry into account as it defines a *shortest-path-tree* based routing strategy as opposite to a *reverse-path-tree* based one. This is an important feature because when routing constraints are introduced links become asymmetric in terms of the quality of service they may offer, thus link costs are likely to be different in each direction. Therefore reverse path routing is not adequate to address Quality of Service Routing.

2   A Model for Multi-class Based Multicast Routing

In this section a new model for implementing a QoS aware Multi-class Multicast Routing is presented. This model supports the Multicast Routing Protocol proposed in this article. Implementation details are given in the next section.

First, a multiple shared tree mechanism is proposed in order to give receivers the ability to joining the group without knowing where are the sources located. Nevertheless, sources are the elements in better conditions to define QoS requirements since they are the ones generating traffic. Having multiple sources per group, with perhaps different QoS requirements, one may have different data flows of different classes of service. In this situation, receivers must join a group with no restrictions in terms of traffic classes they are able to receive. Furthermore, they must be able to receive all classes of all sources, at least in the starting period of group membership.

The multiple shared tree mechanism proposed is inspired in Protocol Independent Multicast-Sparse Mode (PIM-SM)[5] with trees rooted at a Rendez-Vous Point (RP) router. A shared tree per class of service available is needed, in order to give sources the ability to start sending data in any class. It is assumed that the total number of classes of service "available" has a pre-established upper limit and is small when compared to the number of participants.

Data packets originated by sources are sent towards the RP router, previously marked according to source defined QoS parameters. The RP router forwards data packets from sources through one of the shared trees, based on their class of service. Receivers must connect to all of the RP shared trees when joining the group.

At this point, the question lies on how to build several distinct shared trees, one per class of service. Explicit join requests must be sent by the receivers towards the RP router. When RP router receives a join request it must send back to the new receiver an acknowledge message per class through the best unicast path for that class. Routers, along those paths, receiving such acknowledge message may then update their routing tables in order to build new multicast trees branches. Updating is done basically by registering with the multicast routing entry for that tree, the acknowledge message's incoming and outgoing router interfaces.

The multiple RP shared tree mechanism, presented so far, does not really allow receivers to specify their own QoS requirements. Traffic flows from sources to receivers through one of the shared trees, according only to the QoS parameters defined by sources. How can a receiver, after a starting period, specify a given requirement? Can a receiver demand for a reclassification of a source multicast traffic?

This issue cannot be accomplished by a shared tree, but it may be met if the receiver joins a source-based tree. When initiating the join to source procedure, the receiver should include in the join request the desired Class of Service. It is up to the source to decide whether or not to accept the join, knowing that when accepting a join, traffic in the requested class of service must be generated.

In this situation, each source may face several distinct requests of several distinct receivers for different classes of service within the same group. At the limit, for larger groups, there may be requests for all classes. Even with this worst case situation scalability problems do not arise because the total number of different classes will be much smaller than the total number of receivers. In practice this implies one source-based tree per class of service, unless some order relationship between the classes can be established.

When accepting a join for a new Class of Service, a source must generate an acknowledge message, addressed to the corresponding receiver. This procedure is similar to the one described for the construction of the shared trees. But in this situation only one join acknowledge message is generated per join request.

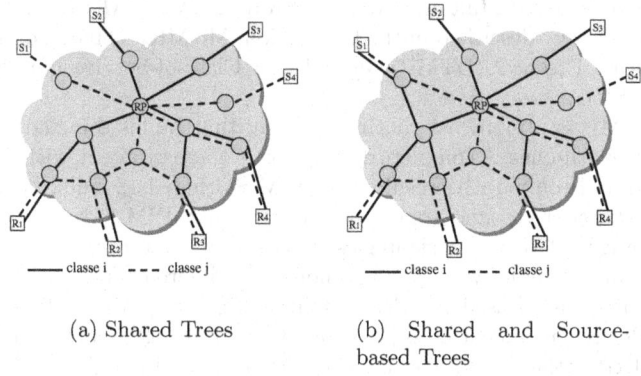

(a) Shared Trees   (b) Shared and Source-
                              based Trees

Fig. 1. QoS Parameters defined by sources and receivers

Figure 1(a) illustrates a scenario with four receivers initially connected to a RP router by two different shared trees, constructed for *class i* and *class j* respectively. There are also four sources, two of them generating traffic marked for *class i* and the other two generating traffic for *class j*. In Figure 1(b) after a short period of time, the receiver R2 decides to join source S1, requesting the class of service i. That single request originates a new source tree, rooted at source S1 for Class of Service i. Note that all the routers along this source tree should stop receiving data from that source through the shared tree in the *class i* in order to prevent duplicate data packets. To accomplish this, a mechanism similar to "prune of source S in shared tree", proposed in PIM-SM specification, must be implemented. In addition, the designated router should stop receiving packets from that source in any other class unless there are other receivers in the same group attached. Therefore the "prune of source S in shared tree" mechanism should be used too when designated router receives the join acknowledge message.

When participants leave a group, additional mechanisms must be implemented to tear down state, and eventually cut out tree branches. As the multicast trees are built from RP or sources towards the receivers, the usual prune mechanism should be modified. To prevent an overload of RP and source nodes and an amount of unnecessary control messages in the de-construction tree process, an additional field should be included in the multicast routing tables, with the identification of the upstream neighbor in the tree. The prunes must be sent directly towards that router instead of being sent to the RP or sources nodes. We believe that this field may be used to implement the periodic tree refresh, too.

3   Multi-class Based Multicast Routing Protocol Implementation

Multi-class based Multicast Routing Protocol (MCMRP) is an implementation of the strategy described in the last section. MCMRP is based on Directed Trees Multicast Protocol (DTMP)[10] and uses Class-of-Service Link State Protocol (CoSLSP).

DTMP is a multicast routing protocol that builds directed trees instead of reverse-path-ones. A complete description of these protocol, with implementation details and comparative results with PIM-SM may be found in [10]. DTMP uses both shared trees and source based trees, like PIM-SM, in order to get the advantages of the both strategies. It is suited for use in asymmetric networks where link costs between any two nodes are different in each direction.

Multi-Class Based Multicast Routing Protocol (MCMRP) extends DTMP in order to implement class based multicast routing. Another major element of MCMRP is the unicast routing protocol in use. Although MCMRP is independent of the underlying unicast routing protocol, it must be a multi-class enabled unicast routing protocol. In other words, the unicast routing protocol must be able to find the unicast routes that can meet the QoS requirements of each Class of Service. In order to build a new tree branch for each Class of Service the multicast routing protocol will search the unicast routing table for the unicast path that is more adequate to satisfy the QoS requirements of each class. To accomplish this new feature, a new unicast routing protocol must be used so an NS-2[11] implementation of CoSLSP has been produced.

3.1   CoSLSP - Class of Service Link State Protocol

CoSLSP aims to provide a class based unicast routing mechanism. The basic idea is to find one route per class-of-service, able to satisfy the QoS requirements of that class. Apart from the goal of satisfying the QoS requirements of each class, this protocol also addresses the problem of optimizing network utilization. Therefore, instead of computing just the routes that might meet the QoS requirements of each class, CoSLSP tries to find the shortest path that might satisfy those requirements.

It is a unicast link-state protocol that uses a modified Dijkstra algorithm capable of finding the shortest path routes, if they exists at all, that can meet the QoS requirements of different classes of service. In few words: the path calculation algorithm starts by finding the shortest path, whose feasibility is then verified against the QoS requirements. If unfeasible, the next shortest path is then iteratively verified, until a feasible path is found or a configured threshold is reached. In this way, a different route is found for each class of service and it is installed in the routing table. The packet forwarding process has been modified too in order to lookup for the appropriate route depending on the class of service of each packet.

CoSLSP has been implemented and evaluated with Network Simulator. The simulations results show that CoSLSP in case of network congestion is able to find "better" routes in respect to the QoS metrics of each class of service.

3.2   DTMP - Directed Trees Multicast Protocol

DTMP is a multicast routing protocol that implements directed trees construction in opposite to usual reverse path ones. The original idea is based on PIM-SM protocol, a widely deployed multicast routing protocol in the Internet. The PIM-SM, as the majority of multicast routing protocols, builds reverse path trees. This fact may lead to poor routes in the presence of asymmetric networks and problems may arise when trying to implement QoS Routing, as links usually have different characteristics in each direction.

Like PIM-SM, DTMP uses both shared trees and source based trees. Receivers begin joining a shared tree, rooted in a pre-defined point called Rendez-Vous Point. After having received a certain amount of data packets from a source, a receiver may switch to a source based tree. The protocol allows for an easy way of constructing a source based tree, pruning unnecessary tree branches within the shared tree.

3.3   MCMRP - Multi-class Based Multicast Routing Protocol

We used CoSLSP and extended DTMP in order to implement the multi-class based multicast strategy proposed in section 2.

When a new receiver decides to join, the designated router uses the shared tree join mechanism proposed by DTMP. A join request message is sent towards the RP. The routers along the way between the new receiver and the RP just forward the join request message and no sate information is introduced in these routers. When the RP receives a join request message from a new receiver it must send one join acknowledge message per class of service. These messages must travel towards the new receiver through the best unicast path per each class of service. Those paths are calculated and installed in the unicast routing table by CoSLSP. All join acknowledge messages should be marked in the corresponding class of service in order to follow the best unicast path per each class of service. When a router between the RP and the new receiver receives one acknowledge message it must create or update the corresponding routing table entry in order to create the new tree branch.

58   Maria João Nicolau et al.

The process of joining the shared tree in MCMRP is detailed in Figure 2, where variables and flags have the same meaning as defined in PIM-SM[5]. In the illustrated scenario there are two different classes of service ($CoS = 1$ and $CoS = 2$) and router A (the designated router of the new receiver) issues a join request message.

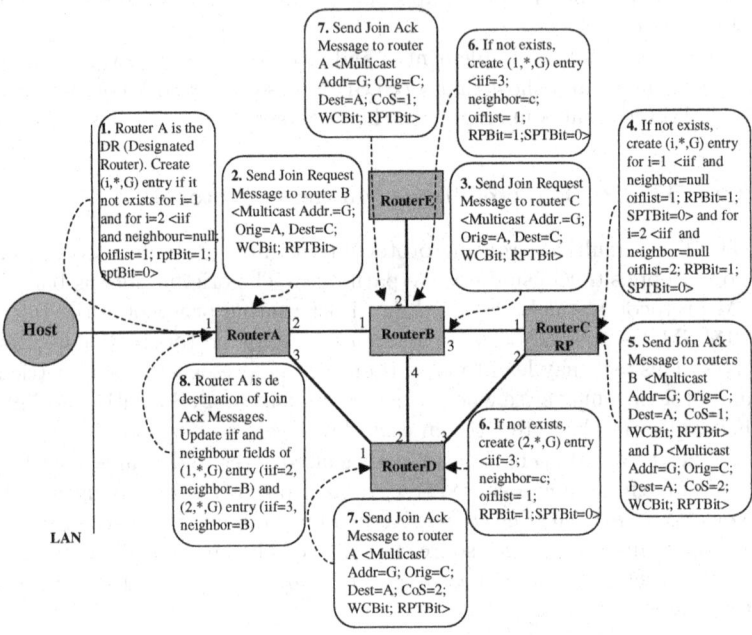

Fig. 2. Set Up Shared Trees Implementation. Actions are numbered in the order they occur

The routing table entries have the same fields as the PIM-SM ones, and an extra one: the upstream neighbor in the tree. This field has been introduced in order to be able to implement the prune mechanism.

The process of commuting to a source based tree is similar to the above described one, with one major difference. When a source receives a join request message, only one join acknowledge message is generated and sent. The join request message is marked in the class of service requested by the receiver. If the source decides to accept this join, a join acknowledge message marked in the same class is generated and sent towards the new receiver following the best unicast routing path for that class. Two different situations may occur. The receiver may decide to switch to a source based tree in the same class used by the source, or it may want to switch to a source based tree requesting a different class of service.

In the first case, when a router in the path between the source and the receiver receives the join acknowledge message, if it is not already in the source based tree it must create a (i,S,G) entry and copy the outgoing interfaces list from the (i,*,G) entry to the outgoing interfaces list of the (i,S,G) new entry. This is because, in the future, packets from source S will be forward based on this new entry. Besides, when a router lying between the source and the receiver starts to receive data from that source, it must issue a prune of that source on the shared tree of that class. This prune indicates that packets of the class of service i from this source must not be forwarded down this branch of the shared tree, because they are being received by means of the source based tree. This mechanism is implemented by sending a special prune to the upstream neighbor in the shared tree of the class i. When a router at the shared tree of the class i receives this type of prunes, it creates a special type of entry (an (i,S,G)RPT-bit entry) closely like a PIM-SM router. In MCMRP the outgoing interface list of the new (i,S,G)RPT-bit entry is copied from the (i,*,G) entry and the interface deleted is the one being used to reach the node that had originated the prune, which may not be the arriving interface of the prune packet. This is because in MCMRP there are directed trees not reverse path ones. These (i,S,G)RPT-bit entries must be updated too when a join acknowledge message arrives in order to allow the join of a new receiver on a shared tree with source-specific prune state established.

When a receiver decides to join a source requesting a different class of service, the process is a little different. When a new (i,S,G) entry is created, the outgoing interface list should not be copied from the (i,*,G) entry, because in this case the other receivers connected through the corresponding shared tree want to receive data packets in the source's default class of service. For the same reason these entries should not be updated when a posterior join to shared tree acknowledge message is received. In addition, the "prune of source in the shared three" mechanism must be triggered by the Designated Router when it receives the join acknowledge message. The prune messages must be sent to the shared trees of all classes except to the shared tree of the class for which the receiver commuted. This is because the receiver will start to receive the source's packets through the source tree in the desired class, so it can not continue to receive it by the shared tree of the source's default class of service.

The process of switching from the shared tree to a source based tree in MCMRP is detailed in Figure 3. In the illustrated situation the receiver decides to switch to a source based tree in class of service 1 ($CoS = 1$), supposing the source's default class of service is 2.

As was referred in the last section the leave group functionality is implemented by means of sending explicit prune requests towards the upstream neighbor in the tree. When the upstream neighbor receives this type of prunes (which are different from the "prune of a source on the shared tree") it must delete the interface used to reach the node that had originated the prune from the outgoing interface list of the corresponding (i,*,G) or (i,S,G) entry. This interface may not be the arriving interface of the prune packet. If the outgoing interfaces

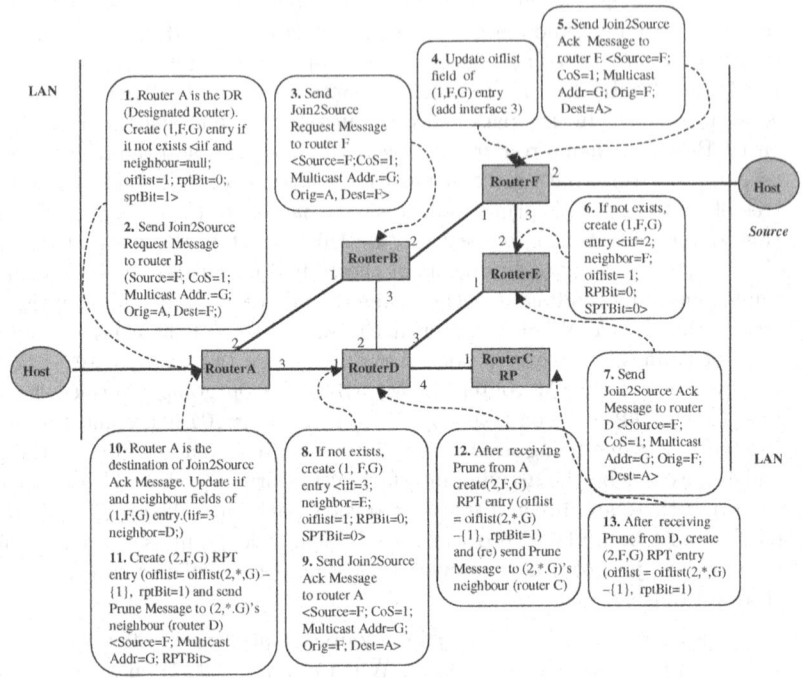

Fig. 3. Switching from Shared Tree to Source Based Tree Implementation

list become empty the entry may be deleted and the prune should be forward to the upstream neighbor in the tree. Thus, although the construction process of the multicast tree was inverted, from RP or source toward the new receiver, the de-construction process is identical to traditional multicast routing protocols, like PIM-SM. This fact saves a lot of unnecessary control messages.

4   Discussion

A new protocol is presented in this paper, MCMRP - a multicast routing protocol that implements multi-class based multicast routing, to be used in a DiffServ environment.

Because class differentiation is inherently unidirectional, we propose the usage of source and shared directed trees instead of typical reverse path forwarding ones. The heuristic is based upon explicit join acknowledges sent by either source or RP routers in response to explicit join requests sent by receivers. Furthermore the multicast framework presented tends to distribute multicast traffic in a evenly fashion as multiple shared-trees will distribute traffic along different links, instead of concentrating traffic on a smaller number of links (those in the single tree). So, although indirectly, this framework is also useful for network traffic engineering purposes as multicast load balancing becomes manageable.

Class differentiation is mainly achieved by means of usual DiffServ mechanisms *plus* routing differentiation, making it possible to use different routes for different Classes of Service. Generic class characteristics and identifications are directly derived from its DiffServ counterparts. Far from conflicting with traditional inside node differentiation strategies, this proposal is their routing-level complement.

The model introduces acceptable changes to node behavior in a DiffServ environment, but it does not introduce additional complexity to node Per-Hop-Behavior, besides normal complexity for simple multicast support. For instance, routing tables changes made to accommodate class information are acceptable within a class-based environment. End-nodes may still use normal join mechanisms, and in addition they may negotiate, after join request, the desired/possible QoS while the multicast application is running.

MCMRP has been implemented in Network Simulator (NS-2)[11] and is perfectly functional. MCMRP performance is currently being evaluated.

References

[1] P. Winter. Steiner problem in networks: A survey. *Networks*, 17:129–167, 1987.

[2] P. Berman and V. Ramaiyer. Improved approximations for the Steiner tree problem. In *Proceedings of Third Symposium on Discrete Algorithms, pp 325-334*, 1992.

[3] Moses Charikar, Chandra Chekuri, To yat Cheung, Zuo Dai, Ashish Goel, Sudipto, and Ming Li. Approximation Algorithms for Directed Steiner Problems. *Journal of Algorithms*, 33(1):73–91, October 1999.

[4] A. Ballardie. Core based trees (CBT version 2) multicast routing. RFC 2189, IETF, September 1997.

[5] D. Estrin, D. Farinacci, A. Helmy, D. Thaler, S. Deering, M. Handley, V. Jacobson, C. Liu, P. Sharma, and L. Wei. Protocol independent multicast-sparse mode (PIM-SM): protocol specification. RFC 2362, IETF, June 1998.

[6] Shigang Chen, Klara Nahrstedt, and Yuval Shavitt. A qos-aware multicast routing protocol. In *INFOCOM (3)*, pages 1594–1603, 2000.

[7] Michalis Faloutsos, Anindo Banerjea, and Rajesh Pankaj. Qosmic: Quality of service sensitive multicast internet protocol. In *SIGCOMM*, pages 144–153, 1998.

[8] A. Mankin, Ed., F. Baker, B. Braden, S. Bradner, M. O'Dell, A. Romanow, A. Weinrib, and L. Zhang. Resource ReSerVation protocol (RSVP) – version 1 applicability statement some guidelines on deployment. RFC 2208, IETF, September 1997.

[9] S. Blake, D. Black, M. Carlson, E. Davies, Z. Wang, and W. Weiss. An architecture for differentiated service. RFC 2475, IETF, December 1998.

[10] Maria João Nicolau, A. Costa, A. Santos and V. Freitas. Directed Trees in Multicast Routing. In *Quality of Service in Multiservice IP Networks QoSIP2003*, February 2003. LNCS 2601, pp 321-333, Ed. Marco A. Marsan et al, Springer-Verlag, 2003.

[11] K. Fall and K. Varadhan. *The NS Manual*, Jan 2001. URL=http://www.isi.edu/nsnam/ns/ns-documentation.html.

ECN-capable Multicast Multimedia Delivery

Robert R. Chodorek

Department of Telecommunications, AGH University of Science and Technology
al. Mickiewicza 30, 30-059 Kraków, Poland
chodorek@kt.agh.edu.pl

Abstract. Explicit Congestion Notification (ECN) is a method of signalling intended to inform end-system(s) of congestion in at least one router along delivery path. In IP networks, congestion build-up is usually detected using active queue management (e.g. RED) and clear indication of congestion can be transferred through the network using ECN bit (the CE codepoint in the IP header). In the paper, ECN-capable multicast multimedia delivery is presented. Described system combines ECN-capability with receiver-driven layered transmission. Experiments show that the use of ECN capable transmission allows to avoid the two main disadvantages of layered transmission scheme: lack of fairness and unexpected packet losses in basic layer[1].

1 Introduction

Layered multicast scheme requires a layered compression, where the input multimedia stream is compressed into several substreams with different QoS requirements. Typically base stream (guaranteed the lowest level of quality with the minimal bandwidth requirements) and several other streams to improve quality are used. Layers can be encoded in cumulative (the complete base stream and some supplementary streams) or non-cumulative manner (a set of complete streams). Layers (substreams) are sending through the network as different multicast groups. Receivers can individually subscribe or unsubscribe to the appropriate multicast group to achieve the best quality signal that the network can deliver. Layers can be joining/leaving only in order of their relevance. In result, end-user achieve transmission with the best QoS that the network can deliver.

The concept of layered multicast transmission was introduced by Turletti and Bolot [13]. This concept was implemented by McCanne [6], who develop receiver-driven layered multicast based on RLM protocol. Experiments, reported in [6], showed the great advantage of layered multicast: a good solution of a network heterogeneity problem. However, RLM-based layered multicast shows also main weaknesses of layered transmission [7], [9]:

- inter-session unfairness – in the case of coexistence of multiple layered sessions in one, common link,

---

[1] This research was supported by State Committee for Scientific Research (KBN) under grant No. 4 T11D 015 24 (years 2003-2005)

M.M. Freire, P. Lorenz, M.M.-O. Lee (Eds.): HSNMC 2003, LNCS 2720, pp. 62-72, 2003.

- TCP unfairness – RTP/UDP traffic is typically non-TCP-friendly and layered transmission isn't TCP-friendly, too,
- packet drops in base layer - packets from the basic layer may be lost which makes receiving higher layers useless,
- necessity of common delivery tree - all layers should follow the same multicast tree even when they are sent separately.

The last problem - usage of common delivery tree – is solved using e.g. active networks technology [14]. Moreover, usually of currently used source-oriented multicast routing protocols (as, for example, DVMRPv3), are stable enough to support multicast transmission which requires common delivery tree.

Although many authors have been addressed the problem of layered multicast transmission, the fairness and (simultaneously) packet dropping problems still remains an unresolved issue. The RLC protocol, designed for TCP-friendly receiver-driven layered multicast, also exhibit pathological behaviours [7].

Other propositions – PLM protocol and SAM – are relatively complex. The PLM protocol [8] uses the packet pair and PGPS scheduling to estimate the available bandwidth. However, the max-min fairness definition used by PGPS cannot be applied to discrete set of rates [10]. Moreover, there is possible misinterpretation problem in the case of MPEG-4 encoding, since the B-VOPs in base layer are usually small enough to be carried in single packet [3]. The possible solution – very small packets – lead to huge overheads.

The SAM mechanism [10] is based on SAPRA protocol, which provides inter-session fairness. However, SAM has two main disadvantages. First, it requires significant changes in the network infrastructure. Second, SAM was intended to use in DiffServ core routers. Because of paradigm of stateless core routers and sender-driven control, there is deep architectural conflict between DiffServ and (receiver-driven) multicasting [12], so (currently) practical implementation of SAM must deal with these problems.

This paper describes an approach to allow receiver-driven layered transmission to minimize packet loss ratio and to maximize the fairness. The proposed approach combines the RTP-based multicast transmission and explicit congestion notification.

The rest of the paper is organized as follows. The second section introduces ECN-capable RTP transport protocol. The third section proposes application of ECN to receiver-driven layered multicast. Section four addresses the evaluation of proposed transmission scheme and compares it with results obtained for congestion indication based on packet drops. Section five summarizes our experiences.

2   ECN-capable RTP Protocol

The congestion avoidance can be provided by transport layer protocol (e.g. TCP) or by application able to adaptive change effective transmission rate. The ECN-capable IP, described in the RFC 3168 [11], was successfully used in both of above cases. Several studies have shown, that application of ECN to TCP results in achieving better goodput when comparing to TCP relying only on packet drops as an indicator of congestion. ECN-capable transmission (based on modified ICMP) was also used for building adaptive video sources, which may reduce the output bit rate according to the available bandwidth [9].

The RTP transport protocol [4] is commonly used for delivery (usually: multicast delivery) of the multimedia streams. However, there is no standardized usage of ECN-based congestion control for RTP yet. The proposition of the ECN-capable RTP protocol is described below.

0 1	2	3	4	5	6	7
DSCP (6 bits)					ECN (2 bits)	

Fig. 1. The structure of DS (Traffic Class) field in the IPv4 (IPv6) header.

Explicit congestion notification is transferred through the IP network using the 8-bit DS field in the IPv4 header (formerly Type of Service, TOS) or the 8-bit Traffic Class field in the IPv6 header [11]. The first 6 bits of DS (and Traffic Class) field is occupied by the DSCP code point (for use to provide various forms of "differentiated service" for IP datagrams). The last 2 bits are assigned for ECN marking (Fig. 1).

ECN-capable RTP sender sets the ECN bits in the IP header to indicate the ECN-capability of the transport protocol end-point. Packet with ECN-Capable Transport codepoint CE(0) (i.e. '10') are sent to the receiver(s) using unicast or multicast transmission. If the congestion is build-up, routers on delivery tree will set the Congestion Experienced (CE) codepoint '11' in the IP header. In result, RTP receiver gets the information about congestion appearing in at least one network node along delivery tree.

The general ECN-capable receiver behaviour, recommended in RFC 3168, suggests that response to obtained CE codepoint should be essentially the same as response to a single dropped packet. RTP generally reacts on packet drops by modification of statistics in RTCP reports. Such a reaction is too weak to ensure effective congestion avoidance. Therefore we propose, that if receiver obtains congestion indication (a single CE packet), the feedback to the sender will be sent. The data receiver informs the data sender, when a CE packet has been received, by sending a new type of RTCP message - ECN-feedback (EFB).

EFB message conveys the information mandatory to RTCP message, as defined in [4], and, additionally, includes reception report blocks (one for each of the synchronisation sources from which this receiver has received RTP data packets). Each reception report block provides ECN-feedback information.

According to the location of traffic controller in end-systems, ECN-capable congestion control can be performed in sender-driven or receiver-driven manner. Sender-driven control can utilise EFB message. If the EFB message is received, the RTP sender will send via API, to the sender application, the request of reducing effective transmission rate (e.g. through change of compression level). Lack of congestion also can be reported to the sender application.

Explicit congestion notification can be also send by RTP receiver to receiver application, via API interface. Receiver application can hold the EFB messages transfer and perform congestion control itself (receiver driven control).

3   ECN-capable Receiver-Driven Layered Multicast

The proposed solution combines network-based explicit congestion notification with the receiver-driven layered multicast scheme. Receivers connect to layers in cumulative manner, in order of their relevance. To discover unknown condition of each network node, ECN capable routers were used. Each network node marks packets (sets CE codepoint) according to RED algorithm.

The RED queue marks packets proportionally to the level of congestion, according to piecewise linear characteristics, i.e. the probability of packet marking increments according to incrementation of average queue size in the network node. In result, if the dangerous of congestion appears in the network node, ECN will be transmitted from the possible point of congestion to the receiver. Based on obtained congestion notification, the receiver takes an autonomous decision about changing (or not) group membership and, in result, about reducing (or not) effective transmission rate.

Because (due to e.g. network latency, buffering, etc.) the receiver is not aware both the current congestion status of the network and available bandwidth, there are three types of timers established to provide suitable rate adaptation,:

- leave-timer T_L, which blocks unsubscription from l^{th} layer,

- join-timers T_J^l, which block subscription to $(l+1)^{th}$ layer,

- relaxation-timer T_R, which activates the relaxation procedure.

There are one one leave-timer, one relaxation-timer and are $(l_{max} - 1)$ join-timers in the system. One join-timer is intended for each layer $l = 1, 2, ..., l_{max} - 1$.

Leave-timer T_L avoids unnecessary multiple unsubscriptions. The timer reflects latency between time of a local unsubscription and the time at which impact of this unsubscription is reflected back to the receiver. The delay value τ_L of leave-timer should be long enough to assure that the congestion caused by $(l+1)^{th}$ layer is over and short enough to assure the proper reaction on the congestion caused by l^{th} layer.

Join-timer T_J^l both avoids unnecessary multiple subscriptions and provides mechanism of learning of the current network state and available bandwidth. The receiver learns the current congestion status, as well as available bandwidth, by experiments. If the join-experiment fails, the delay value τ_J^l of join-timer T_J^l is incremented by the following backoff procedure:

$$\tau_J^l = \min\left(A \cdot \tau_J^l, \ \tau_J^{max}\right), \quad A > 1 \tag{1}$$

where A is a backoff constant and τ_J^{max} is a maximal join-timer (configured).

In the case of stable reception of lth layer, the delay value τ_J^{l-1} of join-timer T_J^{l-1} is decremented by the relaxation procedure given by equation:

$$\tau_J^{l-1} = \max\left(B \cdot \tau_J^{l-1}, \ \tau_J^{min}\right), \quad B < 1 \tag{2}$$

where B is a relaxation constant and τ_J^{min} is a minimal join-timer (configured).

Thus, relaxation and backoff procedures promotes layer, which assures more stable transmission with no congestion reported.

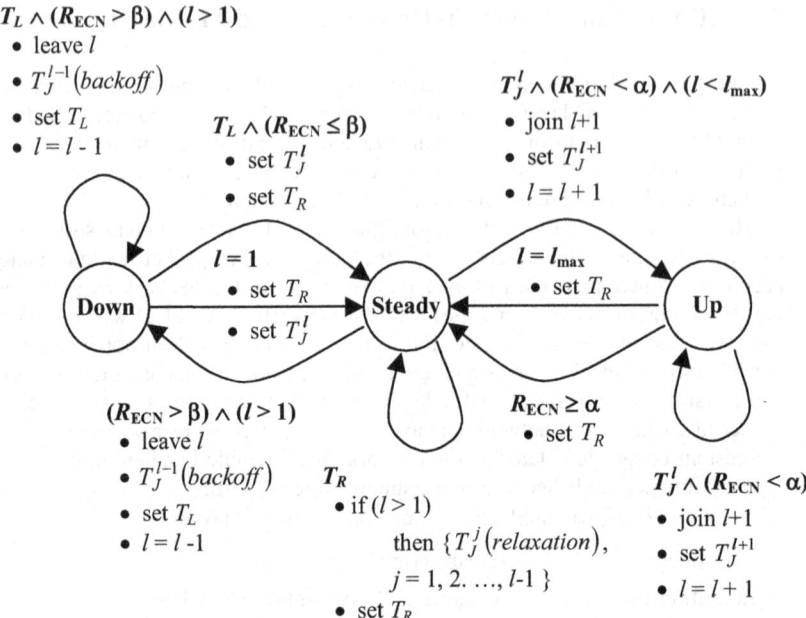

$T_L \wedge (R_{ECN} > \beta) \wedge (l > 1)$
- leave l
- $T_J^{l-1}(backoff)$
- set T_L
- $l = l - 1$

$T_L \wedge (R_{ECN} \leq \beta)$
- set T_J^l
- set T_R

$T_J^l \wedge (R_{ECN} < \alpha) \wedge (l < l_{max})$
- join $l+1$
- set T_J^{l+1}
- $l = l + 1$

$l = 1$
- set T_R
- set T_J^l

$l = l_{max}$
- set T_R

Down   **Steady**   **Up**

$(R_{ECN} > \beta) \wedge (l > 1)$
- leave l
- $T_J^{l-1}(backoff)$
- set T_L
- $l = l - 1$

T_R
- if $(l > 1)$
  then $\{T_J^j(relaxation),$
  $j = 1, 2, ..., l-1\}$
- set T_R

$R_{ECN} \geq \alpha$
- set T_R

$T_J^l \wedge (R_{ECN} < \alpha)$
- join $l+1$
- set T_J^{l+1}
- $l = l + 1$

Fig. 2. Finite state machine of ECN-capable receiver

State transition diagram of ECN-capable receiver is depicted in Fig. 2. Each state transition arc is labelled with the event that caused the transition and with the action taken during the transition. An ECN-capable receiver may be in one of three possible states:
- *Steady* state, when the receiver has subscribed the optimal layer; this is also the initial state of the receiver; *Steady* state provides hysteresis between join and leave operations;
- *Up* state, when the receiver subscribes to the upper layers l, $l = 2, ..., l_{max}$;
- *Down* state, when the receiver unsubscribes from the upper layers l, $l = l_{max}, ..., 2$.

An ECN-capable receiver starts in *Steady* state, where subscribes to the base layer ($l = 1$) and sets the join-timer at this layer (timer T_J^1) as well as the relaxation-timer (timer T_R). The receiver measures the ECN rate (R_{ECN}) with a short-time estimator. R_{ECN} thresholds, α and β, provide hysteresis mechanism to prevent frequent bandwidth oscillations. Action is taken when the estimator exceeds one of configured thresholds (α or β).

If $R_{ECN} < \alpha$ (a small amount of ECNs appears in received stream – i.e. the receiver is connected via lightly congested link), receiver should subscribe to the higher-quality multicast group (if exists). If a layer's join-timer T_J^l expires and the current layer is not the $(l_{max})^{th}$ layer, the receiver will transition to *Up* state. Receiver joins the multicast group, which transfers $(l + 1)^{th}$ layer, and sets the $(l + 1)^{th}$ layer's join-timer T_J^{l+1} to a delay value τ_J^{l+1}. Receiver in *Up* state successively joins layers, in order of their relevance. Periods between successive join operations are determined by join-timers. Receiver returns to the *Steady* state when measured ECN rate R_{ECN} exceeds the lower threshold α or when the receiver joins the highest (l_{max}) layer

If $R_{ECN} > \beta$ (a large amount of ECNs appears in received stream– i.e. the receiver is connected via heavy congested link) the receiver should unsubscribe from the higher-quality multicast group l, to avoid congestion. The receiver will transition to *Down* state if the lth layer isn't the base layer ($l > 1$). Receiver leaves the multicast group, which transfers l^{th} layer, performs the backoff procedure and sets the leave-timer T_L. Receiver in *Down* state successively leaves layers, in order of their relevance. Periods between successive leave operations are determined by leave-timer. Receiver returns to the *Steady* state when measured ECN rate $R_{ECN} \leq \beta$ or when leaves all supplementary layers.

If measured ECN rate $R_{ECN} \geq \alpha$ and $R_{ECN} \leq \beta$, the receiver is in the *Steady* state. The receiver doesn't change the set of subscribed layer $L = \{1, 2, ..., l\}$, and only relaxates join-timers T_j^j, $j \in L - \{l\}$.

The above transmission scheme allows achieving transmission with the best QoS that the network can deliver. The presented algorithm, formally described by the finite state machine depicted in Fig. 2, is flexible enough to be easy adapted to other, than ECN, method of signalling of congestion (e.g. by packet drops). Such adaptation requires only the change of the congestion estimator R, which measures the loss rate (R_{drop}) instead of ECN rate (R_{ECN}).

4   Results and Discussion

Simulation analysis was carried out using an event-driven *ns*-2 simulator [2], developed in U. C. Berkeley. ECN-capability in Berkeley's *ns*-2 covers IP header processing conformable to RFC 3168 and ECN-capable RED queue mechanism. A simulation model of ECN-capable RTP protocol for *ns*-2 was described in [1].

The proposed transmission scheme have been simulated in a large number of topologies and configurations. In the paper five different topologies will be included (Fig. 3), to expose the performance issues as well as scalability. Senders are connected to the router with link at 100 Mbps and 1 µs delay. Receivers are connected to the router through 1 ms delay link. Routers are connected with a link at 5 ms delay. To avoid oscillations, multilevel (three-level) RED queue was used.

Video traffic sources (SV) were modeled as three-layer ($l_{max} = 3$) stream, both CBR and VBR. The CBR streams have thin layers (CBR sources at rates $10 \cdot i$ kb/s, $i = 1, 2, 3$), or thick layers (CBR sources at rates $32 \cdot 2^i$ kbps, $i = 1, 2, 3$). VBR stream streams was generated from realistic *starwars* video traces, encoded as three streams characterised by high, medium and low picture quality. Properties of video traces can be found in [3]. The video streams were sent using ECN-capable RTP protocol and RTP packets have 200 bytes, what is the default value for the MPEG transport stream.

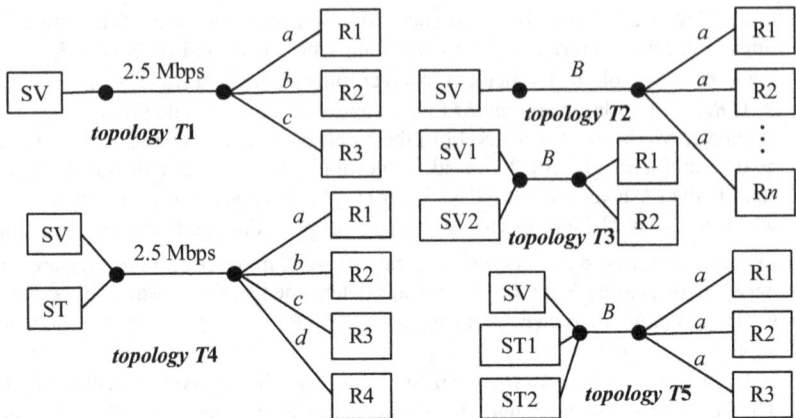

Fig. 3. Simulation topologies.

As the source of elastic traffic (ST), build-in model of FTP source was used. TCP protocol (SACK version) was used in the transport layer. The TCP SACK is currently the commonly used version of TCP (it is used e.g. in MS Windows, Linux, Solaris). TCP packets have a size of 1000 bytes, (default value in *ns*-2). In the case of presence of ECN-capable routers, ECN-capable congestion avoidance was used.

Topology $T1$ was used for adaptability tests. Parameters of topology were set as follows: $a = 11$ kbps, $b = 22$ kbps, $c = 33$ kbps for CBR traffic – thin layers, $a = 36$ kbps, $b = 110$ kbps, $c = 250$ kbps for CBR traffic – thick layers, $a = 0.4$ Mbps, $b = 0.8$ Mbps, $c = 2$ Mbps for realistic VBR traffic.

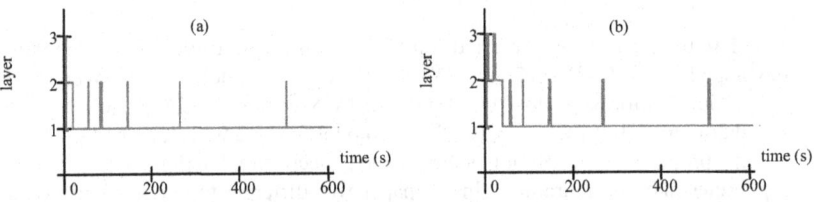

Fig. 4. Adaptability (R1, thin layers): a) ECN-capable indicator, b) packet drops as indicator.

Receiver R3, connected via non-congested link, always was able to receive full video information (layer 1 to 3). Receiver R2 was connected via lightly congested link and always was able to receive layer 2. If the realistic video source was characterized by low-detail, slowly dynamic content, R2 could connect to layer 3. Receiver R1 was connected through heavy congested link. R1 was able to receive layer 1 and, if the *starwars* trace was small enough, could connect to layer 2.

Experiments shows, that adaptability of the ECN-capable system is essentially the same, as obtained for classic, packet-dropping method of signalling (Fig. 4). The only difference is observed in the case of convergence time. In the case of congested links, ECN-capable system faster converge to the optimal layer than the packet-dropping one. This situation has been observed for all tested sequences, both CBR and VBR.

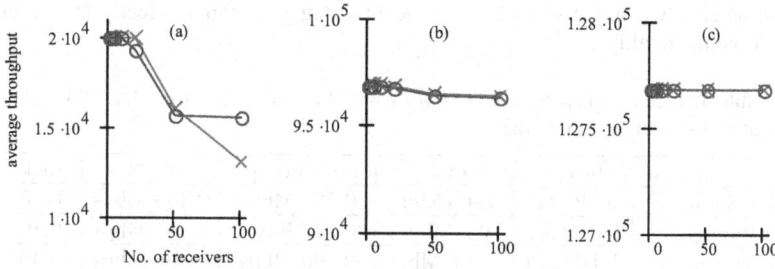

Fig. 5. Session-size scalability: a) thin layers, b) thick layers, c) realistic traffic (*starwars*). Legend: x's – ECN, o's – congestion indication based on packet drops.

Session-size scalability was investigated using topology *T2*. Bandwidth *a* was set to 100 Mbps, *B* was large enough to assure that receivers should connect to layer 2. Results of experiments are depicted in Fig. 5. For thin CBR layers, obtained scalability is very good if number of receiver *n* does not exceeds 20 (Fig. 5a). For large *n* (*n* = 100) scalability is rather poor. Better performance is achievable when ECN-capable congestion indicator is used (Fig. 5a). Scalability is good for thick CBR layers (Fig. 5b) and near perfect in the case of realistic VBR traffic (Fig. 5c). It's worth remarking, that the proposed system hasn't any additional protocol of "shared learning" of network state, as for example RLM.

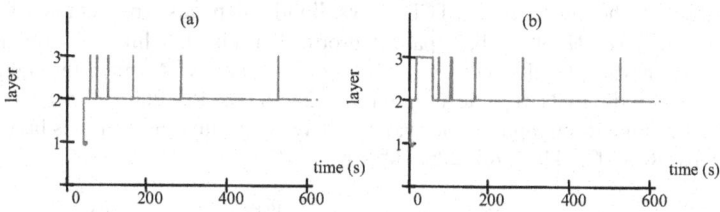

Fig. 6. Inter-session fairness (CBR – thin layers). Topology T3, B = 50 kbps. a) receiver R1 (receives packets from SV1 source), b) receiver R2 (receives packets from SV2 source).

Fairness is an ability of independent transmissions to fairly share network resources. The fairness is usually measured as [5]:

$$F = \frac{1}{N}\left(\sum_i x_i\right)^2 \cdot \left(\sum_i x_i^2\right)^{-1} \tag{3}$$

where *F* is the fairness coefficient, *N* is the number of sources and x_i is the throughput of ith transmission. *F* = 1 denotes the perfect fairness.

If a bottleneck link allows to send the same number of layers in each session, the investigated system always achieved near perfect inter-session fairness (*F* close to 1), independently on methods of congestion indication: ECNs (Fig. 6) and packet drops. Otherwise, ECN-capable layered multicast is more stable – one of sessions join the one more layer, no oscillations are observed. In the case of human end-user, this situation (two stable sessions) is more advantageous than "perfectly fair" oscillations of picture quality.

Table 1. Fairness. Topology $T4$, $a = b = c = 2$ Mbps, d = 0.2 Mbps. R1...R3 receives VBR traffic, R4 receives TCP packets.

Congestion indicator		ECN	packet drops	ECN	packet drops
Maximal	RTP (T_{tr})	0.306 Mbps	0.306 Mbps	0.306 Mbps	0.306 Mbps
throughput	TCP (T_{tt})	0.2 Mbps	0.2 Mbps	0.306 Mbps	0.306 Mbps
Simulated	RTP (T_{sr})	0.306 Mbps	0.306 Mbps	0.306 Mbps	0.306 Mbps
throughput	TCP (T_{st})	0.192 Mbps	0.14 Mbps	0.303 Mbps	0.213
Fairness (F)		0.95	0.879	1	0.969

In the case of all experiments carried out using topology $T4$, ECN-capability allow increase the fairness. However, the maximal possible fairness ($F = 1$) was detected only in the case of ECN-capable receiver-driven multicast. Because of self-limited traffic (as video traffic), perfect fairness can be obtained only if the maximal (theoretical) throughput ratio (T_{tr}/T_{tt}) is equal to 1 (see Table 1).

Other investigations were carried out using topology $T5$. R1 receives VBR stream, R2 and R3 receives TCP packets. Source ST1 starts at $t = 0$ s, ST2 starts at $t = 60$ s and R1 joins the base layer at $t = 20$ s. Bandwidth B was set to 0.8 Mbps. Without TCP backround traffic, R1 was able to receive layer 2 and, if the *starwars* trace was small enough, could connect to layer 3. Results show, that performance of VBR traffic in the presence of TCP flows lightly depends on method of congestion indication (ECN: 99.7·kbps, packet drops: 101 kbps), while performance of TCP flows significantly depends on signalling methodology. Average throughput of TCP streams in the ECN-capable system (R2: 323.1 kbps, R3: 260.3 kbps) was 45% larger than average throughput of the system where congestion indication is based on packet drops (R2: 207.3 kbps, R3: 206.9 kbps).

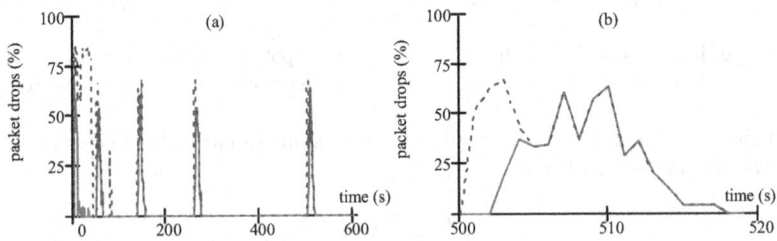

Fig. 7. Percentage loss rate obtained during the adaptability analysis (topology $T1$) a) drops in receiver R1 while joining CBR video stream (thick layers), b) zoom at the last peak. Legend: solid line – packet drops in base layer, dotted line – overall packet drops.

If congestion indication is based on packet drops, packet drops in base layer are caused both by the buffer overflow and by the RED queue properties. Although the average loss rate isn't large (i.e. about 4% in the case of transmission depicted in Fig. 7), the instantaneous loss rate may be close to 90% (see Fig. 7a) and duration of "loss phase", where loss rate exceeds 5% (upper bound of user's acceptability), may be very long (e.g. 12 seconds in Fig. 7b).

No packet drops (in base layer as well as in supplementary layers) was observed during the all simulations, while ECN-capable system was used.

5   Conclusions

Explicit Congestion Notification (ECN) transfers a clear indication of congestion through the network and, therefore, gives a possibility to construct accurate closed-loop control of effective transmission rate. In the paper, ECN-capable multimedia delivery system is presented. The system combines the layered multicast and explicit congestion notification.

Experiments show that the use of ECN capable multicast transmission allows achieving stable transmission of the layered video stream. The ECN-capable multimedia delivery system can learn the state of the network and adapt to different environmental conditions. No significant performance degradation was observed while the session size increased (even in the case of large numbers of receivers).

ECN-capability allows to avoid two main disadvantages of layered transmission scheme: lack of fairness (VBR traffic is typically non-TCP-friendly and layered transmission isn't TCP-friendly, too) and unexpected (not caused by buffer overflow) packet losses in base layer. ECN-capability allow receiver-driven layered transmission to increase the fairness and to achieve TCP-friendly transmission of the video stream, with no packet loss.

References

1. Chodorek, R.R.: A simulation of ECN-capable multicast multimedia delivery in ns-2 environment. Proc. of 14th European Simulation, ESS'2002, Dresden, Germany (2002)
2. Fall, K., Vradhan, K.: The ns Manual. URL http://www.isi.edu/nsnam/ns/doc. April (2002)
3. Fitzek, F.H.P., Reisslein, M:. MPEG-4 and H.263 Video Traces for Network Performance Evaluation. IEEE Network 15, No.6, November/December (2001)
4. Frederick, R., Jacobson, V., Schulzrinne, H., Casner, S.: RTP: A Transport Protocol for Real-Time Applications. RFC 1889. January (1996)
5. Hassan, M., Atiquzzaman, M.: Performance of TCP/IP over ATM networks. Artech House, London (2000)
6. Jacobson, V., McCanne, S., Vetterli, M.: Receiver-driven layered multicast. Proc. of ACM SIGCOMM'96, Stanford, CA (1996)
7. Legout, A., Biersack, E.W.: Pathological Behaviors for RLM and RLC. Proc. of NOSSDAV'2000, Chapel Hill, North Carolina (2000)
8. Legout, A., Biersack, E.W.: PLM: Fast Convergence for Cumulative Layered Multicast Transmission Schemes. Proc. of ACM SIGMETRICS'2000, Santa Clara, USA (2000)
9. Matrawy, A., Lambadaris, I., Huang, Ch.: Comparison of the use of different ECN techniques for IP multicast congestion control. Proc. of ECUMN'02, Colmar, France (2002)
10. Mendes, P. Schulzrinne, H., Monteiro, E.: A Receiver-Driven Adaptive Mechanism Based on the Popularity of Scalable Sessions. Proc. of QofIS/ICQT 2002, LNCS 2511. (2002)

11. Ramakrishnan, K., Floyd, S., Black, D.: The Addition of Explicit Congestion Notification (ECN) to IP. RFC 3168, September (2001)
12. Striegel, A., Manimaran, G.: A Survey of QoS Multicasting Issues. IEEE Communications Magazine, Vol.40, No.6, June (2002)
13. Turletti, T., Bolot, J.: Issues with multicast video distribution in heterogeneous packet networks. Proc. of the Sixth International Workshop on Packet Video. Portland, OR (1994)
14. Yamamoto, L., Leduc, G.: An Active Layered Multicast Adaptation Protocol. Proc. of the 2nd Int. Conference IWAN 2000, Springer LNCS 1942, Tokyo, Japan (2000)

Providing Fault Tolerance for Peer-to-Peer Streaming Service

Sooyong Kang[1], Hyunjoo Kim[2], and Heon Y. Yeom[2]

[1] Dept. of Computer Science Education,
Hanyang University, Seoul, 133-791, Korea
sykang@hanyang.ac.kr
[2] School of Computer Science and Engineering,
Seoul National University, Seoul, 151-742, Korea
{hjkim, yeom}@dcslab.snu.ac.kr

Abstract. Because each node in the peer-to-peer network is autonomous, it is difficult to provide deterministic service on the network. In this paper, we propose a framework for a fault tolerant streaming service on a peer-to-peer network. The proposed framework provides a service migration-based fault tolerance mechanism to cope with both node/link failures and link state changes. Simulation results show that using a small-sized buffer, the proposed framework can provide hiccup-free streaming service and the overhead required to maintain the up-to-date node state information is negligible.

1 Introduction

Due to the increase in demand for streaming services on the Internet many studies are being undertaken to find an efficient scheme for a streaming service. The new network service model, Peer-to-Peer (P2P) service, is a type of reciprocal network service where each node in the P2P network acts both as a client and as a server. Currently, there are two kinds of P2P networks. The first establishes logical relations between nodes to provide service and manage the network. It mainly focuses on the contents distribution from origin node to all the participating nodes. vTrails[1], Allcast[2], SpreadIt[3] and CoopNet[4] are examples. The second does not establish logical relations between the nodes. It mainly focuses on file sharing. Napster and Gnutella[5] are examples. While the P2P service can address the problem of client/server service architecture, i.e., load concentration on the server, it is difficult to provide guaranteed quality of service (QoS) because each node in the P2P network is autonomous. Therefore, for streaming service on a P2P network, a fault tolerant scheme that can cope with node/link failures must be developed.

Previous works on fault tolerance for streaming service on a P2P network can be classified into: 1) data recovery using redundant data, 2) reallocating data sending rate from server nodes, 3) special encoding for graceful quality degradation, and 4) service migration. Leung [6][7][8], used Reed-Solomon Erasure (RSE) correcting code for data recovery. Although such schemes can cope with

M.M. Freire, P. Lorenz, M.M.-O. Lee (Eds.): HSNMC 2003, LNCS 2720, pp. 73–82, 2003.
© Springer-Verlag Berlin Heidelberg 2003

a predefined number of node failures, they require additional network bandwidth
for redundant data. Thinh [9] proposed a dynamic transmission rate adaptation
scheme where multiple server nodes change data transmission rates to the client
node in order to minimize packet loss. Because it assumes that the sum of bandwidths of each node is larger than the necessary bandwidth for a normal playback rate, it is impossible to continue service when the aggregated bandwidth
becomes smaller than the playback rate because of the multiple node failures.
Coopnet [4] proposed Multiple Description Coding (MDC), which enables graceful QoS degradation when packet loss occurs because of node/link failure or link
state change. This scheme encodes a continuous media object into multiple independently decodable substreams so that the client node can continue playback,
despite node/link failures, with degraded quality using only the substreams received. Spreadit [3] used a service migration scheme that finds a new server node
to replace the failed node. However, because this scheme finds a new server node
in the application level multicast tree from the root node, a considerable amount
of time is required to find the new server node.

In this paper, we propose a framework for a streaming service on a P2P network
that provides service migration-based fault tolerance scheme. The fault tolerance
scheme in the proposed framework does not search for a new server node when
a server node fails, but simply selects replacing node(s) from the local node information table that contains the current state of each node, and this minimizes
the service migration overhead.

The organization of the rest of this paper is as follows. In Section 2, the Peer-
to-Peer streaming system model is presented. In Section 3, we describe service
protocols for the proposed framework. We show various simulation results that
reveal the performance of the proposed framework in Section 4 and finally conclude in Section 5.

2   System Model

In a P2P network each node acts as both a client and a server node. A client
node receives data for playback from one or more server nodes. A server node can
provide services to multiple client nodes within the predefined outbound bandwidth. Therefore, a node can receive services from multiple server nodes and can
provide services to multiple client nodes, simultaneously. Assuming no node/link
failures, the service-requesting node should 1) *search:* find nodes that have the
required object, 2) *node selection:* receive available outbound bandwidth information from those nodes and select a suitable number of server nodes that will
actually provide the service, and 3) *scheduling:* assign data segments for transmission to the selected nodes. Because the *search* is beyond the scope of this
paper, we assume that the client node already knows all the nodes that have the
required object. We also assume that media objects are encoded into constant
bit rate data and are sequences of data segments of equal size.

Every node can provide server and client processes for a P2P streaming service.
Figure 1 shows the architecture of the server process. When a service request

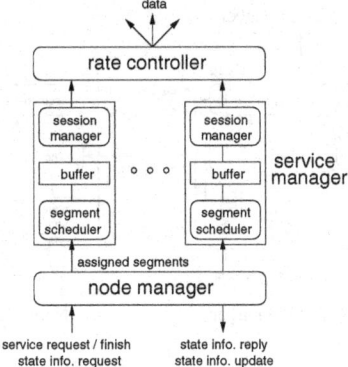

Fig. 1. Server process architecture for a P2P streaming service

arrives from a client node, the server process first advises the client node of the
available outbound bandwidth. On receiving the bandwidth information, the
client process of the client node informs the server process of the server node
whether it is selected as a server node. If selected, the server process of the server
node provides the service to the client, and if not, it sends state update information, whenever the available outbound bandwidth changes, to the client. To
do this the server process consists of: 1) a service manager that assumes the role
of segment scheduling (reading the necessary segments from disk to buffer) and
session management, 2) a node manager that assumes the role of sending state
(bandwidth) information to the client nodes and generating a service manager
when the client selects the node as a server node, and 3) rate controller that
actually transmits the data segments, at the requested rate, to each client node.
The client process receives the streaming service and consists of a data manager,
a node manager, and a player. Figure 2 shows the architecture of the client process. The data manager consists of: 1) a buffer manager that allocates buffers to
store the data transmitted from each server node, and monitors the buffer state
to detect link/node failure or link state change; and 2) a fetch scheduler that
reads data segments from each buffer dedicated to each server node to deliver
them to the player. Because each data segment of a media object can be assigned
to different server nodes for transmission, the fetch scheduler should deliver data
segments read from each buffer in a regular order. Therefore, the fetch scheduler
should know the segment assignment information to each server node.

The node manager selects the initial server nodes, sends request for data transmission and assigns segments to each selected server node, selects a new server
node when a fault signal arrives from the buffer monitor, and sends a request for
data transmission to the selected new server node. Therefore, the node manager
consists of: 1) a node selector that chooses server nodes from the many nodes
that have the demanded object; 2) a segment handler that assigns data segments to each server node for transmission; 3) a service manager that requests

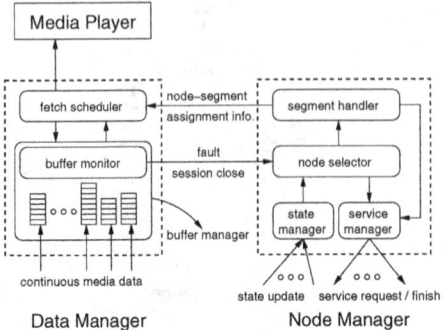

Fig. 2. Client process architecture for P2P streaming service

data transmission from the server nodes and sends a service finish request to the node that should cease data transmission because of the node/link failure or link state change; and 4) a state manager that receives state update information from nodes that are not currently selected as a server node but can be selected later when a server node fails, and transfers that information to the node selector.

3   Service Protocols

In this section, we present protocols for a streaming service on a P2P network. As stated above, we assume that a client node knows all nodes that have the demanded media objects. An object search algorithm should be used to find a set of nodes that have the object before starting our protocol.

3.1   Initial Session Establishment

To start a streaming service the client node selects server nodes that will transmit the data segments between those candidate nodes that have the demanded object. On selecting the server nodes, the client node assigns segments to each selected server node and then sends a start signal to each. On receiving the start signal, the server node establishes a data session between the server and the client node. Figure 3 shows the protocol for the initial session establishment. The state manager of the client node sends a state information request message to all nodes that have the demanded objects. Then the node managers of each server node send a state information reply message that contains currently available outbound bandwidth. On receiving the messages, the state manager stores the bandwidth information of each node and passes it to the node selector. The node selector chooses candidate server nodes based on the available bandwidth information. If we select server nodes with the Larger available outbound Bandwidth First (LBF), the number of server nodes can be minimized, which minimizes the probability of a node/link fault. However, using LBF, the

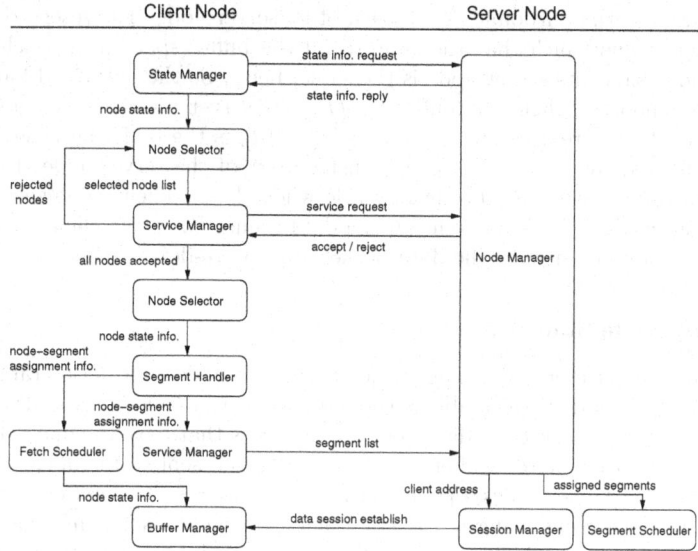

Fig. 3. Initial session establishment protocol

overhead to cope with the fault is large because if a node that serves with a high bit rate fails, it is likely that multiple nodes need to be engaged to replace the failed node. Therefore, the time from failure to recovery can be large. Conversely, if we select server nodes with Smaller available outbound Bandwidth First(SBF), the number of server nodes is maximized, which also maximizes the probability of a node/link fault. However, the overhead to recover from the fault is small because there are many nodes that can replace the failed node. The service manager sends a service request message to each selected node and waits for the reply. The node manager of the server node accepts the request if there has been no state change from when it sent the state information reply message. When all the selected nodes accept the request, the service manager notifies the node selector and the node selector passes the list of server nodes with their available outbound bandwidth to the segment handler. The segment handler assigns data segments to each server node using a suitable assignment algorithm. We used the OTS_{P2P} algorithm proposed by Dongyan [10]. After assigning data segments to each server node, the segment handler passes the node-segment assignment information to both the fetch scheduler and the service manager. The node-segment assignment information is a set of entries that consists of node ID, outbound bandwidth, and assigned segments. Because the fetch scheduler takes charge of passing data segments received from server nodes to the media player, it should know the correct order of the data segments. Therefore, the fetch scheduler stores the node ID and assigned segments. The buffer manager reserves buffer space for each server node. The size of each buffer differs according to the outbound bandwidth of its server node. The reserved buffer size is determined such that the time to fill the buffer space using each outbound bandwidth of its server node is the same. Let r_i be the outbound bandwidth of server node i. Then, the buffer size(B_i) for server node i is determined to be $r_i/s_d \cdot t_p$, where s_d is the segment size, and t_p is the buffering time and can be configured by the user. The session manager of the server node stops sending data to the client and finishes its role when: 1) the client node sends a service finish message, 2) it has sent all the data requested to the client, or 3) there is no acknowledgment of the data packet after a pre-defined time.

3.2   Node State Update

The node selector of the client node maintains a node information table that consists of the address, available outbound bandwidth, and service state (whether it is a server node or candidate node) of all nodes that have the demanded object. A candidate node remembers all client nodes that sent state information request messages to it regardless of whether it actually serves the client or not. When the state of the node changes, the node manager sends a state information update message to each client node so that they can maintain the current state of the node. The candidate node stops informing its state to the client node and removes the client node from the client nodes list when either it receives a service finish message from the node or there is no acknowledgment to the state update message from the node after a pre-determined time.

A node among candidate nodes can fail and should no longer be available for selection as a server node. If the failed node is chosen as a server node by the node selector, the service manager sends a service request message to the failed node. Because there is no reply to the message, the service manager informs the node selector that the node did not reply. Then, the node selector deletes the node from the node information table and the node will no longer be available as a server node.

3.3   Fault Tolerance

We assume that there are two types of fault - failure and state change. Failure means that there can be no more service between server node and client node because of server node shutdown or intermediate link failure. State change means that the actual data transmission rate from the server node to the client node becomes lower than the expected rate because of server overload or network congestion. In this paper, we cope with these in a unified manner.

Before starting playback, the buffer manager of the client node prefetches data segments in each buffer dedicated to each server node. The user can determine the prefetching quantities by configuring the buffering time (t_p) in the player. The quantity of data prefetched in a buffer is determined as $t_p \cdot r_i$, where r_i is the transmission rate of server i. Therefore, different prefetching quantities for each buffer can be defined according to the transmission rate of each server node. Because at least one segment should be transmitted to each buffer before

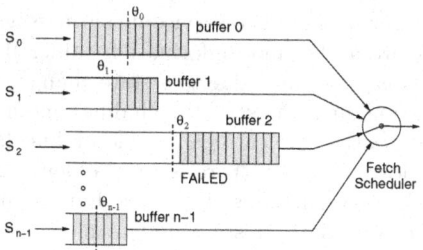

Fig. 4. The state of buffers and their fault detection thresholds

playback starts, the transmission rate of each server node should be no smaller than s_d/t_p, where s_d is the segment size. Therefore, the node selector has to exclude those nodes that have smaller available outbound bandwidth than s_d/t_p from the possible server nodes.

After prefetching data, during the buffering time, the fetch scheduler starts to pass data segments to the media player and playback starts. The volume of data in a buffer does not change significantly unless a fault occurs. However, if a fault occurs, either no more data arrives at the corresponding buffer (failure) or the rate of arrival decreases (state change) while the consumption rate does not change. Therefore, the amount of data in the buffer decreases as time passes. Therefore, we can determine the occurrence of a fault by monitoring the volume of data in a buffer.

The buffer monitor in the buffer manager starts to monitor each buffer when the playback begins. Let δ be the predicted time length from a fault occurrence to when a newly chosen server node starts service. There should be sufficient data for playback during δ in each buffer. Therefore, we can determine the fault detection threshold (θ_i) for *buffer(i)* using the following equation: $\theta_i = \frac{r_i}{s_d} \times \delta$. Figure 4 shows the state of each buffer at a given time. As shown in the figure, the threshold value is proportional to the buffer size.

When a fault is detected, the buffer monitor sends a fault signal containing the corresponding node ID to the node selector. On receiving the fault signal, the node selector chooses one or more replacement server nodes (R-servers) that will replace the failed node and one temporary server node (T-server) that will fill up the corresponding buffer in a short time. To prevent the necessity of segment reassignment to all servers, the aggregated service rate of R-servers is the same as that of a failed node. The segments previously assigned to the failed node will be reassigned mainly to the R-servers and part of the segments will be assigned to the T-server to supplement the data consumed during the time from the fault occurrence to the service migration completion, in a short time. Therefore, the server with the largest available outbound bandwidth is selected as the T-server. Because a relatively small number of segments are assigned to the T-server, it finishes service quickly and becomes one of the candidate servers. After choosing new server nodes the node selector passes the chosen server list to the service manager.

The service manager first sends a service finish message to the failed node and deletes the node from the node information table. If the failed node is still active, which means the fault is due to a state change, it will stop sending data to the client node and finish all service including sending state update messages. If the node is not active, which means node or link failure, the service finish message will be lost; however, there is no problem with the lost message. In the case where the server node is still active but the link is broken, the server node will stop sending data or state update messages to the client node and finish all service if there is no acknowledgment after a pre-defined time. After sending a service finish message to the failed node, the service manager sends service request messages to the R-servers and the T-server. From that time, the remaining procedure is the same as for the initial session establishment process until the T-server finishes sending all its data segments. When the T-server has sent all its data to the client node, the session manager of the T-server sends a session close message to the buffer manager of the client node. Then the buffer manager informs the node selector that the T-server has finished service and the node selector marks it as a candidate node.

3.4   Service Termination

When a server has sent all the assigned data segments to the client node, the session manager sends a session close message to the buffer manager of the client node. Then the buffer manager informs the node selector of the closed session. If all the servers have closed their data sessions, the node selector informs the service manager of service termination with the nodes list and deletes the node information table. Then, the service manager sends a service finish message to all nodes in the list. On receiving the service finish message from the client node, the server nodes (the candidate nodes) delete the client node from their client node list.

4   Simulation

In this section, we present and discuss simulation results. We measured the performance of our framework when using SBF or LBF as the server node selection algorithm and with and without considering link state changes. Therefore, there are four cases - SBF and LBF with or without link state change consideration, respectively (SBF, LBF, SBF_LINK, LBF_LINK).
We assumed total 1000 nodes participate in the simulated P2P network. The initial servers for a client are those nodes that have the demanded object. We fixed the number of initial server nodes at 20. Therefore, initially, the client should select server nodes from those 20 nodes and the remaining nodes become candidate nodes. The predefined outbound bandwidth to provide services to other nodes varies from 30 Kbps to 100 Kbps with 10 Kbps step and they are uniformly assigned to all nodes in the P2P network. We assumed that there are 20 video objects and the object playback rate is 300 Kbps, which is the

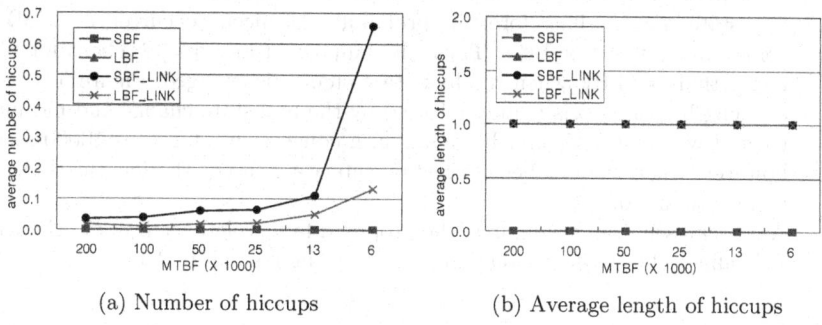

(a) Number of hiccups   (b) Average length of hiccups

Fig. 5. Total and average numbers of hiccups

MPEG-4 encoded object data rate, and the object length is 3600 seconds. The segment size was set to 10 Kbits. Therefore, 30 segments are consumed per second. The initial buffering time(t_p) is five seconds, but this does not affect the performance of the system provided that it is larger than the predicted migration time(δ), which was set as two seconds. We assumed that each node requests an average of one streaming service per day. Therefore, the average request arrival rate is $(1/86400) \times 1000 \sim 0.012$. When we considered the link state change we assumed that each path from a server node to the client node is congested following exponential distribution with mean interval 10000 seconds and the congested state lasts for 50 seconds. For normal state networks the actual migration time follows an exponential distribution with a mean of 0.1 seconds, and for a congested network it follows an exponential distribution with a mean of one second. The simulation was performed for 24 hours. The average node failure interval (MTBF) was varied from 6250 seconds to 200000 seconds. When the MTBF was 6250, $(1000/6250) \times 3600 = 576$ node failures occurred, and when the MTBF was 200000, only a few (exactly 18) nodes failed during the playback. Each of these represent the real world network and the P2P dedicated network, respectively. We made each node to recover from failure after 10 minutes to prevent serious decrement of the number of nodes.

Figure 5-(a) shows how many hiccups occur during playback, and Figure 5-(b) shows the average length of the hiccups. When a node/link fails or a link state changes, the rate of data arrival becomes smaller than the data consumption rate. If this lasts for a long time, a playback pause (hiccup) cannot be avoided because of the lack of data. However, because the client node always has up-to-date node information, the processing time for service migration is generally sufficiently small that most migrations are completed before the corresponding buffer becomes empty. Therefore, the number of hiccups is small. As can be seen from Figure 5-(a), the number of hiccups for a client increases as the MTBF value decreases. When the link state change is engaged, the number of migrations increases more for SBF than for LBF because SBF uses more server nodes than LBF, which means more intermediate links and greater probability of a link state change. Therefore, the probability of hiccup occurrence for SBF becomes larger than for LBF. Thus, the number of hiccups per client for SBF is larger than for LBF when the link state change is engaged. Figure 5-(b) shows the length of hiccup is mainly affected by the link state change and hiccups are treated within 1.0 second. In this figure, congestion interval is 10000 seconds, however, when the smaller congestion interval is used, the length of hiccup is greater than 1.0.

As we can see from the figures, the proposed fault-tolerance framework can provide almost hiccup-free streaming service using a small buffer.

5   Conclusion

In this paper, we proposed a framework to provide fault tolerant streaming service on a peer-to-peer network and showed its performance using simulation results. The proposed framework provides a service migration-based fault tolerant mechanism to cope with both node/link failures and link state changes. It maintains current node state information to minimize the service migration time when a fault occurs. Simulation results show that using a small buffer, hiccup-free streaming service can be provided.

References

1. vTrails, http://www.vtrails.com/.
2. Allcast, http://www.allcast.com/.
3. H. Deshpande, M. Bawa, H. Garcia-Molina: Streaming live media over a peer-to-peer network, Tech. Rep. TR 2001-30, Stanford Database Group, 2001.
4. V. N. Padmanabhan, H. J. Wang, P. A. Chou, K. Sripanidkulchai: Distributing streaming media content using cooperative networking, in *Proc. of NOSSDAV 2002*, (Miami Beach, FL), 2002.
5. Gnutella, http://www.gnutella.com/.
6. W.T.Leung, J. Y.B.Lee: A server-less architecture for building scalable, reliable and cost-effective video-on-demand systems, in *Proc. of Internet2 Workshop on Collaborative Computing in Higher Education: Peer-to-Peer and Beyond*, (Tempe, AZ), Jan. 2002.
7. J. Y. B. Lee, W. T. Leung: Study of a server-less architecture for video-on-demand applications, in *Proc. of the IEEE International conference on Multimedia and Expo.*, (Lausanne, Switzerland), Aug. 2002.
8. J. Y. B. Lee, W. T. Leung: Design and analysis of a fault-tolerant mechanism for a server-less video-on-demand system, in *Proc. of the International conference on Parallel and Distributed Systems*, (Taiwan), Dec. 2002.
9. T. P. Nguyen, A. Zakhor: Distributed video streaming over internet, in *Proc. of the Multimedia Computing and Networking 2002*, (San Jose, CA), Jan. 2002.
10. D. Xu, M. Hefeeda, S. Hambrusch, B. Bhargava: On peer-to-peer media streaming, in *Proc. of International Conference on Distributed Computing Systems*, (Vienna, Austria), July 2002.

Efficient and Scalable Client-Clustering for Proxy Cache

Kyungbaek Kim, Woo Jin Kim, and Daeyeon Park

Department of Electrical Engineering & Computer Science,
Division of Electrical Engineering,
Korea Advanced Institute of Science and Technology (KAIST),
373-1 Kusong-dong Yusong-gu, Taejon, 305-701, Korea
{kbkim, wjkim}@sslab.kaist.ac.kr and daeyeon@ee.kaist.ac.kr

Abstract. Many cooperated web cache systems and protocols have been proposed. These systems, however, require expensive resources, such as external
bandwidth and proxy cpu or storage, while inducing hefty administrative costs
to achieve adequate client population growth. Moreover, a scalability problem in
the cache server management still exists.

This paper suggests peer-to-peer client-clustering. The client-cluster provides a
proxy cache with backup storage which is comprised of the residual resources of
the clients. We use DHT based peer-to-peer lookup protocol to manage the client-
cluster. With the natural characteristics of this protocol, the client-cluster is self-
organizing, fault-tolerant, well-balanced and scalable. Additionally, we propose
the Backward ICP which is used to communicate between the proxy cache and
the client-cluster, to reduce the overhead of the object replication and to use the
resources more efficiently.

We examine the performance of the client-cluster via a trace driven simulation
and demonstrate effective enhancement of the proxy cache performance.

1 Introduction

The recent increase in popularity of the Web has led to a considerable increase in the
amount of Internet traffic. As a result, the Web has now become one of the primary bottlenecks to network performance and web caching has become an increasingly important issue. Web caching aims to reduce network traffic, server load, and user-perceived
retrieval delay by replicating popular content on caches that are strategically placed
within the network.

By caching requests for a group of users, a proxy cache can quickly return documents previously accessed by other clients. Using only one proxy cache has limited
performance, because the hit rate of the proxy is limited by the cache storage and the
size of the client population. That is, if a cache is full and needs space for new documents, it evicts the other documents and it will retrieve the evicted documents from
the Internet for other requests. In Figure 1(a), if the square object is evicted, the proxy
cache obtains it from the Internet. But if the near proxy cache has a square object like
that in Figure 1(b), Proxy 1 can obtain it from Proxy 2 and reduce the latency and the
Internet traffic. According to this procedure, multiple proxies should cooperate with
each other in order to increase the total client population, improve hit ratios, and reduce
document-access latency; that is the cooperative caching.

M.M. Freire, P. Lorenz, M.M.-O. Lee (Eds.): HSNMC 2003, LNCS 2720, pp. 83–92, 2003.

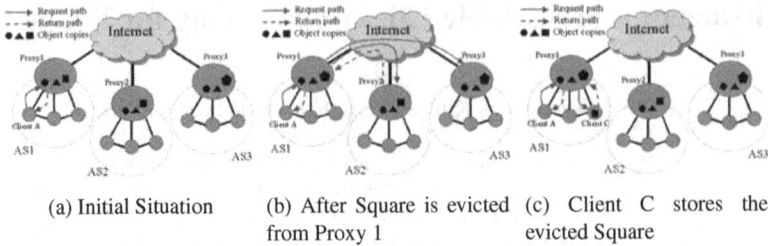

(a) Initial Situation   (b) After Square is evicted   (c) Client C stores the
                         from Proxy 1   evicted Square

Fig. 1. Request and Response path when client A requests the Square object

Various cooperative caching systems have been proposed in [2], [3], [4]. However, these techniques need high bandwidth, expensive infrastructure and high administrative cost. ICP-based cooperative caches communicate with other caches that are connected by busy core-links, which are the inter-proxy links, to find and obtain requested objects in other caches. Even if the requested objects are not in these caches, they spend bandwidth of core-links in order to find the objects. Some cooperative caches use the proxy cluster, as a single large cache so as to be overprovisioned to handle bursty peak loads. However, this approach still needs too much administrative cost for the frequent variation of clients. For example, a growth in client population necessitates increasing the cluster size and updating the cluster information.

In this paper, we suggest a new web caching system which uses the residual resources of clients. In Figure 1(c), not only the proxy cache but also the clients are responsible for storing objects; the proxy cache stores more popular objects and the client-cluster stores evicted objects from the proxy cache. That is, the client-cluster is used as a backup storage for the proxy cache. In this case, Client A can get the square object from Client C, which is inside the network, not outside of it. This behavior reduces the usage of core-links and improves the performance of the proxy cache, in terms of the hit rate, the byte hit rate and the reduced latency. Furthermore, the size of the backup storage of the proxy increases as more clients use the proxy. According to this feature, this approach reduces the administrative cost and makes the proxy cache more scalable.

The client-cluster is composed of the clients' residual resources. Since the clients join and leave dynamically, in order to use its storage efficiently, the client-cluster must be self-organizing and fault tolerant and the load of each client should be balanced. To meet these requirements, we manage the client-cluster by using Distributed Hash Table (DHT) based peer-to-peer protocol. By using this protocol, all clients receive roughly the same load because the hash function balances load with high probability. Additionally, the proxy cache does not need to gather the client information and we reduce administrative cost.

This protocol is responsible for the routing of the object, but it needs to cope with updating the object whenever clients join or leave. Typically, we can replicate the object. However, this approach leads to extremely large traffic overhead and wasted storage. To reduce this overhead, we suggest the *Backward ICP* which is responsible for storing and finding objects in a manner similar to replication. A proxy saves objects to a client-cluster and gets objects from it by using this protocol.

This paper is organized as follow. In section 2, we describe cooperated web caching and peer-to-peer lookup algorithm briefly. Section 3 introduces the detail of the peer-to-peer client-clustering. The simulation environment and the performance evaluation are given in section 4. We mention other related works in section 5. Finally, we conclude in section 6.

2   Background

2.1   Cooperated Web Caching

The basic operation of the web caching is simple. Web browsers generate HTTP GET requests for Internet objects such as HTML pages, images, mp3 files, etc. These are serviced from a local web browser cache, web proxy caches, or an original content server - depending on which cache contains a copy of the object. If a cache closer to the client has a copy of the requested object, we reduce more bandwidth consumption and decrease more network traffic. Hence, the cache hit rate should be maximized and the miss penalty, which is the cost when a miss occurs, should be minimized when designing a web caching system.

The performance of a web caching system depends on the size of its client community. As the user community increases in size, so does the probability that a cached object will soon be requested again. Caches sharing mutual trust may assist each other to increase the hit rate. A caching architecture should provide the paradigm for proxies to cooperate efficiently with each other. One approach to coordinate caches in the same system is to set up a caching hierarchy. With hierarchical caching, caches are placed at multiple levels of the network. Another approach is a distributed caching system, where there are only caches at the bottom level and there are no other intermediate cache levels.

Internet Cache Protocol (ICP) [2] is a typical cooperating protocol for a proxy to communicate with other proxies. If a requested object is not found in a local proxy, the proxy sends ICP queries to neighbor proxies; sibling proxies and parent proxies. Each neighbor proxy receives the queries and sends ICP replies without the existence of the object. If the local proxy receives an ICP reply with the object, it uses that reply. Otherwise, the local proxy forwards the request to the parent proxy. ICP wastes expensive resources; core-link and cache storage. Even if the neighbor caches do not have the requested object, ICP uses the core-links between proxies, which are used for many clients and are bottlenecks of the network bandwidth. Another protocol for cooperated caching is the Cache Array Routing Protocol (CARP) [3], which divides the URL-space among an array of loosely coupled caches and lets each cache store only the objects whose URL are hashed to it. For this feature, every request is hashed and forwarded to a selected cache node. In this scheme, clients must know the cache array information and the hash function, making the management of CARP difficult. Additionally, there are other issues such as load balancing and fault tolerance.

Another problem of CARP, as well as ICP, is scalability of management. Large corporate networks often employ a cluster of machines, which generally must be overprovisioned to handle burst peak loads. A growth in user population creates a need for hardware upgrades. This scalability issue cannot be solved by ICP or CARP.

2.2 Peer-to-Peer Lookup

Peer-to-peer systems are distributed systems without any centralized control or hierarchical organization, where the software running at each node is equivalent in functionality; this includes redundant storage, selection of nearby servers, anonymity, search, and hierarchical naming. Among these features, lookup for a data is an essential functionality for peer-to-peer systems.

A number of peer-to-peer lookup protocols have been recently proposed, including Pastry [5], Chord [6], CAN [7] and Tapestry [8]. In a self-organizing and decentralized manner, these protocols provide a distributed hash-table (DHT) that reliably maps a given object key to a unique live node in the network. Because DHT is made by a hash function that balances load with high probability, each live node has the same responsibility for data storage and query load. If a node wants to find an object, a node simply sends a query with the object key corresponding to the object to the selected node determined by the DHT. Typically, the length of routing is about O(log n), where n is the number of nodes. According to these properties, peer-to-peer systems balance storage and query load, transparently tolerate node failures and provide efficient routing of queries.

3 Peer-to-Peer Client-Clustering

3.1 Overview

As we described in the previous section, the use of only a proxy cache has a performance limitation because of potential growth in client population. Even if proxy caches cooperate with each other to enhance performance, high administrative cost and scalability issues still exist. To improve the performance of the cache system and solve the scalability issues, we exploit the residual resources of clients for a proxy cache. That is, any client that wants to use the proxy cache provides small resources to the proxy and the proxy uses these additional resources to maintain the proxy cache system. This feature makes the system resourceful and scalable.

We use the residual resources of clients as a backup storage for the proxy cache. While a conventional proxy cache drops evicted objects, our proxy cache stores these objects to the backup storage, which is distributed among the client-cluster. When a client sends a GET request to a proxy cache, it checks its local storage. If a hit occurs, it returns the requested object; otherwise, it sends a lookup message to the backup storage and this message is forwarded to the client that has responsibility for storing the object. If the client has the object, it returns the object to the proxy; otherwise, the proxy gets the object from the original server or other proxy caches. This interaction between the proxy cache and the backup storage decreases the probability of sending requests outside the network, reduces the usage of inter-proxy links, and increases the performance of the proxy cache.

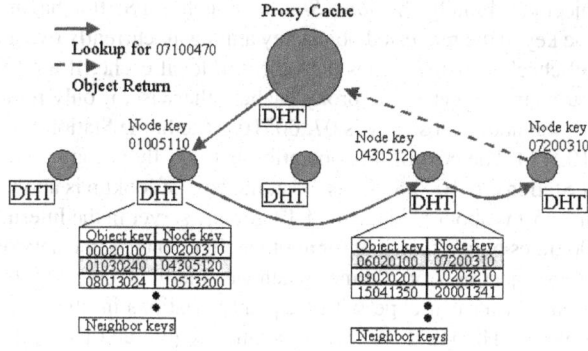

Fig. 2. Basic Lookup Operation In the Client-Cluster. In this Figure, Total Hop count is 3.

3.2 Client-Cluster Management

In our scheme, a proxy cache uses the resources of clients that are in the same network. Generally, if a peer wants to use other peers, it should have information about those. This approach is available when the other peers are reliable and available. However, the client membership is very large and changes dynamically. If the proxy cache manages the states of all clients, too much overhead is created to manage the client information and complex problems such as fault-tolerance, consistency and scalability arise. In consideration of these issues, we establish the proxy cache such that it has no information for the clients and the client-cluster manages itself.

We design the client-cluster by using DHT(distributed hash table) based peer-to-peer protocol [5], [6], [7], [8]. To use this protocol, each client needs an application whose name is *Station*. A Station is not a browser or a browser cache, but a management program to provide clients' resources for a proxy cache. A client can not use resources of a Station directly, while a proxy cache sends requests issued from clients to Stations in order to use resources of a client-cluster. When a Station receives requests from a proxy cache, it forwards requests to another Station or checks whether it has the requested objects. Each Station has a unique node key and a DHT. The unique node key is generated by computing the SHA-1 hash of the client identifier, such as an ip address or an ethernet address, and the object key is obtained by computing the SHA-1 of the corresponding URL. The DHT describe the mapping of the object keys to responsible live node keys for efficient routing of request queries. It is similar to a routing table in a network router. A Station uses this table with the key of the requested object to forward the request to the next Station. Additionally, the DHT of a Station has the keys of *neighbor Stations* which are numerically close to the Station, like the leaf nodes in PASTY or the successor list in CHORD.

The basic operation of the lookup in a client-cluster is shown in Figure 2. When a proxy cache sends a request query to one Station of a client-cluster, the Station gets the object key of the requested object and selects the next Station according to the DHT and the object key. Finally, the *home Station*, which is a Station having the numerically closest node key to the requested object key among all currently live nodes, receives the request and checks whether it has the object in local cache. If a hit occurs, the home Station returns the object to the proxy cache; otherwise, it only returns a null object. In Figure 2, the node whose key is 07200310 is the home Station for the object whose key is 07100470. The cost of this operation is typically O(log n), where n is the total number of Stations. If 1000 Stations exist, the cost of lookup is about 3, and if 100000 Stations, the cost is about 5. Since the RTT for any server in the Internet from one client is 10 or 100 times bigger than that for another client in the same network, we reduce the latency for an object by 2 or 20 times when we obtain the object in the client-cluster.

The client-cluster can cope with frequent variations in client membership by using this protocol. Though the clients dynamically join and leave, the lazy update for managing the small information of the membership changes does not spoil the lookup operation of this protocol. When a Station joins the client-cluster, it sends a join message to any one Station in the client-cluster and gets new DHT and other Stations to update their DHT for the new Station lazily. On the other hand, when a Station leaves or fails, other Stations, which have a DHT mapping with the departing Station, detect the failure of it lazily and repair their DHT. According to this feature, the client-cluster is self-organizing and fault-tolerant.

The proxy cache stores the evicted objects to a particular Station in the client-cluster by using this lookup operation. All Stations have roughly the same amount of objects, because the DHT used for the lookup operation provides a degree of natural load balance. Moreover, the object range, which is managed by one Station, is determined by the number of live nodes. That is, if there are few live nodes, the object range is large; otherwise, it is small. According to this, when the client membership changes, the object range is resized automatically and the home Stations for every object are changed implicitly.

As described, the routing information and the object range are well managed by this protocol. Consequently, after updating the information for variation in the client membership, future requests for an object will be routed to the Station that is now numerically closest to the object key. If the objects for the new home Station are not moved, subsequent requests miss the objects. According to these misses, the performance of a client-cluster decreases remarkably. We can replicate the objects to neighbor Stations to prevent such misses. This approach ensures the reliability of the objects, but leads to serious traffic overhead and inefficient storage usage. To reduce this overhead and use the storage efficiently, we store and lookup objects using the *Backward ICP*. This is described in the next section.

3.3 Backward ICP

The Backward ICP, which is a communication protocol between the proxy cache and the client-cluster, is similar to the ICP used between the proxy caches. However, the Backward ICP uses a local area network rather than an inter-proxy link.

There are two types of messages in the Backward ICP, as shown in Figure 3. One is a *Store* message and the other is a *Lookup* message. A Store message is used to store evicted objects from a proxy cache. The proxy cache sends a Store message and

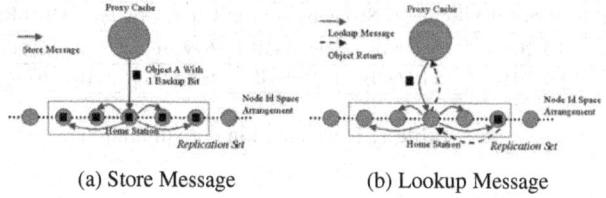

(a) Store Message   (b) Lookup Message

Fig. 3. Two types of Backward ICP Message

the evicted object to the home Station and the home Station replicates the objects to the replication set, which is composed of neighbor Stations. Before sending a Store message for an evicted object, the proxy cache checks the *Backup bit* of the evicted object. This Backup bit is used to prevent duplicated storage of an object that is already in the client-cluster. If the Backup bit is set to 1, the proxy cache knows that the client-cluster has this evicted object and drops this object immediately. If the bit is set to 0, the proxy cache backs up the evicted object to the client-cluster. When the proxy cache gets the object from the client-cluster, this bit is set to 1. When the object is refreshed or returned from the original server, this bit is set to 0.

A Lookup message is used to find objects in the client-cluster. When the proxy cache sends a Lookup message to the home Station, this Station returns the object to the proxy cache if it has the requested object. Otherwise, if a miss occurs, it sends Lookup messages to the replication set simultaneously and waits for a response from any Station. If the object is somewhere among the replication set, the home Station stores this object and returns this to the proxy cache; otherwise, it returns a null object. Following this, the home Station replicates the object to the replication set, except the responding Station.

This protocol replicates objects only at the time when they are stored or a lookup miss occurs. It reduces traffic overhead incurred by object replications. Moreover, it uses storage efficiently by giving more opportunities to retrieve popular objects. The first time when any object is stored, the object is replicated to increase the probability of accessing the object. As time goes by, popular objects are requested more than other objects and they are replicated again to increase the probability.

4 Performance Evaluation

4.1 Traces Used

In our trace-driven simulations we use traces from KAIST, which uses a class B ip address for the network. The trace from the proxy cache in KAIST contains over 3.4 million requests in a single day. We have run our simulations with traces from this proxy cache since October, 2001. We show some of the characteristics of these traces in Table 1. Note that these characteristics are the results when the cache size is infinite. However, our simulations assume limited cache storage and ratios including hit rate and byte hit

Traces	Measuring day	Requests Size	Object Size	Request #	Object #	Hit Rate	Byte Hit Rate
Trace 1	2001.10.08	9.02GB	3.48GB	699280	215427	69.19%	63.60 %
Trace 2	2001.10.09	11.66GB	1.38 GB	698871	224104	67.93%	57.79%

Table 1. Traces used in our simulation

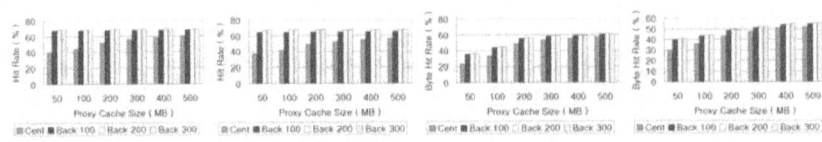

(a) Hit rate for Trace 1   (b) Hit rate for Trace 2   (c) Byte Hit rate for Trace 1   (d) Byte Hit rate for Trace 2

Fig. 4. Hit rate and byte hit rate comparison between only proxy cache(cent) and client-cluster(back-n)

rate cannot be higher than *infinite-hit rate* and *infinite-byte hit rate*, which are the hit rate and the byte hit rate when the infinite cache is used.

4.2   Hit Rate and Byte Hit Rate

Figure 4 shows a comparison of the *hit rate* and the *byte hit rate*. By the hit rate, we mean the number of requests that hit in the proxy cache as a percentage of total requests. A higher the hit rate means the proxy cache can handle more requests and the original server must deal with proportionally lighter load of requests. The byte hit rate is the number of bytes that hit in the proxy cache as a percentage of total number of bytes requested. A higher byte hit rate results in a greater decrease in network traffic on the server side.

In the figures, cent means using only a proxy cache and back n means using the client-cluster with n hundreds clients. The hit rate of only the proxy cache is greatly affected by the cache size, but the hit rate of using the client-cluster achieves nearly an infinite-hit rate without any relationship to the proxy cache size. This is achieved by the plentiful resources provided by the clients. That is, though the proxy cache size is limited, the storage of the client-cluster is sufficient to store evicted objects and the proxy cache gets almost all requested objects from the client-cluster.

For the byte hit rate, we can obtain a similar result as that for the hit rate. However, in this case, using the client-cluster does not yield infinite-byte hit rate, particularly with a small proxy cache size. The reason for this result is the different byte size of the object range, which is roughly the same for each client, because of the different sizes of the objects. Thus some clients that usually have large objects cannot store many objects, and the hit rate and the byte hit rate decrease. In particular, large size objects whose size is bigger than that of one client storage, which is the Station's storage, 10MB, are not stored on the client-cluster and the byte hit rate decreases remarkably.

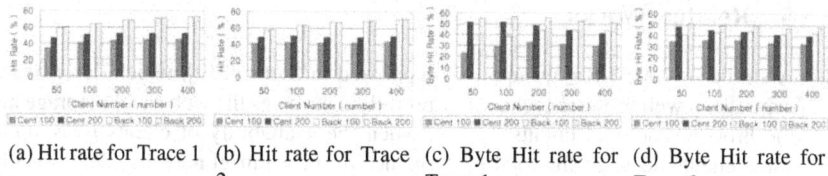

(a) Hit rate for Trace 1   (b) Hit rate for Trace 2   (c) Byte Hit rate for Trace 1   (d) Byte Hit rate for Trace 2

Fig. 5. Hit rate and byte hit rate comparison with various client number

Client #	Mean Req.	Max Req.	Dev.	Mean Byte Req.	Max. Byte Req.	Dev.
100	1024	1369	2.2	13422KB	316805KB	11.1
200	602	733	2.4	6711KB	315158KB	12.1
300	401	510	2.5	4474KB	314197KB	12.9

Table 2. Summary of Client Loads for Trace 1 with the 200MB proxy

4.3   Client Size Effect

In this section, we show scalability of the client-clustering. We assume every 100 clients makes 0.35million requests and simulate with variable client number.

In Figure 5, the hit rate when only the proxy cache is used does not increase markedly. Even in Trace 2, the hit rate decreases. However, when a proxy cache uses the client-cluster, the hit rate increases by 30-40% over that when only the proxy cache is used. Additionally, as the client number increases, the hit rate increases accordingly. For the byte hit rate, when the proxy cache uses the client-cluster, the byte hit rate increases by 20-30% over that when only the proxy cache is employed.

According to these results, when client population grows, using only a proxy cache should take on administrative cost to provide sufficient service to clients. However, using the client-cluster does not need any management cost to handle the growth in client population. Consequently, the client-cluster is scalable.

4.4   Client Load

We examine the client loads, which include the request number, storage size, stored objects, hit rate, etc, to verify that the client-cluster balances the storage and request queries. Table 2 shows a summary of the request number and the sizes of the requested objects. Each client receives roughly the same load, and when the client number increases the load of each client decreases. The properties of DHT-base peer-to-peer protocols account for these findings. For the byte request, we again see the effect of the different sizes of the objects, which we strongly believe account for the performance degradation.

5   Related Works

A similar proposal for our approach appeared in Squirrel [9], which described a de-centralized web browser cache. Squirrel fully distributes the web caches storage among the browser cache of clients. Hence, when the availability of clients is asymmetric, some clients decrease the total performance of the Squirrel network. Additionally, all contents are distributed and it is hard to manage the objects according to the characteristics of web objects. In our scheme, a web object is assigned to the proxy cache or the client-cluster according to the popularity of the object, which optimizes the overall performance of the proxy cache.

6   Conclusions

In this paper, we propose and evaluate peer-to-peer client-clustering, which is used as a backup storage for the proxy cache. The proxy cache with this client-cluster is highly scalable and more efficient, and has low administrative cost. Even if the clients take the load, this load has been verified on a range of real workloads to be low. Moreover, the utility of the client-cluster can be improved by managing objects according to their properties such as size, popularity and update frequency. We can extend the usage of the client-cluster to other proxy systems. If a proxy performs demanding jobs such as encoding/decoding and complex calculation for many clients, it can use the residual resources of the clients to accomplish these tasks.

References

1. P.Rodriguez, C.Spanner, and E.W.Biersack, Web caching architectures:Hierarchical and distributed caching. In proceedings of the 4th International Web Caching Workshop, 1999.
2. A.Chankhunthod, P.B.Danzig, C.Neerdaels, M.F.Schwartz and K.J.Worrell, A hierarchical internet object cache. In proceedings of the 1996 Usenix Technical Conference, January 1996.
3. J.Cohen, N.phadnis, V.valloppillil and K.W.Ross, Cache Array Routing Protocol v1.0. http://www.ietf.org/internet-drafts/draft-vinod-carp-v1-03.txt, September 1997.
4. A.Wolman, G.M.Voelker, N.Sharma, N.Cardwell, A.Karlin and H.M.Levy, On the scale and performance of cooperative Web proxy caching. In proceedings of the 17th ACM symposium on Operating Systems Principles, December 1999.
5. A.Rowstron and P.Druschel, Pastry: Scalable, decentralized object location and routing for large-scale peer-to-peer systems. In proceedings of the International Conference on Distributed Systems Platforms, November 2001.
6. I.Stoica, R.Morris, D.Karger, M.F.Kaashoek and H.Balakrishnan, Chord: A scalable peer-to-peer lookup service for Internet applications. In proceedings of ACM SIGCOMM 2001, August 2001.
7. S.Ratnasamy, P.Francis, M.Handley, R.Karp and S.Shenker, A Scalable Content-Addressable Network. In proceedings of ACM SIGCOMM 2001, August 2001.
8. B.Y.Zhao, J.Kubiatowicz and A.Joseph, Tapestry: An Infrastructure for Fault-tolerant Wide-area Location and Routing. In UCB Technical Report UCB/CSD-01-114, 2001.
9. S.Iyer, A.Rowstron and P.Druschel, Squirrel: A decentralized peer-to-peer web cache. In proceedings of Principles of Distributed Computing'02, 2002.

Diversity Protected, Cache Based Reliable Content Distribution Building on Scalable, P2P, and Multicast Based Content Discovery

Christian Bachmeir[1], Jianxiang Peng[1], Hans-Jörg Vögel[2],
Chris Wallace[3], and Gavin Conran[3]

[1] Technische Universität München, Institute of Communication Networks
bachmeir@ei.tum.de, peng@lkn.ei.tum.de
http://www.lkn.ei.tum.de

[2] The Fantastic Corporation, now with the BMW Group, Munich, Germany
hans-joerg.voegel@bmw.de

[3] The Fantastic Corporation, Zug, Switzerland
{chris.wallace | gavin.conran}@fantastic.com

Abstract. This paper presents a new scalable distributed architecture of collaborating caches. Our approach masks faults in content distribution scenarios towards clients. Basically, in case of a failure, our architecture requests content from distributed caches. When the content is found it is transparently transported to the requesting receiver. Distributed architectures of collaborating caches for fault tolerant content delivery pose a fundamental challenge: The probability to find requested content stored in caches, rises with the number of caches involved. A rising number of caches however implicates more signaling overhead for each query leading to scalability problems. In this work we present a new reliable distributed content discovery architecture that solves the scalability problem. Building on a 2 tier Peer-to-Peer overlay networks in combination with local summary distribution based on Multicast signaling, we provide a fast and scalable signaling architecture for content discovery in large distributed cache networks.

1 Introduction

The focus of our work is on improving fault tolerance—concerning data transport—for networked communicating applications. In this work we concentrate on fault tolerant content distribution in classical client/ server architectures. We present a reliable content distribution overlay network building on the PIRST-ON framework [3], eliminating edge based, single points of failures in communication flows.

PIRST-ON is a framework that transparently reduces packet loss between communicating applications in the Internet. It improves error resilience of data transport by introducing fault tolerance protecting against single node or edge failures through transparent high layer diversity in overlay networks. PIRST-ON builds on the technology of Active and Programmable Networks, which have been discussed in recent years [10], [16]. We utilize proposed architectures (e.g. [15]) as a basis to build trans-

M.M. Freire, P. Lorenz, M.M.-O. Lee (Eds.): HSNMC 2003, LNCS 2720, pp. 93-107, 2003.
© Springer-Verlag Berlin Heidelberg 2003

parent programmable content retrieval overlay networks that improve network performance as perceived by the users' applications.

Transporting data on redundant and diverse paths in overlay networks is a current research topic (see [1], [20], [23]). Applications like Scattercast [11] use caching proxies to enable reliable data transport. However these approaches –to our knowledge– neglect the problem of a fault at one of the communication partner at the edge of the network.

Proxy-caching, combined with transparent cache detection such as Web Proxy Auto-Discovery (WPAD) or Web Cache Coordination Protocol (WCCP) is a well-known and widely-deployed technology to overcome network bottlenecks [5]. There are both, forward caching and reverse caching variants, one to save access bandwidth and enhance local content delivery, the other to reduce server load and enhance server content playout, respectively. Statistical caching had been the first approach to those systems, where popularity of content is directly related to the caching efficiency [21].

Content distribution networks (CDN) such as Akamai and Digital Island haven taken this concept one step further for the public Internet, by placing their caches at strategic co-location facilities of associated ISPs throughout the Internet and proactively pre-populating these caches with their customers' web page content. Thereby, these web pages yield higher download speeds and overall better consumer experience, as content request routing techniques dynamically direct requests to the best available server based on the current load situation in the network.

With increasing content volumes and corporate network size, the same content delivery requirements as on the public Internet also arise on the corporate Intranet. Public CDN offerings are thus complemented by private enterprise CDNs at growing speeds and CDN platforms catering to the specific needs of corporate networks have emerged, e.g. [12].

There have even specified several intercache communication protocols (e.g. ICP, CRP, CARP, WCCP etc. [5]). Collaboration among peers or caches (acting as receivers in a Multicast scenario) during downloads of data in overlay networks is proposed by Byers et al. [8]. However what so far has not been addressed in appropriate breadth and depth is a scalable and reliable signaling architecture that enables collaboration among caches in the discovery process of data, based on fast and scalable decentralized information exchange.

In this work we combine the two research approaches of diversity protection and collaboration, presenting an enhancement to PIRST-ON. We introduce a new diversity protected reliable content distribution network. We propose to mask end-systems failures through replicated surrogate information retrieval and adoption based on distributed and programmable caches. The main contribution of this work is a fast and scalable signaling architecture for data (document) discovery in distributed caches.

This paper is organized as follows: In the next section the PIRST-ON architecture is briefly explained. In the third section we present a new signaling architecture for fast and scalable content discovery in distributed caches.

2   PIRST-ON Architecture

The concept of PIRST-ON presented in [3] is enhanced by this work. We thus begin by summarizing prominent features of PIRST-ON. The basic concept of PIRST-ON is to simultaneously transport redundant data in an overlay network. The overlay network is established on the transport network such as to provide edge- and vertex-disjoint paths. These redundant paths can be dynamically chosen when transporting data through the overlay. This switching decision can be taken based on a number of criteria ranging from statistical metrics such as packet loss ratio up to individual, per-packet decisions protecting against individual packet error or loss. Hence the basic concept of PIRST-ON is "Transparent High Layer Protection Switching".

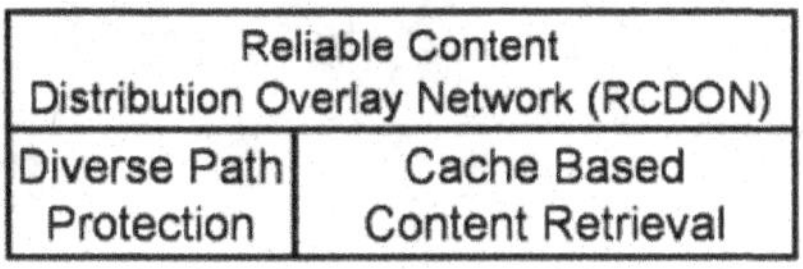

Reliable Content Distribution Overlay Network (RCDON)	
Diverse Path Protection	Cache Based Content Retrieval

Figure 1: RCDON components

The overall goal of our approach is to improve error resilience of communicating applications. However in the basic concept of PIRST-ON there are still some single points of failure (see 2.1). This work introduces a cache based overlay network to complement the basic concept of PIRST-ON (2.2). We use caches to eliminate single points of failure transparently. Hence our work proposes a transparent, reliable content distribution overlay network (see figure 1) building on the PIRST-ON architecture.

2.1 High Layer Transparent Diversity Protection

The basic concept of PIRST-ON [3] is using a simple fault-tolerant technique to provide redundant paths. In terms of network traffic that means using parallel, independent, vertex- and edge-disjoint paths. As shown by Andersen et al. [1] there is physical path redundancy in the Internet even during outages. In our architecture we exploit that basic property. PIRST-ON is an overlay network that is transparent to applications. In case of e.g. a simple Client/Server communication the necessary components of our architecture are shown in figure 2. Two Local Area Networks (LANs) are connected through the Internet. The Internet is presented exemplarily as a meshed network of Autonomous Systems (AS). Client and server are located within the two LANs. "Overlay Access" Points (OAP) are located between the LANs and the Internet. Together with the shown "Overlay Relay" (ORE), the Overlay Access Points build the PIRST-ON architecture. Overlay Relays are located at designated places in the Internet. During a communication between Client and Server, shortly after a data packet is sent out by the Client to the Internet, right at the edge of the network, the packet traverses the first OAP. There, the data packet is duplicated. The OAP then forwards the original, unchanged packet out on the regular path to the Internet. The copy of the original data packet is injected in the PIRST-ON framework. It is guided through an overlay network on a mostly edge- and vertex-disjoint path. The path in the overlay network is determined by the location of the used Overlay Relay. Finally, in the best case, both the original, as well as the copied packet make their way through

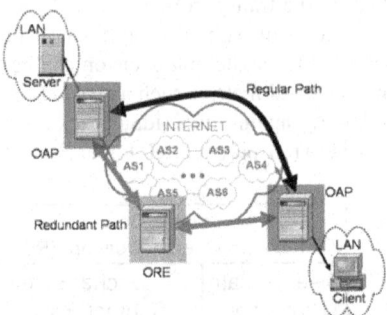

Figure 2: PIRST-ON Components

the Internet and reach the OAP next to the server. Possible redundant data packets are dropped there. Hence the application running on the server only receives one of the two packets. OAPs are transparent and can to some extent be compared to firewalls [3]. Hence we see that client and server are not aware of the PIRST-ON framework, it is also completely transparent to them.

In [2] we show encouraging measurements about the placement and discovery of Overlay Relays which is crucial for provision of redundant paths. We show that our proposed architecture can provide vertex- and edge disjoint paths as targeted.

However there are some limitations: As one of the main goals of our architecture is transparency to end system hosts, there are by definition some single points of failures left in the communication flow. In this work we concentrate on the most obvious one, which is the actual end system host. In case of e.g. a client/ server communication over the Internet this means that if e.g. the server fails, the architecture proposed in [2] cannot mask the failure to the client. Other single points of failures (e.g. OAP) are neglected in the following.

2.2 Distributed Caches

In 2.1 diverse protection was explained. In this paragraph we present the cache based extension to PIRST-ON addressing the yet unsolved problem of origin content server outages. We make the following assumptions:

- Each Overlay Access Point (OAP) or Overlay Relay (ORE) can provide a cache
- Each Overlay Access Point (OAP) should be able to query and use the resources of all available caches in all other OAP or ORE

Hence we propose to build a distributed caching system. Further we assume future wide deployment of this framework. Therefore we require the system to scale from a few, up to millions of OAP or ORE. In Figure 3 the distributed cache extension to PIRST-ON is exemplarily shown. Each of the components known from 2.1 is equipped with a cache. On top to the components necessary in 2.1 an additional Overlay Relay is exemplarily shown, indicating that all available caches in the Overlay Network can be used. Recalling the requirement that there can be a lot of distributed

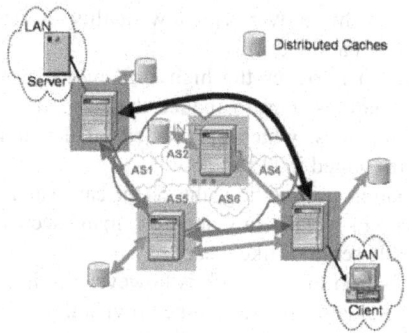

Figure 3: Cache based Extension to PIRST-ON

caches available, and the system should be able to use all of them, we clearly see the scalability problem in inter-cache communication for locating replicated surrogate copies of the origin content. This scalability problem we tackle in chapter 3, proposing a new 2-tier "active signaling" hierarchy.

2.3 Basic Services

In 2.1 and 2.2 we described parts of the basic concept of PIRST-ON. Our framework provides the network with means to react dynamically to topology changes in the Internet. With changes we mean in this context, dynamic changes of topology due to network faults. This level of network services we term as "Basic Services". Another example of a Basic Service would be network support concerning mobility aspects e.g. solving some problems MobileIP imposes on end systems [22]. The common denominator of Basic Services is the application independence of the service. It doesn't matter what kind of communicating applications run at the end systems, all of them could use the Basic Services.

In the following, when speaking of Basic Services we exclusively mean the provision of edge- and vertex disjoint redundant transport of data, supported by distributed caches.

2.4 Additional Application Specific Services

Besides Basic Services our approach is also capable to provide application specific high layer services based on active and programmable networks technology. In [15] transcoding and adaptations of data streams is introduced as a network service for heterogeneous group communication. We see this category of higher layer services also as a reasonable add-on to our proposed architecture.

What could be imagined in a distributed caching environment is the following service:

- A requested movie is only available in a cache with high QoS parameters (e.g. high resolution => high bandwidth)
- A client requests this movie with low quality of service parameters (e.g. low resolution => low bandwidth)

Our proposed solution retrieves the high QoS movie from the cache and does the necessary QoS adaptations (e.g. to reduce the resolution of the movie) using dedicated transcoding modules, which are loaded on demand at chosen overlay nodes (OAP or ORE) as presented in [15].

After the transparent transcoding, the client can watch the requested movie with low QoS parameters. Especially in video on demand scenarios we see a possible wide application of flexible services like these.

The main contribution of this work is however not in high layer services like dynamic transcoding, but concentrates on the provision of Basic Services, namely diversity protected, cache-enhanced error resilient content delivery.

3   Discovery of Cached Data in Overlay Nodes

The data we want to retrieve from caches must be uniquely identified by a URL. In the example of Figure 2 a client requests data from a server. The requested data is uniquely identified by the URL consisting of the server's address and the corresponding path on the server. Each Cache is organized in the same manner:

- Stored Documents can be uniquely identified by an URL
- All the URLs identifying the documents in one cache, are mapped through hash functions, we use a Bloomfilter [6]
- The Bloomfilter describing all the documents stored in the cache is locally recomputed as soon as the cache changes

Based on this cache specific Bloomfilter, in conjunction with the used hash functions, it can be checked with defined probabilities whether a document identified by a URL is located in a specific cache or not.

Bloomfilters were invented in the 1970's and have been used mainly for database applications. Only recently they received widespread attention in the networking literature [13].

The great benefit of the Bloomfilter approach is the possibility to do a fast remote check whether a specific URL is located in a cache or not. Only few bits have to be compared, and with a certain fixed probability it can be said whether a document is stored in a remote cache or not.

As shown in Figure 4 there are basically 3 possibilities when validating the result of a Bloomfilter check. First of all there are the two "good" cases:

1. A document is stored in a cache, and the result of the Bloomfilter check is positive and indicates it correctly.

    2.   A document is not stored in a cache, and the result of the Bloomfilter check is also indicating it, and negative.

We only have one failure case: A document is not stored in a cache; however the Bloomfilter check is positive. That error is termed "false positive". By definition the fourth possible case (document is stored in cache, and Bloomfilter test is negative) cannot happen [6].

	Bloomfilter check: **Positive**	Bloomfilter check: **Negative**
Document in Cache	✔	**Cannot Happen**
Document not in Cache	⚡	✔

Figure 4: Bloomfilter: false positive check possible

The probability of a "false positive" depends highly on the actual implementation of the Bloomfilter. With reasonable effort this probability can be lowered easily down to 2% [7].

    Our proposed architecture builds on work done in the field of distributed caching. In [13] a wide-area web cache sharing protocol is presented. We use the basic principles presented in the architecture, however we concentrate especially on the scalability of distributed cache system. The main contribution of this work is a distributed 2-tier signaling architecture for discovery of cached documents, presented in 3.4.

3.1 Distribution of Cache Specific Bloomfilters in Cache-Clusters

Each Cache in our architecture provides a specific Bloomfilter, representing information about its stored documents. Based on this specific Bloomfilter it can be checked fast whether a document with a specific URL is located in that specific cache.

    In the lower tier of our proposed architecture caches are grouped in clusters. For scalability reasons we limit the number of caches in a cluster and only distribute Bloomfilters within these clusters. Clusters can be formed by caches of local proximity talking to each other through the Cache Array Protocol (CARP) [5].

    Hence, each of the caches in a single cluster can validate, based on a Bloomfilters check, whether a specific document is located in one of the other caches in his cluster.

    To distribute Bloomfilters within clusters we propose to setup intra domain, Multicast based Bloomfilter distribution trees. Building on the digital fountain approach [9] we provide a resource optimized distribution of Bloomfilters within one cluster. In Figure 5 is exemplarily shown how an Overlay Node sends out its Bloomfilter to other Overlay Nodes (OAP and ORE) within their Cache-Cluster. Successively all the other Overlay Nodes also send out their Bloomfilter to the other Overlay Nodes on the Multicast Tree.

Finally after "a while" each of the Overlay Nodes within the Cache Cluster has received all the Bloomfilters from the other Overlay Nodes. Therefore each overlay node can check very fast if a specific document is cached within his Cache Cluster or not. It just has to examine all the Bloomfilters it received, and knows (according to certain probabilities) whether the document is cached within its cluster or not.

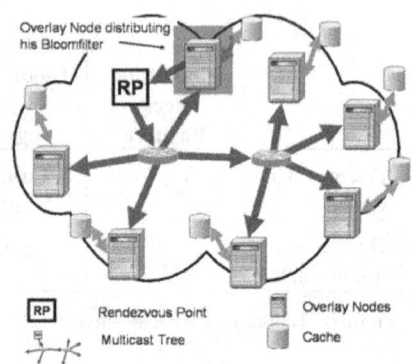

Figure 5: An Overlay Node is distributing his Bloomfilter within a Cache-Cluster

The benefit of the approach to summarize cache information in Bloomfilters and distribute them is obvious: There is virtually no time necessary and network resource used to query a cache directly whether a certain document is available.

3.2 Enhanced Digital Fountain Data Distribution Approach

In 3.1 the Distribution of the Overlay Node specific Bloomfilters was presented in an overview. In this paragraph we focus on the Bloomfilter data transport in the Cache-Clusters in detail.

Whenever a cache set changes, e.g. a new document is stored in the cache; a new Bloomfilter for that specific cache is computed. As the Bloomfilter binary file can be large, for scalability reasons we cannot multicast the new Bloomfilter every time a change in the cache happens.

What also must be taken into account are possible collisions. At the same time different Overlay Nodes from the same Cache-Cluster could intend to multicast their new Bloomfilters to the overlay nodes in their cluster. Simultaneous transmissions like these can be handled by higher layers, and the different Bloomfilters could be separated by the receivers.

However the main problem distributed simultaneous multicast—of different Bloomfilters—imposes on our system, are the inevitable peaks in used bandwidth. Therefore we propose a Multicast data distribution architecture that successively streams Bloomfilters at a constant bandwidth to receivers.

Basically our system builds on a new distributed Multicast-Group Access-Control mechanism. From all Overlay Nodes in the Cluster, only one at a time is allowed to send his Bloomfilter to the Cluster. Based on a priority scheme according to IP Addresses in combination with a fair round robin schedule, one Overlay Node after the other is sending his Bloomfilter to the Cluster. This access control process is managed completely distributed by the receivers themselves, as we dislike for reliability reasons a single management unit.

After the last Overlay Node has finished, sending his Bloomfilter to the Cluster, the first Overlay Node starts over again with a new cycle and sends his current, perhaps new computed, Bloomfilter to the Cluster. Based on that scheme we have a constant data stream of subsequent Bloomfilters in each Cache Cluster.

The necessary signaling for this fair and distributed queuing—leading to an enhanced, i.e. distributed digital fountain—is done "inband" over the existing multicast group. Short signaling packets are injected in between the actual data transmission.

$$BW_{Multicast\,Group} = \frac{N_{Overlay\,Nodes} * L_{Bloomfilter}}{\Delta T_{Cycle}}$$

Figure 6: Bandwidth for continuous Bloomfilter Distribution in cluster

In Figure 6 the formula for the necessary bandwidth is shown. The number N of Overlay Nodes in a cluster multiplied by the average length L of a single Bloomfilter results in the total number of bits that have to be transmitted over the Multicast Group in one cycle. Divided by the update time (for one single cycle), it delivers the minimum transmission bit rate necessary. The two variable parameters, BW and update time, are distributed negotiated and adopted by the Overlay Nodes in the Cluster according to network conditions.

All Overlay Nodes in the Cluster subsequently transmit their Bloomfilters to the Multicast Group based on the negotiated bit rate. Hence receiving OAPs in the Cluster perceive a continuous stream of Bloomfilters.

After the elapse of an update time interval, Bloomfilters of all Nodes have been distributed to all other Nodes in the Cluster and the next cycle starts over. Hence the maximum delay time between the change in a single cache and the distribution of the resulting new Bloomfilter to the Cluster is the update time.

Compared to the "Digital Fountain" (DF) approach [9] we propose some enhancements. DF was originally developed for the distribution of huge files in an unreliable multicast scenario (e.g. asynchronous software updates at millions of clients). Based on error resilient codes [17] a file is constantly distributed to a Multicast group. Based on forward error correction mechanisms, receivers are able to reconstruct the original file if they only received a sufficient number of encoded packets, no matter at what time they started tuning into the stream.

Our proposed enhanced digital fountain does not send the same file continuously. Subsequently new computed Bloomfilters of Overlay Nodes are distributed within the cluster. We also suggest using error resilient codes [17]; hence we introduce some redundancy to reduce packet loss ratios of the data transport over multicast within the cluster. The most obvious enhancement to the digital fountain approach is however the number of senders in the multicast scenario. In our approach all members of the corresponding cluster have to be enabled to distribute their Bloomfilter to the other members. Therefore we introduce a new distributed Multicast Group Access control mechanisms that controls the senders.

To evaluate our enhanced digital fountain based Bloomfilter distribution in a Multicast Cluster, we have an exemplary and representative look at Leibniz Rechenzentrum (LRZ) [18] in Munich. The LRZ is a quite large and exclusive Internet service provider (ISP) for four universities (ca. 100.000 students and staff). Furthermore there are also served some public facilities by LRZ, student housings etc. At LRZ there is a cache installed–in combination with a proxy–that is currently described (Nov. 2002) by the following facts:

- Avg. Nr. of HTTP objects in cache: 18.700.000
- Avg. HTTP request hit rate: 30-35%
- Avg. HTTP byte hit rate: 15-20%

In our architecture we target especially caches at comparable size. According to [7] the necessary size of a Bloomfilter for the whole LRZ cache (with a 2% probability of a false positive) would be in the order of ca. 20 Mbyte. We also include a redundancy of 50% for forward error correction, resulting in the length L of the Bloomfilter of about 30 Mbyte. We limit the size of a Multicast Cluster (Figure 5), to 20 participants. If we target an update time of e.g. about 6 hours, our enhanced digital fountain sends data on the Multicast tree at a constant data rate of about 140kbit/s.

Altogether approximately 2.5 Gbyte of Bloomfilter data would need to be transported per day on the Multicast tree of a cache cluster. Resulting in a monthly overhead of inter-cache information exchange of about 100 Gbyte. If you compare that to the monthly transported amount of data of several tens of thousands of Gbyte (which is e.g. transported at LRZ) the overhead for Bloomfilter signaling can be almost neglected, and imposes for sure no transport problem for current networks.

However the benefit of the distributed cache is obvious: If the HTTP request hit rate (based on distributed caches) can only be raised by about 3% (depending on the average file size of cached documents), the effort already pays off concerning pure data transport, as certain documents can be retrieved from caches close by.

Shared Cache architectures, building on distributed cache summaries as presented in 3.1 and 3.2, are a current research topic [13]. The main contribution of this work lies in the scalable 2-tier signaling architecture presented in 3.4 in combination with the application of caches to improve fault-tolerance of communicating applications.

Originally caches were introduced to save network bandwidth, however our primary target is to use caches for ensuring the fault-tolerant retrieval of content (documents). The situation we basically target with our proposed architecture is the following:

1. In a Client/Server communication the server is not available any more (because of a failure) and a document is requested by the client.
2. The Overlay Node (OAP), close to the client, realizes that, and checks first locally and then with every other Overlay Node available, whether the requested document is cached somewhere, and tries to deliver it to the client.

Obviously the probability, to find a specific document cached somewhere at a remote Overlay Node (cache), increases with the number of caches queried. In our architecture we propose to query as much Overlay Nodes as necessary until we finally discover the requested document. In the worst case all available caches are queried by our architecture. Here we see the difference compared to ordinary caching strategies.

Our basic assumption is that the original document is not available at all, because of a (network) failure. Our framework then tries to retrieve the requested document somewhere in our distributed cache architecture. If the architecture is widely accepted there can be easily millions of Overlay Nodes available. We clearly see a signaling scalability problem arising, which is solved by the new 2-tier discovery architecture presented in 3.4.

3.3 PIRST-ON Service Discovery: A Fault Tolerant 2 Tier P2P Based Signaling Architecture

The PIRST-ON signaling architecture for service discovery is presented in [2]. Based on a scalable, 2 tier signaling approach, vertex- and edge disjoint paths (see 2.1) are discovered. In both tiers, P2P based signaling networks provide a powerful means to discover fast the targeted service.

The connections in the lower tier P2P overlay signaling network are limited to the boundaries of the corresponding Autonomous System.

Few selected peers ("Cluster-Heads", see 3.4) of the lower tier P2P signaling overlay network are also part of the higher tier P2P overlay signaling Network. Peers of the higher tier also form a P2P network. However the connections in that tier are not limited by boundaries. Based on that 2-tier hierarchy and the inherent scalability of P2P systems [19] the signaling architecture scales.

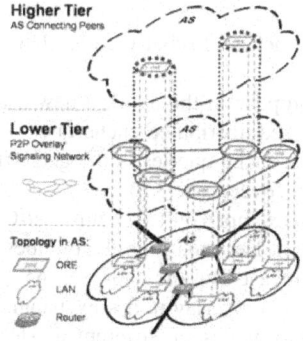

Figure 7: Fault-Tolerant 2-tier P2P based Service Discovery Architecture [2]

The primary goal of the signaling architecture shown in Figure 7 is the fast and fault tolerant discovery of an Overlay Relay that can provide a vertex- and edge-disjoint path (see 2.1).

The PIRST-ON signaling architecture for service discovery is enhanced in this work (3.4) by a scalable content discovery signaling.

3.4 Fast and Scalable Content Discovery in Distributed Caches

The distributed cache system presented in 3.1 and 3.2 clearly does not scale. As the size of a single Bloomfilter is in the order of magnitude of megabytes, the number of overlay nodes, being part of a cluster, is limited to a couple of dozens. The necessary bandwidth to exchange Bloomfilters (Figure 6) limits the number of overlay nodes.

However one of the requirements of our system (see 2.2) is that each Overlay Access Point (OAP) or Overlay Relay (ORE) within the PIRST-ON architecture should

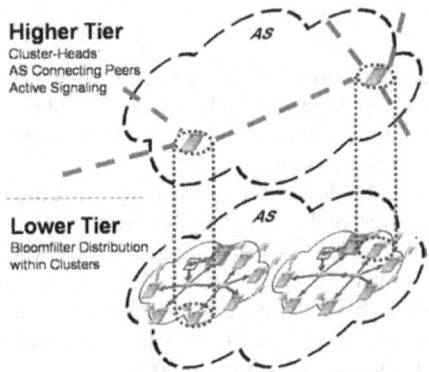

Figure 8: A 2-tier P2P and Multicast-Cluster based signaling architecture for fast distribute cache queries

be able to query all the caches of other Overlay Nodes, not only those being part of their cluster.

For that reason we propose in this work a new scalable 2-tier Peer-to-Peer (P2P) and Multicast-Cluster based distributed cache-query signaling architecture. This new signaling architecture for cache queries is merged with the PIRST-ON signaling architecture for Service Discovery (see 3.3).

In Figure 8 we show exemplarily two Multicast-Clusters of Overlay Nodes in an Autonomous System (AS). Dependant on the number of nodes in an AS there can be several independent Multicast-Clusters within an AS.

Within these clusters, the overlay nodes exchange Bloomfilters (see 3.2 and 3.3). However between overlay nodes of different clusters, no information need be exchanged.

In each cluster a "Cluster-Head" is chosen. Cluster-Heads are overlay nodes, which are part in a Multicast-Cluster and in the higher tier P2P network. The "Cluster-Heads" act as Peers—identical to 3.4—in the higher tier P2P signaling network. The higher tier P2P network is not limited by AS boundaries.

We see that besides the grouping in Multicast-Clusters (Figure 8), all the overlay nodes within an Autonomous System are still in parallel also peers in the lower tier P2P signaling network (Figure 7). Based on that signaling network, Multicast-Clusters (see 3.1) are built among the overlay nodes in the lower tier P2P signaling network. If the maximum allowed number of members in a cluster is exceeded, a new parallel Multicast-Cluster is being set up.

3.5 An Exemplary Cache Look Up

The benefit of the architecture proposed in 3.5 is being elaborated on in this paragraph. We start with the situation mentioned in 3.3: A client requests a document from a server that is currently unavailable because of a (network) failure:

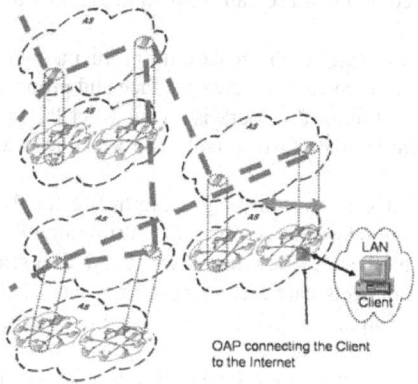

Figure 9: An exemplary setup of the proposed cache query signaling architecture

Figure 9 exemplarily shows 3 interconnected Autonomous Systems (AS). In each AS, Multicast clusters for Bloomfilter distribution among overlay nodes are already set up. The cluster-heads are already chosen and build peers of the higher tier P2P network. We see the higher tier P2P network is not bound to AS boundaries.

A typical cache lookup has the following steps:

1. The OAP that connects the client to the Internet (to an AS) realizes that the requested document cannot be retrieved from the server because of a failure.
2. That OAP first checks in its local cache whether the document is available.
3. In case the document locally is not available, the OAP checks–based on the received Bloomfilters–whether the document is stored inside a cache of its own cluster
4. In case the document is not available within the cluster, the OAP initiates a higher tier scalable active signaling query (Active-PING/PONGs [4]).
5. Based on the higher tier query, other cache-clusters are asked for the requested document in scalable P2P manner.
6. In the best case the requested document is found in a remote cache-cluster.

We clearly see that our approach does not need–due to the signaling overhead for Bloomfilter distribution (3.2)–much signaling for discovery when actually a specific document is searched for. Only few packets have to be sent out to query hundreds of caches. Moreover, based on slim queries, our approach also enables fast responses, if the document is stored in other clusters. Therefore our approach delivers a scalable and fast signaling architecture for discovery of content in distributed caches.

4   Conclusion

This paper presents a new transparent, reliable content distribution overlay network. Building on Transparent High Layer Protection Switching we propose a scalable distributed architecture of collaborating caches. Based on distributed collaborating caches our proposed architecture can mask single points of failure located at the networks' edge.

We especially elaborate on the scalability problem, signaling architectures for discovery in large distributed caches networks face and propose a solution.

The main contribution of this work is a new 2-tier P2P and Multicast based signaling architecture that enables fast, reliable and scalable discovery of content in large overlay networks.

Our approach reduces necessary signaling traffic for discovery of content in distributed caches through summarization and distribution of cache information in cache clusters. Building on these cache clusters we introduce a scalable P2P based signaling network that interconnects cache clusters. Using the P2P signaling network in conjunction with active signaling [4], fast and scalable queries within large overlay networks are possible.

Our signaling architecture for content discovery is fault tolerant against outages in the signaling architecture itself. Based on the P2P nature in combination with the proposed error resilient information distribution within cache clusters through our enhanced digital fountain, we present a new reliable signaling architecture.

As our proposed overlay network builds on programmable and active networks technology it is highly flexible and can dynamically react to new network conditions. Based on this flexibility our architecture can be easily adapted to changes on technology. It is foreseen if there are e.g. advances in error resilient codes, to load dynamically new code modules—without changing the infrastructure— on the overlay nodes, leading e.g. to a reduction of necessary bandwidth for Bloomfilter distribution. Also the active signaling based approach is based on this flexible basic technology.

The work described in this paper has been done as part of the FlexiNet project [14], funded by the German Federal Ministry of Education and Research.

References

1. D. G. Andersen, H. Balakrishnan, M. F. Kaashoek, and R. Morris, "Resilient Overlay Networks", Proc. 18th ACM SOSP, Banff, Canada, October 2001
2. C. Bachmeir, "Fault-Tolerant 2-tier P2P based Service Discovery in PIRST-ON", 10th International Conference on Telecommunications, ICT'2003, Papeete, French Polynesia, February 2003
3. C. Bachmeir and P. Tabery, "PIRST-ONs: A Service Architecture for Embedding and Leveraging Active and Programmable Networks", International Conference on Software, Telecommunications and Computer Networks, SoftCOM 2002, Split, Croatia, October 2002
4. C. Bachmeir and P. Tabery, "Scalable Diverse Protected Multicast as a Programmable Service Leveraging IP-Multicast", 2nd IEEE International Symposium on Network Computing and Applications, NCA'03, Cambridge, MA, USA, April 2003

5. G. Barish and K. Obraczka, "World Wide Web Caching: Trends and Techniques", IEEE Communications, Internet Technology Series, May 2000, pp. 178-185

6. B. Bloom. "Space/time tradeoffs in hash coding with allowable errors", CACM, 13(7):422-426, 1970

7. A. Broder and M. Mitzenmacher, "Network Applications of Bloom Filters: A Survey", 40th Annual Allerton Conference on Communication, Control, and Computing, Allerton Park, Illinois, October 2002

8. J. Byers, J. Considine, M. Mitzenmacher and S. Rost, "Informed Content Delivery Across Adaptive Overlay Networks", ACM SIGCOMM 2002, Pittsburgh PA, USA, August 2002

9. J. W. Byers, M. Luby, M. Mitzenmacher, and A. Rege, "A digital fountain approach to reliable distribution of bulk data", ACM SIGCOMM 1998, Vancouver, Canada, September 1998

10. A. T. Campbell, H. G. De Meer, M. E. Kounavis, and K. Miki, "A Survey of Programmable Networks", ACM SIGCOMM Computer Communications Review, 1999

11. Y. D. Chawathe, "Scattercast: An Architecture for Internet Broadcast Distribution as an Infrastructure Service", PhD Dissertation, University of California at Berkeley, 2000

12. CoreCast eCDN, Enterprise Content Distribution Networking platform, http://www.fantastic.com

13. L. Fan, P. Cao, J. Almeida and A. Broder, "Summary Cache: A Scalable Wide-Area Web Cache Sharing Protocol", IEEE/ACM Transactions on Networking Vol. 8, No. 3, June 2000

14. FlexiNet, a BMBF funded project, http://www.flexinet.de/

15. T. Harbaum, A. Speer, R. Wittmann, M. Zitterbart, "Providing Heterogeneous Multicast Services with AMnet", IEEE Journal of Communications and Networks, Vol. 3, No. 1, March 2001

16. A. Lazar, "Programming Telecommunication Networks", Proc. 5th International Workshop on Quality of Service (IWQOS'97)

17. M. Luby and M. Mitzenmacher, "Irregular Codes for Forward Error Correction" Compaq's Systems Research Center, Nov 1997, http://research.compaq.com/SRC/articles/199711/error_correction.html

18. Leibniz Rechenzentrum http://www.lrz-muenchen.de/services/netz/statistik/

19. R. Schollmeier and G. Schollmeier, "Why Peer-to-Peer (P2P) Does Scale: An Analysis of P2P Traffic Patterns", In Proceedings of the IEEE 2002 International Conference on Peer-to-Peer Computing (P2P2002), Linköping, Sweden, September 2002

20. E. Steinbach, Y. Liang, and B. Girod, "A Simulation Study of Packet Path Diversity for TCP File Transfer and Media Transport on the Internet," 2002 Tyrrhenian International Workshop on Digital Communications (IWDC 2002), Capri, Italy, September 2002

21. Squid Web Proxy Cache, http://www.squid-cache.org

22. P. Tabery and C. Bachmeir, "Advanced Network Services using Programmable Networks", IFIP WG6.7 Workshop and EUNICE Summer School on Adaptable Networks and Teleservices, Norway, September 2002

23. S. Zhuang et al, "Bayeux: An Architecture for Scalable and Fault-tolerant WideArea Data Dissemination", In Proc. of the Eleventh International Workshop on Network and Operating System Support for Digital Audio and Video (NOSSDAV 2001), June 2001

A Measurement Study of Storage Resource and Multimedia Contents on a High-Performance Research and Education Network

Hyun-chul Kim[1], Dongman Lee[2], Joonbock Lee[1],
Jay JungWon Suh[3], and Kilnam Chon[1]

[1] Department of Electrical Engineering and Computer Science ,
[3] Department of Industrial Engineering,
Korea Advanced Institute of Science and Technology,
Daejeon, South Korea 305-701 (Tel. +82-42-869-3554)
{hckim, jblee, jwsuh, chon}@cosmos.kaist.ac.kr

[2] Computer and Information Systems Group,
Information and Communication University,
Daejeon, South Korea 305-732 (Tel. +82-42-866-6113)
dlee@icu.ac.kr

Abstract. With the rapid advent and proliferation of peer-to-peer applications, research and education communities who have high performance networks have started to search for the possibilities of being benefited from the peer-to-peer architecture, in designing and supporting supercomputing applications as well as data-intensive applications. However, surprisingly, although they are mainly concerned with ways to take advantage of edge resources on their high performance network infrastructure, there has not been much work to measure and characterize the amount and usage pattern of the resources. In this paper, we remedy this situation by presenting a measurement study performed over a set of machines in a high performance research and education network, focusing on storage resources, multimedia contents, and availability of machines. We believe that this report will be a good reference to peer-to-peer and/or Grid system designers who have had troubles in getting an estimate for the amount of storage resource and multimedia contents on a high performance network, prior to planning and offering a distributed data service or storage service to research and education communities.

1 Introduction

With proliferation of the Internet and advancement of network technologies, peer-to-peer applications have gained much popularity recently. Although the exact definition of the term "peer-to-peer" is debatable, it generally involves a class of applications that take advantages of resources available at the edges of the Internet. This means, by aggregating and taking advantage of the edge resources, it becomes possible to obtain a huge processing power and build a gigantic data repository or storage space on a scale, otherwise nearly impossible. Among various peer-to-peer applications,

M.M. Freire, P. Lorenz, M.M.-O. Lee (Eds.): HSNMC 2003, LNCS 2720, pp. 108–117, 2003.
© Springer-Verlag Berlin Heidelberg 2003

distributed multimedia file systems such as Gnutella, FreeNet and KaZaA are the most popular ones. Since they all take advantages of edge storage resource to enhance data delivery on the Internet, it is increasingly important to have good information on the amount, usage and usage pattern of the edge resources available on a network.

Recently, network administrators have reported that peer-to-peer applications such as Napster and KaZaA, rather than HTTP traffic, are overwhelming their Internet connection [5, 6, 7, 10]. Although there have been lots of network measurement results which describe how much bandwidth is being consumed by famous peer-to-peer applications, most of those data do not contain information on contents being transferred, such as types, size and popularity of each content. To make matters worse, because new peer-to-peer multimedia applications tend to use control protocols that dynamically assign port numbers for the actual transfer of data, it is getting more difficult to identify traffic generated by peer-to-peer applications. In this paper, as a complementary approach to the current network measurement methodologies, we adopt file system measurement methodology, to provide a detailed view of contents being exchanged on a high-performance network, as well as storage resource usage.

We address the issues of storage resource usage and multimedia contents distributed on a high performance research and education network, by measuring the amount of storage resource, storage resource usage, types and size of file contents, and availability of machines on a high performance research and education network. We try to answer the following questions: How much storage resource do we have on the network? How is the resource being used? What sort of and how much content is browsed and stored into users' disk space? How much multimedia data is there? How many users on the network are keeping large-sized multimedia files in their disk space?

This paper is organized as follows. In section 2 and 3, file system measurement results and machine availability results are reported, respectively. We conclude in section 4 by summarizing the measurement results and discussing their implications.

2   File System Measurement Results

To answer the questions addressed above, we measured file systems, contents in the file systems, and availability of machines on a high performance research and education network. The measurement was performed over a set of machines on KAIST campus network. In KAIST, every building has a multi-gigabit fiber connectivity. In dormitory buildings, students are provided with one 10 Mbps Switched Ethernet port each. In laboratories, 10/100 Mbps or 1 Gbps connectivity is provided to each machine. There are about 9,000 to 10,000 unique IP machines in total.

On the network, we measured a set of Windows file systems to determine the total amount of aggregated disk space and free disk space, the amount of duplicated file contents, and their types and size. For our analysis, we asked students to run a scanning program on their Windows machines that collected file system information from their systems. By this means, from 2001.12.19 to 2002.1.18, we obtained the information on 716 file systems from 306 Windows machines. Besides, to estimate how much untapped storage resource we have on our network, we measured the machine availability. From 2002.1.14 to 2002.1.20, we have measured machine uptimes by pinging 9,846 machines every 30 minutes. A list of 9,846 machines was obtained from the log files of our local DNS name server, in 2001 November.

2.1 File Systems

The total size of the aggregated 716 file systems is 10.2 Terabytes (TB) and the file system size per machine ranges from 0.62 Gigabytes (GB) to 198 GB. The mean file system size is 14.4 GB, that is fourteen times bigger than reported in 1999 [1]. The mean disk size per machine is 33.5 GB and the median disk size per machine is 30 GB. 85% of the surveyed machines have tens of gigabytes of disk storage and only 3% of the machines have more than 100 GB of disk. Figure 1 shows a histogram of machines by their disk size and Figure 2 shows a CDF of the histogram illustrated in Figure 1.
The mean space usage is 66.3%, which is about 13~16% higher than the results of previous studies [1, 2]. Figure 3 shows a distribution of the machines by disk space usage and Figure 4 shows a CDF plot of the histogram illustrated in Figure 3. As shown in Figure 4, about 80% of the scanned machines were equipped with disks more than half full. The median disk utilization is 70%. Compared to the results of previous studies [1, 2], the mean disk utilization has been increased significantly, even though the mean disk size has been increased more than ten times over the last few years. 33.7% of the aggregated disk space, which amounts to 3.41 TB of storage resource, remains free. The size of free disk space on each machine ranges from 251 MB to 112.5GB. The mean free disk size per machine is 11.3 GB. Figure 5 shows a histogram of the machines by free disk size and Figure 6 shows its CDF plot.

2.2 Content Size Distribution

As mentioned earlier, 306 machines are using 6.79 TB of storage as a whole. The machines have 18,807,052 files in total. The average number of files per machine is 61,416, which is about twice larger than reported in [1]. The average file size is 360 KB, which is approximately three to six times bigger than found in [1]. Figure 7 shows two meaningful graphs. One is a distribution of files by size and the other is a distribution of bytes by file size. It is easily noticeable that there are a lot of small sized files but most bytes are consumed by large-sized files. Table 1 explicitly shows that 89% of the used space is consumed by only 2.77% of all files. The median size is 7 KB and 90MB for each plot, which is twice and forty five times bigger than reported in [1], respectively. The forty five times increase in the median size implies that the size of large-sized files has been getting much larger for the last few years. Since the large-sized files take up a considerable amount of disk space, an in-depth analysis on the matters of large-sized files would help in understanding how and for what users on a high performance network use their resource - network bandwidth and disk storage.

Fig. 1. Histogram of machines by disk size   **Fig. 2.** CDF of machines by disk size

Fig. 3. Histogram of machines by disk usage   **Fig. 4.** CDF of machines by disk usage

Fig. 5. Histogram of machines by free disk size   **Fig. 6.** CDF of machines by free disk size

Fig. 7. Distribution of the number of files and distribution of bytes by file size

Table 1. Distribution of large-sized files by size

File size	Counts	Bytes (TB)	Counts(%)	Bytes(%)
1M~10M	460,749	1.56	2.45	22.91
10M~100M	52,535	1.34	0.28	19.78
100M~1G	8,428	3.0	0.04	44.21
1G~10G	61	0.12	0.00	1.83
Total	521,773	6.03	2.77	88.73

Table 2. Top 5 file types sorted by total file size

Types	Counts	Bytes (TB)	Counts(%)	Bytes(%)
video	33,935	2.32	0.18	34.11
audio	471,822	1.06	2.51	15.65
image	5,115,477	0.20	27.20	2.89
compressed	152,799	0.58	0.81	8.56
binary data	260,172	0.80	1.38	11.75
Total	6,034,205	4.96	32.08	72.96

2.3 Content Types

File types are identified by file extensions. Table 2 shows the top 5 file types that have greatest influence on disk usage are video, audio, binary data, compressed, and image files. They account for 72.96% of total disk usage. In this section we elaborate more on large multimedia (e.g., video and audio) data, representing 50% of total disk usage.

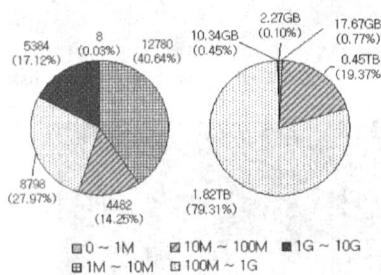 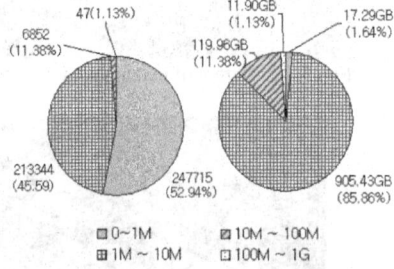

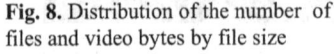

(a) Number of video files (b) Video bytes   (a) Number of MP3 audio (b) MP3 audio bytes
by file size   by file size   file by file size   by file size

Fig. 8. Distribution of the number of   **Fig. 9.** Distribution of the number of video
files and video bytes by file size   MP3 Audio files and audio bytes by file size

Video Files There are 33,935 video files across the scanned machines. The total size of the video files is 2.31 TB, representing 34.1% of disk usage. The mean video file size is 68.26 MB but the median is much smaller, less than 10 MB. Figure 8 shows a distribution of the number of video files by file size and a distribution of video bytes by file size. Video files larger than 100 MB occupy 80% of total video bytes and 17.15% in file count. To find out how many users are keeping how many video files in their disk storage, two distributions were obtained in Table 3 and Table 4. They show a distribution of machines by the number of video files contained, and a distribution of machines by the total size of aggregated video files contained, respectively. As shown in Table 3, about 62.1% of the machines have more than ten video files and about 66.9% of machines have more than one GB of video files. Surprisingly, 13.7 % of machines have more than one hundred video files.

Table 3. Distribution of machines by video file count

Number of video files	Number of machines
0	35 (11.4 %)
1~9	81 (26.5 %)
10~99	148 (48.4 %)
100~999	42 (13.7 %)

Table 4. Distribution of machines by video bytes

Size of video files	Number of machines
Less than 1MB	35 (11.4%)
1~100MB	23 (7.5%)
100MB~1GB	43 (14.1 %)
1GB~10GB	124 (40.5 %)
10GB~100GB	81 (26.4 %)

Table 5. Distribution of machines by MP3 file count

Number of mp3 files	Number of machines
0	9 (2.94 %)
1~10	18 (5.89 %)
11~100	49 (16.0 %)
101~1000	157 (51.3 %)
1001~10000	73 (23.9 %)

Table 6. Distribution of machines by MP3 file bytes

Size of mp3 files(MB)	Number of machines
Less than 1MB	9(2.94 %)
1~10MB	13 (4.25 %)
10~100MB	16 (5.23 %)
100MB~1GB	82 (26.8 %)
1~10GB	165 (53.9%)
10~100GB	21 (6.86 %)

Audio Files The second most influential file type with regard to consuming disk space is audio type. There are 471,822 audio files, representing 15.65 % of total space in use. Figure 9 shows a distribution of the number of audio files by file size and a distribution of audio bytes by file size. As shown in Figure 9, there are two noticeable groups among the audio files, wav files and mp3 files. Most of wav files are Windows system sound files whose size is less than 1 MB. The mean size of all audio files is 2.25 MB, whereas the average mp3 file size is 4.37 MB. The mp3 files account for 47.77% of audio files and 93.37% of audio bytes. To find out how popular they are and how many users are keeping them in their PCs, two distributions were obtained, as in Table 5 and Table 6.

2.4 Duplicate Multimedia Contents

From the file system data we collected, we analyzed the number of duplicated multimedia files, the popularity of those files, and the amount of disk space that could be saved by eliminating duplicated copies.

Video Files For video files, the files with the same size and extension were considered as duplicates. Since our major focus is on large-sized video files, we consider two cases, one for the video files that are larger than 10 MB and one for all video files for the reference. Figure 10 and 11 illustrate the degree of duplications of video files. Among 33,935 video files, there are 16,371 distinct files and 20,486 duplicates. 3,489 files, representing 21.3% of 16,371 distinct files, are duplicated at least once and they generate 20,486 duplicates across the machines. Additional disk space consumed by these duplicates is 0.87 TB, which is equivalent to 37.4% of disk space consumed by all video files. For the video files that are larger than 10 MB, as shown in Figure 10 and 11, the number of duplicated files are much less, but in terms of bytes, there was no significant difference. Among 14,610 video files that are larger than 10 MB, there are 9,382 distinct files and 6,992 duplicates. 1,764 files, representing 18.8% of 9,382 distinct files, are duplicated at least once and they generate 6,992 duplicates across the machines. Additional disk space consumed by these duplicates is 0.86 TB, almost the same as the above. For the video files larger than 10 MB, the degree of duplication is lower than that of small video files, as 80% of duplicated large files are duplicated less than 10 times.

Fig. 10. CDF of video files   **Fig. 11.** CDF of video bytes
by the degree of duplication   by the degree of duplication

MP3 Audio Files For mp3 files, duplication was checked by comparing file size. File name was not considered because it is often likely to be changed by users. It is very probable that two or more files that are exactly the same size are duplicates of each other, especially when they have the same extension, mp3. Among 225,402 mp3 files, there are 89,090 unique mp3 files and 136,312 duplicates. Among 89,090 unique files, 37,584 files are duplicated at least once. Additional disk space consumed by these duplicates is 0.57 TB, representing 58% of total size of mp3 audio files. The degree of duplication and the corresponding number of files as well as size of files are illustrated in figure 12 and 13. 70% of mp3 duplicates are duplicated less than 10 times, but some extremely popular files are duplicated even more than hundreds of times. The ratio of duplicates to all mp3 files amounts to 60.5%, which is much higher than that of video files.

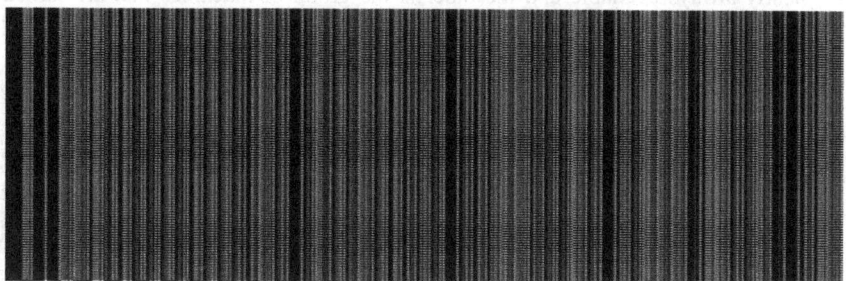

Fig. 12. CDF of audio files by the degree of duplication

Fig. 13. CDF of audio bytes by the degree of duplication

3 Machine Availability Results

In this section, we investigate how many machines are available in terms of duration and frequency, to help in estimating how much untapped storage resource we have within the network. We restricted our analysis to the 7,058 machines that responded to our ping messages at least once during the experiment.

Figure 14 shows plots of the number of responding machines according to time of day and day of the week. From Monday to Thursday, the curves follow the same pattern in accord with the daily cycle of students and faculty members. From Friday afternoon to Sunday, the number of running machines stays decreased. The negative spike on Friday at 14:30 is due to a sudden blackout. Throughout the week, the number of running machines at the same time ranges from 3,548 to 5,478.

Fig. 14. Number of available machines by time and day

Figure 15 illustrates a distribution of machines by uptime interval length. Figure 16 shows a CDF of machines by availability. We found that 3,252 machines, representing 46% of all responding machines, are up more than 80% of the time. We also found that 1,815 machines, representing 25.7% of all responding machines, are always running. As we observe in Figure 16, there are two noticeable groups of machines with regard to uptime interval length. One is the group of machines that are nearly always available and the other is the group of machines that are turned off nightly. This 'uptime consistency' has been observed in the previous work, too [2].

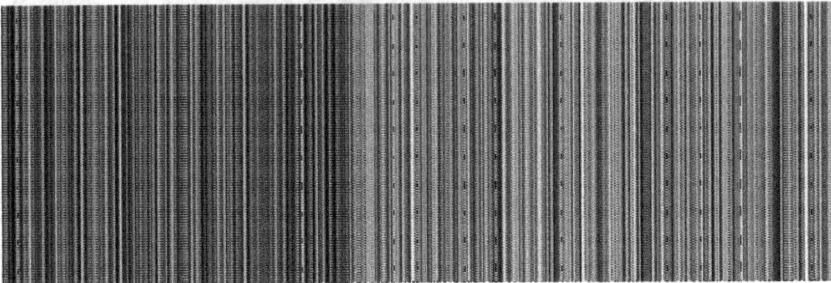

Fig. 15. Distribution of machines by up duration   **Fig. 16.** CDF of machines by availability

4 Summary and Conclusions

In this paper, we have presented a measurement study performed over a set of machines in KAIST campus network and several lessons learned from the results. We collected the data from 716 file systems of 306 Windows machines in KAIST, through voluntary participation of students.

The systems contained 18.8 million files totaling 6.8 TB of data. Since the mean disk size per machine is 33.5 GB and there are 9,000~10,000 machines in KAIST, it is believed that we have tens to hundreds of terabytes of storage resource within our campus network. In other words, we can say that petabyte-scale storage resource has already been deployed around us. Considering that the amount of free disk space is 33.7% of total disk space, there would likely be huge but untapped free disk storage resource in the network. The file systems in our study were about 66% full on average, which is 15 % higher than the results of previous works [1, 2]. About 80% of the scanned file systems were more than half full. According to our analysis, about 89% of used disk space has been consumed by objects larger than one megabyte. Video files and mp3 audio files account for 50% of the disk usage. 70% of the machines have more than one gigabyte of videos, 75% of the machines have more than one hundred mp3 audio files, and nearly all machines have multimedia data in their disk space. Considering that there are 9,000~10,000 machines in KAIST, it is believed that we have tens to hundreds of terabytes of large multimedia data within our campus network. We also found that lots of large multimedia data are duplicated across the network. 21.3% of distinct video files and 42.2% of distinct mp3 audio files are duplicated at least once, consuming 1.44 terabytes of additional disk space. A few extremely popular files are duplicated hundreds of times across the machines. Our contributions in this paper are threefold: First, by measuring and analyzing storage resource, contents, and machine availability, we estimate and present how much untapped storage resource there is and how much multimedia content is being exchanged on a high performance network. This paper will be a good reference to the research and education communities on a high performance network, especially to peer-to-peer system designers who want to get an estimate for the amount of storage resource and multimedia contents distributed on their network, prior to creating and offering a distributed data service or storage service. Also, campus network administrators who are deeply concerned with users' behavior and resource usage on their network will find this one informative. Second, by showing how many multimedia contents are duplicated across the network, we provide a motivation for developing a scalable multimedia content distribution system on a high performance network. And finally, we find that our measurement results are quite different from those of previous work [1, 2] with regard to file system size, file system usage, content size, and content types. With the increase of disk size and network bandwidth as well as the proliferation of peer-to-peer multimedia file sharing applications, file system size, file system usage and size of contents have been increased significantly for the last few years.

Acknowledgement

This research has been supported in part by BANDI(Broadband Application and Network Deployment Initiative) Project at the National Computerization Agency in Korea. We would like to send sincere appreciation to John R. Douceur in Microsoft for giving us initiatives for this work and for helping us to set up the methodology in gathering information on disk contents.

References

1. J. R. Douceur, and W. J. Bolosky, "A Large-Scale Study of File System Contents," in Proc. ACM SIGMETRICS 1999, May 1999.
2. W. Bolosky, J. Douceur, D. Ely, and M. Theimer, "Feasibility of a Serverless Distributed File System Deployed on an Existing Set of Desktop PCs," in Proc. ACM SIGMETRICS 2000, June 2000.
3. S. Saroiu, P. K. Gummadi, and S. D. Gribble, "A Measurement Study of Peer-to-Peer File Sharing Systems," in Proc. Multimedia Computing and Networking 2002, January 2002.
4. B. Krishnamurthy, J. Wang, and Y. Xie, "Early Measurements of a Cluster-based Architecture for P2P Systems," in Proc. SIGCOMM Internet Measurement Workshop 2001, October 2001.
5. H. Kim, J. Lee, J. Suh, and K. Chon, "A Study of End-host behavior on High-Performance Research and Education Networks: Peta-Scale Challenges," APAN Meetings, January 2002.
6. M. Meiss, "It's Not Enough to Have a Big, Fat Pipe: The Case for Resource Management," Internet2 Peer-to-Peer Workshop, January 2002.
7. P. Brunelli, "FlowScan at the University of Wisconsin," Virtual Internet2 Member Meeting, October 2001.
8. I. Taylor, R. Philp, M. Shields, O. Rana, and B. Schutz, "The Consumer Grid," Fourth Global Grid Forum, February 2002.

Deployment of Class-Based Routing in Wide Area Networks: Cost and Performance Assessment

Marília Curado, Orlando Reis, João Brito, Gonçalo Quadros, Edmundo Monteiro

University of Coimbra
Laboratory of Communications and Telematics
CISUC/DEI, Pólo II, Pinhal de Marrocos
3030-290 Coimbra, Portugal
{marilia, oreis, jbrito, quadros, edmundo}@dei.uc.pt
http://lct.dei.uc.pt

Abstract. A QoS routing protocol for the Differentiated Services framework is being developed at the University of Coimbra. The main contribution of this paper is the evaluation of the protocol in wide area networks concerning traffic performance and protocol cost. Many interesting QoS routing proposals have been proposed. However their evaluation has been conducted in majority by simulation of networks. In this paper, we evaluate a QoS routing proposal using a prototype in an emulated Wide Area environment and compare the results with a Local Area scenario. The results show that it is feasible and cost rewarding to use QoS routing in order to improve the performance of QoS aware traffic in the actual existing Internet. The results show that, besides being feasible, the QoS routing strategy proposed plays a major role in traffic performance both at the local and wide area environment, without imposing excessive costs in the network.

1   Introduction

Quality of Service plays a major role in the deployment of communication system for applications with special traffic requirements, such as video-conferencing or Internet telephony. The need to support these types of traffic has motivated the communication research community to develop new approaches. Some of this work resulted in the Differentiated and Integrated Services architectures proposed by the Internet Engineering Task Force (IETF) [1, 2].

Current routing protocols used in the Internet lack characteristics for QoS provision to support emerging new services. All traffic between two endpoints is forwarded on the same path, even if there are other alternative paths with more interesting properties for the requirements of a specific flow or traffic class. Usually, the shortest path is selected, based on a single static metric that does not reflect the availability of resources. In these situations, congestion easily occurs on the shortest path, with the corresponding degradation of traffic performance, despite the underutilization of network resources on alternative paths. This scenario has motivated the development of QoS aware routing protocols.

M.M. Freire, P. Lorenz, M.M.-O. Lee (Eds.): HSNMC 2003, LNCS 2720, pp. 118-127, 2003.

The most significant developments on QoS routing are aimed at communication systems where traffic differentiation is done per flow, as in the Integrated Services [1]. The Differentiated Services framework does not explicitly incorporate QoS routing. It is, thus, essential to develop QoS routing protocols for networks where traffic differentiation is done per class. The Quality of Service Routing strategy of the University of Coimbra (UC-QoSR) was conceived to fulfill this purpose.

The UC-QoSR strategy selects the best path for each traffic class based on information about the congestion state of the network. This strategy extends the Open Shortest Path (OSPF) routing protocol [3] in order to select paths appropriate for all traffic classes as described in [4, 5].

A prototype of UC-QoSR was implemented over the GateD[1] platform, running on the FreeBSD operating system [4]. The evaluation of the UC-QoSR strategy in the Wide Area environment is the main objective of the present paper. The rest of the paper is organized as follows: Section 2 presents some related work; Section 3 describes the UC-QoSR strategy; test conditions and analysis of results concerning local area networks and wide area networks are presented in Section 4; the main conclusions and issues to be addressed in future work are presented in Section 5.

2   Related Work

QoS routing protocols can contribute to improve traffic performance. However, QoS routing introduces additional burden in the network, pertaining to the processing overhead due to more complex and frequent computations and the increased routing protocol overhead. The trade-off between the cost of QoS routing and its performance is an important issue that was evaluated in some works.

The advertisement of quantified metrics, instead of the advertisement of instantaneous values, is a common approach to avoid the excessive communication cost of dynamic routing protocols. The quantification rule can be a simple average of the metric values [6] or can use a moving average with configured timescales [7].

Another approach to reduce the communication cost of QoS routing is the use of trigger policies to control the emission of routing updates [8]. The triggering policies can be classified by the type of trigger used, namely, threshold based, class based and time based. Threshold based triggers control the emission of updates through a threshold. Updates are issued when the relative difference between the last value advertised and the actual value of the metric exceeds the configured threshold. Class based triggers divide the link capacity in classes and trigger the emission of updates when the link capacity changes to a new class. The time based triggers control the emission of updates by some periodic value. An example of such trigger is the hold-down timer used to define the minimum time between updates.

The solutions described above are able to simultaneously reduce communication and processing overhead. This results stems from the fact that once routers receive less update messages, they will not compute paths as often as before. The utilization of the mechanisms described poses the need for a trade-off between the desired

---

[1] <http://www.gated.org>

updated state of the network and the burden this imposes in terms of routing overhead.

Despite the relevant QoS issues addressed, the proposals for QoS routing analyzed lack the analysis of the applicability to a class-based framework and are only evaluated theoretically or by simulation. The use of a prototype approach limits the dimension of the test-bed, however it introduces processing and communication systems dynamics, being closest to a real situation. Furthermore, there is a lack of the evaluation of the QoS routing strategies proposed in both local and wide area environments.

3   The UC-QoS Routing Strategy

In this section the main characteristics of the routing strategy developed at the University of Coimbra (UC-QoSR) are briefly described. A more detailed description can be found in previous publications of the authors [4, 5].

The UC-QoSR strategy was designed for hop-by-hop QoS routing in networks where traffic differentiation follows the class paradigm. This strategy is composed of three main components, as follows:
   a)   A QoS metric that represents the availability of resources in the network;
   b)   Traffic class requirements in terms of QoS parameters;
   c)   A path computation algorithm to calculate the most suitable path for each traffic class, according to the dynamic state of the network expressed by a QoS metric.

The availability of resources in the network is measured through a QoS metric that represents the congestion state of routers interfaces. This metric consists of two congestion indexes, one relative to packet delay (DcI) and other to packet loss (LcI). These indexes evaluate the impact that delay and loss at the router, will have on application performance [9]. The congestion indexes are distributed to all routers in the domain through modified OSPF routing messages (Router Link State Advertisements – R-LSA).

The merging of the congestion indexes origins a value that represents the congestion state of the interface, as it is perceived by traffic belonging to each class. The Dijkstra algorithm is then used to compute the shortest path tree for each traffic class. The UC-QoSR strategy remains fully compatible with original OSPF because the path selection algorithm is not altered, and because the OSPF configured costs are also advertised in R-LSAs. It is thus possible to establish adjacencies among routers running UC-QoSR and OSPF.

QoS routing protocols must contribute to a significant improvement in traffic performance and network resource usage to compensate for the burden they introduce on the network. This overhead is twofold, comprising an increase in the communication load due to routing traffic and a raise in the processing capacity of routers caused by the frequency of path computations. In UC-QoSR, these overheads are controlled by a policy that controls the emission of link state updates. This policy combines metrics quantification and threshold based diffusion. A similar approach was followed by Apostolopoulos et al. but in the flow establishment context [8].

The metrics quantification has two components. In the first step, a logarithmic function is used to smooth extreme instantaneous metric values. In the second step, a moving average of the congestion indexes, with a variable window size. The congestion indexes are monitored every second (the lowest time granularity provided by GateD) and the samples are taken continuously. The filtered values are then presented to the diffusion control module. In this module, the new value is compared with the one that was previously advertised, and will be diffused only if it significantly different. The decision to issue the advertisements is controlled by the value of a defined threshold.

Besides the link state update policy described above, in UC-QoSR, OSPF was modified, in order to control even further the protocol overhead and thus increase the possibility of scalability. In original OSPF, the routing messages denominated Network-LSA (N-LSA) identify the routers connected to the network and its diffusion occurs wherever R-LSAs are issued. In the UC-QoSR strategy, the emission of N-LSAs has been detached from the emission of R-LSAs, because R-LSAs are issued at a higher rate than in OSPF and the information transported in N-LSAs does not change at such a rate. Thus, in the UC-QoSR, the emission of N-LSA remains periodic and dependent on router connectivity, while the emission of R-LSA is controlled through the threshold of the diffusion module. This strategy allows for a significant reduction of routing messages in the network.

The processing cost of a routing protocol is due to the application of the path computation algorithm and to the update of the kernel routing table. These two processes are usually linked, as in the original OSPF. This means, that, as soon as the SPF algorithm is applied, the new routes are flushed to the kernel to update the routing table. In the UC-QoSR the routes are sent to the kernel, only if they are different form the ones that were previously installed. With this approach, the processing overhead associated with the socket communication between the routing daemon and the kernel is significantly reduced.

The policy to control protocol overhead described above contributes also to avoid the number of path shifts that may occur in the network. Combined with these procedures, the UC-QoSR strategy uses a mechanism named class-pinning, that controls the path shifting frequency of all traffic classes [10].

4   Experimentation

In this section the experimentation made to evaluate the cost and performance of UC-QoSR in Wide Area and Local Area Networks are presented and its results are analyzed.

4.1   Test Conditions

The test-bed used for the experiments presented in this section is depicted in Fig. 1. The endpoints 1 to 4 are traffic sources and endpoints 5 to 8 are traffic destinations. Each endpoint only generates or receives traffic of a single class to avoid the influence of endpoint processing on traffic patterns.

The WAN environment was emulated by the use of routers running Dummynet[2]. The routers called Dummynet are responsible for emulating the delays associated with a wide area scenario. These routers run the original OSPF routing protocol to allow for the establishment of adjacencies with the routers running the UC-QoSR protocol.

The routers are PCs with the FreeBSD operating system. The kernel is modified, at the IP level, to include the delay and loss metric modules and to schedule and drop packets according to class sensitivity to these parameters. The monitoring of the delay and loss congestion indexes is needed for the routing decision. The kernel is also modified to interact with the UC-QoSR protocol embedded in GateD. It keeps the routing table with paths for all traffic classes and makes packet forwarding decisions based on destination IP address and Differentiated Services Code Point (DSCP) [2].

The interfaces between endpoints and routers are configured at 100 Mbps. Interfaces between routers are configured at 10 Mbps to introduce bottlenecks. The Wide Area Scenario was emulated though the configuration of Dummynet in order to create a propagation delay of a 10 Mbps connection over 200 Km (a typical distance between two large cities).

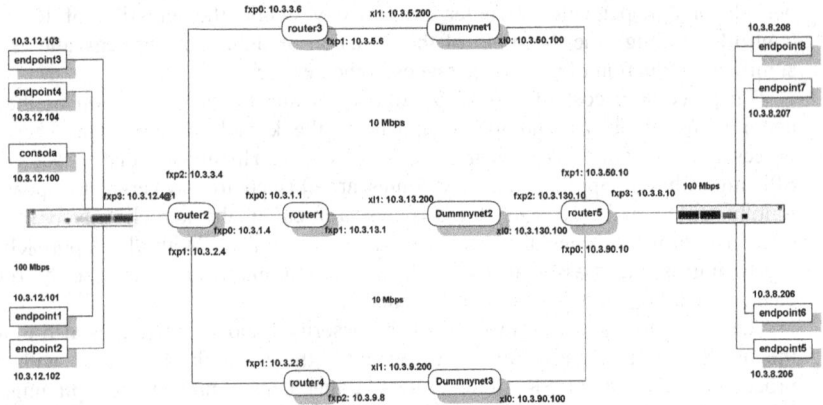

Fig. 1. Experimental test-bed

Traffic was generated and measured with the traffic analysis tool Chariot from NetIQ[3]. Table 1 shows the load distribution that was used in the experiments with 4 traffic classes to attain a total level of load of 24 Mbps. The traffic of all classes is UDP to avoid the influence of TCP flow control in the results. These values were chosen taking into consideration the circulating types of traffic on the Internet[4], with the majority of the traffic being best-effort traffic, which is class 1 traffic.

The experiments for the evaluation of the UC-QoSR strategy was done by varying the parameters that control the emission of routing updates, namely, the moving average window size and the threshold that controls the emission of routing updates.

---

[2] <http://info.iet.unipi.it/~luigi/ip_dummynet>

[3] <http://www.netiq.com>

[4] <http://www.caida.org>

Table 1. Load distribution among classes.

Classes	Class 1	Class 2	Class 3	Class 4
Load (Mbps)	9	7	5	3

The evaluation of cost associated with the UC-QoSR strategy was done by the measurement of protocol indicators. The parameters used to measure the communication cost of the UC-QoSR strategy are the number of routing messages issued and received (Router-LSA and Router and Network[5] LSA).

The processing cost is evaluated by the following parameters:

a)   Number of times the Shortest Path First (SPF) algorithm is applied; this value evaluates the processing cost of the routing daemon due to the application of the path computation algorithm for each traffic class;

b)   Number of path shifts; this value evaluates the processing cost due to the update of the kernel routing table.

The evaluation of traffic performance was made as follows:

a)   Average throughput of all traffic classes – the values shown represent the relation between the obtained throughput and the load generated in each class; this approach was employed to allow for the comparison of the performance of traffic belonging to classes that were generated with different levels of load;

b)   Loss rate of all traffic classes.

Each experiment was carried out for five minutes and was repeated ten times. The results present the averaged values of all tests. The inspection of protocol dynamics was done in all routers using the OSPF-Monitor tool included in GateD. These values were measured by the application Chariot. The plotted results have a degree of confidence of 95%.

4.2   Cost Evaluation Comparison in Local and Wide Area Environments

The comparison of the cost of the UC-QoSR strategy in LAN and WAN scenarios is the subject of this section. The results depicted on the graphics pertain to router 2, where the congestion bottleneck may occur.

Fig. 2 shows the results concerning the communication cost due to the routing information messages distributed in the network. The number of R-LSA issued by router 2 is not significantly different in LAN and WAN scenarios. The difference is only noticeable for a WS of 20 samples. However, in the WAN scenario router 2 receives an important amount of LSA when compared to the LAN scenario. This result is due to the fact that the routers where Dummynet is installed run the original OSPF routing protocol and issue their own R-LSA and N-LSA and participate on the flooding procedure.

The processing cost comparison between LAN and WAN scenarios present some interesting results as depicted in Fig. 3. The number of times the path computation algorithm is applied follows a patterns similar to the one observed with the number of

---

[5] The measure used is the total number of LSAs received, that is, the number of Router and Network LSAs received.

R-LSA. This result is as expected, since the application of the SPF algorithm is triggered by the arrival of R-LSA.

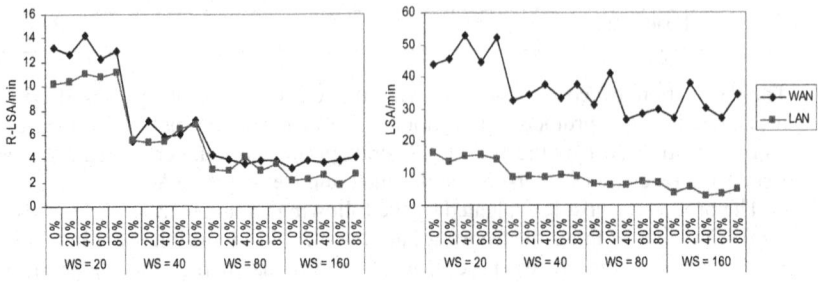

Fig. 2. Communication cost comparison

The number of path shifts in the LAN scenario shows a behavior with a common pattern for all values of the moving average window size. When the threshold that controls the emission of updates is below 40%, the number of paths shifts is smaller than in the WAN scenario. However, when threshold of 60% or above are used, the number of path shifts increases considerably. The same number of SPF produces an increased number of path shifts because the new paths are better than the old ones and are thus installed on the kernel routing table. The reason for this is the selection of paths based on outdated information and can be avoided by using smaller thresholds, keeping the network updated. Even tough the use of high values of the threshold cause instability, the level of instability is controlled by the size of the moving average window.

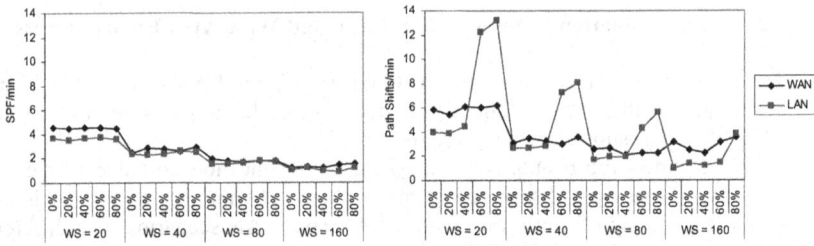

Fig. 3. Processing cost comparison

An interesting observation of Fig. 3 is that the number of paths shifts starts to rise when a WS of 160 samples is used. This is due to the inaccuracy in routing information that is introduced by the excessive smoothing of the metric. In this situation, important changes in network fail to be considered and distributed and thus routers choose paths based on inaccurate information. This will lead to bad paths, which will create congestion and induce the computation of new paths. The problem of QoS routing under inaccurate information was studied, among others, by Chen *et al* and Masip-Bruin *et al*, [11, 12]. The results presented here show that inaccuracy due to metrics quantification can be avoided by a correct parameterization of the quantification rule.

4.3   Traffic Performance Evaluation

In this sub-section the results concerning traffic performance evaluation are presented. The traffic classes considered are presented in Table 2.

Table 2. Traffic classes characterization

Class	Delay sensitivity	Loss sensitivity	Application
1	Low	Low	Best-effort
2	High	Medium	Internet telephony
3	High	Low	Video real-time
4	Medium	High	Video Training

It is clear that the overall performance of all traffic classes is better on the LAN scenario. This is due to the extra delay that is introduced by Dummynet. However, in the WAN environment, class differentiation is done according to class sensitivity to delay and loss, which is a different result from the behavior in the LAN.

Fig. 4 shows the results pertaining achieved throughput ratio and loss rate of traffic of the four traffic classes generated in the WAN scenario. Class 1, the class used by best-effort traffic, achieves the lowest throughput ratio and the highest loss ratio. Classes 2 and 4 show the best throughput and the lowest loss rate, according to their delay and loss sensitivity. Class 3 is treated best than best-effort traffic, but is treated worst than classes 2 and 4 because it has a low sensitivity to delay. These results show that the UC-QoS routing strategy is effective in differentiating traffic classes, through scheduling and routing mechanisms, according to their delay and loss sensitivities.

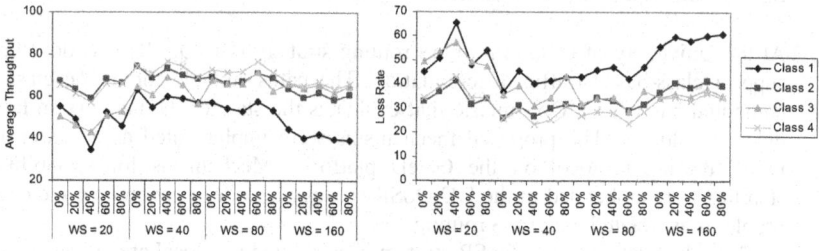

Fig. 4. Performance parameters in the WAN environment

The results also show that the quantification rule is able to contribute to traffic performance, as long as it is correctly configured. When a small moving average window size is used, traffic performance is poor, due to the exaggerated instability in the network caused by frequent distribution of routing messages. On the other side, when the moving average window size is big (over 80 samples), traffic performance is also poor. This is due to the inaccuracy that such a WS introduces in the network.

The results show that the moving average window size must be configured in the range [40, 80] in order to achieve the best traffic performance in the Wide Area environment.

Fig. 5 shows the results pertaining achieved throughput ratio and loss rate of traffic of the four traffic classes generated in the LAN scenario. Then results plotted are better than the ones in the WAN scenario as expected.

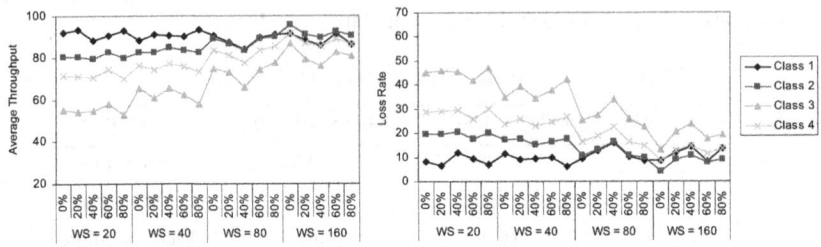

Fig. 5. Performance parameters in the LAN environment

The graphics show that traffic differentiation is achieved and is correctly made among classes 2, 3, and 4. However, the results obtained for class 1 traffic (best-effort traffic) are not consistent with class definition, since this is the best treated class according to throughput and loss rate. This behavior is motivated by two factors: the load distribution among classes and the routing oscillations that occur due to the small timescale inherent to the small sized network. Best-effort traffic stays in the same path because it has low sensitivity to delay and loss and does not require a better path, and any class that tries to share the path with class 1, will swiftly shift to another better path. This behavior is corrected when it is used a moving average window size above 80 samples.

5   Conclusions and Future Work

At the University of Coimbra a QoS routing strategy (UC-QoSR) was developed to support class-based traffic differentiation. The paths suitable for traffic classes are computed based on a QoS metric that evaluates the state of the network in terms of delay and losses. The proposed mechanisms were implemented as an extension to OSPF routing protocol on the GateD platform. Mechanisms for scalability and stability were embedded in the UC-QoSR strategy in order to overcome the common problems associated with QoS routing.

The behavior of the UC-QoSR strategy was studied in a local area network testbed and showed effective differentiating traffic while introducing an overhead that was affordable by the communication system. The focus of this paper was the evaluation of the cost and performance issues of the UC-QoSR in a wide area environment.

The results showed that the mechanisms in the UC-QoSR strategy can be configured to control the overhead introduced in the network both in LAN and WAN environments. The communication overhead remains a function of the network size and is not significantly affected in the wide area scenario. The processing overhead due to the application of the path computation algorithm is also similar in both environments. However, the overhead due to routing table update is higher in the LAN scenario due to instability created by the short timescale scenario.

In the LAN scenario, where the routing timescale is short, a large window size contributes to stability and to increase traffic performance. The inaccuracy introduced is small because updates are distributed fast to all routers in the network. In the WAN scenario the inherent larger timescale limits the window size that can be used. However this is not an issue, since the best performance is achieved

Acknowledgements

This work was partially supported by the Portuguese Ministry of Science and High Education (MCES), under program POSI (Project QoS II and IPQoS) and under the PhD grant PRAXIS XXI/ BD/13723/97.

References

1. R. Braden, D. Clark, S. Shenker, "Integrated Services in the Internet Architecture: an Overview", RFC 1633, Internet Engineering Task Force, June 1994.
2. S. Blake, D. Black, M. Carlson, E. Davies Nortel, W. Weiss, "An Architecture for Differentiated Services", RFC 2475, Internet Engineering Task Force, December 1998.
3. J. Moy, "OSPF Version 2", RFC 2328, Internet Engineering Task Force, April 1998.
4. M. Oliveira, J. Brito, B. Melo, G. Quadros, E. Monteiro, "Quality of Service Routing in the Differentiated Services Framework", Proceedings of SPIE's International Symposium on Voice, Video, and Data Communications, Boston, MA, USA, November 5-8, 2000.
5. M. Oliveira, J. Brito, B. Melo, G. Quadros, E. Monteiro, "Evaluation of a Quality of Service Routing Strategy for the Differentiated Services Framework", Proceedings of the International Conference on Internet Computing (IC'2001), Las Vegas, Nevada, USA, June 25-28, 2001.
6. A. Khanna, J. Zinky, "The Revised ARPANET Routing Metric", Proceedings of SIGCOMM'89, Austin, Texas, USA, September 19-22, 1989
7. B. Lekovic, P. Van Mieghem, "Link State Update Policies for Quality of Service Routing", Proceedings of Eighth IEEE Symposium on Communications and Vehicular Technology in the Benelux (SCVT2001), Delft, The Netherlands, October 18, 2001.
8. G. Apostolopoulos, R. Guerin, S. Kamat, and S. Tripathi. "Quality of Service Based Routing: A Performance Perspective", Proceedings of SIGCOMM'98, Vancouver, British Columbia, USA, September 1998.
9. G. Quadros, A. Alves, E. Monteiro, F. Boavida, "An Approach to Support Traffic Classes in IP Networks", Proceedings of the first International Workshop on Quality of future Internet Services (QofIS 2000), Berlin, Germany, September 25-26, 2000.
10. M. Curado, O. Reis, J. Brito, G. Quadros, E. Monteiro, "Stability and Scalability Issues in Hop-by-Hop Class-Based Routing", Proceedings of the 2nd International Workshop on QoS in Multiservice IP Networks (QoS-IP 2003), Milan, Italy, February 24-26, 2003.
11. S. Chen, K. Nahrstedt, "Distributed QoS Routing with Imprecise State Information", Proceedings of 7th IEEE International Conference on Computer, Communications and Networks (ICCCN'98), pp. 614-621, Lafayette, LA, USA, October, 1998
12. X. Masip-Bruin, S. Sánchez-López, J. Solé-Pareta, J. Domingo-Pascual, "A QoS Routing Mechanism for Reducing the Routing Inaccuracy Effects", Proceedings of the 2nd International Workshop on QoS in Multiservice IP Networks (QoS-IP 2003), Milan, Italy, February 24-26, 2003.

Prediction-Based Dynamic QoS Assurance for Multicast Multimedia Delivery

Agnieszka Chodorek

Department of Telecommunications and Photonics, Kielce University of Technology,
al. Tysiąclecia Państwa Polskiego 7, 25-314 Kielce, Poland,
a.chodorek@tu.kielce.pl

Abstract. The RSVP protocol provides signaling service for resource reservations. RSVP version 1 protocol allows flexible reservations for multicast transmission, even for large multicast sessions. The key features of new RSVP protocol, described in RFC 3175, include aggregation for IPv4 and IPv6 reservations and predictive reservations. However, predictive reservation methodology, policy and detailed system architecture are not defined in this specification. The paper proposes prediction-based dynamic QoS assurance for multicast distribution of MPEG-encoded video traffic. Dynamic bandwidth allocation uses extended RSVP signaling protocol and prediction-based bandwidth renegotiation module. Computer simulations confirmed that the proposed solution lead to better utilization of network resources than fixed (non-predictive) service[1].

1 Introduction

The QoS assurance is based on a priori reservation of network resources. In IP network, two alternative resource reservation architectures were developed and standardised by IETF: the Integrated Services (IntServ) architecture, working in absolute reservation mode, and the Differentiated Services (DiffServ) architecture performed reservations in relative manner.

Integrated Services, based on RSVP version 1 signaling protocol, allows flexible reservations for multicast transmission, even for large multicast sessions. However, at the end of nineties, scalability concerns for large IntServ networks was reported. From the other side, the newest publications report a deep architectural conflict between DiffServ and multicast transmission, which caused difficulties in simple integration of DiffServ and multicasting [8]. In result, the large-scale real-time multimedia traffic, multicastly distributed through the network, shouldn't use IntServ reservations and cannot use DiffServ reservations. One of recently proposed solutions of this problem is to use aggregated IntServ reservations.

IntServ architecture, based on RSVP version 1 protocol [2], doesn't allow aggregation of individual reserved sessions into a common class. The RFC 3175 [1]

---

[1] This research was supported by State Committee for Scientific Research (KBN) under grant No. 4 T11D 015 24 (years 2003-2005)

M.M. Freire, P. Lorenz, M.M.-O. Lee (Eds.): HSNMC 2003, LNCS 2720, pp. 128-135, 2003.

introduces aggregation of RSVP for IPv4 and IPv6 reservations in a manner conceptually similar to the use of Virtual Paths in an ATM network. This solution is intended to make RSVP suitable for large-scale networks.

The other main feature of new RSVP is possibility of predictive reservations. However, reservation methodology, policy and detailed system architecture are not defined in this specification and still remains an unresolved issue.

The aim of the paper is to propose prediction-based QoS assurance for multicast multimedia delivery. This solution combine extended RSVP signaling protocol, able to transfer predictor's parameters, and prediction-based bandwidth renegotiation module.

The rest of the paper is organized as follows. Section 2 introduces the concept of prediction-based dynamic QoS assurance for multicast distribution of MPEG-encoded video traffic. Simulational experiments and their results are presented in Section 3, while Section 4 concludes the paper.

2   Prediction-Based Dynamic QoS Assurance for MPEG-encoded Video Traffic

Prediction-based dynamic QoS assurance requires at least two components: a fast, effective traffic predictor and a dynamic bandwidth allocation method. The proposed dynamic bandwidth allocation is performed using extended RSVP signaling protocol and prediction-based bandwidth renegotiation module (PRM).

2.1   System Overview

QoS mechanisms base typically on the Leaky Bucket algorithm. The user sends only set of simple parameters to the node, such as peak and mean value of bandwidth. The network, which makes QoS decision using Leaky Bucket must assume worst-case traffic patterns conforming to these parameters. Therefore the sufficient QoS results in under-utilization of network resources.

Prediction-based dynamic bandwidth allocation uses QoS-aware nodes with PRM module implemented inside. Before the transmission is performed, the predictor is setup using only a few parameters. Future bandwidth requirements for each video stream are predicted during the transmission. Network node forecasts total bandwidth occupancy as a sum of predicted values of all transmitted video streams (e.g. sum of predicted values obtained from all instances of prediction engine). Total bandwidth reserved in a network node is calculating using the following formula:

$$B(t) = \sum_{i=1}^{N} b_i(t),\qquad(1)$$

where $B(t)$ is a bandwidth reserved in node, $b_i(t)$ is a predicted bandwidth (for i^{th} stream).

In the proposed system, predictor's parameters are sending to nodes using signaling protocol RSVP. Because objects defined in RSVP cannot be used for carrying such a data, the new RSVP *PSpec* (Predictor Specification) Object has been introduced.

A *PSpec* Object is intended to carrying parameters needed for setting up prediction engine. The Object contains type of predictor, P flag, number of predictor's parameters and a list of predictor's parameters. In the case of regressive predictor, list of parameters is composed of regression coefficients. Each parameter is stored as an IEEE single- or double-precision floating-point number, conformable to RFC 1832 [7]. The precision of the parameter depends on the P flag.

The sender (application) prepares predictor parameters together with the typical reservation parameters and sends them in prediction-capable *Path* message (*pPath*). Receiver sends back extended reservation request *pResv* to each network node, along the delivery path, using typical RSVP mechanisms.

Both, *pPath* and *pResv* messages, contains *PSpec* object as well as subset of the typical *TSpec* (Traffic Specification) parameters. If:

• the network node do not support prediction, or
• the predictor's type is unknown, or
• critical error occurs (e.g. the video stream is out of synchronism),

the SENDER_TSPECs transferred in PATH messages and the TSPECs transferred in RESV messages (as a part of FLOWSPEC) are used to perform an appropriate resource reservation.

If network node supports prediction and is able to accept the reservation according to *TSpec* parameters, the new instance of PRM will be created and set up using *PSpec* parameters. One PRM is dedicated for one traffic stream and setting up according to properties of video traffic.

Prediction-based dynamic bandwidth allocation bases on the ability of RSVP to renegotiation of reservation after it is originally set up. In the case of prediction-capable RSVP routers, this renegotiation is based on the forecasted bandwidth. The renegotiation is performed internally in the router (by the PRM) and doesn't propagate to other routers. The new reservation is checked by the admission control module.

The prediction-capable RSVP is able to service both unicast and multicast traffic. It supports merging of flow specifications, as "typical" RSVP do. It allows RSVP to scale for very large multicast groups. The prediction-capable RSVP supports fixed filter (FF) style of reservations.

The PRM is associated with the WFQ queue. The WFQ allocates multiple queues, servicing each queue in bit-by-bit round-robin manner. The queue emulates round-robin server by scheduling packets in the increasing order of their departure times. The departure time T_F of the ith packet p of the jth flow can be computed as follows:

$$T_F\left(p_j^i\right) = \max\left[v\left(A\left(p_j^i\right)\right), T_F\left(p_j^{i-1}\right)\right] + \frac{l_j^i}{b_j(t)}, \quad i \geq 1, \quad T_F\left(p_j^0\right) = 0, \tag{2}$$

where $A\left(p_j^i\right)$ is the arrival time of the ith packet p of the jth flow, l_j^i is a size of a packet p_j^i and $v(t)$ is defined as:

$$\frac{dv(t)}{dt} = \frac{B_l}{\sum_k \beta_k(t)},$$ (3)

where B_l is the capacity of the hypothetical round-robin server and β_k is an instantaneous bandwidth of a flow which is an element of a set of backlogged flows at time t (including bandwidth of the best-effort service).

Instantaneous reserved bandwidth depends on predicted value of the next video frame. Of course, this mechanism lead to perfect bandwidth allocation only if prediction error is equal to zero (predicted value is equal to the real value). If predicted value is less than the real one, differences will be buffered. If the predicted value is larger than actual one, buffer will be emptied. Because the mean value of reservations are equal to the mean rate of the video stream, we obtain variable-bit-rate version of well-known bandwidth allocation strategy based on mean (Mean Rate Allocation, MRA).

2.2   Bandwidth Renegotiations and Error Control

Bandwidth renegotiations, performed in PRM module, are based on one-step prediction of unknown size of the next (successive) video frame. The PRM module includes measurement module, predictor and decision module. Prior to prediction, on-line measurement of video stream is performed. The measurement module evaluate a size l_j^i of a packet p_j^i and calculate the sum $r_j^f(t)$ of all the received packets of the current video frame f:

$$r_j^f(t) = \sum_{i=i_{0f}}^{i_{cf}} l_j^i,$$ (4)

where i_{0f} is the sequential number of the first packet in the current video frame and i_{cf} is the sequential number of the current packet. The prediction requires computation of the size $R_j^f(t)$ of the current video frame which is also calculated as the sum over i of the received packets, where i ranges from i_{0f} to the sequential number i_{nf} of the last packet in the current video frame.

To evaluate unknown size of the next video frame, one-step linear predictor of MPEG video traffic have been used. The prediction method combines decomposition according to regions in phase space and linear regression [3]. An MPEG video traffic piecewise linear prediction, based on above decomposition, consists in partition the space into 6 regions, each with different linear predictor. Each local linear predictor is described by its linear transfer function. In the case of regressive predictor, linear transfer function is a weighted sum of current value and $(q-1)$ previous values of time series.

Thus, predicted size $P_j^{f+1}(t)$ of the next video frame is defined as:

$$P_j^{f+1}(t) = \sum_{k=1}^{6} \delta_{k,S} \left(a_{0S} + a_{1S} R_j^f(t) + a_{2S} R_j^{f-1}(t) + \ldots + a_{qS} R_j^{f-q+1}(t) \right) \qquad (5)$$

where $a_{0S}, a_{1S}, \ldots a_{qS}$ are regression coefficients, S is the sequential number of a current cluster in the phase space and $\delta_{k,S}$ is the Kronecker delta function.

The predictor (5) was previously tested using MPEG-1 and MPEG-2 video traces, as well as MPEG-4 video traces. Results show, that the predictor is accurate (evaluation of prediction accuracy can be found in [3][4]).

The decision module takes decision about reservation change and the value of new reservation. The bandwidth $b_j^{f+1}(t)$ needed for the real-time transmission of the next video frame is computed as follows:

$$b_j^{f+1}(t) = \min\left[\frac{8}{\Delta T} \left(P_j^f(t) + C_j \right), \xi_j \right], \qquad (6)$$

where ΔT is the frame generation period (usually 40 ms or 33 ms) and ξ_j is the peak rate (in bps) of the jth video stream, C_j - constant. To determine whether new reservation can be made, admission control module is employed

The mean value of prediction error is equal zero, because bandwidth underestimations are compensated by overestimations. Unfortunately, the overestimation errors do not cumulate during successive renegotiations and the underestimation errors cumulate as the unnecessary buffer occupancy. This bias error of bandwidth underestimation causes larger delays and may cause buffer overflow. Thus, to eliminate a bias error, a small constant value C_j may be added. Value of C is chosen arbitrally, but either possible overestimations cannot cumulate or the video stream cannot use more bandwidth than limited by frame sizes. However, very large C (e.g. $C_j \approx \xi_j$) can lead to resource underutilization.

Furthermore, to retain assumed reservation accuracy in the case of gross error (e.g. due to unexpected scene change), the decision module provides on-line observation of the reservation behavior. If the incoming video traffic will exceed assumed threshold, the definition of reservation can be modified on-line. Decision about correction is taken based on the instantaneous value of the sum $r_j^f(t)$, the predicted value $P_j^f(t)$ and parameters from policy and admission control:

$$b_j^f(t) = \begin{cases} \min\left[\dfrac{8}{\Delta T} \left(P_j^f(t) + C_j \right), \xi_j \right], & r(t) \leq thresh \cdot \left(P_j^f(t) + C_j \right) \\ \min\left[\dfrac{8 \cdot \mu}{\Delta T}, \xi_j \right], & r(t) > thresh \cdot \left(P_j^f(t) + C_j \right) \end{cases} \qquad (7)$$

where μ is the mean frame size and *thresh* is a threshold value.

3   Experiments

Simulation analysis was carried out using an event-driven ns-2 simulator [5], developed in U. C. Berkeley. Although simulator incorporates various network protocols, including RSVP, both additional predictor modules and new RSVP TSPEC Object were created.

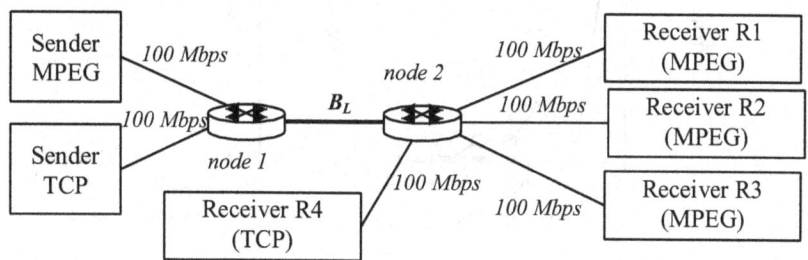

Fig. 1. Network topology.

The proposed transmission scheme have been simulated in a topology depicted in Fig. 1. A network simulation model is composed of two network nodes (prediction-capable RSVP routers) with finite capacity (200 kB) buffers, an 100 Mbps Fast Ethernet links and multicast MPEG connections. Bandwidth of the bottleneck link (B_L) depends on parameters of the transmitted MPEG stream and is defined as:

$$B_L = \frac{8(\xi + \sigma_\varepsilon)}{0.04} \cdot 1.05 \cdot 2 \tag{8}$$

where ξ is the maximum frame size (in bytes) and σ_ε is the standard deviation of prediction error. To assure that even the worst-case reservation will be accepted by admission control module, 5% of bandwidth was added. Reserved bandwidth will occupy no more than 50% of network resources.

Video traffic consists of 24 video traces generated from movies (*diehard*, *lambs*, *starwars*, *startrek*), sport events (*formule1*, *ski*), static camera (*cam*), videoclips (*vclips*). Each video was encoded for high (hq), medium (mq) and low (lq) picture quality. Statistical properties of video traces can be found in [6] and prediction errors for regressive predictor (phase space decomposition) can be found in [4]. The RTP protocol was used in the transport layer and the RTP packet size was set to 200 bytes.

As the background *best-effort* traffic, FTP source was used. The most commonly used TCP version – TCP SACK protocol – was applied in the transport layer. TCP packets have 1000 bytes.

Fig. 2 and Fig. 3 compares the dynamic bandwidth allocation strategies with the fixed service: Mean Rate Allocation (MRA) and Peak Rate Allocation (PRA). In the Fig. 2, frequencies of the loss rate are depicted. As the figure shows, MRA is comparable with the worst-case biased dynamic reservations. Both strategies 6 times (of 24) exceed the 5% threshold and they never achieve 0% loss rate (at least during the experiments).

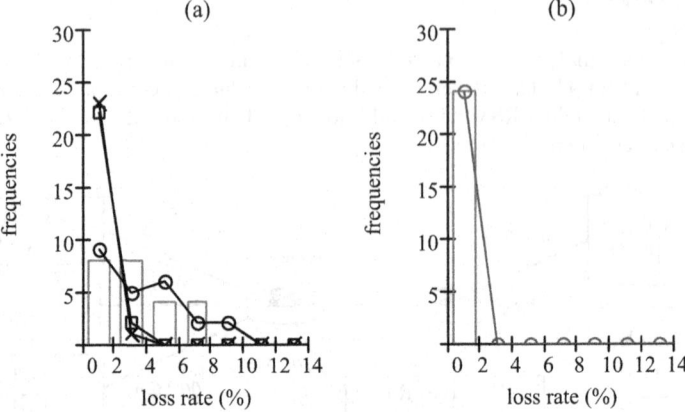

Fig. 2. A frequencies of loss rate (sample size – 24 movies): a) MRA reservations (bars) vs. biased ($C = 0$) dynamic reservations (solid lines), where thresholds: *thresh* = 1 (x's), infinite threshold (boxes), *thresh* = 1.5 (o's), b) PRA reservation (bars) vs. unbiased dynamic reservations (solid line, o's) for $C = \sigma_\varepsilon$ and large threshold (*thresh* = 3).

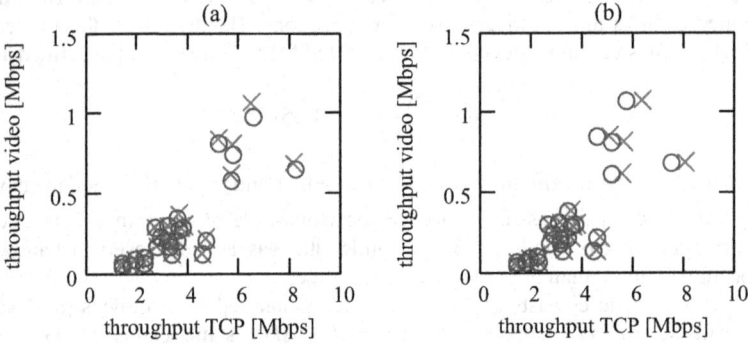

Fig. 3. Throughput of video data vs. throughput of TCP (sample size – 24 movies): a) unbiased ($C = 0$) dynamic reservations, *thresh* = 1.5 (x's) and MRA reservations (o's), b) biased dynamic reservations for $C = \sigma_\varepsilon$, *thresh* = 3 (x's) and PRA reservations (o's).

The biased dynamic reservation with *threshold*=1.5 is comparable with the best-case dynamic reservation (Fig. 2a) and allows to achieve 0% loss rate (10 movies of 24 in the case of *threshold*=1, 4 movies of 24 in the case of *threshold*=1.5). Loss rate is usually less than 1%.

Results of unbiased reservations are similar to results obtained for PRA strategy (Fig. 2b). However, loss rate for PRA reservations are always equal to zero, while dynamic reservations usually allows to achieve 0% loss rate (4 times of 24 loss rate have been larger than 0% but wasn't larger than 1%).

Fig. 3 illustrates that dynamic bandwidth allocation allows to achieve better utilization of network resources than the fixed service. Fig. 3a shows that biased dynamic reservation gives comparable or larger throughputs of video than the MRA strategy, while the TCP throughput remains the same. This tendency is shown even if the worst-case dynamic reservation is performed (not included in Fig. 3). Similar situation is depicted in Fig. 3b. Fixed (PRA) and dynamic service achieve maximal throughput of video stream, although unbiased dynamic reservation allows to achieve larger TCP throughputs (improvement ranges from 1.8 kbps to 0.6 Mbps).

4   Conclusions

Two main contributions have been made in this paper. First, the general concept of decentralized prediction-based QoS assurance was proposed. The each network node takes autonomous decision about the bandwidth renegotiation. No centralized control is necessary and no transfer of additional, control information along delivery tree is required. In result, time intervals between reservations are not upper-limited by round-trip-time, what in turn enables the usage of one-step predictors.

Second, the prediction-based bandwidth renegotiation module (PRM) was proposed. The module includes measurement module, predictor and decision module. The proposed solution gives a variable-bit-rate strategy of reservation close to the Mean Rate Allocation (MRA) strategy. Simulations, carried out in *ns*-2 environment, demonstrated that proposed VBR-MRA reservations doesn't cause excessive packet loss, as classic CBR-MRA reservations do. Moreover, addition of small constant (chosen proportionally to the standard deviation of the prediction error) allows both achieve results similar to usage of bandwidth allocation strategies based on peak and avoid (typical for PRA) under-utilization of network resources.

References

1. Baker, F., Iturralde, C., Le Faucheur, F., Davie, B.: Aggregation of RSVP for IPv4 and IPv6 Reservations. RFC 3175. September (2001)
2. Braden, R. (Ed.), Zhang, L., Berson, S., Herzog, S., Jamin, S.: Resource ReSerVation Protocol (RSVP) – Version 1 Functional Specification. RFC 2205. September (1997)
3. Chodorek, A., Chodorek, R.R.: An MPEG 2 video traffic prediction based on phase space analysis and its application to on-line dynamic bandwidth allocation. Proc. of ECUMN'02, Colmar, France (2002)
4. Chodorek, A.: A fast and efficient model of an MPEG-4 video traffic based on phase space linearised decomposition. Proc. of 14th European Simulation, ESS'2002, Dresden, Germany (2002)
5. Fall, K., Vradhan, K.: The ns Manual. URL http://www.isi.edu/nsnam/ns/doc. April (2002)
6. Fitzek, F.H.P., Reisslein, M:. MPEG-4 and H.263 Video Traces for Network Performance Evaluation. IEEE Network 15, No.6, November/December (2001)
7. Srinivasan, R.: XDR: External Data Representation Standard. RFC 1832. August (1995)
8. Striegel, A., Manimaran, G.: A Survey of QoS Multicasting Issues. IEEE Communications Magazine, Vol.40, No.6, June (2002)

A QoS Based Routing Algorithm for Multi-class Optimization in DiffServ Networks[1]

Wenpeng Zhou, Peng Zhang, Xiaole Bai, and Raimo Kantola

Networking Laboratory of Helsinki University of Technology
Otakaari 5A, Espoo, FIN 02015, Finland
Tel: +358 9 451 5454, Fax: +358 9 451 2474
{wzhou, pgzhang, xbai, kantola}@netlab.hut.fi

Abstract. DiffServ has been proposed as a scalable model to offer various quality of services (QoS) in the Internet. It supports diverse traffic classes with different priorities. However, recent work has discovered that high priority classes (e.g., EF class) have significant impact on the performance of low priority classes (e.g., BE class) when traditional shortest path (SP) routing algorithms are applied. This phenomenon is also called inter-class effect. In this paper, we propose a simple QoS based multi-class routing scheme called PERD to relieve the problem. The essence of the scheme is to enable routing optimisation for each class by applying different algorithms for different classes. Through analysis and simulation study, we prove that the proposed scheme is able to improve the performance of all classes, especially the low priority classes. Moreover, the scheme produces comparable cost as other QoS routing algorithms. We believe that the proposed mechanism is beneficial for providing a scalable, multi-service solution in future IP networks.

1 Introduction

In today's rapidly growing networking environment, more and more diverse traffic is conveyed over networks where IP protocol plays an important role. Since traditional IP networks only provide best-effort service, Differentiated Services (DiffServ) has been proposed to offer various QoS and achieve scalability [1]. The DiffServ model aims to achieve scalability through simplifying functions in network core while keeping complicated operations only in network boundary. The services provided by the DiffServ architecture can be classified into three main categories: Expedited Forwarding (EF) [2], Assured Forwarding (AF) [3] and Best Effort (BE).

Recent work found that high priority classes (e.g., EF) have significant impact on the performance of low priority classes (e.g., BE) when traditional shortest path (SP) routing algorithms are applied [4][5]. Notably, this phenomenon is often called inter-class effect. In order to solve the problem, recent studies employed hop-by-hop QoS based routing algorithms to fairly distribute traffic over whole network so as to alleviate the inter-class effect [4]. However, we notice that neither this solution nor

---

[1] This work is supported by IRoNet project carried out at Networking Laboratory, Helsinki University of Technology.

M.M. Freire, P. Lorenz, M.M.-O. Lee (Eds.): HSNMC 2003, LNCS 2720, pp. 136–145, 2003.

traditional routing schemes are able to solve the problem successfully because of the following reasons.

First, different classes may possess different traffic characteristics and different QoS requirements. For example, real-time traffic carried by EF class naturally requires smaller delay while ftp traffic carried by BE class naturally requires larger throughput. However, it is difficult to achieve routing performance optimization for every class if all classes use a same routing tree as traditional routing schemes work.

Second, when a network is congested at a link by EF class for example, it is impossible for BE class to avoid the link since all classes use a same routing table. In such case, the performance of BE class is still significantly degraded by EF class.

In other words, it is difficult and inefficient to achieve the performance optimisation of all classes if a single routing tree is used. In this paper, we propose a simple QoS based routing scheme called Per-class Routing Based on Per-class Dissemination (PERD). The essence of the scheme is to enable routing optimisation for each class by applying different algorithms for different classes. With this algorithm, traffic can be evenly distributed within networks according to not only the offered traffic of each class but also the network state information of each class. In this paper, we investigate the algorithm through theoretical analysis and simulation study.

The rest of the paper is organized as follows. In section 2, we present the related work. In section 3, we depict the PERD algorithm and its implementation. In section 4, we describe our simulation environment and present simulation results and performance analysis in Section 5. We give conclusions and future work in the final section.

2   Related Work

Nowadays, QoS routing has been regarded as an enhancing mechanism for providing QoS in IP networks [6]. The study on QoS routing has attracted more and more attention. In [6], Chen, et al, presented an overview on QoS routing algorithms for future IP networks. In [7], Apostolopoulos, et al, developed QoS extension to OSPF and investigated its performance and cost.

In [8], Faucheur, et. al. introduced the concept of per-class Traffic Engineering, which is related to our paper. However, their work only has overall description, lacking deep considerations and solutions. Our work is also related to the work done by Wang et al., recently [4]. The authors explored two simple QoS routing algorithms to find optimal routes for premium class traffic in DiffServ networks. Our work shares a common interest in improving the performance of BE class, but our approach is distinct from theirs in such way that we apply different routing optimization for each class, which is not addressed in their paper. In addition, as we discussed in the Introduction, their approach is not capable of achieving the optimization of all classes.

3 Routing Algorithm

3.1 PER-class Routing Based on Per-class Dissemination (PERD)

With traditional routing algorithms, all classes use a same routing tree at each node. This is difficult to achieve the routing optimization of all classes at the same time. In this section, we propose a simple routing scheme PERD to solve the problem.

The PERD computes different routes for different classes through applying different routing algorithms for different classes. We describe the PERD with two classes (i.e., EF and BE class) as shown in Fig. 1. Notably, the PERD is not limited to the number of classes. For clarification, the PERD contains a set of combinations of routing algorithms, each of which is for a class. A combination is denoted by (R_1, R_2,..), where R_i is the routing algorithm for class i.

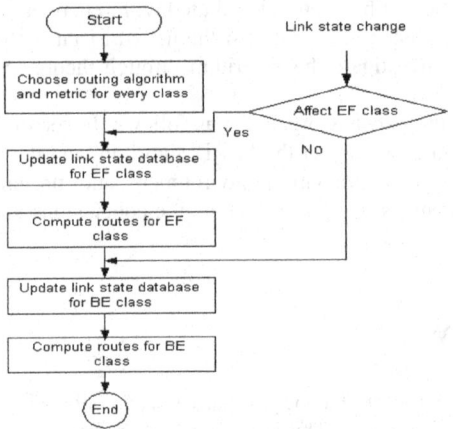

Fig. 1. PERD algorithm

According to the QoS requirements and optimization of each class, a specific routing algorithm and its parameters are chosen for each class. Note that the PERD does not specify the choice of routing algorithms, that is, the routing algorithms can be independently chosen. Then, the routing algorithm for EF class starts to compute routes for EF class according to the link state information of EF class. Note that the PERD does not specify the choice of link state information either, that is, the link state information can be independently considered too. For example, if an amount of bandwidth is provisioned for EF class at each node beforehand, the link state information can be the residual bandwidth of EF class, i.e., the provisioned bandwidth for EF class minus the bandwidth used by EF class.

After the routes for EF are computed, the link sate information should be updated and might be broadcasted. Then, the routing algorithm for BE class starts to compute routes for BE class based on the newly updated link state information. After that, the link state information is updated and might be broadcasted.

In particular, we emphasize some considerations supporting the PERD as follows.

1) Different classes may have different QoS requirements. For example, EF class supporting voice and video services is more delay sensitive and BE class supporting email and ftp services is more throughput sensitive.

2) PERD is suitable for the DiffServ model that provides support for various traffic classes from network architecture to network mechanisms. Migrating single-class routing schema into multi-class routing schema requires only a few changes on the DiffServ networks.

3) A DiffServ network is normally a policy-based network, which means routing changes should be infrequent, e.g., hours, days. Thus, the cost of applying PERD is likely less critical as traditional networks. Furthermore, the implementation of PERD can be either centralized or distributed, which means the cost of the PERD can be reduced by various ways.

3.2 Implementation

The PERD can be implemented by extending OSPF as illustrated in Fig. 2, that is, every node in the network carries out route computation for each class based on a link state database consisting of the link states of each class.

In the figure, each node has such function blocks as local link state pre-processor (LLSP), per-class routing block (PCRB), per-class routing tree (PCRT), per-class topology database (PCTD) and per-class link state trigger (PCLST). One of the key functions of the LLSP is to transform various local link state information into variables that can be used by routing. The PCTD maintains the link state information of each class. The PCRB is to find routes for specific class based on the PCTD and stores the routes in the PCRT for routing. The PCLST determines when the PCTD advertises its link state information to the network. In addition, advanced trigger mechanisms can be applied by the PCLST in order to reduce advertisement costs [10].

In this paper, the link state of a class on a link in the PCTD is denoted by a duplex (B_{pro}, B_{av}), where B_{pro} is the bandwidth provisioned for the class and B_{av} is the available bandwidth of the class, and $B_{pro} >= B_{av}$. Notably, as we described in previous subsection, various link state information can be applied in accompany with the PERD.

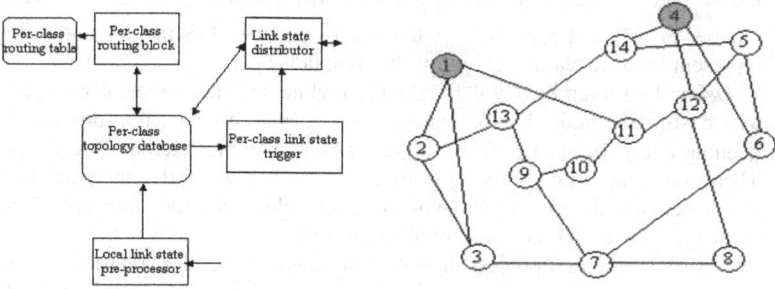

Fig. 2. Implementation of PERD   **Fig. 3.** Simulated network

4 Simulation Environment

In the section, we describe the simulation environment in details.

4.1 Assumptions

In the simulations, we study a DiffServ MPLS network where requests for setting up label switched paths of three traffic classes (i.e., EF, AF and BE) are arisen. In the network, we evaluate the performance of every class in terms of throughput and delay when PERD is utilized in comparison with that under the shortest path (SP) algorithm and the widest bandwidth (WB). The SP algorithm is the conventional routing algorithm in the Internet. The WB algorithm selects the path that has the widest bandwidth [10]. In particular, since the PERD allows different routing algorithms for different classes, in the paper we let PERD use WB algorithm for EF class and AF class and SP algorithm for BE class. Notably, as we described in Section 3, various routing algorithms can be applied under PERD.

In our simulations, network resources in the network are provisioned for each class beforehand so that each class can achieve acceptable QoS while the amount of real-time traffic on a link can be restricted. In the simulations, the following provisioning principle is abided by: EF class allocation amounts to 20% of the capacity of a link and AF accounts for 30% of the capacity of a link. The rest of the capacity is left for BE traffic. It is reasonable to have this principle because in reality BE traffic will still take a big portion of whole network traffic and EF traffic should not take too much portion as premium traffic. Particularly, we intend to guarantee that the BE class is never completely blocked by EF and AF classes.

4.2 Metrics

In this paper, we consider the following metrics for performance evaluation of the classes.

Throughput: To get the average network throughput, we log the number of received packets of each class at the destination node during simulations. We define the average throughput of each class with such formula: $N_i * L_i / T$, where N is the number of received packets, L is the size of packets, T is the simulation time and *i* represents service class. The unit of throughput is bps.

Delay: End-to-end delay is the duration while a packet travels from a source node to a destination node. It is composed of propagation delay, transmission delay and queuing delay. In practice, the number of hops may be different for different routes. Therefore, delay might vary from time to time because different routes are chosen. We calculate the average delay of each class by the formula: $\sum$delay per class/$\sum$packets per class. The unit of delay is ms.

Cost: We use total processing time consumed by the PERD during the simulation time to represent its cost. We adopt the settings of the processing time of each routing action same as [10]. The processing time of each action is shown in Table 1:

Table 1. Cost of each routing action

No.	Cost(us)	Action Description
1	1500	Find next hop
2	1500	Compute QoS path
3	500	Update local topology database
4	200	Broadcast link state information
5	100	Broadcast a message packet

4.3 Simulation Environment

To carry out the study, we make use of QoS Routing Simulator (QRS) [12]. In the QRS simulator, traffic flows from source nodes and sinks into destination nodes.

We apply an ISP network as shown in Fig. 3. Notably, we also investigate various network topologies that are described in [5].

In order to simplify our analysis, we consider both node1 and node4 as boundary nodes while node1 is the source node and node4 is the destination node. We assign the capacity of each link along the shortest path node1->node11 -> node12 -> node4 as 3 Mbps. The capacity of other links is 2 Mbps. We should note that the capacities are chosen for efficient simulations and simplicity. We have made tests with bigger link capacities and got similar simulation results. In other words, the unit of link capacity is independent from our simulation results.

In Fig. 3, we notice that the minimal cut between node1 and node4 has three links (link4-14, link4-12 and link4-6) with the total capacity of 7 Mbps. Obviously, the total throughput should be at most 7Mbps. Considering the provisioning principle mentioned in Section 4.1, the provisioned bandwidth of EF class, AF class and BE class are 1.4Mbps, 2.1Mbps and 3.5Mbps, respectively.

During simulations, we increase traffic load by 10% each time, namely, we initially generate 0.7Mbps traffic and increase that to 1.4Mbps, and so on. This process lasts until 100% traffic load is reached. We run simulations for over 100 times and 10000s for each simulation. The simulation time is much larger than traffic duration so that simulation results are insensitive to traffic variation.

5 Performance Analysis

In the section, we present and analyze the simulation results.

5.1 Throughput Vs. Load Percentage

Fig. 4 shows the total average throughput of all classes under PERD, WB and SP algorithms. The throughput of each class under the routing algorithms is shown in Fig. 5– Fig. 7.

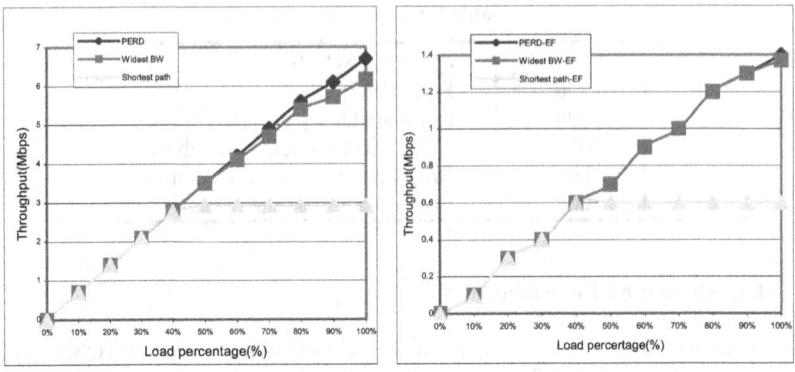

Fig. 4. Total throughput   **Fig. 5.** Throughput of EF class

As shown in Fig. 4, the total throughput of SP algorithm is rather low after the load increases to a threshold. This is because the SP only uses a single path, i.e., the shortest path. In comparison with the SP, WB and PERD achieve much better throughput. Moreover, when the traffic load is relatively light, e.g., less than 60%, there is no obvious difference between PERD and WB. The advantage of PERD shows up along the increase of traffic load. The total throughput of PERD is 6.23 Mbps when the traffic load is 90%, which leads to efficiency 6.23/7=89%. In contrast, the total throughput of the WB algorithm is 5.67 Mbps, whose efficiency is 5.67/7=81%.

Fig. 5 shows EF class throughput under the three routing algorithms. Similar to Fig. 4, both WB and PERD perform better than SP. However, WB and PERD have little difference even in high load, which means both PERD and WB can guarantee the performance of EF class.

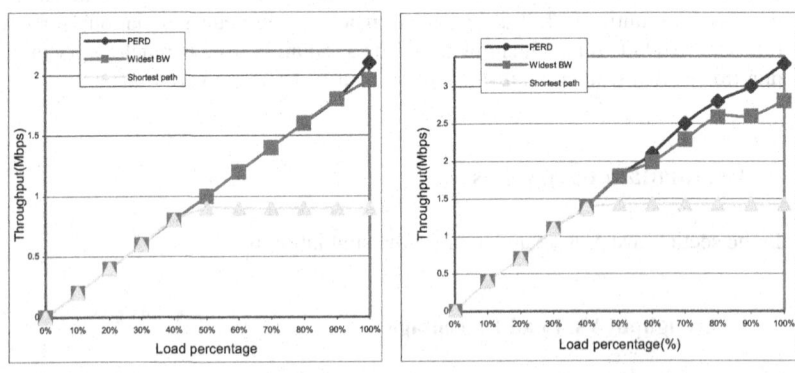

Fig. 6. Throughput of AF class   **Fig. 7.** Throughput of BE class

Fig. 6 shows the throughput of AF class under the three different routing algorithms. Similar to Fig. 5, both PERD and WB work better than SP while PERD achieve slightly better throughput than WB only in very high load, e.g., larger than 90%.

The advantage of PERD becomes more obvious when observing the throughput of BE class under three different routing algorithms as shown in Fig. 7. This figure shows that PERD achieves clearly better performance than WB. For example, when load is 90%, PERD results in 3Mbps of BE class, while WB results in 2.6Mbps. In comparison with Fig. 5 and Fig. 6, Fig. 7 shows that PERD can achieve significantly better performance of BE class than WB and SP.

In summary, we find that PERD can improve total throughput and per-class throughput as well, especially for low priority class traffic. This is because PERD can achieve the route optimization of each class. High priority traffic can be more evenly distributed over the network while low priority traffic can avoid links congested by high priority traffic. As a result, the probability of congestion is reduced that leads to the increment of throughput.

5.2 Delay Vs. Load Percentage

We present the delay performance of each class under the three routing algorithms between Fig. 8 and Fig. 10.

We show the average delay of EF class under the three routing algorithms in Fig. 8. Overall, the delay increases when traffic load increases and SP achieves the smallest delay. Obviously, this is because SP uses the shortest path with the smallest number of hops. In comparison with WB, PERD achieves better delay performance than WB, for example, when the load is 90%, PERD results in 92ms delay while WB results in 116ms.

Fig. 9 shows the average delay of AF class under different routing algorithms. Similar to Fig. 8, SP achieves the best delay performance while PERD achieves similar delay performance for AF traffic as WB.

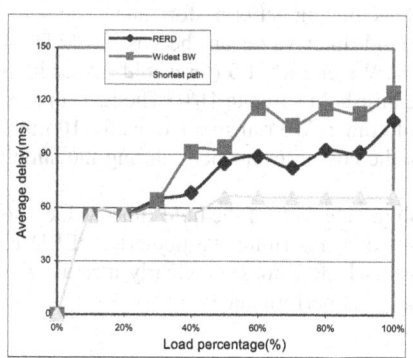
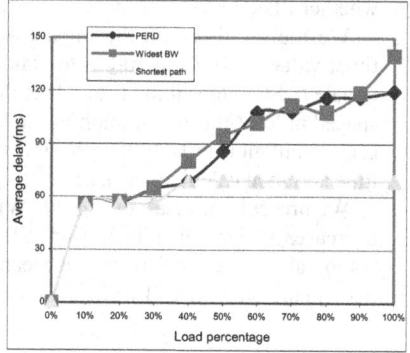

Fig. 8. Delay of EF class   **Fig. 9.** Delay of AF class

We draw BE class delay under the three routing algorithms in Fig. 10. The figure clearly shows that PERD is much better than WB when traffic load exceeds 60%. Particularly, PERD achieves comparable delay performance as SP.

As proved in above figures, PERD can achieve better delay performance than WB, especially for low priority classes. This is mainly because the amount of real-time traffic is overly distributed on the whole network so that EF traffic traversing bottleneck links decreases and the queues of EF class become shorter, which leads to the smaller delay of other classes.

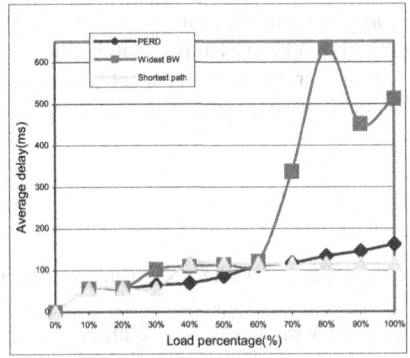
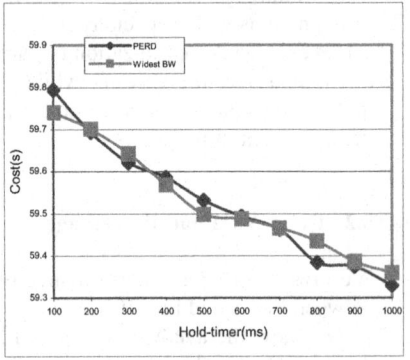

Fig. 10. Delay of BE class   **Fig. 11.** Cost vs. hold-timers

5.3 Cost Vs. Hold-Timer Value

In this sub-section, we compare the cost of PERD and WB algorithm to investigate whether PERD produces more cost while achieving better performance.

We mainly focus on the impact of hold-timer value on the cost [10]. The hold-timer values vary from 100ms to 1000ms. We employ TB (threshold based) link state update (LSU) algorithm [10] and set the threshold value to 10%. The LSU updates are spaced at least for the duration of the hold timer. We run simulations for 10 times and each simulation lasts 1000s. We record the cost in every node during the simulation time and then calculate the sum.

We present our result in Fig. 11. With the increase of the hold-timer value, the cost decreases under either PERD or WB routing algorithm. Particularly, PERD results comparable costs as WB, which means that PERD does not clearly increase the cost in comparison with WB while achieving better performance.

6 Conclusions

In this paper, we investigated the inter-class effect and explained that traditional routing algorithms are unable to achieve the performance optimization of all classes in DiffServ networks. Then, we proposed PERD algorithm to solve the problem in a heuristic way. We described PERD and presented its implementation by extending OSPF.

Furthermore, we choose to simulate a scenario in which the offered traffic is directed rather differently from the one assumed at network design. Under this imbalance through simulations, we found that:

(1) Both throughput and delay of EF class service can be guaranteed until the offered traffic exceeds the provisioned capacity under PERD and WB algorithm.

(2) PERD can result in better throughput of each class than WB and SP, especially for low priority classes, e.g., BE class.

(3) PERD can result in better delay performance than WB for both high priority classes and low priority classes.

(4) PERD produces comparable cost as WB algorithm.

The better performance achieved by PERD is mainly because PERD can achieve the performance optimization of every class based on the link state information of each class. In our future work, we aim to develop a sort of global optimization objectives and routing algorithms for achieving global network optimization as well as the performance optimization of each class.

References

[1] S. Blake, et al. An Architecture for Differentiated Service. IETF RFC 2475, December 1998.
[2] B. Davie, et al. An Expedited Forwarding PHB. IETF RFC3426, March 2002
[3] J. Heinanen, et al. Assured Forwarding PHB Group. IETF RFC2597, June 1999.
[4] J. Wang and K. Nahrstedt. Hop-by-Hop Routing Algorithms For Premium-class Traffic in DiffServ Networks. IEEE Infocom'2002.
[5] W. Zhou. Provision and Route Optimization in DiffServ Networks. Master thesis. Helsinki University of Technology, October 2002.
[6] S. Chen and K. Nahrstedt. An Overview of Quality of Service Routing for Next-Generation High-Speed Networks: Problems and Solutions. IEEE Networks. November/December 1998.
[7] G. Apostolopoulos, et al. Implementation and Performance Measurements of QoS Routing Extensions to OSPF. IEEE Infocom'99, Volume: 2, 1999 Page(s): 680 -688 vol.2.
[8] F. Le Faucheur, et. al. MPLS Support of Differentiated Services. IETF RFC3270, May 2002
[9] J. Kleinberg, et al. Fairness in Routing and Load Balancing. 40th Annual Symposium on Foundations of Computer Sciense, 1999, pp. 568-578
[10] M. Zhansong, P. Zhang and R. Kantola, Influence of Link State Updating on the Performance and Cost of QoS Routing in an Intranet. HPSR'2001, April 2001
[11] D. Bertsekas and R. Gallager, Data Networks. Prentice-Hall, Inc. 1992
[12] P. Zhang and R. Kantola. Designing a New Routing Simulator for DiffServ MPLS Networks. 2001 SCS Symposium on Performance Evaluation of Computer and Telecommunication Systems (SPECTS'2001). July 2001

An Open Modular Router with QoS Capabilities*

Giorgio Calarco and Carla Raffaelli

D.E.I.S. - University of Bologna, Viale Risorgimento 2 - 40136 Bologna – ITALY
Phone: +39 51 2093776, Fax: +39 51 2093053
{gcalarco,craffaelli}@deis.unibo.it

Abstract. This paper describes the design, implementation, and testing of an edge router supporting flow-based classification functions for real time traffic. Protocol and statistical analysis of application flows is performed to provide EF treatment to multimedia traffic without any user signaling. These functions take advantage of the modular Click environment and implement per flow traffic recognition and SLA management. Sample measurement shows the effectiveness and feasibility of the proposed approach as a step beyond in the field of open routing design.

1 Introduction

The enormous growth of the Internet and its progressive extension to new application environments requires to re-consider routing architectures and procedures to meet the new needs. Today users ask forever increasing bandwidth and especially require services with quality of service guarantees. Being the network built on a set of different sub-networks, service access control is necessary through procedures coordinated among different domains and quality of service requires to be managed during information. To this end new routing and queuing techniques must be investigated and new functionalities to manage different application flows must be introduced within the network [1], [2]. As regards the international scientific community, the IETF has defined models for quality of service management in the Internet and in particular the Differentiated Services model, which is interesting for scalability aspects. This model requires some functions to be implemented in the edge routers, such as packet assignment to service classes on the basis of explicit signaling or classification mechanisms, and class management in the core routers.

Solutions for Differentiated Services implementation are available by main router manufacturers as proprietary solutions that are difficult to modify and optimize. Recently open routing approaches have been developed with the aim to use standard hardware platforms to support free and open software [1]. The main aim of this new router design strategy is the definition of flexible and modular design environment and tools that allow fast router design and modification in order to meet user and context needs. Some proposals have been recently made most of which are suitable for

* This work was partially funded by the Italian Ministry of Education, Universities and Research through the EURO project 2002098329.

M.M. Freire, P. Lorenz, M.M.-O. Lee (Eds.): HSNMC 2003, LNCS 2720, pp. 146-155, 2003.
© Springer-Verlag Berlin Heidelberg 2003

the Linux environment and assume standard PCs as hardware platforms. Here the Click modular approach [3] is assumed as a starting point to develop flow-based classification of real time services and to demonstrate a viable design procedure to support new multi-service router functionalities.

The focus is on the edge router where users are required to register as willing to generate real time traffic: this information is stored at the edge router as Service Level Agreements (SLA) and then used for on line authentication. The main target of the Quality of service (QoS) function is to recognize real time flows without explicit user signaling on the basis of the protocol used or, as an alternative, on the basis of statistical analysis of user traffic. The classification procedures require modification of the reference Click router diagram and new output queue management modules.

The new functionalities have been evaluated in terms of latency and classification effectiveness. Comparisons of performance are presented to show the processing overhead introduced by classification.

2 Click Modular Environment

The large number of hardware producers, low costs of PCs, and the continuous progress in performance are important factors which are making the design of a packet switch based on a free and open-source platform more attractive [1][2]. Another important demand is nowadays the modularity of the software structure, which would help network manufacturers' revision and design of new functionalities in a router, according to different types of needs. For instance, edge routers, contrary to core routers, usually need more specialized tasks, like packet filtering and classification for Quality of Service. The Click Modular Router is a new Linux-based software framework developed by the MIT [3]. It permits the design of PC routers or other packet processors offering an extensive library of simple modular components. The principal advantages of such a modular system are flexibility and extensibility: the designer can easily create various services simply connecting the basic modules, called elements. The standard libraries can also be enhanced by developing new functionalities. In fact, each Click object is an instance of an associated C++ class, containing the appropriate source code, and always derived from the pre-defined root class "Element". Having the template of a new class already available, the programmer can simply focus in the methods' implementation. From the designer point of view, things are even simpler: using a plain declarative language, a configuration file has to be created. This must contain a set of commands, at first checked by the Click environment and then used to initiate and connect the elements (thus determining how packets move among them). An IETF RFC-1812 router was proved quite simple to realize, since only 16 click elements must be employed, as described in [4]. This standard configuration can be a starting point for the implementation of new router functionalities: for instance, packet filtering, web caching, quality of services, or others. Even if performance is not the main goal of the project, Click can be dynamically linked as an object to the Linux kernel, taking advantage of the kernel-space execution priority. Several optimization tools are also available, which offer perceptible performance improvement. Moreover, some network cards can be managed with polling drivers, instead of using the more expensive interrupt-based technique [5], eliminating the livelock problem and improving the forwarding rate. Combining an Intel Gigabit Ethernet card with a 1.6 GHz AMD Athlon MP processor on a 64-bit/66 MHz PCI motherboard, an optimized Click router has shown to reach a maximum forwarding rate of 740,000 64-byte packets/s [6]. The standard library also contains an effective support for measurements: the *SetCycleCount* and *CycleCountAccum* elements can be inserted anywhere in the Click configuration, counting the number of CPU-cycles necessary to a packet to move between them. We have used them extensively for obtaining the performance evaluation graphs contained in section 4.

3   Real-Time Flow Classification

In this section, the approach to allow QoS unaware users of multimedia tools to take benefit of network QoS is described. The new service is introduced into the edge router and consists in a classifier that, according to a given set of SLAs, performs both protocol and statistical analysis on the traffic incoming from the stub network. The new functionality and its prototype implementation are called *Real Time Classifier* (RTC). Figure 1 depicts the modules inserted in the Click framework to realize the RTC. Comparing it with the RFC1812 router described in [4], the RTC replaces here the simple FIFO-based output queuing scheme, being it inserted between the basic router and the output device interface.

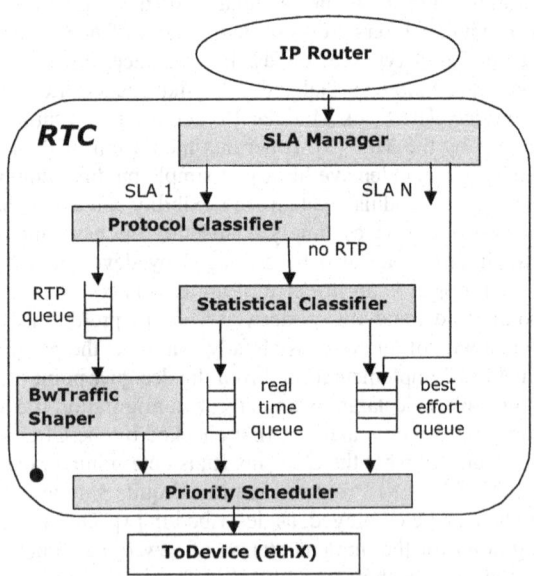

Fig. 1. The RTC internal structure

The RTC is designed for interactive multimedia applications and, at this moment, is able to recognize and mark that kind of traffic. In terms of DiffServ PHB, RTC marks the traffic recognized as belonging to real-time multimedia streams as EF, setting the IP packet DSCP field. The number of packets required for classification can be chosen independently for each classification algorithm with the aim to optimize the classification delay and failure rate trade-off. With reference to figure 1, the SLA Manager module is dedicated to identify the traffic belonging to a certain SLA. For our purposes, a 7th-tuple as shown in the table 1 defines a SLA format.

Table 1. The SLA format implemented

ID	SRC IP	Mask	BW	Shared	DSCP	Policy

The ID parameter is the unique SLA identifier. The fields IP and MASK are used to identify the host/network belonging to the SLA. The BW parameter is the bandwidth allowed for the considered SLA. The Policy parameter can take different values according with the policy adopted for the out-of-profile traffic of the considered SLA. Finally, Shared is used to specify the degree of fairness to among flows belonging to the same SLA. The value of the field ranges between 0 and 100, and represents the percentage of the bandwidth used on a FCFS basis, with zero meaning that all the bandwidth is equally split between the flows and 100 meaning all bandwidth used on a FCFS basis. The SLA Manager is implemented using an existing Click element, *IPClassifier*, which performs a pattern-based filtering to examine the source IP address and checking if it pertains to a specific SLA. If so, the packet is passed to the Protocol Classifier, which is as a new Click compound element designed and added to the library; otherwise, it is pushed into the BE (low-prioritized) output queue. The Protocol Classifier, depicted in Figure 2, is able to filter the RTP-marked traffic flows. The IETF RFC1889 [7] establishes that the RTP packet must always contain a 32-bit field called SSRC (Synchronization SouRCe identifier), which is kept constant and distinct for each single flow. The *GetSSRC* element extracts these useful bits from the RTP header and passes them to the *RTPClassifier*, which is able to hook each distinct RTP flow if obtaining N occurrences of its SSRC value in a T-seconds interval of time. Once a flow is identified, an internal table keeps the flow in the "classified" state, deleting it only after 30s of inactivity. The *SetIPDSCP* element is then involved in marking the TOS field of the IP header. The presence of the RTP protocol in the analyzed flow is considered a sufficient, but not necessary, condition to classify it as a multimedia stream. For this reason, the Statistical Classifier does an additional analysis. Figure 2 also depicts the structure of this other new compound element. The statistical classification algorithm adds classification capability in the case of real time applications, which are not RTP compliant. It takes into account the flow rate and the packet size as main parameters for the classification process. Typically, these parameters depend on the source encoding used and bandwidth, as mentioned in [8]: for instance, a flow can be considered an interactive multimedia flow if the packet rate is greater than 15 packets/s and the packet size is less than 200 bytes. Once sufficient information is collected, the flow is classified as real-time. Obviously, since no SSRC field is present in this case, miscellaneous flows cannot be distinguished from each other. The *SplitFirst(J)* block is destined to redirect (in the BE queue) the leading J packets: this mechanism should guarantee the cascading modules to receive stable data. *CheckAverageLength(K)*, instead, is able to monitor the mean size of the last 15 received packets: if greater than K bytes, the current packet is passed to the BE queue.

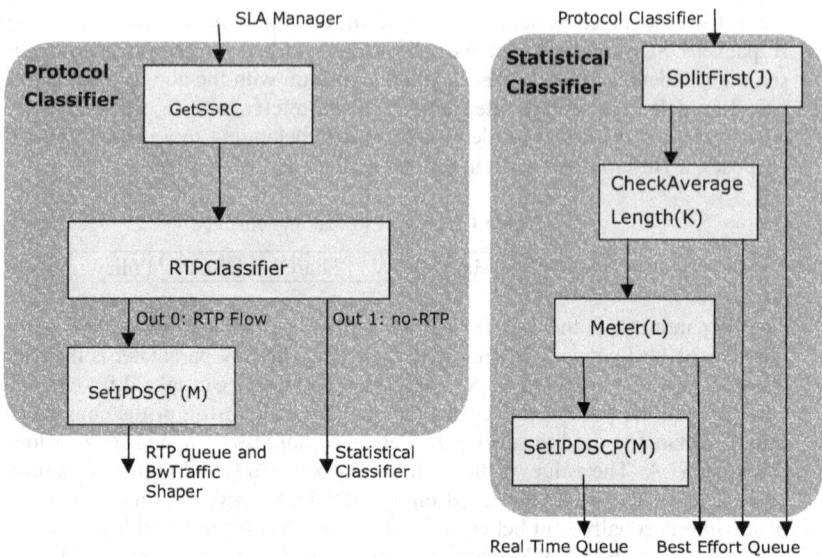

Fig. 2. Protocol based and statistical classification

Otherwise, it is pushed in the *Meter(L)* element, which measures the packet rate and classifies the real-time flow, when that is greater than L packets/s. Accordingly to the SLA "BW" and "Policy" parameters, another new block was designed to manage the out-of-profile traffic with more flexibility, the *BwTrafficShaper*, similar to the standard BandwidthShaper, but with a secondary output dedicated to the out-of-profile traffic. While the in-profile traffic is shaped as required, it allows to apply various policies to the out-of-profile one: besides being discarded, this can be redirected elsewhere (for instance, to the BE queue).

4 Experimental Evaluation

In order to perform quality of service trials, a testing configuration was designed to emulate functions of a real network environment and to offer real time services with quality of service. Figure 3 shows the test-bed layout, which consists of four PC-based systems, connected through a Gigabit Ethernet layer2-switch. The edge router (*Alpha*) is equipped with a 1.6 GHz Pentium IV Processor. The other PCs (*Beta, Gamma,* and *Delta*) are exclusively utilized for traffic generation and analysis and have an on-board 1Ghz–Pentium III processor. Every PC is equipped with the Intel PRO1000XT-Server network adapters. On our router, we plugged two of them on the 32-bit/33 MHz PCI bus, even if they would be ready to work with the more advanced 64-bit/133 MHz PCI-X bus. The choice of this NIC was led by the necessity of using the same polling-based driver already developed by the MIT for the Intel PRO1000 family cards.

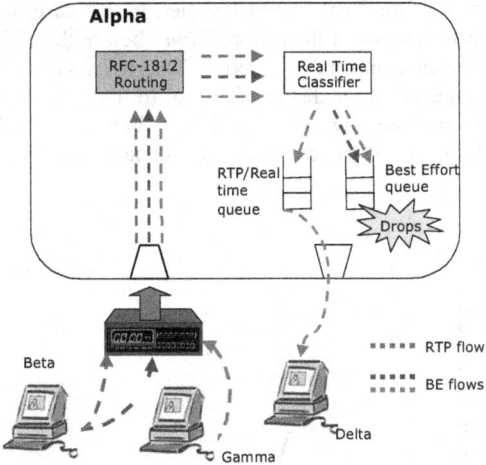

Fig. 3. Functional diagram of the test-bed layout

All the PCs were installed with the 2.4.9 version of the Linux operating system and Click release 1.2.4 (with the Intel Pro1000 4.3.15 driver added). The edge router performs the quality of service functions. To this end, it offers RTP-based and statistical classification of multimedia traffic, and SLA management. When necessary, the output link of the router was also tightened to work at 10 Mbit/s, so that it can be easily saturated. *RUDE*, a traffic generator, was installed on Beta and Gamma, which were used for injecting three distinct flows of traffic into the input port of the router. Specifically, these are a real time flow, a non real-time flow, and a best effort flow (at 16 Mbit/s, thus sufficient to saturate alone the output port of the router). Access to the router by Beta and Gamma is obtained through the Gigabit Ethernet switch. A traffic receiver, *CRUDE*, is set up on Delta: it collects information about the packets coming from the output interface of the router, helping us to verify if the real time flow was correctly treated. Other applications were also useful for generating the real time flows and evaluating how the system can significantly improve the quality of the communication under a human perspective. Examples of these are the popular Microsoft "NetMeeting" and RAT. Other more general measurements were done using Click installed on *Beta* and *Delta* as a traffic generator and collector. Figure 4 shows performance offered by the described hardware platform. The router can manage a maximum loss-free forwarding rate of 120,000 packet/s with the interrupt-based drivers and 370,000 packet/s using the polling technique. The main performance figures of interest for a QoS capable router, however, are the packet delay and the time jitter. Figure 5 depicts the average delay time of an RFC-1812 polling-based router, at different input packet rates with 60 s runs of traffic. The main contribution to the global delay is due to the output queue term (a FIFO with 100 elements), while the routing process alone requires about 1.2 μs. Under these conditions, no packet loss is observed. It is to mention that 10 elements FIFOs were also tested: the global delay is much smaller (about 2-3 μs), but packets drops are observed when coming up to the maximum input rate. More detailed analyses were done for the QoS capable router, after the insertion of the Real Time Classifier. In this case, its output link was tightened to 10Mbit/s, inserting a *BandwidthShaper* before the *ToDevice* block (which interfaces the Click environment to the NIC). The *RUDE*s installed on Beta and Gamma were used for injecting three distinct flows of traffic into the input port of the router. Specifically, a real time flow, a non real-time flow (at 512 Kbit/s), and a best effort flow (at 16 Mbit/s, thus sufficient to saturate alone the output port of the router).

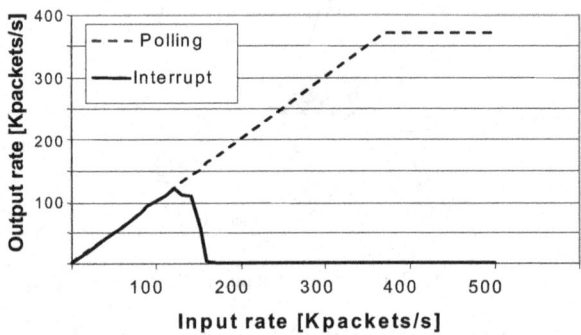

Fig. 4. Forwarding rate as a function of input rate for a Click-based RFC-1812 router using interrupt and polling techniques (64-byte packets)

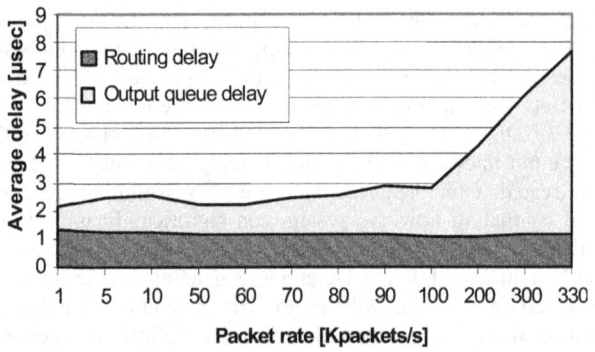

Fig. 5. Average delay time for a Click-based RFC-1812 router as a function of input rate (64-byte packets and 60 seconds runs)

Table 2 illustrates the average delay time for the RTP and the best-effort traffic, and the maximum output queues length reached during the runs (the output queues are 100 elements FIFOs). As expected, the RTP traffic is forwarded with a much smaller delay ($\approx$32 μs) than best effort traffic (typically 5 ms).

Table 2. Average delay time and maximum output queues length for a RTP 512 Kbit/s flow in the presence of a 16 Mbit/s best effort flow over a 10 Mbit/s link

Traffic	Average IP Routing Delay	Average RTC Delay	Average Click Delay	Max Queue Length
RTP	1.19 µs	30.75 µs	31.94 µs	13
Best Effort	1.19 µs	> 5000 µs	> 5000 µs	Overflow

With the same contour conditions, an additional evaluation was done about the end-to-end delay of the RTP traffic. This is feasible since RUDE marks any packet with a sequential time-stamp, making possible to determine the total delay of the packets, due to the path from the generator to the receiver. This measurement is influenced by all the delay factors inside the test-bed (the traffic generator and collector inner delays, the switch latency, the Click delay, and the NIC-to-Click transit time). Figure 6 shows how the end-to-end delay for the RTP flow is about 120 µs. It is determined in the presence of the implemented functions and compared with a wired generator-to-receiver connection. The latency introduced by all the functions inserted in the Click environment is denoted with Tclick and is given by

$$Tclick = Trouting + Trtc, \qquad (1)$$

where Trouting is the delay introduced by the RFC1812 router part, and Trtc is the delay due to the RTP classifier blocks. The values of these contributions were measured through the Click support. The end-to-end lag can be resumed as

$$Tdelay\_with\_click = Tgen + 2*Tsw + 2*Tnic + Tclick + Tcoll, \qquad (2)$$

where Tgen is the time spent by the traffic generator to put the packets on the wire, Tsw is the switch latency (2,5 µsec), Tnic is the NIC-to-Click transfer time, and Tcoll is the time spent by the traffic collector to retrieve the packets from the wire. The direct wire connection instead is

$$Tdelay\_with\_wire = Tgen + Tsw + Tcoll . \qquad (3)$$

Thus, knowing that Tclick = 31.94 µsec, Tdelay_with_click =123 µsec, Tdelay_with_wire= 58,2 µsec, it is possible to estimate the value of

$$Trouter \equiv Tnic + Tclick + Tnic = 62,3 \text{ µsec} ; \text{ Tnic} \approx 15,18 \text{ µsec}. \qquad (4)$$

A point to mention regards the graphed data in figure 6: it is possible to notice a few high delay peaks in the picture. The same spikes were also observable in the case of the wire connection delay, not reported in this paper. This makes us believe that they are not due to an odd behavior of the router, but more probably to some extraneous activity on the traffic generator and collector systems. An additional analysis of the transmission delay (inside the Click environment) is presented in figure 7 and 8. Figure 7 shows the distribution of the delay for the RTP and BE flows, Figure 8 depicts the temporal jitter for the same kinds of traffic. Most of the values of the jitter for real-time traffic are acceptable being within 100 µs after the flow has been classified. As regards the jitter for non real time traffic, it is limited to some hundreds of microseconds only because almost all non-real time traffic is dropped and the small percentage of packets that enters the queue typically finds it full.

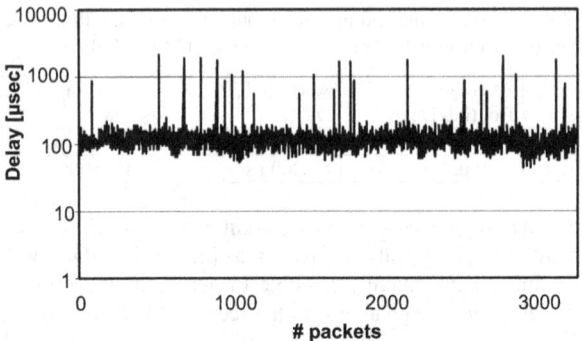

Fig. 6. End-to-end delay for a RTP 512 Kbit/s flow in the presence of a 16 Mbit/s best effort flow over a 10 Mbit/s link

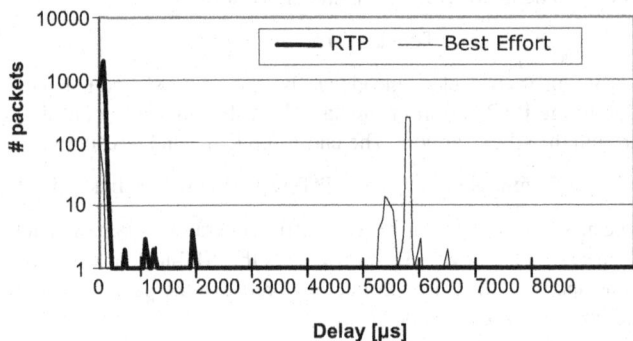

Fig. 7. Delay time distribution for a RTP 512 Kbit/s flow in the presence of a 16 Mbit/s best effort flow over a 10 Mbit/s link

5 Conclusions

In this paper the design, implementation and testing of a flow based real time classifier called RTC have been described. RTC uses different methodology to perform its function, based on protocol analysis and traffic patterns. Being it flow-oriented, it can perform functions such as SLAs management and bandwidth usage measurement. This can be fruitfully used in dynamic bandwidth management (i.e. bandwidth broker support). The results show effectiveness of RTC in recognizing real time flows and in guaranteeing bandwidth as limited delays for these kinds of applications.

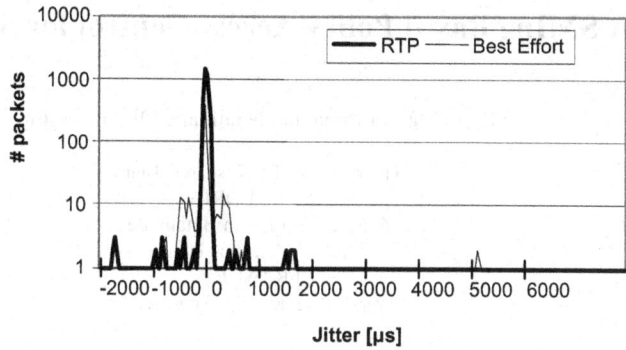

Fig. 8. Jitter distribution for a RTP 512 Kbit/s flow in the presence of a 16 Mbit/s best effort flow over a 10 Mbit/s link

References

1. Keshav S., Sharma R.: Issues and trends in router design. IEEE Communication Magazine, vol.36, n.5, pp.144-151, May 1998
2. Xipeng Xiao, Ni L.M: Internet QoS: a big picture. IEEE Network , Volume: 13 Issue: 2 , March/April 1999 Page(s): 8 –18
3. Click Modular Router, http://www.pdos.lcs.mit.edu/click/, MIT, Cambridge, MA
4. E.Kohler, R.Morris, B.Chen, J.Jannotti, M.F.Kaashoek: The Click modular router. ACM Trans. Computer Systems 18, August 2000
5. J.C.Mogul, K.K.Ramakrishnan: Eliminating receive livelock in an interrupt-driven kernel. ACM Trans. Computer Systems 15, August 1997
6. E.Kohler, R.Morris, B.Chen: Programming language optimizations for modular router configurations. ACM SIGPLAN Notices, Volume 37, October 2002
7. http://www.cis.ohio-state.edu/cgi-bin/rfc/rfc1889.html - RTP, Real Time Protocol
8. G.Calarco, R.Maccaferri, G.Pau, C.Raffaelli: Design and Implementation of a Test Bed for QoS Trials. QOS-IP 2003, Lecture Notes in Computer Science, Vol. 2601 pp.606-618, February 2003

A SMIng Based Policy Access Control for SNMPv3

Radu State, Emmanuel Nataf, and Olivier Festor

The MADYNES Research Team
INRIA-LORIA
615, Rue du Jardin Botanique
54600, Villers-les-Nancy
FRANCE
{Name.Surname}@loria.fr

Abstract. The recent advances toward mobility enhanced services and infrastructures require new conceptual solutions for the underlying management plane. This paper investigates an extension to the standard management framework based on a new access control mechanism. We propose a policy based approach for an agent side access control. We integrate the policy specifications and management information (MIB) within the recently proposed Structure of Management Information Version framework.

1 Introduction

During the last few years, attention has been brought to novel information modelling techniques, management services and protocols. Results from these efforts are very different in nature mostly because they emerge from different communities with very different requirements (e.g., backward compatibility with a legacy approach or technology conformance). The ubiquitous internet and the enhanced user mobility witnessed over the past few years, raise new challenges for the network management community. The network management community addressed the issues related to the management of fixed elements located within the same management domain.

Mobile users and networks connecting seamlessly to the Internet using different and dynamic network access points require a new approach for management. Management operations must be performed over various management domains, requiring an enhanced configurability of the management stack. We consider in this paper the issue of a flexible management stack capable to have a high degree of configurability. We propose a policy based management approach for the management of the management stack. Until recently, the two conceptual different management approaches, the policy based management one vs. the standard SNMP one, could have either considered as competing technologies or as rather disjoint (SNMP for monitoring and Policy Based Management - PBM for the configuration). We propose in this paper an integration of the two approaches trough a meta-management approach.

Our paper starts in section 2 with an introduction to new requirements faced by current management paradigms. Next, it provides an enhanced access control module based on authorization policies and discusses similarities and differences with respect

M.M. Freire, P. Lorenz, M.M.-O. Lee (Eds.): HSNMC 2003, LNCS 2720, pp. 156-164, 2003.

to the existing SNMPv3 standard. Section 3 proposes a unified information modeling solution for the management plane. This integration is based on the use of the recently proposed SNMP Structure of Management Information Version 2 (SMIv2) [4] specification. Section 4 illustrates how this unified view can be implemented within an SNMP agent, while related work is described in section 5. Finally, section 6 concludes the paper with conclusions and pointers to future work.

2   Extended Access Control in SNMP Agents

The current SNMPv3 specification proposes an authentication and privacy extension to the SNMPv1&2 standards called User Security Module (USM) [14]. The major functionality of this module is to provide authentication for the manager as well as the privacy (encryption/decryption) of the management traffic. The complement of these security functions, concerns the access control for the agent MIB. This is done through the use of several tables (a separate extension to the MIB2 is defined to content these tables). The access control model, which is also called View Access Control Module (VACM) allows to specify views, which are collections of subtrees in the MIB, and their access rights (read/write, read and write) for a group of management applications. The basic architecture of the VACM processing can be summarized as follows:

1. Individual Management Applications are associated to one or several pairs (security name, security model). Access control is defined per groups. Each such pair can be mapped to a group via a table (vacmSecurityToGroup). All elements within a group have identical access rights.
2. The information about where the targeted management object is found can be obtained from another table, vacmContextTable.
3. Information about the protection of the SNMPv3 message can be retrieved from the vacmAccessTable.
4. For each type of operation read/write a collection of subtrees is defined allowing this particular operation within a given context. Information about these collections are represented in another table (vacmViewTreeFamiliy).

A process is defined based on these tables, in order to implement an access control enforcement. Without detailing, this process in this paper, we point out the cumbersome configuration requested in order to correctly configure this access control plane. We started our work motivated to reduce the complexity for the access control configuration and willing to enhance the flexibility of the access control mechanism. While the SNMP (v1, v2, v3) framework is the de facto standard for network management, its first two versions (v1, v2, v2c) provide trivial security mechanisms, while the third version is relatively rigid and difficult to use.

With respect to the SNMPv3 architecture, we propose an extension which stems from two key observations. The first one is a commodity based one. The correct configuration of the access plane is difficult and error prone. Since many tables are used to   implement the VACM, a simple miss-configured entry could potential either be a major security hole, or on the contrary deny legitimate access to management applications.

The second motivation for our extension is triggered by the need to refine access control rights with respect to the local context of the agent as well as additional constraints. Existing access control scheme in the SNMPv3 framework allow to statically allow/deny access to MIB objects for a management applications. The more and more nomadic and mobile environments of modern users demand new approaches suited to:

1. Allow context-driven management based on the current users/equipment location. For instance, one might allow his enterprise manager to manage his/her laptop whenever the latter is connected to the enterprise network, but this management should be not allowed in any other cases.
2. Perform conditional management. For instance, one user could allow to an unknown manager to perform management if and only if there seems to be errors on some network interface.
3. Integrate within the current management paradigms any extension needed for the two previous points. This means, that no new management protocols should be invented.

Since current SNMPv3 approaches do not allow this type of management. We propose an extension to the SNMPv3 View Access control which is based on 2 major contributions.

The first one is related to a policy based [11] access control which allows to specify context-driven and conditional management. The second contribution is related to the use of SMIng in order to map these policies into implementation specific policy based management.

The framework for the access control specification of the management actions can be described [16] in a formal way, as follows:

1. A set S represents all possible subjects requesting access to objects. In our case, these are all managers: For instance in terms of the previously described simple scenario.
2. The set of all possible objects is O. This corresponds to all OIDs in the MIB.
3. A is the set of access modes permitted on objects. $A = \{read, write\}$.
4. There is the notion of context, c, representing the location of the agent. The set of contexts is C. A particular context is given by the collection of ipaddress/netmask/DNS used on each network interface. In this paper, we will use the term context having this definition in mind. The VACM aware reader should not confuse this term with the one used to specify a MIB view in SNMPv3.
5. A permission is either to grant or to deny access. The set of permissions is Perm = {grant, denied}.
6. A set FM of formulas. An individual formula f is a logical conjunction of equalities and/or inequalities. For instance $t>18$ means current time after 18h. An equality or inequality is constituted of constant terms (string or numbers) as well system accessible variables. System accessible variables are all variables in the MIB. Other system specific variables might also be presented. If a formula holds, then the authorization policy is active (see in the following for the definition of an authorization policy).

The configuration of the access control scheme is based on providing a set of authorization policies.

$Auth\,\Pr \subset O \times S \times A \times C \times Perm \times FM$. An authorization policy, for instance is: $(1.3.4.21.^*, EMP, read,$

$context\,(address\ = 194.224.3.23, netmask\ = 255.255.255.255, dns\ = 195.224.3.1),$

$grant\,, time\ > 18) \in AuthPR$

modeling the fact that : Manager EMP is allowed to read all elements under the subtree 1.3.4.21, if the agent is connected with IP address 194.2234.3.23, netmask 255.255.255.255 and DNS server 194.224.3.1, and current time is past 18h,

An authorization request is a 4-tuple, $ar = (o, s, a, c) \in O \times S \times A \times C$, meaning that action a in context c is to be performed s on object o. For the previous example, such a request might look like:

$(1.3.4.21.^*, EMP, read,$

$context(address\ = 194.224.3.23, netmask\ = 255.255.255.255$

$, dns\ = 195.224.3.1))$

This request models the read operation on OID starting with 1.3.4.21, performed by manager EMP, where the current connectivity configuration of the laptop is given by the address, netmask and DNS.

For every authorization request, an authorization decision is computed based on the set of authorization policies. Basically, a decision is to either grant or deny an action. An example for a decisions follows:

$decision = (1.3.4.21.^*, EMP, read,$

$context(address\ = 194.224.3.23, netmask\ = 255.255.255.255$

$, dns\ = 195.224.3.1), grant)$

This decision allows the access for EMP to read all objects in the subtree 1.3.4.21, if the agent is on a network (IP address of the agent=194.224.3.23 with netmask 255.255.255.255.

3   Access Control Specifications with SMIng

SMIng (Structure of Management Information next generation) is a proposal that was submitted to the SMIng IETF working group [6], [7], [8]. This proposal is not the sole candidate for standardisation (SMI-DS *Data Structure* is an example of another possible approach) but has the advantage of being object-oriented like, and not being bound to any underlying approach while offering compatibility with both SNMP-SMI and SPPI [5]. While SMIng is described in the related drafts, we shortly present its structure through an example (see code excerpt below). It contains the definition of management information which model statistical measures of active application executions and together with policy rules used to decide if an active application could be launched.

SMIng is designed for the definition of data interfaces. Thus, there is no procedural or functional statement support but only data oriented specifications. SMIng provides a set of basic data types like OctetString, Unsigned32 etc. From these types, new ones can be defined through the use of the typedef statement as shown in the following excerpt.

```
(1)      typedef  SecModelName{
(2)          type OctetString(255);};
(3)      typedef  SecName{
(4)          type OctetString(64);};
(5)      typedef  IPAddress{
(6)          type OctetString(4);};
(7)      typedef AccessMode{
(8)          type OctetString(5);};
(9)      typedef OID{
(10)         type OctetString(255);};
(11)     class Subject{
(12)         attribute SecModelName  scnmodname;
(13)         attribute SecName scname;};
(14)     class Context{
(15)         attribute IPAddress ipaddr;
(16)         attribute IPAddress dnsaddress;
(17)         attribute IPAddress netmask;}
(18)     class PolicyRule{
(19)         attribute OctetString(10) name;
(20)         attribute Subject   subject;
(21)         attribute OID oid;
(22)         attribute Context ct;
(23)         attribute  AccessMode am;
(24)         attribute  Formula fm;};
(25)     snmp{
(26)         table{vacmSecurityToGroupTable{
(27)         oid vacmMIBObjects.2;
(28)         index(1);
(29)         implements Subject {
(30)             object 2 scnmodname;
(31)             object 3 scname;};};
(32)     copspr{
(33)         prc SNMPPolicyRule {
(34)         oid vacmPIBObjects.10;
(35)         pibindex(1);
(36)         implements PolicyRule{
(37)             object 2 name;
(38)             object 3 subject.scnmodname;
(39)             object 4 subject.scname;
(40)             object 5 oid;
(41)             object 7 ct.ipaddress;
```

```
(42)                    object 8 ct.dnsaddress;
(43)                    object 9 ct.netmask;
(44)                    object 10 fm;};};
```

Examples of such statements are shown in lines 1 to 9; for instance we define the type IPAddress to be an octetstring with four bytes.

SMIng provides a class statement to define object classes that are composed of attribute and event statements (as well as simple inheritance (not shown in this paper).

For instance, the class context regroups three IP addresses, one for the DNS, one for the netmask and one for the used IP address. For the sake of simplicity, we considered only the use of a single-homed agent, but the generalization to a multi-homed one is straightforward.

In a similar manner, we can express the elements of an access policy (see lines 18-24).

The core of SMIng is protocol independent and can be used for both network and policy management as well as other domains. As these approaches strongly rely on dedicated information models, albeit sometimes very similar, and specific protocols, SMIng offers a facility to express the specification of a mapping from classes and their attributes to protocol specific information.

As an example, we show both a SNMP (lines 25 to 31) and a COPS-PR (lines 32 to 44) mapping specifications. Each mapping specifies which SMI table or SPPI provisioning class of the existing MIB and PIB of the management agent is implementing some SMIng object class.

The oid part gives the global object identifier (other SMIng constructs allow a full definition of the object identifiers for the extended Agent MIB and associated Agent PIB. Following is the index column(s) specification of the table or PRC and the implemented SMIng class (lines 29 and 35).

The object statement maps a column identifier to an SMIng class attribute. If attribute is itself a class, a dotted notation is used to go until a simple value attribute is found.

Line 26 shows how the Subject class could be mapped to an entry of the existing vacmSecurityGroupTable. This shows on one hand that our approach is capable to specify the access policies implemented in the existing standard. On the other hand, we can map these policies to COPS-PR [13] specific implementation and conceive a policy based management solution for the management stack. This extends the existing access module and allows for a more flexible and powerful management solution.

4 The Extended SNMP Agent

This section describes the architecture of an extended SNMP agent. The block functional architecture (based on [15]) is illustrated in figure 1. The extension proposed in our approach lies firstly in the enhanced Access Control Module. This Module based on the authorization policies introduced previously behaves as a Policy Enforcement Point (PEP) [12] with respect to these policies. The configuration of these policies is done using the COPS-PR protocol. The SMIng compliant management application acts in the role of a Policy Decision Protocol (PDP) with respect to the PEP Policies concerning access rights being provisioned on the management agent. The SMIng aware management application manages the management agent also via the SNMP protocol. The advantage of a SMIng based solution is twofold. Firstly, SMIng allows to express management information in an implementation independent manner. As shown previously, we can model the whole MIB2 as well as access policies within the same language and next use the SMIng defined mappings for SNMP and respectively COPS-PR specific implementations. This allows to use COPS-PR/COPS for the policy based specific (which is the main reason for the existence of these protocols) part and the SNMP for the standard management. Secondly, we can show how these two protocols can be integrated within the same management framework in a very complementary manner.

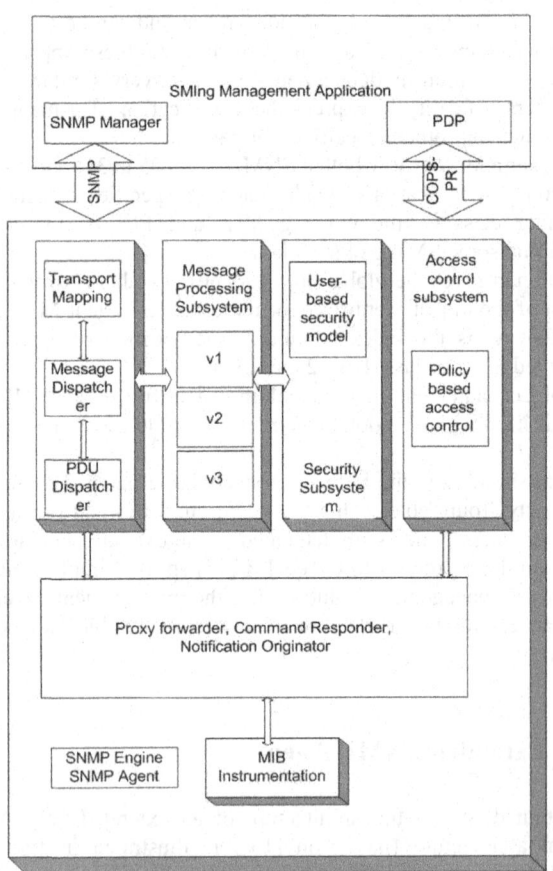

Fig. 1. Extended SNMP v3 Agent

5 Related Work

Policy based management has been the focus of tremendous recent research efforts. Due to space limitations we can not cover all this work. For a good introduction, the reader can consult [11]. Most of the work in policy based management considered the control of traffic in Intserv or Diffserv enabled networks. Our work is different since we address the issue of configuring the management plane within a policy based framework.

The object oriented network modeling is well described in [1]. The concept of Meta Managed Objects [9] contains the same base elements as those proposed by SMIng with a separate definition of data and their different representations. Other mappings exists from objects to TMN or SNMP management information [10]. The *libsmi* project of the Technical University of Braunschweig provides a library to access SMI information. A component of this library is an SMIng parser that allows a syntax and semantical analysis of modules. An HTML version can be tested on line at the Simple Web site. An API provides access to MIB and PIB modules information to ease the development of management applications. The design and development of applications that combine policy manipulation and MIB object access is much more convenient within a common framework. This has been also demonstrated while our group developed management applications for an active network [2] environment.

6 Conclusions and Future Work

We addressed in this paper the issue of supporting novel access control mechanism in SNMPv3 agents. We started with the observation that current standardized network management frameworks do not allow enhanced agent autonomy. This is due to an access control module which is difficult to configure and incapable to allow dynamic access decisions. We argue that current SNMPv3 specification provide an excellent authorization and access control mechanism for a fixed environment. This is the case with most existing target environments. However, nomadic environments where more and more users are mobile require new management frameworks. We addressed this issue by assuming the standard management protocol SNMPv3 and we proposed an extension of the SNMPv3 management framework. A new access control mechanism based on the policy based management paradigm is proposed in our paper

Our management framework is based on access policies for the dynamic configuration and execution of the access control. One access policy is more general than the existing SNMP V3 (VACM), allowing to define policies based on local the context (IP connectivity) of the agent, as well as additional constraints. The policy based management of management access can be implemented with the existing COPS protocol.

We integrate the definition of the access policies and the managed information within the unique specification framework offered by the Structure of Management Information V2. Our approach generalizes the View based Access Control subsystem proposed in the SNMPv3 architecture, without requiring changes at a SNMPv3 protocol level. Thus, our extension is transparent for already existing management applications.

References

1. S. Bapat: Object-Oriented Networks. Models for architecture, operations and management. PrenticeHall, 1994.
2. E. Nataf, O. Festor, G.Doyen: A SMIng centric approach for integrated monitoring and provisioning. Accepted in Proc IEEF/IFIP Symposium on Integrated Management, IM2003, Colorado, USA 2003.
3. T.R. Chatt: TMN/C++: An object-oriented API for GDMO, CMIS, and ASN.1. In Integrated Management V. IFIP, Chapman & Hall, May 1997, pages 177–191, 1997.
4. F. Strauss J. Schoenwaelder: Next generation structure of management information for the internet. In R. Stadler & B. Stiller, editor, Active Technologies for Network and Service Management, DSOM'99.Zurich, Switzerland, pages 93 – 106. Lecture Note in Computer Science, IFIP/IEEE, Springer, October 1999.
5. K. McCloghrie, M. Fine, J. Seligson, K. Chan, S. Hahn, R. Sahita, A. Smith, and F. Reichmeye: Structure of Policy Provisioning Information (SPPI), RFC3159, August 2001.
6. K. McCloghrie, D. Perkins, and J. Schoenwaelder: Conformance Statements for SMIv2, April 1999. IETF, STD58, RFC 2580.
7. K. McCloghrie, D. Perkins, and J. Schoenwaelder: Structure of Management Information Version 2 (SMIv2), April 1999. IETF, STD58, RFC 2578.
8. K. McCloghrie, D. Perkins, and J. Schoenwaelder: Textual Conventions for SMIv2, April 1999. IETF, STD58, RFC 2579.
9. J. Seitz: Meta managed objects. A. Lazar, R. Saracco, and R. Stadler, editors. Integrated Management V. IFIP, Chapman & Hall, May 1997. pages 650 – 660
10. N. Soukouti and U. Hollberg: Joint Inter Domain Management: CORBA, CMIP and SNMP. In Integrated Management V. IFIP, Chapman & Hall, May 1997. pages 153–164, 1997.
11. D. Verma: Policy-Based Networking. New Riders Publishing.2000.RFC 3159. Structure of Provisioning Information (SPPI). IETF. 2001
12. RFC 2748. The COPS (Common Open Policy Service). IETF. 2000
13. RFC 3084. COPS Usage for Policy Provisioning (COPS-PR). IETF.2001.
14. W. Stallings: SNMP, SNMPv2, SNMPv3 and RMON1 and 2. Addison-Wesley Pub Co; 3rd edition 1998
15. W. Stallings: Network Security Essentials, Prentice Hall, 2nd edition 2002.
16. M. Kuda, S.Hata: XML Document security based on provisional authorization, 7th ACM Conference on Computer and Communication Security (CCS 2000), Nov. 2000.
17. V. Konstantinou, Y. Yemini, and D. Florissi: Towards Self-Configuring Networks. DARPA Active Networks Conference and Exposition (DANCE), May 2002, San Francisco, CA.

An Innovative Resource Management Scheme for Multi-gigabit Networking Systems

George Kornaros[1] and Ioannis Papaefstathiou[2]

[1] Ellemedia Technologies
Science & Technology Park, Vassilika Vouton, GR71110, Iraklio, Crete, GREECE
kornaros@ellemedia.com, Tel: +302810391947
[2] ICS-FORTH, P.O. Box 1385, GR71110, Iraklio, Crete, GREECE

Abstract. One of the hardest problems faced by today's multi processor networking devices is the scheduling of the different hardware and software events so as to process network traffic streams at rates of multiple gigabits per second. In this paper we present a novel scheme for resource management in such Network Systems-on-a-Chip (SoCs), that we claim can deal with resource management in a very flexible way, while attacking the sources of performance degradation using sophisticated techniques. The presented architecture supports efficiently both high and low priority requests with a hybrid scheme which is greatly effective, since it has a very high performance to cost ratio, while also being very flexible by supporting different scheduling algorithms, depending on the application needs. Finally, performance results of the hardware implementation of this scheme are demonstrated.

1 Introduction

Nowadays network devices must employ special schemes in order to handle wire speed cell packet processing at 2.5Gbps and higher line rates, that take advantage of the state-of-the-art semiconductor technology and advanced circuit design techniques. In addition, besides best-effort applications, today's and future applications require from the network servers to guarantee them particular performance bound and delay guarantees. The service level that an application enjoys principally depends on how efficiently a network component applies a scheduling discipline to allocate different bandwidth to connections. Thus, in every network embedded system, special resource management schemes are needed to facilitate packet processing in a fair, balanced way and at the same time should not be expensive it terms of hardware complexity.

In this paper we present such a resource manager, which reduces to the absolute minimum the off-chip memory accesses, while at the same time has a relatively low hardware complexity. The scheme supports two different priorities equivalent to the ones that most of the networking devices support: wire-speed and best-effort. The main objective is to make the high priority scheduling as efficient as possible at the cost of more expensive hardware (mainly on-chip memory), while keeping the performance of the low priority scheduler at acceptable levels and its hardware cost low. Hence, the presented scheme is a hybrid one comprising of both a very efficient scheduler, and a low cost one.

M.M. Freire, P. Lorenz, M.M.-O. Lee (Eds.): HSNMC 2003, LNCS 2720, pp. 165-175, 2003.

Solutions to coherent protocol processing and high-speed resource management appear in the literature (e.g. [5], [6]), but are insufficient or even not applicable in protocol processing of the "fast path" data flow; this is also analyzed in [3]. The same applies for the scheduling algorithms as they have been proposed and studied for traffic scheduling in data networks [7], [9]. On the other hand, there are several commonalities between our protocol processor environment and the context within each of these algorithms. One first observation is that pre-emptive scheduling algorithms in modern Network Processors are not efficient since this would stall the pipelined operation of the embedded processing cores required, and cause extensive overhead due to context switching (it is also discussed in [6]). Another observation stems from the fact that even state-of-the-art Network Processors offer limited support for internal resource-allocation mechanisms making the problem of context switching in the case of advanced scheduling schemes even worse [7]. Moreover, the implementation of advanced scheduling algorithms is very resource consuming, leaving narrow margins for the use of other packet processing functions [8].

The following sections describe the implementation of our resource manager along with its performance. We analyze the requirements of resource management in a real networking system and we outline 2 already implemented scheduling schemes.

2   Resource Management Inside a Network Processor System

The PRO3 is a network processor[1] ([4]) which is capable of executing network layer protocol functions together with the most time consuming operations of transport protocols in a TCP/IP as well as in an ATM network environment, either in a stand-alone fashion or in collaboration with a host system that executes other higher layer functions and applications. The PRO3 processor provides substantially high throughput for a range of complex applications such as packet filtering, statefull inspection and proxy applications in a Firewall [4], or a signalling controller. In order to meet its performance goals it is evident that software implementations do not suffice for such types of applications. Due to these constraints PRO3 follows a different approach than typical Network Processors that follow more or less a brute force approach based on massively parallel architectures (e.g. architectures described in [3]). The PRO3 alleviates processing load related to specific packet processing tasks by incorporating fixed hardware accelerators (e.g. for functions at the network interface like the ATM/AAL5 protocols), configurable modules that respond to specific commands like the Data Memory Management and schedulers and software programmable engines (e.g. for wire speed header parsing and packet classification with external Ternary CAM based search engine support). Complex protocol processing are executed at the RPMs (re-programmable RISC Cores), which have access to protocol state stored in a separate control RAM (CRAM). Thus PRO^3 differs substantially from typical computing system architectures. The notion of the system memory does not exist, nor is the PRO^3 controlled by a software operating system.

---

[1] PRO3 is operable at 200MHz, was fabricated in UMC's 0.18u CMOS process and prototyped in Q2-2002; it is supporting up to 512K flows (using per flow queues) at 2.5Gbps.

The requirement though for scheduling of processing tasks (regarding packet processing) still exists. Scheduling in such an environment is used in order to resolve contention for processing resources in a fair manner. This problem though, cannot be formulated as in the case of typical processor architectures, due to the requirements of coherent protocol processing and pipeline control of the PRO3 processor. Therefore, a novel scheduler is employed that can accommodate the diversity needs of this protocol processor. The scheduler is detailed in [1] and it is outlined here so as to demonstrate its advantages and disadvantages from the proposed architecture.

Mainly there are 32 scheduling queues supported, which are used for sharing the processing resources of PRO3 in a Weighted Fair Queueing manner. Each of these queues is associated with one of the possible internal destinations of packets within PRO3 and a specific handler protocol that will be executed on the data of this flow. Obviously, more than one data queues will share the same scheduling queue. The multiplexing of multiple flows in one scheduling queue (flow group) is done in a Round-Robin way. Thus, all the flows that hash into the same scheduling queue will share equally among them the portion of internal processing resources (in terms of service opportunities) that is allocated to this queue. The allocation of resources to the different queues is done according to some pre-configured weights.

The 32 scheduling queues are hierarchically organized. The first queue is treated with strictly highest priority over the others (it is mainly used to schedule traffic with low delay requirements for processing by the cores of the PRO3). The remaining 31 scheduling queues can either be treated with the same priority level and be serviced in a Weighted Round Robin fashion, or (determined upon configuration) they can be hierarchically organized in two sets with strict priority of the first set of queues over the second. The scheduling queues of the same priority/set are served in a WRR way.

2.1   Active Flow Identifiers for Scheduling

Another scheme for resource management, which is based on "Active Flow Identifiers", has been described in [2]. The architecture presented in this paper, is using a variation of this "active flow" based scheme, as one of its components, and thus the "active flow scheme" is briefly outlined.

The key idea of this novel high-speed scheduling mechanism is the "active" flow identifier. An internal tag of a connection is not a plain number that is assigned based on a scheduling scheme. On the contrary, a flow identifier can be "active" in the sense that it represents its priority level. In fact, it is an encoding way that associates one flow ID to a position in a large list of connections, each one with its own set of parameters, and QoS level. Thus, thousands of flows are managed in a compact way, which results in high-speed handling, saving off-chip accesses and extra space.

The gains of this organization are attributed to this property, and to several techniques to enhance flexibility and configurability for easy deployment to OC-192 routers. Well-defined interfacing and modular approach allows for easy adaptation to different scheduling policies and tailoring to match diverse needs at the same time (accelerate service, save on area, differentiate flow treatment). The key advantage of the proposed architecture is its reduced off-chip memory bandwidth and latency.

3   Proposed Architecture

The proposed Resource Management architecture is shown in Fig. 1. The service data queue (SIDQ) Manager is the coordinator that handles the priority queues, and schedules commands to the four potential processing units. The major enhancements to this architecture are located in the modules with a bold outline. Besides the Resource Manager, a Traffic Scheduler (TRS) is integrated, which orders the ATM cells or IP packets to be transmitted to the output network interface performing a shaping function in terms of peak-rate policing. Whenever the output data queues are active the TRS sends commands for transmission respecting the contracted peak rate for flows that are amendable to specific traffic contracts and service level agreements.

The Control and Update Unit (CU) is responsible to collect configuration and update commands from the Classifier, the Data Memory Manager (DMM) and the RISC cores (via the internal bus) and redirect them to the appropriate manager. Finding the right destination necessitates access to the Context Table Memories.

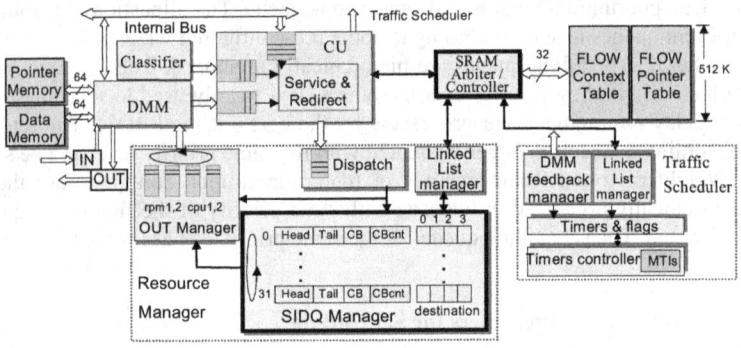

Fig. 1. Organization of the Resource Management Scheme.

Our Resource Manager supports a light, yet powerful set of commands, summarized in Table 1. These are mainly used for flow management and overall control of the command path from the CPU modules to the Data Memory Manager.

Obviously, it is critical to prioritize the commands that are coming from the CPU and should be serviced at the highest priority, because otherwise the processing of the system would have to stall. Taking also into account possible pending commands inside the FIFOs (causing additional latency), we allowed the Resource Manager to deliver one additional command to the DMM without getting a status acknowledge. The packet status for each flow that is eligible is pre-computed and shadowed inside the resource manager, and we wait for the DMM confirmation, before we update the external context tables with the actual status. The following sub-section describes in detail this implemented enhancement.

Table 1. The Resource Manager commands

Source Block	Command	Description
CPU/RPM/Classifier	INIT_DQ	Initialize a Scheduling Memory entry of a specific DQ
CPU	INIT_SIDQ	Initialize Service Queue
DMM/RPM/CPU	INS_PACKET	Arrival of a new packet belonging to a specific DQ
DMM	UPDATE_QS	Update scheduler's memory regarding number of packets of a DQ stored in the DMM's data memory
DMM	MORE	Inform the scheduler about the status of a packet in order to continue sending more commands.
CPU	DEL_FLOW	Delete a flow
RPM/CPU	FIN_PACKET	The packet in a CPU module finished processing.
RPM/CPU	MOVE_FLOW	Move a flow from a source SIDQ to another SIDQ.
RPM/CPU	FWD_COM	Forward a command from a CPU to the DMM

3.1   Speculative Service

The packet memory manager (DMM) utilizes fast off-chip SRAMs to store the needed data structures. In particular, both linked lists of segments and of packets are maintained per flow. In order to support a large number of flows, and since we have to do packet-buffering at wire speed, many bits are used for segment and packet pointers in addition to extra fields such as segment length and special flags (the data pointer memory bus is 64 bits wide). Moreover, visiting off-chip memories causes latencies that are not negligible when special situations arise, such as a single flow conveying a 2 Gbit per second traffic stream. The turn-around time between the Resource Manager transmitting a command to the DMM and collecting the queue status so as to decide whether it is eligible again, should be kept under 128 ns in order to sustain such a high-speed service of the flow.

To overcome these situations, we adopted a very compact representation of the number of packets per flow, along with a speculative service discipline. A two-bit wide counter, called "QSTAT" hereafter, is enough to depict the packet status out of the queue of a specific flow: it denotes whether there are zero, one, or more than one packets. This representation is based on the time window delay that the DMM reply lays on. The Resource manager now, has to make decisions and issue commands based on the information provided by the "QSTAT" field. In addition, a small cache is required. The purpose of utilizing a cache area is to record the information block of the last two transmitted commands; a delayed update might be needed in the associated priority queues (both internally and externally), due to the delayed response from the DMM. If our Manager issues commands for two or more different flows, then the delayed acknowledgement of the DMM regarding the packet status is considered on time and before we have to re-schedule the same flow. The hazard appears if the same flow is eligible for a second time and our manager guesses the "QSTAT" value, without having received the real "QSTAT" from the DMM. Hence, careful handling of all possible situations was performed so as to alleviate all the undesirable effects such as:

i) Issuing a command to the DMM regarding a flow without any packets,
ii) Reinsertion of the serviced flow back to the linked list with a false value, causing complex treatment in order to re-estate the right values.
In Fig. 2 we illustrate an example scenario, where we assume that for the depicted time interval only one high-bandwidth flow is eligible. The Resource Manager speculates the next value of QSTAT and acts appropriately: sends the command to the DMM, decrements the QSTAT value and deletes this flow from the SIDQ when empty. The DMM announces the actual value of QSTAT to the Resource Manager, which makes the analogous correction. Meanwhile, another pending command may reside in the DMM incoming FIFO. The asterisk indicates the time that a correction is required, since a command for the last packet has already been transmitted.

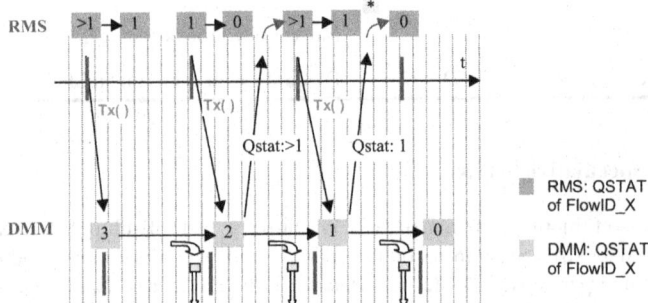

Fig. 2. Single Flow service: coordination between Resource and Data Memory Manager

3.2   Transparent Integration of On-Chip and Off-Chip Scheduling Tables

One essential enhancement we employed inside the Resource Manager (RMS) aims to reduce the latency of off-chip accesses for high-speed connections while also providing superior flexibility. Those are achieved by utilising a caching system (if configured to operate as such), which adds negligible implementation complexity. In addition, it facilitates stand-alone operation, without the external SRAMS, assuming that 2K flows suffice in a network environment. These enhancements, shown in Fig. 3, are integrated so as the resource manager is not aware of any intricacies due to the additional structures. The interface remains the same, while the only observable difference is the reduced response time when managing some specific flows.

The SRAM controller is responsible to access the off-chip Context and Pointer Tables, while at the same time synchronizes the system and the external devices clock domains. The bandwidth provided by the ZBT SRAMs (4.27Gbps) is sufficient for the performance of most of the networking devices. However, a significant percentage of the latency per command is due to going out of the chip, especially when considering that the average number of accesses per command is 2.5.

An innovative lookup technique is employed in order to economize both silicon area and lookup time. The novel idea is that a single bit is enough to distinguish if a flow resides on the flexible cache area or externally. The flow identifier itself is used to locate this configuration bit inside the lookup table. The 10 most significant bits of the flow identifier are the index to read a whole word from the lookup table, while the 6 least significant ones are used to locate this configuration bit. In the same time that this memory block is accessed, the decoding of the 6 low-order bits occurs. Thus, only one additional cycle is required and only a 64kbit lookup table is employed.

The latency is reduced from nine clock cycles to two when we are handling the on-chip high-priority flows (improvement by almost 60% if we also take into account the three additional clock cycles for arbitration (and service) among the rest of the ports), and to three when we need to access the flows belonging to the flexible cache table (improvement by 50%). The width of the embedded pointer tables remains the same (19 bits). This allows for addressing of all the memory space up to 512K.

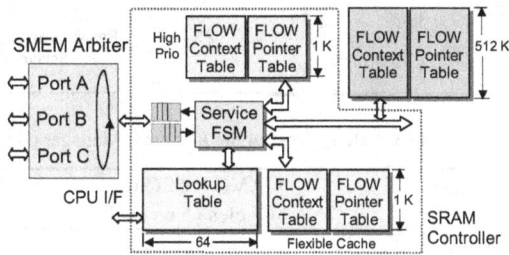

Fig. 3. The enhanced organization of the Controller of the RMS Tables

Hence, this scheme is flexible enough to inter-mix flows from both on-chip and external memory in the same priority queue with no side effect. This configuration is essential if the CPU desires to accelerate some flows, moving them to the flexible cache table. The ways of transferring a flow context to the on-chip fast memory are:
1. assigning a flow in the range 0-1023 (on-chip fast flows) by a INITDQ command,
2. commanding MOVE_FLOW to assign a different flow identifier to a connection,
3. setting the LOOKUP table for a specific flow in the range (0 – 64K).

4 Design Implementation and Performance

The design complexity of the optimized Resource Manager components is summarized in Table 2. The reference CMOS technology is UMC's 0.18 micron.

The only block that is affected significantly is apparently the SMC: the initial area was 0.14 mm^2, while by embedding the compiled SRAMS, now occupies 1.7 mm^2 in total, including 166 Kbits of compiled SRAM. The size of each compiled memory block is depicted in the table as a point of reference. The logic to implement the speculative service is under 1Kgates. The clock cycle is 4.7 ns, as the Synopsys design compiler reports, meeting the specifications. The plot demonstrates the relative increase in area caused by our enhanced RMS version. It also shows a third scheme that incorporates the "Active Flows Scheduling" scheme for reasons of completeness.

The next table lists the latency of the main commands executed by the Resource Manager that occur in high frequency during normal operation. In addition, the number of accesses to the Memory Modules in the worst case is shown.

Table 2. Implementation complexity of the proposed architecture (Enhanced RMS)

Block	# Logic Gates	Area (mm²)
SP-SRAM (pointers: 1024x19)		0.2
SP-SRAM (context: 1024x32)		0.23
RMS	37.8K	0.67
CU	9.7K	0.22
SRAM Arbiter (SMC)	90K	1.72
Total	137.5K	2.6

Table 3. Latency cost of the Resource Manager commands

Command	AVG # of Clock Cycles (5 ns each)	# of Memory Accesses (worst case)
INS_PACKET	21	3
FIN_PACKET	16	2
UPDATE_QS	18	4
SERVICE	17	3
MOVE_FLOW	16	2

Our original Resource Manager is designed to meet the specifications underlining the maximum supported traffic rate of 2.5 Gbps. The reasons for being able to perform at such high speeds are :

1. The latency to access the external SRAMs is visible only when a read is activated; the write operations are instantly acknowledged, and a FIFO holds the pending accesses. If a read of the context and the pointer is required (even in pre-fetching), they are issued back-to-back, called a "burst", so as to save arbitration latency.
2. The latency of the commands presented in Table 3 is not accumulated when many commands have to be completed, since the commands are pipelined in the following way: The Control and Update unit is responsible to access the Context Table to discover the SIDQ one flow belongs, and consequently the appropriate manager: Resource Manager or Traffic Shaper. At the same time, other commands may be in process inside these units. Thus, for example an INS_PACKET command may spend 18 clock cycles for pre-processing and 8 additional cycles inside the Resource Manager.
3. The operations of the SIDQ Manager and the OUT Manager sub-blocks inside the RMS device are independent, and hence are proceeding in parallel, without stalls.

The Resource Manager subsystem however, is not work conserving in the sense that only 2 commands per Protocol Processing Engine may be outstanding, since this rate is the upper bound set by the capacity of these processing modules and the data memory manager.

4.1   Performance Measurements

The VHDL models of the original RM scheme and the optimised one have been extensively simulated. Upon dispatching a command, the SIDQ Manager is triggered and executes it; the rest are queued until the current one is completed (with the exception of the "MORE" command that bypasses the standard flow, in order to allow a previous one to complete). One apparent important factor that influences the rate of commands processed is the delay response of the SRAM controller. The Figure below shows this effect in two extreme scenarios: all the flows reside in the external SRAM versus the best case of accessing only the internal context and pointer tables. Of course in a real situation the percentage of the Resource Manager sitting idle lies in the middle and depends on the traffic mix of the flows.

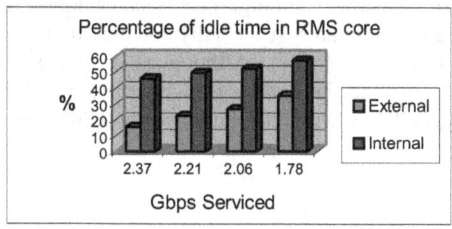

4.2   Integrating the Active Flows Scheduler with the RMS

In order to further enhance the RMS system, we have complemented the SIDQ Manager with the Active Flows Scheduler (AFS), described previously, in the following way: the dispatcher identifies the appropriate block to handle a command. The AFS requires also a Context Table to maintain the same information as the RMS, but is free from the Linked List Manager sub block shown in Fig. 1, since the round-robin service is inherent in the AFS principle of operation. The distinguishing feature of the AFI Scheduler is that allows the enqueue commands to proceed in parallel with the service process as long as these are manipulating two different priority queues.

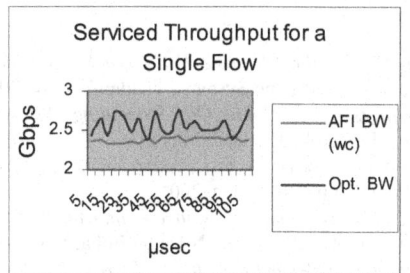 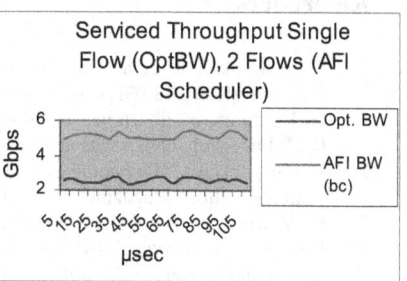

The Scheduler designed in [2], which is based on the idea of Active Flow Identifiers (AFI), is enhanced with an on-chip context table, much in the same way as in our enhanced version. The additional latency after selecting an eligible flow is about 5 clock cycles of 3.2 ns. The figure above (left) plots the results of a worst-case simulation scenario of this scheduler (accessing all the 8 words comprising a Priority Queue before discovering the eligible flow), versus a single high-speed connection serviced by our new enhanced Resource Manager. The fluctuations observed in the latest case are due to other commands serviced in the same time, without however affecting significantly the serviced bandwidth. Instead, the AFI scheduler does not include the functionality featured by the RMS and thus the serviced bandwidth is almost flat. In the second plot we compare the service of a single flow conveying high-speed traffic by the enhanced Resource Manager that incorporates also the AFI Scheduler operating with the same system clock of 200 Mhz. For the latter case two flows are configured each in a different priority queue in order to take advantage of the independent pipelined Finite State Machines (one handling enqueues and the other dequeues). It is obvious that such high performance connections are more susceptible to bursty arrivals of commands (especially for the commands destined to our RMS, whose service time is variable). Although the external SRAMs provide ample bandwidth (4.27Gbps) the simulations show that it is possible to sustain a 2 Gbps rate of commands by the RMS, while demanding only 0.76 Gbps of memory bandwidth.

5 Conclusions

In this paper we presented a resource management architecture that can be used in multi-gigabit networking devices, while at the same time it eliminates the need for external memory. The latter is considered a main advantage since it results in smaller Printed Cards (PCBs) and lower power consumption. A simpler version of our scheme can reduce the external memory requirements in terms of throughput/latency, leaving more available memory throughput to the packet memory manager. The scheme comprises of two simpler mechanisms that are integrated together so as to provide both high speed processing for the high priority tasks and low cost processing for the low priority ones.

References

1. I. Papaefstathiou, et al. *"An Innovative Scheduling Scheme For High Speed Network Processors"* ISCAS'03, IEEE Int. Symp. on Circuits and Systems, Thailand., May 2003.
2. G. Kornaros, et al. *"Active Flow Identifiers For Scalable, Qos Scheduling"* ISCAS'03, IEEE Int. Symp. on Circuits and Systems, Bangkok, Thailand, May 2003.
3. W. Bux, et al. *"Technologies and building blocks for fast packet forwarding"*, IEEE Communications Magazine , Vol. 39, Issue: 1, pp. 70 –77 Jan. 2001.
4. K. Vlachos et al. *"Processing and Scheduling Components in an Innovative Network Processor Architecture"*, 16th IEEE Int. Conf. in VLSI design, N.Delhi, India, Jan. 2003.
5. R. Gopalakrishnan, G. Parulkar, *"Bringing Real-Time Scheduling Theory And Practice Closer For Multimedia Computing"*, Proc. of ACM SIGMETRICS Int. Conf. on Measurement and modeling of computer systems, Philadelphia, USA, 1996.
6. K. Ramamritham, J. A. Stankovic, *"Scheduling algorithms and operating systems support for real-time systems"*, IEEE proceedings, vol.82, no.1, pp.55-67, Jan. 1994.

7.   A. Srinivasan et al. "*Multiprocessor Scheduling in Processor-based Router Platforms: Issues and Ideas*", Workshop on Network Processors, 9th Int. Symp. on High-Performance Computer Architecture, Anaheim, California, USA, Feb. 2003.
8.   I. Paul, et al *"Efficient Implementation of Packet Scheduling Algorithm on High-Speed Programmable Network Processors"*, Proc. of the 5th IFIP/IEEE Int. Conf. on Management of Multimedia Networks and Services, MMNS, S.Barbara, USA, Oct. 2002.
9.   D. Stephens, J. Bennett and H. Zhang, *"Implementing Scheduling Algorithms in High-Speed Networks"*, IEEE Journal on Selected Areas in Communications, Vol. 17, pp. 1145-1158, Jun. 1999.

Rate-Based Active Queue Management with Token Buckets

Andreas Kind and Bernard Metzler

IBM Zurich Research Laboratory
CH-8803 Rüschlikon, Switzerland
{ank,bmt}@zurich.ibm.com

Abstract. Active queue management (AQM) is applied in IP routers to protect routing resources, improve link utilization, and limit end-to-end delay. This paper proposes a rate-based AQM scheme based on adaptive token buckets per aggregated traffic flows. The approach is different from queue-occupancy-based AQM schemes because drop probabilities are not directly linked to the average queue size. In the proposed system, probabilistic dropping at routers is controlled by token buckets with committed information rates (CIR) adapted to the current router congestion status. The paper shows that this approach is better suited to the multi-modal traffic mix of short-lived responsive and long-lived non-responsive flows prevalent in the Internet.

1 Introduction

The Internet is based on the principle of statistical sharing of resources, which may lead to congestion at routers when bandwidth demand exceeds what the available resources can provide. Together with end-to-end flow control mechanisms, active queue management (AQM) aims to control such overload situations. This paper describes a new rate-based AQM scheme that achieves better link utilization and delay behavior for typical Web traffic (i.e., short-lived TCP flows with long round-trip times mixed with a growing fraction of non-responsive UDP traffic) than queue-occupancy-based AQM such as RED and its variants.

AQM systems typically use a feedback signal to control the drop probability of a class of packets. If a packet enters a router, the drop probability of the packet class is used to decide whether the packet is discarded or forwarded. To which class a packet belongs is determined by a classifier, for instance, depending on information in the packet header. The basic idea behind such probabilistic dropping is to avoid queue overflow, which has undesirable effects on the behavior of end applications. Large buffers (in the range of many megabytes) deployed in today's high-speed routers potentially lead to packet delays of up to hundreds of microseconds at a single intermediate node. Furthermore, if a packet is dropped due to overflowing buffers (i.e., tail drop), consecutive packets of a single flow are also likely to be dropped. Such consecutive drops cause some transport protocols to drastically back off in terms of the transmission rate (e.g., slow start with

M.M. Freire, P. Lorenz, M.M.-O. Lee (Eds.): HSNMC 2003, LNCS 2720, pp. 176–187, 2003.
© Springer-Verlag Berlin Heidelberg 2003

TCP). In certain round-trip time scenarios such backoffs can even lead to global synchronization problems and, thus, to severely underutilized networks.

AQM schemes can be divided into *queue-occupancy based* and *rate-based* schemes. Queue-occupancy based schemes use the level of queue occupancy (typically measured as average queue length) to control drop probabilities. Random early detection (RED) [1], the most prominent queue-occupancy based AQM scheme, uses a linear function between minimum and maximum queue thresholds (q_{min_thr}, q_{max_thr}) for determining the drop probability. No packets are dropped below q_{min_thr} and all packets are dropped above q_{max_thr}. A drawback of queue-occupancy-based AQM systems is that the actual transmitted rates and delays cannot be controlled accurately [2]–[4]. The dilemma is that, if thresholds are set high, burst can be accommodated but delays are long, whereas if thresholds are set low, delays are acceptable but bursts are cut off. In other words under varying offered loads queue-occupancy-based AQM systems are difficult to configure for optimal network utilization and delay.

Rate-based AQM schemes address the configuration problems by determining drop probabilities depending on the actual offered rates. If the actual net rate (i.e., the offered rate minus the rate of dropped packets) of a class of packets is below a certain threshold (i.e., a minimum guaranteed rate) the drop probability is reduced until the guaranteed rate has been reached. If the actual net rate is above the threshold and no excess bandwidth is available, the drop probability is increased. A further requirement addressed with rate-based AQM is that drop probabilities converge to values that lead to a fair sharing of excess bandwidth, e.g., according to max-min fairness. A rate-based AQM system is for instance proposed by *Bowen et al.* [5].

The assumption with queue-occupancy based AQM schemes is that the most dominant type of traffic in the Internet consists of responsive flows. Responsive flows (e.g., TCP flows) interpret packet drops as network congestion and reduce transmission rates. RED drops can, therefore, be regarded as a way to communicate with the end devices to reduce the sending rates.

Two trends in the Internet require us to rethink the assumption that responsive traffic is predominant. First, the amount of non-responsive traffic has been growing since the advent of multi-media applications (e.g., streaming). Second, responsive traffic in the Internet is increasingly driven by Web traffic, i.e., short-lived HTTP/TCP flows with long round-trip times for which packet drops as a means of congestion notification to end-hosts is too slow [4, 6, 7]. Hence, not only is the proportion of non-responsive traffic growing compared to responsive traffic, responsive traffic also behaves at core routers—as an aggregate—increasingly like *non*-responsive "mega flows" despite the fact that each participating TCP flow is itself responsive. Given this trend and the configuration dilemma of queue-occupancy-based schemes described above, it is in fact questionable whether RED and queue-occupancy-based AQM schemes in general improve the performance of Internet core routers [3, 7, 8].

This paper proposes a new rate-based approach to active queue management that provides protection of routing resources, minimum rate guarantees, and the fair allocation of excess bandwidth even during severe overload situations. The drop probability of a traffic class is controlled by a token counter with an adaptive committed information rate (CIR). The CIR is decreased exponentially to a minimum threshold if the router is congested or, otherwise, increased linearly to a maximum threshold. Extensive simulations with the Omnet++ [9] network simulator showed that the scheme achieves better link utilization and delay behavior for typical Web traffic than existing queue-occupancy-based AQM systems do. Also, compared with other rate-based AQM schemes, the proposed approach requires less state and fewer configuration parameters.

The paper describes in detail the functionality (Section 2) and simulation (Section 3) of the token bucket control queue management mechanism. The approach is compared with related work and discussed in Section 4. Finally, a conclusion is drawn in Section 5.

2   Rate-Based AQM with Token Buckets

This section describes the use of token buckets for queue management at routers. Token buckets are typically used for traffic policing and shaping [10]. A token counter T is continuously incremented with a rate referred to as the CIR (committed information rate). The upper limit and initial value of the token counter is called PBS (peak burst size). If a packet arrives and the token counter is less than the packet size, the packet is either dropped or marked as being *not within* the profile of the token bucket. Otherwise, the token counter is decremented by the length of the packet, and the packet is forwarded or marked as being *within* the profile of the token bucket.

With traffic policing and shaping the CIR is typically a constant configuration parameter. However, for queue management purposes we specify that the rate of token increments is variable. To recognize this feature the variable $C(t)$ is introduced in place of the CIR. Furthermore, probabilistic dropping is added to the token bucket technique. The drop probability P is used to decide whether a packet is enqueued in a queue Q or dropped (see Fig. 1). In a first approach the drop probability is determined by $P(t) = 1 - sig(T)$. If the token counter T is zero, packets are dropped. Otherwise, packets are enqueued. One or more flows can be controlled in this way. To accommodate more than one flow, the index i is used; hence the variable increment rate is C_i, the token counter is T_i, and the drop probability is P_i.

A key aspect of the AQM scheme based on token buckets is to automatically adapt the committed information rates C_i according to the current congestion status of the router. The aim is to let each C_i converge to a value such that $\sum C_i$ is equal to the outgoing link rate r_l. The token buckets are used for shaping aggregate traffic flows according to adaptive profiles that consider the available link capacity, fair distribution of excess bandwidth, and potential minimum/maximum rate limits ($f_{i,\min}$, $f_{i,\max}$). The value of $C_i(t)$ is updated with a fixed period dt:

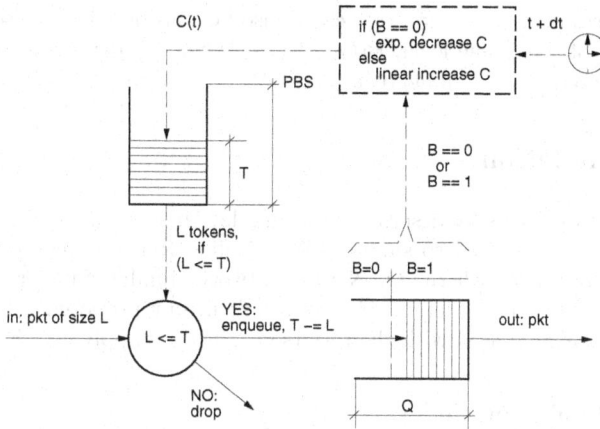

Fig. 1. Using token buckets for queue management

$$C_i'(t+dt) = \begin{cases} C_i(t) + f_{i,\mathrm{max}}/w_1 & \text{if} \quad B(t) = 1 \\ C_i(t) * (1 - 1/w_2) & \text{otherwise} \end{cases} \tag{1}$$

$$C_i(0) = f_{i,\mathrm{min}} \tag{2}$$

$$C_i(t) = \max(f_{i,\mathrm{min}}, \min(f_{i,\mathrm{max}}, C_i'(t))) \tag{3}$$

According to Equation (1), if feedback from a queue or processor indicates excess bandwidth, C_i' is increased linearly; otherwise it is decreased exponentially. The control mechanism of linear increase and exponential decrease is also referred to as AIMD (additive increase, multiplicative decrease). The update amount is determined by $w1$ and $w2$ relative to the current C_i value and the maximum value $f_{i,\mathrm{max}}$ of C_i. C_i is limited by $f_{i,\mathrm{min}}$ and $f_{i,\mathrm{max}}$, see Equation (3). The rate limits specify minimum and maximum rate guarantees. In steady state, the aggregate traffic will not contribute more than with a rate of $f_{i,\mathrm{max}}$ to the outgoing traffic. Likewise, the aggregate traffic will contribute at least with a rate of $f_{i,\mathrm{min}}$ (or up to the offered load if it is below $f_{i,\mathrm{min}}$) to the outgoing traffic. The initial committed information rate at $t = 0$ is the minimum guaranteed rate $f_{i,\mathrm{min}}$ (3).

If the sum of all minimum guaranteed rates does not exceed the outgoing link rate, the queue is protected against overflow in steady state. In order to protect the queue also with regard to incoming bursty traffic, the total peak bust size $\sum \mathrm{PBS}$ is equal to the maximum queue length.

$B(t)$ is defined as a binary excess bandwidth signal: $B(t) = 1$ if excess bandwidth is available, otherwise $B(t) = 0$. Excess bandwidth could be determined by the average router processor load or by the average queue level. In the latter case, the queue depletition rate could also be considered in the sense that, independent of the queue level, $B(t) = 1$ even when the depletion rate is above the total offered load of all aggregate flows.

3   Simulation

This section starts by describing the simulation setup, including the traffic and protocol models used to simulate Web traffic. It then presents the simulation results obtained with the OmNet++ network simulator under various network traffic conditions in detail. The results from our proposed token-based AQM scheme are compared with the results obtained by applying RED.

3.1   Simulation Model

We developed a simulation model that allows us to investigate the dynamic behavior of AQM schemes under tightly controlled traffic, network, and protocol conditions.

The simulation setup consists of a group of independent web-client applications connected to a group of web-server applications. Each client and each server resides on a distinct host system, thus, no local interaction is assumed (see Fig. 2). The client host systems are connected via private 1 MBit/s links to a forwarding system A, which forwards the traffic via a link with adjustable capacity to the next intermediate system B, which distributes the traffic to the appropriate peer hosts. In this setup, the inner link is the bottleneck resource, as the vast majority of traffic is produced by the server systems, feeding the network with HTTP replies containing requested objects. The resource is protected by an AQM system located in forwarding system B.

The links to which the client and server systems are attached, are further defined by a fixed transfer delay equally distributed between 3 and 50 ms one-triptime each. Because it is a equally shared resource, no fixed delay for the inner 'backbone' link was assumed. Assuming an uncongested network, with this setup the round-triptime per connection is in the range of $[12, 200]$ ms. During simulation, additional variable delay occurs that is due to tentative packet queueing in system B and to the limited bandwidth of all links.

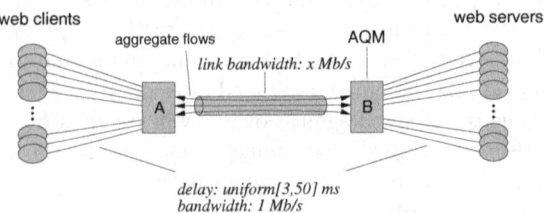

Fig. 2. Basic simulation scenario

The pattern of Web traffic is determined by both user behavior and web content transferred. To create a realistic scenario, we parametrized our model based on the work presented in [11, 12] and assumed the usage of HTTP/1.1. The Web traffic mix is parametrized as follows:

- *objects per page*: The number of HTTP objects forming a web page. If a web page is downloaded, all objects must be fetched.
- *interobject time*: The time the server system needs to start sending an object after it has been requested. This number strongly depends on the server's cache hit ratio and on whether the objects are static or created dynamically.
- *interpage time*: The time a user will wait after a web page has been successfully received before requesting the next web page (also called *user think time*).
- *server persistence*: Number of consecutive pages requested from the same server. Because the HTTP/1.1 protocol reuses a persistent TCP connection as long as the server is not changed, this parameter controls the TCP connection setup rate.
- *object size*: Size of an object embedded within a web page.

For all attributes a probability distribution must be assigned and parametrized. Except for server persistence and interobject time, we used the parameter settings presented in [11]: *interpage* (pareto: mean 50 s, shape 2), *interobject* (pareto: mean 0.2 s, shape 1.5), *objects on page* (pareto: mean 4, shape: 1.2), *object size* (pareto: mean 12 KBytes, shape 1.2), and *server persistence* (approx. from CDF given in [13]: mean 2.5).

The pareto distributed *interobject time* given in [11] with a mean of 0.5 and a shape of 1.5 appeared to be rather pessimistic – with this parameter set no faster response time than 167 ms can be generated. We have chosen a mean of 200 ms, resulting in a minimum response time of 67 ms.

As all distributions are parametrized to have a finite mean, we can directly compute the average number of payload bytes transferred on an established TCP stream. For our setup, we obtain 120 KBytes plus HTTP header overhead – significantly more than when using HTTP/1.0, where this number would be controlled only by the average object size. Nevertheless, owing to the heavy-tailed behavior of the Pareto distribution, with the parameters given objects of several tens of megabytes are to be downloaded sometimes.

Unlike other previous work, we did not employ a given TCP/IP simulation model to instantiate client and server protocol stacks, but took a 'real-life' end host kernel implementation of TCP and 'implanted' it without any changes to its logical flow of control into a dedicated execution environment. We have taken a recent version of the *NewReno* TCP implementation of the FreeBSD kernel.

Unless stated otherwise, simulation results are collected during a 60 min time interval, after running a simulation warm-up phase of 1000 s. The maximum wire packet length including TCP/IP/MAC header was set to Ethernet MTU.

Before starting our simulation, we first estimated some basic characteristics of our traffic model. Setting the link bandwidth of the bottleneck link to infinite and varying the number of peers, we collected the mean offered link load over the simulation lifetime, the peak link load averaged over one second, as well as the average total user level throughput at the socket level (i.e., goodput). The results are shown in Fig. 3. As expected, both the offered load and the goodput increase linearly with the number of connected peers. The gradient of the resulting curve suggests an average bandwidth contribution of about 0.625 KBytes/s per flow. The burstiness of the aggregated TCP flows clearly depends on the number of peers – the peak-to-average ratio (PAR for one-second intervals) is more than 10 with 100 users, and still above 1.5 for 2000 users.

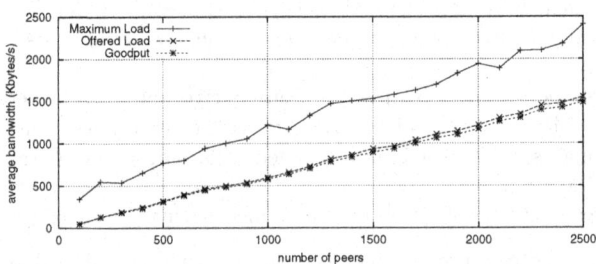

Fig. 3. Offered load as a function of the number of users

3.2   Single-Flow Scenario

For the initial simulations, the bottleneck link bandwidth was set to 10 MBit/s and the number of client/server pairs was varied to create different load scenarios. The mean offered load was adjusted in a range from temporary congestion situations caused by tentative traffic bursts exceeding the link bandwidth to clear overload due to a mean load exceeding the link bandwidth by 25%. In Fig. 3, this corresponds to 500 to 2500 peers.

We applied our token bucket agorithm and the well-known RED with settings according to the current guidelines of the RED inventors accessible at [14], conclusions drawn from similar experiments discussed in [7] as well as from own experiments: $qlen = 256$ pkts, $q_{min\_thr} = 30$ pkts, $q_{max\_thr} = 90$ pkts, $w_q = 0.002$, and $max_p = 0.1$.

For the token bucket algorithm, we set the same maximum queue size as for RED, corresponding to 256 full-sized packets. The other parameters were choosen to allow for full line occupancy for the single aggregated flow: $w_1 = 64$, $w_2 = 64$, $qlen = 360$ KBytes, $f_{min} = 8$ MBit/s, $f_{max} = 10$ MBit/s, $B = 72$ KBytes.

Fig. 4 shows average results for offered load, link utilization and application throughput (i.e., goodput) for both RED and our AQM scheme. Clearly, both schemes behave quite similarly for all scenarios that do not produce link loads higher than the available line speed. In terms of offered load, RED behaves slightly better in overload scenarios (number of peers exceeding 1900). Owing to

TCP flow adaptivity, the random early dropping algorithm is able to slow down the sending side better than the other scheme does. Both algorithms enable perfect link utilization.

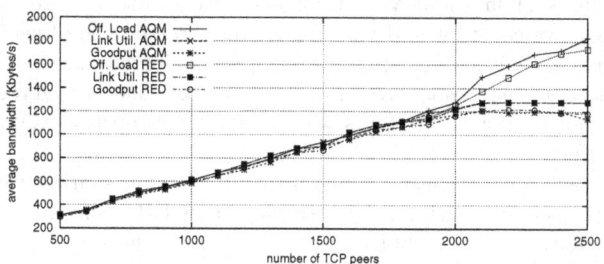

Fig. 4. Offered load, link utilization and throughput for token-based AQM and RED

The examination of the average output queue length reveals, however, a different picture. With RED, the queue grows up to a value determined by max_{th}, whereas the token-based AQM is able to bound the average queue length to a maximun, when overload is actually encountered. If the load further increases, then because of frequent oscillations of the controlled token rate between f_{min} and f_{max}, more packets get dropped before entering the queue. Whereas the token-based AQM scheme as well as RED yield perfect link utilization, our algorithm performs much better in overload conditions (see Fig. 5). In fact, decreasing the average queue length with increasing input overload results in better ressource utilization because there is no risk of the queue becoming empty.

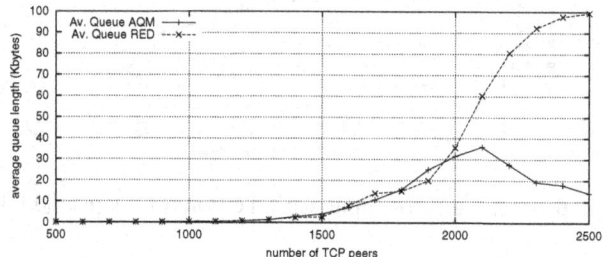

Fig. 5. Average queue length for token-based AQM and RED

3.3 Multiple Flow Scenarios

As introduced in Section 1, the current Internet traffic consists of a mix of responsive flows with often rather short lifetimes and nonresponsive flows with varying burstiness and lifetimes. To test our AQM scheme under such conditions, we conducted simulations with traffic mixes from both Web-generated traffic and nonresponsive constant and variable bit-rate traffic. The objective was to show that our scheme is able to protect ressources dedicated to responsive traffic from being used by nonresponsive traffic. This was done by aggregating traffic of similar characteristics into flows, and applying appropriate AQM parameters for each aggregate.

We started with constant-bit-rate (CBR) traffic sharing the bandwidth of the bottleneck link with our Web traffic. The CBR traffic was set to an offered load of 640 KByte/s, the linkspeed to 10 MBit/s, and the number of TCP peers was varied between 100 and 2000. In two simulation runs, our AQM scheme and RED were applied. Whereas for RED, the parameters were the same as before, for the TCP and CBR aggregates different parameter sets were chosen in order to control the bandwidth share of both flows: $qlen = 360$ KBytes, $w_1 = w_2 = 64$, $B = 72$ KBytes, $f_{TCP,min} = 7$ MBit/s, $f_{TCP,max} = 10$ MBit/s, $pbs_{TCP} = 288$ KBytes, $f_{CBR,min} = 1$ MBit/s, $f_{CBR,max} = 5$ MBit/s, $pbs_{VBR} = 72$ KBytes.

Fig. 6 shows the resulting application-level throughput for this simulation. Whereas in overload conditions, the token-based AQM gracefully degrades the throughput of both flow aggregates down to its intended per-flow f_{min}, RED is unable to protect the TCP flows against the nonresponsive CBR traffic. A preference of one flow over another can also be achieved with a weighted variant of RED; however, it is not possible to guarantee a minimum rate for varying offered loads.

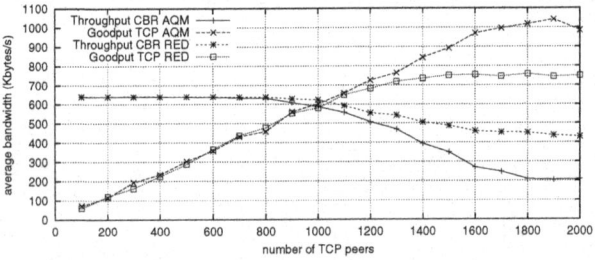

Fig. 6. Average throughput with TCP and background CBR traffic

As a third traffic scenario, we mixed our Web traffic with traffic generated by sources having variable bit rates. To achive a VBR traffic load of 50% of the available link bandwidth (i.e., 640 KBytes/s), we aggregated the traffic of independent Pareto-On/Off sources. The parameter settings for the Pareto-On/Off sources are *peak rate* $= 256$ pkts/s, *mean inactivity time* $= 360$ ms, *mean burst* $= 10$ pkts,

$\beta_{on} = 1.9$, and $\beta_{off} = 1.3$. With a constant packet size of 512 Bytes and 51 activated sources, we produce self-similar, bursty VBR traffic offering the targeted mean load to the bottleneck link.

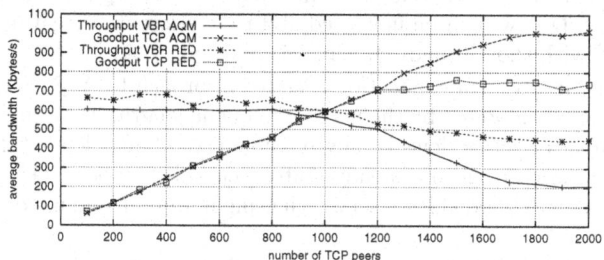

Fig. 7. Average throughput with TCP and background VBR traffic

Figure 7 shows results that are quite similar to the CBR case. Again, RED is unable to protect the TCP flows against the non responsive traffic. As we set f_{max} of the VBR flow to its mean bandwidth value and only provided a peak burst size of 72 KBytes, the VBR flow becomes penalized with longer bursts even without overload conditions. Setting a higher *pbs* would avoid this – intended – behavior.

4   Related Work and Discussion

The problem of configuring AQM systems has been addressed by related work, which is summarized and compared with the proposed approach in this section.

A number of existing AQM systems have attempted to adapt RED parameters automatically. The basic idea is to determine whether parameter settings are too aggressive by observing the average queue length [4]. If the average queue length is around q_{min_th}, than RED operation is too aggressive and max_p is reduced. However, if the average queue length is around q_{max_th}, parameter settings would be too conservative and max_p is increased. The adaptation is exponential in both cases. In a variation of adaptive RED [15] this is changed to AIMD.

Firoiu and Borden [16] model RED as a feedback control system and derive recommendations for configuring RED and congestion control techniques in general. The study assumes a constant number of long-lived TCP flows. However, due to the dominance of Web applications, today's traffic consists of a quickly changing number of short-lived flows and an increasing number of non-responding UDP flows.

FRED [8] performs selective dropping based on the number of active connections using buffer space at a router. The goal is to improve fairness between responsive flows with different round-trip times and between responsive and non-responsive flows.

A more lightweight implementation of dropping depending on the number of active connections is proposed by SRED [2]. An incoming packet is compared with a randomly chosen packet that has been previously enqueued. This simple test delivers information about the number of active flows and about potential misbehaving flows. With this information the drop probability for potential misbehaving flows can be increased and the preferential treatment of TCP connections with short round-trip times is reduced.

We believe that a connection-oriented approach to AQM requires too much state even when bound by the maximum queue length. An accurate prediction of the number of active flows is only possible if the buffer loaded. Hence the delay is compromised even in a steady state overload situation. The approach is not concerned with bandwidth reservation using minimum and maximum guaranteed rates.

Feng et al. [6] propose to increase or decrease the drop probability linearly according to queue occupancy levels. *Bowen et al.* [5] extend the idea of incremental drop probability updates using minimum and maximum rate thresholds and AIMD (additive increase, multiplicative decrease) updates. The resulting rate-based AQM scheme is similar to what is described in this paper. However, using token buckets to shape the incoming traffic aggregates according to min/max rate specification and the maximum burst capacity of the scheduler queue is an entirely different technique that provides much tighter control of the allocation of router resources. Moreover the amount of state needed for each aggregate flow is smaller with the token-based approach presented here.

The AQM scheme proposed in this paper has a number of advantages over other AQM approaches:

- The amount of state to be held for each aggregated flow is small. Only two 32-bit variables for the variable increment rate C_i and the token counter T_i are required per flow i.
- Specifying minimum and maximum bandwidth allocations is easy. That is, $f_{i,\min}$ and $f_{i,\max}$ are given in bits-per-second for each traffic flow.
- The amount of computation per packet is low. For each packet a token counter T_i is checked and decremented if nonzero.
- The amount of periodic computation per dt is low. An excess bandwidth signal B is computed and the $C_i(t)$ is updated depending on the excess bandwidth signal B. Furthermore, the token counter is incremented according to the actual C_i. The token counter is only decremented when traffic arrives. Relative to mechanisms with computationally costly updates even in the absence of traffic, this is an advantage for intermittent or low bandwidth flows.
- Even during severe overload the approach can assure minimum guaranteed rates plus a fair share of the excess bandwidth.
- In steady overload situations buffer occupancy is low because drop probabilities are mainly determined by rate thresholds and not by buffer occupancy thresholds.

5   Conclusion

We have presented a rate-based queue management approach with token buckets which leads to improved delay and link utilization compared to queue-occupancy-based schemes. The committed information rate of the token buckets is automatically adapted according to minimum/maximum rate specifications and fair sharing of excess bandwidth per aggregate flow. The paper focusses on a subset of the results obtained from a large number of simulations with the proposed AQM system. In particular, burst behavior and fairness have not been discussed in detail so far, but will be topic of future work.

References

[1] S. Floyd and V. Jacobson. Random early detection gateways for congestion avoidance. *ACM Trans. on Networking*, August 1993.

[2] T. J. Ott, T. V. Lakshman, and L. H. Wong. SRED: Stabilized RED. In *Proceedings of INFOCOM '99*, volume 3, pages 1346–1355, 1999.

[3] M. May, J. Bolot, C. Diot, and B. Lyles. Reasons not to deploy RED. In *Proc. of 7th Int. Workshop on Quality of Service (IWQoS '99)*, London, June 2000.

[4] W. Feng, D. D. Kandlur, D. Saha, and K. G. Shin. A self-configuring RED gateway. In *Proc. of INFOCOM '99*, pages 1320–1328, March 1999.

[5] E. Bowen, C. Jeffries, L. Kencl, A. Kind, and R. Pletka. Bandwidth allocation for non-responsive flows with active queue management. In *Proceedings of International Zurich Seminar on Broadband Communications*, Lecture Notes in Computer Science. Springer, Berlin, 2002.

[6] W. Feng, D. Kandlur, D. Saha, and K. G. Shin. BLUE: A new class of active queue management algorithms. Technical Report CSE-TR-387-99, University of Michigan, 15, 1999.

[7] M. Christiansen, K. Jaffay, D. Ott, and F. D. Smith. Tuning RED for Web traffic. In *SIGCOMM*, pages 139–150, 2000.

[8] D. Lin and R. Morris. Dynamics of random early detection. In *SIGCOMM '97*, pages 127–137, Cannes, France, September 1997.

[9] A. Varga. The OMNeT++ discrete event simulation system. In *Proceedings of the European Simulation Multiconference (ESM'2001)*, June 2001.

[10] J. Heinanen and R. Guerin. A single rate three color marker. RFC 2697, IETF, September 1999.

[11] A. Feldmann, A. C. Gilbert, P. Huang, and W. Willinger. Dynamics of IP traffic: A study of the role of variability and the impact of control. In *SIGCOMM*, 1999.

[12] G. Iannaccone, C. Brandauer, T. Ziegler, C. Diot, S. Fdida, and M. May. Comparison of tail drop and active queue management performance for bulk-data and Web-like internet traffic. In *Proceedings of IEEE ISCC*, July 2001.

[13] B. Mah. An empirical model of http network traffic. In *Proc. of INFOCOMM'97*, April 1997.

[14] http://www.icir.org/floyd/REDparameters.txt, 1997.

[15] S. Floyd, R. Gummadi, and S. Shenker. Adaptive RED: An algorithm for increasing the robustness of RED, 2001.

[16] V. Firoiu and M. Borden. A study of active queue management for congestion control. In *INFOCOM (3)*, pages 1435–1444, 2000.

Towards Web-Based Information and Knowledge Management in Higher Education Institutions

Joel J.P.C. Rodrigues[1] and Maria Joaquina Barrulas[2]

[1] Department of Informatics, University of Beira Interior
Rua Marquês d'Ávila e Bolama, 6201-001 Covilhã, Portugal
joel@di.ubi.pt
[2] INETI – Instituto Nacional de Engenharia e Tecnologia Industrial
Estrada do Paço do Lumiar, 1649-038 Lisbon, Portugal
joaquina.barrulas@ineti.pt

Abstract. This paper is about knowledge management (KM) in organizations and reports the results of a research project carried out in the Department of Informatics (Computer Science) of the University of Beira Interior – Portugal. The study aimed at to identify and to understand knowledge generation, knowledge transfer and knowledge sharing among the actors of a university department. Based upon the study findings, a knowledge management model aimed at to facilitate personal interaction and knowledge sharing within the department is proposed.

1 Introduction

This paper is a follow up of a study undertaken in the Department of Informatics (DI) of the University of Beira Interior (UBI) - Portugal, as part of a research project carried out in 2001.

The main objective of the study was to understand the process of knowledge creation, transfer and use in the context of the DI/UBI and to design a Knowledge Management Model to improve knowledge sharing in this university department.

The case study approach was chosen to carry out the project, using triangulation of methods (questionnaire survey, participant observation and document research), for data collection [1].

Through a questionnaire survey, data on research activities, qualifications and specific scientific domains of all the academic staff of the DI were collected.

Through participant observation informal relationships and communication flows in common working areas as well as, in order socialization spaces, were identified.

Through desk and documentation research relevant administrative and staff related documents were collected and information flows identified.

Base upon data collected, a KM model and KM system structure was designed as described in section 3 to 5.

The project raised sufficient interest among interested parties in the University and moved forward to an implementation phase. Through a benchmarking process it is expected to improve the KM system with other content subjects and to extend the KM process to other departments, as described in section 6 of this paper.

M.M. Freire, P. Lorenz, M.M.-O. Lee (Eds.): HSNMC 2003, LNCS 2720, pp. 188-197, 2003.
© Springer-Verlag Berlin Heidelberg 2003

2 Knowledge Management and Knowledge-Based Societies

Disparate definitions of the information/knowledge society have filled hundreds (thousands) of pages written by social scientists, "hard scientists", technologists as well as by politicians, in the last decades. In spite of diverging in specific formulations by emphasising the economic, social or the technological element, it is indisputable that the pillars of such a knowledge society are **the enabling technologies (ICT)** and the **human capacity to create, transfer and use knowledge** in every aspect of their day live activity.

As it is pointed out by Castells [2], "in the last quarter of this [20th] fading century, a technological revolution, centered around information, has transformed the way we think, we produce, we consume, we trade, we manage, we communicate, we live, we die, we make war and we make love. A dynamic global economy has been constituted around the planet, linking up valuable people and activities from all over the world, while switching off from the networks of power and wealth, people and territories dubbed as irrelevant from the perspective of dominant interests".

In Europe, the European Commission and the governments of various member countries have set up "Information Society initiatives" aimed at to improve information and communication infrastructures and, at the same time to prepare the citizens and the organizations to make better use of their knowledge assets. Under the 5th Framework Program, (the umbrella of R&D initiatives in Europe) a specific Information Society Technologies sponsored a great number of technology driven projects as well projects user oriented in response to concrete needs of citizens and business.

One of the most quoted statements of the Lisbon European Council (2000), is that the Europe should became by 2010, "the most competitive and dynamic knowledge-based economy in the world, capable of sustainable economic growth with more and better jobs and great social cohesion".

Peter Drucker was one of the first authors to call attention to the importance of knowledge work and people doing such work in any organization and it is nowadays accepted not only by theorist but also by businesspeople that "knowledge work is in at the heart of innovation, which is itself the key to long-term organizational sustainability and growth" [3]. Not surprisingly, Knowledge Management (KM) became a popular topic abundantly discussed in the management literature. However, the interest of academia and the research community by KM has grown fast in the last decade or so and the topic became recognized as an area of study in several disciplines, from Management to Cognitive and Computer Sciences [4, 5, 6, 8, 9, 10, 11, 12].

The essence of KM is considered by some authors [13, 14] as the understanding of how knew knowledge is created and generated within an organization. Others take KM as the process that involves activities devoted to the creation, or generation, codification, storage, dissemination and incorporation of knowledge within an organizational environment. Leif Edvinsson [15] who was appointed the world's first director of intellectual capital at Skandia[1] considers KM only a fraction of intellectual capital.

The "hidden" intangible assets of the firm that need to be identified, valorized and to made visible in the company's balance sheets became to be designated as the intellectual capital, prior that the concept was clearly defined.

Thomas Stewart [16] probably the most recognized among the authors dealing with the subject gives a wide scope definition: " intellectual capital is knowledge, information, intellectual property and experience that can be used to create organizational wealth", while Edvinsson [15] in a condensed definition stresses the learning dimension: "intellectual capital is the output of accelerated learning at the organizational level".

Intellectual capital and Knowledge Management can be seen as part of a management approach that seeks to improve competitiveness and foster innovation in any organization.

KM is not about technologies, leading authors agree. However, technological development, in particular in collaborative and web-based tools, was an important factor that extended KM discussion to a wider audience.

3   The University as a Knowledge-Based Organization

Higher Education establishments can be defined as truly knowledge-based organizations. The university is an organization whose mission is to foster knowledge creation and knowledge diffusion among communities of students, scholars and researchers. Through research and teaching activities, Universities have been throughout the years (centuries) knowledge-production and knowledge-sharing centers. In recent times, more and more universities feel the need to establish close links with the communities they belong be it enterprises, public and private organizations and individual citizens in order to complete the "knowledge cycle": from creation to use through incorporation in activities, products and services.

New strategies, techniques and processes to improve learning and apprenticeship have been devised, for the benefit of the society as a whole.

In Europe, recent strategies towards preparing the citizens for the knowledge society, such as the "Lifelong learning" [2] or "e-learning initiative" [3], place new challenges to the University. One of them is for sure the need to implement new management processes to become agile, flexible and competitive organizations. A

---

[1] Skandia, a financial services company based in Sweden is acknowledged to be the first enterprise to set up a coherent strategy to manage its intellectual capital. In 1991, Leif Edvisson's mission was to develop a coherent, practical and commercially powerful means of looking at the issue of intellectual capital. The knowledge and expertise within Skandia was uncoordinated, misunderstood and mismanaged and as a result it was largely worthless or unvalued. By 1995 this company was the first to make public a report on intellectual capital and to present the Navigator Management and Reporting Model, described as new economics model and a new economics taxonomy.

[2] Communication CE (COM 678 final) November 2001

[3] www.elearningeuropa.info

KM approach to a university department is the underlying proposal of the present study.

The choice of an academic department was deliberately assumed as a challenge, taking into account that most of the published literature focuses on enterprises or business type organizations. However, if we take researchers, it is relevant, even a priority, to understand the underlying processes of such an activity, as well as to identify the mechanisms that facilitate knowledge sharing among the various actors.

4 Knowledge Management Model for the DI/UBI

A picture of what we call the "intellectual capital" of the Department of Informatics (DI/UBI) was created, based upon the analysis of data collected. The concept of intellectual capital, borrowed from the management literature is defined above.

Fig. 1 represents the main dimensions chosen to characterize both the existing human resources – the academic staff – and the information assets of DI/UBI.

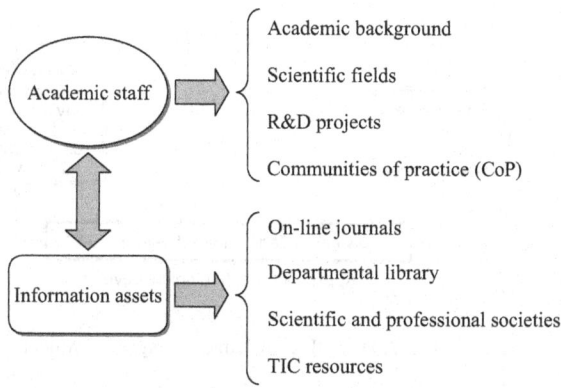

Fig. 1. DI/UBI "Intellectual Capital"

The proposed Knowledge Management Model for the DI/UBI represented in Fig. 2, is built taking into account Nonaka's approach of the dynamic aspects of knowledge creation in organizations. Knowledge is dynamic and it is created in social interactions among individuals and organizations, via a continuous process.

The process of knowledge creation in organizations occurs converting tacit[4] into explicit knowledge[5] [13], in four modes: socialization, externalization, combination and internalization (the SECI model). Socialization (tacit to tacit) is the process of

---

[4] Tacit knowledge is rooted in action, routines, values and emotions, is individual and hard to formalize

[5] Explicit knowledge can be expressed in formal and systematic language and shared in the form of written or codified data

converting new tacit knowledge through shared experiences. Individuals learn by observing and imitating others, being exposed to hands on experiences. Externalization is the process of articulating tacit knowledge as explicit knowledge. It is a process of concept creation, the basis of new knowledge. Combination is the process of converting explicit knowledge into systematic sets of explicit knowledge. Finally, internalization is the process of embodying explicit knowledge into tacit knowledge, it is closely related to learning by doing.

As Nonaka points out, knowledge needs a context to be created, and expands in spiral (the spiral of knowledge) as much as it is shared among individuals working in teams within organizations, and inter-organizations [14]. Managers are more and more aware of the importance to create working environments and appropriate conditions to favor a knowledge sharing culture in the organization.

In the proposed model for DI/UBI these aspects are addressed. Considering the intervention at the organizational level, two main issues were identified: the need to implement information management procedures and the need to develop a "positive knowledge behavior". To support the KM process a technology-based KM System is designed.

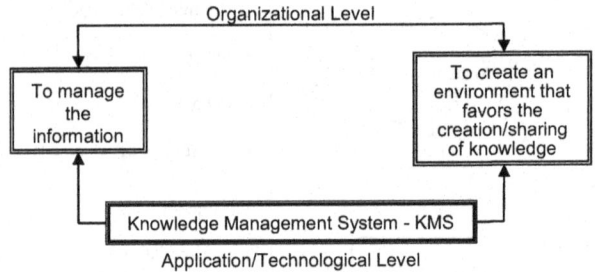

Fig. 2. DI/UBI Knowledge Management Model

5   Managing the Information

Information Management (IM) procedures and methods and a document management database (which will integrate administrative, scientific and pedagogical information), are considered in the KMS described in section 6. It is obvious that appropriate IM practices are beneficial to any organization. In the case of DI/UBI will contribute to improve secretarial work efficiency and to facilitate academic staff interaction with internal bureaucracy, as well as will help the integration of new staff, curricula development, R&D activities.

5.1 Creating a Knowledge Sharing Environment

The success of a KM strategy in any organization is dependent upon the fully commitment of the top management, but requires also that the members of such organization have to share a common vision and develop a common sense of belonging to the same community.

In the case of DI/UBI some aspects that emerged from the present study and can contribute to create the appropriate conditions for a successful KM strategy, are mentioned bellows:

Encourage the establishment of communities of practice (CoP), both related to pedagogical issues and organized by scientific areas. Within CoPs, tacit knowledge is shared and conditions for generating new knowledge are created. At the same time, CoPs contribute to improving the competencies of the academic staff [17];

Stimulate the creation of discussion *fora* or e-groups, allowing, also, the participation of people that are temporarily out of the University;

Register and Disseminate the "good practices" namely, related with pedagogical aspects; network and information systems administration; hardware and software problem resolution, etc. developed in the Department.

Other discussion *fora* that may be created are concerned to issues of different interest to the academic staff, such as: hobbies, holidays, sport, etc. This space allows the motivation of the participants, stimulating their familiarization with the system.

6 KM System

The KM System proposed takes into account tendencies mentioned in the KM support technology literature and considers also the constraints and characteristics of the DI/UDI .The platform chosen to implement the system is based on Internet technologies. A fully description of the system is given in an earlier paper [18].

The general structure of the KM System (Fig. 3), shows the main functionalities of the system and respective relationship, at the present state, and includes new functionalities that were introduced after the first implementation tests. These are mainly those related with the need to facilitate public access to the students to the specific areas of the information repository.

The system has four different user profiles: (1) visitor user, (2) administrative staff, (3) academic staff – the main user of the application and referred in this paper, only like a user –, and (4) the system administrator.

The intuitive and friendly user interface offers help online. The dynamic portal allows the user to login the system (after doing Login and Password) and to customize and personalize his own interface. To customize the interface, the user can, namely, select the scientific areas of his own interest and the information that he wants to receive. To do so, we created a database that not only saves the user profile, but also registers its system logs.

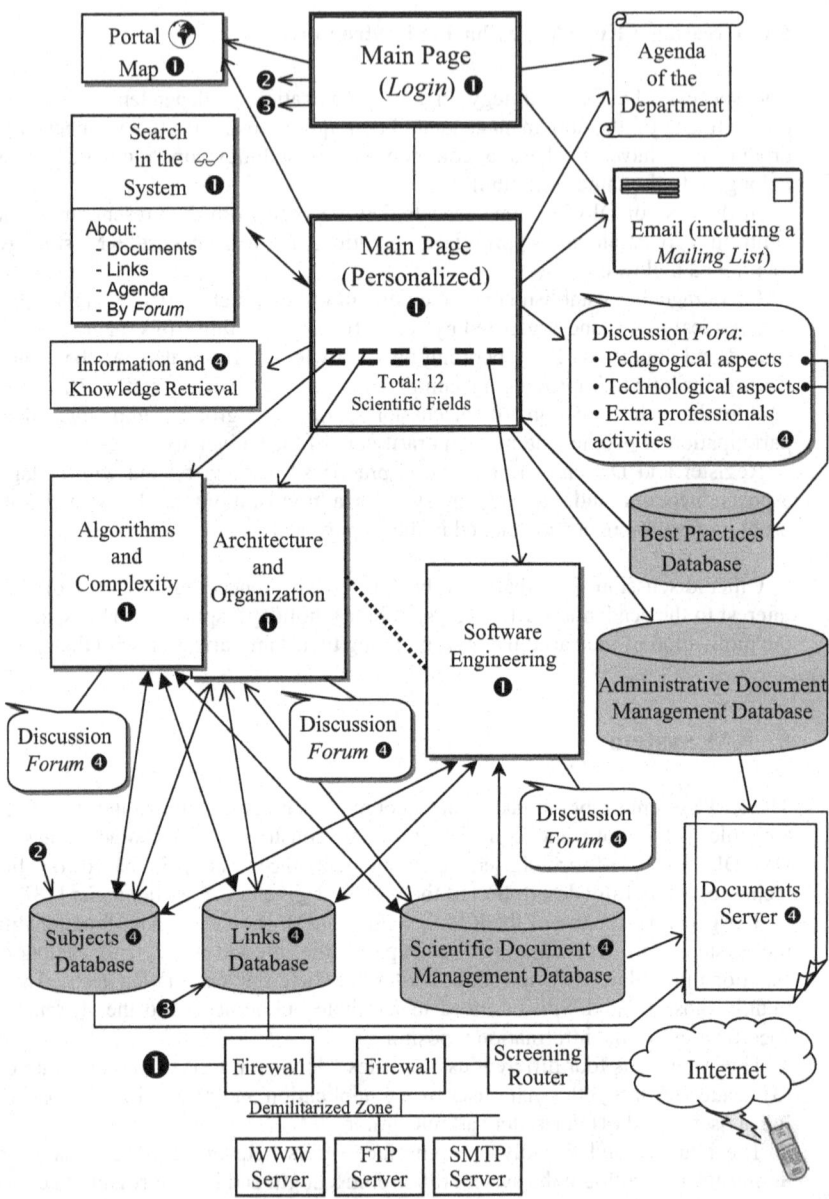

Fig. 4. General Knowledge Management System Structure

The user can also select and define the sending of short messages to his own mobile phone, to know that there are new participations in the system, for example:

sending a new message to a forum that the user is member, place a new scientific document, diffusion of an administrative message, etc. This functionality can be implemented using the WML language (Wireless Markup Language), which belongs to the WAP protocol (Wireless Applications Protocol), using Internet resources [19].

The main portal page presents the intranet of the DI/UBI, facilitates the Internet access as any other page (signed by ❶ in the figure), and allows the authentication of the user and his login to the system. After the authentication, the user enters in the second page, called the main page (personalized). We consider this page also as main page, because is from there that the system is organized. As said before, its in this page that the user can define his own areas of interest, by personalizing the interface. In every portal page it is possible to go directly to the main page (personalized) and logout from the system.

We expect the creation of a best practices database from de discussion fora of pedagogical and technological aspects.

As can be shown in Fig. 3, without authentication in the system, the Department's students, mainly, can easily consult information about their subjects (signed by ❷ in the figure) and download documents associated, visit links database (signed by ❸ in the figure), portal map, and agenda of the Department.

The administrative staff profile allows the utilization of all functionalities defined to visitors and the issues related with administrative (insert events in the agenda and administrative documents).

The administrator profile has the general activities normally considered to this user: management of user accounts, analyses system logs, etc.

7 Further Developments

A new functionality under implementation is an information retrieval tool to search knowledge and information stored in the databases, document files and discussion *fora* of the system (signed with ❹ in Fig. 3) and to answer automatically to multiple questions.

Another important feature to be developed in future work is the integration of E-learning facilities in this platform. However, the implementation of these functionalities is dependent upon the availability of a high-speed network at the University. The bandwidth of the Local Area Network is at present not enough to guarantee quality of service.

Nevertheless, as said above, the new challenges of the universities are related with the capacity to extend their activity beyond their internal walls, and distance learning is becoming a priority issue.

8 Conclusions

A Knowledge Management system's model based upon an integrative approach that considers Information Management, Knowledge Sharing and Cooperative work, fundamental axes of the working environment, was developed within the project carried out at the Department of Informatics of UBI.

The proposed model incorporates results obtained through a study undertaken, which looked at barriers to information flow and knowledge sharing in a knowledge-based organization. The novelty of the approach is related with the identification of existing "intellectual assets" that should be taken into consideration within a global management strategy of the department and the organization (university) as whole.

It was not a purpose of this research to study in depth the technology related issues, on the contrary, the intention was deliberately to show, through the use of available technologies, that a simple, suitable application to a concrete organization, can be a driver for change.

The KM System, now in its implementation phase, is a proof of concept to further incorporate new facilities and to provide new services, as far as the potential of high-speed networks permits.

Acknowledgements

Part of this work has been supported by the Group of Communications Networks and Multimedia of the Institute of Telecommunications at Coimbra, Portugal. The authors also acknowledge Prof. Mário M. Freire the collaboration in this work.

References

1. Yin, R.: Case Study Research: design and methods. Sage Publications, 2nd Edition, 1994.
2. Castells, M., The Information Age: Economy Society and Culture. Vol 1, The Rise of the Network Society. Blackwell Publishers, Oxford, 1996.
3. Davenport, T. H. et al. The mysterious Art and Science of Knowledge-Worker performance. MIT Sloan Management Review. Fall (2002) 23-30.
4. Shaw, W.J.: Knowledge Management. A Project Presented to the Faculty of California State University Dominguez Hills in partial fulfillment of the requirements for the Degree Master of Science. California State University Dominguez Hills, 1999.
5. Knowledge Management Programs at GW. http://km.gwu.edu/km/programs.cfm. George Washington University, 2001 (in 10th March 2003).
6. Knowledge Technology Centre. http://psychology.notthingham.ac.uk/research/ktc/. University Of Notthingham, 2001 (in 21st November 2002).
7. Centre for Knowledge Management. http://luton/ac/uk/depts/know_man/courses.shtml. University Of Luton, 2001 (in 20th December 2002).
8. Knowledge Management Courses. http://www.uts.edu.au/fac/hss/Departments/DIS/km/course.htm. University of Technology - Sydney, 2001 (in 1st December 2002).
9. Olscheske, T.J.: Knowledge Creation and Discovery Learning Teams: A Case Study Exploring the Dynamics of Knowledge Creation, Utilization, and Transfer in Bio-Technology R&D Groups. PhD Thesis. University of Wisconsin – Madison, 1999.
10. Thompsen, J.A.: A Case Study of Identifying and Measuring Critical Knowledge Areas as Key Resource-capabilities of an Enterprise. A Dissertation submitted to Walden University in partial fulfillment of the requirement of the degree of Doctor of Philosophy. Walden University, 1999.

11.Kalman, M.: The Effects of Organizational Commitment and Expected Outcomes on the Motivation to Share Discretionary Information in a Collaborative Database: Communication Dilemmas and Other Serious Games. A Dissertation Presented to the Faculty of Graduate School of The University of Southern California in partial fulfillment of the requirements for the Degree Doctor of Philosophy. University of Southern California, 1999.

12.Bontis, N.: Managing an Organization Learning System by Aligning Stocks and Flows of Knowledge: An Empirical Examination of Intellectual Capital, Knowledge Management, and Business Performance. A Dissertation submitted to the Faculty of Graduate Studies of The University of Western Ontario in partial fulfillment of the requirements for the degree of Doctor of Philosophy. University of Western Ontario, 1999.

13.Nonaka, I.: The Knowledge-Creating Company. Harvard Business Review. November-December (1991) 96-104.

14.Nonaka, I., Takeuchi, H.: The Knowledge-Creating Company: how Japanese companies create the dynamics of innovation. Oxford University Press. New York, 1995.

15.Edvinsson, L.: Corporate longitude. Financial Times. Prentice Hall. London, 2002.

16.Stewart, T. A.: Intellectual Capital – The New Wealth of Organizations. Nicholas Brealey Publishing Ltd, 1998.

17.Wenger, E.: Communities of Practice: Learning, Meaning, and Identity. Cambridge University Press. Cambridge, 1998.

18.Rodrigues, J. J. P. C., Freire, M. M., Barrulas, M. J.: Information and Knowledge Sharing in Higher Education Institutions Using Internet Technologies. In M. Boumedine (Ed.): Proceedings of the IASTED International Conference on Information and Knowledge Sharing (IKS'2002), St. Thomas, US Virgin Islands, November 18-20, 2002, 77-82.

19.Dreier, T.: The Wireless Intranet Part III: WML, the Language of the Wireless Web, Intranet Journal. http://www.intranetjournal.com/articles/200008/uw_08_30_00a.html. 2000 (in 25th March 2003).

A Bi-initiation-Based Path Restoration Mechanism for Wavelength-Routed WDM Networks

Jun Zheng and Hussein T. Mouftah

School of Information Technology and Engineering
University of Ottawa
Ottawa, Ontario K1N 6N5, Canada
{junzheng, mouftah}@site.uottawa.ca

Abstract. This paper proposes a bi-initiation-based path restoration mechanism for surviving single-link failures in wavelength-routed WDM networks. This mechanism allows the source node and the destination node of a broken connection to respectively initiate a path restoration process in the event of a link failure and uses the destination node to coordinate between the two processes. The purpose is to reduce the path restoration time so that a backup path can be provisioned faster for each broken connection that traverses the failed link. Based on this mechanism, a fast path restoration protocol is also presented and its performance is evaluated through simulation experiments.

1 Introduction

The emergence of wavelength division multiplexing (WDM) technology has tremendously increased the usable transmission capacity of optical fibers. WDM allows multiple optical signals to be transmitted simultaneously and independently over a single optical fiber and can therefore meet the ever-increasing bandwidth demand of network users. With the advent of reconfigurable optical devices, such as optical add/drop multiplexers (OADMs) and optical cross-connects (OXCs), WDM is evolving from a point-to-point transmission technology towards a networking technology. The wavelength-routed WDM network has been considered to be a promising network infrastructure for future large transport networks [1]. However, this also presents some potential problem. Since each fiber link offers a huge capacity of bandwidth to carry user traffic, a single network failure may cause a large amount of data loss in the network, which would severely degrade and even disrupt network services. To guarantee network services, the network must provide survivability capabilities to survive various types of network failures, such as a fiber cut or a node fault. Although the higher layers (e.g. IP, ATM, SONET) may have their own protection and restoration mechanisms, optical-layer survivability is still attractive because of its fastness and efficiency as well as some other advantages [2].

Optical-layer survivability has been extensively studied for wavelength-routed WDM networks and a variety of protection and restoration mechanisms have been proposed in the literature [2-5]. The objective is to recover network services fast and utilize network resources efficiently. All these mechanisms are based on two basic

M.M. Freire, P. Lorenz, M.M.-O. Lee (Eds.): HSNMC 2003, LNCS 2720, pp. 198-206, 2003.
© Springer-Verlag Berlin Heidelberg 2003

survivability paradigms: static protection and dynamic restoration [4-5]. In general, static protection is faster in service recovery but less efficient in resource utilization, while dynamic restoration is more efficient in resource utilization but slower in service recovery. For this reason, fast provisioning of service recovery has been a big challenge in dynamic restoration. In this paper, we propose a bi-initiation-based path restoration mechanism for surviving single-link failures in wavelength-routed WDM networks. The proposed restoration mechanism allows the source node and destination node of a broken connection to respectively initiate a path restoration process in the event of a link failure and uses the destination node to coordinate between the two processes. The purpose is to provision a backup path faster for each broken connection that traverses the failed link. Based on this mechanism, a fast path restoration protocol is further presented and its performance is evaluated through simulation experiments.

We consider a wavelength-routed WDM network that consists of routing nodes interconnected by point-to-point WDM links in an arbitrary mesh topology. Each routing node consists of an OXC that performs wavelength routing and switching optically, and an electronic controller that controls the OXC. Each controller maintains global network state information (e.g. network topology and wavelength usage). An access device may be connected to each routing node, which is used as an interface between the optical network and its client networks. In the context of this paper, an access node and its associated routing node is, as a whole, referred to as a network node or simply a node. Each WDM link consists of a pair of unidirectional fiber with a certain number of optical channels (or wavelengths) on each fiber. The controllers communicate with each other over one dedicated optical channel on each fiber link or via a dedicated IP network. In such a network, traffic is delivered over lightpaths. Two lightpaths must use different wavelengths on a common fiber link. If each node does not have wavelength converters, a lightpath must use the same wavelength on all fiber links it traverses, which is known as the wavelength-continuity constraint. This constraint may largely decrease the wavelength utilization and increase the request blocking probability. To overcome this constraint, wavelength converters must be used at network nodes. However, the cost of wavelength converters is still considerably high and will remain as so in the short term. For clarity and ease of exposition, we assume no wavelength conversion at each network node hereafter.

The remainder of the paper is organized as follows. In Section 2, we discuss dynamic path restoration and related work. In Section 3, we present the proposed path restoration mechanism and fast path restoration protocol. In Section 4, we evaluate the performance of the protocol through simulation experiments. In Section 5, we present our conclusions.

2   Dynamic Path Restoration

In dynamic path restoration [5], the source and destination nodes of each broken connection that traverses a failed link dynamically establish a backup path on an end-to-end basis in the event of a link failure. If no backup path can be established for a broken connection, the connection will be blocked. To establish a backup path, existing path restoration mechanisms usually use the source node of a broken connection to initiate a path restoration process. In the restoration process, either a forward reservation protocol (FRP) or a backward reservation protocol (BRP) is used to make wavelength reservation. With FRP [6], when the source node (S-node) receives a restoration request for a broken connection, it first performs a routing algorithm to compute a new route and select an available wavelength for the broken connection based on the global network state information it maintains. Once a route is decided and a wavelength is selected, the source node uses a forward control message (i.e. *REQ*) to reserve the selected wavelength at each intermediate node along the decided route on its way to the destination, as shown in Fig. 1a. When the destination node receives the *REQ* message, it will send a backward control message (i.e. *ACK*) back to the source node along the reverse route to configure the OXC at each intermediate node. If the *ACK* message reaches the source node, a backup path has been established successfully for the broken connection. Fig. 1a illustrates the forward reservation process. The shaded area represents the period during which wavelengths are reserved but not in use. Obviously, FRP wastes a lot of bandwidth on the reserved wavelength during the reservation period, which would largely decrease the resource utilization in the network. A simple way to address this problem is to employ BRP, as shown in Fig. 1b.

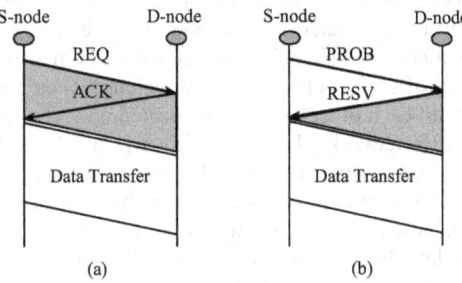

Fig. 1. Wavelength reservation: (a) Forward reservation; (b) Backward reservation

With BRP [6], the source node first performs a routing algorithm to compute a new route for the broken connection based on the global network state information it maintains, and then uses a forward control message (i.e. *PROB*) to collect the wavelength usage information on each link along the decided route. When the destination node receives the forward control message, it selects an available wavelength based on the collected information and then uses a backward control message (i.e. *RESV*) to reserve the selected wavelength and simultaneously configures the OXC at each intermediate node along the reverse route. Obviously, this can significantly reduce the bandwidth waste. A detailed description of FRP and BRP can be found in [6], which also concludes that BRP generally performs better than FRP.

It is obvious that both BRP and FRP take a two-way delay to establish a backup path. A forward control message (i.e. *REQ* or *PROB*) must first be sent to the destination node followed by a backward control message (i.e. *ACK* or *RESV*) sent back to the source node. This may not be the most efficient way for path restoration. In path restoration, the destination node is able to have a record of information about each broken connection, such as the connection identifier, the source address, and the wavelength used, during the establishment of each connection. Accordingly, the destination node also has the capability to initiate a path restoration process. This makes it possible to take a one-way delay to establish a backup path and can thus significantly reduce the path restoration time. Based on this observation, we have proposed a destination-initiated path restoration mechanism in [7] and have shown that it can significantly reduce the path restoration time as compared with the source-initiated restoration mechanism. However, there still exist some particular cases in which the destination-initiated mechanism may result in longer restoration time than the source-initiated mechanism.

3   Bi-initiation-Based Path Restoration Mechanism

To further reduce the path restoration time, we propose a bi-initiation-based path restoration mechanism. This mechanism allows the source node and the destination node of a broken connection to respectively initiate a path restoration process in the event of a link failure and uses the destination node to coordinate between the two processes. The basic idea behind is to combine the advantages of both source-initiated and destination-initiated mechanisms so that the path restoration time for each broken connection can be significantly reduced. Based on this mechanism, a fast path restoration protocol is described as follows. We consider a single-link failure scenario as shown in Fig. 2.

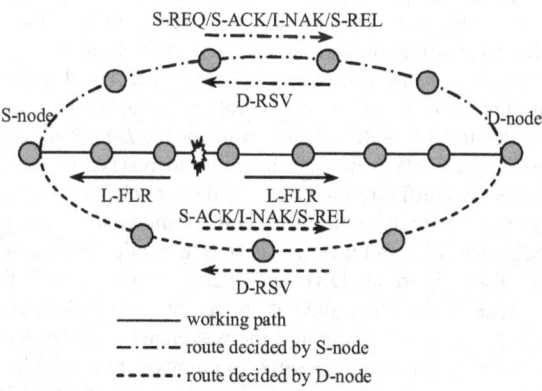

Fig. 2. Bi-initiation-based path restoration

- Once the end nodes of the failed link detect the failure, a link failure (*L-FLR*) message is sent to the source node and destination node of a broken connection, respectively, along the working path of the connection, as shown in Fig. 2. The *L-FLR* messages will disconfigure all the OXCs and release the wavelength reserved for the broken connection at each intermediate node.

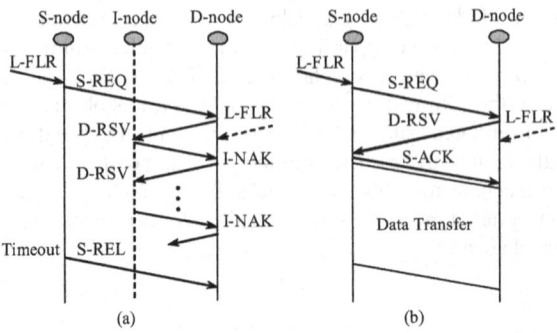

Fig. 3. Source-initiated process: (a) Unsuccessful; (b) Successful.

- Once the source node receives the *L-FLR* message, it initiates a path restoration process. In the restoration process, it first performs a routing algorithm to compute a new route for the broken connection based on the global network state information it maintains, and then sends a request (*S-REQ*) message to the destination node along the decided route. The *S-REQ* message does not reserve any wavelength on its way to the destination node. Instead, it just collects the wavelength usage information on each link along the route. When the *S-REQ* message reaches the destination node, the destination node will check if it has already received the *L-FLR* message and sent out a *D-RSV* (see below) message. If a *D-RSV* message has been sent out, the destination node will simply store the *S-REQ* message and wait for the next control message. Otherwise, it will select an available wavelength based on the collected information and then send a reservation (*D-RSV*) message back to the source node along the reverse route. Meanwhile, it will also store the *S-REQ* message and then wait for the next control message. If there is no wavelength available, the destination node will just wait for the *L-FLR* message. At each intermediate node, the *D-RSV* message attempts to reserve the selected wavelength and simultaneously configure the OXC. If the wavelength can be reserved, the *D-RSV* message is forwarded to the next hop. Otherwise (see Fig. 3a), a negative acknowledgement (*I-NAK*) message is sent to the destination node. The *I-NAK* message will disconfigure the OXC and release the wavelength already reserved by the *D-RSV* packet at each intermediate node. When the destination node receives the *I-NAK* message, it will reattempt the wavelength reservation on another available wavelength (if any) along the same route or on an available wavelength along another computed route (if any), whichever route is shorter. If the *D-RSV* message reaches the source node, it implies that a backup path has been established successfully (see Fig. 3b) for the broken connection. In response, the source node will send an acknowledgement (*S-ACK*) message to the destination node to confirm the reservation success and meanwhile to terminate the restoration process at the destination node.

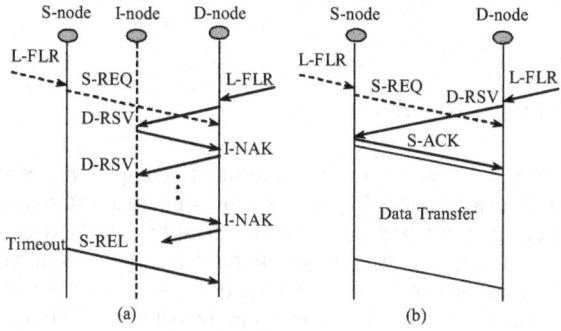

Fig. 4. Destination-initiated process: (a) Unsuccessful; (b) Successful.

- Once the destination node receives the *L-FLR* message, it also initiates a path restoration process. In the restoration process, the destination node first checks if it has already received the *S-REQ* message and sent out a *D-RSV* message. If a *D-RSV* message has been sent out, the destination node will just wait for the next control message. Otherwise, it will also perform a routing algorithm to compute a new route and select an available wavelength for the broken connection based on the global network state information it maintains. Once a route is decided and a wavelength is selected, the node sends a *D-RSV* message to the source node along the reverse route. At each intermediate node, the *D-RSV* message attempts to reserve the selected wavelength and simultaneously configure the OXC. If the wavelength can be reserved, the *D-RSV* message is forwarded to the next hop. Otherwise (see Fig. 4a), an *I-NAK* message is sent to the destination node. The *I-NAK* message will disconfigure the OXC and release the wavelength already reserved by the *D-RSV* message at each intermediate node. When the destination node receives the *I-NAK* packet, it will reattempt the wavelength reservation on another available wavelength (if any) along the same route or on an available wavelength along another computed route (if any), whichever route is shorter. If the *D-RSV* message reaches the source node (see Fig. 4b), it implies that a backup path has been established successfully for the broken connection. In response, the source node will send an *S-ACK* packet to the destination node to confirm the reservation success and meanwhile to terminate the restoration process at the destination node.

As mentioned above, in the event of a reservation failure, the destination node will reattempt the wavelength reservation on an available wavelength along the same route or along another computed route. This would obviously increase the path restoration time. To control the restoration process, the source node can use a timer and set it to the maximum allowed restoration time upon the receipt of the *L-FLR* message. If the timer times out without receiving a *D-RSV* message, the source node can send a release (*S-REL*) packet to the destination node to terminate the restoration process and meanwhile block the broken connection. Note that the particular routing and wavelength assignment algorithms used in the protocol is beyond the scope of this paper.

The readers are referred to [8] for a variety of routing and wavelength assignment algorithms.

4   Simulation Results

In this section, we present simulation results to compare the bi-initiation-based path restoration mechanism (BRM) with the source-initiated restoration mechanism (SRM) and the destination-initiated restoration mechanism (DRM), respectively. We use the request blocking probability and the path restoration time as the performance metrics. The request blocking probability is defined as the ratio of the successful connection requests to the total connection requests in the network. The path restoration time is defined as the time taken from the instant the link fails to the instant a backup path is established successfully, which mainly includes the propagation delay on each fiber link, the message processing delay at each intermediate node, the routing time for making a routing decision, and the wavelength reservation time at each intermediate node. For SRM, we only consider BRP as it usually performs better than FRP [6]. In comparison, we assume that all the three restoration mechanisms use the same routing algorithm.

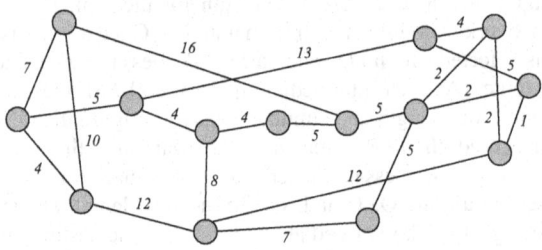

Fig. 5. 14-node NSFnet backbone topology

The simulation experiments are performed on a 14-node NSFnet backbone topology, as depicted in Fig. 5. Each node maintains global network state information (i.e. network topology and wavelength usage on each link), which is dynamically updated on a periodical basis. The number on each link represents the weight factor of the propagation delay. The connection request arrives at each node based on a Poisson process. The holding time of each connection is exponentially distributed. The destination of each connection request is uniformly distributed. Without loss of generality, we assume fixed-alternative routing with first-fit wavelength assignment [8], and three alternate routes between each pair of source and destination nodes. These routes include the first three shortest paths, which are pre-computed and stored in the routing table at each node. A backward reservation protocol is used to establish lightpaths for regular connection requests. Any blocked request is dropped and no retrying is considered. In each execution, 100,000 connection requests are processed and a link failure is generated randomly with a uniform distribution on each link. To give some numerical results, we assume that the number of wavelengths on each link is 10. The packet processing time is 0.01 *ms*. The routing time is 1 *ms*. The unit propagation delay on each link is 0.5 *ms*. The wavelength reservation time is 0.01 *ms*. The mean holding time of each connection is 500 *ms*.

Fig. 6 shows the average request blocking probability with SRM, DRM, and BRM, respectively. It is seen that BRM does not result in larger blocking probability than SRM and DRM. Under light traffic load, the blocking probability is very small. With the arrival rate increasing, the blocking probability increases remarkably.

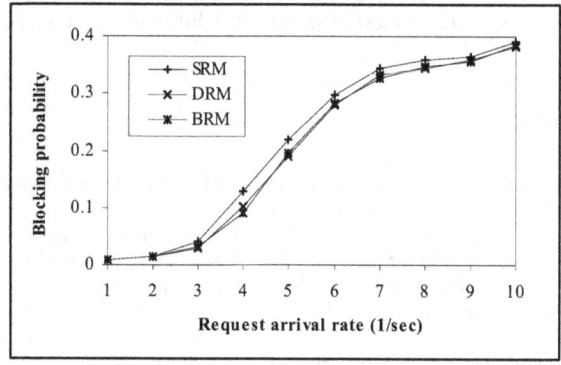

Fig. 6. Request blocking probability

Fig. 7 shows the average connection restoration time with SRM, DRM, and BRM, respectively. Obviously, the restoration time with DRM is smaller than that with SRM while the restoration time with BRM is further smaller than that with DRM. Under light traffic load, the restoration time increases with the arrival rate increasing. This is because more longer-routes are likely chosen. However, with the arrival rate further increasing, the restoration time decreases. This is because under heavy traffic load, the network becomes more congested and longer routes are less likely chosen.

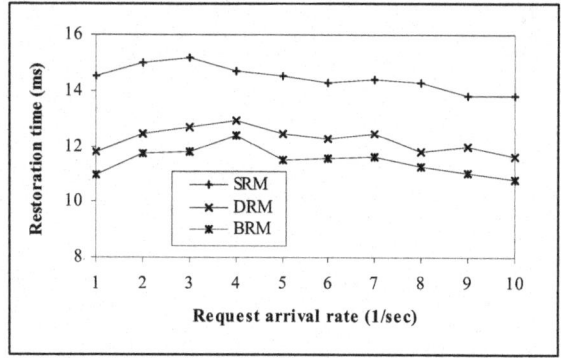

Fig. 7. Path restoration time

5 Conclusions

In this paper, we proposed a bi-initiation-based path restoration mechanism for surviving single-link failures in WDM-routed WDM networks. This mechanism differs from existing path restoration mechanisms in that it allows the source node and destination node of a broken connection to respectively initiate a path restoration process and uses the destination node to coordinate between the two processes. The simulation results have shown that it can significantly reduce the path restoration time as compared with the source-initiated and destination-initiated restoration mechanisms without increasing the request blocking probability in the network.

References

1. Ramaswami, R. and Sivarajan, K. N.: Optical Networks-A Practical Perspective. Morgan Kaufmann Publishers, San Francisco (1998)
2. Gerstel, O. and Ramaswami, R.: Optical Layer Survivability: A Services Perspective. IEEE Communications Magazine, Vol. 38, No. 3. (2000) 104-113
3. Gerstel, O. and Ramaswami, R.: Optical Layer Survivability: An Implementation Perspective. IEEE Journal on Selected areas in Communications, Vol. 18, No. 10. (2000) 1885-1899
4. Ramamurthy, S. and Mukherjee, B.: Survivable WDM Mesh Networks, Part I—Protection. Proc. of IEEE INFORCOM'99, Vol. 2. New York (1999) 744-751
5. Ramamurthy, S. and Mukherjee, B.: Survivable WDM Mesh Networks, Part II—Restoration. Proc. of IEEE ICC'99, Vol. 3. Vancouver, Canada (1999) 2023-2030
6. Saha, D.: A Comparative Study of Distributed Protocols for Wavelength Reservation in WDM Optical Networks. SPIE Optical Networks Magazine, Vol. 3, No. 1. (2002) 45-52
7. Zheng, J. and Mouftah, H. T.: A Destination-Initiating Path Restoration Protocol for Wavelength-Routed WDM Networks. IEE Proceedings-Communications, Vol. 149, No. 1. (2002) 18-22
8. Zang, H., Jue, J. P., and Mukherjee, B.: A Review of Routing and Wavelength Assignment Approaches for Wavelength-Routed Optical WDM Networks. SPIE Optical Networks Magazine, Vol. 1, No.1. (2000) 47-60

A Resource Efficient Optical Protection Scheme for IP-over-WDM Networks

Noélia S.C. Correia and Maria C.R. Medeiros

Universidade do Algarve,
Centro de Electrónica, Optoelectrónica e Telecomunicacões,
Campus de Gambelas, 8000-117 Faro, Portugal
ncorreia@ualg.pt, cmedeiro@ualg.pt

Abstract. In this work, we propose a novel protection strategy for IP-over-WDM networks. This new strategy maximizes the amount of protected traffic while providing fast recovery times. It assumes coordination between the IP and the WDM layer provided by GMPLS in a peer model. IP LSPs aggregated into a lightpath (high capacity LSP) are protected together, as a unity, using spare capacity of edge-disjoint lightpaths whenever necessary. While protection is provided at the lightpath level offering fast recovery times, this scheme also allows the use of the spare capacity of working lightpaths.

Keywords: Optical WDM Networks, IP-over-WDM, Survivability, GMPLS.

1 Introduction

Due to the feasibility of new emerging optical devices, such as *optical cross-connects* (OXCs), the optical layer of *wavelength division multiplexing* (WDM) networks is not only able to provide capacity but also to implement some network functionalities, leading to an evolution from point-to-point WDM transmission systems towards *wavelength routed networks* (WRN). Wavelength routing techniques enable the routing of high-capacity optical signals according to their wavelengths without opto-electronic conversion or processing allowing, via appropriate routing and wavelength assignment, the establishment of lightpaths between network node pairs that are geographically far apart.

In WRNs routing is done only at the lightpath level. Although presenting several advantages, this strategy becomes inappropriate in a network scenario where traffic is heterogeneous in the sense that traffic can consist of several subrate data streams (e.g. OC-3, OC-12, OC-48, OC-192, 100/1000 Ethernet, 1.0 Gb/s fiber channel, etc). Under this scenario, to render the network efficient and profitable, it is necessary to groom the low rate data streams onto high capacity lightpaths. This is known in the literature as traffic grooming [6]. Traffic grooming reduces the number of lightpaths (and therefore wavelengths) required in the network and avoids the waste of bandwidth in lightpaths that rises from the mismatch between the traffic demand and the lightpath capacity.

M.M. Freire, P. Lorenz, M.M.-O. Lee (Eds.): HSNMC 2003, LNCS 2720, pp. 207–216, 2003.

While WDM optical groomed networks may carry large volumes of traffic between users, they also have some potential problems. The most serious is the network survivability, that is, the capacity of the network to provide continuous service in the presence of failures. With the ultra-high-capacity fiber cables and OXCs, fiber cuts or OXC failures can be catastrophic, causing severe service loss unless rapid restoration of service is an integral part of the network design and operation strategy [2]. Since networks are becoming more IP data centric, and it is widely accepted that transporting IP traffic directly over WDM will lead to more cost efficient networks, how to provide survivability to these networks becomes a fundamental issue.

The *generalized multi-protocol label switching* (GMPLS) is the proposed signaling and control plane for IP-over-WDM networks. The optical WDM core network consists of GMPLS capable OXCs interconnected by optical links. On top of the optical WDM core network the IP network has a collection of *label switching routers* (LSRs). An LSR can employ GMPLS to set up an optical connection, called *label-switched path* (LSP), from itself to another LSR in the network. The LSR routers can perform the aggregation of lower rate LSPs onto higher capacity lightpaths [7].

By assuming coordination between the IP and the WDM layer provided by GMPLS, we propose here a protection scheme that provides fast recovery times while using network resources efficiently. This is possible since our scheme provides aggregated WDM protection to lightpaths whenever possible. When full lightpath protection can not be provided, our scheme protects the traffic in the lightpath, in an aggregate way, using spare capacity in other working lightpaths. The next sections are organized as follows. Section II describes the facilities provided by GMPLS to support the proposed protection strategy. Section III discusses fault management schemes currently used and presents our protection strategy. The maximum throughput problem is presented and formulated in section IV. Section V discusses results and section VI summarizes the work.

2   GMPLS Network Architecture

The GMPLS architecture extended MPLS to include LSRs whose forwarding plane is not capable of processing individual IP packets. Such LSRs include devices where the forwarding decision is based on time slots, wavelengths or physical ports. An LSP can be established between interfaces of the same type. In the context of WDM optical networks we consider *lambda switch capable* (LSC) interfaces, that forward data based on the wavelength on which the data is received, where an LSP is also called lightpath [7]. A lightpath from an ingress port in an OXC to an egress port in a remote OXC is established by setting up suitable cross-connects in the ingress, the egress and a set of intermediate OXCs such that a continuous physical path exists from the ingress to the egress port. The IP/MPLS routers that have direct physical connectivity with the optical network are referred to as *edge routers*. Edge routers have *packet switch capable* (PSC) devices and can only communicate through lightpaths [10].

2.1   Interoperability Models

Two models emerged for interoperability between the IP and the optical layer: the *overlay model* and the *peer model*. In the peer model the IP and optical networks are treated together as a single integrated network from a control plane point of view. The optical layer control information can be transferred to the IP layer, which may assume end-to-end control, that is, an edge router can create lightpaths with specific attributes, delete or modify lightpaths as it creates LSPs. The general idea is that the overlay model is architecturally more direct and simplified while the peer model needs additional communication between the IP and optical layer, although allowing better resource utilization. In the proposed survivability scheme, since protection requires topology information from both layers and may involve virtual links we assume a peer model [3].

2.2   Forwarding Adjacency

An LSR uses GMPLS *traffic engineering* (TE) procedures to create and maintain an LSP. The LSR may then announce this LSP as a TE link into the same instance of the GMPLS control plane as the one that was used to create the LSP. In a peer model this is used to realize LSP hierarchy. Such link is called a *forwarding adjacency* (FA). We refer to this LSP as *forwarding adjacency LSP* (FA-LSP). An FA is therefore a TE link between two GMPLS nodes whose path crosses zero or more GMPLS nodes in the same instance of the GMPLS control plane [9]. For details on the procedures and signaling aspects used to constructing FAs out of LSPs see [9].

The concept of forwarding adjacency can be used to specify virtual links. Once a lightpath is established between two edge routers it can be advertised as a forwarding adjacency (a virtual link) in a link state protocol. A node, when performing route computation, is able to use conventional and virtual links since they appear in the IS-IS/OSPF routing database [10]. This will enable our protection scheme to use the bandwidth available on working lightpaths for backup purposes because working lightpaths are announced as TE links.

3   Suggested Protection for IP-over-WDM Networks

Until very recently two fault management schemes have been discussed for IP-over-WDM network where the two layers were not aware of each other [5]:

1. *WDM protection* - Protection is performed at the physical level where lightpaths are re-mapped to new physical links after a failure making the failures invisible to upper layers. This scheme reacts very fast to failures.
2. *IP restoration* - Involves rerouting the disrupted traffic around the failed area. The IP network is overprovisioned so that operational links can carry all the traffic. The recovery times are slower then WDM protection but resources are better utilized. Since fast recovery is a key concern in WDM networks this scheme becomes inadequate.

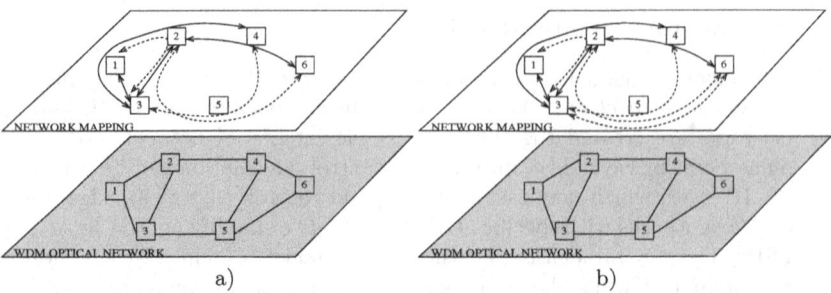

Fig. 1. Network example using: a) WDM protection; b) Our protection.

With GMPLS, integrated survivability can be provided by incorporating network state information from both layers. In this context, the *integrated protection* scheme has been discussed in [4]. In this scheme, for each IP LSP request, bandwidth is both reserved in a primary (working) and a in backup path. The primary and backup paths are placed on lightpaths in a way that they use disjoint sets of physical links. In [4] this scheme is compared with WDM protection and results show that it can accommodate more requests than WDM protection. The advantage of WDM protection is that it provides aggregate protection to all IP LSPs in a lightpath while integrated protection protects individual IP LSP. Not that both WDM and integrated protection schemes can use dedicated and shared resources. In GMPLS the SRLGs are used for resource sharing between backup paths that have link-disjoint working lightpaths [10,7].

The scheme we suggest uses, if necessary, spare bandwidth of working lightpaths to provide end-to-end-protection to other lightpaths. This is illustrate in figure 1 where working lightpaths are represented by solid lines and backup lightpaths by dashed lines. In figure 1a) WDM protection is used while in figure 1b) our protection scheme is used. Considering that just two wavelengths were available at each link, only the lightpaths between the node pairs (3,4), (2,6) and (1,3) were protected using WDM shared protection. The lightpath (2,3) could not be protected. The protection lightpaths of working lightpaths (1,3) and (2,6) can share the physical link (2,3) because they are link-disjoint. For the same scenario, using our scheme, the traffic of lightpath (2,3) could be protected using lightpath (2,6) since there is enough spare bandwidth available. For that to be possible the backup lightpath (6,3) must be activated when lightpath (2,3) fails. Wavelength sharing can be used by backup lightpaths in physical link (3,5) since the corresponding working lightpaths are link-disjoint. This kind of scheme is feasible because we assume the use of GMPLS and, as explained earlier, lightpaths can be announced as links to the network. Thus, the routing algorithm can include the lightpath (2,6) in the backup route of lightpath (2,3). Note also that lightpath (2,6) can be used to protect lightpath (2,3) because they are link-disjoint. This can be controlled in GMPLS because an FA contains the SRLGs for the path taken by the lightpath.

4   Problem Formulation

The problem considered is called *maximum throughput* (MT) problem and is defined as follows. For comparison we formulate and solve this problem for the integrated and proposed protection schemes since they both use GMPLS.

Definition 1 (MT Problem). *Given an all-optical WDM physical network* $\mathcal{G}(\mathcal{N}, \mathcal{L})$*, where* $\mathcal{N}$ *is the set of nodes and* $\mathcal{L}$ *is the set of links, and a set of connection requests* Λ*, each having a specific bandwidth requirement and all requiring end-to-end protection, find the virtual topology and connection routing on the virtual topology such that the total throughput is maximized.*

4.1   Network Assumptions and Notation

The WDM network consists of physical edges connecting nodes equipped with *wavelength division multiplexers* (WDMs) and *wavelength cross connects* (WXCs) with conversion functionality. A physical edge includes two links (optical fibers) for transmission in both directions and an edge failure affects both links in it. Therefore, working and backup routes must be edge-disjoint. The set of edge IP routers must establish a set of IP LSP connection requests, each with a bandwidth requirement and end-to-end protection. The set of possible bandwidth requirements (a portion of the total bandwidth of a lightpath) considered is {OC-3,OC-12,OC-48,OC-192} where the bandwidth of an OC-n channel is approximately $n*51.84$ Mb/s [6]. The notation used for connection requests closely follows [6]. We assume the following inputs:

$\mathcal{G}(\mathcal{N}, \mathcal{L})$	all-optical WDM physical network, where $\mathcal{N}$ is the set of nodes and $\mathcal{L}$ is the set of links.
$\mathcal{Z}$	set of lightpaths, already mapped, that can become part of the virtual topology. The source and destination nodes of a lightpath $z \in \mathcal{Z}$ is given by $s(z)$ and $d(z)$ respectively.
δ_{ij}^{z}	one if the lightpath $z \in \mathcal{Z}$ uses the link $ij \in \mathcal{L}$; zero otherwise.
$\mathcal{F}$	set of physical edges, possible faults, where the physical edge $f \in \mathcal{F}$ connecting nodes i and j includes both links ij and $ji \in \mathcal{L}$.
$\mathcal{P}_f$	set of primary lightpaths in Z affected by fault $f \in \mathcal{F}$.
$\mathcal{Y}$	set of granularities of connection requests: $\mathcal{Y} = \{3, 12, 48, 192\}$.
Λ	traffic matrix set: $\Lambda = \{\lambda_y\}$ where $y \in \mathcal{Y}$. The number of OC-y connection requests (LSPs) from the source node s to the destination node d is given by $\Lambda_y^{s,d}$.
W	number of wavelength channels available on each link.
C	bandwidth of a lightpath; assumed to be equal to OC-192.

Variables common to ILP1 and ILP2:

σ^z	one if lightpath $z \in \mathcal{Z}$ belongs to the virtual topology; zero otherwise.
$\phi_{y,t}^{s,d}$	one if the tth OC-y connection request from node s to node d has been successfully established; zero otherwise.
$\beta_{z,y}^{s,d,t}$	one if the tth OC-y connection request from node s to node d uses lightpath $z \in \mathcal{Z}$ in its primary route; zero otherwise.

$\alpha_{z,f,y}^{s,d,t}$ one if the tth OC-y connection request from node s to node d will have bandwidth reserved for backup in lightpath $z \in \mathcal{Z}$ when fault $f \in \mathcal{F}$ occurs; zero otherwise.

Variables specific to ILP1:

$\epsilon_{z,y}^{s,d,t}$ one if the tth OC-y connection request from node s to node d uses lightpath $z \in \mathcal{Z}$ in its backup route; zero otherwise.

Variables specific to ILP2:

$\nu_{z'}^{z}$ one if the backup route of lightpath $z \in \mathcal{Z}$ uses lightpath $z' \in \mathcal{Z}$; zero otherwise.

θ_{ij}^{z} one if the backup route of lightpath $z \in \mathcal{Z}$ includes physical link $ij \in \mathcal{L}$; zero otherwise.

4.2 Integer Linear Programming (ILP) Formulations

The goal of the two ILPs is to maximize the total network throughput. This is achieved by the following objective function.

$$Maximize \sum_{s,d \in \mathcal{N}} \sum_{y \in \mathcal{Y}, t \in [1, \Lambda_y^{s,d}]} y * \phi_{y,t}^{s,d} \tag{1}$$

Integrated Protection Constraints (ILP1) The following constraints will choose a virtual topology (a set of lightpaths), and find a primary and a backup route on the virtual topology for each IP LSP.

– Routing of IP LSPs primary routes:

$$\sum_{z \in \mathcal{Z}:s(z)=i} \beta_{z,y}^{s,d,t} - \sum_{z \in \mathcal{Z}:d(z)=i} \beta_{z,y}^{s,d,t} = \begin{cases} \phi_{y,t}^{s,d}, \ if \ s=i \\ -\phi_{y,t}^{s,d}, \ if \ d=i \\ 0, \ otherwise \end{cases},$$
$$, \ \forall s,d,i \in \mathcal{N}, \forall y \in \mathcal{Y}, \forall t \in [1, \Lambda_y^{s,d}] \tag{2}$$

– Routing of IP LSPs backup routes:

$$\sum_{z \in \mathcal{Z}:s(z)=i} \epsilon_{z,y}^{s,d,t} - \sum_{z \in \mathcal{Z}:d(z)=i} \epsilon_{z,y}^{s,d,t} = \begin{cases} \phi_{y,t}^{s,d}, \ if \ s=i \\ -\phi_{y,t}^{s,d}, \ if \ d=i \\ 0, \ otherwise \end{cases},$$
$$, \ \forall s,d,i \in \mathcal{N}, \forall y \in \mathcal{Y}, \forall t \in [1, \Lambda_y^{s,d}] \tag{3}$$

$$\beta_{z,y}^{s,d,t} * \delta_{ij}^{z} + \epsilon_{z',y}^{s,d,t}(\delta_{ij}^{z'} + \delta_{ji}^{z'}) \le 1 \ , \ \forall z, z' \in \mathcal{Z}, \forall s, d \in \mathcal{N}, \forall y \in \mathcal{Y},$$
$$, \ \forall t \in [1, \Lambda_y^{s,d}], \forall ij, ji \in \mathcal{L} \tag{4}$$

– Limitation of wavelengths used and bandwidth available on lightpaths:

$$\sum_{s,d \in \mathcal{N}} \sum_{y \in \mathcal{Y}, t \in [1, \Lambda_y^{s,d}]} (y * \beta_{z,y}^{s,d,t} + y * \alpha_{z,f,y}^{s,d,t}) \le C * \sigma^{z}, \forall z \in \mathcal{Z}, \forall f \in \mathcal{F} \tag{5}$$

$$\alpha_{z,f,y}^{s,d,t} \geq \beta_{z',y}^{s,d,t} + \epsilon_{z,y}^{s,d,t} - 1 \ , \ \forall z \in \mathcal{Z}, \forall f \in \mathcal{F}, \forall z' \in \mathcal{P}_f,$$

$$, \ \forall s,d \in \mathcal{N}, \forall y \in \mathcal{Y}, \forall t \in [1, \Lambda_y^{s,d}] \quad (6)$$

$$\sum_{z \in \mathcal{Z}} \sigma^z * \delta_{ij}^z \leq W \ , \ \forall ij \in \mathcal{L} \quad (7)$$

– Integer and binary assignments:

$$\sigma^z, \beta_{z,y}^{s,d,t}, \epsilon_{z,y}^{s,d,t}, \phi_{y,t}^{s,d}, \alpha_{z,f,y}^{s,d,t} \in \{0,1\} \quad (8)$$

Constraints 2 and 3 are responsible for routing of IP LSPs primary and backup routes respectively guaranteeing flow conservation. Constraint 4 ensures edge-disjointness of the IP LSPs primary and backup routes. Constraint 5 limits the bandwidth used in each lightpath, where the first term is the bandwidth consumed by primary routes of the IP LSPs and the second is the bandwidth consumed by backup routes of the IP LSPs. Constraint 6 forces bandwidth reservation for backup in lightpath $z \in \mathcal{Z}$, due to fault $f \in \mathcal{F}$, if the primary route of the IP LSP has been affected by fault $f \in \mathcal{F}$ and the backup route of the IP LSP uses lightpath $z \in \mathcal{Z}$. Finally, constraint 7 limits the number of wavelengths used by lightpaths in each physical link.

Our Protection Constraints (ILP2) The following constraints will choose a virtual topology (a set of lightpaths), find backup routes for each lightpath on the virtual topology and route the IP LSPs primary routes on this virtual topology. The backup routes of lightpaths can use basic TE links and FAs.

– Routing of IP LSPs primary routes:

$$\sum_{z \in \mathcal{Z}:s(z)=i} \beta_{z,y}^{s,d,t} - \sum_{z \in \mathcal{Z}:d(z)=i} \beta_{z,y}^{s,d,t} = \begin{cases} \phi_{y,t}^{s,d}, \ if \ s=i \\ -\phi_{y,t}^{s,d}, \ if \ d=i \\ 0, \ otherwise \end{cases} ,$$

$$, \ \forall s,d,i \in \mathcal{N}, \forall y \in \mathcal{Y}, \forall t \in [1, \Lambda_y^{s,d}] \ (9)$$

– Backup routes of virtual topology lightpaths:

$$\sum_{j:ij\in\mathcal{L}} \theta_{ij}^z + \sum_{z'\in\mathcal{Z}:s(z')=i} \nu_{z'}^z - \sum_{j:ji\in\mathcal{L}} \theta_{ji}^z - \sum_{z'\in\mathcal{Z}:d(z')=i} \nu_{z'}^z =$$

$$= \begin{cases} \sigma^z, \ if \ s(z)=i \\ -\sigma^z, \ if \ d(z)=i \ , \ \forall z \in \mathcal{Z}, \forall i \in \mathcal{N} \\ 0, \ otherwise \end{cases} \quad (10)$$

$$\sigma^z * \delta_{ij}^z + \theta_{ij}^z + \theta_{ji}^z \leq \sigma^z \ , \ \forall z \in \mathcal{Z}, \forall ij, ji \in \mathcal{L} \quad (11)$$

$$\sigma^z * \delta_{ij}^z + \nu_{z'}^z(\delta_{ij}^{z'} + \delta_{ji}^{z'}) \leq \sigma^z \ , \ \forall z, z' \in \mathcal{Z}, \forall ij, ji \in \mathcal{L} \quad (12)$$

– Limitation of wavelengths used and bandwidth available on lightpaths:

$$\sum_{s,d\in\mathcal{N}} \sum_{y\in\mathcal{Y}, t\in[1,\Lambda_y^{s,d}]} (y * \beta_{z,y}^{s,d,t} + y * \alpha_{z,f,y}^{s,d,t}) \leq C * \sigma^z, \forall z \in \mathcal{Z}, \forall f \in \mathcal{F} \ (13)$$

$$\alpha_{z,f,y}^{s,d,t} \geq \beta_{z',y}^{s,d,t} + \nu_z^{z'} - 1 \; , \; \forall z \in \mathcal{Z}, \forall f \in \mathcal{F}, \forall z' \in \mathcal{P}_f,$$

$$, \; \forall s, d \in \mathcal{N}, \forall y \in \mathcal{Y}, \forall t \in [1, \Lambda_y^{s,d}] \quad (14)$$

$$\sum_{z \in Z} \sigma^z * \delta_{ij}^z + \sum_{z \in \mathcal{P}_f} \theta_{ij}^z \leq W \; , \; \forall ij \in \mathcal{L}, \forall f \in \mathcal{F} \quad (15)$$

– Integer and binary assignments:

$$\sigma^z, \theta_{ij}^z, \beta_{z,y}^{s,d,t}, \phi_{y,t}^{s,d}, \nu_{z'}^z, \alpha_{z,f,y}^{s,d,t} \in \{0,1\} \quad (16)$$

Constraint 9 is responsible for routing of LSPs primary routes guaranteeing flow conservation. The flow conservation of backup routes is ensured by constraint 10 where basic TE links and FAs can be used. Constraint 11 ensures that the edges used by the backup are different from the ones used by the lightpath being protected and constraint 12 ensures that the edges used by FAs are different from the ones used by the lightpath being protected. Constraint 13 limits the bandwidth used in each lightpath. The first component is the bandwidth consumed by primary routes of the IP LSPs and the second is the bandwidth consumed by backup routes of lightpaths. Constraint 14 forces bandwidth reservation for backup in lightpath $z \in \mathcal{Z}$, due to fault $f \in \mathcal{F}$, if the primary route of the IP LSP has been affected by fault $f \in \mathcal{F}$ and the backup route of the lightpath used by the primary route of the IP LSP uses lightpath $z \in \mathcal{Z}$. Constraint 15 limits the number of wavelengths used in each physical link considering sharing the wavelengths between lightpaths with edge-disjoint primary routes.

If we ignore protection, the MT problem becomes a RWA problem, known to be NP-complete [6]. Thus, the MT problem with protection is also NP-complete.

5   Results

The following results were obtained, using CPLEX 8.0, for the network in figure 1. The traffic matrices used for OC-3, OC-12, OC-48 and OC-192 connection requests were randomly generated using different uniform distributions as in [6]. Uniformly distributed random numbers between 0 and 16 were generated for OC-3, between 0 and 8 for OC-12, between 0 and 4 for OC-48, and between 0 and 2 for OC-192. The set of lightpaths $\mathcal{Z}$ that can become part of the virtual topology includes a lightpath for each node pair using the shortest path.

The time necessary for a network to recover from a failure is representative of potential data loss. Here we compare the recovery times of the protection schemes discussed using the GMPLS signaling described in [8]. The RSVP is used to distribute labels and reserve appropriate wavelengths. Every node will keep track of the set of labels that need to be enabled when a failure occurs. When an edge fails multiple RSVP messages will be sent, by the node detecting the failure, to the nodes of the affected lightpaths responsible for recovery. When a node receives an RSVP message to activate a certain path, it will also activate all other paths related to that failure. If the node receives further RSVP messages that request the activation of those paths, it forwards the message to the next

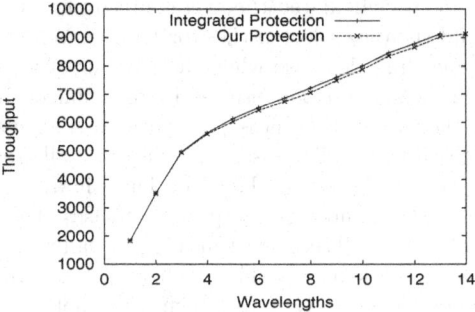

Fig. 2. Throughput vs wavelengths.

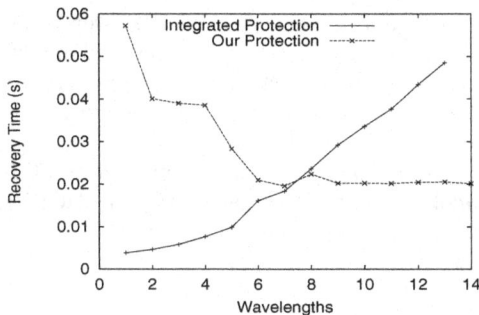

Fig. 3. Recovery time vs wavelengths.

node in the protection path taking no further action. This speeds the recovery. We assume a control network with the same configuration of the data network.

For recovery time calculations we assume a message processing delay of 0.3ms at each node and a propagation delay of 0.5ms for each link traversed, for a fiber length equal to 100 km, as in [5]. The time to detect a failure and to configure and test a cross-connect is 0.1ms and 5ms respectively, as in [1] (these are not referred in [5] and are independent of the protocol). For queueing delay we consider the maximum queueing delay that a message can expect at a node.

Figure 2 shows the throughput of the two protection schemes. The integrated protection presents the best throughput and accommodates all IP LSP requests using 13 wavelengths. Our protection scheme has a throughput very close to the integrated protection and can accommodate all IP LSP requests with 14 wavelengths. Thus, although protecting IP LSPs in an aggregated way our scheme can utilize the network capacity efficiently.

Figure 3 shows the recovery times. These are the worst times obtained from all edge failures. That is, for our scheme, we calculated the average recovery time of a lightpath for all edge failures and then we selected the worst value. For the integrated scheme we calculated the average recovery time of an IP LSP for all edge failures and then we selected the worst value. With our protection scheme the recovery times first decrease when the number of wavelengths increase but then stabilize. This is due to the discussed cross-connect time benefit that exists when multiple path activation messages travel on the network. That is, when a node receives the first RSVP message, it will make all cross-connect operations for all backup routes affected by the fault. Thus, in average, the recovery times will be smaller as the number of lightpaths increases. The integrated protection scheme presents very small recovery times for a small number of IP LSPs accommodated at the network but as this number increases the recovery times also increase due to queueing delay. This scheme does not scale well.

6   Summary

This article presents a protection scheme for IP-over-WDM networks using GM-PLS. The performance of this scheme was analyzed and results show that it can provide fast recovery times, since aggregated protection is provided, while using resources efficiently since spare bandwidth on working lightpaths can be used.

Acknowledgment: This work was supported by FCT (Foundation for Science and Technology) from Portugal within the DOPNET-POSI/CPS/42073 project.

References

1. S. Ramamurthy and B. Mukherjee: Survivable WDM Mesh Networks, Part I - Protection. Proc. IEEE INFOCOM'99, Vol 2 (Mar 1999) 744–751.
2. Dongyun Zhou and Suresh Subramaniam: Survivability in Optical Networks. IEEE Network, Vol. 14, No. 6 (Nov/Dec 2000) 16–23.
3. Krishna Bala: Internetworking between the IP and the Optical Layer. Optical Networks Magazine (May/Jun 2001) 16–18.
4. Yinghua Ye, Chadi Assi, Sudhir Dixit and Mohamed A. Ali: A Simple Dynamic Integrated Provisioning/Protection Scheme in IP over WDM Networks. IEEE Communications Magazine (Nov 2001) 174–182.
5. Laxman Sahasrabuddhe, S. Ramamurthy and Biswanath Mukherjee: Fault Management in IP-Over-WDM Networks: WDM Protection Versus IP Restoration. IEEE JSAC, Vol. 20, No. 1 (Jan 2002) 21–33.
6. Keyao Zhu and Biswanath Mukherjee: Traffic Grooming in an Optical WDM Mesh Network. IEEE JSAC, Vol. 20, No. 1 (Jan 2002) 122–133.
7. Eric Mannie et al.: Generalized Multi-Protocol Label Switching (GMPLS) Architecture. Internet Draft, draft-ietf-ccamp-gmpls-architecture-02.txt (2002).
8. Richard Rabbat et al.: Fault Notification and Service Recovery Protocol. Internet Draft, draft-rabbat-fault-notification-protocol-00.txt (2002).
9. Kireeti Kompella and Yakov Rekhter: LSP Hierarchy with Generalized MPLS TE. Internet Draft, draft-ietf-mpls-lsp-hierarchy-08.txt (2002).
10. Bala Rajagopalan, James Luciani and Daniel Awduche: IP over Optical Networks: A Framework. Internet Draft, draft-ietf-ipo-framework-03.txt (2003).

A Service and Network Management Framework for Providing Guaranteed QoS IP Services over WDM

Dimitrios Kagklis, Lampros Raptis, Yiorgos Patikis, Giorgos Hatzilias,
Michalis Ellinas, Dimitris Giannakopoulos, and Efstathios Sykas

National Technical University of Athens,
9, Heroon Polytechniou, 15773 Zografou, Athens, Greece
{kaglis, lraptis, gpatikis, gchatzi, ellinm, dgianna,
sykas}@telecom.ntua.gr

Abstract. IP-based applications are the prevailing trend of the telecommunications market, but the path towards the "IP over everything" target is not unhampered. The main shortcoming of the IP protocol is its lack of providing guaranteed Quality of Service (QoS), although significant effort is spent within different standardization bodies and organizations. At the same time, the tremendous increase of traffic, mostly data traffic, has drained the available deployed fibers resources. The introduction of the Wavelength Division Multiplexing (WDM) technology has relieved this problem, however the usage of an additional transport technology increased the complexity of network operation and management. The proposed service and management framework allows the provisioning of guaranteed QoS IP services of WDM networks, by integrating service and network management layers.

1   Introduction

Today telecommunications market is highly driven by IP-oriented applications and technologies. This is a completely different situation in respect of what happened in the past when almost all the traffic of telecommunications networks was voice. This tremendous proliferation of the Internet made the volume of data traffic close to that of voice traffic. As a result, a shift is occurring to the direction of technologies that initially were designed to serve merely data traffic but now they extend to employ other services such as voice, video or multimedia.

The move by telecom operators' corporate customers into the IP world, and the need for interoperability between private and public networks, drives the telcos to adopt IP in their core networks as a mean of unifying traffic types that are compatible with their customers' networks.

Nevertheless, the need for deployment of value-added IP services has yielded a thorough research on how to provide QoS for network applications. QoS means providing consistent, predictable data delivery service, in simple terms, satisfying customer application requirements. But "best effort" can make no guarantees about when data will deliver, or how much it can deliver. Increasing the bandwidth, which is the obvious solution, is costly; as such, the need for efficient protocols, providing differentiated high quality services, still remains and significant efforts are exerted by

M.M. Freire, P. Lorenz, M.M.-O. Lee (Eds.): HSNMC 2003, LNCS 2720, pp. 217–226, 2003.
© Springer-Verlag Berlin Heidelberg 2003

standardisation organisations and equipment vendors to give data networks the means to support QoS requirements.

But quality of service is only the one side of the problem. In fact, the volume of traffic has grown so much that it is necessary to look for more transport capacity, since existing technologies combined with the exhaustion of deployed fibers are not adequate themselves to address the problem. The advent of the WDM technology, which allows the multiplexing of many optical signals using different light-waves into the same fiber, solved this problem by multiplying the available capacity of existing transport networks. Although the introduction of one more technology layer increases the complexity of deployed networks, gradually all technologies will converge towards IP over WDM networks, following an evolution process.

In that respect, it seems apparent that IP and WDM as well as advanced QoS techniques need to interact to fully exploit the network resources and at the same time provide services with the required levels of quality. The purpose of this paper is to propose a management framework that allows the provisioning of differentiated IP services over WDM networks. The provided services will be based on Service Level Agreement (SLA) that will be requested and negotiated between customers and the Internet Service Provider (ISP). At the same time, the ISP and the Network Service Provider (NSP) will also negotiate in an automatic way on the provided Network Level Agreement (NLA).

Significant effort has been spent in proposing architectures for the integrated management of different network technologies like ATM and SDH [1] or IP and WDM [2] and at the same time, different approaches are proposed towards the creation and negotiation of SLA as well as the provisioning of guaranteed QoS services. The proposed management framework extends relevant work in the two previous areas and is a step towards not only the horizontal integration of different network technologies (IP and WDM) but also the vertical integration between the network management layer and the service management layer.

The structure of the paper is the following. Section 2 describes the business environment where the proposed framework can be deployed, focusing on the relationships between the identified entities. Then, in section 3, the architecture of the proposed framework is presented, followed by the description of a four-steps scenario, where interactions between the different components are further elaborated. The paper closes with the main conclusions including items for future work.

2   Business Model

Business entities, which abstract users and producers of services in today's information market, may play different business roles. The following types of business roles ([3]) were identified as having some kind of interaction, either directly or not, with the system:

- Customers and end-users. Customers are legal entities, humans or companies, which have contracts with Value Added Service Providers (VASPs) about the right to use telecommunications services and the obligation to pay for this right and the usage of these services according to the tariffs. End-users are entities, which interact with the VASPs to obtain the effect of the service. End users may be humans, or an automated piece of application software.

- Value Added Service Providers (VASPs) whose role is oriented towards customer management and value adding. Customers buy services from VASPs, which act as retailers of telecommunications services, providing other services than connectivity. Examples include VPN and VoIP SPs.
- Network Service Providers acting both as Network Providers and Network Management Providers. Their role is to support VASPs to provide their services, acting basically as connectivity providers. They provide an interface to VASPs, which enables them to request connections between arbitrary end-points in the global network. Network Providers are responsible for managing resources involved in service and network provision. The services offered by the Management Service Providers aim at fulfilling the management needs of their customer organizations, such as VASPs and business customers.

The different roles are placed in Fig. 1 in a left-to-right direction according to the identification of role played, i.e. Customers/End Users, Value Added Service Providers and Network Service Providers. Note the central role that the Inter-domain Network Management System (INMS) takes in this figure.

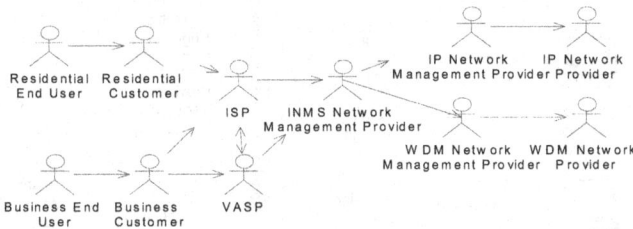

Fig. 1. Business Environment

For our model we assume that a number of 2 or more ISP that supply guaranteed QoS IP services utilize the network resources of one Network Provider that supports the management of IP over WDM. Each ISP makes a forecast of the demand of each class of service the ISP supports. According to the location and the network resources needed, the ISP makes a deal with NSP for specific network resources (Label Switched Paths – LSPs with specific characteristics) and location. At the same time, the ISP categorizes customers according to classes of service and the customers' traffic is routed to the respective LSPs allocated by the NSP. On the other hand, the NSP is obliged to inform the ISP about network disorder affecting the allocated LSPs.

It should be noted that the policies, enforced by both NSP and ISP, are irrespective. These decisions will be taken according to available bandwidth, cost, evaluation of statistical information concerning the usage of network resources and network malfunction. Finally, our model is dynamic in the sense that the ISP could request changes to network resources using a negotiation procedure as well as the NSP to allocate the requested resources by using relative mechanisms.

3   Architecture

The proposed architecture covers the service and network management layers of the TMN pyramid. It subsumes the Service Management System (SMS), the Integrated Network Management System (INMS) and the IP and WDM NMSs.

The main functionality of the SMS is to satisfy the customer needs on a service level, providing an advanced and flexible negotiation mechanism, and to interact with the network layer in order to instruct the latter to provide the necessary resources, independent of the transport network technology. Such instructions can only be given after the mapping of the services requirements to the network parameters.

The framework should be also flexible enough to handle a variety of diverse transport layers. The requests that are issued by the SMS typically do not have any dependencies on a particular network technology. The network management system should receive such requests, interpret the abstract terms that the SMS uses to define the new service and as a result, issue the appropriate commands that are native to the infrastructure that is currently employed.

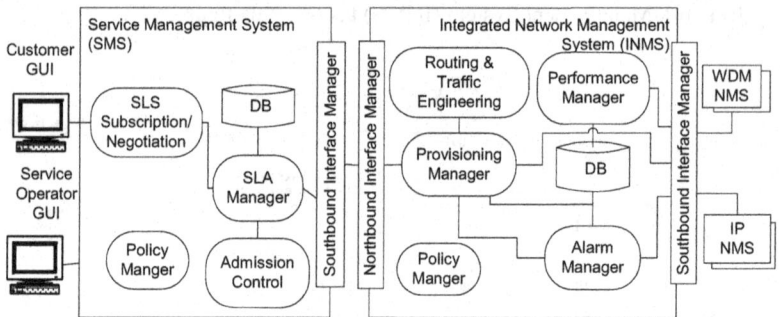

Fig. 2. System Functional Architecture

Such functionality is provided by the INMS, whose role is to provide a technology-agnostic interface that the SMS can use to request the creation of generic connection-oriented services. The end result of this process is a set of commands that are issued by the INMS towards the lower layers. These lower layers can be any connection-oriented network technology like SDH, ATM, MPLS or WDM, but in our case we will focus only on the IP/MPLS and the WDM technologies.

As it is depicted in Fig. 2, the commands issued by the INMS are forwarded to a set of network specific NMSs. While INMS is independent of the underlying network technology, this is not the case for the WDM and IP-NMS. Their role is to receive INMS requests and configure the WDM and IP sub-networks accordingly.

The INMS, IP-NMS and the WDM-NMS subsystems are based on a common detailed architecture [4]. The main differences between the components of the various NMSs (INMS, IP-NMS and WDM-NMS) are the data that they handle, since the special features of each technology domain should be taken into consideration.

Each ISP will employ a SMS in order to interact with the NSP, which itself uses the INMS. The proposed framework can support multiple ISPs, which can communicate with multiple NSPs. For simplicity reasons, in the rest of the paper, we will assume the existence of one ISP and one NSP.

In the following two subsections the main components of the SMS and the INMS subsystems are described.

3.1   SMS Components

SLS Subscription/Negotiation: This component performs, through a negotiation mechanism between the customer and the provider, the dynamic creation of a SLA. The dynamic creation of a SLA is in simple terms the procedure through which a customer can electronically specify the characteristics of the service he wishes to have and the network will decide whether it can accommodate the customer or not. The interaction between ISP and customer must be done through a standard based SLS-template [5], called *"service template"* form. The Negotiation mechanism accepts user requirements, support the negotiation procedure and delivers a deal or conflict deal. The usage of a negotiation protocol allows users and ISPs to negotiate for SLAs and pursue an agreement on the content of a specific service proposal. With the use of this negotiation protocol the service provider will accept, reject or counter-propose an SLA. The customer will accept or reject the service provider offer or will create an alternative SLA request.

SLA Manager: The SLA Manager supports software mechanisms for mapping SLAs to network parameters, allocating resources, and storing the resulted SLAs to a central repository. It holds all the credentials of the authenticated customers registered to the specific ISP in the customer repository of the central repository. Moreover, the SLA Manager decides the supported QoS Classes and is acquainted with the available traffic trunks described by the location of the ingress, egress and the respective QoS Class. The available resources per traffic trunk of the network are stored in the resource repository of the system.

Policy Manager: The Policy Manager through automated transformation and refinement of policies will enforce SLAs and support policies integrity. It evaluates the information provided by the SLA Manager and taking into account the available resources, the QoS Classes and the network parameters described by the SLAs, it defines policies in order to best satisfy the customers demands.

Admission Control: The main role of this component is to maximize the number of admitted services and the QoS they enjoy, thus maximizing network utilization while preventing QoS degradation caused by overloading the network [6]. The Admission Control component according to the available resources of each traffic trunk and the signed SLAs, decides if a signed SLA can be best served. In cases of failure to reach the agreed level of QoS, either the customer is not served or receives the service in a lower-quality QoS Class.

Southbound Interface Manager: The Southbound Interface Manager is the component that is responsible from the SMS side to coordinate the interaction of the ISP with more than one NSP, while translating at the same time the service specific parameters to the appropriate requests that the NSP is expecting, in order to allocate the necessary resources for each LSP.

Service Operator/Customer Graphical User Interface (GUI): The Service Operator GUI is a set of graphical tools that the service operator uses to interact with the system. The Customer GUI provides the customer with information about the available services as well as a mechanism to select the service characteristics.

3.2   INMS Components

Northbound Interface Manager: The Northbound Interface Manager implements a single point of entry, for the communication between the SMS of the ISP and the INMS of the NSP. There are two distinct flows of information passing through Northbound. One originating from the upper layers, and carries the new connectivity requests and one that carries alarms or performance data, asynchronously back to the upper layers.

Provisioning Manager: The Provisioning Manager interprets the incoming requests and analyses them into a sequence of simpler commands that are issued toward the rest of the components. This makes Provisioning manager the central component inside the INMS that has the task of coordinating the actions of the rest.

Routing & Traffic Engineering: The Routing & Traffic Engineering component handles the design of the new connections. The routing functionality varies between the NMS systems, in order to take into consideration the specific characteristics of each network technology. So while in the IP-NMS the routing decisions can be simply forwarded to the IP routing protocols, in WDM the routing functionality of the component must implement a solution for the Routing and Wavelength Assignment (RWA) problem. The traffic engineering functionality allows the aggregation of the customer traffic that belongs to the same QoS class into the respective traffic trunk, thus permitting better utilization of the NSP resources.

Repository: The Repository component provides persistency for the rest of the systems by storing information relevant to the network topology. It stores two schemas, the physical, which describes the network topology and the logical, which depicts the connections that have been implemented by the system.

Alarm Manager: One of the objectives of the system architecture is to provide robust means of communication for its users. The first step towards achieving this goal is identifying the root cause of network problem and such functionality will be implemented inside the Alarm Manager component. The Alarm Manager listens for alarms originating from lower layers of the system and by correlating them, decides upon the cause of network malfunction. When the component identifies the root cause of the problem, it notifies both the administrator of the NSP as well as the SMS by forwarding appropriate notifications to the upper layers.

Performance Manager: The Performance Manager monitors the quality of service parameters inside the network, thus making sure that their values are inside the ranges that are acceptable by the SMS and there is no violation for the agreed levels. The measurements taken are forwarded to the upper layers of the system in order to verify whether the NSP complies to the NLA that has with the ISP.

Policy Manager: The Policy Manager enables the dynamical change of the behavior of the system. This is achieved by creating a set of generic rules that define how the system will react in each situation.

Southbound Interface Manager: The Southbound Interface Manager provides abstraction from the characteristics of the network infrastructure. Its role is to translate the commands that are issued by the various components into a format that can be understood by the lower layers.

4   High Level Scenario

The purpose of this section is to present, through a four -steps scenario, all the possible phases that are taking place in order for the ISP to provide QoS guaranteed IP services over a WDM network. The description of the four steps permits a deeper understanding of the components functionality that was described in section 3.

The scenario phases are the following:

- Phase 0: Network Topology Generation according to the "anticipated" SLAs
- Phase 1: Network Configuration by the NSP according to the NLAs
- Phase 2: SLA Creation and Service Activation
- Phase 3: Dynamic Network Topology Re-configuration

4.1   Phase 0

The ISP that is willing to supply IP added-value services initially makes a business plan, which defines the target group of the market, the categories of the IP services that are going to be supplied as well as the expected customers for each IP service category. On completion of the business plan, the SLA Manager of the SMS has to make the essential estimation of network requirements per service category indicated by the number of contracts, the level of QoS needs to be guaranteed for each service category as well as the location of available servers and Internet gateways. This procedure will result in a number of traffic trunks.

Due to the lack of extended network infrastructure, ISPs have to make NLAs with the NSPs in order to fulfill their business plan. Such agreement or contract will specify the allocated network resources, their level of availability and survivability, performance, operational as well as financial and legal aspects.

ISP and NSP will come to an agreement with respect to the NLA through traditional human-to-human communication. Once the contract is signed the ISP is responsible for accommodating the customers demands in service level while the NSP is responsible to satisfy the ISPs demands in a network level. The network configuration by the NSP is described in the following sub-section.

4.2   Phase 1

The ISP after making an initial estimate of the network resources that are required to accommodate the user needs forwards a new service request to the NSP. Each request for connectivity that is issued by the SMS of the ISP is accompanied by a set of QoS parameters that the NSP must implement. The receiving of such a command results in the following series of steps that aim at making the appropriate configuration in the core network.

Firstly, the SMS request is received by the INMS Northbound Interface Manager of NSP, which forwards the request to the Provisioning Manager for further processing.

Inside the Provisioning Manager the request undergoes a series of transformations. The abstract terms that are used by the SMS to describe the new request are translated into terms that have meaning for the NSP core network. After this initial analysis the request is decomposed into a set of commands that are issued towards the rest of the components. The Provisioning Manager based on the NSP policies may choose between creating a separate LSP for each incoming request or to perform service aggregation.

Then, the Provisioning Manager interacts with the Routing & Traffic Engineering component. For each incoming connectivity request, the Routing & Traffic Engineering component has the task of designing the appropriate path according to the QoS constraints that defined by the SMS of the ISP. For this task it utilizes the network topology information that resides in the repository. If the network does not have the necessary resources that are needed to accommodate the new service the Routing & Traffic Engineering component rejects the request, otherwise it returns to the Provisioning Manager the path of the new connection.

Upon the successful completion of the design for the new connection the Provisioning Manager initiates the process of allocating the necessary resources in the network. Such initiation is done by making the necessary requests to the lower layers, through the Southbound Interface Manager. In the case of INMS the lower layers are the WDM-NMS and IP-NMS subsystems, while in the case WDM-NMS and IP-NMS they are the network elements themselves.

A notification is passed to the Provisioning Manager through the Southbound Interface Manager indicating the end status of the creation process. In case of a failure in the network the SMS is informed through the INMS Northbound Interface Manager. If the process succeeds the network representation in the repository is updated in order to reflect the new changes, the SMS is also notified about the successful creation of the new service.

The Performance Manager set-ups measurement points inside the network in order to monitor QoS parameters. The measurements are forwarded through INMS Northbound Interface Manager to the SMS Southbound Interface Manager.

4.3   Phase 2

After the successful network configuration, the ISP can provide to its customer different services depending on their needs. Firstly, through the GUI, the customer submits its personal information in order to be authenticated. On successful authentication through the Subscription/ Negotiation component, the ISP provides the customer with a *service template* form. This form contains significant information, like the names and a short description of the services, which are currently available by the ISP, and such information is stored in the customer repository. In case that some services have been modified or new services are available by the ISP since the last time the customer logged on to the ISP, they are provided to the user.

Secondly, the customer specifies dynamically the characteristic of the service he wants to subscribe to. This is performed through the supplied GUI environment, which provides a step-by-step guidance procedure in terms of completing the *service template* form and avoiding and/or correcting any mistakes.

Then a negotiation starts between the customer and the ISP in order to result to a specific SLA. The requested SLA is passed from the Subscription/Negotiation component to the SLA Manager component. The SLA Manager examines the customer's requirements and maps them to network requirements. The SLA Manager in cooperation with the Admission Control decides whether the service, described by the received service template, can be supported by the current network configuration. That decision may be based on the information stored in the customer, network and resource repositories.

According to the result of the admission control and the availability of network resources, the SLA Manager accepts or rejects the customer's demands. Also, if this specific service proposal cannot be accommodated, the SLA Manager through the Subscription/Negotiation component negotiates by creating and sending an alternative suggestion to the customer. The customer has the ability to accept or reject the ISP's offer of alternatives and to create another service proposal according to the alternatives proposed values, which is then submitted to the ISP. The negotiation continues until an agreement is reached or one side decides to withdraw. If the negotiation phase ends up with a mutual agreement, then the last service proposal becomes a contract (SLA) between the customer and the ISP and both sides store the agreement in their respective repositories. After that, the agreed service is available according to the terms of the contract (time of day, continuous, etc).

After the agreement of the SLA, the service should be activated in order the customer to use it. Firstly the Policy Manager after examining the terms of the SLA must decide and enforce the policy that will fully or best satisfy the customer's requirements. Then it stores the specific SLA in the repository, which holds the SLAs that can be activated, and informs the Admission Control.

The Admission Control accesses the repository and through a time-schedule mechanism traces the contracts that should be activated according to time and date parameters. Each time that the Admission Control locates one SLA that has to be activated informs the INMS to aggregate the traffic injected by the customer to the specific LSP that the contracted SLA belongs to and informs the SLA Manager for the activation of the SLA. Finally the SLA Manager updates the repository for network operation and accounting purposes.

4.4   Phase 3

The proposed Dynamic Network Topology Reconfiguration mechanism in cases of network malfunction is responsible for creating or modifying the already existing network paths in order to satisfy the supplied levels of QoS specified with the NLA.

In case of network failure, the INMS takes the appropriate actions in order to recover the affected services. If there are no available resources or there are multiple faults in the network and the service cannot be restored then the SMS is notified about the unavailability of the services. Any modifications to the existing network configuration are transparent to the SMS.

Moreover, in the typical scenario that the ISP wishes to modify the NLA with the NSP, a negotiation mechanism similar to the one described in phase 1 should exist.

The appropriate enhancements in the negotiation protocol need to be done in order to perform peer-to-peer negotiation between the ISP and the NSP. By this protocol, the ISP can negotiate the modification of the terms of the NLA in cases the ISP wished to expand, shrink or modify its business plan.

5   Conclusions

This paper gives an overview of a novel service and network management framework, which allows the provisioning of guaranteed QoS IP services over WDM network. The proposed framework not only integrates horizontally two different technologies, namely the IP and the WDM, but also integrates vertically the service and the network layer of the TMN. The implementation of the proposed framework is being carried out in a distributed way (component platform) using the Java technology as the main programming language. The evaluation of the system, which will take place in the near future, will be done in a real network environment.

Acknowledgments

The authors would like to thank all TEQUILA and WINMAN colleagues who have also contributed to the ideas presented here.

References

1. Berdekas, K., et. al.: Enabling Accounting, Configuration and Fault Management for Multi-technology, Broadband Connections among Operators through X-type Interface. PDPTA 99, June 28 - July 1, Las Vegas, USA (1999)
2. Raptis, L., et. al.: An Integrated Network Management approach for managing hybrid IP and WDM networks. To be appeared on the IEEE Network Magazine, May/June issue, (2003)
3. Raptis, L., et. al.: An Integrated Approach for the Management of IP connectivity over WDM transport networks. International Conference on Telecommunications, Telecom 2000, 11-13 October, Varna, Bulgaria (2000)
4. Raptis, L., et. al.: Integrated Management of IP over Optical Transport Networks. IEEE International Conference on Telecommunications, 4-7 June 2001, Bucharest, Romania (2001)
5. Goderis, D., et. al.: Service Level Specification semantics, parameters and negotiation requirements: Internet Draft, Work in progress, June (2001)
6. Mykoniati, E., et. al.: Admission Control for Providing QoS in DiffServ IP Networks: The TEQUILA Approach. IEEE Communications Magazine, Vol.41 No.1 January (2003)

The Study on the Traffic Modeling with PI and the Design for the All Optical Network Modeling with WDM in Korea

Moonjong Jang and Hyocheon Choi

Korea Electric Power Research Institute
Munji 103-16 Yusong, Daejeon, ROK
mjjang@kepri.re.kr
http://www.kepri.re.kr/index.html

Abstract. Recently, data traffic is rapidly exceeding voice traffic for the increasing demand from the Internet in Korea. And, it's also known that some of the traffics are due to the mobile subscribers such as PCS, PDA, and so on. To meet this terrific demand on the backbone network, it's better to use existing optical fibers fully than to install more optical fibers simply. For this reason, All Optical Network System with WDM is spotlighted nowadays.

In this paper, PI(Population-Information factor) method will be introduced to make a modeling which is fit to the environment of Korea, and the telecommunication model with WDM for Korea Electric Power Corporation(KEPCO) will be designed. For this purpose, a simulation tool to design the telecommunication network for KEPCO was developed with Visual C and this is used to analyze the designed model. This result can be used to design and simulate functions and performance when All Optical Network with WDM is constructed.

1 Introduction

To accept various multimedia services properly such as mobile data, video and Internet traffic that are expected to explode in the 21st-century IT (Information and Telecommunication) era, there is a need to increase the capacity of the backbone network greatly. For this purpose, high-speed broadband telecommunication network is under construction with Korean government's strong drive. After this project in 2005, All Optical Network is installed nationwide and the speed between backbone nodes will be tens of gigabits per second. But, to support tens of gigabits per second high transfer rate, the circuit distribution multiplexer processing thousands of gigabits per second in each node is needed. It's not economical to implement this circuit distribution capacity for thousands of gigabits bandwidth with the existing electric signal processing method, so to solve this problem more effectively, a lot of advanced researchers are focusing on the All Optical Network with WDM (Wavelength Distribution Multiplexing) method recently [1].

M.M. Freire, P. Lorenz, M.M.-O. Lee (Eds.): HSNMC 2003, LNCS 2720, pp. 227–234, 2003.
© Springer-Verlag Berlin Heidelberg 2003

Therefore, in this paper, how to configure the structure of AON with WDM reflecting Korean environment and government's plan in high-speed communication network construction project, make a model to accept the presumed traffic in the future, and design the network to accept increasing traffic each year will be shown.

2   Configuration Scheme of All Optical Network in Korea

The first thing in designing AON in Korea is to decide the number of the nodes and their locations. The whole areas are divided into 6 parts with the consideration of the previously installed topology of the network, the topographical characteristics and population distribution by region. After that, the most populous city is selected as the representative node within the partition. And, mesh structured AON is constructed between the nodes.

In figure 1, the diagram for the main transportation network as a high-speed communication network is shown. According to this, nationwide spread 144 points are interconnected. Therefore, it's desirable that AON consist of 6 cities in order to absorb this plan. The chosen cities as the leading nodes in each group are Seoul, Daejon, Daegu, Pusan, Kwangju and Chunchon, and they'll be used in the traffic modeling.

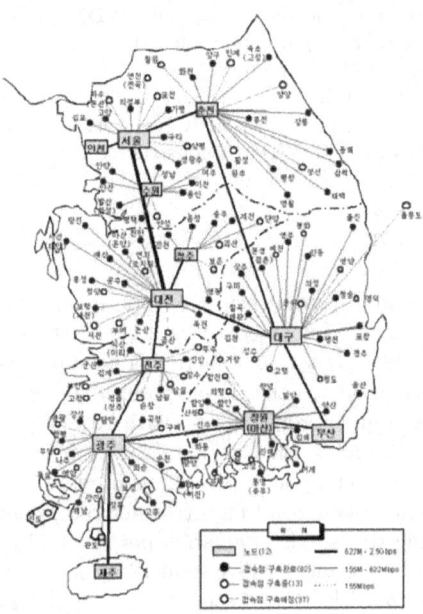

Fig. 1. The diagram of the backbone network for high-speed communication in Korea

3   Traffic Modeling

Secondly, the traffic should be calculated that is necessary for the backbone network with the six cities. Because real traffic statistics are not reported yet in Korea, estimates are usually used to calculate the needed traffic.

For this purpose, there are various traffic modeling schemes. One of the simplest methods is to estimate the amount of the send/receive data with the ratio of population distribution. Because this simple population ratio based estimating has lots of errors, RACE group in Europe suggests traffic calculation method including distance and population distribution in a COST 239 project. Another method is adding an error-calibrating factor to the population ratio and distance [2]. Besides these, many other modeling schemes have been suggested.

In this paper, new modeling scheme for network traffic that uses population ratio and information index to compute expected traffic guessing is introduced. Previously suggested modeling scheme uses distance as one of the factors, but that is ignored in this scheme. In the future traffic, almost all the data will be generated by Internet and mobile communication, and the common feature in these services is that they are free from the distance. Hence, the variation in traffic due to the distance factor could be neglected unlike the former one.

PI based traffic modeling is to take a calculation with the population ratio related directly in traffic generation. Thus, a numerical expression is as follows.

$$\text{Traffic}(s,d) = k \times IP(s) \times IP(d) \qquad (1)$$

$\text{Traffic}(s,d)$ means the traffic between source s and destination d, and k is a pertinent constant value. $IP(i)$ represents Informative Population(IP) generating traffic directly in node i. It is determined as following expression.

$$IP(i) = \text{Information Index}(i) \times \text{Population}(i) \qquad (2)$$

Table 1 shows traffic generation ratio produced with the factor of the estimated population and presumed information index in 2005. This estimated population is based on the data reported by Korea National Statistical Office, and estimated information index is from the result of the research on the information index estimation by region conducted by Korea Information Society Development Institute (KISDI) [3].

About 60 Gbps communication line has been installed between Seoul and Daejeon in 1997, and if the capacity is enough to accept current network traffic, then possible constant value, k, is assumed 1000, which is calculated with the population from the estimated population and the population index in 2005. Figure 2 shows the estimated traffic value in 2005.

4   All Optical Network Design

A simulation program was implemented to design the AON, and the program accepts node, link and traffic matrix as input, produces the designed AON link

Table 1. Traffic generation ratio with the estimated population and information index in 2005

Receiving Node	Sending Node	Informative Population Distribution	Percentage In Group	Total Percentage
Seoul	Daejeon	3,754,265	18.31%	9.43%
	Daegu	4,658,211	22.72%	11.70%
	Pusan	6,659,016	32.49%	16.73%
	Kwangju	4,464,302	21.78%	11.22%
	Chunchon	962,792	4.70%	2.42%
Daejeon	Seoul	21,764,042	56.52%	5.02%
	Daegu	4,658,211	12.10%	1.07%
	Pusan	6,659,016	17.29%	1.54%
	Kwangju	4,464,302	11.59%	1.03%
	Chunchon	962,792	2.50%	0.22%
Daegu	Seoul	21,764,042	57.88%	6.38%
	Daejeon	3,754,265	9.98%	1.10%
	Pusan	6,659,016	17.71%	1.95%
	Kwangju	4,464,302	11.87%	1.31%
	Chunchon	962,792	2.56%	0.28%
Pusan	Seoul	21,764,042	61.13%	9.63%
	Daejeon	3,754,265	10.54%	1.66%
	Daegu	4,658,211	13.08%	2.06%
	Kwangju	4,464,302	12.54%	1.98%
	Chunchon	962,792	2.70%	0.43%
Kwangju	Seoul	21,764,042	57.58%	6.08%
	Daejeon	3,754,265	9.93%	1.05%
	Daegu	4,658,211	12.32%	1.30%
	Pusan	6,659,016	17.62%	1.86%
	Chunchon	962,792	2.55%	0.27%
Chunchon	Seoul	21,764,042	52.70%	1.20%
	Daejeon	3,754,265	9.09%	0.21%
	Daegu	4,658,211	11.28%	0.26%
	Pusan	6,659,016	16.12%	0.37%
	Kwangju	4,464,302	10.81%	0.25%

Table 2. The estimated network traffic value in 2005

Node	Seoul	Daejeon	Daegu	Pusan	Kwangju	Chunchon
Seoul	-	94.3	117.0	167.3	112.2	24.2
Daejeon	50.2	-	10.7	15.4	10.3	2.2
Daegu	63.8	11.0	-	19.5	13.1	2.8
Pusan	96.3	16.6	20.6	-	19.8	4.3
Kwangju	60.8	10.5	13.0	18.6	-	2.7
Chunchon	12.0	2.1	2.6	3.7	2.5	-

capacities as output. The algorithm used to design the AON is categorized into Heuristic-Sequential RWA method and Exhaustive RWA method [4], [5]. In the case of the former, either fixed method or unconstrained method can be used for routing, and in the case of wavelength assignment, most-used-wavelength-first method and first-fit-wavelength-first method can be used.

Figure 2 shows the user interface where a fixed method as routing is selected and a most-used method as wavelength assignment.

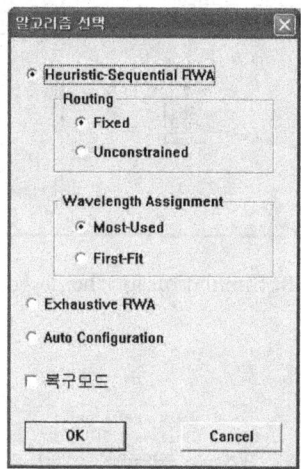

Fig. 2. User interface for selecting the algorithm

In figure 3, network topology that has upper and lower rings as the physical link with 6 nodes is shown. Estimated value of traffic generation in 2005 (Table 2) is used as a traffic matrix.

Figure 4 shows how much capacity is needed by link in the AON according to the result of the simulation. The values in each row can be translated as follows.

$$\text{Source-destination : line speed} \times \text{needed number of the line} \qquad (3)$$

Figure 5 shows how many channels are required by link according to the needed capacity in a link. In the figure, it's shown that estimated traffic between Seoul and Daejeon is the largest one. If the AON with the estimated population and information index in another year is designed with this method, it can be inferred how many wavelengths are allocated by link while the network is upgraded in stages. It will be helpful to invest in the expansion of the network economically.

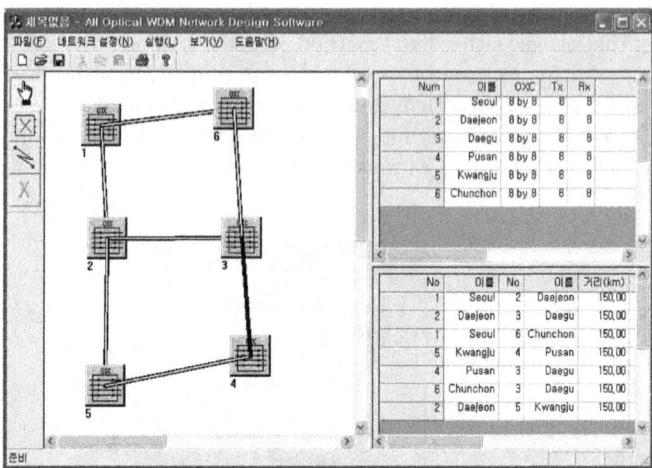

Fig. 3. Simulation for the design of the AON

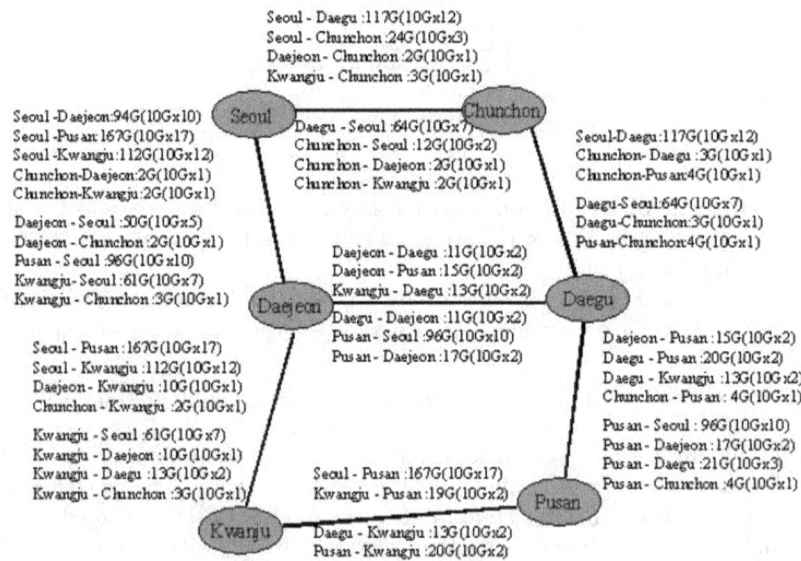

Fig. 4. AON configuration with the 10 Gbps wavelength channel (Estimated population and information index in 2005)

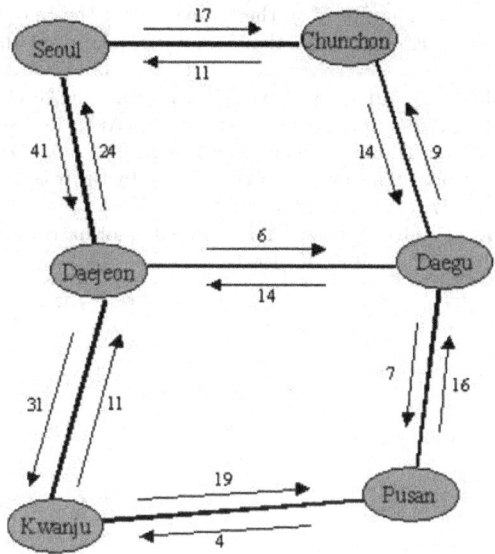

Fig. 5. Channel allocation diagram with unidirectional wavelength by link

5   Conclusion

Once backbone network is installed, it's used for a long time, so when it's deployed, it's already been designed to embrace large capacity. But, if the traffic is estimated for the too far future, it will be inefficient at the network-upgrading point. Therefore, it will be more economical to maintain the network with the change of the traffic by 5 or 10 year.

Hence this is considered in this paper, consequently, the topology of the domestic backbone network and the modeling scheme for network traffic with topographical characteristics and distribution of the population are suggested. And the AON in 2005 is designed in order to prepare for the evolution to the future backbone network.

From comparing the designed AONs in other points, it will be calculated how many channels should be installed additionally. Also, with the development of the technology, 2.5 Gbps base will move to 10 Gbps base in the near future. So, it will be possible to accept expanding traffic without extra fiber cores.

References

1. M. Jang, et al.: KEPCO All Optical Network Project (Interim Report). Korea Electric Power Research Institute, Daejeon ROK (Jan., 2000)
2. M. C. Sinclair : Improved model for European international telephony traffic. Electronic Letters, Vol. 30, No. 18 (Sep., 1994), 1468-1470

3. D. Choi, et al. : The Study on the Estimation of the Information Index in Major Region, Korea. Korea Information Society Development Institute, Daejeon ROK (1996)
4. Ahmed Mokhtar : Adaptive Wavelength Routing in All-Optical Networks, Vol.6, No.2 IEEE/ACM transactions on networking (Apr., 1998)
5. N. Jung., et al.: Traffic Modeling and Design of An All-Optical WDM Backbone Network in Korea. The Journal of the Korean Institute of Communication Sciences Vol. 24, No. 6B, 1165-1173 (Jun., 1999)
6. K. Jung, et al.: The Indicators for Regional Informatization I. National Computerization Agency, Seoul ROK (1997)

Multihoming with Mobile IP

Christer Åhlund [1] and Arkady Zaslavsky [2]

[1] Luleå University of Technology, Centre for Distance-spanning Technology,
Department of Computer Science, SE-971 87 Luleå, Sweden
christer@cdt.luth.se
[2] School of Computer Science & Software Engineering, Monash University,
900 Dandenong Road, Caulfield East,
Vic 3145, Melbourne, Australia
a.zaslavsky@monash.edu.au

Abstract. Mobile IP is the standard for mobility management in IP networks. With today's emerging possibilities within wireless broadband communication, mobility within networks will increase. New applications and protocols will be created and Mobile IP is important to this development, since Mobile IP support is needed to allow mobile hosts to move between networks with maintained connectivity. This article describes multihomed Mobile IP enabling mobile hosts to register multiple care-of addresses at the home agent, to enhance the performance of wireless network connectivity. Flows can be load-balanced between care-of addresses to achieve a more reliable connectivity. A prototype is also described.

1 Introduction

In future wireless local area networks (WLAN), connectivity to access points (AP) by different technologies and different providers will be a reality. Technologies like 802.11 [1], Bluetooth [2] and HiperLAN [3] will support wireless network connectivity to wired network infrastructures, to reach the Internet and for other types of services. WLAN-technologies are becoming efficient enough to support network capabilities for applications running in desktop computers.

With the use of WLANs, new challenges arise and mobile hosts (MH) will face multiple APs with possibly different capabilities and utilization.

The work described in this article is based on 802.11b technology. In 802.11b, there are two different Basic Service Sets (BSS) for connectivity: infrastructure BSS and independent BSS. In infrastructure mode the association with an AP is based on link-layer mechanisms using the signal quality. The selection is invisible to upper layer protocols and one association at a time is possible. In independent BSS a network interface can communicate with all others within communication range without association and this is the mode used in ad hoc networks [4].

The selection of which AP to associate with should also be available for higher level protocols, the applications and the users. It might be that the signal quality is somewhat better to one AP but the overall performance is better at another. Then it is reasonable to use the AP with the best overall performance. Wireless connections are

M.M. Freire, P. Lorenz, M.M.-O. Lee (Eds.): HSNMC 2003, LNCS 2720, pp. 235-243, 2003.

prone to errors and by using multiple simultaneous connections to APs, a more reliable connectivity is achieved.

In the largest study so far [21], a university campus equipped with WLANs is evaluated. 476 APs are spread over 161 buildings divided into 81 subnets. 5,500 students and 1,215 professors are equipped with laptops. The study shows that 17% of the sessions involves roaming and that 40% of it is between different subnets, causing the IP traffic to fail. MHs sometimes perform frequent handovers between APs while being in the same place.

For mobility and maintained network connectivity for an MH that moves between APs, the Extended Service Set (ESS) can be used. The ESS manages handover in the datalink layer, so it is restricted to the same Local Area Network (LAN) or Virtual LAN (VLAN). An MH doing handover between APs in different networks (ESS) will break flows. To manage handover between networks without disrupting flows, the Mobile IP (MIP) [5] is proposed and partly deployed. For an MH connected to the home network, the IP will operate normally. If the MH disconnects from the home network and connects to a foreign network, the MIP will manage network mobility which will be transparent for the protocol layers above the network layer and to the user of the MH. There are two versions of MIP: MIPv4 [6] and MIPv6 [7].

The study [21] shows the MIP requirements and the potential to associate with multiple APs simultaneously to avoid breaking and disrupting sessions.

An MH disconnecting from the home network and connecting to a foreign network will request a care-of address or a co-located care-of address. A care-of address is usually used in MIPv4 if there is a foreign agent (FA), and all packets to and from the MH are sent through the FA. A co-located care-of address is used when the MH can receive a topology-correct address without an FA by using the Dynamic Host Configuration Protocol (DHCP) [8] both with MIPv4 and MIPv6. In MIPv6 another possibility to get a co-located care-of address is to use stateless auto-configuration managed by Neighbour Discovery (ND) [9]. The term care-of address will be used to describe both types and it will be clear from the context which one is intended. The MH sends information about the care-of address to its home agent (HA) at the home network. The HA will install a tunnel [10] with the care-of address as the tunnel end-point. A correspondent host's (CH) packets to the MH home address will be forwarded (tunneled) by the HA to the current location of the MH. Packets from the MH are sent directly to the CH if possible because of ingress filtering [11], otherwise a reverse tunnel to the HA where the HA forwards the packets to the CH can be used. To make the routing more efficient, route optimization can be used. The CH is then informed of the care-of address used by the MH and can send packets directly to that address without using the HA.

To enhance performance and reliability in network connectivity, host-based multihoming can be used. A host can be multihomed by using two interfaces configured with different IP addresses, or by using two IP addresses for the same network interface.

Host-based multihoming is usually managed by a Domain Name Server (DNS) [12]. For a multihomed host the name-to-address binding binds multiple IP addresses to a single host name. The DNS can return the IP addresses in a round robin fashion upon name resolution requests. Another option is that multiple IP addresses are returned and the host selects which address to use.

The work in this article describes an approach to enhanced network connectivity to MHs connecting to WLANs. The MIP is extended to support multihomed connectivity where multihoming is managed by MIP. A real prototype developed is also described below. This will enable the AP selection on other criteria than just the signal-to-noise ratio and hereby avoid rapid re-associations. Traffic to and from an MH can be sent using multiple APs.

Section 2 describes multihomed MIP. In section 3 related work is presented and section 4 concludes the paper and discusses future work.

2 Multihomed Mobile IP

Multihomed MIP enhances the performance and reliability for MHs connecting to WLANs. Wireless connections are prone to errors and changing conditions which must be considered to enable applications for desktop computers to be usable on MHs connecting wireless.

The multihoming is managed by the MIP and hidden from the IP routing, keeping IP routing protocols like the Routing Information Protocol (RIP) [13] and Open Shortest Path First (OSPF) [14] unaware. For a sender, multihomed MIP can be considered an any-cast approach [15] where a sender relies on the network protocol to use the best available destination for the packets. The available destination will be one of possibly multiple care-of addresses used by an MH. In IPv6, an any-cast address is used to reach the best available destination (server) among multiple destinations supporting the service required. The approach in this paper for a sender to any-cast address an MH, is that the MH's home address is used to locate the best care-of address. The difference from the any-cast approach in IPv6 is that it is address-based instead of server-based and the destination will be the same host.

The MH keeps a list of all networks with valid advertisements and registers the care-of address at the HA (and the CH if MIPv6 route optimization is used) for the networks supporting the best connectivity. To evaluate the connectivity, the MH monitors the deviation in arrival times between advertisements and calculates the metric based on this information (see formula 1). This metric is used to describe the MH's connectivity to foreign networks. A small metric indicates that agent advertisements sent at discrete time intervals arrive without collisions and without being delayed by the FA. This indicates available bandwidth as well as the FA's capability to relay traffic to and from the MH. Among the care-of addresses registered at the HA, the FA with the smallest metrics will be installed as the default gateway in the MH.

$$\text{SampleDelta} = \text{CurrentArrivalTime} - \text{LastArrivalTime}. \tag{1}$$

$$\text{MeanDelta} = \text{SampleDelta} \times \delta - \text{MeanDelta} \times (1 - \delta).$$

$$\text{Metric} = (\text{SampleDelta} - \text{MeanDelta})^2 \times \mu + \text{Metric} \times (1 - \mu).$$

The selection of which care-of address to use for an MH is based on the delay between a CH or the HA and the MH, where the delay includes wireless links. In IP routing with protocols like RIP and OSPF a wireless last hop link is not considered in the route calculation. A hop count of 1 is used in the RIP protocol, and a static link cost in OSPF based on the link (usually Ethernet) connecting the APs. In multihomed MIP, IP routing is used to the care-of address selected but the selection of what care-of address to use is managed by MIP. The HA makes its own selection and the CH does the same if route optimization is used.

Before informing the HA and CHs about the current location of the MH, the MH must decide which foreign networks to register with. An MH receiving advertisements from foreign networks will monitor the available networks and calculate the deviation in arrival times. This is recorded for each sender and the networks with the smallest metric calculated from the deviation are registered at the HA. An MH is configured with the maximum number of care-of-addresses to register.

Since the MH may register multiple associations with foreign networks, the HA can have multiple bindings for an MH's home address. Based on the round trip time (RTT) between the HA and the MH, one of the care-of addresses will be installed as the tunnel end-point to the MH. The measuring of RTTs is based on the registration messages sent between the MH and the HA.

A CH sending packets to an MH without route optimization will send them to the MH's home network, where the HA will make the selection of which care-of address to use to forward the packets. With route optimization the CH will send the packets to the MH without using the HA and based on the MIP version used it will either tunnel the packets (MIPv4) or use the routing header (MIPv6). Route optimization is managed by the HA (MIPv4) or the MH (MIPv6), sending the CH information of which care-of address to use. In multihomed MIP multiple care-of addresses may be sent. The selection by the CH for which care-of address to use can be based on:

-   longest prefix match
-   the first address received
-   delay

Considering the proposal made to MIPv4 for route optimization without explicitly measuring the RTT (e.g sending ICMP echo requests) between the CH and the MH, longest prefix match and the arrival order are the options available. With the proposal for route optimization made to MIPv6 the care-of address selection made by the CH is managed the same way as by the MH. However, instead of the MH sending the RTT time delayed by one registration request, the CH itself measures the RTT by monitoring the time between sent binding refresh update messages and binding update response.

The choice of care-of address is based on individual selections by the HA, the CH and the MH for packets sent by them. In a scenario where an MH has registered three care-of addresses and there are two CHs, one using the HA to communicate with the MH and the other using route optimization, three different APs may be used: one by the HA, another by the CH using route optimization and the third by the MH to send packets (see figure 1).

The metrics for the selection of care-of address made by the HA and CH (if route optimization is managed by the MH) is based on the Jacobson/Karels algorithm [16] (se algorithm 2). A small value is preferred.

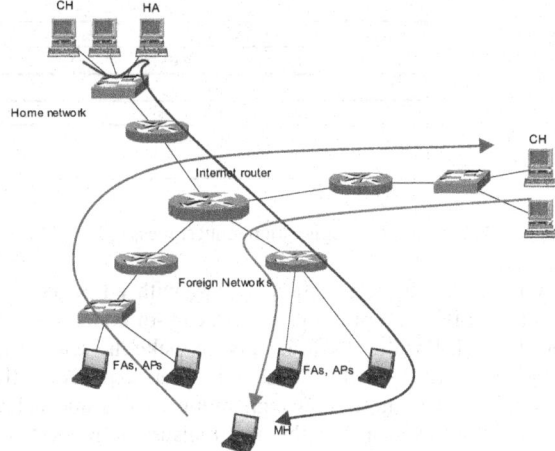

Fig. 1. A multihomed connectivity scenario where the HA, CH and MH make their own selections of which care-of address to use.

$$\text{Difference} = \text{SampleRTT} - \text{EstimatedRTT}. \tag{2}$$

$$\text{EstimatedRTT} = \text{EstimatedRTT} + (\delta \times \text{Difference}).$$

$$\text{Deviation} = \text{Deviation} + \delta(|\text{Difference}| - \text{Deviation}).$$

$$\text{Metric} = \mu \times \text{EstimatedRTT} + \phi \times \text{Deviation}.$$

To avoid rapid changes resulting in flapping of the care-of addresses and the default gateway because of metrics close in value, a new care-of address or gateway is only chosen if its value is less than the value used minus a threshold.

2.1 The Prototype

This section describes the prototype and the changes made to MIP. MIPv4 is used as the framework and the use of an FA is assumed. Route optimization is handled by MIPv4 and MIPv6 in different ways; In MIPv4 route optimization messages are sent by the HA to CHs. In MIPv6 the MH informs CHs about its address. To add this behavior to MIPv4 as well, both types of route optimization are considered.

To register a care-of address at the HA, a registration request is sent, and to enable the HA to distinguish between a non-multihomed and a multihomed registration, an N-flag is added to the registration request (see figure 2).

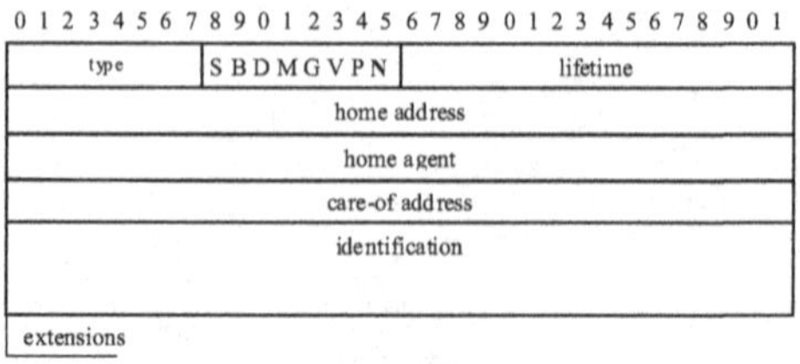

```
0 1 2 3 4 5 6 7 8 9 0 1 2 3 4 5 6 7 8 9 0 1 2 3 4 5 6 7 8 9 0 1
```

type	S B D M G V P N	lifetime
home address		
home agent		
care-of address		
identification		

extensions

Fig. 2. The modified registration request message with the added N-flag.

An HA receiving the registration request with an N-flag will keep the existing bindings for the MH. One of the registered care-of addresses will be used to forward packets to the MH. For the HA to be able to make the selection, the RTT to the MH through the different care-of addresses is measured. The MH monitors the time between registration requests and registration replies and calculates the RTT. The RTT is added as an extension in the next registration request. The HA will maintain all registrations for an MH and based on the metrics it will install a tunnel into the forwarding table with the care-of address with the smallest metrics.

With a care-of address advertised by an FA, the MH is not allowed to use the Address Resolution Protocol (ARP) [17]. This will confuse other hosts connected to the network and may cause problems when the MH disconnects and moves to another network. To avoid this in MIP, the MH monitors the MAC address in the frame containing the agent advertisement, and installs the binding between the FA's MAC address and the IP address in the ARP table, for the FA registered with. When a packet is sent using the default gateway, an entry in the ARP table will already be available and no ARP request is needed. In multihomed MIP, the MH will maintain multiple registrations with different FAs as well as keep control of available FAs not registered with. All IP addresses for the FAs are installed in the forwarding table, and the bindings between the IP and the MAC addresses are installed in the ARP table.

We propose two changes for route optimization, considering both the proposal for MIPv4 as well as how MIPv6 manages route optimization. For MIPv4 route optimization, the binding update sent from the HA to a CH is shown in figure 3. For MIP multihoming, multiple packets must be sent to inform the CH of multiple care-of addresses. The binding update is extended with an N-flag to signal multihomed binding updates. The first binding update clears the N-flag to erase the binding cache in the CH from possibly stale entries. The rest of the binding updates have the N-flag set. The CH will install a tunnel to the MH in its forwarding table based on the information in the binding updates. The decision of which care-of address to install as the tunnel end-point in the forwarding table is based on the selections described earlier. When an MH performs a handover between networks and changes from one care-of address to another, the binding update needs to express both the new and old care-of address, so that the HA and the CH knows which binding to update. In the case of a single-home binding, only the new care-of address is included.

When a binding is about to expire, CH sends a binding request message to the HA. The binding request must include the care-of address for the binding (see figure 4) so that the HA knows which binding to respond with. Without the care-of address included, binding updates are requested for all care-of addresses. An HA will respond with care-of addresses for all available bindings for an MH.

```
0 1 2 3 4 5 6 7 8 9 0 1 2 3 4 5 6 7 8 9 0 1 2 3 4 5 6 7 8 9 0 1
```

type	A I M G N reserved	lifetime
mobile host home address		
care-of address		
identification		
replaced care-of address (optional)		

Fig. 3. The modified binding update message with the added N-flag and the optional care-of address.

```
0 1 2 3 4 5 6 7 8 9 0 1 2 3 4 5 6 7 8 9 0 1 2 3 4 5 6 7 8 9 0 1
```

type	reserved
mobile host home address	
identification	
requested for care-of address (optional)	

Fig. 4. The modified binding request message with the optional care-of address that the request is sent for.

If a binding request is sent for one care-of address and multiple bindings are maintained, the binding update will have the N-flag set. This will inform the CH whether other bindings are maintained as well. If the care-of address requested in the binding request message has no binding in the HA, the HA will respond with a binding update with a lifetime set to 0.

To manage route optimization where an MN sends binding updates (instead of the HA) to the CHs as in MIPv6, the same messages is used as described above (see figures 3 and 4). The advantage of this method for route optimization is that RTT can be measured by the CH by monitoring the departure time of binding requests and the arrival of binding updates. The selection of the care-of address to install as the tunnel end-point is based on formula 2.

3 Related Work

In MIPv4, an option for simultaneous bindings is proposed for sending packets to multiple care-of addresses for an MH. Packets will be duplicated at the HA and one copy sent to each registered care-of address, so that packets can be received through multiple APs. This option was proposed to decrease the number of dropouts of packets during handover, and for an MH with bad connections to APs to receive the same packet through several APs, with an increased probability of a success. The solution does not enable the network layer to decide which connection to use and it will waste resources in the WLAN.

In the current specification of MIPv6, all traffic uses the same care-of address. This prevents the dynamics of the MIP from fully utilizing the dynamics in WLANs and should be altered.

In [18], an approach to multihoming for survivability is proposed, managed at the datalink layer and based on radio signalling. This approach restricts the selection of APs to the datalink layer and is not available to higher levels.

In [19], a transport layer protocol is proposed striping data between multiple links to achieve bandwidth aggregation. The work presented in this paper instead aims to evaluate multiple connections and how to use the best available connection(s) to forward packets.

Another transport layer solution is presented in [20] for multihomed hosts. Here the sender selects one of the host's IP addresses as the destination address for the packets. If the IP address becomes unavailable due to network failure, the protocol will switch to another IP address for the same destination host with maintained connectivity at the transport layer. The approach does not address mobility within networks and delays considering a wireless last hop link.

4 Conclusion and Future Work

The work here described extends the MIP to manage multiple simultaneous connections with foreign networks. Based on the registered care-of addresses, multiple paths can be used for packets to and from an MH. The approach will also prevent MHs from flapping between foreign networks due to the fact that an MH has similar quality of connectivity to multiple APs.

Enhanced throughput and a more reliable connection are achieved. The current prototype is based on MIPv4 but will in the next phase be deployed on MIPv6 as well.

A study will be performed on the impact of the delay between the measure of the RTT and the time the HA receives the information, since the RTT is sent one registration request later than when it was measured.

An MH can connect to multiple APs simultaneously and to manage this, the network interfaces are configured in independent BSS mode. Another option is to use two or more interface cards in infrastructure BSS mode, but still the association is made in the datalink layer. The association should be made available to higher protocol layers and provided through an Application Programmer's Interface (API). Future work will look into possible solutions to achieve this.

We are currently measuring the performance of our implementation.

References

1. Gast, M.S.: 802.11 Wireless Networks, The Definitive Guide. O'Reilly (2002)
2. Bhagwat, P.: Bluetooth Technology for Short-Range Wireless Apps. Internet Computing Volume 5, No. 3 (2001)
3. van Nee, R.D.J., Awater, G.A., Morikura, M., Takanashi, H., Webster, M.A., Halford, K.W.: New High-Rate Wireless LAN Standards. IEEE Communications Magazine, Volume 37, No 12 (1999) 82-88
4. Perkins, C.E.: Ad Hoc Networking. Addison-Wesley (2001)
5. Perkins, C.: Mobile IP. IEEE Communications Magazine (May 2002) 66-82
6. Perkins, C.: IP Mobility Support for IPv4, revised. IETF RFC3220 (2002)

7. Johnson, D.B., Perkins, C.E.: Mobility Support in IPv6. draft-ietf-mobileip-ipv6-18.txt (2002)
8. Droms R.: Automated Configuration of TCP/IP with DHCP, Volume 3, No 4. (1999) 45-53
9. Thomas, N.: Neighbour Discovery and Stateless Autoconfiguration in IPv6. IEEE Internet Computing, Volume 3, No 4. (1999) 54-62
10. Peterson, L.L., Davie B.S.: Computer Networks, a system approach, second edition. Morgan Kaufman Publisher (2000) 279-280
11. Park, K., Lee, H.: On the effectiveness of route-based packet filtering for distributed DoS attack prevention in power-law internets. Proceedings of the conference on applications, technologies, and protocols for computer communications. (2001) 15-26
12. Mockapetris, P.V., Dunlap, K.J: Development of the Domain Name System. ACM SIGCOMM Computer Communication Review, Volume 25 Issue 1 (1995) 112-122
13. RIP http://www.cisco.com/univercd/cc/td/doc/cisintwk/ito_doc/rip.htm
14. OSPF http://www.cisco.com/univercd/cc/td/doc/cisintwk/ito_doc/ospf.htm
15. Metz, C.: IP Anycast Point-to(Any) Point Communication. Internet Computing, Volume 6, No 2 (2002) 94-98
16. Peterson, L.L., Davie, B.S: Computer Networks a Systems Approach. Morgan Kaufman Publishert (2000) 391-392
17. Stevens, W.R.: TCP/IP Illustrated, Volume 1: The Protocols. Addison-Wesley (1994) 53-64
18. Dahlberg, T.A, Jung, J.: Survivable Load Sharing Protocols: a Simulation Study. Wireless Networks, Volume 7, Issue 3. (2001) 283-296
19. Hsieh, H.-Y., Sivakumar, R.: A Transport Layer Approach for Achieving Aggregate Bandwidths on Multi-homed Mobile Hosts. Mobicom (2002) 83-94
20. Stewart, R., Metz, C.: SCTP: New Transport Protocol for TCP/IP. Internet Computing Volume 5, No 6 (2001) 64-69
21. Kotz, D., Essien, K.: Analysis of a Campus-wide Wireless Network. Mobicom (2002) 107 - 118

Dynamic Proportional Delay Differentiation Scheduling over IEEE 802.11 Wireless Network

Kyungae Yoon and JongWon Kim

Networked Media Lab., Department of Information and Communication
Kwang-ju Institute of Science and Technology(K-JIST)
Gwangju, 500-712, Republic of Korea.
{kayun,jongwon}@kjist.ac.kr

Abstract. The deployment of wireless local area networks (WLANs) in corporate environments along with the increasing demand for quality of service (QoS) support create a need for controlled sharing of wireless link. To satisfy the QoS demand, an on-going standardization work of IEEE 802.11e defines modifications to IEEE 802.11 MAC (medium access control). However, existing MAC scheduling for IEEE 802.11 WLAN focuses majorly on static QoS differentiation. It does not allow the network operator to proportionally adjust QoS classes independent of network load. In this paper we propose a MAC scheduling mechanism that enables dynamic and proportional differentiation of QoS classes in terms of delay. Simulation results show that the proposed mechanism improves proportional delay differentiation in spite of network load variation.

1   Introduction

During past few years, the enormous growth of the Internet coupled with universal market demands has given sharp rises to different types of wireless and mobile services supporting real-time multimedia applications. Especially, the wide-spreading deployment of wireless local area networks (WLANs) and the emergence of wireless Internet providers create an ever-increasing need to control link sharing and support quality of service (QoS). In case of IEEE 802.11 [1], MAC (medium access control) scheduling plays a key role in delivering various QoS classes over WLAN links. In fact, an on-going standardization work of IEEE 802.11e [2] defines modification to IEEE 802.11 MAC to enable effective transport of voice/audio and video. Manipulation parameters such as backoff, inter frame space (IFS) and fragmentation size are being utilized to differentiate as in [3]. Thus, in order to deploy a high-quality low-latency continuous media transport over the IEEE 802.11 WLAN environment, an adaptive media delivery framework should be established by effectively leveraging the differentiation tools.

For wireless networks in general, recent results in MAC scheduling have shown how to achieve fairness (or weighted fairness) and how to provide relative delay differentiation of each class in the presence of link errors [6]. For example, a scheduling scheme attempts to provision each class with minimum

M.M. Freire, P. Lorenz, M.M.-O. Lee (Eds.): HSNMC 2003, LNCS 2720, pp. 244–253, 2003.
© Springer-Verlag Berlin Heidelberg 2003

bandwidth share of link capacity [8]. To provide relative class-based delay differentiation, people have proposed schedulers such as packet-based version of generalized processor sharing (GPS), class-based queuing (CBQ), and others. However, one major challenge in scheduling is that slight change in network load affects the resulting delay dramatically. Furthermore, modifications to the IEEE 802.11 WLAN have been proposed to better explore a number of differentiation mechanisms. In [3], it is concluded that the most superior scheme is to use an approach based on DIFS (distributed coordination function IFS). He applied different DIFS value to each class while keeping backoff scheme unmodified to retain the desirable stability. However, existing efforts focus majorly on providing static differentiation among QoS classes. They lack in supporting relative QoS differentiation among classes independent of network load fluctuation.

In this paper, we are addressing proportional delay differentiation scheduling that support wide range of network load dynamically. While leveraging lessons learned from previous works as much as possible, in this paper, we present a MAC scheduling mechanism that enables dynamic and proportional delay differentiation for the IEEE 802.11 WLAN environment. The proposed scheduling extends the waiting time priority (WTP) scheduling proposed in [5]. The proposed mechanism dynamically adjusts the waiting time of each class so that delay differentiation among classes can be well controlled[1].

The remainder of this paper is organized as follows. Section 3 explains the original MAC of IEEE 802.11 WLAN along with the concept of proportional differentiation service. The proposed scheduling follows in Section 4 with simulation results in Section 5. Finally we summarize paper in Section 6.

2   Differentiation Service Model over the IEEE 802.11 WLAN

2.1   IEEE 802.11 MAC and Differentiation

First we briefly present the basic access method in IEEE 802.11 MAC focusing on the commonly adopted DCF (distributed coordination function) [1]. As shown in Fig. 1 (note that this figure is for the case of IEEE 802.11e enhanced MAC), it is based on carrier sense multiple access with collision avoidance (CSMA/CA) scheme that works like a "listen before talk". A station which intends to transmit a frame must sense the medium and ensure that the medium is idle for the specified DIFS duration before transmitting. To avoid collision, CSMA/CA performs a random backoff procedure. If a station to transmit initially senses the channel to be busy, then the station waits until the channel becomes idle for the DIFS period, and then computes a random backoff time to wait before sensing again to verify a clear channel on which to transmit. If the channel becomes busy before time out, the station freezes its timer. This process is repeated until the waiting time approaches zero and the station is allowed to transmit.

---

[1] Currently, we only consider delay differentiation leaving other aspects of QoS (i.e., loss and bandwidth) to future works.

Also, in IEEE 802.11e [2], HCF (hybrid coordination function) stands for a queue-based service differentiation that combines both DCF and PCF (point coordination function) enhancements. HCF thus covers two access mechanisms: contention-based channel access tied with enhanced DCF (EDCF) for prioritized QoS and controlled channel access with polling addition for parameterized QoS. These two accesses are applied in combination during both CFP (contention free period) and CP (contention period). To enable further differentiation towards statistical QoS guarantees, IEEE 802.11 MAC is modified based on the following differentiation parameters that vary according to the associated priority levels (a.k.a., access category or class) [3]:

1. Backoff Increase Function: Each priority level has a different backoff increment function.
2. DIFS: Each priority level is assigned a different DIFS, after which it can transmit its RTS or data packet.
3. Maximum fragment size: Each priority level has a different maximum frame length allowed to be transmit at once.

For example, in IEEE 802.11e terminology, arbitration IFS (AIFS) is used. The AIFS for a given access category should be a DIFS plus some (possibly zero) time slots. Access category with the smallest AIFS will have the highest priority as shown in Fig. 1. Similarly contention window size that are linked with backoff varies, too.

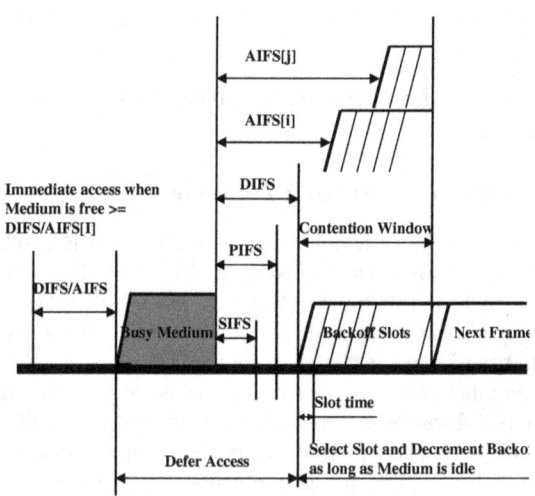

Fig. 1. Enhanced MAC access scheme for IEEE 802.11.

Note here that the scope of MAC modification in the standardization work of IEEE 802.11e is limited to protocol aspects. As a result several algorithmic issues including scheduling and admission control for HCF are open to implementation-dependent choices.

2.2   Proportional Differentiation Service Model

Now we describe the proportional differentiation service model suggested in [4][5]. For example, the differentiation can be based on appropriate pricing (i.e., higher classes are more expensive), on capacity provisioning (i.e., higher classes get more bandwidth relative to their expected loads), or on static class prioritization. However, such mechanisms cannot always provide consistent QoS differentiation, because the relative QoS differentiation among classes varies with the network loads. In a practical setting, network operators want to have something like tuning knobs through which they can adjust the QoS difference among classes. Thus, the main idea behind proportional differentiation model is that "performance metrics of certain class should be proportional to the differentiation parameter that the network operator chooses". Network performance can be measured in terms of queuing delay and loss ratio. Better class performance means lower queuing delays and/or lower loss probabilities.

In [5], it is assumed that $\tilde{q}_i(t, t + \tau)$ is the measure of performance for class i during the time interval $[t, t + \tau], \tau > 0$. Classes are ordered such that a class receives a better service than the previous classes $(< \tau)$. The following relation is defined among classes:

$$\frac{\overline{q_i(t, t + \tau)}}{q_j(t, t + \tau)} = \frac{c_i}{c_j}, \tag{1}$$

where $c_1 < c_2 < \cdots < c_N$ (if N classes are defined) are the QDPs (quality differentiation parameters). The relation $\frac{c_i}{c_j}$ between classes is called quality ratio. They remain fixed even if the quality level of each class (i.e., the class performance) changes according to the class load. These ratios express the proportional relation among classes. This model does not propose strong guarantees. It only assures that a class will receive a service that will be a fraction of the service proposed by another class. This model can be used for both delay and loss differentiation.

So far, for wireless networks, several researches have been performed on scheduling algorithms to provide relative differentiated services [7]. As discussed, in this paper, we apply this proportional model for delay differentiation. The algorithm proposed is designed in an attempt to emulate this proportional differentiation service model in [5] using WTP scheduling in IEEE 802.11 wireless network. Two issues are worth noting. First, the proposed scheme for delay differentiation can be extended to loss and others. Second, the implementation of the proposed approach involves somewhat different modification from that of [5] (to be discussed later in Section 4).

3   Dynamic Proportional Delay Differentiation Scheduling

The proposed dynamic and proportional delay differentiation relies on scheduling based on the proportional differentiation service model [5] and existing differentiation service model in the IEEE 802.11 MAC [3].

Remark 1 The dynamic and proportional delay differentiation scheduling borrows on WTP scheduling idea of transmitting the packet whose priority is highest at the head of the queue first.

Remark 2 A dynamic proportional delay differentiation scheduling approach for determining the highest priority is employed, extending the DIFS of IEEE 802.11 MAC. The essential idea is to choose a DIFS interval that is proportional to the priority of packet to be transmitted.

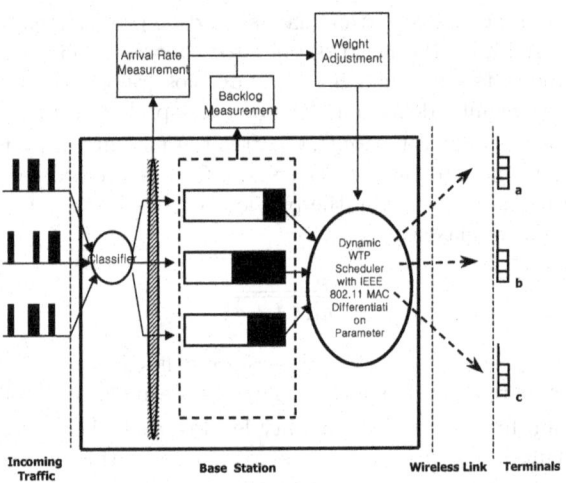

Fig. 2. Proposed delay differentiation scheduling.

Now, let's describe the proposed approach in detail. In IEEE 802.11 WLAN, a base station has a classifier, a scheduler, and a buffer manager in order to control traffic flows. The classifier classifies incoming packets into a number of classes/flows. The scheduler, which can be priority based (i.e., waiting time priority based) then serves packets based on traffic contracts of flows/classes. We employ WTP in scheduler and make modifications on it [4][5]. Here, we assume the buffer is infinite in the base station and packet drop is not considered as of now. In this extended model, we measure the arrival time of incoming packets to each class. A backlog monitor is designed to measure the amount of backlog in each class. These measurement results will feed into a process to adjust the weights of classes in the WTP scheduler. The weight of each class will be periodically updated according to the packet arrival rate and buffer occupancy. The proposed model is shown in Fig. 2.

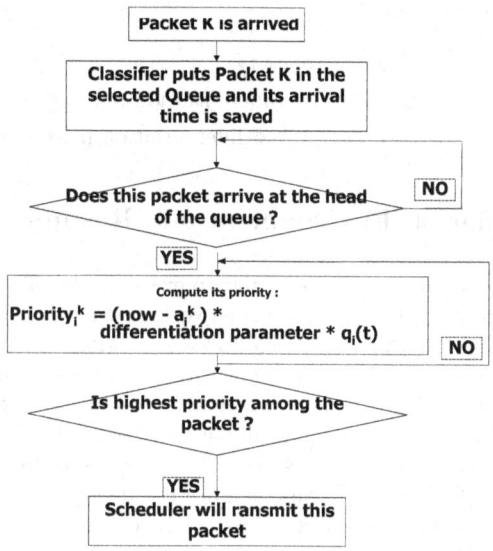

Fig. 3. Proposed scheduling algorithm extending WTP scheduler.

We suppose that class i is backlogged at time t and $w_i(t)$ is the head waiting time of class i and then normalized head waiting time of class i at time t is $w_i(t) = w_i(t) \div \delta_{i,\delta}$. Besides, every time a packet is to be transmitted, WTP scheduler selects the backlogged class j with the maximum normalized head waiting time.

$$1 = \arg \; max_{i \in B(t)} w_i(t). \tag{2}$$

Also, the described algorithm is shown in Fig. 3. When the packet k arrives, the classifier puts this packet in the selected queue i and its arrived time a_i^k is saved. When this packet arrives at the head of the queue, its priority was computed as follows.

$$priority_i^k = (now - a_i^k) \times \text{differentiation\_parameter} \times q_i(t). \tag{3}$$

Where differentiation parameters such as DIFS, backoff, fragmentation size are considered. Also, 'now' represents the current time, a_i^k is the arrival time of packet k at the head of the queue i, $(now - a_i^k)$ represents the queuing delay of packet k in the queue i, and $q_i(t)$ is the weight associated with the queue i.

The scheduler will transmit the packet with the highest priority among the packet at the head of the queue first. This scheduler meets the requirement of the proportional delay differentiation.

$$\frac{d_i}{d_j} = \frac{\delta_i}{\delta_j} \Longleftrightarrow \frac{d_i}{\delta_i} = \frac{d_j}{\delta_j}. \tag{4}$$

If the following constraints are verified, $q_i = \frac{1}{\delta_i}$. And the proportional delay differentiation equation is

$$d_i \times q_i = d_j \times q_j \Leftrightarrow$$
$$(\text{now} - a_i^k) \times \text{differentiation\_parameter} \times q_i$$
$$= (\text{now} - a_j^k) \times \text{differentiation\_parameter} \times q_j. \tag{5}$$

4   Simulation Environment and Results

Intensive simulations are conducted to examine the effectiveness and efficiency of the proposed scheduling. *NS2* network simulator is used as the simulation platform. Fig. 4 shows the network topology adopted. A base station generates data traffic to three wireless stations through wireless channel. Incoming packets are classified into three classes where class 1 is the lowest priority and class 3 is the highest priority. We assume all packets of class 1 are entered into station(0), packets of class 2 belong to station(1) and packets from class 3 are classified into station(2). Moreover, we configure the delay differentiation among classes as 4:2:1. The base station connects to three wireless stations by a full-duplex link with 5Mbps bandwidth each and 2ms delay.

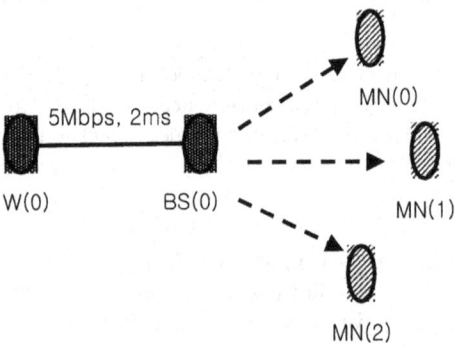

Fig. 4. Simulation topology.

To verify the performance of the original MAC in delay differentiation, source node generates CBR traffic to destination nodes in the first simulation. The traffic loads on three service classes are the same and packet size is set to be 1100 bytes for all classes. The simulation time lasts for 250 seconds. Fig. 5 shows average delay of each class for original MAC. This result shows that original MAC

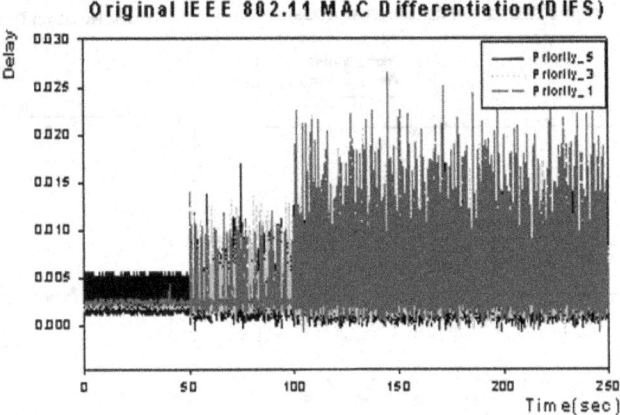

Fig. 5. Original IEEE 802.11 MAC differentiation (DIFS).

delay differentiation mechanism achieves delay differentiation of each class very well. But they are not proportional to their predefined ratios.

To show the effectiveness of the proposed approach, we test and compare the difference between average delay. Note that to emulate more realistic situation, more traffics are generated in this case. In other words, we generate different levels of load in simulation network topology as follows.

- Light load = 20 CBR connections sending 1100 byte packets at 4 packet per second.
- Heavy load = 30 CBR connections sending 1100 byte packets at 7 packet per second.

Other parameters remain the same. The results for two cases are shown and compared in Fig. 6 and Fig. 7, respectively.

Fig. 6(a) shows the result by applying original MAC delay differentiation. We can learn that the differences between the average delays of each class are not proportional to their predefined ratios. On the other hand, as shown in Fig. 6(b), the results improves a lot by employing proposed scheduling. We adjust the weights, i.e., service rates, of each class dynamically according to arrival rate and buffer occupancy so that the delay time can be more predictable and controllable. Also, the results meet the specified requirements in the traffic contracts.

Fig. 7(a) and Fig. 7(b) show the results under heavy load. By comparing these figures, we can verify that the proposed scheduling performs much better. Interestingly, under heavy load, the delay differentiation ratios among classes become more accurate, since WTP serves classes based on the predefined ratios while all classes have backlog packets.

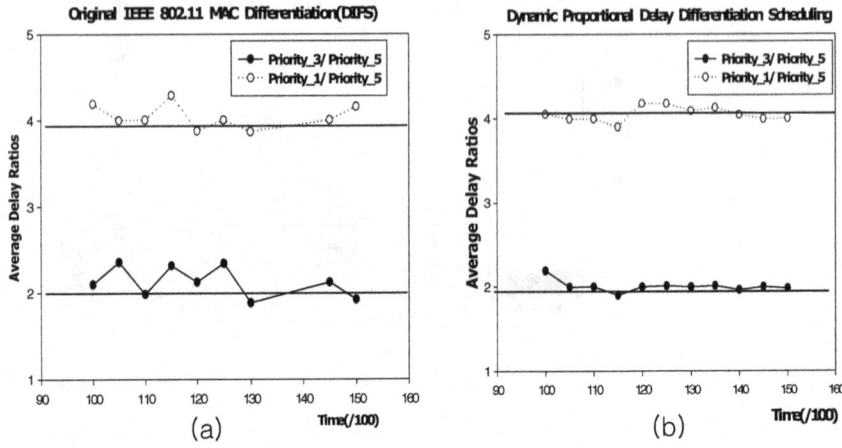

Fig. 6. Short-term delay ratios under light network load.

5   Conclusions

We presented a dynamic and proportional delay differentiation scheduling based on extension of WTP scheduling for IEEE 802.11 WLAN. By adjusting the service rate of each class dynamically according to the proportional differentiation service model, we can provide the desired differentiation independent of network fluctuation. Note however the proposed approach only illustrates the possibility of proportional differentiation. More in-depth investigation should be performed before real-world usage.

Acknowledgement

This work is supported in part by the Korea Research Foundation grant (KRF-2002-041-D00448) and in part by BK-21 program.

References

1. IEEE 802.11 standard working group, "Wireless LAN medium access control (MAC) and physical layer (PHY) specifications," (1997).
2. IEEE 802.11 standard working group, "Medium access control (MAC) enhancement for quality of service (QoS)," IEEE 802.11e/D3.0 draft, (2002).
3. I. Aad and C. Castelluccis, "Differentiation mechanisms for IEEE 802.11," in *Proc. IEEE INFOCOM '2001*, (2001).
4. C. Dovorlis and D. Stiliads, "Relative differentiated services in the Internet: Issues and mechanisms," *ACM SIGMETRICS Performance Evaluation Review*, vol. 27, no. 1, (1999), pp. 204–205.

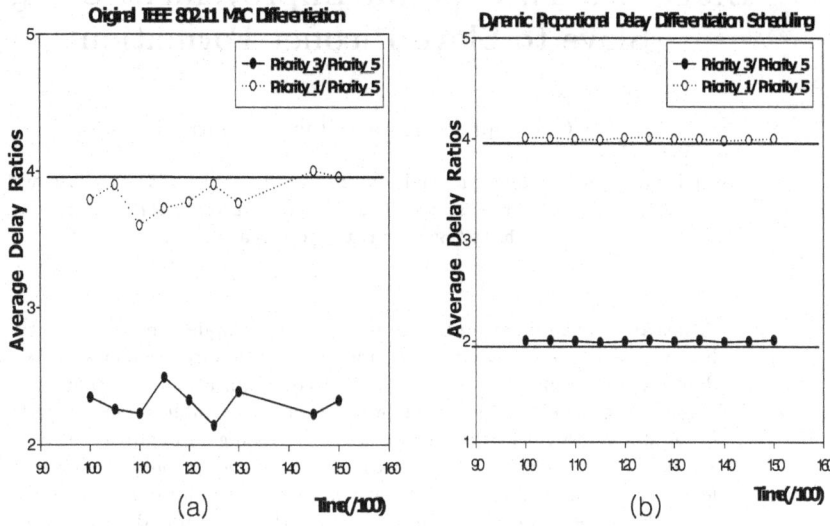

Fig. 7. Short-term delay ratios under heavy network load.

5. C. Dovorlis, D. Stiliads, and P. Ramanathan, "Proportional differentiated services: Delay differentation and packet scheduling," in *Proc. ACM SIGCOMM '99*,(1999).
6. S. Lu, V. Bharghavan, and R. Srikant, " Fair scheduling in Wireless Packet Networks," *In Proceeding of ACM SIGCOMM'97*, Cannes, France, (1997).
7. J. M. Ryong, K. Kentaro, M. Hiroyuki, and A. Tomonori, " A wireless scheduling method for relative delay differentiated service," in *Proc. Multi-Dimensional Mobile Communications, MDMC2001*, (2001), pp.310-317.
8. N. Vaidya, P. Bahl, and S. Gupta, "Distributed fair scheduling in a wireless LAN," in *Proc. ACM MOBICOM'00*, Boston, MA, (2000).
9. G. Bianchi, "Performance analysis of the IEEE 802.11 distributed coordination function," *IEEE Journal on Selected Areas in Communications*, vol. 18, no. 3, pp. 535–547,(2000).

Bluetooth Throughput Improvement Using a Slave to Slave Piconet Formation

Christophe Lafon and Tariq S. Durrani

University of Strathclyde, DSP Division, 204 george street g11xw, Glasgow UK.
`christophe@spd.eee.strath.ac.uk, durrani@strath.ac.uk`
`http//www.strath.ac.uk/eee`

Abstract. This paper addresses issues for the establishment of multi-hop ad-hoc networks based on Scatternet formation using bluetooth. We describe a new approach of inter-piconet communication. Differing from existing protocols, the design allows the slave to establish contact with other slaves present in the piconet without passing through the master. All new piconet clock synchronization will depend on only one master leader. This will increase the capacity of slave to switch from one piconet to another every slot, increasing consequently the traffic data transfer. We perform a simulation that provides evidence of improving average throughput.

1 Introduction

At the original state, all bluetooth units are in the standby, i.e. they are not associated with any piconet. A bluetooth device uses the inquiry process to discover other devices. It will learn about the identity of other units (the address is unique for each bluetooth device) and their clock phase. In the page processes, a device explicitly contacts another unit to join the piconet in which the inviting unit will become the Master and the other its Slave. After connection between Master and Slave, they communicate using a Time Division Duplex (TDD) slot structure. TDD is strict alternation of slots between the Master and Slaves. The Master can only send packets to a Slave in even slots while the Slave can only send packets to the Master in odd slots. This implies that the scheduling occurs in pairs of slots. (The channel is divided into time slots, each $625\mu s$ in length). Usually one time slot is enough to transmit a package but in some cases (when the package is longer) the package is transmitted in 3 or 5 slots. Packets can carry synchronous information (voice link) or asynchronous information (data link); in the following presentation, only data links are discussed A bluetooth piconet consists of one master up to seven slaves. Frequency hopping allows multiple concurrent Bluetooth communications within radio range of each other, without adverse effects due to interference. This facilitates high densities of communicating devices, making it possible for dozens of piconets to co-exist and independently communicate in close proximity without significant performance degradation. Co-existence and Intercommunication between piconet form a Scatternet. As a Bluetooth can participate in more than one piconet, the basic

M.M. Freire, P. Lorenz, M.M.-O. Lee (Eds.): HSNMC 2003, LNCS 2720, pp. 254–263, 2003.

idea is that the unit may act as a Share Slave in two piconets. In fact, in our schedule all different piconets part of the scatternet will be perfectly synchronize. Where the slave could be part in one piconet and for the next slot in another one. While the basic idea is simple, a number of challenging problems will be developed and solved before this becomes a reality. In Section II, we discuss the relevant research on Bluetooth Scatternet. In Section III, we propose an overview an efficient topology formation algorithm called SSPF (Slave to Slave Piconet Formation). In section IV explain all the new configuration of roles to nodes. Then see the consequence of the clock drift in such algorithm and explain how we could avoid it with a meeting point time. We provide simulation results, and analysis in Section V. Finally in Section VI, we conclude with remarks on future simulation work.

2   Related Work

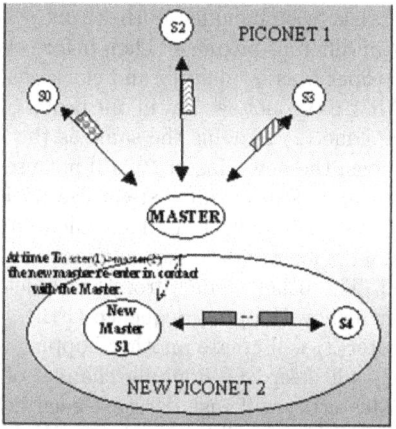

Fig. 1. Slave (S1) becomes a new master in a new Piconet.

Due to special characteristics of such networks, many theoretical and practical questions regarding the scatternet performance have been raised. Nevertheless, only a few aspect of the scatternet performance have been studied. In [5], [6], [7], the scatternet formation algorithm is introduced. In this formation, the objective is to try to reach as many as possible nodes present in the area and interconnect to each other. In our protocol, we just split the existing piconet, to form smaller piconets to ensure ease of transfer of data. This is similar to the TDD challenge in terms of performance in a Piconet as proposed by [3], [4];

where the high system throughput and fairness is determined by the scheduling TDD slots efficiency.

3   Preliminaries

3.1   Investigation to Form Two Piconet from One Piconet Schedule

In order to increase the exchange rate inside a piconet, a slave (1) will have the possibility to indicate to the Master that an important transfer will occur between itself and another Slave present in the piconet. This can be achieved by using a special bit in the payload header, (a) 1 for high traffic and, (b) 0 for low traffic. After agreement between the two Slaves and the Master, a Slave will become a Master in a new Piconet. Data are now sent by two different bandwidths, which have to goal to increase the data traffic. In order to make faster jumps between different piconets feasible, we change the bluetooth specifications to allow the new master to conserve the same phase and hopping channel as the precedent one. No guard time has to be included in the traffic scheduling to account for the slot misalignment of different piconets. Then before changing piconets, the node has to select the proper Master identity and clock offset to synchronize with the desired piconet. After a piconet switch, in our protocol, the new synchronization clock of the new Piconet(2) remains the same as the initial Master clock of the first Piconet(1). Thus, the new Master(2) will not use its Native Clock (CLKN: the clock of the current device) but instead use its Estimate Clock (CLKE: a slaves estimate of the masters clock used to synchronize the Slave device to the Master). Hence, if a device wants to switch from one piconet to another, no slot delay is generated. The other change from the bluetooth specification [1], [2], remains on the frequency Hopping Sequence (FHS). If another piconet is created, the new Master(2) will create another hopping sequence. In our schedule, the new Master(2) will keep the hopping channel of Master(1), known by all slaves. The new Master(2) will just decrease each hop frequency of Master(1) by say 10 times the Address of the slave creating the new piconet. (AM-ADDR: 3 bits address to distinguish between slave units participating in the piconets). With only seven AM-ADDR possible and with the communication channel represented by a pseudo random sequence through the 79 channel, decreasing FHS by 10 times AM-ADDR will avoid interference from the Piconet(1). For example a predictable hop sequence generated by the Master(1) between itself and Slaves could be: 32, 41, 30, 26, 36, 39 leading to a new Piconet(2) hopping sequence with AM-ADDR=1 : $(32-10*1) \rightarrow$ 22, 31, 20, 16, 26, 29 generated by Master(2) (Slave 1). Figure 2 illustrates this example. A meeting time Tmaster(1)$\rightarrow$master(2) will be chosen and explain later on to allowed the master S1 to re-enter in contact with the Master to exchange information. To increase the performance of this schedule, the new master will enter in discovering communication (Inquiry and Page nodes in the area). Then previous Slaves will be in both piconets with the same clock time phase but with different FHS to avoid any interference.

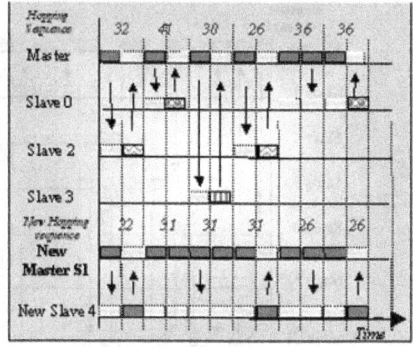

Fig. 2. Slots traffic of 5 Slaves sharing both Piconet.

4   Performance Evaluation of Scatternet Formation Protocol

All Slaves listen to one Master and during the next slot perform a new hops frequency to listen to the other Master. Slaves can switch quickly from one Master to the other in only one slot time, due to clock synchronisation between the two piconets. For example using the TDD scheme, if Slaves 2 and 3 do not receive data on the even slot from the Master, instead of entering in sleep mode on the next odd slot, they can switch to the other piconet and listen to the Master(2). They perform it by decreasing their initial FHS by 10 and enter directly to the new piconet. Thus as shown in figure 4, if Slave 4 receives data from Master(1), it will reply to Master(1) on the next odd slot keeping the same FHS. At the same odd slot, all slaves listen to Master(2), and Master(2) can talk to Slave 5 without interfering with other communications. Slave 5 will reply to

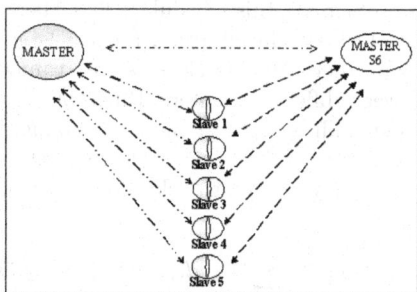

Fig. 3. Configuration of 5 Slaves sharing both Piconets.

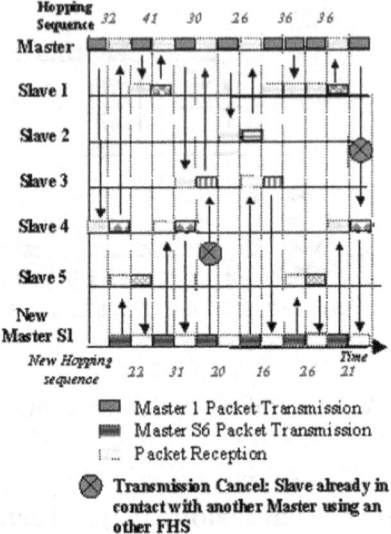

Fig. 4. New Slot Traffic with Slaves switching between both piconets.

master NMS1 and the other Slave will switch to Piconet1. In case Master(1) is already in communication with Slave 3, Master(2) cannot contact Slave 3, its transmission will be cancel without collision (not the same FHS), thus Master(2) will wait until the next even slot to transmit data to Slave 3. The same case could happen with Master(1). Traffic priority is made from the first packet send on the piconet.

4.1   Inconvenient of This Protocol

One of the major problems of this schedule is that Master(1) and Master(2) needs to have the same clock synchronisation. Each master has a clock determining the timing of its piconet. As this clock is free running, the clock speed may differ slightly between different Masters. Bluetooth allows a clock drift of max: ± 20 ppm (parts per million) against the ideal timing during activity. Thus two piconets may drift against each other with up to 40 ppm in active mode. The absolute packet transmission timing of slot boundary must fulfill the equation(1).

$$T_k = [\sum_{i=1}^{k}(1 + d_i)T_N] + jk + offset \qquad (1)$$

Where TN is the nominal slot length ($625\mu s$), jk denotes jitter ($|jk| \leq 1\mu s$) at slot boundary k, and, dk, denotes the drift $|dk| \leq 20$ppm within slot k. The jitter and drift may vary arbitrarily within the given limits for every slot, while offset is an arbitrary but fixed constant. The typical value the mutual clock drift of Bluetooth devices could be up to 40 ppm (parts per million. Thus the master has to send packets to the slaves at least every 0.25 seconds in order to synchronize them to the piconet, since the size of the slave's receive window in active mode is $10\mu s$. If we assume that the master sends packets to the Slaves in the piconet more frequently than 0.25 seconds, the receive window can be smaller than 10 μs: (0:25 s * 40 ppm = $10\mu s$). To avoid this, a meeting time is

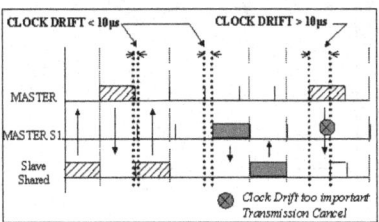

Fig. 5. Description of Clock Drift.

required between the two Masters to permit at Master(1) to readjust its clock from Master. The rendezvous point, is a pre-arranged slot that both Masters agree. After establishing the rendezvous point it will be periodically honoured for the duration of the connection. Rendezvous points are supported in the bluetooth specification [1] [2] by using the sniff mode. Rendezvous point allows the easy development and application of inter-piconet scheduling algorithms (IPS).

4.2   Advantage of This Scatternet Protocol

Since an extra piconet is formed, Slaves will have two different bandwidths to transfer heavy data. They could easily switch from one piconet to another every slot time. This will result in more fluid traffic compare to a Single Piconet Formation (SPF). Another significant advantage of this schedule allows Master to communicate to Master, in case one Master loses communication with a slave, the other Master will have the possibility to reach the concerned Slave and continue the communication by forwarding the data; which is impossible via a SPF schedule.

5   Simulation

In order to evaluate the performance of our approach, a bluetooth simulation has been developed with the use of the Network Simulator (NS-2) [8] and the Bluehoc patch [7], developed by IBM Labs in India. The Bluehoc package allows the modeling and performance assessment of various TCP/IP-based applications running over Bluetooth connections. However, in Bluehoc, the applications send traffic only in the Master to Slave direction and the scatternet formation has been developed only with the Hold mode under Bluescat [9].

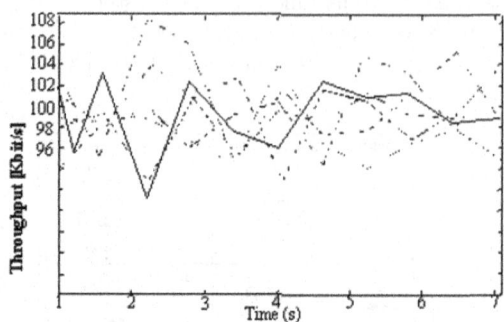

Fig. 6. Throughput for all Slaves sharing both Masters.

5.1   Performance Evaluation

The ACL link allows the use of 1, 3 or 5 slots data packets. In symmetric data efficiency depends on the number of slots it occupies. In type DH1 (with no FEC coding data transmission), which represent 1 slot time, the throughput is 173Kb/s. For DH3 (3 slots) 384 Kb/s, and for DH5 (5 slots), the most efficiency is 432 Kb/s. The packet type is determined through a random distribution leading to an average throughput of 330 Kbits/sec. If seven slaves are presents in the piconet, the performance of the symmetric throughput will be divided by 7 which gives us an average of 47 Kbits/s for each slave in a Single Piconet Formation. For example, to improve throughput, one Slave (s7) will enter into communication with other slaves present in the piconet. At the beginning the Master will send packets between all its slaves to inform the presence of a new piconet forming by slave 7, having the same clock time and a decreasing hop frequency of 70 for each FHS. Then all Slaves will proceed to enter the new Piconet(2) by still remaining in Piconet(1). Both Masters will decide a meeting point to readjust their time clock synchronisation. In our case the meeting time will occur every 0.125sec (200 slots) for an average data transfer of 33Kbit/s. This will have the advantage of Slaves belongs to two piconets, thus two bandwidths to share, except when the two masters communicate together. Consequently two times one sixth of this throughput, (100Kbits/s) per slave, is expected from a fair distribution of bandwidth, which is a noticeable increase compare to the SPF (47 Kb/s). Results are shown for simulation runs lasting 6 seconds of traffic. We simulate bi-directional CBR data transfer between Master-Slaves, with regard to the traffic

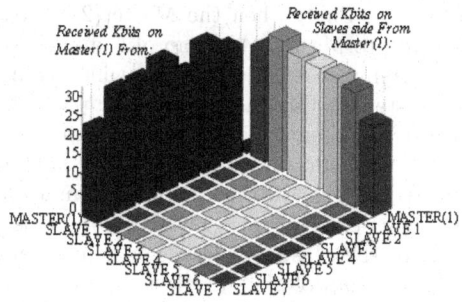

Fig. 7. Number of Bits Sent and Received For all devices using SPF during 1sec.

generated. We assume all slaves are in communication mode after 1 second. All nodes remain connected and no data transfer failed (only when both Master communicate to the same slave). Figure 6 shows the throughput of all slaves

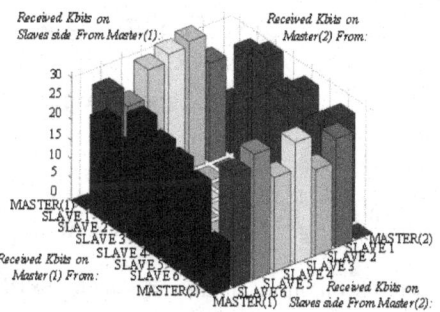

Fig. 8. Number of Bits Sent and Received for all devices using SSPF during 1sec.

sharing both Piconets. The bandwidth is distributed in a fair manner among the six links. All nodes present have an average throughput around 99Kbits. Figure 7 and 8 show two graphs comparing the number of bits transmitted between Masters to Slaves during one second, figure 7 using SPF, and figure 8 using the SSPF schedules. We can clearly see the contribution of Master(2) to increase the number of transmit and receive packets at all nodes. In addition, Figure 9 compares the two different schedules, where the SSPF significantly increases the overall throughput of all the nodes. Numerical throughput values obtained from longer simulation (Not depicted here) show that the maximum average rate of 660 Kbits/s is not reached. They actually reaches 641Kbits/s. This decrease

is due to two reasons. First, when the Master(2) leaves or comes back to its
Master role to listen to Master(1), a gap of slots are lost. Secondly, when the
Master wants to communicate to one Slave, which is already transferring data
with the other Master. In this case the Master packets will not interfere with
the other piconet transmission, different hop frequency, but will lost two slots
before reaching the next odd slot, where it will be able to transmit again to the
Slaves (Not depicted here) show that the maximum average rate of 660 Kbits/s
is not reached. They actually reaches 641Kbits/s. This decrease is due to two
reasons. First, when the Master(2) leaves or comes back to its Master role to
listen to Master(1), a gap of slots are lost. Secondly, when the Master wants
to communicate to one Slave, which is already transferring data with the other
Master. In this case the Master packets will not interfere with the other piconet
transmission, different hop frequency, but will lost two slots before reaching the
next odd slot, where it will be able to transmit again to the Slaves.

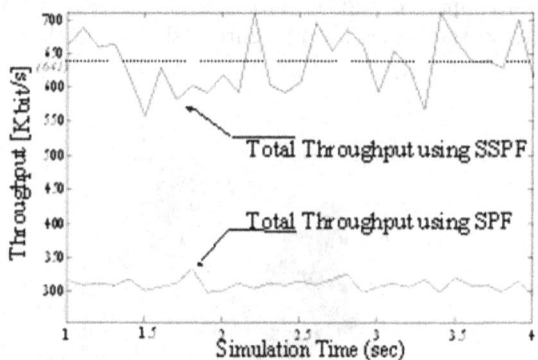

Fig. 9. Total Throughput at all nodes using SSPF and SPF Schedule.

It is clear that the probability of this transmission failing will increase as the
number of Slaves decrease. Figure 10 shows and confirm this characteristic by
comparing the total throughput function of the number of slaves sharing the two
piconets. It is clear that the throughput is improving over 75% in a configuration
of two Masters sharing more than two slaves comparing to SPF.

6   Conclusion and Further Work

This paper has described a scatternet formation algorithm SSPF for small networks constructed for devices communicating using bluetooth. The method is
specially designed to facilitate inter-piconet scheduling. We have introduced a
new scatternet algorithm to obtain a significant improvement in throughput.

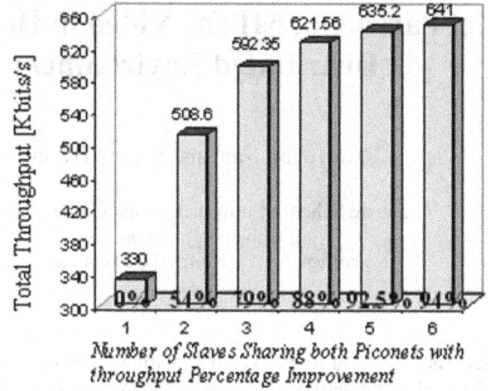

Fig. 10. Percentage of throughput improvement using SSPF depending on Number of Slave Shared.

Our simulations show that scatternet structure and inter-piconet communication have significant impact on the fluidity of traffic compared to a single piconet model. The work is the first approach towards scatternet performance with a small number of devices (8). The simulations show that the throughput increases with the number of Slaves present in the piconet, and it will be important to look at scatternet formation for an higher number of devices.

References

1. Specification of the Bluetooth System, Ver.1.1. February 22:
   http://www.bluetooth.com
2. Bluetooth Special Interest Group: http://www.bluetooth.com.
3. Kalia,M.,Bansal,F.,Shorey,R.:MAC SchedulingPolicies for Power Optimizations in Bluetooth: A Master Driven TDD Wireless System IEEE Vehicular Technology Conference 2000, Tokyo, Japan.
4. Johansson,N.,Alriksson,F.,Jonsson,U.: JUMP Mode A Dynamic Window-Based Scheduling Framework for Bluetooth Scatternets, SwitchLab, Ericsson Research 2001.
5. Tan,G.,Miu,G.,Guttag,J.,Balkrishnan,H.: Forming Scatternets From Bluetooth Personal Area Networks, MIT Laboratory October 2001.
6. Law,C.,Siu,K-I: A Bluetooth Scatternet Formation Algorithm, Massachusetts Institute of Technology, IEEE Symposium on Ad Hoc Wireless Networks 2001, San Antonio, Texas, USA, November 2001.
7. Bluehoc: Bluetooth performance evaluation tool.
   http://oss.software.ibm.com/developerworks/opensource/bluehoc/
8. Network Simulator (NS): version 2.1b8a Manual. In http://www.isi.edu/nsnam/
9. Bluescat: Bluetooth scatternet scenario in NS.
   http://www.IBM.com/developworks/oss/cvs/bluehoc/bluescat0.6/bluescat/src/

Parallel Parsing of MPEG Video in Heterogeneous Distributed Environment

Yunyoung Nam and Eenjun Hwang

Graduate School of Information and Communication,
Ajou University, Suwon, Korea
{youngman, ehwang}@ajou.ac.kr

Abstract. As the use of digital video is getting popular, there is an increasing demand for efficient retrieval of video. To do that, effective video indexing should be incorporated. One of the most fundamental steps in video indexing is decompose video stream into shots and scenes by parsing. Generally, it takes long time to parse video by traditional sequential computers due to the huge amount of computation. In order to solve this problem and speed up the process, we propose three different parallel scheduling algorithms for heterogeneous distributed multicomputers and compare their performance using extensive simulations. We report some of the results in terms of speedup and load balancing.

1 Introduction

Last few years have witnessed explosive growth in the usage of digital media. Especially, digital video is increasingly popular with the advent of high-speed networks, powerful yet cheap computers, and various compression standards. With this explosive growth, there has been a steady demand to store, index, and retrieve digital video efficiently.

Digital video requires more storage and network bandwidth than traditional data. To relieve this resource requirements, digital compression standards for video has been developed by the Moving Pictures Experts Group (MPEG) [1] committee. There are currently several MPEG standards: MPEG-1, MPEG-2, MPEG-4, and MPEG-7. MPEG-1 is the standard on which such products as Video CD and MP3. MPEG-2 is for digital television such as DVB/ATSC and digital storage such as DVD. MPEG-4 is for the standard for multimedia for the fixed and mobile web, adopts object-based coding approach fitting many applications. MPEG-7 is the standard for description and search of audio and visual content by using Descriptors (D) and Descriptor Schemes (DS). The MPEG video is the basis of many current and future communications and multimedia applications such as Video-On-Demand (VOD), Movie-On-Demand (MOD), Digital Video Disc (DVD), High Definition Television (HDTV), and Digital Library.

---

* This work was supported by grant No. R05-2002-000-01224-0 from the Basic Research Program of the Korea Science & Engineering Foundation.

M.M. Freire, P. Lorenz, M.M.-O. Lee (Eds.): HSNMC 2003, LNCS 2720, pp. 264-274, 2003.

Although digital video has many advantages over conventional analog video, including bandwidth, compression, and ease of manipulation, few systems that can index, browse, and search large volumes of video efficiently. To advance the technology of indexing and retrieval of visual information in large archives, content-based indexing would complement the text-based search. Multimedia systems must successfully combine digital video and audio, text animation, graphics and knowledge about such information units and their interrelationships in real time [12].

One of the challenges in digital video processing is to decompose a video sequence into elementary parts (shots and objects). We consider a video sequence a collection of shots, where a shot is a group of frames, and each frame is composed of objects. A shot is a sequentially recorded set of frames representing a continuous action in time and space by a single camera. There are two video segmentation techniques, which are temporal segmentation and spatial segmentation. The temporal segmentation generally refers to finding shot boundaries, where various edit efforts such as cuts, dissolves, fades, and wipes are used. The usually spatial segmentation corresponds to extracting of visual objects from each frame and tracking them (e.g. face detection, edge detection, text extraction). For the segmentation, it is necessary to compute content-based indexing features for the extracted shots, scenes, or objects. Some of the visual features are based on color histograms, representative color frames, types of camera motion directions.

Since the use of video structure enables faster access than an unstructured raw video data, video parsing (i.e. temporal segmentation and spatial segmentation) plays an important role. However, traditional sequential algorithms take a lot of time in parsing video due to the huge amount of computation. Particularly, the discrete cosine transform (DCT), the motion estimation (ME), and motion compensation (MC) are computationally intensive. For example, MPEG-1 video (3477 frames, 320 × 240 pixels, IBPBPBPBPBPBPP pattern) took 1,086 seconds to detect shot boundaries on SUN Sparc Ultra-60 by one of the sequential algorithm was developed. Namely, we had to process 3.4 frames per second.

Real-time processing is required for many applications such as HDTV and digital library. However, some applications may require "faster-than-real-time" performance. For example, suppose one wanted to analyze 1,000,000 video titles in a digital library. If each title requires one hour for parsing, it would require more than 100 years to complete the project using real-time analysis. "Faster-than-real-time" analysis could reduce this process to several months [8].

In this paper, we propose three different scheduling algorithms for parallel parsing of MPEG video in a heterogeneous distributed environment, which all reduced the parsing time a lot.

The rest of this paper is organized as follows. Section 2 gives an overview of the MPEG compression, video parsing, and parallel video parsing. Section 3 shows parallel video parsing model. In section 4, we describe three different scheduling strategies, and show that they can reduce the parsing time a lot. Section 5 presents some of the experimental results and finally, the last section concludes this paper and discusses future work.

2 Related Works

2.1 MPEG Overview

Each MPEG video sequence consists of a series of Groups of Pictures (GOP). A GOP is composed of a sequence of pictures (frames). A picture is subdivided into slices, each of which defines a fragment of a row in the picture. A slice is made up of a series of macroblocks, and a macroblock is composed of 6 blocks for 4:2:0 video material. MPEG video compression relies on two basic techniques: block-based motion compensation for reduction of temporal redundancy and DCT-based compression for the reduction of spatial redundancy. The motion information is computed using 16 × 16 pixel blocks (called macroblock) and is transmitted with the spatial information. As mentioned earlier, a macroblock contains 6 blocks, which are 4 blocks for luminance (Y) and 2 blocks for chrominance (U and V). The Y content is broken up to 4 blocks of 8 × 8 pixels, and both the U and V planes are made up of 8 × 8 pixels.

MPEG divides the compressed video frames into three types: I-frame, P-frame, and B-frame. I-frame, the intra-coded frame, is encoded without reference to other frames, exploiting only the spatial correlation within a frame. P-frame, the predictive-coded frame, is encoded using motion compensated prediction from a past I-frame or P-frame. The bidirectionally-predictive coded frame, or B-frame, requires both past and future reference frames (I-frame or P-frame) for motion compensation. I-frame has the highest data rate and the lowest motion artifacts. The typical data rate of an I-frame is 1 bit per pixel while that of a P-frame is 0.1 bits per pixel and for a B-frame, 0.015 bits per pixel. Obviously, the use of P-frame and B-frame yields a much lower data rate.

Frames of the MPEG video sequence are compressed as an I, P, or B-frame. This pattern of I, P, and B-frame usually repeats itself throughout the video sequence. An example of a pattern of frames is IBBPBBPBBI. MPEG video sequence, several consecutive frames are combined to form a structure known as a GOP. By definition, a GOP must contain at least one I-frame. The first frame must be an I-frame or a B-frame, and the last frame in a GOP must be an I-frame or P-frame. If the first frame is an I-frame or a B-frame that does not depend on the frames of the previous GOP, then the GOP is defined as a closed GOP and it can be decoded independently.

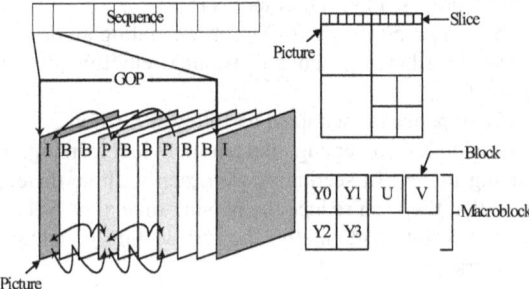

Fig. 1. An example of a video sequence with the I-frames, P-frames, and B-frames

2.2 Video Parsing

Video parsing refers to video segmentation such as the detection of shot/scene changes, special effects, camera motion. Video segmentation is composed of temporal segmentation and spatial segmentation.

The temporal segmentation, or shot change detection, involves identifying the frames where a transition takes place from one shot to another. In case this change occurs between two frames, it is called a cut or a break [13].

Examples of transitions that occur gradually over several frames include fades, dissolves, wipes, and other special effects in the video stream. These shots may be further classified according to the camera motion such as pans and zooms.

Segmentation using macroblock information exploits the inter-frame coherence that exists in a video stream. This technique can be applied to any type of MPEG sequence consisting of I, P, and B-frames. Any algorithm employing pure DCT information can be used to detect the shot changes.

As mentioned before, an MPEG stream contains I, P, and B-frames. If a P-frame contains primarily intra-coded macroblocks, this suggests that these macroblocks could not be predicted from the previous reference frame, and that there is a very high probability of a shot change having occurred somewhere between the previous I/P-frame and the current P-frame. If in a B-frame, majority of the macroblocks is forward predicted from the previous I/P-frame, then there is a high probability that a shot change will occur between the current frame and the next I/P-frame. If majority of the macroblocks in a B-frame is backward predicted, then the probability of a shot change having occurred between the previous I/P-frame and the current frame is high. Within any two reference frames, the B-frames on either side of a shot change must behave according to these observations. That is, for all B-frame prior to the shot change, the first observation must hold true, and for all B-frames after the shot change, the second observation must hold true. The tests for the presence of these features are employed in the detection process.

2.3 Parallel Video Parsing

The units of parallel parsing could be slice, frame, or GOP as follows [6] [12] [14].

•Slice-level approach: The scan process puts the slices in a task queue. The worker processes grab the slices, decode them and compute the sum of the DC values in the macroblock. All processes working on the same frame coordinate or communicate with each other.

•Frame-level approach: The worker processes gets n adjacent frames. If process does not have I-frame or P-frame, it must be communicate with other processes.

•GOP-level approach: If GOP is closed, each process does not need to communicate with others. Since the GOP is independent of other frame, the results can be handled easily.

The GOP-level approach takes low communication overhead than the other two approaches. Many researchers have reported that the GOP-level speedup is higher than slice-level and frame-level speedup [12] [14]. In this paper, we used the GOP-level approach for better performance.

3 Parallel Video Parsing Model

This section describes overall system architecture for parallel video parsing, which takes a classic master-slave model. In the figure 2, the system is composed of network storage, one master and several slaves. The network storage may take hierarchical architecture not only to store digital video, but also to support proper organization and management [11]. The master is operated by a scheduler that manages tasks and slaves. The scheduler has three queues: input queue, output queue, and slave queue. The input queue is for delivering tasks to slaves and output queue is for storing the parsing results from slaves. The slave queue stores the information about slaves.

The master is responsible for preparing parsing units and communicating with slaves for parallel processing. The slaves communicate with the master for acquiring a parsing unit and return the result. The master reads a video sequence from the disk into the memory. The video is then scanned for splitting into parsing units. In the meantime, video information such as frame size, number of GOP, average bit-rate is extracted. The parsing units are placed into the input queue. The slave reads a parsing unit from the input queue and performs the segmentation using a parsing algorithm. The segmentation results by the slaves are placed into the output queue. However, the order of parsing units in the output queue could be different from that in the input queue due to the different performance of slaves (see section 4). Therefore, parsing units in the output queue should be rearranged for the correct ordering. It may happen that some slaves do not respond to the master request, nor return the results. To handle such cases, we incorporated the time-out mechanism. That is, if the time expires, the master closes connection to the corresponding slave and assigns the task to another slave.

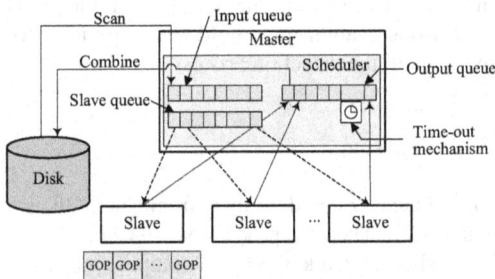

Fig. 2. The Overall System Architecture

4 Scheduling Algorithms

In this section, we introduce three different scheduling algorithms for efficient video parsing. They are Round Robin, Size-Adaptive Round Robin, and Dynamic Size-Adaptive Round Robin scheduling algorithm. In addition, we explain about our policy on the workload distribution and communication between master and slaves.

4.1 Round Robin

Round Robin scheduling is one of the simplest, fairest and most widely used scheduling algorithms. Figure 3 represents the Round Robin scheduling. As mentioned in the
previous section, all runnable slaves are kept in a slave queue. The scheduler goes
around this queue, allocating tasks to each slave for a time interval of one quantum.
The scheduler picks up the first task from the slave queue, sets a timer for interrupt-
ing, and dispatches the task to the slave.

For example, suppose we have one master (M) and three slaves (S_1, S_2, S_3) as in
figure 3. When S_1 is communicating with M, the other slaves are waiting. If S_1 finishes communication with M at time T+i (i>0), S_2 and then S_3 will communicate M
according to the order in the queue. However, since S_3 finishes computation first, S_3
sends back the result to M.

If one slave takes more time than others, it will cause other slaves to stay idle. In
addition, if no slaves send results, it will cause to take more time than optimal time. In
order to solve this problem, Round Robin scheduling must be improved. We will
describe improved Round Robin scheduling in next section.

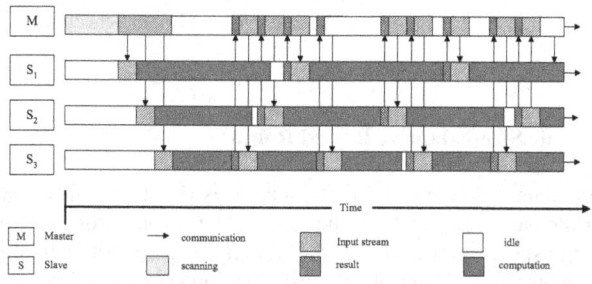

Fig. 3. Round Robin Scheduling

4.2 Size-Adaptive Round Robin Using Sampling

Slaves may show different response time depending on their performance. For example, the response time can be affected by factors such as CPU clock, the number of
processors, memory size. In addition, slaves may have different network bandwidth
in heterogeneous network environment. However, the master cannot know these
factors, It just prepares fixed-size tasks and allocates them to the slaves. Due to this
reason, the Round Robin scheduling suffers from performance down fall. To improve
this situation, slave's performance and network bandwidth should be considered. This
is the main motivation of Size-Adaptive Round Robin scheduling.

Figure 4 shows the Size-Adaptive Round Robin scheduling. The master distributes
a small sample video stream of equal size to all the slaves. When the master received
the results from the slaves, it can estimate the performance and network bandwidth of
the slaves. Using this estimation, the master splits the video stream into different size
of parsing unit and distributes them to slaves.

The Size-Adaptive Round Robin scheduling is more efficient than the Round Robin scheduling. However, both master and slave may be idle due to lack of data. At the master, idle time may be avoided by using load-balancing technique. At the slaves, they are idle while other slaves preempt or communicate with the master. This idle time can sometimes be avoided by structuring a program so that the slaves perform other computation while waiting for the master.

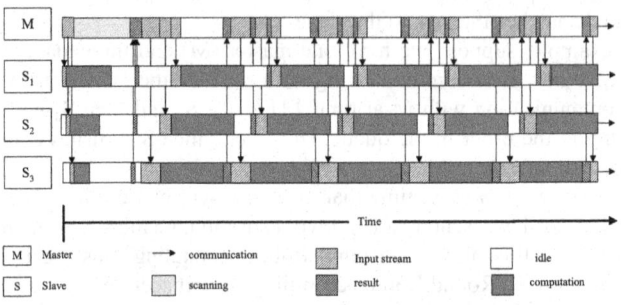

Fig. 4. Size-Adaptive Round Robin Scheduling

4.3 Dynamic Size-Adaptive Round Robin

In the previous algorithm, the first problem is due to the fact that the master itself waits for the parsed results from the slaves. The second problem arises main from the fact that the slave itself waits for the master to receive the parsing data. In order to solve these problems, a non-blocking strategy must be considered.

For the master, sufficient number of slaves could solve the first problem of idle time at the master. Unfortunately, an excessive number of processors are useless and waste of resources, because it causes a large number of slaves to stay idle. The sampling makes an initial estimate on the slaves' computational workload and network bandwidth at first; it adjusts each job size. When the master stays idle, the scheduler increases the number of slaves or the master execute a parsing task. When a lot of slaves stay idle, the scheduler decreases the number of slaves in low performance order. As a result, It adjusts the number of slaves accordingly. This can reduce idle time and minimize redundant or wasted effort in the slave.

5   Experiments

In this chapter, we describe several experiments we performed and show some of the results. In the experiments, SUN Sparc Ultra-60 and 10 slave machines connected via Ethernet performed. Also, the slaves have a different computation performance and network throughput; it is varied from 0.8 GHz to 1.8 GHz for the CPU clock and from 10Mbps to 100Mbps for network bandwidth. That is to say, the machines are typically heterogeneous distributed multicomputers.

Table 1. Test MPEG video sequences characteristics

Sequence	Format	Frames	Resolution (pixels)	Keys/ GOPs	File size (Kbyte)
News1	MPEG-1	3477	320 × 240	298	19,730
News2	MPEG-1	5158	320 × 240	308	29,296
Music Video	MPEG-4	6413	640 × 360	54	68,898
Sports	MPEG-4	11756	640 × 480	131	126,996
Movie	MPEG-4	195934	640 × 480	3568	737,165

In order to compare the performance of three scheduling algorithms, we chose five different video sequences, which are compressed using MPEG-1 or MPEG-4. In addition, these sequences are stored in RAID (redundant array of inexpensive disks) storage system. Table 1 summarizes features of these video sequences.

In the table, News1 has 12 frames per GOP with the frame pattern of IBPBPBPBPBPP. On the other hand, a sequence of News2 had 18 frames per GOP, which had a frame pattern of IBBPBBPBBPBBPBBPBB. The other three Sequences were compressed using MPEG-4 with 120, 90, 72 frames per key frame respectively.

Generally, communications among heterogeneous computers are achieved using compatible data representations and message-passing protocols. In our system, we used XML (Extensible Markup Language) [2] for data representations and SOAP (Simple Object Access Protocol) [2] for message-passing protocols. SOAP is a light-weight protocol for exchange of information in a distributed environment. It is an XML based protocol, which acts as a glue between heterogeneous software components. SOAP can potentially be used with a variety of other protocols.

We define the execution time of a parallel program as the time that elapses from when the first slave starts executing a task to when the last slave completes execution. This definition may not be entirely adequate for a timeshared parallel computer but suffices for our purposes. During the execution, each slave is computing, communicating, or idling, as illustrated in figure 3 and 4. T_{comp}^i, T_{comm}^i, and T_{idle}^i are the time spent computing, communicating, and idling, respectively, on the ith slave. Hence, the total execution time T can be defined.

(i)   as the sum of computation, communication, and idle times on an arbitrary processor j. That is

$$T = T_{comp}^j + T_{comm}^j + T_{idle}^j \qquad \qquad (1)$$

(ii)   as the sum of these times over all processors divided by the number of processors P. That is,

$$T = \frac{1}{P}(T_{comp} + T_{comm} + T_{idle})$$
$$= \frac{1}{P}(\sum_{i=0}^{P-1} T_{comp}^i + \sum_{i=0}^{P-1} T_{comm}^i + \sum_{i=0}^{P-1} T_{idle}^i)$$
$$(2)$$

Figure 5 shows the computation, communication, and idle times of slaves to detect shot boundaries for News2 using the Round Robin scheduling algorithm. As the number of machines increases, the amount of time required to parse video sequence decreases with minimum at eight machines. A single machine took 221.2 seconds by the sequential parsing. However, total parsing time was 30.5 seconds for the eight machines using the parallel parsing. This indicates that parallel parsing was about 7.1 times faster than sequential parsing. Total parsing time of six machines is longer than that of five machines, because any slaves may be idle due to the lack of data. Over eight machines, total parsing time increased linearly, because excessive slaves wasted resources and causes other slaves to stay idle. Therefore, eight was optimal number of slaves in this case.

To evaluate the performance of the presented scheduling algorithms, we used two measures: speedup and efficiency, where

$$speedup = \frac{time\ for\ sequential\ parsing}{time\ for\ parallel\ parsing} \tag{3}$$

$$efficiency = \frac{speedup\ for\ N\ machines}{N} \tag{4}$$

Figure 6 shows the speedup where several different video sequences and Round Robins scheduling were used. As we can see, News2 was parsed up to 7.1 faster using eight machines, and music video was parsed to 7.3 faster using ten machines. The parallel video parsing yielded more than seven times faster than sequential video parsing in all cases.

Figure 7 indicates the speedup and the efficiency when both Round Robin and Size-Adaptive Round Robin scheduling were used for the MPEG-4 movie. As we can see, the Size-Adaptive Round Robin scheduling (SARR) performed better than Round Robin scheduling (RR). In figure 7(a), the speedup is nearly linear to the number of machines and the Size-Adapted Round Robin scheduling achieves very good speedup. When the number of machines were eleven, the speedup of the Round Robin was 7.0 and the Size-Adaptive Round Robin scheduling yielded a 7.6 times better speedup than sequential parsing. In addition, the Size-Adapted Round Robin scheduling works much more efficiently as shown in figure 7(b). However, the speedup will not improve beyond the optimal number of machines as we can see from figure 6. This is mainly because excessive machines cause too much communication and idle time.

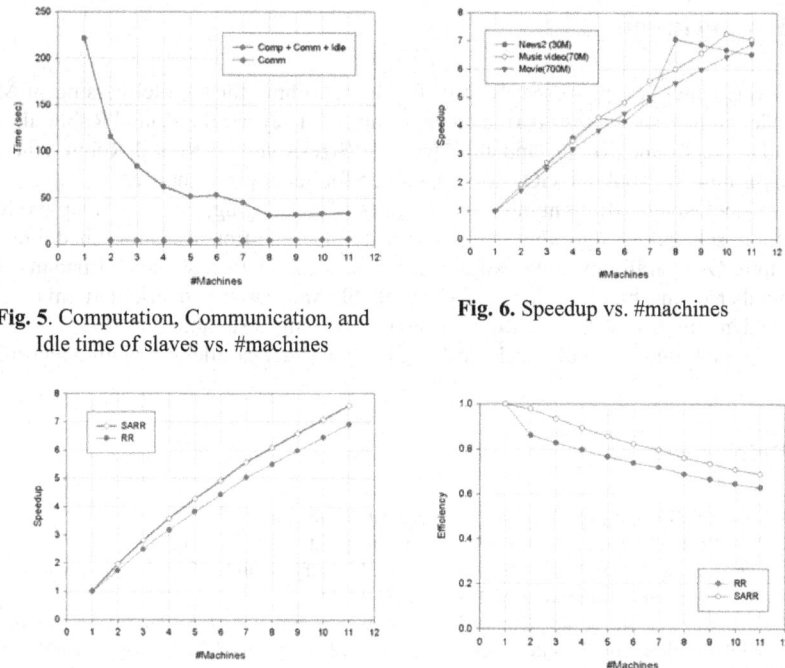

Fig. 5. Computation, Communication, and Idle time of slaves vs. #machines

Fig. 6. Speedup vs. #machines

(a) Speedup vs. #machine

(b) Efficiency vs. #machines

Fig. 7. Speedup and Efficiency vs. #machine

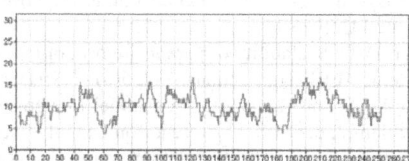

Fig. 8. #machines vs. Time (available slave machines are 20)

Figure 8 shows the number of slaves involved according to time with the Dynamic Size-Adaptive Round Robin scheduling. If some of the machines have low perform-ance and network bandwidth, it will take long time to complete video parsing. There-fore, the master would look for more volunteer machines in order to achieve in the parsing and reduce the number of slow machines. On the other hand, if some of the machines have high performance and network bandwidth, the master would maintain the fast machines and discard the slow machines.

6 Conclusion

In this paper, we proposed three different algorithms for parallel parsing of MPEG video in heterogeneous distributed environment. They are the Round Robin, the Size-Adaptive Round Robin, and the Dynamic Size-Adaptive Round Robin scheduling algorithm. We took the GOP-level approach for better performance.

Conclusively, if the number of machines is unchanging, the Size-Adaptive Round Robin scheduling algorithm performed better than the Round Robin scheduling algorithm. Our parallel parsing exhibits a 7.6 times faster than sequential parsing. If the number of machines is changing in unreliable and variable distributed environment, the dynamic Size-Adaptive Round Robin scheduling is suitable.

In the future, we will develop efficient and optimal parallel scheduling algorithm.

References

1. The MPEG home page, http://mpeg.telecomitalialab.com/
2. World Wide Web Consortium (W3C) home page, http://www.w3.org/
3. Sun, X.H. and Ni, L.:Scalable Problems and Memory-Bounded Speedup, Journal of Parallel and Distributed Computing, Vol. 19. (1993) 27-37
4. Grama, A., Gupta, A. and Kumar, V.: Isoefficiency Function: A Scalability Metric for Parallel Algorithms and Architectures. IEEE Parallel & Distributed Technology, Vol.1(9). (1993) 12-21
5. Hwang K.: Advanced Computer Architecture: Parallelism, Scalability, Programmability, McGraw-Hill (1993)
6. Kevin L.G. and Lawrence A.R.: Parallel MPEG-1 Video Encoding. the Picture Coding Symposium (1994)
7. Moore, J. et al.: Optimal parallel MPEG encoding. Department of Computer Science 4130 Upson Hall, Cornell University.
8. Sun, X.H., Rover, D.T.: Scalability of parallel algorithm-machine combinations, Parallel and Distributed Systems, IEEE Transactions, Vol. 5(6). (1994) 599-613
9. Shen, K., Rowe, L. A. and Delp, E. J.: A Parallel Implementation of an MPEG1 Encoder: Faster than Real-Time!, the SPIE Conference on Digital Video Compression (1995)
10. Foster, I.: Designing and Building Parallel Programs, Addison-Wesley (1995)
11. Lin, Y.D., et al.: A hierarchical network storage architecture for video-on-demand services, 21st Conference on Local Computer Networks (1996)
12. Bilas, A., Fritts, J. and Singh, J. P.: Real time parallel MPEG-2 decoding in software. 11th International Parallel Processing Symposium (1997)
13. Kobla, V. and Doermann, D.: Indexing and Retrieval of MPEG Compressed Video. Journal of Electronic Imaging, Vol. 7(2) (1998) 294-307
14. Suchendra M., et al.: Parallel Parsing of MPEG Video. International Conference on Parallel Processing (2001)
15. Rao, K.R. et al.: Multimedia Communication Systems, Prentice Hall (2002)

User-Assisted Segmentation and Tracking of Video Objects+

Sung-Hoon Hong[1] and Mike Myung-Ok Lee[2]

[1] Department of Electronics, Computer & Information Engineering, Chonnam National University, 300 Yongbong-Dong, Puk-Ku, Gwangju, 500-757, Korea
hsh@chonnam.ac.kr
[2] School of Information and Communication Engineering, Dongshin University, 252 Daeho-Dong, Naju, Chonnam 520-714 Republic of Korea

Abstract. This paper introduces a semi-automatic segmentation method which can be used to generate VOP for object based coding schemes and multimedia authoring environment etc. Semi-automatic segmentation can be thought of as a user-assisted segmentation technique. A user can initially mark objects of interest around the object boundaries. Then the user-guided and selected objects are continuously separated from the unselected areas though time evolution in the image sequences. Our proposed method shows very promising results and this encourages the development of objects based video editing.

1 Introduction

Segmentation and tracking of moving objects in a video sequence are basic task for several applications, e.g., video monitoring system, intrusion surveillance, airport safety and video editing tools. In order to support the philosophy of the MPEG-4 Video standard, especially, each image of video sequences should be represented in terms of VOPs to be encoded, that is, the objects to be encoded in image sequences should be prepared before the encoding process starts. The MPEG-4 Video has committed to providing an import tool to support for the object-based handling of video data though There is no MPEG-4 Video standard; the MPEG-4 part dealing with video coding is called Visual.

However, the current technologies for automatic segmentation are somehow premature to obtain desirable segmentation results because automatic segmentation itself is an open-issue and ill-posed problem. Nevertheless, there is a more interesting and attractive approach to image segmentation which is semi-automatic [1][2]. The semi-automatic segmentation is a user-assisted segmentation technique. A user can initially mark objects of interest around the object boundaries. Then the user-guided and selected objects are continuously separated from the unselected areas though time

+ This research is partially supported under RRC-HECS in CNU, and is partially supported by Masters & PhD Education Program under the MOCIE, Korea. The support of IDEC CAD tools and equipments in this research are also gratefully acknowledged.

M.M. Freire, P. Lorenz, M.M.-O. Lee (Eds.): HSNMC 2003, LNCS 2720, pp. 275-283, 2003.
© Springer-Verlag Berlin Heidelberg 2003

evolution in the image sequences. This user-assisted segmentation is a much more practical in generating VOPs of moving objects. This paper is organized as follows: Section II addresses our proposed a user-assisted segmentation technique. The validity of the proposed method is presented with experimental results in Section III, and the Section IV concludes the paper.

2 User-Assisted Segmentation

The proposed user-assisted video object segmentation algorithm is depicted in Figure 1. It consists of two processing steps: intra-frame segmentation and inter-frame segmentation. First, the intra-frame segmentation is applied to the first frame of the image sequence or to the frames which contains only newly appeared video objects or scene change. A user manually defines or segments the newly appeared video objects in the image. Then inter-frame segmentation is applied to the consecutive frames following the first frame or a frame with a newly appeared object or scene change. In the inter-frame segmentation, the user-defined video objects are segmented automatically by object tracking [3]. Therefore the resulting partition can achieve the temporal coherence of object labeling *i.e.* object correspondence and maintain segmentation similarity between successive frames.

During the inter-frame segmentation process, when a new object appears and the user wants to include it into his video object plane, he can stops inter frame segmentation process and go to an intra-frame segmentation mode to define region of interest for the newly appeared object. The intra-frame segmentation algorithm is described in section II.1 and the inter-frame segmentation algorithm in section II.2.

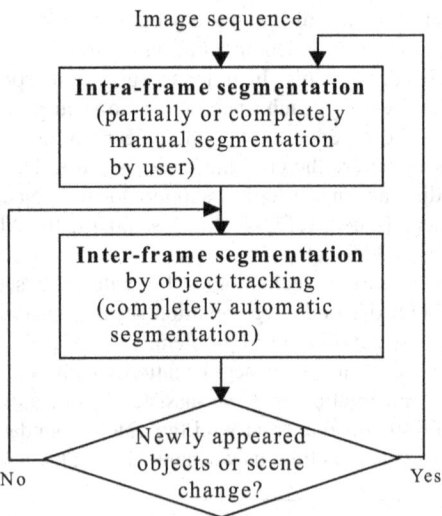

Figure 1. Overall scheme of the proposed user-assisted segmentation method

The proposed method takes advantage of initially precise boundary information for an object of interest to be segmented before the inter-fame segmentation starts. Therefore a more reliable segmentation results can be obtained compared to those with automatic segmentation methods.

2.1 I-frame Segmentation by User Assistance

The goal of user assistance is to provide an approximation of the object boundary using an input device, e.g., a mouse. A good user interface could allow a user to identify and portray the initial object boundary easily and precisely. In order for a user to define an object of interest in the image, a graphical user interface (GUI) is provided as shown in Figure 2. Supposed the user is interested in extracting an object, a person called AKIYO, with precise boundary. The user can mark the entire object all the way around AKIYO using a mouse with a user defined pixel width. A marked swath made by the mouth constitutes an uncertainty area in which the real object boundary exists. A boundary detection algorithm is then applied in the uncertainty area so that the real object boundary can be obtained and used as input to the inter-frame segmentation module. Note and meaning of the I-frame segmentation is no direct relation that with I-frame coding because no coding is involved here.

Figure 2. A graphical user interface for supporting intra-frame segmentation

2.2 Inter-frame Segmentation by Object Tracking

Typically image sequences are greatly correlated between successive frames. To efficiently exploit the temporal redundancy, a coherent segmentation through time is required. Thus, a tracking technique is applied in the consecutive frames after the manual segmentation of the first frame as long as there is no important change in scene contents. The tracking algorithm is composed of motion-compensated temporal projection of the previous segmentation $S(t-1) = \cup_{i=1}^{n} O_i(t-1)$ and boundary fitting, where $S(t-1)$ is the segmentation mask of the $(t-1)$th frame and $O_i(t-1)$ is a video object in the $S(t-1)$. Figure 3 shows the proposed segmentation algorithm by object tracking. The projection constructs $\hat{S}(t)$, the prediction for $S(t) = \cup_{i=1}^{n} O_i(t)$ using $S(t-1)$ and motion information. Then a boundary-fitting process refines the boundaries of video objects using the brightness information of the current frame.

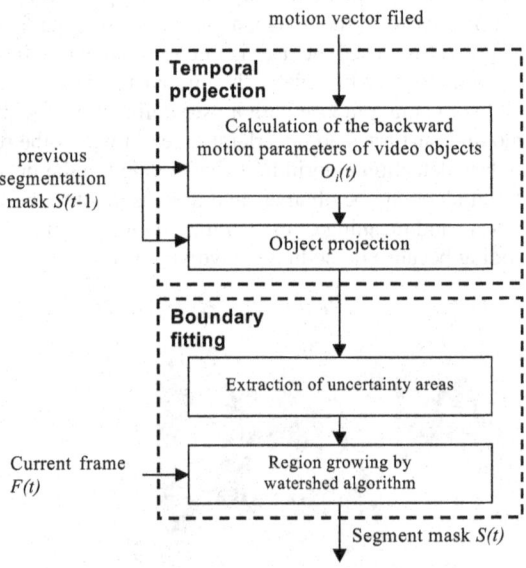

Figure 3. The block diagram of the inter-frame segmentation algorithm by object tracking

A. Motion field estimation

To obtain the dense motion field from the input image sequence, a block-matching algorithm (BMA) and a bilinear interpolation technique are used. At first, sparse block vectors are estimated at every 4×4 pixel distance by the BMA. Block size is 9×9, and the center of the block is placed at the current point. Then, the generated vectors are median-filtered to eliminate noisy vectors. Finally, the dense pixel-wise vectors are computed from four-neighbor block vectors using bilinear interpolation.

B. Temporal projection

To project each video object in $S(t-1)$, the backward motion that represents the motion of $O_i(t-1)$ to the tth frame are required. However, the forward motion that represents the motion of $O_i(t)$ from the $(t-1)$ th frame should be computed first, because only a forward motion vector field can be available. The supporting area for the estimation of the forward motion between the $(t-1)$ th and tth frames is $O_i(t)$. Unfortunately, $O_i(t)$ is the goal of the process and is unknown in advance. Thus the motion is initially estimated in $O_i(t-1)$ assuming that a large area of $O_i(t-1)$ is overlapped with $O_i(t)$ and a dominant motion can be constituted. To describe the motion of each video object, the affine motion model having six parameters is used. The affine motion model is described in Eq. (1)

$$u(x,y) = a_1 + a_2 x + a_3 y$$
$$v(x,y) = a_4 + a_5 x + a_6 y$$

$$(1)$$

where $\{a_i; i = 1,...,6\}$ are the affine motion parameters and $[u(x,y), v(x,y)]$ is the motion vector generated by the motion parameter. The accuracy of the estimated motion depends on the number of the outlier vectors. Thus a few iterations are required to reject outlier vectors in estimating the motion. The decision on the outlier vectors in each iteration is based on the following condition:

$$\sqrt{(u-\hat{u})^2 + (v-\hat{v})^2} > 2\sigma \qquad (2)$$

$$\sigma = \frac{\sum_o \sqrt{(u-\hat{u})^2 + (v-\hat{v})^2}}{\sum_o 1} \qquad (3)$$

where σ represents the averaged deviation between the estimated motion vectors in the supporting area and those computed from the motion parameter estimated at the previous iteration.

C. Boundary fitting

Imperfection of the temporal projection results in ambiguities in video objects' boundaries of $\hat{O}_i(t)$. To remedy this, the pixels within a predefined small width from the boundaries of $\hat{O}_i(t)$ are marked as uncertainty pixels in addition to the unlabelled (uncovered) or multi-labeled (overlapped) pixels generated in projection process. The determination of the width depends on the accuracy of the projection and the magnitude of the motion. In the range of a relatively moderate motion, 3-pixel width will be sufficient for QCIF format.

The object allocation for the uncertainty pixels is achieved based on the brightness information in the current frame. Region growing using the watershed algorithm [4] is utilized to merge the uncertainty pixels. In this case, each projected video object $\hat{O}_i(t)$ is composed of a seed region, i.e., a local minimum. Seed characteristics such as an average brightness are computed in each seed region. Then the initialization and flooding process merges the whole pixels in uncertainty areas based on the similarity measure in view of brightness.

3　Experimental Results

This section first shows the segmentation results using the proposed video object extraction technique for several video sequences and then introduces the video editing tool performing video object extraction, composition and encoding operations. Figure 4 shows the segmentation results by object tracking for 5 QCIF color sequences by the proposed method. The first "Akiyo" sequence has a slow motion. However the motion is non-rigid body motion because the human body may contain moving and still parts at the same time. User wants to extract the human body. The second "Foreman" sequence has a medium level motion, and the camera is moving as well. The user intends to extract the human face. The third "mother and daughter" sequence and the user intends to extract the two humans sitting in front of a still background. The Fourth "hall monitor" sequence and the user want to extract the moving human. The last sequence is "container" sequence and the user interest focuses on the slowly moving container ship.

　　The segmentation results exhibit quite accurate contours of the objects and the whole regions of objects were declared as foregrounds. Mostly these nice object contours are possibly obtained via object tracking using previous object mask.

Foreground　　　　　　　　　　Background

Akiyo, (58th frame, started from 1st frame)

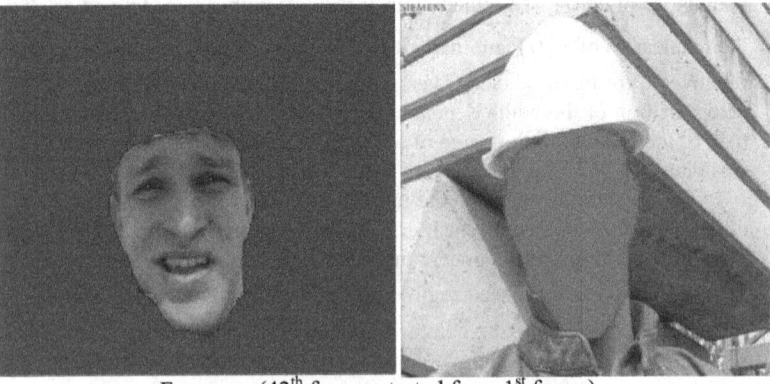

Foreman, (42th frame, started from 1st frame)

Foreground   Background

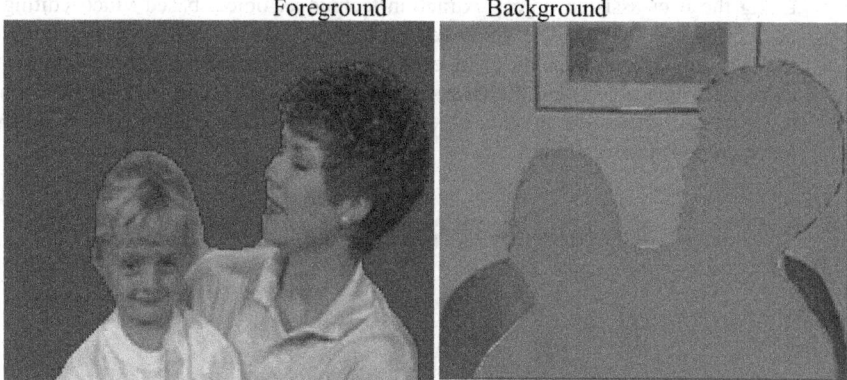

Mother & daughter, (56th frame, started from 1st frame)

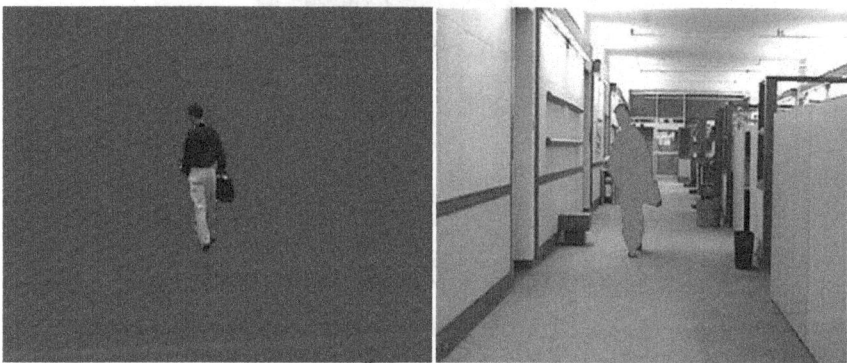

Hall monitor, (76th frame, started from 50st frame)

Container, (204th frame, started from 151st frame)

Figure 4. Experimental results for 5 QCIF sequences

Using the user assisted object extraction technique, object based video editing tool has been implemented. The video editing tool includes several other functions, e.g., moving object extraction by change detection [5], frame based composition of the extracted video object and the user selected background video, and MPEG-4 encoding. Figure 5 shows the moving object extraction operation, and Figure 6 shows the video composition operation.

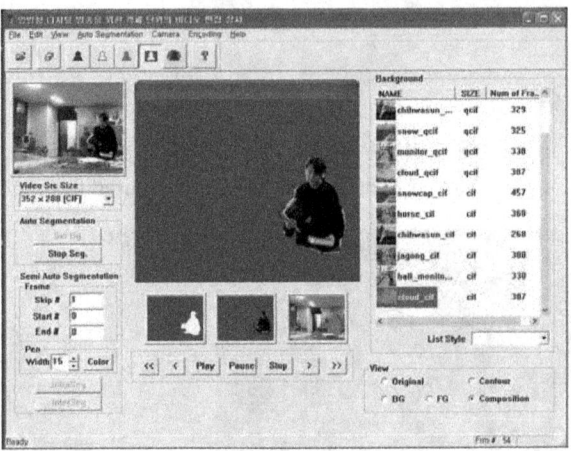

Figure 5. Moving object extraction

Figure 6. Composition of moving object and user selected background

4 Conclusion

We proposed the concept of the semi-automatic segmentation of VOP relying on user's assistance and object tracking. For the segmentation of the first frame, a user can initially mark or define the video objects. Subsequent frames were segmented using an object tracking method to provide temporal coherency. Through experimental results, it was observed that the proposed method gives stable and efficient results.

References

1. Jae Gark Choi, Munchurl Kim, Jinsuk Kwak, Myoung Ho Lee, Cheituek Ahn; User-assisted video object segmentation by multiple object tracking; ISO/IEC JTC1/SC29/WG11 MPEG97/m3349, March, 1998.

2. C. Gu, M-C Lee, "Semiautomatic segmentation and tracking of semantic video objects," *IEEE Trans. Circuits Syst. Video technol.*, Vol. 8, No. 5, Sept. 1998

3. S. W. Lee, J. G. Choi, S-. Kim, "Scene segmentation using a combined criterion of motion and intensity", *Optical Engineering*, vol.36, No. 8, pp. 2346-2352, August 1997.

4. P. Salembier and Montse Pardas, "Hierarchical morphological segmentation for image sequence coding," *IEEE Transactions on Image Processing*, vol. 3, no. 5, pp. 639-651, 1994.

5. T. Aach, A. Kaup, R. Mester, "Statistical model-based change detection in moving video", *Signal Processing*, vol. 31, No. 2, pp. 165-180, March 1993.

An Efficient Rate-Distortion Analysis Model for MPEG Video[+]

Mike Myung-Ok Lee[1] and Sung-Hoon Hong[2]

[1]School of Information and Communication Engineering, Dongshin University, 252
Daeho-Dong, Naju, Chonnam 520-714 Republic of Korea
mikelee@dsu.ac.kr
[2]Department of Electronics, Computer & Information Engineering, Chonnam National
University, 300 Yongbong-Dong, Puk-Ku, Gwangju, 500-757, Korea

Abstract. In this paper, we propose a rate-distortion estimation method for
MPEG-2 video, which enables us to predict the amount of bits and the distortion generated from an encoded picture at a given quantization step size and
vice versa. The proposed estimation method has some outstanding advantages.
First, the computational complexity is small because its major operation is just
to obtain a histogram or weighted histogram of the DCT coefficients from an
input picture, and the final form of the proposed estimation model is simple.
Second, its results are very accurate enough to be applied to practical video
coding applications. Simulation results show that the estimation errors for rate
and distortion do not exceed 2.5% and 1%, respectively.

1 Introduction

In general, video coding standards that perform the video encoding with MC-DCT
like MPEG-2 [1] control the output bit rate or picture quality by adjusting the quantization step size (QS). Therefore, accurate estimation of the rate and the distortion
corresponding to the applied QS is helpful to the efficient and precise control of video
encoding. Here, QS is a function of quantization parameter (QP); let the nth QP be
denoted as QP_n (generally, QP_n = n) and the corresponding QS be denoted as QS_n ,
then the relationship between QP and QS is usually $QS_n = 2 \times QP_n$ and $QP_n < QP_{n+1}$.
lthough several studies [3]-[5] concerning rate-distortion estimation have already
been published, the proper method for the standard video coding scheme, especially
MPEG-2, has not been fully explored in view of accuracy and complexity. In this
paper, therefore, we propose a practical rate-distortion estimation method for MPEG-
2 video and show its results to verify the accuracy of the proposed estimation. By this
rate-distortion estimation, we can predict the amount of bits and the distortion generated from an encoded picture at a given QP and vice versa. We will use MPEG-2
TM5 [2] as MPEG-2 encoding scheme in our experiments.

[+] This research is partially supported under RRC-HECS in CNU, and is partially supported by
Masters & PhD Education Program under the MOCIE, Korea. The support of IDEC CAD
tools and equipments in this research are also gratefully acknowledged.

M.M. Freire, P. Lorenz, M.M.-O. Lee (Eds.): HSNMC 2003, LNCS 2720, pp. 284-293, 2003.
© Springer-Verlag Berlin Heidelberg 2003

2　Bit Estimation of MPEG-2 Video

The output information of MPEG-2 video consists of side information, such as motion vector and headers, and signal information from DCT coefficients that are composed of intra-DC and other DCT components. The components directly influenced by change of QP level are DCT coefficients except intra-DC, and most of the output bits from the encoder are from DCT coefficients in case of high bit rate video coding applications. The coding procedure of the DCT coefficients is as follows. First, quantization process is performed. The quantization and the de-quantization processes in MPEG-2 are classified into intra (I) and non-intra (N) depending on the coding type of MB (MacroBlock). The quantizer suggested in MPEG-2 TM5 [2] is

$$\overline{ac}_{qt}(i,j) = \left(16 \times ac(i,j)\right) // W_{qt}(i,j),\qquad(1)$$

$$QAC_{qt}(i,j) = \left\{\overleftarrow{ac}_{qt}(i,j) + \delta_n(i,j)\right\} / \left(2 \times QP_n\right),\qquad(2)$$

$$\delta_n(i,j) = \begin{cases} sign\left(\overline{ac}_I(i,j)\right) \times \left((3 \times QP_n) // 4\right) & \text{for intra} \\ 0 & \text{for non - intra} \end{cases},$$

where $ac(i,j)$ is input DCT coefficients except intra-DC, and $W_{qt}(i,j)$ is (i,j)th component of quantization matrix for quantization type $qt \in \{I, N\}$. The operator '$//$' is integer division with rounding to the nearest integer and the operator '$/$' is integer division with truncation of the result toward zero. The quantization for $ac(i,j)$ is first to perform the visually weighted quantization by individual quantization factors, namely, the components of the quantization matrix as expressed in (1), and then the coefficients (i.e. $\overline{ac}_{qt}(i,j)$) are quantized by QP as expressed in (2).

On the other hand, MPEG-2 de-quantization is performed with the de-quantizer represented in (3) [1].

$$REC_{qt}(i,j) = \left\{\left(2 \times QAC_{qt}(i,j) + \Theta(i,j)\right) \times W_{qt}(i,j) \times QS_n\right\} / 32$$

$$\Theta(i,j) = \begin{cases} 0 & \text{for intra blocks} \\ sign\left(QAC_N(i,j)\right) & \text{for non - intra blocks} \end{cases}\qquad(3)$$

Ignoring the quantization matrix effects, Fig. 1 shows the quantization characteristics obtained from (2) and (3) when the applied QP is QP_{n-1} and QP_n. Note that the quantization results for the input components lying in the gray region are not zero when QP= QP_{n-1}, but are zero when QP= QP_n. After quantization, the quantized DCT coefficients are ordered along a zig-zag scanning path and runs of zeros are identified. In order to further increase the compression efficiency, variable length coding (VLC) using Huffman like table is used to code events corresponding to a pair (zero-run, level). The number of the events denoted as (zero-run, level) is equal to the number of non-zero coefficients (NZC) of the quantized DCT coefficients except intra-DC.

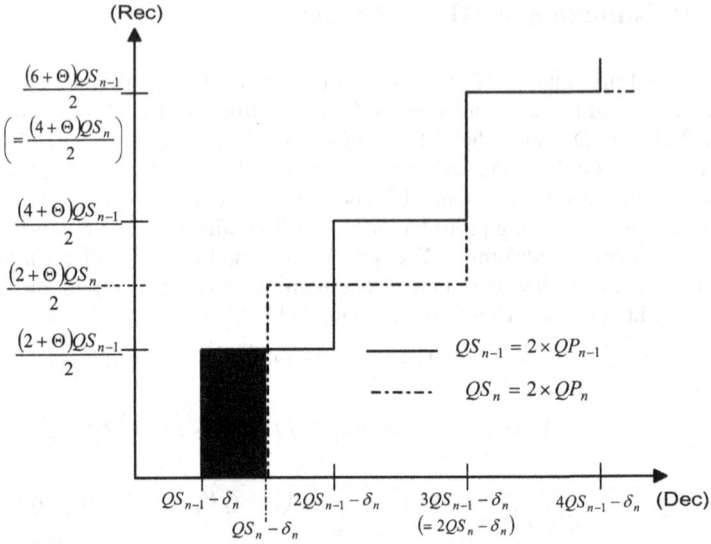

Fig. 1. MPEG-2 quantization characteristics.

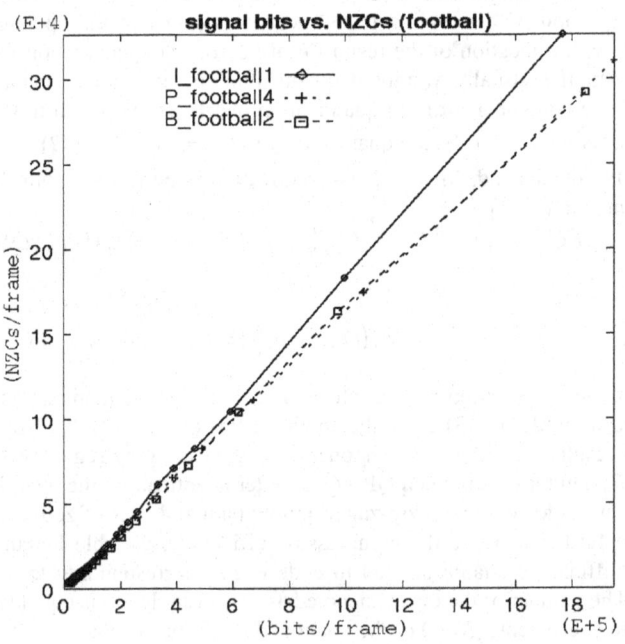

Fig. 2. Relationship between the number of *NZC*s and bit amount generated per frame as increasing the quantization parameter from 1 to 31 for I, P, and B picture.

The coefficients is proportional to the number of *NZC*s. If the average code length for the events according to the applied QP is constant, then the number of bits generated from the DCT coefficients is linearly proportional to the number of *NZC*s. Fig. 2 shows the relationship between the number of bits and the number of *NZC*s from the DCT coefficients per frame as the applied QP level is increased from 1 to 31. We used the same QP level to quantize all MBs in a frame, and fit the P or B frames with their anchor frames (I or P) coded with QP=10. These results tell us that the number of the *NZC*s is relatively linearly proportional to the number of bits generated from DCT coefficients, which is independent of picture coding type and picture content, even though VLC is used. Therefore, the number of bits to be generated from the DCT coefficients in a current picture at a given QP level, denoted as $Sbit(QP)$, will be estimated by counting the number of the *NZC*s corresponding to the QP level, and it can be expressed as

$$Sbit(QP_n) = \sum_{qt \in \{I,N\}} \left(\alpha_{qt} \times NZC_{qt}(QP_n) \right). \tag{4}$$

In this equation, $NZC_{qt}(QP_n)$ is the number of *NZC*s from the DCT coefficients quantized with the *qt* type quantizer within current picture when the applied QP is QP_n. And α_{qt} is the proportional coefficient between bit amount and the number of the *NZC*s generated from DCT coefficients quantized with *qt* type quantizer. In our experiment, we found this coefficient by using linear regression analysis and the formula is

$$\alpha_{qt} = \sum_{i=1}^{P} \left(Sbit_{qt}^{i} \times NZC_{qt}^{i} \right) \bigg/ \sum_{i=1}^{P} \left(NZC_{qt}^{i} \right)^{2} \tag{5}$$

where P is the number of frames observed in the past. $Sbit_{qt}^{i}$ and NZC_{qt}^{i} are the signal bits and *NZC*s generated from DCT coefficients quantized with *qt* type quantizer in the previous *ith* frame.

When DCT coefficients are quantized with the quantizer suggested by MPEG-2 TM5, we can easily calculate the number of *NZC*s corresponding to the applied QP by the following procedure, and also easily estimate the bit amount generated from DCT coefficients by inserting this result into (4).

S1) obtain the histogram of $UQP_{qt}(i,j)$, such that

$$NZC\_hist_{qt}[UQP_{qt}(i,j)]++ \tag{6}$$

where $UQP_{qt}(i,j) = clipping[\alpha \times |\overline{ac}_{qt}(i,j)| + \beta]$, $clipping [\cdot]$ is an operator that changes an input to the truncated integer value limited from 0 to 31, and α and β are constants derived from (2), which are (α=0.8, β=0.4) for intra quantizer and (α=0.5, β=0) for non-intra quantizer. That is, $UQP_{qt}(i,j)$ indicates the QP level that makes the absolute value of the (i,j)th components of the quantized DCT coefficients into integer one. In case of the non-intra quantizer, the QP level that makes $|QAC_N(i,j)|$ into integer one is $QP = 0.5 \times |\overline{ac}_N(i,j)|$, so α=0.5 and β=0. As a result, $NZC\_hist_{qt}[QP_n]$ stores the decreasing number of *NZC*s due to QP level increment from QP_n to QP_{n+1} in the quantization process with qt type . For example, $NZC\_hist_{qt}[QP_{n-1}]$ is the number of the input components lying in the gray region in Fig. 1.

S2) accumulate the $NZC\_hist_{qt}[QP]$, such that

$$NZC_{qt}[QP_n] = \sum_{QP=n}^{31} NZC\_hist_{qt}[QP], \ 1 \leq n \leq 31 \qquad (7)$$

From (7), the number of generated NZCs is stored in $NZC[QP_n]$ when $QP = QP_n$.

Consequently, the number of NZCs corresponding to the given QP level can be easily obtained by (7), and the number of bits to be generated from the DCT coefficients in a coding unit can be estimated by applying the $NZC_{qt}[QP]$ into (1). Furthermore, we can also predicted the total number of bits to be generated from a current picture according to the applied QP, such that

$$Tbit(QP_n) = Sbit(QP_n) + Obit$$

(8)

where $Obit$ is the amount of bits generated from the side information that is not directly influenced by change of QP level, which is obtained by performing the bit count only once.

3 Estimation of MPEG-2 Video

The distortion estimation proposed in this section is based on two facts. First, distortion in terms of mean squared error (MSE) is proportional to the square of the applied QS to the quantization. Typically, a uniform quantization is often used in a practical video coding system. If the quantization process is an ideal uniform quantization and the input signal into the quantizer is uniformly distributed, the distortion (MSE) due to the quantization with QS_n is $QS_n^2/12$. In MPEG-2 quantization, quantization matrixes are used to consider the psychovisual effect. Considering the quantization matrix effect, the distortion increment is proportional to $(QS_n^2 - QS_{n-1}^2) \times W^2(i,j)$ as QS is increased from QS_{n-1} to QS_n. Second, when the applied QS increases one step from QS_{n-1} to QS_n, the quantized DCT coefficients that were zero at $QS = QS_{n-1}$ do not affect the distortion increment, and only non-zero components of the DCT coefficients quantized with QS_{n-1} affect the distortion increment due to the QS increment. Based on these facts, we estimate the distortion in terms of MSE corresponding to the QP level applied to the MPEG-2 quantization.

To consider the quantization matrix effect, the proposed distortion estimation uses the weighted histogram and its cumulative value, which are achieved by following procedure. S1) obtain the weighted histogram of $UQP_{qt}(i,j)$ as

$$QM\_hist_{qt}[UQP_{qt}(i,j)] + = W_{qt}^2(i,j) \qquad (9)$$

where $UQP_{qt}(i,j)$ was defined in (6), and $W_{qt}(i,j)$ is the squared value of (i,j)th element of the qt type quantization matrix. S2) accumulate the $QM\_hist_{qt}[QP]$, as

$$QM\_NZC_{qt}[QP_n] = \sum_{QP=n}^{31} QM\_hist_{qt}[QP], \ 1 \le n \le 31 \tag{10}$$

$QM\_NZC_{qt}[QP_n]$ obtained from (10) stores the sum of the squared quantization matrix elements corresponding to $NZCs$ of the quantized DCT coefficients when applied QP to the qt type quantization process is QP_n. The distortion estimation model proposed in this section is derived from the assumption that the $NZCs$ existing between the adjacent decision levels are uniformly distributed.

Ignoring the quantization matrix effect, input signal within $[k \times QS_n - \delta_n, (k+1) \times QS_n - \delta_n)$ is reconstructed to $(2k + \Theta) \times QS_n/2$ when applied QS is QS_n $(n > 1)$. Therefore, if the input signal into the MPEG-2 quantizer is uniformly distributed between the adjacent decision levels, the distortion (MSE) generated by the quantization with QS = QS_n is

$$UD_{qt}(QP_n) = \frac{1}{QS_n} \int_{k \cdot QS_n - \delta_n}^{(k+1)QS_n - \delta_n} \left(x - \frac{(2k + \Theta)}{2} QS_n \right)^2 dx \tag{11}$$

(refer to Fig. 1). Thus, when the applied QS is increased by one step from QS_{n-1} to QS_n, the sum of the increased distortion for the $NZCs$ greater than $(QS_n - \delta_n)$ is approximated by

$$\Delta E_{qt}(QP_n) = \{UD_{qt}(QP_n) - UD_{qt}(QP_{n-1})\}$$
$$\times \frac{QM\_NZC_{qt}[QP_n]}{16^2} \tag{12}$$

And the distortion increment for the uniformly distributed input signal within $[QS_{n-1} - \delta_{n-1}, QS_n - \delta_n)$ is

$$\Delta UR_{qt}(QP_n) = \frac{1}{(QS_n - \delta_n) - (QS_{n-1} - \delta_{n-1})}$$
$$\times \int_{QS_n - \delta_n}^{QS_n - \delta_n} x^2 dx - UD_{qt}(QP_{n-1}) \tag{13}$$

Therefore, the sum of the increased distortion for the $NZCs$ within $[QS_{n-1} - \delta_{n-1}, QS_n - \delta_n)$ is

$$\Delta RE_{qt}(QP_n) = \Delta UR_{qt}(QP_n) \times \frac{QM\_hist_{qt}[QP_{n-1}]}{16^2}. \tag{14}$$

Consequently, when the QS is increased from QS_{n-1} to QS_n, the sum of the increased distortion due to the qt type quantization can be estimated by

$$\Delta D_{qt}(QP_n) = \Delta E_{qt}(QP_n) + \Delta RE_{qt}(QP_n), \tag{15}$$

and the distortion generated at QS = QS_n can be expressed as

$$\hat{D}_{qt}(QP_n) = D_{qt}(QP_{n-1}) + \Delta D_{qt}(QP_n)/p\_num_{qt}, \tag{16}$$

where p_num_{qt} is the number of pixels quantized with qt type quantizer.

On the other hand, since quantization result for the input signal within $[0, QS_1 - \delta_1)$ is zero, the distortion for this signal is

$$\Delta UR_{qt}(QP_1) = \frac{1}{(QS_1 - \delta_1)} \int_{\delta_n}^{QS_1 - \delta_1} x^2 \, dx \qquad (17)$$

Therefore, the initial distortion for the NZCs can be expressed as

$$\hat{D}_{qt}(QP_1) = \left\{ DC_e^2 + \Delta UR_{qt}(QP_1) \times QM\_hist[0] \right. \\ \left. + \Delta UD_{qt}(QP_1) \times QM\_NZC[QP_1] \right\} / \left(16^2 \times p\_num_{qt}\right) \qquad (18)$$

where DC_e^2 is the sum of the distortion from the intra-DC components. If the distortion estimation is performed per frame unit, the distortion estimation formula (16) for non-intra quantization should be modified because some MBs in P or B frame may be coded with intra coding mode. And the distortion estimation results are slightly dependent on the coding type and input image characteristics. To solve this problem, (16) is modified by

$$\hat{D}(QP_n) = \hat{D}(QP_{n-1}) + \sum_{qt \in \{I,N\}} \left\{ d_{qt} \times \Delta D_{qt}(QP_n) \right\} / p\_num \qquad (19)$$

where p_num is the number of pixels in a frame, and the proportional coefficient d_{qt} is the ratio between the actually generated distortion and the estimated distortion. In our experiment, we found this coefficient by using linear regression analysis and the formula to find d_{qt} is

$$d_{qt} = \sum_{i=1}^{P} \left(D_{qt}^i \times \hat{D}_{qt}^i \right) / \sum_{i=1}^{P} \left(\hat{D}_{qt}^i \right)^2 \qquad (20)$$

where P is the number of frames observed in the past. D_{qt}^i and $\hat{D}_{qt}^i$ are the measured and estimated distortion generated from DCT coefficients quantized with qt type quantizer in the previous ith frame. Fig 3 shows the relationship between the estimated distortions by (19) and the measured distortions when the 'football' images are encoded with I, P, and B picture coding types, respectively, and the applied QP level is increased from 1 to 31. These results indicate that the estimated distortions are also linearly proportional to the measured distortions and their slopes are almost '1' regardless of the picture coding types.

4 Simulation Results

To evaluate the performance of the proposed estimation, we carried out simulations with four standard MPEG video sequences of CCIR601 format (*flower garden, football, mobile,* and *popple*), and compared the estimated values with actual coded values. Each test sequence is coded with fixed GOP structure, that is IBBPBBPBBPBB, at a bit rate of 4.5 Mbps.

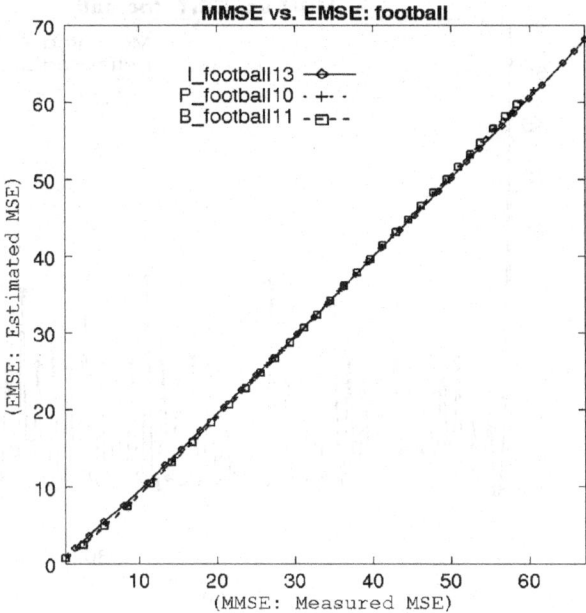

Fig. 3. Relationship between measured distortion (MMSE) and estimated distortion (EMSE) from (19) for '*football*' image.

In our simulation, we use the same QP level for all the MBs in a picture, and the level corresponds to the estimated bits closest to the picture target bits, which is calculated by the algorithm in TM5 [2].
Fig. 4 shows the comparative results between the estimation values and the actual coded values for '*football*' sequence. These results indicate that the estimated values are almost same as the actually measured values, which are independent of picture coding types. Table I presents the bit estimation results of the four test video sequences at the bit rate of 4.5 Mbps. From this, the estimated bits are very similar to the actual coded bits, and there is no significant estimation error (Maximum *Diff* for any sequence is not exceed 4 %). Here, *Diff* is

$$Diff = \frac{|Measured - Estimated|}{Measured} \times 100 \quad (\%).$$

Table II presents the distortion estimation results of the four test video sequences. From this, the estimated distortions keep very similar values of the measured distortions, and there is also no significant estimation error (Maximum *Diff* for any sequence is not exceed 5 %).

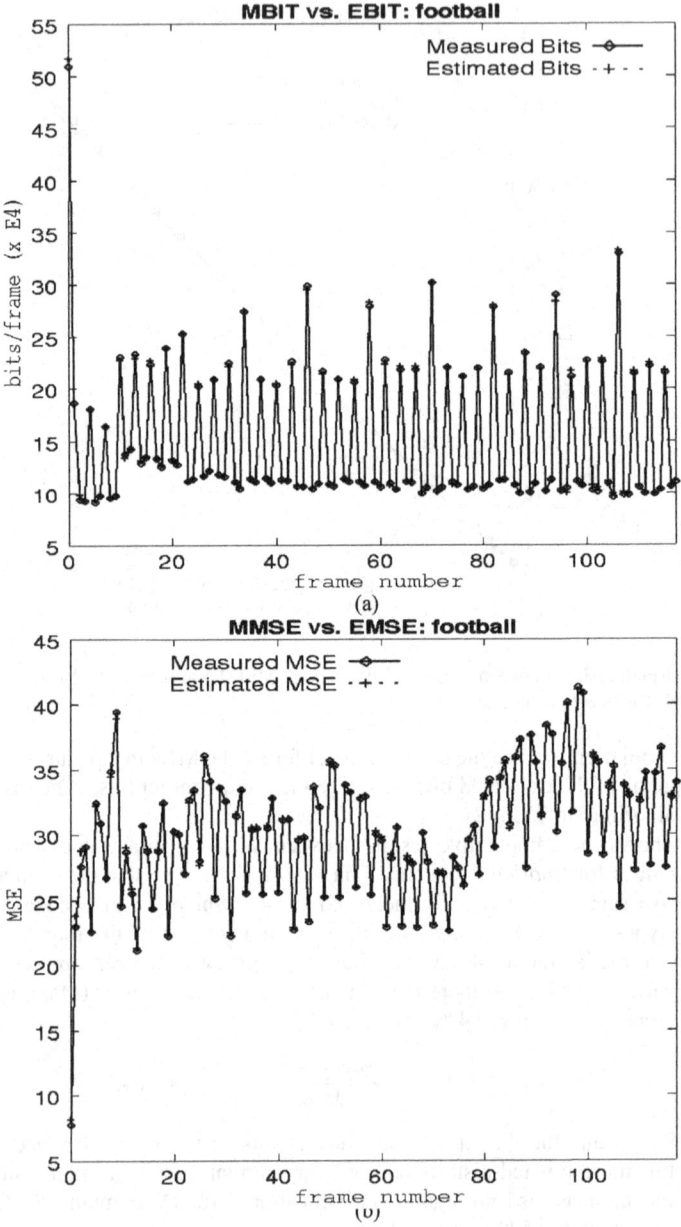

Fig. 4. Estimation Results of (a) bits and (b) MSE for '*football*' sequence.

TABLE I. Bɪᴛ Eꜱᴛɪᴍᴀᴛɪᴏɴ Rᴇꜱᴜʟᴛꜱ (MBITS: Mᴇᴀꜱᴜʀᴇᴅ Bɪᴛꜱ, EBITS: Eꜱᴛɪᴍᴀᴛᴇᴅ Bɪᴛꜱ).

	Average MBITS	Average EBITS	Maximum Diff (%)
flower	153957.8	153896.3	3.77
football	153643.4	153716.1	1.49
mobile	154359.1	154524.1	1.63
popple	153033.8	153679.3	1.28

TABLE II. Distortion Estimation Results (MMSE: Measured MSE, MSE: Estimated MSE)

	Average MSE	Average EMSE	Maximum Diff (%)
flower	54.92	54.94	3.11
football	30.00	30.03	4.3
mobile	68.64	68.75	2.35
popple	21.41	21.39	4.98

5 Conclusion

In this section, we proposed an estimation method for the rate and the distortion generated from a coded picture at a given QP. The proposed rate-distortion estimation method has some outstanding advantages. First, the computational complexity is small because its major operation is just to obtain a histogram or weighted histogram of the DCT coefficients from an input picture, and the final form of the proposed estimation model is simple. Second, its results are accurate enough to be applied to practical video coding applications. Our simulation results show that maximum estimation error for rate and for distortion are not exceed 4% and 5%, respectively. Furthermore, the proposed estimation procedure can be employed in other standard video coding schemes such as H.261, H.263 and MPEG-1.

References

1. ISO-IEC/JTC1/SC29/WG11, "Generic coding of moving pictures and associated audio information: Video," ISO-IEC 13818-2, Nov. 1994.

2. Document ISO-IEC/JTC/SC29/WG11,"Test Model 5," Draft, Apr. 1993.

3. T. Berger, *Rate Distortion Theory.* Englewood Cliffs, NJ: Prentice Hall, 1971.

4. N. S. Jayant and P. Noll, Digital Coding of Waveforms. Englewood Cliffs, NJ: Prentice Hall, 1984.

5. Hsueh-Ming Hang and Jiann-Jone Chen, "Source Model for Transform Video Coder and Its Application – Part I: Fundamental Theory," *IEEE Trans. Circuits Syst. Video Technol.,* vol. 7, no. 2, PP. 287-298, Apr. 1997.

Multiple Description Coding for Quincunx Images. Application to Satellite Transmission

Manuela Pereira*, Annabelle Gouze, Marc Antonini, and Michel Barlaud

I3S laboratory of CNRS, University of Nice-Sophia Antipolis
Bâtiment Algorithme/Euclides, 2000 route des Lucioles
06903 Sophia Antipolis Cedex, France
{pereira, gouze, am, barlaud} @i3s.unice.fr

Abstract. A way to improve image resolution is to combine a pair of
CCD linear arrays in a quincunx arrangement. Because each CCD array
yields a classical image according to a square grid the systems using such
acquisition model are tempted to treat each image isolated, disregarding
the highly redundancy between them.
We propose two different methods of joint source-channel coding that
takes into account the redundancy between the two images in source
and/or channel coding. The proposed methods use the satellite channel characteristics when performing the source-channel coding. The first
method process the quincunx sampled image with a well-suited transform
to reduce the redundancies. After this step, we use the MDC method
proposed in [1, 2] adapted for the case of satellite models. In the second
method the redundancy between the two images is used to find a robust
scheme. More precisely the different dyadic images are used to generate
the two different descriptions in a MDC scheme and the difference between these two images are joined to both descriptions. This results in a
highly robust scheme.

1 Introduction

The increasing demand of satellite images (for regional planning, plane cartog-
raphy and restitution of the relief, ecological monitoring, follow-up of the vege-
tation, etc...) justify the continuous efforts in order to improve the image quality
provided. A way to improve image resolution is to combine a pair of CCD linear
arrays in a quincunx arrangement. For instance, the earth observation satellite
of CNES, SPOT5[3], provides a quincunx sampling image by using two different
CCD linear arrays, shifted each other by 0.5 pixel in the direction of linear arrays, and $n + 0.5$ pixels ($n \in \mathbb{N}$) in the satellite motion direction (see figure 1).
The emergence of such sampling techniques is due to the Modulation Transfer
Function (MTF) of satellites equiped with CCD instruments. This MTF corresponds roughly to a low pass filter and has a frequency support close to the
quincunx one [4]. The double linear arrays make a denser sampling grid with
an optimal frequency support for this kind of acquisition scheme. Each CCD

---

* Research partially supported by PRAXIS XXI grant SFRH/BD/1234/2000

M.M. Freire, P. Lorenz, M.M.-O. Lee (Eds.): HSNMC 2003, LNCS 2720, pp. 294–303, 2003.
© Springer-Verlag Berlin Heidelberg 2003

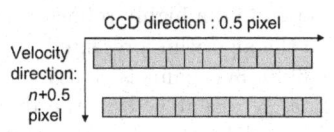

Fig. 1. Representation of the two CCD linear arrays of a SPOT5 type acquisition system.

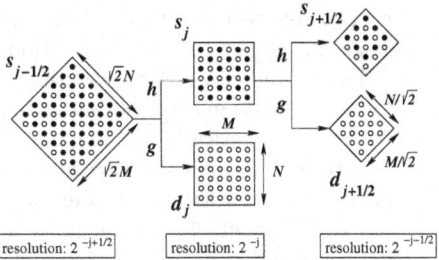

Fig. 2. Quincunx multiresolution analysis.

linear array generates an image sampled on a square grid. This is the principal reason, why models using such acquisition system process independently each of the two images. Traditionally, such kind of scheme performs Forward Error Correction (FEC) for each image independently to combat channel failures. For instance, SPOT5 uses Reed-Solomon channel codes more precisely RS(239,255) with interleaving. The drawback in such kind of model is that the dependencies between the pixels of two images are not taken into account neither in source neither in channel coding [4].

We propose to perform joint source-channel coding to get the best image quality after transmission over satellite channel. Taking into account the redundancy between the two CCD arrays when performing joint source-channel coding results in a good trade off rate-quality-robustness.

A particular joint source and channel coding method, known as multiple description coding (MDC), has proven to be an effective way to provide error resilience with a relatively small reduction in compression ratio. In the MD problem (reduced to the simplest case of two descriptions), a source is described by two descriptions with side rates R_1 and R_2. These two descriptions individually lead to reconstructions with side distortions D_1 and D_2, respectively; the two descriptions together yield a reconstruction with central distortion $D_0 \leq D_1$ (and D_2).

2   Main Contributions of the Paper

We propose two different MDC schemes for quincunx images. In the present work we design it for application to satellite image transmission. The two methods take into account the dependencies between the pixels of the two CCD arrays and uses the noise characteristics, to be adapted to the satellite channel model, when performing the source-channel coding.

In the first MDC approach the quincunx sampled image is performed with a suited transform to reduce the redundancies. After this step we use the MDC method proposed in [1, 2]. It was shown in [1] that high compression efficiency is achieved even when comparing with SDC compression schemes in noiseless case.

In the second model we use the redundancy of the two CCD arrays to find a robust scheme. More precisely, the different dyadic images are used to generate the two different descriptions in a MDC scheme. The difference of these two images are joined to both descriptions in order to find a highly robust scheme.

For redundancy control we use the ideas in the algorithm presented in [5] for BSC and Gaussian channels and extended in [6] for 3G channels. This algorithm controls automatically the amount of redundancy dispatched on the different descriptions by taking into account the channel model and state. Here we extend the algorithm for satellite channels.

Using channel information and source redundancy when designing joint source channel coders results in a robust and efficient compression scheme.

The paper is organized as follow. Section 3 introduces the general MDC scheme. Method I and II are presented in sections 4 and 5, respectively. Results are presented in section 6 and we conclude in section 7.

3   General MDC Scheme

The proposed methods use MD schemes based on the Discrete Wavelet Transform (DWT) and an efficient bit allocation technique. Our goal is to find an optimal trade-off between efficient compression and robustness to errors due to communications using unreliable channels. For that, we propose to control automatically the amount of redundancy dispatched on the different descriptions by taking into account the satellite channel model and state (figure 3). The use of the Scan-Based DWT transform presented in [7, 8] allows the development of a stripe-based MDC and so, to use different redundancies to take into account changes in channels state while coding.

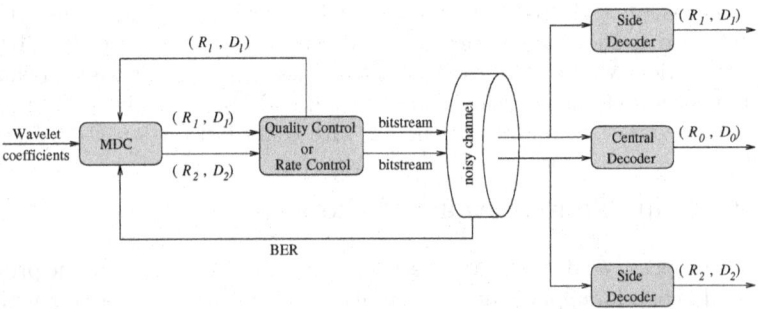

Fig. 3. General scheme with the MD Bit Allocation system taking into account the channel state when performing the bit allocation (computing the quantification steps $q_{i,j}$).

The objective of both methods is to find, for a given redundancy between the descriptions, which combination of scalar quantizers across the various wavelet coefficients subbands will produce the minimum total central distortion while satisfying the side bit rates R_l, and side distortions constraints D_l. This allocation problem is a constrained problem which can be solved by introducing the Lagrange operators. The different beginning point of the two methods (4, 5) results in different expressions of Lagrangian functional. Therefore, below we expose each method into a dedicated section.

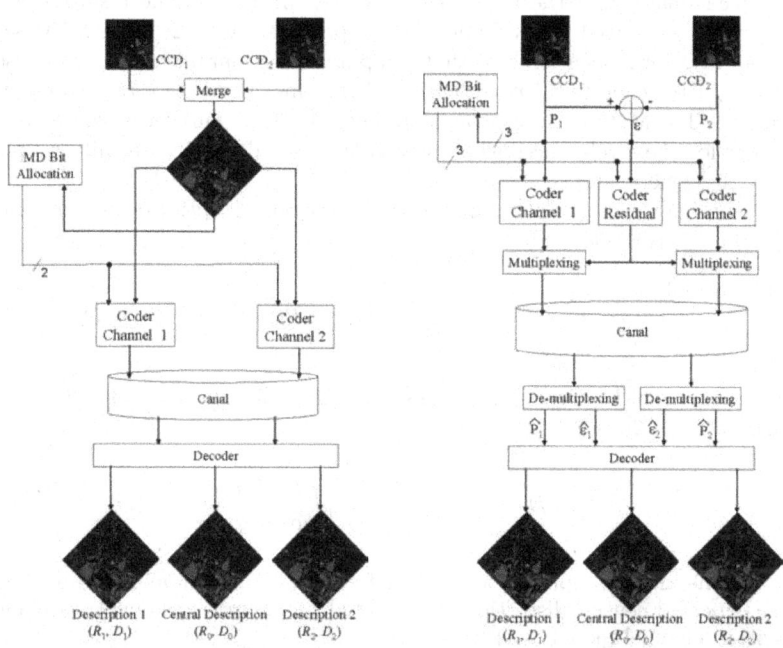

Fig. 4. MDC for quincunx images - Method I.

Fig. 5. MDC for quincunx images - Method II.

4 MDC for Transmission of Quincunx Images - Method I

The optimal way to reduce the redundancies is to process the quincunx sampled image with a well-suited transform. In the case of quincunx sampled images, we start from a semi-level of resolution and we must have a quincunx compressor, in order to avoid processing the two images separately. The used transform is a quincunx lifting scheme [9, 10] and the quincunx multiresolution is defined by adding an intermediate half resolution (see figure 2). The difference in resolution between two successive image approximations is equal to a factor $\sqrt{2}$ for the quincunx case [11] and a factor 2 for the common separable case. Meyer showed that only one wavelet is necessary and not three like in the separable case [12].

Thus, wavelet transform decomposes signal into two subbands and not four. The factor of resolution differs from the bidimensional separable case. For a Mallat decomposition this factor is equal to 2, and for the quicunx case it is identified by the function L, which is a linear transform checking $L(x,y) = (x+y, x-y)$. One can observe that $L \circ L = 2Id$.

Taking the previous considerations, in this method we perform the quincunx sampled image with the transform presented in [9, 10]. The resulting wavelet coefficients are used in the MDC scheme proposed in [1, 2]. This MDC scheme uses a MD Bit Allocation bloc that computes the scalar quantizers to be used by the coder to generate the two different bitstreams. These steps are represented in figure 4. The MD Bit Allocation is presented in [1, 2]. Furthermore, we point the reader for these references when details are desired and in the suite we present only the general steps.

The Lagrangian functional for this constrained optimization problem, as given in [1] is the following:

$$J(\{q_{i,1}, q_{i,2}\}) = D_0 + \sum_{j=1}^{2} \lambda_j (R_j \le R_l) + \sum_{j=1}^{2} \mu_j (D_j \le D_l) \qquad (1)$$

For a source with Generalized Gaussian (GG) distribution [13], D_0 has been written in [1, 2] as (2).

$$D_0 = \sum_{i=1}^{\#SB} \Delta_i \sigma_{i,0}^2 D_{i,0} \left(\frac{q_{i,1}}{\sigma_{i,1}}, \frac{q_{i,2}}{\sigma_{i,2}} \right) \qquad (2)$$

In (2) the Δ_i is an optional weight for frequency selection and in this approach the expected central distortion is estimated based on the channel state and the a priori channel model as follows.

$$D_{i,0} \left(\frac{q_{i,1}}{\sigma_{i,1}}, \frac{q_{i,2}}{\sigma_{i,2}} \right) = \frac{1}{\sigma_{i,0}^2} \frac{1}{1+r_N} \left[min \left(\sigma_{i,1}^2 D_{i,1}, \sigma_{i,2}^2 D_{i,2} \right) + r_N \times max \left(\sigma_{i,1}^2 D_{i,1}, \sigma_{i,2}^2 D_{i,2} \right) \right] \qquad (3)$$

The $\sigma_{i,j}^2 D_{i,j}(\frac{q_{i,j}}{\sigma_{i,j}})$ is the Mean Square Error for the ith subband in the case of a GG distribution. r_N is the weighting parameter associated to the redundant subbands, called redundancy parameter. The amount of redundancy, i.e., the importance of the redundant subbands, depends on the channel BER. Taking into account the Shannon theorem 10 of [14] it is proposed in [5] to compute the redundancy parameter as $r_N = \frac{H_y(x)}{max(H(x))}$, where $H(x)$ is the entropy of the input and $H_y(x)$ the conditional entropy. The resulting system for a two channels scheme ($j \in \{1,2\}$) that provides the optimal sets of quantization steps $\{q_{i,1}\}, \{q_{i,2}\}$, as given in [1], is the following.

$$\begin{cases} \dfrac{\partial D_{i,j}}{\partial R_{i,j}} \left(\dfrac{q_{i,j}}{\sigma_{i,j}} \right) = \dfrac{-\lambda_j a_i}{\Delta_i \sigma_{i,j}^2 (C_{i,j} + \mu_j E_j)} & \text{(a)} \\ \sum_{i=1}^{\#SB} a_i R_{i,j} \left(\dfrac{q_{i,j}}{\sigma_{i,j}} \right) - R_l = 0 & \text{(b)}. \end{cases} \qquad (4)$$

The a_i coefficient is the quotient of the size of the subband divided by the size of the whole image (e.g., $a_i = \frac{1}{2^{2i}}$ in the dyadic case); $E_j = 2 \times (D_j - D_l)$ if $D_j > D_l$ or 0 otherwise; and $C_{i,j}$ is $\frac{1}{1+r_N}$ if $min(\sigma_{i,1}^2 D_{i,1}, \sigma_{i,2}^2 D_{i,2}) = \sigma_{i,j}^2 D_{i,j}$ or $\frac{r_N}{1+r_N}$ otherwise. Solution for the expression of $\frac{\partial D_{i,j}}{\partial R_{i,j}}\left(\frac{q_{i,j}}{\sigma_{i,j}}\right)$ can be found in [7].

5   MDC for Transmission of Quincunx Images - Method II

In this model we use the redundancy of the two CCD arrays to reach robustness. More precisely, the different dyadic images are used to generate the two different descriptions in a MDC scheme and the difference of these two images are joined to both descriptions. Let us call $P1$ and $P2$ the two different CCD arrays, and ϵ their difference. As can be seen in figure 5, one description contains $P1$ and ϵ, while the other contains $P2$ and ϵ. In this model we have always two different ways to recover an information: ϵ is coded twice; $P1$ can be recovered from description 1 or from $P2 + \epsilon$, and finally, $P2$ can be recovered from description 2 or from $P1 - \epsilon$. This results in a highly robust scheme.

In this model, the redundancy parameter is associated to the residual image ϵ. This parameter is computed in the same way as in the former method, i.e., using r_N equation as proposed in [5]. In this approach we propose to apply the redundancy parameter to the residual image, because the use of the residual image by the decoder is dependent of the transmission losses.

The Lagrangian functional for this constrained optimization problem, is given by equation (5).

$$J\left(\{q_{i,1}, q_{i,2}, q_{i,\epsilon}\}\right) = D_0 + \sum_{j=1}^{2} \lambda_j (R_j \leq R_l) \tag{5}$$

For a source with GG distribution, D_0 in equation (5) can be written as

$$D_0 = \sum_{i=1}^{\#SB} \Delta_i \sigma_{i,0}^2 D_{i,0}\left(\frac{q_{i,1}}{\sigma_{i,1}}, \frac{q_{i,2}}{\sigma_{i,2}}, \frac{q_{i,\epsilon}}{\sigma_{i,\epsilon}}\right), \tag{6}$$

where Δ_i is an optional weight for frequency selection.

Here we express $D_{i,0}\left(\frac{q_{i,1}}{\sigma_{i,1}}, \frac{q_{i,2}}{\sigma_{i,2}}, \frac{q_{i,\epsilon}}{\sigma_{i,\epsilon}}\right)$ as

$$\frac{1}{\sigma_{i,0}^2}\frac{1}{1+r_N}\left[\sigma_{i,1}^2 D_{i,1} + r_N\left(\sigma_{i,2}^2 D_{i,2} + \sigma_{i,\epsilon}^2 D_{i,\epsilon}\right) + \sigma_{i,2}^2 D_{i,2} + r_N\left(\sigma_{i,1}^2 D_{i,1} + \sigma_{i,\epsilon}^2 D_{i,\epsilon}\right)\right] =$$

$$\frac{1}{\sigma_{i,0}^2}\left[\left(\sigma_{i,1}^2 D_{i,1} + \sigma_{i,2}^2 D_{i,2}\right) + \sigma_{i,\epsilon}^2 \frac{2r_N}{1+r_N}D_{i,\epsilon}\right] \tag{7}$$

$(R_{j=1,2} < R_l)$ has to be defined for each descriptor. For the different descriptors $j = 1, 2$, we write it as a constraint.

$$Q_j = \left(\sum_{i=1}^{\#SB} a_i\left(R_{i,j}\left(\frac{q_{i,j}}{\sigma_{i,j}}\right) + R_{i,\epsilon}\left(\frac{q_{i,\epsilon}}{\sigma_{i,\epsilon}}\right)\right) - R_l\right) \tag{8}$$

where, $R_{i,k}(q_{i,k})$, is the bit rate in bits per sample for the ith subband.

Considering (6) and the constraint (8) the Lagrangian functional (5) can be rewritten as

$$J\left(\{q_{i,1}, q_{i,2}, q_{i,k}\}\right) = \sum_{i=1}^{\#SB} \Delta_i \sigma_{i,0}^2 D_{i,0}\left(\frac{q_{i,1}}{\sigma_{i,1}}, \frac{q_{i,2}}{\sigma_{i,2}}, \frac{q_{i,\epsilon}}{\sigma_{i,\epsilon}}\right) + \sum_{j=1}^{2} \lambda_j Q_j \qquad (9)$$

Solution of (9) is obtained when $\frac{\partial J(\{q_{i,1}, q_{i,2}, q_{i,3}\})}{\partial q_{i,k}} = 0$ for $k = 1, 2, \epsilon$. This derivative is detailed below.

Deriving equation (8), the Lagrangian functional (9) becomes,

$$\Delta_i \sigma_{i,0}^2 \frac{\partial}{\partial q_{i,k}} D_{i,0}\left(\frac{q_{i,k}}{\sigma_{i,k}}, \frac{q_{i,2}}{\sigma_{i,2}}, \frac{q_{i,\epsilon}}{\sigma_{i,\epsilon}}\right) + A_k a_i \frac{\partial}{\partial q_{i,k}} R_{i,k}\left(\frac{q_{i,k}}{\sigma_{i,k}}\right) = 0 \qquad (10)$$

For $k = 1, 2 : A_k = \lambda_k$; and for $k = \epsilon : A_k = \lambda_1 + \lambda_2$; By deriving equation (7) the Lagrangian functional (10) is written in (11).

$$\Delta_i \sigma_{i,k}^2 C_k \frac{\partial}{\partial q_{i,k}} D_{i,k}\left(\frac{q_{i,k}}{\sigma_{i,k}}\right) + A_k a_i \frac{\partial}{\partial q_{i,k}} R_{i,k}\left(\frac{q_{i,k}}{\sigma_{i,k}}\right) = 0 \qquad (11)$$

In (11), for $k = 1, 2 : C_k = 1$ and for $k = \epsilon : C_k = \frac{2r_N}{1 + r_N}$. Simplifying (11) (for $j \in \{1, 2\}$ and $k \in \{1, 2, \epsilon\}$) for a two channels scheme.

$$\begin{cases} \frac{\partial D_{i,k}}{\partial R_{i,k}}\left(\frac{q_{i,k}}{\sigma_{i,k}}\right) = \frac{-A_k a_i}{\Delta_i \sigma_{i,k}^2 C_k} \\ \sum_{i=1}^{\#SB} a_i \left(R_{i,j}\left(\frac{q_{i,j}}{\sigma_{i,j}}\right) + R_{i,\epsilon}\left(\frac{q_{i,\epsilon}}{\sigma_{i,\epsilon}}\right)\right) - R_l = 0 \end{cases} \qquad (12)$$

Resolution of system (12) gives us the optimal sets of quantization steps $\{q_{i,1}\}$, $\{q_{i,2}\}$ and $\{q_{i,\epsilon}\}$.

6   Results

6.1   Scan-Based DWT Coder

For spatial decomposition in the first method the coder uses (6,2) nonseparable lifting scheme and performs a seven level decomposition [9]. In the second method the coder uses 9-7 biorthogonal filter [13] and performs a three levels decomposition. Quincunx transform adds an intermediate resolution level between two successive levels in the separable case, and then allows a twice as accurate multiresolution analysis as the separable one. Thus, the difference of resolution between two succesive levels has the value 2 in the bidimensional separable case, and a value $\sqrt{2}$ in the nonseparable case. One can observe that the resolution of the quincunx sampling images is $\sqrt{2}$ times higher than the resolution of CCD1 and CDD2. To obtain the same resolution for all low frequency images, a n level separable decomposition have to correspond to a $2n + 1$ level nonseparable decompositions.

The frames of the video sequence are acquired and processed on the fly to generate the wavelet coefficients and the data are stored in memory only until these coefficients have been encoded [7]. The bit allocation procedure is followed by a simple scalar quantization and the encoding of each subband uses context-based arithmetic bit-plane coder [15]. In order to provide synchronization and minimize the error propagation in the case of errors due to satellite communication, each spatio-temporal subband is divided into blocks. Then, arithmetic coding is synchronized on each block. For error detection, we use the Smart Arithmetic Coding method presented in [6]. As satellite channel simulator we use the model proposed by Chee and Sweeney for LEO satellite channels [16].

6.2   Satellite Channel Model

We compute the LEO satellite communication channel proposed in [16]. They show that for elevation angles of 23° and 52°, the burst statistics can be described by a two good state single error state Frichman model while a three-good state, single error state Frichman model can accurately describe the measured statistics for the rest of the elevation angles. Fritchman's partitioned Markov chain model is a generalization of Gilbert's model partitioned into k error free states and $N-k$ error states [17]. In this model, the interval length distribution between the errors is described by the sum of k exponentials, while the error burst distribution is described by the sum of $N - k$ exponentials. The derived transition probabilities for the three good state Fritchman model can be found in [16].

6.3   Simulations

We use a 352×704 quincunx Nimes image for method I and two 352×352 dyadic Nimes image for method II. Each test was performed 10 times. Table 1 presents the average PSNR obtained by the side decoders and the central decoder, for method I and II at different bit rates and for different redundancies. We can conclude from this table that method I his better suited for lesser redundancies (less noise), while method II is better suited for higher redundancies (more noise). Figures 6 and 7 presents one of the simulations at 2 bpp.

7   Conclusions

We propose two models of joint source-channel coding for quincunx images. The presented models are designed to get the best image quality after transmission over satellite channel.

Systems using a pair of CCD linear arrays in a quincunx arrangement to improve resolution treat each image independently, disregarding the highly redundancy between them. In the present work we take into account the redundancy between the two CCD arrays when performing joint source-channel coding. Furthermore, taking into account the satellite model characteristics presents a good trade off quality-robustness comparing with standard methods using forward error correction.

$r_N = 0.01$	Side PSNR	Central PSNR
2 bpp		
Method I	32.71	40.26
Method II	31.29	38.74
3 bpp		
Method I	33.04	42.27
Method II	31.62	37.82

$r_N = 0.5$	Side PSNR	Central PSNR
2 bpp		
Method I	33.92	37.76
Method II	31.88	39.48
3 bpp		
Method I	32.77	39.60
Method II	31.84	40.12

Table 1. PSNR values for Nimes image when considering transmission at an elevation angle of 40°.

References

[1] M. Pereira, M. Antonini, and M. Barlaud, "Channel adapted multiple description coding scheme using wavelet transform," in *IEEE ICIP*, Rochester, NY, US, Sept. 2002.

[2] ——, "Low complexity multiple description coding scheme using wavelet transform," in *EUSIPCO*, Toulouse, France, Sept. 2002.

[3] C. Lambert-Nebout, C. Latry, G. Moury, C. Parisot, M. Antonini, and M. Barlaud, "Image compression for future high resolution optical remote sensing missions," in *SPIE*, San Diego, 2000.

[4] C. Latry and B. Rougé, "Spot5 thr mode," in *SPIE VCIP*, USA, 1998.

[5] M. Pereira, M. Antonini, and M. Barlaud, "Multiple description coding for noisy-varying channels," in *IEEE DCC*, Snowbird, US, March 2003.

[6] ——, "Multiple description image and video coding for wireless channels," *EURASIP Signal Processing: Image Communication, Special issue on Recent Advances in Wireless Video*, submited, 2003.

[7] C. Parisot, M. Antonini, and M. Barlaud, "3D scan-based wavelet transform and quality control for video coding," *EURASIP Special Issue Multimedia Signal Processing*, vol. 2003, no. 1, pp. 56–65, January 2003.

[8] C. Parisot, M. Antonini, M. Barlaud, C. Lambert-Nebout, C. Latry, and G. Moury, "On-board stripe-based wavelet image coding for future space missions," in *IEEE IGARSS : Special Session on Remote Sensing Compression*, Honolulu, Hawaii, Juillet 2000.

[9] A. Gouze, M. Antonini, and M. Barlaud, "Quincunx lifting scheme for image compression," in *IEEE ICIP*, vol. 1, Vancouver, septembre 2000, pp. 665–668.

[10] A. Gouze, M. Antonini, M. Barlaud, and B. Macq, "Optimized lifting scheme for two-dimensional quincunx sampling images," in *IEEE ICIP*, vol. 2, Thessaloniki, Greece, October 2001, pp. 253–258.

[11] J. C. Feauveau, "Analyse multirésolution pour les images avec un facteur de résolution $\sqrt{2}$," *Traitement du signal*, vol. 7, no. 2, 1990.

[12] Y. Meyer, *Wavelets and Operators*. Cambridge University Press, 1992.

[13] M. Antonini, M. Barlaud, P. Mathieu, and I. Daubechies, "Image coding using wavelet transform," *IEEE Trans. on Image Proc.*, vol. 4, no. 8, pp. 1053–1060, Aug. 1992.

[14] C. Shannon, "A mathematical theory of communication," *The Bell System Technical Journal*, vol. 27, pp. 379–423, 623–656, July, October 1948.

Fig. 6. Method I. From left to right: channel 1, channel 2 and channels 1 and 2.

Fig. 7. Method II. From left to right: channel 1, channel 2 and channels 1 and 2.

[15] C. Parisot, M. Antonini, and M. Barlaud, "Ebwic: A low complexity and efficient rate constrained wavelet image coder," in *ICIP*, Vancouver, Canada, Sept. 2000.

[16] V. Chu and P. Sweeney, "Channel modelling and error control strategies for the leo satellite channel," in *ISCTA*, Ambleside, UK, July 1999.

[17] B. Frichman, "A binary channel characterisation using partitioned markov chains," *IEEE Transactions in Information Theory*, vol. IT-13, pp. 221–227, April 1967.

Base Station Joint Scheduling for Downlink Throughput Maximization in CDMA Packet Data Networks

Christian Makaya and Sonia Aïssa

INRS-Telecommunications
800, de la Gauchetiere W., Suite 6900
Montreal, QC, H5A 1K6, CANADA
{makaya,aissa}@inrs-telecom.uquebec.ca

Abstract. In this work, we address the problem of CDMA downlink packet scheduling. Our goal is to maximize data throughput and fairness among mobile users. We formulate packet scheduling as a constrained integer optimization problem, modelling the constraints arising from data rate requirements, power budgets and interference limitations. Given the objective of maximizing the overall carried traffic in a given sector of a cell and power limitations in the neighboring sectors, joint optimization of resource utilization to control packet flow among the interdependent neighboring sectors is considered, and shown to provide higher performance compared to separate optimization in which each sector attempts to maximize the utilization of the available resources under in-cell and out-of-cell power limitations, without taking into account the traffic load among the adjacent sectors.

1 Introduction

In the upcoming third-generation wireless systems, resource management mechanisms will play a key role in guaranteeing the quality of service (QoS) required by multimedia applications. For the downlink, such efficient mechanisms are of particular importance due to the fact that the increasing demand is expected to result in an asymmetric data traffic with the bulk directed from the base station to mobile terminals. Given limited radio resources, performance in terms of the amount of traffic carried and fairness in serving the different users, heavily depends on the efficiency of the applied resource management schemes, including multiple access, call admission, power control, flow control, and congestion control. In this paper, our focus is on the design of a flow control algorithm for packet data transmission on the downlink of a Code Division Multiple Access (CDMA) system. The performance of CDMA systems depends on the success in managing the interference arising from both inter-cell and intra-cell transmissions. Therefore, managing the interference generated by packet transmissions is expected to improve performance both in terms of throughput and fairness.

The control of downlink packet flow at the base stations of power controlled CDMA wireless networks is constrained by the transmit power available at each

M.M. Freire, P. Lorenz, M.M.-O. Lee (Eds.): HSNMC 2003, LNCS 2720, pp. 304–315, 2003.
© Springer-Verlag Berlin Heidelberg 2003

base station (BS) and interference limitations and has two conflicting objectives to be optimized, namely throughput and fairness among the mobiles. We previously proposed [1], [2] a packet scheduling algorithm, referred here as Individual Rate Assignment algorithm (IRA), for downlink packet transmission. In the previous study, based on radio resource limitations that are communicated between adjacent BSs, the flow control problem is formulated as a constrained optimization problem and each BS performs its optimization independently of the traffic load in the neighboring BSs. However, in situations where the traffic load is highly unequal between adjacent BSs, this may result in patently unfair service between users of these interdependent BSs. In this paper, we propose a flow control algorithm that schedules packet transmissions within each cell so as to maximize throughput and ensure fairness among its users, while maintaining the interference to neighboring cells at a minimum level through efficient use of the radio resources available in order to enhance the performance both in terms of throughput and fairness in the adjacent cells as well. The proposed packet scheduler, termed Joint Rate Assignment algorithm (JRA) allows enhancing the system's performance while improving service in the loaded cells.

The remainder of this paper is organized as follows. Sect. 2 provides a description of the system topology and sector subdivision into zones based on the average packet resource requirements. In Sect. 3, we formulate the optimization problem and describe the algorithm proposed. We then present a solution to reduce the complexity of the algorithm. In Sect. 4, performance analysis and comparisons are provided. Concluding remarks are presented in the last section.

2   System Model and Analysis

2.1   System Model

We consider a hexagonal cell geometry as illustrated in Fig. 1. A cell is divided into three $120°$ sectors with transmissions to a pair of regions each consisting of n_z zones. Transmissions to each region generates interference to mobiles served by the BS opposing it. Refer to a sector by the corresponding BS and consider BS_0 as the target, the neighboring BSs are BS_1 and BS_2. An example of this configuration is shown in Fig. 2 with four zones per sector. Based on such a configuration, three adjacent sectors identify a cluster of interdependent BSs and our purpose is to schedule packet transmission through joint optimization of the radio resources available in the cluster. Our analysis focuses on three facing sectors, however, it can easily be generalized to any cluster in the system.

Let U be the number of users in the system and U_l ($l = 0, \cdots, L - 1$), the number of users served by BS_l. We denote by $d_{u,l}$ the distance between user u and BS_l, and $h_{u,l}$ the link gain between user u and BS_l. We assume that the path loss is given by $h_{u,l} = 10^{(s_{u,l}/10)} d_{u,l}^{-4}$, where $s_{u,l}$ is the log-normal shadowing with zero mean and standard deviation σ_s. The shadowing is correlated between BSs, i.e., is serial and site-to-site correlated. This effect is modelled by considering the shadowing as a sum (in dB) of a component common to all base stations and a component specific to BS_l [3].

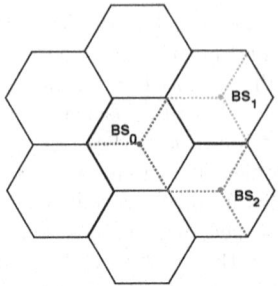

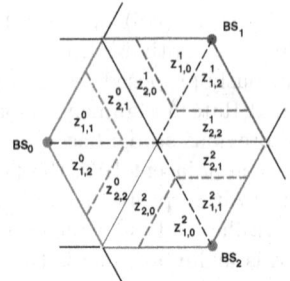

Fig. 1. Hexagonal cell geometry   **Fig. 2.** Partitioning a sector into zones

2.2   Resource Requirement Based Sector Subdivision

The QoS on the downlink can be measured by the Signal-to-Interference (SIR) ratio at the mobile terminals. Compared to the uplink, the interference experienced by the mobile on the downlink comes from a few sources (BSs) but the interfering power is relatively high. As the interference experienced by a mobile terminal depends on its path loss to all BSs, all users experience different interference levels depending on their locations [4].

Let p_u, $u = 1, ..., U_l$, be the power transmitted to user u by BS_l. The total transmitted power for BS_l is then given by $P_l = P_{pilot} + \sum_{u=1}^{U_l} p_u$. This power has to be lower than the available transmit power $P_{max,l}$ at the corresponding BS. Given this power constraint, each user has to be assigned enough power so as to maintain its SIR at the target level Γ. The SIR for user u can be expressed as follows:

$$SIR_u = \frac{G_b}{r_u} \frac{h_{u,l} p_u}{I_{u,l}^{ic} + I_{u,l}^{oc} + \eta_0 W} \tag{1}$$

where G_b is the processing gain relative to the basic transmission rate R_b, r_u is the number of packets transmitted to user u during a time slot, η_0 is the background noise power spectral density at the mobile unit and $I_{u,l}^{ic} = \delta \sum_{u'=1, u' \neq u}^{U_l} p_{u'} h_{u,l} = \delta(P_l - p_u) h_{u,l}$ is the in-cell (IC) interference term, with δ the orthogonality factor. An average value for $\delta = 0.06$ for microcellular pedestrian applications will be used in our simulations. The main interference though is the out-of-cell (OOC) interference resulting from transmissions in the adjacent cells and is given by $I_{u,j}^{oc} = \sum_{l'=0, l' \neq l}^{L} P_{l'} h_{u,l'}$.

We group users in each sector based on the average resource requirements needed to transmit a packet to a given user depending on its location. Indeed, users near the BS may require less transmit power from the serving BS than those who are closer to the cell boundary. Such a subdivision of sectors into zones is illustrated in Fig. 2 with $2n_z$ zones per sector. Separation lines between zones are found by means of mean squared error minimization which is described in details in [5]. Considering such a subdivision, we determine the average transmit power per packet $\bar{p}_z$ for users in each zone z. Using minimum power assignment, the transmit power per packet to user u connected to BS_l is adjusted to attain the target SIR Γ. Then the average transmitted power for zone z is given by

$$\bar{p}_z = \frac{\Gamma}{G_b + \delta\Gamma} P_l \left(\delta + \sum_{l'=0, l' \neq l}^{L} \frac{P_{l'}}{P_l} E \left[\frac{h_{u,l'}}{h_{u,l}} \right]_{u \in z} \right) \qquad (2)$$

where z refers to a zone (i,j) of BS_l.

For the remainder, we note the three interdependent sectors by the corresponding BS index, that is $S = \{0,1,2\}$. Considering $2n_z$ zones per sector, the set of average power values corresponding to a sector $l \in S$ are denoted $\alpha_{i,j}^l$ where $i = 1, \cdots, n_z$ and $j \in FB_l = S - \{l\}$ refers to the facing BSs. To calculate the average OOC resource requirements per transmitted packet, consider that an additional packet is transmitted to a mobile in zone (i,j) of BS_l facing BS_j. To overcome the interference generated by this packet transmission and keep the required SIR level for its users, BS_j has to increase its transmit power by an amount $\beta_{i,j}^l = \sum_{uj \in BS_j} \Delta P_{uj}$. A simple equalization of the SIR's of a user uj in BS_j before and after the packet transmission in BS_l yields

$$\Delta P_{uj} = \frac{\Gamma}{G_{uj}} \alpha_{i,j}^l \frac{h_{uj,l}}{h_{uj,j}}, \qquad (3)$$

where G_{uj} is the processing gain of user uj. Depending on the position of this user, an average value for $\frac{h_{uj,l}}{h_{uj,j}}$ has been found to be equal to $\gamma_{in} = 0.08$ if the mobile is located in an inner zone of BS_j and $\gamma_{out} = 0.62$ if the mobile is located in an outer zone [5]. Let N_{in} and N_{out} be the respective throughput values, expressed in terms of number of packets per time slot of the users in the inner and outer zones of the region in BS_l facing zone (i,j), the average increase in the transmit power at BS_j due to the transmission of an additional packet to zone (i,j) of BS_l can be expressed as follows

$$\beta_{i,j}^l = \frac{\Gamma}{G_b} \alpha_{i,j}^l (N_{in}\gamma_{in} + N_{out}\gamma_{out}). \qquad (4)$$

3 Packet Scheduler Design

3.1 Problem Statement

Consider that each sector is subdivided into $2n_z$ zones. Packets destined for mobiles in each sector are grouped into different queues, one for each zone of the sector. The scheduler objective is to determine the best transmission assignment per time slot, to mobiles requesting packet transmission, given the time varying resource availability, mobility and time-varying transmission demands. The main resource, available at each time slot, correspond to the BS power budget $P_{budget} = P_{max} - P_{pilot}$. The interaction between neighboring sectors implies that each BS has to devote a certain amount of power to overcome the interference generated by packet transmissions in the adjacent BSs. Thus, part of the available power budget is used to transmit packets within the target sector and the remaining resources are used to overcome the interference generated by transmissions in the facing adjacent sectors. Hard power margins may be used as in [1] but these margins may result in wasted resources. Indeed, let W_l^k be the power budget for IC packet transmissions at BS_l during time slot k and denote by $OC_{\{j \in FB_l\}}^k$ the power margins available at the facing BSs as counter-measure. These margins are hard limits specifying the levels of interference that can be generated by packet transmissions in the target sector without giving rise to excessive outage in the facing sectors. These power margins are predicted based on measurements of the carried traffic in each sector and communicated between adjacent BSs. In this case, and following the approach described in [1], the resource constraints for $BS_{l \in S}$, at time slot k, are expressed as follows:

$$
\begin{aligned}
&\sum_{i=1}^{n_z} \sum_{j \in FB_l} \alpha_{i,j}^l n_{i,j}^l(k) \leq W_l^k , \\
&\sum_{i=1}^{n_z} \beta_{i,j}^l n_{i,j}^l(k) \leq OC_j^k , \quad j \in FB_l \\
&0 \leq n_{i,j}^l(k) \leq N_{i,j}^l(k); \quad i = 1, \dots, n_z, \; j \in FB_l ,
\end{aligned}
\tag{5}
$$

where for each $l \in S$, $n_{i,j}^l$ is the number of packets allocated to users in zone (i,j) of the sector served by BS_l and $N_{i,j}^l(k)$ is the number of packets queued for these users at time slot k. Under these resource constraints, the scheduling algorithm proposed in [1] finds the assignment vector $\mathbf{n}^l$ (denoting the numbers of packets allocated to the different zones of BS_l), which optimizes the resource utilization in each sector of the cluster individually, the only information considered from the adjacent sectors being the limits on the power margins. We refer to this algorithm by the Individual Rate Assignment (IRA) and propose a more efficient scheduling scheme which we call Joint Rate Assignment (JRA) algorithm.

3.2 Joint Rate Assignment Algorithm

The IRA algorithm is optimal when the load is equally balanced between sectors. However, if this is not the case, such a scheduling scheme may lead to wasted radio resources. In fact, setting hard power margins in each BS to overcome the OOC interference generated by packet transmissions in the facing sectors would be ineffective if these sectors are not heavily loaded. As the load in each sector varies with time, an efficient use of the available resources among each three interdependent sectors is expected to enhance the overall system's performance. For this purpose, the JRA algorithm jointly determines at each time slot the best assignment matrix $\mathbf{n}(k) = \{\mathbf{n}^0(k), \mathbf{n}^1(k), \mathbf{n}^2(k)\}$, where $\mathbf{n}^l(k)$ is the assignment vector corresponding to BS_l. This is done by using the available resources at each BS, namely $P_{budget,l}^k$ to support IC packet transmissions and to overcome the OOC interference generated by packet transmissions in the facing sectors depending on the variable load of each sector of the cluster.

We formulate the problem as a constrained integer optimization problem following the approach in [1]. The formulation uses an objective function composed of a weighted sum of throughput, fairness, and a function which quantifies the proximity to the available remaining resources. The resource constraints for the cluster of interdependent sectors at time slot k, can then be expressed as follows

$$\sum_{i=1}^{n_z} \sum_{j \in FB_l} \left(\alpha_{i,j}^l n_{i,j}^l(k) + \beta_{i,l}^j(\mathbf{n}^*(k-1)) \, n_{i,l}^j(k) \right) \leq P_{budget,l}^k \quad \forall \, l \in S$$

$$(6)$$

$$0 \leq n_{i,j}^l(k) \leq N_{i,j}^l(k), \, \forall \, l \in S; \; i \in \{1, \ldots, n_z\}, \; j \in FB_l.$$

where, in time slot k, $P_{budget,l}^k$ is the power budget available at BS_l after support of ongoing stream services, and $\mathbf{n}^*(k-1)$ is the optimal assignment matrix of the previous time slot. The resource availability associated with a transmit assignment vector $\mathbf{n}^l$ for BS_l at time slot k can be expressed as

$$RW_l^k(\mathbf{n}) = P_{budget,l}^k - \sum_{i=1}^{n_z} \sum_{j \in BF_l} \left(\alpha_{i,j}^l n_{i,j}^l(k) + \beta_{i,l}^j(\mathbf{n}^*(k-1)) \, n_{i,l}^j(k) \right). \quad (7)$$

We differentiate three sets of remaining resources associated with each sector BS_l (one IC and two OOC) associated with an assignment matrix $\mathbf{n}$ as follows

$$\begin{aligned} RIC_l^k(\mathbf{n}) &= RW_l^k(\mathbf{n}) \, , \; l \in S \\ ROC_j^k(\mathbf{n}) &= RW_j^k(\mathbf{n}) \, , \; j \in FB_l. \end{aligned} \quad (8)$$

and use a proximity function that measures the maximum number of additional packets that could be transmitted to zone (i, j) of BS_l

$$\bar{n}_{i,j}^l(\mathbf{n}) = \min \left\{ \left\lfloor \frac{RIC_l^k(\mathbf{n})}{\alpha_{i,j}^l} \right\rfloor, \left\lfloor \frac{ROC_j^k(\mathbf{n})}{\beta_{i,j}^l(\mathbf{n}^*(k-1))} \right\rfloor \right\}, \quad (9)$$

where $\lfloor \cdot \rfloor$ denotes the integral part of a number. Generalizing over all zones, the resource proximity function corresponding to the assignment $\mathbf{n}^l(k)$ is that of the zone with least spare resources and is defined as

$$\mathcal{P}_{\mathbf{n}^l}(k) = \min_{i,j} \bar{n}_{i,j}^l(\mathbf{n}). \quad (10)$$

The joint control of packet data flow investigated for the set of interdependent sectors consists in finding, at each time slot k, the transmit matrix $\mathbf{n}(k) = \{\mathbf{n}^0(k), \mathbf{n}^1(k), \mathbf{n}^2(k)\}$ which jointly maximizes throughput and fairness among the different zones, while ensuring that the resource constraints for all BSs are not violated. To provide fair allocation of resources among users so that they experience equitable levels of service while maintaining an acceptable throughput, we define the optimization criterion as the maximization of the functional $\mathcal{J}_{\mathbf{n}}(k)$ corresponding to an assignment matrix $\mathbf{n}(k)$:

$$\mathcal{J}_{\mathbf{n}}(k) = \mathcal{T}_{\mathbf{n}}(k) + \mathcal{P}_{\mathbf{n}}(k) + \underline{\lambda} \cdot \mathcal{F}_{\mathbf{n}}^T(k), \quad (11)$$

where in time slot k, $\mathcal{T}_{\mathbf{n}}(k) = \sum_{l \in S} \mathcal{T}_{\mathbf{n}^l}(k)$ is the throughput in total number of packets transmitted, $\mathcal{P}_{\mathbf{n}}(k) = \min_{l \in S} \mathcal{P}_{\mathbf{n}^l}(k)$ is the proximity function which measures the resource availability resulting from assignment $\mathbf{n}(k)$, $\mathcal{F}_{\mathbf{n}}(k)$ is the fairness metric and the coefficient vector $\underline{\lambda} = (\lambda^0, \lambda^1, \lambda^2)$ is chosen to tune the trade-off between throughput and fairness. $\mathcal{T}_{\mathbf{n}^l}(k)$ and $\mathcal{P}_{\mathbf{n}^l}(k)$ designate respectively the throughput and proximity function associated with BS_l. $\mathcal{F}_{\mathbf{n}^l}(k)$ measures the intra-cell fairness in sector BS_l and is expressed as function of the variance of the delay on the remaining head-of-queue packets. The optimization problem reduces to finding the optimal assignment matrix $\mathbf{n}^*(k)$ which maximizes the objective function (Eq. 11) under the joint constraints (Eq. 6). Note that the IRA algorithm can be seen as a particular case of JRA where instead of maximizing the functional given by Eq. 11 under the constraints specified by Eq. 6, we maximize the functional $\mathcal{J}_{\mathbf{n}^l}(k) = \mathcal{T}_{\mathbf{n}^l}(k) + \mathcal{P}_{\mathbf{n}^l}(k) + \lambda^l \mathcal{F}_{\mathbf{n}^l}^l(k)$, $\forall\, l \in S$, under the corresponding constraints (Eq. 5).

For a given vector $\underline{\lambda}$ and an initial assignment matrix $\mathbf{n}^{(iter=0)}(k)$, the algorithm iteratively updates the assignment matrix , increasing index $iter$ until the stopping criterion is met and the optimal assignment matrix $\mathbf{n}^*(k)$ is reached. As long as the resource constraints are satisfied and the objective function (Eq. 11) increases, the algorithm iterates on $iter$ following a *steepest ascent* strategy. At each iteration, the algorithm selects up to $6n_z$ possible assignments that include one additional packet to be transmitted from non-empty queues. The packet that maximizes the objective function is selected and added to the assignment matrix and the process continues until the optimal assignment is reached. Based on this assignment, the average power increments (β's) are computed, and new sets of resource limits are obtained for use in the next time slot.

3.3 Complexity Reduction

The complexity of the JRA algorithm is dominated by the requirement for the number of zones $nz = 2n_z$ in each sector. Increasing the number of zones achieves higher throughput at the cost of additional complexity. When the resources vary slowly in time, the complexity may be reduced by using the previous assignment matrix as the starting point for the current time slot. Indeed, in finding the optimal assignment matrix $\mathbf{n}^*(k)$, we used the steepest ascent strategy and assumed that the starting matrix $\mathbf{n}^{(iter=0)}(k)$ satisfies the resource constraints. If that condition is not satisfied, the search for $\mathbf{n}^*(k)$ is performed by iteratively decrementing the component of the current matrix to which the resource utilization is most sensitive until the available resources become adequate. More specifically, given that the throughput value of the initial matrix $\mathbf{n}^{(iter=0)}(k)$ is $\mathcal{T}_{\mathbf{n}^{(iter=0)}}(k)$, for a throughput of value $\mathcal{T}_{\mathbf{n}^{(iter=0)}}(k) - 1$, define up to $6\, n_z$ ($2\, n_z$ in the case of the IRA algorithm) possible assignment matrices that include one less packet that could be transmitted to a particular zone, find the corresponding objective function values and select the transmit matrix that minimizes the objective function. If a resource constraint is irrelevant to transmission to a particular zone, it can be ignored in calculating the minimum. Once, the starting point that satisfies the resource constraints found, the algorithm performs the search for the optimal assignment matrix following steepest ascent. Consequently, the scheduling algorithm provided can be executed in a sequential fashion by selecting, for a given time slot k, the assignment matrix of the previous time slot as the starting matrix when searching for the current one i.e $\mathbf{n}^{(iter=0)}(k) = \mathbf{n}^*(k - 1)$.

4   Results and Analysis

The operation of the algorithms has been studied for a wide range of parameters, arrival models as well as distribution of mobile users. Herein, we consider the four-zone subdivision of a 120° sector, 10 users in each inner zone and 4 users in each outer zone. Packets destined for transmission to each terminal follow a Poisson arrival process during a packet arrival interval of 100 time slots with an average load per terminal of 3 packets per time slot. For mobility, we consider a directional random walk model and assume correlated shadowing at subsequent positions. The performance of each algorithm is evaluated by collecting statistics for each three-sector cluster. Results are provided for the central cluster of the network and expressed in terms of average throughput, fairness, and maximum delay at the head of each queue. The average throughput is defined as a moving average over a time frame. In addition, a time-to-completion measure, defined as the number of time slots required to transmit all packets corresponding to the arrival interval, is used for comparison purposes. Results provided correspond to the traffic load exceeding the available resources both in IC and OOC. As for the fairness multipliers, we provide results for equal values, i.e., $\lambda^l = \lambda$, $l \in S$ and focus on the extreme cases for fairness: $\lambda = 0$ for throughput maximization only, and λ approaching ∞ for extreme importance assigned to fairness. The resource budget in each sector correspond to the maximum power available after accounting for the pilot power [7]. This is the power budget available in the case of JRA optimization. For IRA, this budget is the sum of IC and OOC resource limits. The latter defined by a percentage of the IC resources. A value of 5% is chosen [6]. The main simulation parameters are summarized in Fig. 9.

We represent in Fig. 3 the average throughput results for both algorithms. During the packet arrival interval, the average throughput decreases as λ increases. Compared to throughput maximization only, this decrease is traded-off for an increase in fairness as illustrated in Fig. 4 for BS$_0$. However, as can be seen in Table 1, throughput reduction for a given value of λ is less important for the JRA scheme compared to IRA. Indeed, comparison of the results show that JRA yields an increase in throughput (Fig. 3), and a higher fairness level (Fig. 4). For a given λ, we observe how the JRA algorithm allows efficient resource utilization to increase throughput and considerably decrease the completion time as can be seen in Table 1. Analysis of the results provided in this table show that the JRA algorithm allows maximum achievable fairness with a throughput loss (calculated with respect to $\lambda = 0$) of 14%, whereas this loss is of 39% for IRA. Considering throughput maximization only, higher fairness can be obtained using JRA (Fig. 4), with a gain in throughput of 14% compared to IRA. The maximum achievable fairness using JRA is higher than its IRA counterpart with a gain in throughput of 40%.

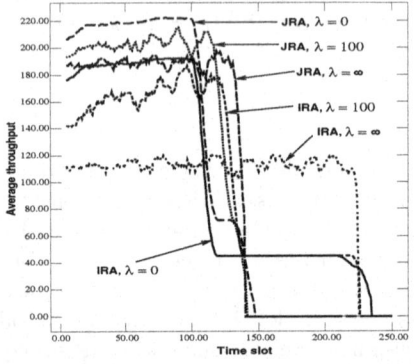

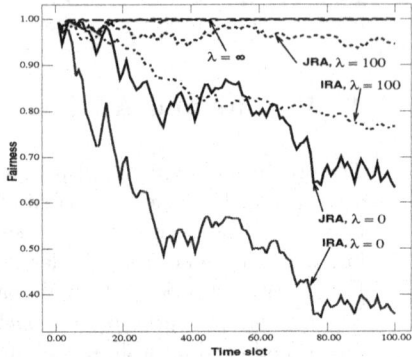

Fig. 3. Comparison of the average throughput for JRA and IRA algorithms for different values of λ

Fig. 4. Comparison of the fairness achieved using JRA and IRA algorithms for different values of λ

Table 1. Time-to-completion and throughput loss as function of λ

λ	Time-to-completion		Throughput loss		Throughput loss
	JRA	IRA	JRA	IRA	IRA vs. JRA
0	147	235	--	--	14%
100	141	226	9%	15%	20%
∞	140	225	14%	39%	40%

The improvement in fairness is achieved by striving to equalize the delays of the head-of-queue packets. Delay equalization is indeed improved as λ increases, as can be seen in Fig. 6 showing the maximum delay at the head of each queue using $\lambda = \infty$ for BS_0 and implementation of the JRA algorithm, compared to the results corresponding to $\lambda = 0$ and shown in Fig. 5. Compared to the results corresponding to case using IRA, provided in Fig. 7 ($\lambda = 0$) and Fig. 8 ($\lambda = \infty$), we observe how the JRA scheme yields lower delay values, and consequently lower time-to-completion values as can be seen in Table 2.

As previously mentioned, the complexity of the JRA algorithm can be reduced through the use of the previous assignment matrix as the starting point for the current time slot. Under this mode of operation, the number of iterations, needed for the algorithm to find the final matrix can significantly be reduced. Consider, throughput maximization only and the central cluster. In Fig. 10 we

Table 2. Comparison of the algorithm time-to-completion for BS_0

Algorithm	$\lambda = 0$	$\lambda = 100$	$\lambda = \infty$
IRA	$(111, 229)$	$(130, 222)$	$(220, 220)$
JRA	$(111, 139)$	$(122, 136)$	$(135, 133)$

show the difference in number of iterations needed for convergence, between the zero starting matrix and the non-zero one. As we can see, the complexity of the algorithm can be reduced without affecting its optimality. Indeed, throughput results for both modes of operation correspond to the number of iterations needed when the algorithm starts from the zero assignment matrix.

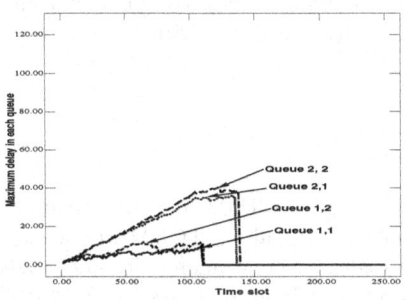

Fig. 5. JRA algorithm: maximum delay at the head of each queue for $\lambda = 0$

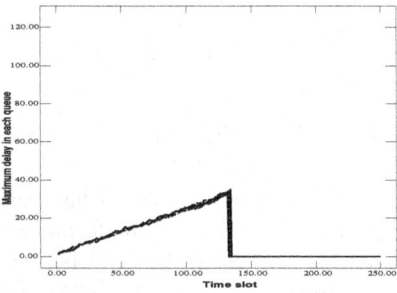

Fig. 6. JRA algorithm: maximum delay at the head of each queue for $\lambda = \infty$

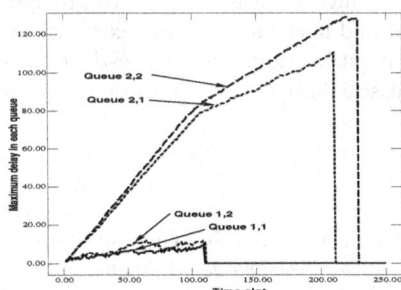

Fig. 7. IRA algorithm: maximum delay at the head of each queue for $\lambda = 0$

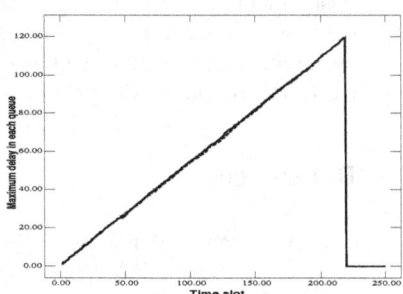

Fig. 8. IRA algorithm: maximum delay at the head of each queue for $\lambda = \infty$

Item	Symbol	Value
System bandwidth	W	5 MHz
Carrier frequency	f_c	2 GHz
Cell radius	R	1000 m
Slot length	TS	10 ms
Frame length	TF	10 TS
Speed	υ	3.6 Kmph
Basic rate	R_b	38.4 Kbps
Orthogonality factor	δ	0.06
Path loss exponent		4
Handoff margin		4 dB
Standard deviation	σ_s	8 dB
BS maximum power	P max	10 W
Power control step	Δ	0.5 dB
Target SNR	Γ	6.5 dB

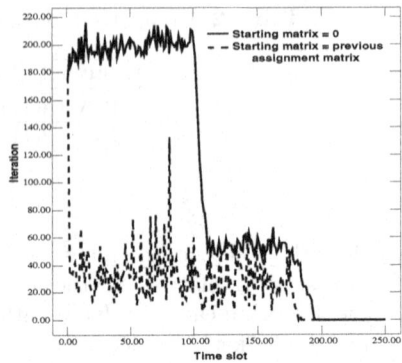

Fig. 9. Main simulation parameters and their values

Fig. 10. Number of iterations for zero and non-zero starting matrix using the JRA algorithm with $\lambda = 0$

5   Conclusion

A scheduling algorithm has been proposed for CDMA downlink packet data transmission and its performance evaluated in a multi-cell CDMA network. Joint optimization of the available resources is conducted among clusters formed by interdependent sectors. Through the proposed Joint Rate Assignment (JRA) algorithm, we showed that higher performance can be achieved both in terms of throughput and fairness compared to the case when optimization of the radio resources is performed individually in each sector through the Individual Rate Assignment (IRA) scheme [1]. The JRA algorithm is designed to provide adequate compromise between throughput and fairness, adapts to existing resource availability and results in high network utilization. Under investigation is the use of the proposed algorithm for joint scheduling and base station assignment.

References

1. S. Aïssa and P. Mermelstein, "Downlink Flow Control for Wireless CDMA Packet Data Networks", *IEEE Trans. on Vehicular Technology*, vol. 51, no. 5, pp. 1193-1205, September 2002.
2. F. Beaulieu and S. Aïssa, "Position-Based Packet Data Scheduling for Multi-Class CDMA Downlinks", *IEEE International Conference on Telecommunications*, Papeete, French Polynesia, February 2003.
3. A. J. Viterbi, *CDMA Principles of Spread Spectrum Communications*, Addison-Wesley, 1996.
4. C. Mihailescu, X. Lagrange and Ph. Godlewski, "Soft Handover Analysis in Downlink UMTS WCDMA System", *IEEE International Workshop on Mobile Multimedia Communications*, San Diego, USA, November 1999.

5. A. Maaref, S. Aïssa and S. Affes, "Combined Flow Control and Interference Cancellation for Packet Data Transmission in Wideband CDMA Systems", *In Proc. IEEE International Conf. on Communications*, Anchorage, Alaska, May 2003.
6. S. Kandala and P. Mermelstein, "Integrated Voice and Video Services in Microcellular CDMA Systems - Downlink Power-Based Call Admission", *Mobile Multimedia Communications*, Plenum Press, New York, pp. 51–57, 1997.
7. D. Kim, Y. Chang and J. W. Lee, "Pilot Power Control and service coverage support in CDMA mobile systems", in *Proc. VTC*, pp. 1464–1468, Houston, TX, May 1999.

Implementation of Digital Transceiver for Multiple CDMA Signals

Jae Ho Jung, Kwang Chun Lee, and Deuk Soo Lyu

Electronics and Telecommunications Research Institute (ETRI),
Mobile Telecommunicaton Research Laboratory
161 Gajeong-Dong, Yuseong-Gu, Daejon, 305-350, Korea
jhjung@etri.re.kr

Abstract. In this paper, we have presented the improved IF transceiver architecture and its implementation results on re-configurable transceiver based on
digital IF for multiple wideband CDMA base stations, which have been implemented as ADC, DAC with high speed and resolution and high performance
FPGA. The implemented digital IF transceiver has been designed to support
multiple frequency allocations and multiple standards by only modifying the
programmable software not its hardware as the software defined radio concept.
The digital complex quadrature modulation technique has been used for the
digital IF transmitter, which is able to combine multiple frequency bands in
digital processing block not RF block and to reject the image frequency signals.
Also, this method is possible to apply to the baseband digital adaptive predis-
tortion technique. And, the bandpass sampling technique has been used for the
digital IF receiver to reduce the sampling rate of ADC. As the implementation
results, the FIR and interpolation/decimation halfband filters over 200 taps,
digital mixers and digital synthesizers has been implemented on FPGA with
200 million gates for the digital IF transceivers in wideband CDMA base stations. This paper has presented the experiment results on the frequency response and constellation of the implemented digital IF transceiver through
back-to-back combining a transmitter with a receiver using a simplified
16QAM physical channel model.

1 Introduction

Recent advances in analog to digital converter (ADC) or digital to analog converter
(DAC) with high sampling rate and high bit resolution above to 100Msps and 16bits
respectively are possible to implement directly the digital signal frequency conversion
scheme on intermediate frequency (IF) to baseband in digital domain [1-3]. Also, as
the high speed field programmable gated arrays (FPGA) operating up to about
100MHz can be available on the cellular base station systems, the software defined
radio (SDR) system on which is useful for reconfigurable communication systems
supporting the multiple modes or multiple standards only by modifications of its
software is realizable to implement. Because of the above reasons, digital IF technologies are very important for implementation on SDR systems or reconfigurable
base station systems to improve the performance of already installed systems without

M.M. Freire, P. Lorenz, M.M.-O. Lee (Eds.): HSNMC 2003, LNCS 2720, pp. 316-325, 2003.

modifications of hardware. Moreover, digital IF technologies have advantage to reject the mismatch of in-phase/out-phase (IQ) signals and DC offset problems that can be easily generated on the conventional heterodyne system, because the IF modulators and demodulators in digital IF transceivers are composed on digital and have the identical performance. And these technologies are able to combine the multiple frequency allocations on digital domain using the complex quadrature modulation and demodulation technique for multicarrier systems.

In this paper, we present the reconfigurable digital IF transceiver architecture for supporting multiple wideband code division multiple access (CDMA) signals. Especially, on the presented digital IF transmitter, the digital IQ modulation structure for the rejection of image frequency components can be applied to the digital baseband adaptive predistorter in which has been commercialized [4]. The simulations and experiments using a simplified 16QAM physical channel structure have been performed to certify the presented transceiver architecture structure by back-to-back connection of digital IF transmitter and receiver. And, we have implemented on the presented digital IF transceiver with only single FPGA chip and high performance ADC and DAC.

Here, the implemented digital IF technologies are the bandpass sampling technique for reduction of the sampling rate of ADC, the decimation or interpolation halfband filter technique with the polyphase type and digital complex quadrature modulation technique for rejection of the image frequency signals, etc. Many literatures are published about efficient digital filters [5-6] and channelizer/dechannelizer using the polyphase multirate system [7-8] for SDR systems.

This paper is organized as follows. In the second section, we describe the architecture of digital IF transceiver available on wideband CDMA base station systems. And we show the validity of the presented transceiver architecture by simulation on the simplified 16QAM physical channel structure in the third section. In the forth section, the digital IF transceiver module implemented on PCB boards with single FPGA, ADC and DAC and its experiment results on the frequency response and constellation are described. A conclusion remark is presented in the last section.

2 Architecture of Digtal IF Transceiver

2.1 Structure of Digital IF Transmitter

The presented architecture of digital IF transmitter supporting 2 FA bands in wideband CDMA base stations is shown in Fig. 1. The IQ signals received from a physical channel modem corresponding to each multiple FA are injected into the digital IF transmitter as the sample rate of 3.84Msps defined by chip rate in our system. And, zeros are inserted by two times of chip rate to interpolate to higher sample rate. These zeropadded complex multiple FA signals are filtered by the root raised cosine (RRC) filters whose coefficients are extracted by WCDMA specification [9], and then are filtered by the finite impulse response (FIR) filters using Park-MacClellan algorithm. The band limited complex baseband signals filtered by RRC and FIR are interpolated as much as 16 times of chip rate via three halfband filters to fit to the recommended

sample rate of a commercial adaptive baseband predistorter [4]. Each filter is implemented as polyphase type to reduce the number of multipliers [2].

In general, the complex IQ baseband signals through the RRC filter can be directly
upconverted to IF or RF signals using the analog or digital quadrature modulator.
But, in this paper, the digital complex quadrature modulation technique instead of the
digital quadrature modulation that is able to reject image frequency components is
used for digitally combining the baseband signals of multiple FAs and for applying to
the baseband digital adaptive predistorter to increase the RF system's linearity. Even
if the four digital mixers, two numerical controlled oscillators and two summers
should be used for one digital complex quadrature modulator, the increase of gates on
FPGA is ignorable.

First, the complex baseband signal passed by digital filters corresponding to the
first FA is upconverted to –2.5MHz center frequency, and its image frequency component exists on +2.5MHz. Similarly, in case of the second FA, the complex baseband signal is upconverted to +2.5MHz, and its image frequency component exists on
–2.5MHz. These complex signals of each FA after digital complex quadrature modulation are summed to be the complex signal with multiple FA bands. Therefore, the
desired multiple FA signals are combined with its image signals on baseband, and
then these signals can be injected into the baseband adaptive predistorter to distort as
much as RF system's nonlinearity. The digital complex baseband signal of two FAs is
again upconvertered to 8.56MHz by the complex quadrature modulation method
before used. To obtain the digital IF signal of 70MHz, we have used a commercial
DAC chip [10] made in Analog Devices, in which are including three interpolation
filters, NCOs and dual DACs with high sample rate close to 400Msps, because it is
difficult to operate on FPGA over 140Msps as Nyquist sampling rate. The image
frequency components generated by the combination of FAs can be rejected using the
quadrature modulation in DAC chip. The digital IF signal with 245.76Msps data rate
interpolated by two halfband filters in DAC chip is converted into 70MHz analog
signal and is transmitted to RF boards and antennas.

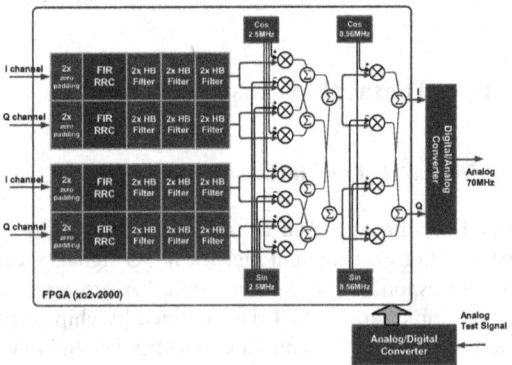

Fig. 1. Architecture of digital IF transmitter

2.2 Structure of Digital IF Receiver

The presented architecture of digital IF receiver for two FA bands in wideband CDMA base stations is shown in Fig. 2. As generally known, this structure consists of wideband, high speed and high resolution ADC, digital mixers, NCOs, decimators and digital filters. In our structure, the received analog IF signal whose center frequency is 70MHz, bandwidth is 10MHz corresponding to two FA bands is digitized by wideband and high resolution ADC. The available ADC is AD6645 made in Analog Devices inc. whose specifications is 80Msps sampling rate and 14bit resolution [11]. In our digital IF receiver, the ADC's clock rate is 61.44MHz and the center frequency of digital IF is 8.56MHz, because the frequency down conversion is performed by bandpass sampling technique. The received signals are again downconverted to baseband as digitally mixing with the output signals of NCO of 6.06MHz and 10.06MHz for each FA. And, this signals are filtered by FIR and RRC filter whose stopband attenuation is about 82dB similar to transmitter. So even though the low pass filter on the RF block should be roughly used, this is sufficiently possible to distinguish the desired signal from other signal interferences. The filtered signals are interpolated to 30.72MHz, eight times of chip rate, to search pilot signals at physical channel modem.

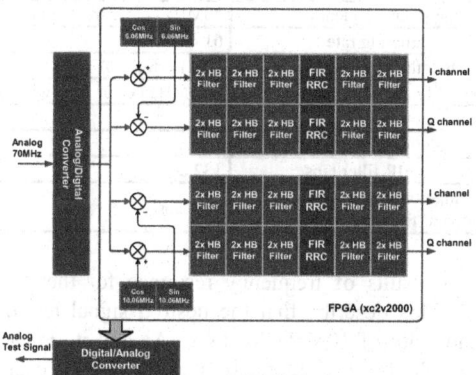

Fig. 2. Architecture of digital IF receiver

3 Simulation Results

In this section, the computer simulation results are shown to certify the previously proposed structure of the digital IF transceiver for wideband CDMA base stations. The simulation is performed with the simplified physical channel structure which is composed of QAM mapper, channelizer and scrambler and implemented by MATLAB software.

To verify the presented digital IF transceiver, the simulation for wideband CDMA is performed with simulation conditions shown in Table 1 and 2. As shown in table 1, the number of coefficients of digital filters in digital IF transmitter is 257 taps and the interpolation rate is 64. Also, the transmitted digital IF signal has the 70MHz center frequency and the sample rate of 245.76Msps.

Table 1. Simulation parameters for digital IF transmitter

Contents	Specifications
Digital IF frequency	70MHz center freq. with 2FA
DAC's sampling rate	245.76MHz
Bandwidth	10MHz for 2FA
Interpolation rate	64
RRC and FIR filter taps	132 taps
Interpolation halfband filter taps	125 taps (DAC's 62 taps included)

Similarly, in order to simulate the digital IF receiver, the digital filters with 237 coefficients is used and the bandpass smapling is performed to down convert to baseband from 70MHz analog IF signal as ADC with the rate of 61.44Msps.

Table 2. Simulation parameters for digital IF receiver

Contents	Specifications
Analog input frequency	70MHz center freq. with 2FA
ADC's sampling rate	61.44MHz
Bandwidth	10MHz for 2FA
Digital IF signal	8.56MHz center freq. with 2FA
Decimation rate	4
Interpolation rate	2
RRC and FIR filter taps	132 taps
Decimation/interpolation halfband filter taps	105 taps

The simulation results of frequency response for the digital IF transmitter are shown in Fig. 3. This describe that the desired signal has the center frequency of 70MHz, the bandwidth of 10MHz for two FAs and its image signal has the center frequency of 52.88MHz. The attenuation difference of desired signals and image signals is about -80dBc. The spectral density of image signals can be more reduced as the number of taps of half band filters is more increased. As shown in Fig. 3, the characteristics of passband ripple are similar to that of RRC filter because the passband ripple of other filters such as FIR and halfband filters is very small.

4 Experiment Results

The implemented digital IF transmitter and receiver modules are shown in Fig. 5 and Fig.6 respectively, which are comprised ADC, DAC and single FPGA for each module. Two modules have been fabricated as a transmitter and receiver respectively, but these modules have the same structures and devices except the block for interface to the physical channel modem. A system clock is 61.44MHz, which is provided by a

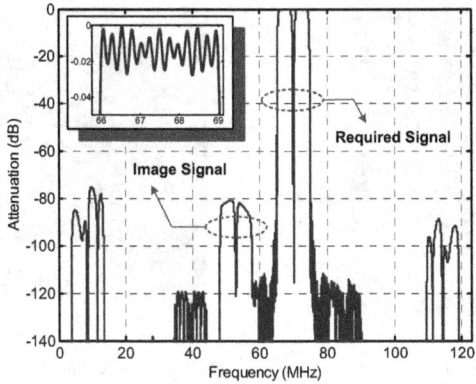

Fig. 3. Frequency response of digital IF tranmitter

The simulated frequency response of digital IF receiver is shown in Fig. 4. The stopband rejection is about −85dBc at 2.5MHz. This is sufficient to extract the desired signal from the adjacent signals of multiple band signals without the loss of bit error rate.

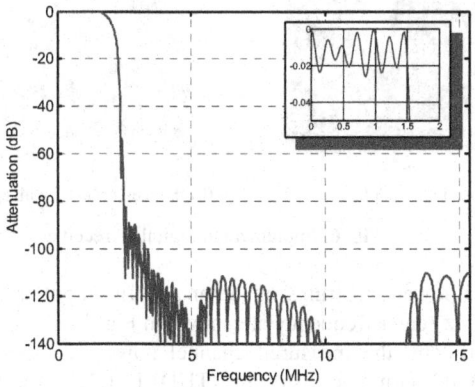

Fig. 4. Frequency response of digital IF receiver

voltage controlled crystal oscillator (VCXO). A single FPGA modeled as Xilinx's XC2V2000 BG575 [12] was used for a digital IF up or down conversion VHDL core which is composed of digital filters, NCOs and digital mixers, etc. The Analog Devices' AD 9777 was employed as the DAC which has features as 16bit resolution, 160/400Msps input/output data rate, selectable 2×/4×/8× interpolating filters, programmable gain control and digital quadrature modulation capability [10]. Also, the Analog Devices' AD6645 was used as ADC [11].

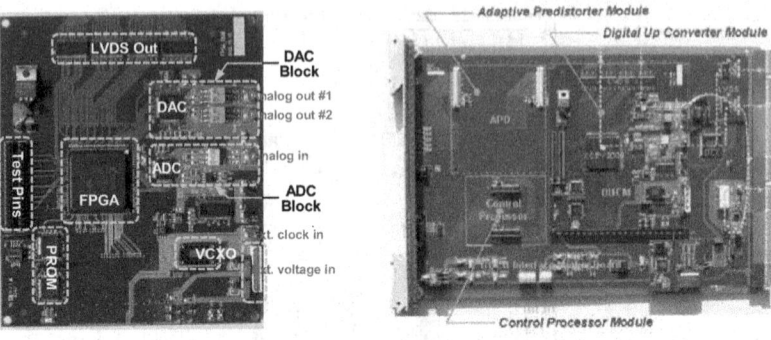

(a) digital IF transmitter module   (b) IF transmitter board with (a) for base station

Fig. 5. Implemented digital IF transmitter

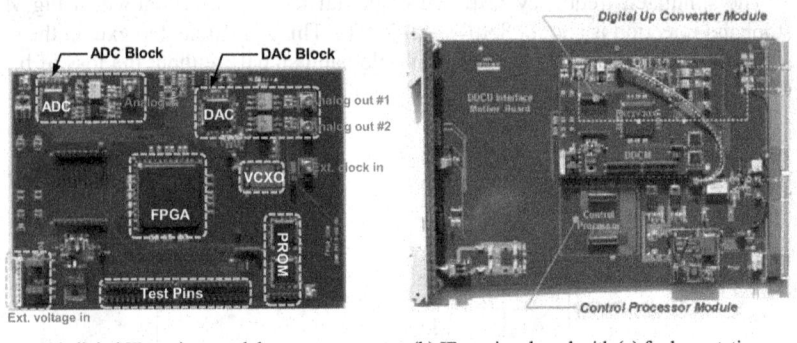

(a) digital IF receiver module   (b) IF receiver board with (a) for base station

Fig. 6. Implemented digital IF receiver

The measured power spectrums of the analog IF output and digital IF output for two FAs at 70MHz center frequency are shown in Fig. 7.

At this experiment, the measured channel power is about −14dBm at 10MHz bandwidth, the total harmonic distortion (THD) is 1.33% and the dynamic range is about 60dB. And, Fig. 8 describe the power spectrum of digital IF output shown in Fig. 7, which has the span of 50MHz to inspect the image signal power. The spectral density of image signal is as low as −55dBc than the desired signal. This image signal power can be reduced if the system clock for DAC is more stable.

The responses of the transmitted baseband signal at analog IF module and the received baseband signal at digital IF receiver module are shown in Fig. 9. Here, the received baseband analog signal form the digital IF receiver module is measured by employing the extra DAC embedded in receiver module for test only.

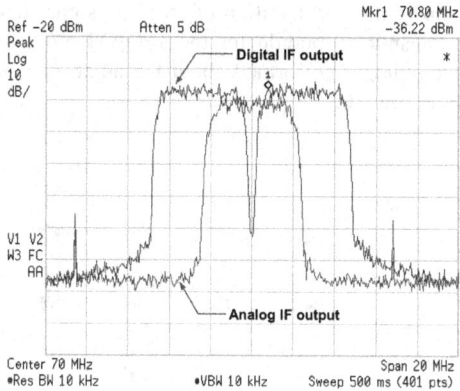

Fig. 7. Comparison of digital IF and analog IF output power spectrum

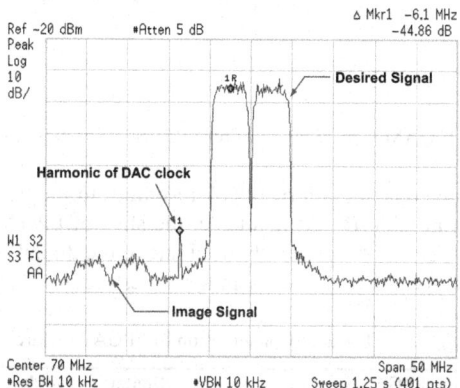

Fig. 8. Response of desired signal and image signal spectrum

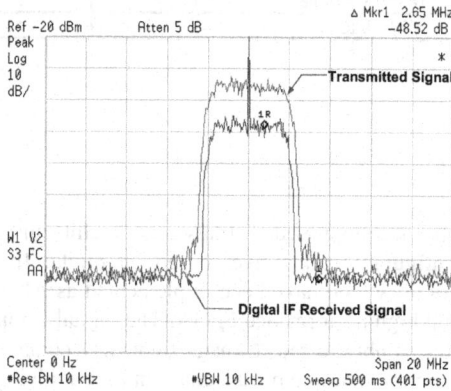

Fig. 9. Response of transmitted baseband signal at analog IF module and received baseband signal at digital IF receiver module

The Fig. 10 shows the constellation of received signal into the digital IF receiver from digital IF transmitter module for the 16QAM modulation. The demodulation process can be completely performed about the adjacent multiple wideband CDMA signals as known in Fig. 10.

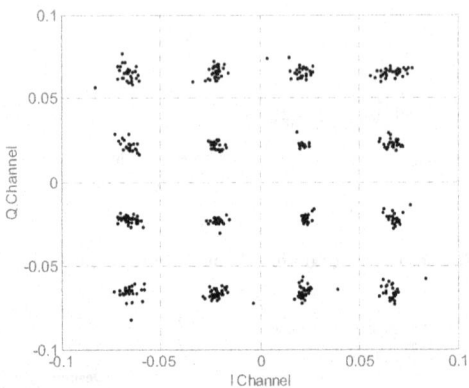

Fig. 10. 16QAM Constellation of received signal at digital IF receiver module

The logic gate consumption of FPGA resources to implement the digital IF transceiver is shown in table III. At this table, the slice of FPGA is used about 60% and the multiplier in Vertex^{TM} –II is fully used due to the digital filters of polyphase type. The block RAM is more used in transmitter to restore the 16QAM test signal vectors.

Table 3. Consumption of FPGA Resources

FPGA resources (XC2V2000)	Digital IF modules	
	Transmitter	*Receiver*
Slice	60%	61%
18×18 Multiplier	100%	92%
Block RAM	82%	53%

5 Conclusions

We have presented the improved IF transceiver architecture and its implementation results on re-configurable transceiver based on digital IF for multiple wideband CDMA base stations, which have been implemented as ADC, DAC with high speed and resolution and high performance FPGA. The digital complex quadrature modulation technique that is able to reject image frequency components has been used for digitally combining the multiple band signals and for applying to the baseband digital adaptive predistorter to increase the RF system's linearity in our digital IF transmitter architecture. Also, the bandpass sampling technique has been applied in our receiver architecture and the digital filters such as RRC, FIR and halfband filter with high dynamic range have been designed to extract the desired signal from the adjacent FAs. We have developed the digital IF transceiver module of which is composed single FPGA, ADC and DAC. The RRC, FIR and interpolation/decimation halfband filters over 200 taps, digital mixers and NCOs has been implemented on single FPGA with 200 million gates. This paper has presented the experiment results on the frequency response and constellation of the implemented digital IF transceiver using a simplified 16QAM physical channel model. The results have been obtained that the dynamic range is about 60dB at 70MHz IF center frequency.

References

1. David B.Chester, "Digital IF Filter Technology for 3G Systems : An Introduction," IEEE Commun. Mag., pp. 102-107, Feb. 1999.
2. Sungbin Im, Woncheol Lee, Chonghoon Kim, Yoan Shin and Seung Hee Lee, "Implementation of SDR-Based Digital IF Channelizer/De-Channelizer for Multiple CDMA Signals," IEICE Trans. Commun., vol. E83-B, no.6, pp.1282-1289, June 2000.
3. J.Mitola, "The software radio architecture," IEEE Commun. Mag., vol.33, pp.26-38, May 1995.
4. PMC-Sierra inc., Digital Guide for Integrating the PM7800/PM7815 PALADIN-10/15 Reference Design, Feb. 2001, available at < www.pmc-sierra.com >.
5. Hyuk J.Oh, Sunbin Kim, Ginkyu Choi and Yong H. Lee, "On the Use of Interpolated Second-Order Polynomials for Efficient Filter Design in Programmable Downconversion," IEEE Journal on Selected Areas in Commun., vol.17, no.4, pp.551-560, April 1999
6. Alan Y.Kwentus, Zhongnong Jiang and Alan N. Willson, "Application of Filter Sharpening to Cascaded Integrator-Comb Decimation Filters," IEEE Trans. on Signal Processing, vol.45, no.2, pp.457-467, Feb. 1997
7. Kambiz C.Zangi and R. David Koilpillai, "Software Radio Issues in Cellular Base Stations," IEEE Journal on Selected Areas in Commun., vol. 17, no.4, pp.561-573, April 1999
   Weng Ho Yung, Ming Jian and Yew Wee Ho, "Polyphase Decomposition Channelizers For Software Radios," ISCAS2000, pp.353-356, May 2000
8. 3GPP, Technical specification group radio access networks; UTRA (BS) FDD; Radio transmission and reception, 3GPP TS25.104, v3.5.0, Dec. 2000.
9. Analog Devices Inc., AD9777 Technical Data ; 16-Bit, 160Msps 2×/4×/8× Interpolating Dual TxDAC+D/A Converter, Jan. 2002, available at < www.analog.com >.
10. Analog Devices Inc., AD6645 Preliminary Technical Data ; 14-Bit, 80Msps A/D Converter, Jan. 2002, available at < www.analog.com >.
11. Xilinx Inc., VertexTM –II Platform FPGAs : Introduction and Overview, Sep. 2002, available at <www. xilinx. com>

The Implementation of 256 QAM CDMA Modulator

Joon Woo Shin, Hyeong Jun Park, Dae Soon Cho, Chang Wan Yoo, Yoon Ok Park, and Deuk Soo Lyu

Modem Architecture Research Department
Mobile Telecommunication Research Laboratory
Electronics and Telecommunications Research Institute, Korea
joonoos@etri.re.kr

Abstract. We implemented 256 Quadrature Amplitude Modulation (QAM) Code Division Multiple Access (CDMA) modulator with Field Programmable Gate Array (FPGA). In this paper, we describe the implemented modulator specifications and structures. With Modem Analysis Tool (MAT), we confirm that the implemented modulator functions without error. From fixed-point simulation, we show that this modulator bit error rate performances are almost equal to the theoretical QAM bit error rate and know how fading influence modulator performance. We recommend that the implemented 256 QAM CDMA modulation methods can be employed in high-speed mobile environment, if only the exact fading compensation is possible.

1 Introduction

Recently, To more efficiently utilize limited bandwidth resources in high speed mobile transmission, Quadrature Amplitude Modulation (QAM) which can send more bits per symbol is regarded as one of the best solution [1]. Although we agree that higher modulation level QAM definitely increase transmission capacity, we could not increase modulation level easily. As more bits are assigned to each symbol, so the minimum Euclidean distance between symbols is decreased. As a result, transmission systems are more sensitive to fading and noise in mobile environment [2]. This is why high-level QAM methods are less employed in mobile communications. In these latter days, 64 QAM, which allots 6 bits per symbol, is used in [3] and 16 QAM is commercially used. Grafting 256 QAM, which assigns 8 bits per symbol, into Code Division Multiple Access (CDMA), we suggest 256 QAM CDMA modulator structures, implement it with Field Programmable Gate Array (FPGA), and verify implemented 256 QAM CDMA modulator's performances. In this paper, part II describes 256 QAM CDMA modulator structures and its implementation specifications, and part III shows 256 QAM CDMA modulator performances using Modem Analysis Tool (MAT) and fixed-point simulator, which has the same structure with the implemented modulator.

M.M. Freire, P. Lorenz, M.M.-O. Lee (Eds.): HSNMC 2003, LNCS 2720, pp. 326–332, 2003.

2 Modulator Specifications and Structures

256 QAM CDMA modulator specifications are accordant to table 1. Modulator input, and output frame size is 2 ms. Using 16 Orthogonal Variable Spreading Factor (OVSF) codes, we can deploy 16 distinguishable channels (one for pilot channel and the others for traffic channels). If all 15 traffic channels are allotted to one user, the implemented modulator transmits maximally 28.8 Mbps with 5 MHz bandwidth.

Table 1. 256 QAM CDMA Modulator Transmission Specifications.

Unit Frame Size	2 ms
Bandwidth	5 MHz
Modulation Level	256 QAM
Chip rate	3.84 Mcps
Mapper	Gray Encoder
Multicode	16 × 16 OVSF
Scrambling	3 GPP Specification [4]
Physical Channel	16 (1:Pilot, 15:Traffic)

Fig 1 shows the implemented modulator structures. Randomly generated data are segmented into 2 ms frames, and these frames go through channel coding unit, which is built up at other board. Modulation part in Fig 1, which we implemented as 256 QAM CDMA modulator, takes channel-encoded frames. In this modulation part, by Gray encoding rule, mapper translated every 8 bits input into appropriate symbol. As like signal constellation in Fig 4, all the mapped symbols are elucidated in rectangular coordinate system. So we can express mapped symbols in I, Q coordinates. To accommodate modulator output power, gain control block adjusts mapped symbol powers. In order to deploy 15 distinct channels, serial to parallel (S/P) block arranges serial symbols into 15 parallel symbols. Channelization block scrambles each parallel symbol with its Orthogonal Variable Spreading Factor (OVSF) code. According to the 3GPP(3rd Generation Project Plan)[4], from this process, each parallel symbol, which has same OVSF code, is easily classified. In addition to channelization function, OVSF code spreads 16 times.

These distinct 15 channel symbols are added up in chip level summation block. Chip level means each symbol is summed up chip by chip. In case of pilot, its initial values are all '0'. To comply with traffic channel chip rate (3.84 Mcps), pilot data rate before scrambling is 240 kbps. For the sake of discriminating between pilot and traffic, we scramble pilot with OVSF code as like traffic data. Finally, the complex spreading block scrambles one pilot and fifteen traffic channels together, and adds them up. From the above process, 256 QAM CDMA modulator completes its operation. If employ this modulator in real mobile system, we transfer these modulated data to RF part.

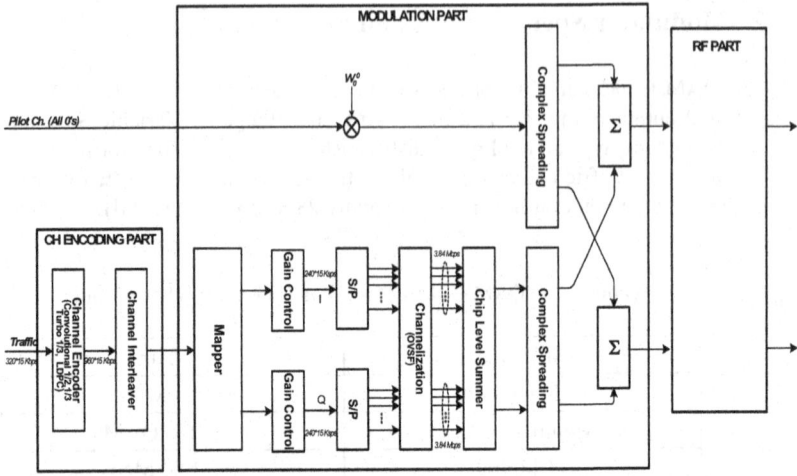

Figure 1. Block Diagram of 256 QAM CDMA Modulator

Fig 2 shows the implemented 256 QAM CDMA modulator board with Xilinx XCV2000E, the modulation part in Fig 1 is incorporated in this Field Programmable Gate Array (FPGA). Each I, Q output data from 256 QAM CDMA modulator is expressed in 15 bits (from – 16,384 to 16,383). Therefore we carefully design modulator, its output magnitude does not exceed this range. When we place and route 256 QAM CDMA modulator into Xilinx XCV2000E, this modulator module's maximum operating frequency is 33.209 MHz, and it occupies 242 IOBus, 3634 slices.

Fig 3 shows the integrated transmitter. The rightmost daughter board is 256 QAM CDMA modulator which we implemented, the middle one is channel encoding part with TMS320C6416 Digital signal processor (DSP), and the leftmost one is Cell Element Processor (CEP) with which we manage DSP and control DSP, FPGA interface.

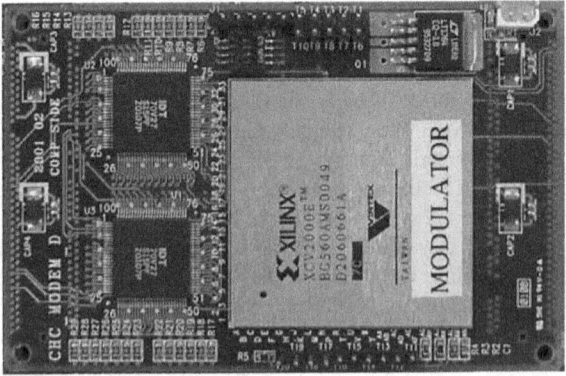

Figure 2. 256 QAM CDMA Modulator FPGA modules.

Figure 3. The integrated 256 QAM CDMA transmitter board.

3   Modulator Performances

The best way to analyze the implemented 256 QAM CDMA modulator performances is field test with demodulator units, which is correspondent to the implemented modulator. But on account of several latent difficulties, we make use of Modem Analysis Tool (MAT) made by ETRI. Modem analysis tool receives modulator digital output directly without channel, executes synchronization process, demodulates the transmitted data, compute bit error rate, and display the signal constellation.

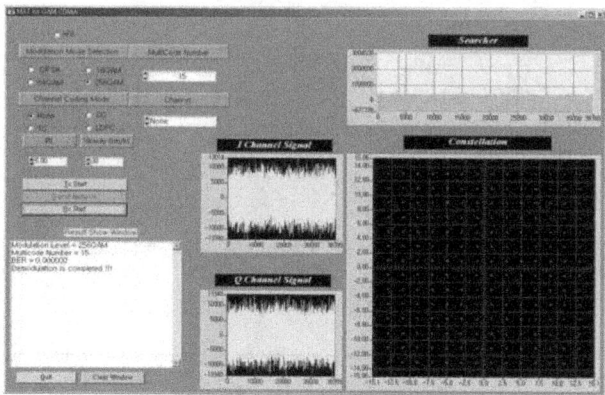

Figure 4. Modem Analysis Tool Outputs.

Fig 4 is the displayed results from Modem Analysis Tool. The right upper side figure shows synchronization process with scrambling codes (modulator use the same codes). Middle lower figure and right lower side one are transmitted I, Q signal and their signal constellation, respectively. From I, Q signal figures, we recognize that average signal magnitude is around 10,000, but if we regard this fact and allot 14 bits to modulator output, then output signal range is from –8,192 to 8.192. This makes some of the modulator output signal to be clipped. As modem Analysis Tool captures the modulator output directly, so there is no error and fading effect. In other words, modulator output signal does not undergo channel. Therefore every symbol from modulator is located exactly one point where each symbol has to be, without any scattering.

To measure the 256 QAM CDMA modulator performances in mobile environment, we use fixed-point simulator. This simulator works exactly the same structure as the implemented modulator. That is to say, if same frame is inputted to simulator and implemented modulator, then the outputs are coincident. Fig 5 indicates modulator performances in Additive White Gaussian Noise (AWGN) channel. At 10^{-3} bit error rate, the Eb/No difference between QPSK and 16 QAM is 4 dB, 16 QAM and 64 QAM is 4.5 dB, and 64 QAM and 256 QAM is 5 dB. This results are correspondent to theoretical QAM modulator performances [5,6], and confirms that the implemented modulator functions correctly.

Knowing how fading influences 256 QAM CDMA modulated signals, we change fading velocity to 3 km/h, 30 km/h, and 60 km/h. Fig 6 – 1, 2, 3 show the simulation consequences. As the number of allocated bits per symbol increases, the Euclidean distance between symbols decreases. Systems are more sensitive to phase variation. So fading and noise influence system performance fatally. This explains why the implemented 256 QAM CDMA modulator Eb/No at 10^{-2} bit error rate is 26 dB, when fading velocity is 60 km/h. These bit error rate performance makes it hard to employ 256 QAM modulation method commercially. Therefore, if the implemented 256 QAM CDMA modulation can be used in high speed mobile environment, complete fading compensation is essential.

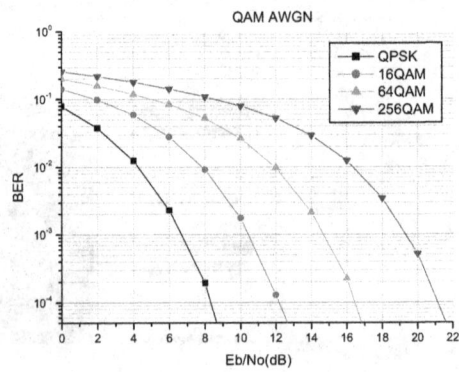

Figure 5. The BER performance of 256 QAM CDMA modulator in AWGN Channel condition.

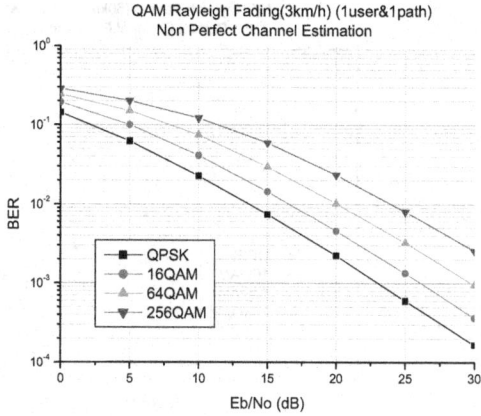

Figure 6-1. The BER performance of 256 QAM CDMA modulator in Rayleigh Fading (3 km/h) Channel.

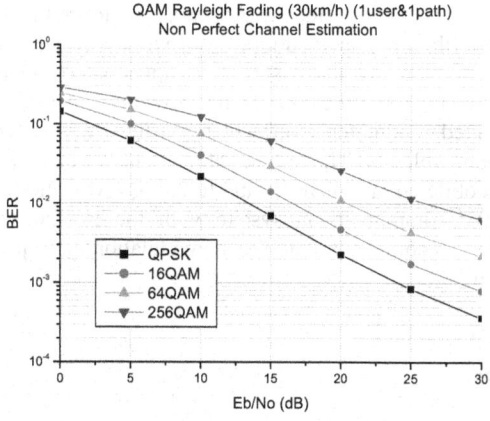

Figure 6-2. The BER performance of 256 QAM CDMA modulator in Rayleigh Fading (30 km/h) Channel.

4   Conclusions

In this paper, to increase frequency utilization effieciecy, we employ 256 Qadurature Amplitude Modulation(QAM). By combing 256 QAM and Code Division Multiple Access(CDMA), we suggest 256 QAM CDMA modulator sturucture and implement it with FPGA.

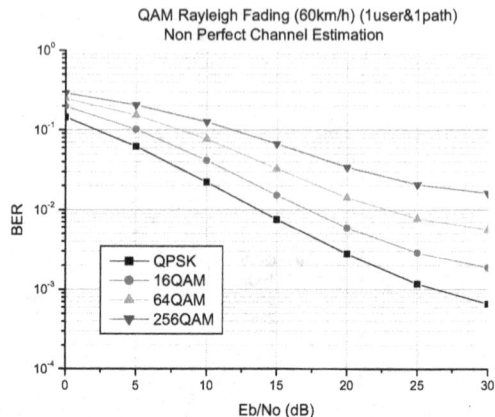

Figure 6-3. The BER performance of 256 QAM CDMA modulator in Rayleigh Fading (60 km/h) Channel.

To measure the implemented 256 QAM CDMA mdulator performanes, we excute several tests. First, with Modem Analysis Tool(MAT). The results from MAT confirm us that the implemented modulator work correctly. Second, with fixed point simulator. From this, we make sure the implemented modulator performances are approachting to the theoretical QAM bit error rate. And furthermore, to know how the implemented modulator is affecte by fading, we perform the simulation with changing fading velocity. The fading velocity change simulation shows that fading in high speed mobile environment is fatal to 256 QAM CDMA modualtor. Therefore if employing the communciation system with the implemented 256 QAM CDMA modulator, we recommand that the demodulation part prepares complete fading compensation.

References

[1] W.T. Webb, "QAM: the modulation scheme for future mobile radio communications.", *Electronics And Communication Engineering Journal*, Aug 1992, pp. 167-176.
[2] S. Sampei, T. Sunaga, "Rayleigh Fading Compensation for QAM in Land Mobile Radio Communications.", *E Trans. Veh. Technol.,Vol. 42, No. 2*, May 1993, pp.137-144.
[3] A. Doufexi, S. Armour, M. Butler, A. Niz, D. Bull, J. McGeehan, "*A Comparison of the HIPERLAN/2 and IEEE 802.11a Wireless LAN Standards.*", *IEEE Communication Magazine*, May 2002, pp. 172-180.
[4] 3GPP, 3G TS 25.213: *"Spreading and Modulation (FDD)"*.
[5] B. Sklar,*"Digital Communications Fundamental and Applications."*, *Prentice Hal PTR*, pp 565.
[6] Richand van Nee, Ramjee Prasad, *"OFDM for Wireless Multimedia Communications."*, *Artech House Publishers*, pp. 60-62.

HIDRA: HIstory Directed Routing Algorithm for IP Networks

Paraskevi Fafali, Charalampos Z. Patrikakis, and Emmanuel N. Protonotarios

Telecommunications Laboratory
National Technical University of Athens,
Heroon Politechniou 9, Zographou, Greece 15773,
tel: +30 210 7721513, fax: +30 210 7722534
{pfafali,bpatr}@telecom.ntua.gr

Abstract. The need for making optimal use of the available resources in IP networks is of crucial importance as multimedia communications become part of our everyday activities. Inspired by this problem, we are presenting HIDRA, a routing algorithm which targets at two long-standing optimization objectives. The first one is pertaining to routing incoming traffic while preserving as much as possible resources for future demands. The second goal is to maximize the amount of traffic served. The main idea upon which our traffic engineering framework is built is to allocate resource assets online, directed by history monitoring information and Service Level Agreements (SLAs) so as to steer traffic through network in the most effective way. The simulation experiments conducted show that our routing scheme surmounts traditional routing algorithms such as shortest path and widest-shortest path in terms of blocking effects and total bandwidth passed.

1 Introduction

As the Internet evolves into a standard communications network, new techniques must be introduced for the management of the available assets. That is why nowadays traffic engineering is of paramount importance, aiming at respecting customers requirements for quality, while at the same time utilizing resources in a more economical way. The prevailing routing protocol used across the LANs is OSPF (Open Shortest Path First) [1]. It is a link state protocol based on shortest path algorithm. It develops and maintains a full knowledge of network routers and their interconnections via the exchange of Link-State Advertisements (LSAs). OSPFs functionality has been enhanced by QoS extensions as described in RFC2676 [2]. The specified additions allow supporting best effort and bandwidth guaranteed traffic through the pre-computation of a minimum hop count path with the maximum available bandwidth for every destination (i.e. widest-shortest path algorithm).

During the last decade, intensive research effort has been carried out on aspects of QoS routing. The variety of the topics tackled confines our reference only to those that are related to our work. A recently proposed scheme, referred

M.M. Freire, P. Lorenz, M.M.-O. Lee (Eds.): HSNMC 2003, LNCS 2720, pp. 333–342, 2003.
© Springer-Verlag Berlin Heidelberg 2003

to as MIRA [3], takes into account the notion of an ingress-egress pair's interference with other source-destination pairs. Despite the innovation spurred by that idea, its computational overhead exacerbates its performance delivery. Moreover, it is oblivious of any information regarding history traffic measurements. Policy-Based Routing (PBR) [4] refers to another interesting approach aware of total expected bandwidth for all source-destination pairs. PBR pre-allocates link resources to aggregates of requests based on the multicommodity network flow problem whose objective is to maximize the amount of flow sent through the network. Therefore, it is prone to splitting traffic between a source-destination pair into multiple flows. So, though it pays off concerning load balance, it proves insufficient in routing high bandwidth demands.

The motivation of our work is to touch upon aspects related to traffic engineering and specifically to address the issue of establishing bandwidth guaranteed paths. The primary objective is to efficiently route traffic demands by including in the path selection process subcontracted SLAs and history traffic measurements. We will uncover how the legacy IP interior gateway protocols such as OSPF can be enriched with feedback information stemming from statistics collected from the operational network. Traffic statistics, pertaining to the interval in which bandwidth demands oscillated, can be essential for driving path calculation process towards maximizing the number of accepted requests and throughput. Our impetus is to prove the importance of allocating network resources, not only regarding network topology infrastructure, but also in the face of past routing information collected.

Most of the past research work [3] [4] previously reviewed has been built upon MPLS-based architectures. In our study, we develop and evaluate a routing scheme without adhering to a specific networking technology. The suggested framework can be applied to any connection-oriented architecture that is facilitated with the feature of explicit path routing such as MPLS or the current OSPF routing protocol supplied with QoS extensions.

The rest of the paper is organized as follows: Section 2 presents the assumptions on the basis of which the routing algorithm was developed along with its detailed analysis. Section 3 describes the simulation environment used. In section 4, simulation results are provided along with a performance evaluation report. Section 5 presents the conclusions and gives insights for future directions.

2   Improving Traffic Management Based on History Monitoring Information and SLAs

Before we proceed in the elaboration of the algorithm developed, we should lay emphasis on the assumptions taken. To begin with, the algorithm can be characterized as online, and there is no a priori knowledge of future traffic. It is assumed that requests should be routed on a single path, without splitting. We also make the hypothesis that after a connection establishment, the resources allocated to a source-destination pair are committed for the total duration of the session examined.

2.1   HIstory Directed Routing Algorithm (HIDRA)

The major contribution of our work is the incorporation of history monitoring information into path selection procedure. Owing to the offline nature of past information analysis, there is no time duration or labor computation constraint. As indicative metrics of past monitoring information we consider maximum and minimum values of bandwidth requested between all discrete source-destination pairs.

Our approach is not based on the certainty that the traffic to appear will be close to what occurred in past. Though traffic demands cannot be easily predicted, macroscopically, traffic profile in communication networks depends on the period of the day. One reason for this dependency is that most of the traffic carried during the day is professional traffic while residential traffic dominates in the evening [9]. In this context, the notion is to try to identify in general how bandwidth between source-destination pairs ranged in connection requests submitted between the same endpoints. It is necessary that our online routing algorithm can function irrespectively of history traffic measurements. Those values should only act as controlling factors of traffic manipulation and must not lead to performance degradation in cases where incoming traffic is completely different to what has been provisioned. That goals are fulfilled in the framework of the algorithm that will be elaborately described next.

HIDRA Offline Phase. Suppose that past monitoring information pertaining to source-destination pairs and their bandwidth requirements has been collected. We are given a fully specified network topology composed of nodes and bi-directional links. We are interested in information regarding the maximum (Max_i) and minimum (Min_i) bandwidth values that have been requested for every source-destination pair indexed i. Suppose that according to traffic measurements there are n different source-destination pairs, sorted in descending order based on their Max_i. In this case, Max_n refers to the pair with the minimum value of maximum bandwidth requested.

The inceptive step is to solve the problem of finding paths for the concurrent satisfaction of the greatest bandwidth requests (Max_i) for each source-destination pair. Specifically, given the past maximum bandwidth requests, and based on the hypothesis that all these requests have to co-exist in the network, the exact paths for their routing should be specified. In that computation, the additional objective of selecting the shortest one among all feasible paths is also taken into consideration. This procedure of calculating the maximum number of concurrent shortest paths will be mathematically stated later on. The choice of shortest path routing for accommodating requests is coherent. Since offline phase focus is to reserve highly capacitated paths, flows are discouraged from long paths that lead to worthless resource consumption.

In each iteration step of the offline phase, we run the list of sorted bandwidth values bottom to top in order to select the maximum bandwidth value M_{si} to change. As M_{si} value of the selected pair we use the respective Max_i value reduced by 10%. Once the whole list has been passed through, the process starts again increasing the reduction percentage by 10%. The above procedure can be modeled to the following equation:

$$M_{si} = \begin{cases} Max\_r & \text{if } Max\_r > Min_i \\ Min_i & \text{otherwise} \end{cases} \qquad (1)$$

where $Max\_r = Max_i - 0.1 \cdot int\left(\dfrac{s+i-1}{n}\right)$, $i = 1, 2, ..., n$. Parameter s denotes the step of iteration of paths calculation procedure and M_{si} stands for the maximum bandwidth value of pair i at iteration step s. The pre-computed paths extracted from the aforementioned process are stored and the network resources dedicated to them are left intangible until online algorithm resolves the appropriate timing to allot them.

The concept upon which function (1) was formulated is that our routing algorithm intention is to encourage the potential for supporting large bandwidth demands and hence, achieve maximum network throughput. Thus, we have chosen to reduce a unique M_{si} value by a specified percent (10%) starting initially from the minimum Max_i. Also, the selection of Min_i value as a low limit is made under the consideration that the network will always have the potential to accommodate at least the minimum bandwidth request of every discrete source-destination pair. In addition, the primary goal is to give boost to network traffic increase which is in our approach basically achieved by reserving the maximum feasible bandwidth paths.

So far, we have not dealt with the issue of how SLAs can be incorporated in our routine. Specifically, SLAs can be basically translated in terms of source-destination pairs and their respective bandwidth demands. The required resources for their accomplishment should be reserved throughout the SLA active period and the admissible paths for SLAs should be determined so as to be all simultaneously running. Paths for SLAs fulfillment can be calculated by taking the same mathematical model of the phase of maximum value paths computation. At this point, the offline phase of the algorithm is accomplished.

Computation of Concurrent Paths for Maximum Bandwidth Demands and SLAs. Lets assume a network topology defined as a capacitated, undirected graph $G(V,E)$, where V is the set of nodes and E is a collection of bi-directional transmission links. Let C_{ij} are the capacity and $cost_{ij}$ the cost of link directed from node i to node j. Note that links (i,j) and (j,i) are considered symmetric, meaning that they are characterized by the same parameters (capacity, propagation delay) in both directions. The number of users' requests is K and each has bandwidth requirement b_k. Every demand $k \in \{1, ..., K\}$ is described by the triple (s_k, d_k, b_k), where s_k, d_k are special nodes of the graph expressing the source and the destination of the demand respectively.

The problem of computation of concurrent shortest paths for maximum bandwidth demands and for SLAs is twofold. It can be defined as finding feasible paths so as to route simultaneously K requests with the additional objective of selecting the shortest ones, while not exceeding the capacities on the network links.

The mathematical model of the aforesaid linear optimization problem is given as follows. The decision variables are:

$$Y_k = \begin{cases} 1 & \text{if request } k \text{ is routed} \\ 0 & \text{otherwise} \end{cases} \tag{2}$$

$$F_{ijk} = \begin{cases} 1 & \text{if request } k \text{ uses link } (i,j) \\ 0 & \text{otherwise} \end{cases} \tag{3}$$

The problem comprises of two different objectives. The first is the objective of maximizing the number of requests that can be simultaneously satisfied and is given by:

$$max \sum_k Y_k \tag{4}$$

The second objective of deciding on the shortest path is given by the equation:

$$min \sum_{k,\,(i,j)\in E} cost_{ij} F_{ijk} \tag{5}$$

The first set of constraints comprises the flow conservation constraints.

$$\sum_{(i,j)\in E} F_{ijk} b_k = \sum_{(j,m)\in E} F_{jmk} b_k \quad \forall (i,j),(j,m)\in E,\ j \neq s_k, d_k \tag{6}$$

$$\sum_{(i,j)\in E} F_{ijk} b_k - \sum_{(j,i)\in E} F_{jik} b_k = -b_k Y_k \quad \forall (i,j),(j,i)\in E,\ j = s_k \tag{7}$$

Equation (7) indicates the supply of flows at source nodes.

$$\sum_{(i,j)\in E} F_{ijk} b_k - \sum_{(j,i)\in E} F_{jik} b_k = b_k Y_k \quad \forall (i,j),(j,i)\in E,\ j = d_k \tag{8}$$

Equation (8) denotes the traffic that should be moved to demand nodes. Capacity constraints should also be imposed on every link of the network graph.

$$\sum_k (F_{ijk} b_k \leq C_{ij}) \quad \forall (i,j) \in E \tag{9}$$

Furthermore, in order to enforce loop avoidance, requests are not allowed to pass by the same link or node twice. The above formed problem was implemented in AMPL modeling language [5].

HIDRA Online Phase. It is assumed that requests arrive one at a time. Our intention is not to select a unique routing algorithm but to apply a different routing strategy based on the magnitude of the requested bandwidth (b_i). This means that upon a request arrival, its bandwidth demand is compared to thresholds heuristically introduced. These thresholds are functions of past traffic measurements (i.e. Min_i, Max_i) that divide the interval $[Min_i, Max_i]$ of past (s_i, d_i) pairs into three equal subintervals. According to the subinterval in which b_i belongs to, there are three different path selection options that are followed, as it is depicted in Fig 1.

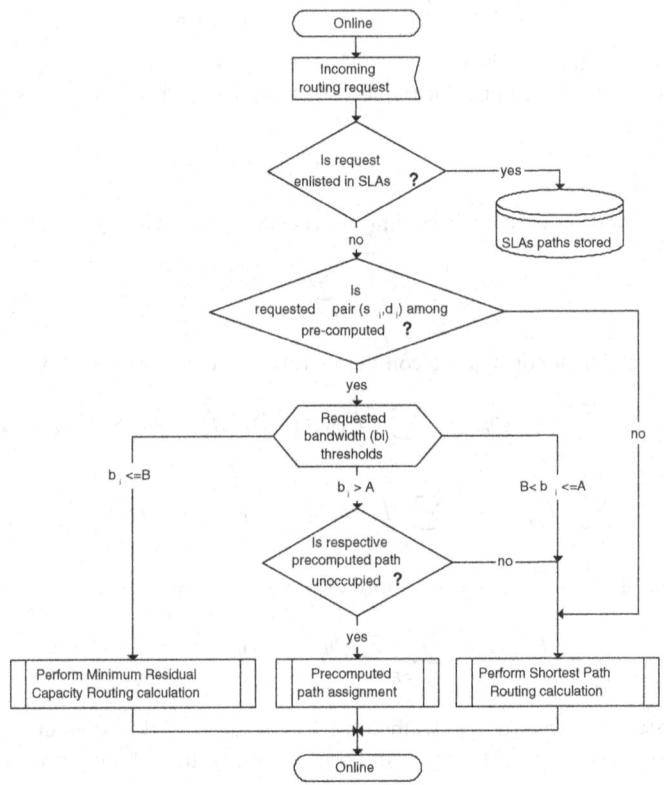

Fig. 1. Online routing algorithm flowchart

Particularly, we discriminate the following cases:

Case I: $b_i > A = \dfrac{2Max_i + Min_i}{3}$

The request is assigned the pre-computed path found for the corresponding pair, on the premise that sufficient resources are unoccupied. If the pre-computed path resources have already been allocated, then a new shortest path should be estimated for request routing.

Case II: $b_i > B = \dfrac{2Min_i + Max_i}{3}$ and $b_i \leq A$

The request is forwarded through a shortest path that is estimated.

Case III: $b_i \leq B$

A path with the minimum residual capacity, i.e. that its links residual capacity is as close as possible to the requested bandwidth, will be picked. Our intent is to fill in small unused portions of links capacity and to leave wider paths intact for future exploitation.

Case IV: In case an incoming request is pertaining to a pair that does not appear in history monitoring information, then it is routed through the shortest path.

Finally, if a request belongs to cases II or III and cannot be satisfied, then it is designated resources of the pre-computed paths.

3   Simulation Environment

This section is devoted to the simulation environment employed to assess our routing algorithm juxtaposed with the fundamental OSPF shortest path routing algorithm and with the one introduced in QoS routing extensions to OSPF which brings together OSPF and explicit path pre-computation feature.

The environment of our simulation experiments was created by the BRITE synthetic topology generator [6]. A Waxman model of 20 nodes and 40 edges was produced. In detail, the model parameters that were input to the generator are: a plain of size 1000 by 100; heavy tailed node placement; preferential connectivity both, incremental growth type; bandwidth exponentially distributed between 1Mbps and 10Mbps. The cost of each link is designated as one, such that shortest path algorithm is reduced to minimum hop count. On the purpose of our simulation experiment, we consider that history information obtained through monitoring is depicted in the following table.

Table 1. History demands information

(S, D)	max	min	B	A
(14,15)	2	0.01	0.673	1.33
(15,17)	2	0.1	0.733	1.30
(18,13)	2	0.1	0.733	1.30
(6,3)	2	0.2	0.8	1.27
(9,11)	2	0.01	0.673	1.33

In the experiment conducted, we generated a sequence of 46 individual requests arriving one at a time, most of them between the source-destination pairs of Table 1 and others that were not included in history metrics in an effort to prove that our algorithm can tackle even unpredicted combinations of ingress-egress couples. Requested bandwidth for every source-destination pair scales between minimum and maximum values presented in Table 1, while some of them were deliberately selected to exceed those limits in order to avoid biasing the results in favor of our scheme. The above problem was submitted to the NEOS optimization server [8]. To allow evaluation of the results of HIDRA, the same simulation tests were executed in Network Simulator NS2 [7] which includes implementation both for link-state Dijkstra based protocol similar to OSPF and for QoS routing extensions [2].

4   Experimental Results

The results acquired through the simulation tests were processed thoroughly, to assess HIDRAs performance. As a first indication of its behaviour, Figure 2 illustrates the bandwidth of accepted requests for the three algorithms examined.

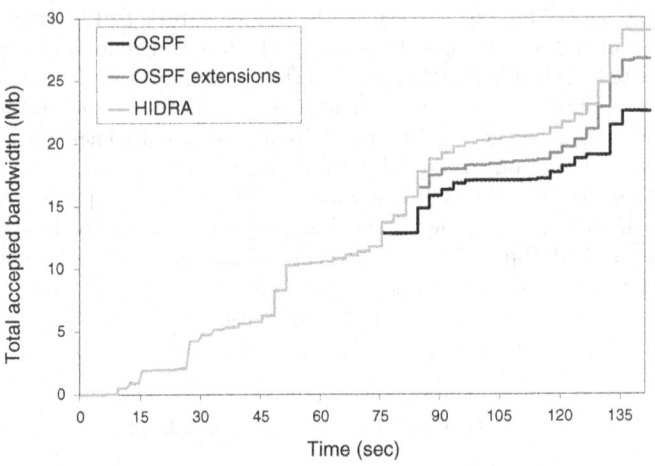

Fig. 2. Total bandwidth of accepted requests

It is obvious, from the results drawn, that HIDRA outperforms widest-shortest path algorithm. As expected, shortest-path routing is the one that shows the poorer performance in relation to the other two algorithms. More precisely, the improvement in terms of total bandwidth routed and the number of rejected requests is depicted in Table 2.

As it can be observed, HIDRA surpasses OSPF shortest path and OSPF extensions widest-shortest path in a percent of 22% and 7.7% respectively regarding the total bandwidth passed. Another performance measure looks at the number of blocked requests. In the case of shortest-path routing, the essence of the number of rejected requests is inapplicable due to the fact that shortest-path implementation in NS2 doesnt support explicit path routing. Because of this limitation, some requests are accepted for transmission although the network has insufficient resources and thus, when routers queues become full, the packets following next are dropped.

Table 2. HIDRA performance compared to OSPF and OSPF extensions

	OSPF	OSPF extensions	HIDRA
Total accepted bandwidth	22.587	26.754	28.988
Percent of improvement	22%	7.7%	-
Number of rejected requests	Inapplicable	3	1

The results obtained come up to our expectations. The outcomes demonstrate that our algorithm favors great bandwidth claims. While predominant routing schemes fail to respond to higher bandwidth demands, our proposed algorithm reacts very successfully. Having history as a benchmark for deciding on the technique applied to the path selection process and depending on the magnitude of the request, we make efficacious use of network resources. However, even without the certainty that history occurred will be in all respects repeated tomorrow, HIDRA algorithm retains pre-computed paths for high demands but doesn't reserve them in the strict notion. The tactic followed in case of small bandwidth requests is to fill in the little gaps of unused links capacity so as to diminish the probability of standing in the way of newly arriving requirements, whereby maximizing the potential for traffic growth.

5   Conclusions and Future Work

The major contribution of this paper is the detailed description, development and evaluation of a new routing algorithm (HIDRA) for providing bandwidth guaranteed paths. Its distinctiveness rests in that its baseline is history monitoring information. The appropriate data extracted from past day traffic are used in an offline mode and pre-processed in order to delineate the course of action that will be traced in the path selection process. Except for taking history into account, our algorithm provisions for how SLAs can be treated towards their contentment. The online phase of the routing algorithm proposed is not computationally expensive.

We have compared the performance of HIDRA with classical shortest-path and widest-path routing algorithms in large Internet-like topologies. The experiments executed and the analysis done leads us to the conclusion that the suggested framework of embedding history into routing procedure appears too promising. Last, but not the least, our scheme can be well fitted to the routing mechanisms that are widely deployed.

An investigation and assessment of how HIDRA performs in larger and more complicated network topologies is a significant area of future work. In addition, an immediate extension to this research is to increase the number of requests that will be loaded to the system. In that context, it would be really illuminating to observe how fast our system reaches its saturation point at which no more requests can be accommodated. Moreover, this metric is of great importance as it will reveal the maximum bandwidth the network can admit and will probably give as insight on how further and under what circumstances its limits can be stretched.

Another topic for further study is to explore how the thresholds A and B selected for deciding about the routing traffic treatment will be ameliorated. In line with what already described in the algorithm section, the heuristics selected and their relation to the bandwidth requested each time judge whether the shortest route will be calculated or the minimum residual bandwidth path. One possible scenario to be examined is to project our algorithm's behavior for a wide range of values around the proposed thresholds. Through the performance indications obtained, we can possibly come up to more sophisticated values for the decision thresholds. In the case of minimum residual capacity path, it is important to investigate the conditions under which an additional constraint regarding the number of hop counts should be enforced. That constraint could be possibly be related to the requested bandwidth values, the routing domain size or even the aggregated traffic the network experienced in past scenarios. Eventually, as the main direction of our dynamic routing algorithm is history monitoring metrics, it would be interesting enough to study how deviating from history is reflected to the profit gained. In other words, we will weigh the trade-off between how close to past requested traffic is and our framework's performance.

References

1. Cisco Press Publications: IP Routing Fundamentals (2001)
2. G. Apostolopoulos and et. al: QoS Routing Mechanisms and OSPF extensions. IETF RFC 2676 (August 1999)
3. M. Kodialam, and T. Lakshman: Minimum interference routing with applications to MPLS traffic engineering. In proceedings of INFOCOM (2) (2000)
4. S. Suri, M, Waldvogel, and P. Warkhede: Profile-Based Routing: A New Framework for MPLS Traffic Engineering. Computer Communications (2002)
5. Robert Fourer and David M. Gay: Expressing Special Structures in an Algebraic Modeling Language for Mathematical Programming. ORSA Journal on Computing 7 (1995) 166-190
6. BRITE topology generator: http://www.cs.bu.edu/brite
7. UCL/LBNL/VINT Network Simulator ns (ns 2): http:// www-mash.cs.berkeley.edu/ns/ns.html
8. NEOS optimisation server: http://www-neos.mcs.anl.gov/neos/
9. W. Ben-Ameur: Multi-hour design of survivable classical IP networks. International Journal of Communication Systems (June 2002)

A Dimensioning Strategy for Almost Guaranteed Quality of Service in Voice over IP Networks

Sanaa Sharafeddine[1], Anton Riedl[1], and Jürgen Totzke[2]

[1] Institute of Communication Networks, Munich University of Technology
Arcisstr. 21, 80290 Munich, Germany
{Sharafeddine, Riedl}@ei.tum.de
[2] Siemens AG
Schertlinstr. 8, 81359 Munich, Germany
Juergen.Totzke@siemens.com

Abstract. Providing hard quality of service guarantees for Voice over IP traffic in multi-service IP networks is quite costly in terms of network resources. However, if one is willing to slightly soften the guarantees and to accept a small probability of service degradation, the amount of capacity necessary for voice traffic can be greatly reduced. In this paper, we investigate the tradeoff between quality of service and the required bandwidth for voice traffic in IP networks taking into account different scheduling schemes. We propose a dimensioning strategy, which allows the worst-case packet delay to exceed a desired threshold with a certain probability. Based on simulations, it can be demonstrated that bandwidth is reduced while the quality of service is assured in most cases.

1 Introduction

Today's computer networks were originally designed to support a single type of service treating all kinds of traffic as belonging to one traffic class. However, with ongoing convergence of information technology and telecommunications, new applications are evolving, which generate traffic with various characteristics and which also demand different Quality of Service (QoS) criteria. Thus, the existing IP network architecture needs to be upgraded in order to support a variety of services ranging from non-real-time traffic such as ftp and email to real-time traffic such as interactive voice and video. Over the past years, several technologies and mechanisms have been developed, which allow the realization of QoS-enabled multi-service networks. One fundamental prerequisite for these types of networks is the capability to differentiate between packets of different traffic streams and to forward the packets appropriately, each with the desired QoS. This requires that for the various traffic streams, separate queues are set up within routers, which are then served according to a certain scheduling scheme. Doing so, each traffic stream receives a certain share of the available bandwidth, which if insufficient leads to quality degradation. The two most important QoS frameworks specified by the IETF – Integrated Services (IntServ) [i] and Differentiated Services (DiffServ) [ii] – rely on the capability of packet differentiation. In

M.M. Freire, P. Lorenz, M.M.-O. Lee (Eds.): HSNMC 2003, LNCS 2720, pp. 343-352, 2003.
© Springer-Verlag Berlin Heidelberg 2003

IntServ, traffic differentiation is proposed on a per-flow basis, while DiffServ suggests that only a few traffic classes be defined, which are then treated differently (i.e., differentiation on a traffic-aggregation basis). However, the proposed mechanisms can only achieve good QoS if sufficient bandwidth is provisioned.

In this work, we investigate the tradeoff between voice QoS, which is correlated to packet delay, and the amount of bandwidth given to voice traffic. We specifically consider the maximum possible packet delay whenever several connections share a single link and show that the amount of required bandwidth can be drastically decreased if only a small percentage of all connections are allowed to be negatively affected. We also investigate the delay of packets in multi-service networks as a function of the employed scheduling schemes.

In the next section, we provide a brief overview about QoS-related issues of Voice over IP (VoIP) traffic. Section 3 presents the network model adopted in our work and discusses the considered scheduling schemes. In Section 4, we introduce network dimensioning strategies based on worst-case delay scenarios. In Section 5, the proposed dimensioning strategy is studied quantitatively and compared to other models. Section 6 concludes the paper.

2   Voice over IP Traffic and Quality of Service

The characteristics of a traffic stream sent out by a VoIP source are determined by the type of encoder, which is used to convert voice samples into IP packets. The most common voice coders nowadays are constant bit rate (CBR) coders that transmit a fixed-size IP packet every constant interval of time. A G.711 coder, for example, might generate a 200-byte packet every 20 ms, resulting in an IP data rate of 80 kbps.

For Voice over IP to become widely accepted, it will have to provide a quality level comparable to conventional telephony systems. One crucial factor for the perceived quality of voice communication is the end-to-end delay of voice samples between the speaker and the listener. In VoIP systems, this delay consists mainly of encoding and decoding delays as well as packet transfer times between the sender and the receiver. Furthermore, in order to equalize delay jitter, which arises from traffic variations within the network, a playback buffer is employed in the receiver. Incoming packets whose interarrival times might vary are temporarily stored and played out in equidistant time intervals just as they were sent out by the original sender. This playback buffer time also contributes to the overall delay budget. Altogether, the one-way end-to-end delay value should be less than 150 ms for interactive communication [iii].

Having a rather constant coder and playback buffer delay, one can derive a certain maximum threshold for the network delay. Thus, for IP networks to be able to appropriately support VoIP services, network latency has to be kept lower than this threshold. As the main contribution to latency in IP networks is queuing delay, which occurs at network nodes during congestion phases, this delay component increases with each hop. Thus, we can derive a certain per-hop delay limit in a way that the total delay of the maximum number of hops in the network is below the given threshold. Based on this per-hop delay limit, the network links can be dimensioned.

3 Network Model

Fig. 1 depicts a general IP network model with several nodes, each of which supports a set of traffic classes by implementing separate queues per output port. In this work, we consider all voice traffic to be treated as one class giving it a separate queue, while other queues may contain any other kind of traffic. In order to account for a general network model with various network topologies, traffic at every hop is assumed to be independent from other hops.

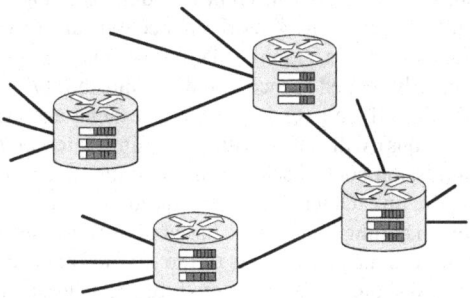

Fig. 1.   General IP network model

In our investigations, we focus on one hop and analyze the multiplexing process of several incoming lines onto one outgoing port. We assume that K voice connections are active and that the corresponding VoIP packets need to be forwarded onto the same output link with capacity C. The traffic of each voice connection is generated by a CBR encoder without silence suppression, i.e., packets of length L are sent out with a periodicity of T seconds, resulting in an average rate $r = L/T$. For simplification, we assume that the K traffic streams reach the router over different input lines. This way, it is possible that K incoming VoIP packets arrive at the router at almost the same time and being instantaneously put into the output buffer, but the queuing delay of each packet should not exceed a threshold D. The maximum packet size of the other traffic classes is assumed to be equal to the output link's maximum transfer unit (MTU).

The scheduling algorithms used in the routers are priority queuing (PQ) and class-based weighted fair queuing (CB-WFQ). Priority queuing assigns priority levels to the different queues. Packets in a lower priority queue are not processed until all packets of higher priority queues are serviced and the corresponding output buffers are empty. A pre-emptive type of PQ aborts transmission of a lower priority packet upon the arrival of a higher priority one, whereas a non-pre-emptive type allows the completion of the transmission. PQ has been proposed as an adequate scheduling for the expedited forwarding per-hop behavior EF-PHB [iv], which grants premium service to a defined aggregate of traffic in the DiffServ model and has been introduced to support critical real-time traffic such as voice. Voice traffic is normally given the highest priority as it is also assumed in this work. With PQ, however, it is possible that traffic classes with the highest priority take up the whole bandwidth and push out lower-priority traffic. An alternative to PQ is CB-WFQ, which allocates a weight to each class or queue and shares the link capacity among the busy queues in direct proportion to their assigned weights. Thus, no traffic class is capable of seizing the whole link at congestion times.

4 Bandwidth Considerations and Dimensioning Strategies

In this section, we investigate different link dimensioning strategies for VoIP traffic. Assuming that a maximum of K VoIP connections are forwarded to one output link, we need to find the link's required bandwidth that provides a certain QoS. In our case, QoS is directly related to a certain delay threshold D at each node. Furthermore, assuming that all VoIP sources implement the same encoders, K packets (belonging to the K connections) will arrive within any time interval T. During network operations, a call admission control scheme has to assure that not more than K connections are allowed on the link. Otherwise, the required QoS cannot be provided.

The first dimensioning approach is based on worst-case considerations, which give hard QoS guarantees, i.e., all packets of the K voice connections are definitely served within a delay threshold of D irrespective of the load situation. Deterministic upper bounds on queuing delays in packet-switched networks are derived in [v,vi] and they correspond to the case when K IP packets arrive all at exactly the same time instance. It then has to be assured that the packet, which happens to be put into the buffer last and which has to wait longest, is still sent out within time D. Thus, $K \cdot L$ bytes have to be sent within D requiring a rate of $K \cdot L / D$. This dimensioning concept is referred to as worst-case dimensioning or hard-guaranteed dimensioning.

Instead of deterministic delay bounds, statistical delay values can be considered. Taking into account that the K packets usually arrive in some way distributed over the time period T, a smaller bandwidth seems to be sufficient. This way, softer QoS guarantees are given and the dimensioning strategy is referred to as average-case dimensioning or statistical-guaranteed dimensioning. However, one has to be aware that in some cases, not all of the packets can be serviced within the time threshold D if statistical-guaranteed dimensioning is used.

The opposite extreme of worst-case dimensioning would be best-case dimensioning. This approach corresponds to a scenario where every packet arrives at the moment when the previous packet has just been sent out. Based on this scenario, the required capacity is at least L/D. In any case, the minimum required capacity is the mean rate of the K connections. Fig. 2 illustrates the bandwidth range between the two extremes, for $L = 200$ bytes, $T = 20$ ms, and $D = 5$ ms. For each of these extreme expectations, we plot the required link capacity assuming that the network supports only voice services or employs pre-emptive PQ. As the number of connections or active users K increases, the range gets broader. It is also shown that worst-case dimensioning requires rates much higher than the mean rate of the active users causing very low link utilization values (e.g., for $K = 10$, the link utilization is $10 \cdot 80/3200 = 0.25 = 25\%$). In contrary, best-case dimensioning starts slightly higher than the mean rate and then coincides with it at $K = 4$, causing a 100% link utilization.

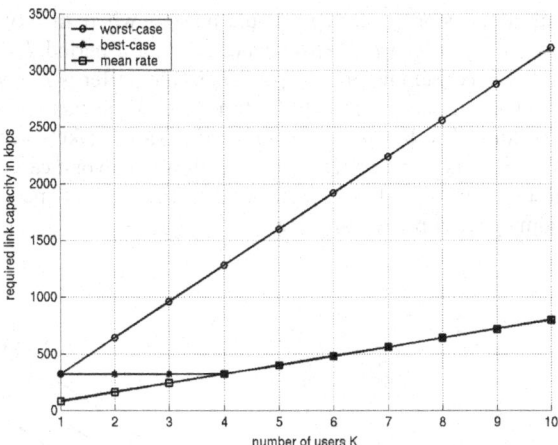

Fig. 2.   Worst-case vs. best-case dimensioning in voice-only networks

While best-case dimensioning certainly does not achieve satisfactory QoS in most cases (too many active connections would exceed their delay budget), worst-case dimensioning is considered a highly pessimistic assumption [vii]. Here rises the question, how necessary it is to dimension according to the worst-case scenario and how frequent this case exists. To compute the probability of this case, $P_{worst\ case}$, we assume a slotted time interval T where each slot is equal to the service time of one packet. All packet arrivals occur at the beginning of a slot and are uniformly distributed over all available slots in the time interval T. Having periodic sources, only one packet per active connection appears every T interval. If link utilization is 100%, i.e. the number of users K equals the number of time slots in T, the probability for the worst-case is

$$P_{worst\ case} = \frac{1}{K^{K-1}}.$$ (1)

Obviously, for lower link utilization, $P_{worst\ case}$ is even less. Setting $K = 10$ users, $P_{worst\ case} \leq 10^{-9}$. Therefore, we would be wasting 75% of the link capacity (see Fig. 2) just to account for a case that occurs once every 10^9 times. For comparison, the probability of the best-case scenario, $P_{best\ case}$, is computed with 100% link utilization as:

$$P_{best\ case} = \frac{K!}{K^K} = P_{worst\ case} \cdot (K-1)!.$$ (2)

$P_{best\ case}$ evaluates much higher than $P_{worst\ case}$ for high K values. Furthermore, for lower link utilization, $P_{best\ case}$ is even higher. Setting $K = 10$, $P_{best\ case} \geq 3.6 \cdot 10^{-4}$. However, if dimensioning is done according to the best case, the desired QoS would not be achieved in at most $(1 - 3.6 \cdot 10^{-4})$ of all cases. It is clear that dimensioning according to either extreme is not realistic. While one approach wastes a lot of bandwidth, the other one leads to service degradation of most voice connections. A practical satisfactory dimensioning strategy should lie somewhere in between.

We define *(K-i)-packet worst cases* where during a period T, for K active voice connections, the maximum number of packets in the buffer is $K-i$, with $i = 0, 1,..., K-1$. In other words, the maximum waiting time over all packets is $K-i$ times the individual service time. The last packet waits until $(K-i-1)$ packets in front of it are serviced in addition to its own service time. Therefore, the worst case corresponds to $i = 0$ and the best case to $i = K-1$. Fig. 3 shows the required link speeds for a voice-only network assuming $(K-i)$-packet worst cases.

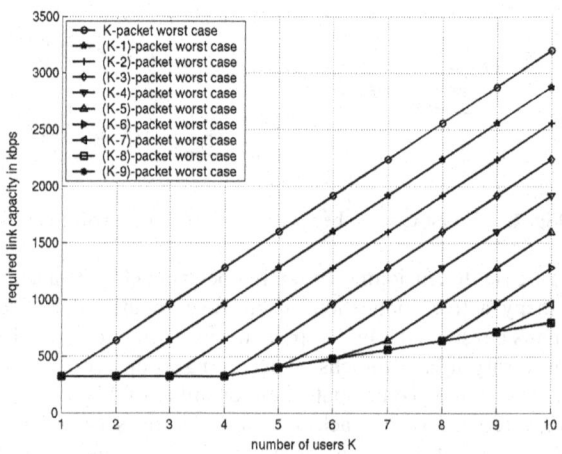

Fig. 3. $(K-i)$-packet worst case

If dimensioning is carried out according to the $(K-2)$-packet worst case, 20% of the bandwidth can be saved as compared to worst-case dimensioning, leading to service degradation only in $(K-0)$- and $(K-1)$-packet worst cases, which arise with a very low probability.

In a network supporting several traffic classes as depicted in the general network model in Fig. 1, $(K-i)$-packet worst-case dimensioning depends on the employed scheduling scheme. For the commonly-used PQ and CB-WFQ, Table 1 presents the link capacity and bandwidth share, respectively, which are needed to satisfy a certain per-hop delay limit D using $(K-i)$-packet worst-case dimensioning. Using this dimensioning concept, we can guarantee that in most cases (up to a certain probability) no packet has to wait more than the predefined delay threshold. Only in a few "unfortunate" cases, the threshold is exceeded.

In the next section, the correlation between the capacity C and the probabilities of $(K-i)$-packet worst cases is investigated by simulation. The $(K-i)$-packet worst cases are identified by the respective maximum waiting times. Furthermore, we propose a dimensioning strategy, which takes into account these waiting times.

Table 1. Required bandwidth for all $(K\text{-}i)$-packet worst cases (L = voice IP packet size, D = per-hop delay limit, r = voice coder IP rate, C = link capacity, $i = 0,\ldots, K\text{-}1$)

	Best case	$(K\text{-}i)$-packet worst case	Worst case
Voice-only / Pre-emptive PQ	$\max\left(\dfrac{L}{D}, K \times r\right)$	$\max\left(best\ case, (K\text{-}i)\times \dfrac{L}{D}\right)$	$K \times \dfrac{L}{D}$
Non-pre-emptive PQ	$\max\left(\dfrac{L}{D}, K \times r\right)$	$\max\left(best\ case, \dfrac{(K-i)\times L + MTU}{D}\right)$	$\dfrac{K \times L + MTU}{D}$
CB-WFQ	$\max\left(\dfrac{L}{D}, K \times r\right)$	$\min\left(C, \max\left(best\ case, \dfrac{(K-i)\times L}{D - \dfrac{MTU}{C}}\right)\right)$	$\min\left(C, \dfrac{K \times L}{D - \dfrac{MTU}{C}}\right)$

5 Investigation of Waiting Time

The probabilities of the above-mentioned "unfortunate" cases are evaluated by means of simulation. To do so, we generate arrival scenarios of K VoIP connections within a time interval of length T, which is equal to the coder period. The setup time of each connection is uniformly distributed over $[0, T)$. For each generated scenario, the average and the maximum waiting times are computed, which can be directly converted into the average and maximum number of packets that are available in the buffer and being in service.

The results are compared with an N*D/D/1 queuing system, which models a number of equi-periodic sources serviced at a constant rate by one server [viii]. This model is applicable to CBR voice traffic of equal coder rate multiplexed on one link [vii,ix]. While voice flows lose their strict periodic behavior in multi-service networks, it is preserved in voice-only networks and, therefore, modeling voice flows as N*D/D/1 is an appropriate approximation.

In Fig. 4a, we plot the complementary cumulative distribution function (CCDF) of the maximum waiting time encountered for 30 active users in comparison with the average waiting time and the N*D/D/1 model, for various values of link utilization (which correspond to different link capacities). We observe, as expected, that the average waiting time curve is bounded between the curves of the maximum waiting time and the N*D/D/1 model. For a fully utilized link, the CCDF of the average waiting time matches very closely the N*D/D/1 model. This is clear knowing that the average waiting time averages the delay over all packets; whereas, the N*D/D/1 model computes the time average, where times of empty queues lower the average. By having a fully utilized link, the queue is always occupied and, thus, both CCDFs match. In case the N*D/D/1 model is used for dimensioning, it would suggest that a link speed of 3.2 Mbps (= 75% utilization) would be sufficient to keep the average per-hop delay below 4.2 ms for $(1-10^{-4})$ of the cases. However, the CCDF of the maximum waiting time model at 4.2 ms is $4\cdot10^{-3}$. This means that in 4 out of 1000 cases, not all of the active VoIP connections experience the desired QoS.

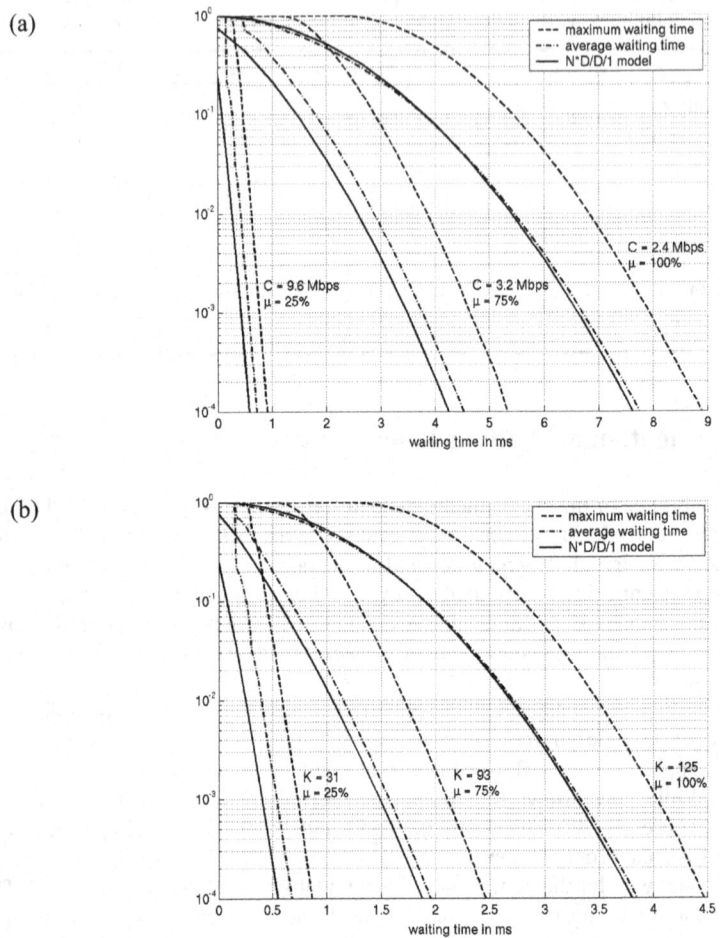

Fig. 4.   CCDF of some waiting time models (rate = 80 kbps, link utilization μ = 25%, 75%, and 100%) (a) K = 30 users (b) Link speed = 10 Mbps

Fig. 4b shows the considered waiting time models for a link speed of 10 Mbps and different link utilizations (which now correspond to different numbers of active users). On a 10 Mbps link, 125 active users could be multiplexed at one time (100% utilization) and a delay limit of 4.5 ms is guaranteed up to $(1-10^{-4})$ of the cases. Using the worst-case dimensioning approach with hard QoS guarantees and a per-hop delay threshold of 4.5 ms, the capacity of 10 Mbps would already be required for 28 active users leading to an effective utilization of 22.4%. In a different perspective, the 125 active users would require around 44 Mbps to have a hard guaranteed per-hop delay of 4.5 ms. This is due to the fact that worst-case dimensioning is a 125-packet worst case assuming that all 125 users arrive at the queue at the same instant and so the last packet queued has to be serviced within the delay limit. On the other hand, the maximum waiting time model shows that a maximum of 28 packets are queued at one time for $(1-10^{-4})$ of the cases and it corresponds to 28-packet worst case dimensioning. As a result, dimensioning VoIP networks based on maximum waiting time model provides 'almost' guaranteed QoS for rather low costs.

For an IP network, which supports various traffic classes, it is important to study the performance of voice in the general network model of Fig. 1. We assume highly congested network conditions where queues of all traffic classes excluding voice are constantly filled up with *MTU*-sized packets. Fig. 5 presents the CCDF of the maximum waiting time of voice packets belonging to 30 active voice connections and awaiting service from a link of capacity C. Results are shown for each of non-preemptive PQ and CB-WFQ.

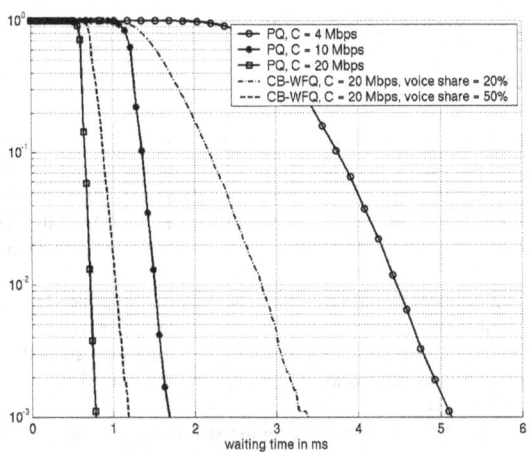

Fig. 5.   CCDF of maximum waiting time

It is observed that 4 Mbps link capacity is sufficient to provide a deterministic delay threshold of around 5.2 ms for $(1-10^{-3})$ of the cases if non-preemptive PQ is used; whereas, using worst-case dimensioning, 11.5 Mbps link capacity is required if the same delay threshold is requested for all possible cases. A lower delay threshold is granted when the same amount of bandwidth is allocated for voice in a network using CB-WFQ. That might not be directly intuitive but easily understood when knowing that in non-preemptive PQ, any packet of other classes, which could have been in transmission while a voice packet arrived, is serviced with the link speed which is 4 Mbps. However, in CB-WFQ, any packet of other classes, which could have been in transmission when a voice packet is *scheduled* for service, is serviced with the link speed which is 20 Mbps and, thus, faster. However, with the link speed of 20 Mbps, PQ outperforms CB-WFQ even when 50% capacity share is allocated for voice.

6 Conclusions

As voice services require certain QoS guarantees in order to perform well over IP networks, large resources should be allocated for this traffic class. However, we have shown that providing hard performance guarantees to voice services is extremely costly and unaffordable.

Based on the concept of statistical worst-cases, we investigated the tradeoff between allocated network resources and the probability of quality guarantees. Based on simulations where we derived the average and maximum delay values of packets during periods when the voice queue is busy, we have shown that the amount of bandwidth can be reduced if only a certain probability of service degradation is allowed. Furthermore, we have illustrated that the dimensioning strategy which is based on the maximum waiting time model offers 'almost' guaranteed QoS with rather low costs.

References

i. Braden, R., Clark, D., Shenker, S.: Integrated Services in the Internet Architecture: An Overview. Request for Comments RFC 1633. Internet Engineering Task Force (June 1994)
ii. Blake, S., Black, D., Carlson, M.: An Architecture for Differentiated Services. Request for Comments RFC 2475. Internet Engineering Task Force (December 1998)
iii. ITU-T Recommendation G.108: Application of the E-model: A Planning Guide. (September 1999)
iv. Jacobson, V., Nichols, K., Poduri, K.: The Virtual Wire 'Per-Domain Behavior': Analysis and Extensions. Internet Engineering Task Force (July 2000)
v. Parekh, A.K., Gallager, R.G.: A Generalized Processor Sharing Approach to Flow Control in Integrated Services Networks: The Single-Node Case. IEEE/ACM Transactions on Networking (June 1993)
vi. Parekh, A.K., Gallager, R.G.: A Generalized Processor Sharing Approach to Flow Control in Integrated Services Networks: The Multiple Node Case. IEEE/ACM Transactions on Networking (April 1994)
vii. Mandjes, M., van der Wal, K., Kooij, K., Bastiaansen, H.: End-to-End Delay Models for Interactive Services on a Large-Scale IP Network. 7th IFIP Workshop on Modeling and Evaluation of ATM/IP Networks (1999)
viii. Roberts, J., Mocci, U., Virtamo, J.: Broadband Network Teletraffic: Final Report of Action COST 242. Springer-Verlag, Berlin Heidelberg New York (1996)
ix. Bonald, T., Proutiere, A., Roberts, J.W.: Statistical Performance Guarantees for Streaming Flows Using Expedited Forwarding. INFOCOM 2001 (April 2001)

An Admission Control Scheme for Voice Traffic over IP Networks*

Hung Tuan Tran and Thomas Ziegler

Telecommunications Research Center Vienna (ftw.)
Donaucity Strasse 1, 1220, Vienna, Austria
{tran,ziegler}@ftw.at

Abstract. The paper deals with the admissibility of voice traffic flows with QoS requirement in terms of packet delay and packet loss. A two-stage CAC approach based on the rate envelope multiplexing principle along with a simplified reference model is proposed. One concrete realization of such a CAC mechanism that utilizes the Chernoff bound based effective bandwidth and the recently stated negligible jitter conjecture is constructed and analyzed. This approach for admission rules is discussed and explored by considering both, an analytical model as well as realistic simulation scenarios.
Keywords: VoIP, admission control, M/GI/1/K vacation queue

1 Introduction

One of the most popular application over the Internet that could be offered with guaranteed QoS is streaming, particularly voice application. For this real time application (often referred to as Voice over IP), strict end-to-end delay, jitter and loss should be delivered (less than 150ms end-to-end delay, 1% packet loss rate). The question is how to do that in an efficient and scalable way given the fact that voice traffic is normally mixed with other kind of traffic. This raises two important design issues concerning both the data plane and control plane of the would-be QoS architecture. First, in the data plane, appropriate traffic control mechanisms (e.g. packet scheduling, queue management) should be worked out. For example, in the DiffServ architecture, it is recommended that real-time traffic should be treated in an expedited forwarding manner [5], i.e. being stored in a high priority queue apart from the queue of other traffic. Second, in the control plane, an adequate call admission control (CAC) scheme should be applied to voice flows to keep the QoS at the acceptable level. From engineering aspects, the CAC should remain as simple as possible, while being still able to make judicious admission decisions with regard to the current traffic load in the network.

The topic of the present paper falls into the category of the second issue. We propose a two-stage CAC approach for voice traffic flows with loss and delay

---

* This work has been performed in the context of the Austrian Kplus program and the IST project Moby Dick

M.M. Freire, P. Lorenz, M.M.-O. Lee (Eds.): HSNMC 2003, LNCS 2720, pp. 353–364, 2003.
© Springer-Verlag Berlin Heidelberg 2003

requirements. The CAC approach combines the concept of rate envelope multiplexing [7] and the idea of using a simplified reference model. We provide one concrete realization of the proposed approach, when rate envelope multiplexing is ensured with the Chernoff bound based effective bandwidth concept. The simplified reference model is obtained by exploiting the recently divulged negligible jitter conjecture [4] coupled with the implication of an M/GI/1/K queue with exhaustive service and multiple vacation. We elaborate computational methodologies enabling the numerical assessment of the relevant quantities (effective bandwidths, percentile of delay, packet loss probability). Moreover, we build up simulation runs reflecting realistic network scenarios to examine and verify the merit of the proposed CAC mechanism with respect to analytical results.

The paper is organised as follows. In Section 2 we describe the proposed two-stage CAC mechanism. Several aspects are presented including the motivations, the basic operation, the theoretical background and the realization model. The computational procedures for relevant performance parameters are also explained in details in this section. In order to evaluate the merit of the model used in the CAC scheme, we perform both analytical and simulation analysis. Section 3 contains the description of analytical and simulation scenarios, the obtained results and their discussions. Finally, Section 4 ends the paper.

2   The Two-Stage CAC Scheme

2.1   Informal Description

In [4] the authors state the so called NJ (negligible jitter) conjecture that provides a useful methodology for traffic engineering of EF traffic in DiffServ networks. The NJ conjecture sketches that if: *i)* the network realizes priority queueing for EF traffic at each router; *ii)* EF flows have negligible jitter at the ingress with respect to a Poisson process with MTU packet size; and *iii)* at every multiplexing stage (router) within the network the sum of input rates is less than the service rate, then throughout the network the EF flows behave better than a Poisson stream with MTU packet size, i.e the EF flows can be replaced by a Poisson process for dimensioning rules. The effect of jitter then is ignored while applying engineering rules to the flows. The statistical bound for the queue length (and so for the queueing delay) therein is provided by the expression

$$P(Q > x) \leq \begin{cases} 1 & x < x_{min} \\ ke^{-rx/MTU} & x \geq x_{min} \end{cases}, \tag{1}$$

where Q is the queue length, r is a root of the equation $\rho(e^r - 1) - r = 0$, $k = \dfrac{1 - \rho}{\rho^2 e^r - \rho}$, $x_{min} = \dfrac{-MTU}{r} \log \dfrac{1}{k}$ and ρ is the utilization of the assimilated *infinite queue*. The NJ conjecture has been affirmed with both theoretical arguments based on considerations of stochastic ordering and with simulation results. However, only the case when the EF traffic is generated by CBR sources with constant packet size was dealt in details, leaving the case of VBR traffic with different packet size touched at the mentioning level.

Suppose now that we have to perform the admission control for *heterogenous* voice flows at a given output link of a given node in the network. We split the CAC functionalities into two modules in sequence. The first module ensures that the rate of the aggregate voice traffic only exceeds the capacity of the output link with a small probability (called rate overloading probability). Moreover, whenever rate overload takes place, it discards the excess traffic. *Our motivation of introducing such the first module is to make the NJ conjecture applicable* (refer to the *(iii)* condition) and thus to facilitate further analysis needed in the second one for loss and delay related requirements of the aggregate voice traffic. Consequently, when a new voice flow requesting admission arrives, a two-stage CAC procedure is performed as follows.

- Decision 1: if the new flow does not make the rate overloading probability increase beyond the predefined one (denoted by $e^{-\gamma}$), it is admitted by the first module and is passed to the second module. Otherwise, the flow is rejected and the CAC procedure ends.
- Decision 2: if the new flow is admitted to the second module, a numerical analysis is done to check further delay and loss metrics of the voice flows. The computation procedure for the assimilated model (see later in Section 2.3) is achieved to check the delay metric $d_{current}$ and the buffer overflow probability $p_{current}$ taking into account also the load produced by the new flow. Let d_{req} and p_{req} be the delay and loss requirements of the voice flows. If $d_{req} > d_{current}$ and $p_{req} > p_{current} + e^{-\gamma}$, the new flow is accepted, otherwise it is rejected.

From engineering aspects, rate envelope multiplexing (REM)[7] is appropriate to be applied for the first module. The REM module ensures that the rate overload probability determined as $\dfrac{E(\Lambda_t - C)^+}{E(\Lambda_t)}$, where C is the output link capacity, Λ_t is the aggregate input rate and $(.)^+ = max(0, .)$, is below the predefined threshold $e^{-\gamma}$. Note that it is also the loss rate induced by the REM module, because no burst-scale buffer is provided for the excess traffic. For the second module, an analytical model is needed. The application of the NJ conjecture in the second module will lead to the analytically simplified model with a Poisson arrival process (therefore we refer to this module as simplified reference module SRM). In fact, we get a *finite* $M/GI/1/K$ vacation queue modelling the behaviour of the aggregate voice traffic in the presence of the background traffic.

2.2   Model of the REM Module

To achieve rate envelope multiplexing we resort to the Chernoff bound based effective bandwidth concept presented in [7]. The reason for this choice is because the Chernoff bound approach can give a tight upper bound on the rate overload probability. Moreover, it is capable to deal with multiple classes of ON-OFF input traffic sources, which is typically the case of voice traffic stemming from different codecs.

Suppose that we have J types of independent ON-OFF traffic sources generating traffic to an output link of capacity C. In accordance with DiffServ philosophy, we assume that the network operators have a priori information on the traffic pattern of each traffic class, i.e. the mean rate m_j and the peak rate r_j of a source of type j are known.

Given the threshold for the rate overloading probability $e^{-\gamma}$ and a traffic mix $n = (n_1, n_2, \dots n_J)$, the effective bandwidth of a source type j is then defined as

$$\alpha_j = \frac{\log\left[1 + \frac{m_j}{r_j}(e^{s^* r_j} - 1)\right]}{s^*}, \tag{2}$$

where $s^* = \arg\inf_{s>0} f(s) = \arg\inf_{s>0}\left[\sum_{j=1}^{J} n_j \log\left(1 + \frac{m_j}{r_j}(e^{s r_j} - 1)\right) - sC\right]$. When a new flow arrives, the first CAC decision is made by checking the validity of the inequality $\sum_{j=1}^{J} n_j \alpha_j + \frac{\gamma}{s^*} \leq C$. If the condition is fulfilled, the new flow can pass the REM module and becomes a subject to the second acceptance decision in the SRM module. Otherwise, the new flow is rejected.

Note that the concrete value of s^*, and in turn the value of the effective bandwidth of each type of sources, naturally depends on the choice of a feasible initial traffic mix, i.e. the choice of the values n_j, $j = 0, 1, \dots J$. This means that for different choices of the traffic mix we may have different CAC regions. In general, given a feasible traffic mix $n = (n_1, n_2, \dots n_J)$, by making the first derivative of $f(s)$ zero, one has to solve a transcendental equation to determine s^*. A general computational procedure is shown in Fig. 1.

---

1. Choose an appropriate initial trafic mix $n = (n_1, n_2, \dots n_J)$

2. Solve the trancendent equation $\dfrac{df(s)}{ds} = 0$ to get s^*

3 Compute $\alpha_j, j = 1, 2, \dots, J$ based on (2)

4. Check the feasibility of the initial traffic mix:

   If $\displaystyle\sum_j n_j \alpha_j + \frac{\gamma}{s^*} \leq C$, END the procedure;

   Otherwise, choose another initial trafic mix, GO TO Step 2

Fig. 1. General calculation of effective bandwidths

The transcendental equation and efforts for its solution, however, can be avoided if the initial traffic mix contains only one type i of sources, i.e. n_j is set to 0 for all $j \neq i, j \in [1, J]$, because the equation $\dfrac{df(s)}{ds} = 0$ then gives the close form for s^*. The general computational procedure then degenerates to the one shown in Fig. 2.

We have implemented both the above numerical computational procedures. With our set of input parameters (see later in Section 3), the obtained CAC regions do not exhibit a significantly difference. Thus, the simpler computational procedure seems reasonable to be applied.

---

1. Choose source type i, set $N = C/m_i$
2. Compute s^* and α_i:
   DO
   - Compute $s^* = \dfrac{1}{r_i} \log \left[\dfrac{C(1 - m_i/r_i)}{m_i(N - C/r_i)} \right]$
   - Compute α_i from (2)
   - $N = N - 1$
   $WHILE\ (N\alpha_i + \frac{\gamma}{s^*} > C)$

---

3. Using s^*, compute $\alpha_j, j = 1, 2, \ldots, J, j \neq i$, based on (2)

Fig. 2. Simpler calculation of effective bandwidths

2.3   Model of the SRM Module

By employing the REM module, we may now assimilate the aggregate voice traffic with a Poisson process with the same load. We adopt a queueing model where voice packets are fed into a *finite buffer* and served by a server representing the output link.

The operation of the server is considered in a manner of exhaustive service and multiple vacation scenario. That is the server delivers voice packets in the finite buffer until it becomes empty. At the finishing instant of the service, if the server finds the queue empty, it takes vacation. If there are still no packets in the queue when the server returns from its vacation, it takes another vacation and so on. Note that the vacations of the server correspond to the situation when the output link is occupied by the best effort traffic. The assumption of multiple vacation implies that the offered load of the best effort traffic is sufficiently high to immediately utilize the link capacity whenever no voice packet is present. The vacation time is assumed to be the time needed for transmission of a best effort packet with MTU size (worst-case assumption). In effects, we obtain a finite $M/GI/1/K$ queue with exhaustive service and multiple vacation.

We solve the steady state distribution of this queue based on the work available from [6] and accomplish some further derivations which enable the calculation of important statistical measures. Specifically, the following parameters are considered:

— *Mean queueing delay:* This parameter is calculable by means of Little's law

$$d_{avg} = \frac{\text{Mean queue length}}{\lambda(1 - p_{loss})}, \qquad (3)$$

where λ is the mean packet arrival rate, p_{loss} is the loss probability given by expression (7).

— *p-percentile of queueing delay:* Although the mean queueing delay is definitely of interest, the p-percentile of delay variable could be a better parameter to characterize the end-to-end delay behavior of the voice connection, because it provides statistical information on the upper-bound of jitter of the voice connections. Having the delay value d of the p-percentile, the probability that the queueing delay is larger than d is at most $1 - p$, i.e.

$$P(delay \geq d) \leq 1 - p. \qquad (4)$$

In general, the p-percentile of queueing delay can be determined exactly, if the density function of the queueing time is known. Unfortunately, the density function in the time domain is unavailable. Therefore, we propose here the solution derived from the Laplace domain analysis. In [6], the LST (Laplace-Stieltjes transform) of the queueing time distribution (which is identical to the Laplace transform of the density function) is given as

$$W(s) = S(s)^K \sum_{j=0}^{K} \pi_j \left(\frac{\lambda}{\lambda - s}\right)^{K+1-j} + \frac{\lambda \pi_0}{1 - h_0} \frac{\left[1 - \left(\frac{\lambda S(s)}{\lambda - s}\right)^{K+1}\right](V(s) - 1)}{\lambda - s - \lambda S(s)},$$

(5)

where π_j is the steady state probability that j voice packets are left in the system at a departure epoch, $S(s)$ and $V(s)$ are LSTs of the service and vacation time, respectively. To transform back this expression into the time domain is very hard, if not impossible. Thus, in order to obtain the p-percentile for a given p, we resort to an approximation using the Chernoff inequality in probabilistic theory, which gives

$$P(delay \geq d) \leq \inf_s \frac{W(-s)}{e^{ds}}.$$

(6)

To find the infimum of the right hand $G(s) = \dfrac{W(-s)}{e^{ds}}$ of the inequality (6) we have to solve the transcendental equation $\dfrac{dG(s)}{ds} = 0$. As one can recognize from equation (5), the expression for $G(s)$ is quite complicate and so is its derivation. The best suitable numerical method we are aware of in this case is the Secant method [2]. In fact, this method has been chosen to be implemented in our work. Another observation is that the computation can only be done in such a way, that the value d must be given as an input parameter, based on which the value $p = 1 - \inf_s G(s)$ is calculated. This is in contrast with the original intention according to which p should be given as an input parameter and d is the output parameter. However, this contradiction can be resolved by a computational procedure presented in Fig. 3, where d_{step} stands for the increment with a sufficient granularity to reach the required p. It should be pointed out, however, that to make the complexity reasonably low, a binary search may be involved instead of the linear search shown in Fig. 3. This is particularly useful, when new flows arrive frequently, leading to frequent executions of the calculation procedure to conduct admissibility decisions.

– *Packet loss probability due to buffer overflow:* From [6]

$$p_{loss} = 1 - \frac{(1 - h_0)\lambda^{-1}}{E(V)\pi_0 + E(S)(1 - h_0)},$$

(7)

where $E(V)$, $E(S)$ are the mean service time and mean vacation time, h_0 is the probability that no voice packet arrival occur during a vacation time V, π_0 is the steady state probability that no voice packet is left in the system at a departure epoch.

---
1. Set an appropriately, small initial d, and set $p = 0$
2. $WHILE$ $(p < p_{need})$
   3.1. $d = d + d_{step}$
   3.1. Find $s^* = \arg\inf_s G(s, d)$
   3.2. Compute $p = 1 - G(s^*, d)$
3. Return d and p

Fig. 3. Calculation procedure for the delay percentile

3   Analytical and Simulation Discussions

To get insights into the goodness of the proposed model used for the CAC scheme, we perform both analytical and simulation analysis. We consider voice sources having typical ON-OFF nature. During the ON period, voice packets of identical length are generated periodically, while no packets are produced over the OFF period. The packet length and the periodicity of packet generation depends on the type of voice codec applied at the source. We take three types of voice codecs into consideration (see Table 1): G723.1 (type 1), G726 (type 2) and G729 (type 3). The ON-OFF voice sources have the mean time of ON period 0.35s and the mean time of OFF period 0.65s.

Table 1. Characteristics of voice codecs used in simulative and numerical investigations

Codec	Packet size (payload + 40 bytes RTP, UDP, IP header)	Packet interval-time during ON period	Peak rate during ON period
G723.1	64 byte	30.5ms	16.78Kbps
G726	120 byte	20ms	48Kbps
G729	60 byte	20ms	24Kbps

A dumbbell topology shown in Fig. 4 is used for the ns-2 [1] simulation runs[1]. Voice sources send traffic from node h_1 to node h_6 through the route h_1-r_1-r_2-h_6. Each node-router link has a capacity of $500Mbps$. The bottleneck link between the router r_1 and r_2 has a capacity of 1.5Mbps. We have implemented the non-preemptive, priority scheduling scheme for voice and background traffic at the router r_1, where the queueing delay of voice packets is monitored. Simulation runs are performed with the web-like TCP background traffic, which is generated according to a realistic model from [3]. The background packet sizes are set to MTU (1500 bytes). Note that the web server is placed in the node h_2 and the client is placed in node h_4 ensuring that the file download direction is from left to right. To achieve a sufficiently heavy load of the web traffic on the bottleneck link, 500 web sessions are simultaneously established.

First we demonstrate the effect of applying the CAC decision in the REM module. Results reported below use the effective bandwidths calculated with the

---
[1] Each simulation run lasts for 5000 seconds in simulation time.

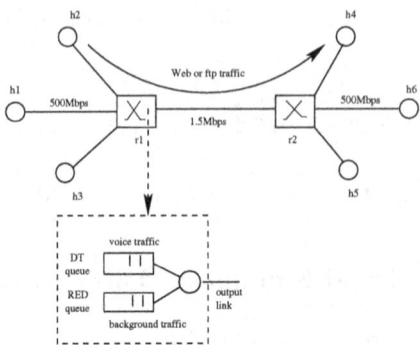

Fig. 4. Simulation scenario

procedure presented in Fig. 2. Two of its calculating alternatives were performed, where the selected source type i (see Step 1 in Fig. 2) was chosen to be $G723.1$ and $G726$, respectively. From now on, we refer to them as SCENARIO 1 and SCENARIO 2. This implementation leads to two CAC regions for each prede-fined rate overloading threshold γ as shown in Table 1. Note that the acceptance region is defined by a plane crossing three points $(n_1, n_2, n_3) = (n_{1,max}, 0, 0)$, $(0, n_{2,max}, 0)$ and $(0, 0, n_{3,max})$. For the aim of demonstration, we also report the CAC region obtained with the general calculation presented in Fig. 1, when the initial traffic mix consists of 50% type 1, 30% type 2 and 20% type 3 sources (SCENARIO 3). Table 2 indicates that with our input parameters, there is no significant bias between the CAC regions produced by the REM module when applying different calculation procedures. As expected, making the over-load requirement more stringent (i.e. increasing γ) reduces the number of ad-missible sources. As a consequence, the achievable link utilization also decreases as demonstrated in Table 3 and Table 4.

We now turn to the investigation of the second module, where the simplified reference model was introduced by utilizing the NJ conjecture. We take two approaches for defining the packet size of the assimilated Poisson stream. In the first approach, packet size is considered as the mean value computed over all the packet sizes belonging to the source types in the system. This is the *mean packet size* approach. In the second one, we simply set the packet size to the value of MTU as proposed by the original NJ conjecture in [4]. Note that in both cases, the M/GI/1/K vacation queue becomes a M/D/1/K vacation queue. The main question we would like to answer is how good and tight approximation the simplified reference model offers from the aspect of system dimensioning. We examine this question with respect to the chosen packet size approach, the number of voice sources and the buffer size (measured in the number of packets whose length is defined according to the mean packet size approach).

The typical behavior of the 99-percentile delay obtained with simulation and numerical solution of the M/D/1/K queue is presented in Figs. 5 – 8. For com-

Table 2. CAC regions after the REM module for different scenarios

γ	SCENARIO 1			SCENARIO 2			SCENARIO 3		
	$n_{1,max}$	$n_{2,max}$	$n_{3,max}$	$n_{1,max}$	$n_{2,max}$	$n_{3,max}$	$n_{1,max}$	$n_{2,max}$	$n_{3,max}$
3	206	59	138	201	62	137	206	58	137
6	189	51	124	184	53	123	186	53	124
9	176	46	114	172	47	113	167	47	111
12	166	42	106	163	43	106	148	42	98

Table 3. Attainable link utilization versus overloading threshold γ, SCENARIO 1

SCENARIO 1				
# G726 = 0, # G729 = 0		# G726 = 25, # G729 = 15		
γ	Max. #G723.1	link utilization	γ	Max. #G723.1	link utilization
3	206	0.806559	3	97	0.743787
6	189	0.739998	6	74	0.653735
9	176	0.689099	9	57	0.587174
12	166	0.649945	12	45	0.540190

Table 4. Attainable link utilization versus overloading threshold γ, SCENARIO 2

SCENARIO 2				
# G723.1 = 0, # G729 = 0		# G723.1 = 12, # G729 = 10		
γ	Max. #G726	link utilization	γ	Max. #G726	link utilization
3	62	0.694400	3	54	0.707784
6	53	0.593600	6	45	0.606984
9	47	0.526400	9	40	0.550984
12	43	0.481600	12	36	0.506184

parative purposes we also compute the delay bound of the original NJ conjecture provided by expression (1) (referred to as "NJ bound" in the figures). The obtained results allow some main findings as follows.

Firstly, results from the simplified analytical model are indeed upper bounds for those from the simulation. The bounds are very tight when the mean packet size is used for the assimilated arrival process instead of MTU packet size.

Secondly, the original NJ conjecture suggests that the assimilated Poisson input process could have MTU (1500 bytes) packet size. According to our experiences, this leads to a too coarse bound for the 99-percentile of delay. As the figures show, it is true both when we apply the original NJ conjecture and compute the bound (1) and when we compute the bound with our analysis based on the finite M/D/1/K queue. Thus, in case of voice traffic with packet sizes significantly smaller than MTU, it is more advisable that the packet size of the assimilated Poisson process remains in a commensurate range with the average size of all packet sizes belonging to the source type being in the system. For instance, if currently only sources from G723.1 type are present, the assimilated packet size should be set to 64 bytes. In case all the three source types are present, the assimilated packet size should be $(64+120+60)/3 \approx 82$ bytes.

Observe that in Figs. 5 – 8, we only increase the number of voice sources until the value comparable to the admissible threshold defined by the REM module with the most stringent overloading probability $e^{-\gamma} = e^{-12}$ (see again Table 3

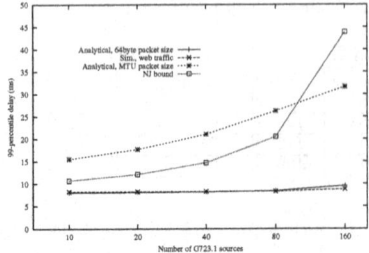

Fig. 5. 99-percentile queueing delay versus number of voice sources, SCE. 1, #G726=0, #G729=0, buff.=100 packets

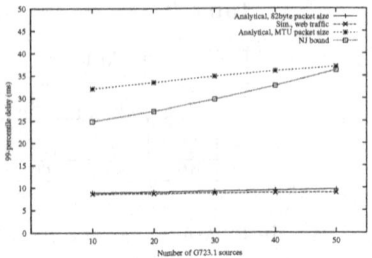

Fig. 6. 99-percentile queueing delay versus number of voice sources, SCE. 1, #G726=25, #G729=15, buff.=100 packets

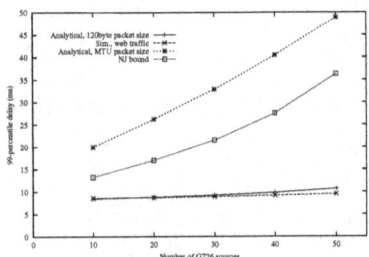

Fig. 7. 99-percentile queueing delay versus number of voice sources, SCE. 2, #G723.1=0, #G729=0, buff.=100 packets

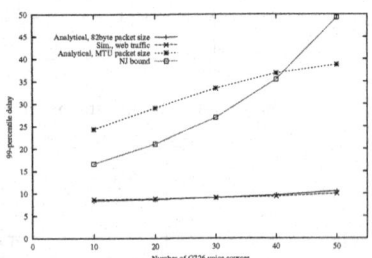

Fig. 8. 99-percentile queueing delay versus number of voice sources, SCE. 2, #G723.1=12, #G729=10, buff.=100 packets

and Table 4). Within the chosen region, the actual delay percentile exhibits quite slight increasing tendency. Of course, by relaxing the overloading constraint of the REM (by decreasing γ), more and more voice sources can be admitted to the second module SRM. Fig. 9 plots the delay percentile evolution for different buffer sizes while further increasing the number of voice sources. It is verified again that the delay curves of simulation and analytical model match each other quite closely. It is interesting to see that at a very high load of voice traffic (more than 100%), the delay percentile becomes constant due to the fact that the buffer is always full. Moreover, if the buffer size is small (e.g. 15 packets) this constant value is even smaller than the delay observed in low load situations. This is due to the effect of heavy loaded best effort traffic. When the load of voice traffic is low, the high priority queue for voice packets may be empty, allowing best effort packets to have a chance to occupy the link. Consequently, an arriving voice packet has to wait not only for the service completion of other voice packets in front of it in the queue, but also for the service completion of the best effort packet currently in service (because of the non-preemptive discipline). When the load of voice traffic is very high, the high priority queue is practically never empty, so that the delay of a given voice packet is solely the time to complete service of voice packets in front of it in the queue. Given that the length of

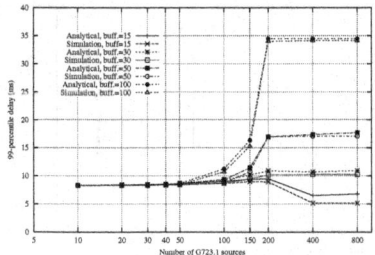

Fig. 9. Delay evolution for different buffer sizes (#G726=0, #G729=0)

best-effort packets (1500 byte) is considerably large compared to that of voice packets (64 byte), the beforementioned delay evolution is experienced.

Figures 10- 13 show the evolution of the packet loss probability due to buffer overflow in both the simplified model and in simulation. One can observe that the analytical results match the simulation results very well, if the mean packet size approach is used. Again, using MTU packet size for the assimilated model leads to unreasonably coarse bounds. We note that setting the buffer to a small value may be preferable from the aspect that we can keep the maximum queueing delay reasonably low at heavy loads. To evade a possibly significant packet loss rate due to buffer overflow in the SRM module, the rate overload probability of the REM module should be set sufficiently small. For example, setting $\gamma = 12$ leads to the required rate overload probability $e^{-\gamma} \approx 6 * 10^{-6}$. If we fix the number of G723.1 and G729 voice sources to 12 and 10 respectively, then the maximum admissible number of G726 sources (at the REM module) is 36 (see Table 4), which produces the packet loss rate due to buffer overflow in a range of 10^{-3} as shown in Fig. 13.

4   Conclusions

In this paper, the issue of QoS provisioning for VoIP traffic has been tackled. A two-stage CAC scheme has been worked out based on the combination of the rate envelope multiplexing concept and the negligible jitter conjecture. As a consequence, an analytical model for conducting CAC decisions has been built and a methodology to calculate delay and loss metrics of voice traffic based on a M/GI/1/K vacation queue has been developed.

Analytical and simulation analysis have validated that our constructed model gives tight predictions on the delay and loss metrics of voice traffic. Therefore, one can indeed rely on the model to compute these QoS measures in order to make CAC decisions.

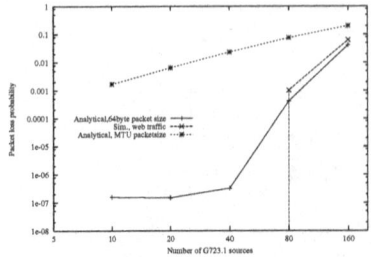

Fig. 10. Packet loss behavior, SCE. 1, #G726=0, #G729=0, buff.=15 packets

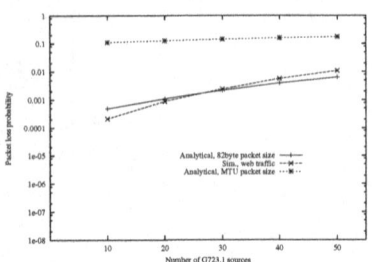

Fig. 11. Packet loss behavior, SCE. 1, #G726=25, #G729=15, buff.=15 packets

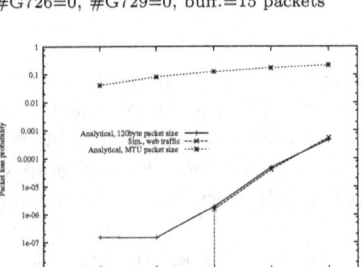

Fig. 12. Packet loss behavior, SCE. 2, #G723.1=0, #G729=0, buff.=15 packets

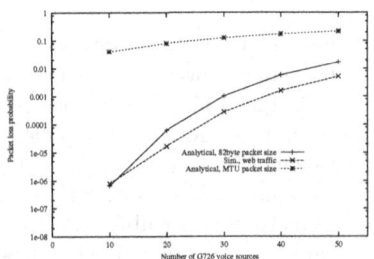

Fig. 13. Packet loss behavior, SCE. 2, #G723.1=12, #G729=10, buff.=15 packets

References

[1] Ns Simulator Homepage. http://www.isi.edu/nsnam/ns.

[2] Numerical Recipes in C- Book on-line. www.library.cornell.edu/nr/bookcpdf.html.

[3] P. Barford and M. E. Crovella. Generating representative Workloads for Network and Server Performance Evaluation. In *Proceedings of ACM SIGMETRICS*, pages 151–160, 1998.

[4] T. Bonald, A. Proutiere, and J. W. Roberts. Statistical Performance Guarantees for Streaming Flows using Expedited Forwarding. In *Proceedings of IEEE INFOCOM*, volume 2, pages 1104–1112, 2001.

[5] B. Davie et al. An Expedited Forwarding PHB (Per-Hop Behaviour). RFC3246, March 2002.

[6] A. Frey and Y. Takahashi. A note on an M/GI/1/N queue with vacation time and exhaustive service discipline. *Operations Research Letter*, 21(2):95–100, 1997.

[7] J. Roberts, U. Mocci, and J. Virtamo, editors. *Broadband Network Traffic: Final report of Action COST 242*. 2nd Edition, Springer-Verlag, 1996.

IP Concatenation: The Method for Enhancement of IPsec Performance

Junghwan Moon and Heon Y. Yeom

School of Computer Science and Engineering,
Seoul National University,
Seoul, 151-744, South Korea
{jhmoon, yeom}@dcslab.snu.ac.kr

Abstract. IPsec provides security services at the IP layer. The performance of IPsec is markedly decreased when it handles small packets. In this paper, we propose a method, IP packet concatenation (IPConc), to improve throughput of small packet processing. Our proposal reduces the number of packets and overall load for packet processing and IPsec processing. We implemented IPConc with Linux 2.4.17 and FreeS/WAN 1.95. The system which is enhanced by our proposal performed significantly better than original version. The throughput with 64 byte packets was increased as much as 250%.

1   Introduction

The VPN (Virtual Private Network)[5] is a private data network that makes use of the public telecommunication infrastructure, maintaining privacy through the use of tunneling protocols and security procedures. The main purpose of a VPN is to give the company the same capabilities as private leased lines at much lower cost by using the shared public infrastructure.

IPsec(IPsecurity architecture)[12] provides security services at the IP layer. It can be used to protect paths between a pair of hosts, between a pair of IPsec gateways, or between a IPsec gateway and a host (IPsec gateway is the term to refer to a gateway that implements IPsec protocols). IPsec has some advantages that it outperforms all other popular schemes that try to accomplish secure network communications and is transparent to applications and users[3].

The performance of IPsec is of paramount interest and it has been reported in [3]. It was observed that the performance of IPsec degrades rapidly with decreasing packet size. The speed of encryption/decryption of packet is proportional to the size of packet. The core of this degradation is not the speed of encryption/decryption but overhead in initializing encryption/decryption. The system consumes an amount of resources to begin processing each packet. Basically, the packet processing needs communication with hardware devices (NIC, hardware accelerator). The cost of communication is proportional to the number of packets.

In this paper, we investigate the performance of the IPsec implementation and propose some techniques to improve the performance of processing small

M.M. Freire, P. Lorenz, M.M.-O. Lee (Eds.): HSNMC 2003, LNCS 2720, pp. 365–374, 2003.

packets in the IPsec gateway. Our key idea is to reduce the number of packets by concatenating several packets into one. All the performance results presented in this paper have been obtained through experiment with the system implemented on FreeS/WAN 1.95 and Linux kernel 2.4.17.

Experimental results show that our system works well without imposing too much overhead. The system which is enhanced by our proposal performed significantly better than the original version. The throughput with 64 byte packets was increased as much as 250%. The rest of the paper is organized as follows. Section 2 gives some information of IPsec and FreeS/WAN. Section 3 describes problems and our proposal. We describe the implementation details in section 4 and presents the performance results of our implementation in section 5. Finally, we draw conclusions in section 6.

2   IPsec and FreeS/WAN

IPsec[12] provides protection for the traffic as it passes between "trusted" networks via an "untrusted" one. IPsec is used for constructing Virtual Private Network(VPN). Outgoing data from some host to other hosts through Internet is encrypted while it passes a IPsec gateway. The IP packet is encapsulated in new IP header, IPsec headers and IPsec tails. The source address of the changed data is IPsec gateway's IP address and the destination is peer IPsec gateway's IP address. The original source and destination is encrypted and included in its payload. When the data arrives at its destination, IPsec gateway decapsulates the data, verifies its origin and decrypts it. Passing these process, the data takes back its original form. IPsec provides the set of security services for access control, connectionless integrity, data origin authentication, protection against replays, confidentiality, and limited traffic flow confidentiality at the IP layer of the network protocol stack. AH(Authentication Header)[14], ESP(Encapsulating Security Payload)[13], IKE(Internet Key Exchange)[7] are protocols for these services.

FreeS/WAN[6] is an implementation of the IPSEC and IKE for Linux. It is composed of two main parts, KLIPS and Pluto. KLIPS implements AH, ESP, and packet handling within the kernel. Pluto implements IKE, negotiating with other systems. These two modules communicate with each other through PF_KEY[11], and exchange the information of SA(Security Association)[12].

When an IP packet arrives at `ip_input()`, `ipsec_ rcv()` will be called if the protocol number of arrived packet is ESP (50) or AH (51). In `ipsec_rcv()`, the packet is decapsulated, verified, and decrypted. When a packet is handed to the IP module for transmission, a lookup is made in Linux routing table. If a SA had been established, its information was reflected in the routing table with a routing entry. If a packet route through the routing entry which added by establishing SA, `ipsec_tunnel_start_xmit()` will be called. Figure 1 shows the overall flow of packets.

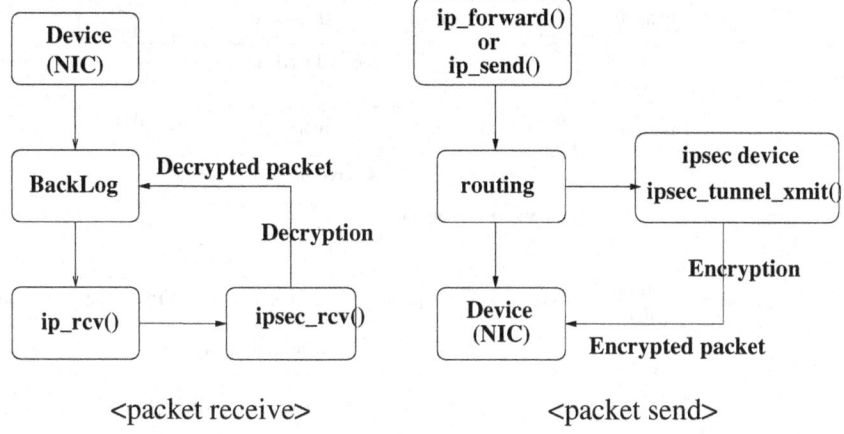

<packet receive>   <packet send>

Fig. 1. Packet Flow in Linux with FreeS/WAN

3 Problems and Enhancement

3.1 Problems

We measured the packet forwading rate of IPsec gateway with tunnel mode configuration, and observed the fact that the rate is very low when the packet size is small. This fact was be affirmed in other work[3] as well. We have learned some facts from the comparison of our result of tests and the graph from previous work[3]. The important fact is that the number of packets have an significant influence on the performance of packet processing. Actually, the performance of the packet forwarding rate of small packets is importance because many VPN equipments use small packets when they exchange some informations for network and tunnel management.

Our focus is on describing implementation details to improve the throughput of small packet processing in IPsec tunnel mode and how much the throughput improved through experiments. (The details of overall processing of our methods is described in Internet-Draft[1].)

3.2 Enhancement

We propose two schemes to improve small packet processing rate. The key idea is reducing the number of packets by concatenating multiple packets into one whenever possible. Based on this idea, we have devised two techniques to improve IPsec performance.

---

[1] This draft was announced as an individual document with a filename 'draft-moon-ipsec-ipconc-00.txt'.

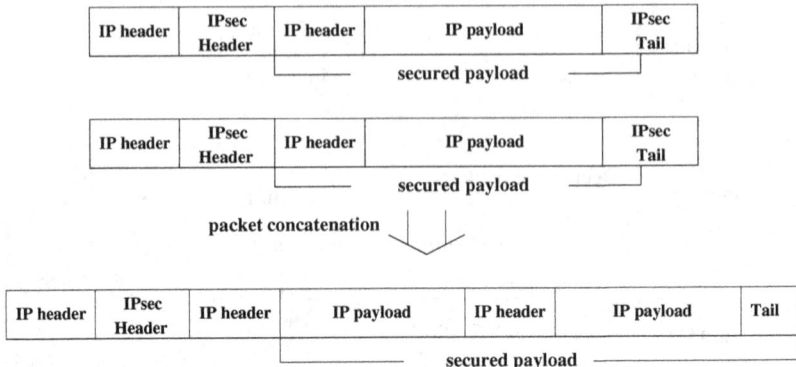

Fig. 2. The shape of concatenated socket buffer

The first is multiple queuing and batch processing. The queueing mechanism provides some policies to determine whether a packet is enqueued or processed immediately. We allocate queue per the SA and transport layer protocol. If a packet is destined for hosts within an IPsec channel, the packet be enqueued to the appropriate SA and transport layer protocol of the packet. It helps improving IPsec performance because there is no need to fetch SA information for each packet if they are from the same queue. The SA information is fetched if the new packet is not from the same queue where the last packet is fetched. We batch IPsec procedure periodically using softtimer[2].

The second is IP concatenation(IPConc). IPConc has two phases: concatenation of outbound IP packets("concatenation") and separation of inbound packets("separation"). The concatenation of outbound IP packets must be applied to packets that have the same destination and the same transport layer protocol. Processing of outbound IP packets must be done before any IPsec processing, such as encryption and authentication. In contrast, the separation of inbound IP pakcets must be done after the completion of all IPsec processing.

The concatenation procedure should be applied to small packets, and their combined size MUST be smaller the the MTU. This method change some small packets into one packet with a large IP payload. The separation procedure must not affect packets that are sent without the concatenation procedure of IPConc. It will be performed when the size of the packet is larger than the size stated in the IP packet header.

Figure 2 shows the concatenation procedure intuitively.

4   Implementation

As previously mentioned, FreeS/WAN is composed of mainly two parts, KLIPS and Pluto. We only modified KLIPS module because Pluto is concerned only with IKE and the processing of packets was solely handled in KLIPS.

For multiple queuing , we added and modified some data structures. The data structure `eroute`, encapsulation route, have a pointer to a radix tree entry and a pointer to SAID. A radix tree is a data structure for network information of IPsec gateway and its peers. We added a variable to `struct eroute` for assigning a queue per each `struce eroute`. Because the return value of `ipsec_findroute()` is a pointer of `struct eroute`, the system can immediately find which queue a packet should be enqueued without additional work. We also added the structure `queue_per_eroute`. This data structure is for referring to `struct eroute` and for managing queue per protocol. The structure has a set of queues and a pointer to corresponding `struct eroute`. When the packet is arrived at the IPsec device, it is evaluated to find appropriate SA and queue and then enqueued. In the function, `ipsec_do_xmit()` which is called periodically by softtimer, enqueued packets were handled. The size of packet is compared along with the size of the next packet and concatenation is performed if possible. The resulting packet is sent to the encryption module. Before concatenating packets, we expanded the `sk_buff` by allocating new space as much as MTU, copying original data of `sk_buff` and change the value of tail which is the variable defined in `sk_buff`. The concatenation is completed through copying the portion of data of later `sk_buff` on earlier `sk_buff`'s tail. Memory copying was occurred on each concatenating procedure.

Originally, FreeS/WAN processes the part concerned IPsec as soon as the packet is arrived at IPsec device. Outgoing packet going through the IP stack leads the system to call a function, `ipsec_tunnel()`, if the destination of packet is IPsec device through looking up the routing table. In `ipsec_tunnel()`, the packet needs to be processed by IPsec and changed to secured packet. Incoming packet is processed in `ipsec_rcv()` which was called in `ip_rcv()` if the protocol number stated in IP header was 50 (ESP), 51 (AH), or 108 (IPCOMP). We mainly modified two files, `ipsec_tunnel()` and `ipsec_rcv()`, for batch processing. In case of `ipsec_tunnel()`, we modified it to check arrived packet's protocol if it was UDP or ICMP. If the protocol was UDP or ICMP, the packet would be enqueued and returned. The packet of which protocol was others would be immediately processed by IPsec. Enqueued packets were processed periodically. The part which processes enqueued packets is `ipsec_do_xmit()`. This function had been registered in softtimer's handler. In this function, we dequeue a packet and compare its size. As proposed, packets would be concatenated or processed without concatenation. The processing of IPsec, encryption, authentication, and so on, is done in `ipsec_tunnel_real_xmit()`.

The `ipsec_rcv()` which undertook decryption, verification, and decapsulation of packets was modified to be able to process concatenated packets. After doing original function's duties, the packet would be recovered original packet before processing by IPsec at source part's IPsec gateway of packet IPsec gateway. We must decide whether a escaped packet from protection is concatenated or not. We interpreted that the packet had been concatenated if its size (the size of `sk_buff`) is greater than the size stated in IP header of it. If the size was same with the size stated in IP header, we passed it to the upper protocol stack. We

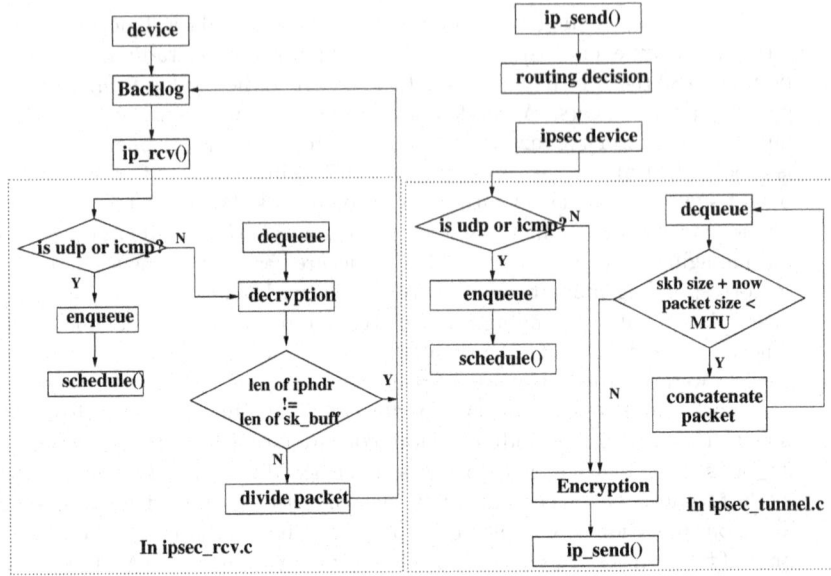

Fig. 3. the IPsec processing with IPConc

separate the concatenated packet in the following manner. The size stated in IP header (`iph->tot_len`) is the size of first IP packet in the concatenated packet. First, we copy `sk_buff`. Copied `sk_buff` was called `new_skb` in this section. To process first IP packet, we changed `sk_buff` into `sk_buff` whose size is the same as the size of first IP packet by trimming off the rest, and forward it to upper layer. To process concatenated IP packets without first packet, we pulled `new_skb` as much as the size of first IP packet using `skb_pull()`. These process was repeated with `new_skb` until the size of `sk_buff` be the same the size stated in IP header.

Figure 3 shows the flow of packet processing equipped with IPConc.

5   Evaluation

5.1   Model

We arranged a series of performance benchmarks to verify the effect of packet concatenation proposed in this paper. The experimental setup consists of a total of four Intel Pentium PCs running Linux. One of them is source host(packet generator). The packet generator can generate up to 110,000 64-byte UDP packets per second using UDPGen module of Click[1]. Another of them is destination host. The remain two PCs, the subject of our experiment, running Linux 2.4.17

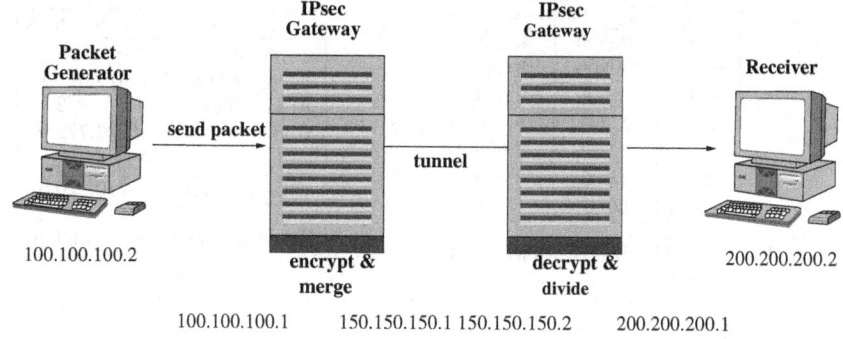

Fig. 4. Environment

with modified FreeS/WAN 1.9.5, is configured as IPsec gateways, and we established VPN tunnel between two IPsec gateways(Figure 4).

The packet generator and receiver are 600MHz Intel PIII machines with 128MB of registered PC100 SDRAM, 3c905B 100Mbps network adapters. The IPsec gateways are 800MHz Intel PIII machines with 128MB of registered PC100 SDRAM, and two 3c905B 100Mbps network adapters. They are connected by point-to-point full-duplex 100Bast-T links. Figure 4 shows the network configuration and the overview of experimental setup.

Our focus was to gain performance advantages on processing small packets. No system can fully support 100Mbps with 64byte packets. So we only considered and examined half-duplex traffic. Modern operating systems such as UNIX and its descendents depend on interrupt mechanism to pay the least attention in controlling I/O peripherals. In Linux, the kernel masked IRQ and jumped to interrupt handling routine if the interrupt was occurred on processing packet transmission and reception. During this procedure, the interrupt which could be occurred by another NIC would be blocked. The packet processing would be delayed, and it could affect the system performance. If the network traffic was full-duplex, this situation would be more profound than in half-duplex traffic.

We used one-way communication for our testing. Strictly speaking, although the result of this experimental was not the maximum throughput of IPsec, we could measure the performance gains of the system which had been implemented our proposed scheme compared with original system.

5.2   Packet Forwarding Rate

Our experiments took into consideration six sizes of packets: 64, 128, 256, 512, 1024, and 1400 bytes. The maximum size of packet is 1400 bytes because the MTU of Ethernet is about 1500 bytes and the size of AH header and ESP header is a little less than 100 bytes. We measured the maximum forwarding rate of each sized packet. Table 1 shows the maximum throughput of original IPsec gateway

pkt size	orig (pps)	mod (pps)
64	18,000	45,000
128	15,800	29,000
256	11,900	16,000
512	7,800	8,000
1024	4,700	4,600
1280	4,000	3,800
1400	3600	3500

Table 1. Maximum forwarding rate

System	min/avg/max
Orig.	0.3/0.3/0.5
Mod. (200us)	0.5/0.6/1.1
Mod. (500us)	1.1/1.4/2.1
Mod. (1000us)	2.2/2.7/2.9
Mod. (10000us)	20.7/20.9/22.0
without VPN	0.2/0.2/0.3

Table 2. Response time(ms)

and modified IPsec gateway. The throughput stated in table 1 was calculated by (measured pps / maximum pps). The precise maximum forwarding rate may be a little greater than shown value because we didn't consider the size of AH and ESP header. The cost of encryption/decryption is directly proportional to the total volume of data. If we consider only the volume, the throughput of packet processing must be irrelevant to the size of packet. But we observed the performance was obviously declined in case of small packets. It means that the number of packets is significant factor to determine the system performance. In this paper, we proposed and implemented the method to reduce the number of packets. In case of small packets, our proposed scheme, packet concatenating, provided large performance gains. We observed 250% improvement compared to original FreeS/WAN on 64 bytes, 80% on 128 bytes, 40% on 256 bytes, and 2% on 512bytes. But if the size of packet was lager than about 700 bytes, the performance was slightly degraded since the overhead is greater than the gain.

The reason that the proposed method show performance gain is that our proposal removed the load to process packets, context switching, DMA transfer or communication with PCI, by reducing the number of packets.

In view of the results, we assured that the number of packets is very significant factor of IPsec performance and improved throughput. The packet forwarding rate was decreased at a point about 512 bytes. It can be explained as follows. As the size of packet gets larger, the system is more affected by the load for copying memory than the load for packet processing. Though the number of packet was reduced by packet concatenating, the concatenating procedure had overheads. For large sized packet than 1024 byte, our implementation performance dropped about 5%. There is a threshold of performance gain. We have implemented so that two packets be concatenated if the sum of two packet's size is smaller than MTU-64. If we change the value 64 into the threshold value, we can remove the degradation.

Considering the network response, our system might get sluggish. To examine the influence about the response time in modified system, we have measured RTT of ICMP packets using `ping`. As expected, the latency of our system increased in proportion to the interval. Table 2 shows the result of testing response time. The result shows that when the interval of softtimer is 200μs, the response time jumps upto 300-600 μs, and when the interval is 500μs, the increase is about 800-1400 μs. The packet must pass through two IPsec gateways, so the response time can be increased twice. The increase of response time is proportional to timer interval. The `ping` can send about 3,000 packets per second in flooding mode. The comparison one packet per second mode `ping` and flooding mode give us some information that there is overhead for concatenating packets, and memory copying. When the timer interval is 200 μs, the difference of response time is little because the packet is arrived at IPsec gateway on each 300 μs. This means the concatenation is not occurred. However, the latency which modified system have is bearable and adjustable to system requirement and purpose.

To sum up, our proposal brought noticeable improvement of small packets processing and performed stably under heavy network load. Though there is disadvantage in the latency aspect, the latency can be adjusted by tuning the interval of the softtimer and the number of packets how much enqueue and to be enqueued.

6   Conclusion

The processing caused by IPsec is CPU bounded job. Encryption/decryption uses CPU for all their procedure. Many people think that the major portion which have an effect on the throughput is the encryption and decryption. The result of the previous work and our experiments informs that the number of packets is very significant factor for determining the performance of IPsec. Our key idea is based on this fact. We thought that the reduction of the number of packets could help with elevating throughput of IPsec. We implemented the packet concatenating methods and measured the performance. As expected, proposed scheme gained maximum of 250% improvement.

The system which uses interrupt to communicate with peripheral device can't help context switching. The context switching is very expensive procedure. The more the number of packet, the overhead occurred during packet processing is larger. We introduced new scheme which concatenates packets if possible. The scheme reduces the number of packets to process, so that the number of raising interrupt was decreased.

For concatenating packets, we implemented batch processing using multiple queues. Batch processing led the system to drop packets earlier if the CPU usage is too high to process the packets and incurred the increase of response time. Though the increase couldn't be removed completely, we could adjust it by controlling the interval of softtimer.

If the system is equipped with a hardware accelerator for encryption and decryption, the improvement of performance may be greater than our experiments. The reason is because we implemented multiple queue. This method can reduce the number of communication with peripheral device, hardware accelerator. IPsec procedure must pass the data which will be encrypted or decrypted and the SA which will be used for encryption or decryption per packet. But there is no necessity for passing SA to the device on every time the packet is passed to the device using our system implements multiple queue. On time the queue is changed, the SA will be passed.

We implements our system to drop a packet which can't be processed at IP layer. If we use timer mode device driver which proposed in our previous work[4], which can limit the receiving rate of packets at device layer, the throughput will be enlarged.

IPCOMP(IP payload COMPression) is a protocol to reduce the size of IP payload. This protocol increases the overall communication performance between a pair of communicating hosts/gateways by compressing the IP payload. Compression on small buffers does not usually work as well as on fast links since the time it takes to compress is longer than the time to transport the data[9]. Therefore, if our proposal is applied to small buffers which are not big enough to be compressed, the overall communication performance would be increased. We have confidence that the mixed solution of IPCOMP and IP concatenation which we proposed in this paper, will bring the better performance to IPsec.

References

1. E. Kohler, R. Morris, B. Chen, and J. Jannotti: The Click Modular Router. ACM Transactions on Computer Systems, 18(3):263-297, 2000
2. Mohit Aron and Peter Druschel: Soft Timers - Efficient Microsecond Software Timer Support for Network Processing. ACM Transactions on Computer Systems, 18(3):197-228, 2000
3. Stefan Miltchev, Sotiris Ioannidis and Angelos D. Keromytis: A Study of the Relative Costs of Network Security Protocols. The proceedings of the USENIX Annual Technical Conference, Jun 2002.
4. Ilhwan Kim and Junghwan Moon and Heon Y. Yeom: Timer-Based Interrupt Mitigation for High Performance Packet Processing. International Conference on High-Performance Computing in the Asis-Pacific Region, Sep 2001.
5. Virtual Private Network Consortium. http://www.vpnc.org/.
6. FreeS/WAN - Linux IPsec Implementation. http://www.freeswan.org/
7. D. Harkins and D. Carrel: RFC 2409 The Internet Key Exchange (IKE).
8. D. Maughan, M. Schertler, M. Schneider, and J. Turner. RFC 2408 Internet Security Association and Key Management Protocol (ISAKMP).
9. R. Pereira: RFC 2394 IP Payload Compression Using DEFLATE.
10. A. Shacham , B. Monsour, R. Pereira, and M. Thomas: RFC 3173 IP Payload Compression Protocol (IPCOMP).
11. D. McDonald, C. Metz and B. Phan: RFC 2367 PF_KEY Key Management API, Version 2.
12. S. Kent and R. Atkinson: RFC 2401 Security Architecture for the Internet Protocol.
13. R. Atkinson: RFC 1827 IP Encapsulating Security Payload (ESP).
14. R. Atkinson: RFC 1826 IP Authentication Header (AH).

Analysis Tool for a Video-on-Demand Service Based in Streaming Technology

Xabiel G. Pañeda[1], David Melendi[1], Manuel García[2], Víctor García[1],
Roberto García[1], and Enrique Riesgo

Computer Sciece Department, University of Oviedo
Campus Universitario de Viesques. Sede Departamental Oeste
33204 Xixón-Gijón Asturies, Spain
Telephone: 985 18 33 70 - Fax: 985 18 19 86
[1]{xabiel, melendi, victor, roberto}@correo.uniovi.es,
[2]manuel@atc.uniovi.es

Abstract. This paper describes the tool developed in order to analyse a video-on-demand streaming service. The aim of this work is to provide a powerful system to help both the service providers and the communication operators to configure this sort of services. Distributing the contents, developing redistribution routes, creating new contents in the most popular subjects and increasing or decreasing the length of information depending on the subscribers' behaviour can improve the quality of the service. However, these decisions must be taken based in service performance. This tool tries to fill the gap in this field and provide the necessary analysis to configure these services. The quality of the tool has been evaluated by the www.lne.es, which is one of the most successful digital news sites in Spain. Its multimedia section offers a large number of videos on demand with several subjects, lengths and qualities. During the last months an analysis process has been performed to improve the service by using this analysis tool. This work is included in a project about analysis, modelling and configuring of interactive multimedia services.

1   Introduction

The emergence of World Wide Web has changed the Internet world. This service has become an important communication medium. Daily, an important number of web accesses is produced and a big volume of information is delivered. Due to the rising of the number of users, a large sum of money has been invested by companies of several sectors such as telecommunications, TV, Newspapers, sales, etc.

One of the groups of companies, which has bet widely on the Internet world, has been the Newspapers. They have built an important number of web sites with different types of news, interviews and reports. Reaching the first position in the ranking of visits has become the main goal of these enterprises. However, providing good news is not enough to get visited, it is necessary to offer contents in an attractive format. First the pictures, and afterwards the animations were added to the digital news sites successfully. Nowadays, a new format has appeared in Internet: the video.

M.M. Freire, P. Lorenz, M.M.-O. Lee (Eds.): HSNMC 2003, LNCS 2720, pp. 375-384, 2003.
© Springer-Verlag Berlin Heidelberg 2003

Thanks to the streaming technology, news on video format can be reproduced by a subscriber without a previous download. Only few seconds are loaded in a client buffer to avoid deficiencies in the broadcast. The advantages of video streaming and the expectations created in the subscribers are important, however this technology presents some problems. Video delivering consumes an important bandwidth in the network and requires a constant quality of service. To maintain the quality of service under control and select the most interesting content, making use of good analysis systems is basic.

These analysis systems must provide the necessary information to configure the streaming services correctly. Two different parts appear when a service must be configured. The first one is related to the service provider, who must improve the service working on contents. The second one is linked to the network operator, who has to manage the service architecture, the routing, and the bandwidth.

In this paper, a tool to configure a video-on-demand service based in streaming technology is presented. The aim is to reach the best configuration for both the service provider and the network operator. To achieve the excellence of service, the provider should boost the most visited subjects increasing the number of videos, or modifying the length of videos depending on the subscribers' preferences. To obtain a good quality of service, the network operator should allocate enough bandwidth and improve the architecture using proxies to balance the workload. In every case, an analysis process is necessary, and to make use of a tool can facilitate the job. The goal of this analysis tool is to make the analysis process easier and to help managers to configure the service.

The multimedia section of *La Nueva España Digital* has been studied to validate the developed tool. This digital news service is one of the most visited in Spain, reaching the 8th position in the most visited ranking. Its multimedia section appeared in 2001 and has got an important number of subscribers due to the quality of its own production.

The rest of the paper is organized as follows: In section 2 other related works are analysed. A general description of the tool will be done in section 3. Tool's architecture will be revised in section 4. The two different processes to load data from the server will be revised in section 5. Section 6 will summarize the results provided by the tool. The case of study used to check the analysis system will be introduced in section 7. Finally, conclusions and future works will be presented in sections 8 and 9.

2   Related Works

Several works about streaming service analysis have been appearing over the last years. Some of them did not study any streaming specific information [1,2], and others [3,4,5,6] processed more characteristic information of this type of services such as inter-interaction times, forward and backward jumps, session lengths, etc. All of them used typical http analysis tools [7, 8], network analysis tools or generic mathematical tools. None of these analyses were supported by an automatic analysis tool for streaming systems. Recently, tools like [9] have begun to provide analyses for multimedia services. However, several important parameters are not considered in its results. For example, quality of transmission, bandwidth consumed or interactions made. The specialization of these tools is still low.

The tool developed tries to cover the lack of specific access analysis tools for streaming services. The main goal is to build a tool to generate automatic reports of streaming performance. These reports are being used to configure real services (*La Nueva España*, *Corvera TV*, etc), to make analysis of real systems like [10,11,12] and to develop simulation models to predict future performances.

3   General Description

The developed tool is a powerful instrument to analyse the performance of a video streaming service. This tool is capable of extracting information from the log of the streaming sever, process it and generate graphical and textual reports. Through two loaders, the system can collect service information automatically and periodically, and process it. Several analyses can be performed with just one click using its web environment. Regularly, the evolution of the service can be monitored and its parameters corrected. This condition turns the tool into a valuable device for a continuous test of the service.

This tool tries to cover the hollow in this field and help both service providers and network operators to make configuring decisions. The analysis process is transformed into an automatic task, based on simple observations.

Starting from its results, conclusions about several parameters can be obtained directly; anyway, the tool provides the possibility of extracting numerical information to be introduced in more specific tools or simulation models.

4   Tool Architecture

The analysis tool presents a complex architecture with several modules in charge of different tasks.

The tool uses two different modules to load the performance information from the server, one for on-line loads and other

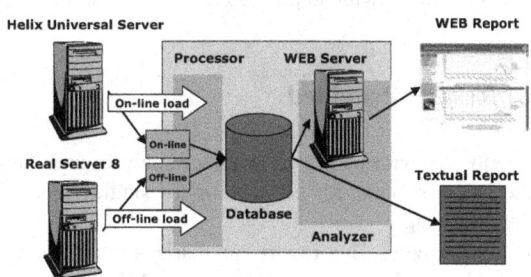

Fig. 1. Tool architecture

for off-line loads. These loaders retrieve the data from the server log and structure them in order to be introduced in a database.

The main element of the system is a database that stores all the necessary information to perform the analyses. Its use is very important to allow a continuous update of data. The database management system used is **MySQL**.

The tool provides textual reports, mainly oriented to generate input data for other tools and performance models. Nowadays, some of the results are being used to validate a video-on-demand simulation model. This task has been programmed using shell scripts, basically.

The tool also generates graphical reports through a web system. By using several **php** scripts the tool is able to process the information stored in the database and to generate graphics with different types of analysis. To present the graphics, the **Easy-Charts** applet is used and the web server to retrieve the reports is **Apache**.

The architecture is shown in figure 1.

5 Load Process and Analyzed Data

The analysis tool obtains the performance information from the log system of the streaming server. This system provides a lot of data about clients' behaviour and video delivering [13,14]. There are two possibilities to retrieve the information from the log system: an on-line load, and an off-line load.

The on-line load, allows us to recover log information immediately after an event is produced. By using this type of load the tool offers the advantage of a just-in-time analysis. However, it only can be used with Helix Servers. Several possibilities to extract performance information are available: sockets, http post requests or UDP packets. To receive the information sent by the streaming server a program has been developed. This software reads the socket and adds the received data to the database.

The off-line method retrieves the information from the log files where the streaming server saves the events produced by user accesses. A program that parses these files and adds the information in the database has been designed. Due to this method, a just-in-time analysis is impossible, however, several scripts have been designed to automate the download process from the streaming server every night.

6 Results Provided

The tool provides a great variety of analyses and reports, which can be generated for the whole service, for sections or for single videos. The most important reports are the following:

- **Summary**. This report summarizes the current number of accesses, number of stored videos, number of sections, MB delivered, date of last request, date of first request, number of valid requests, number of fast leavings, number of mistaken requests, etc. With this analysis the manager will be able to obtain a general perspective of the current status of the service.
- **Access evolution**. This report shows the evolution of accesses in the last month and week. Accesses can also be visualized divided into sections and qualities.

- **Media delivered time**. The evolution of the average, minimum and maximum media delivered percentages and a graphic with media delivered time histogram are represented together. This report shows how much time of the video is visualized by users. This information allows the manager to know whether the video is successful (high percentage) or not (low percentage). A media delivered time histogram is displayed in figure 2.
- **Session length**. The purpose of this report is mainly scientific. The maximum, minimum and average length evolutions, and session length histogram are shown. This analysis is extremely important if the user behaviour must be modelled.
- **Interactions**. This report shows the average number of interactions, the percentages of each type of interaction, and the interaction histograms. This analysis combined with session length and media delivered time, altogether, provide the necessary information to characterize the typical user behaviour.
- **Deliver quality**. In this reports graphics with the resent packets, failed resents, delayed packets, and unordered packets evolution are presented. This analysis provides the manager information about how the quality is evolving. One of the quality evolution graphics is shown in figure 3.
- **Fast leaving**. To conform this report a bound has been fixed for the necessary time a user has to reproduce a video to be aware of its content. A displayed time less than 10 seconds is considered an out of interest reproduction. The reason can be caused by a low quality reproduction or a disappointing video. This kind of reproductions is quite dangerous for the service, because the subscriber is dissatisfied. Figure 4 shows the evolution of fast leavings in video reproductions.
- **Mistaken reproductions**. The reproductions with a delivered time of zero seconds are considered mistaken reproductions. In these cases, users cannot visualize the video. The main problem is usually the lack of a suitable plug-in to reproduce de video on the client computer. As happened with fast leavings, these reproductions are bad for the service. A misinformed subscriber can feel annoyed. Figure 4 shows the evolution of mistaken reproductions.
- **Platforms' and subscribers' information**. The operating system, the plug-in type, the user language and the processor type are presented. This report allows the manager to know the profile of the typical subscriber.
- **Loyalty study**. One of the most important parameters to evaluate a service is the loyalty of its subscribers. The provider must try to get users who usually request the service. Figure 5 shows a loyalty representation. Getting a convex line must be a goal for the service manager.
- **Output bandwidth used in the server**. This analysis shows the consumed bandwidth in the sever output. The aim is to know the maximum consume to report the network provider. If there were too much consumed bandwidth it would be necessary to improve the service architecture with proxies. Figure 6 shows the consumed bandwidth per minute in a week.
- **Popularity study**. This analysis compares the popularity of videos of the real service with the theoretical Zipf-like distribution. This comparison is very important to simulate the subscribers' content selection. Moreover, an ordered list with the most popular videos is presented.

Some of the reports are general and they can also be found in other tools. However, a system that tries to perform a whole analysis cannot lack them. Other analyses have the scientific purpose to design the behaviour pattern for the typical user.

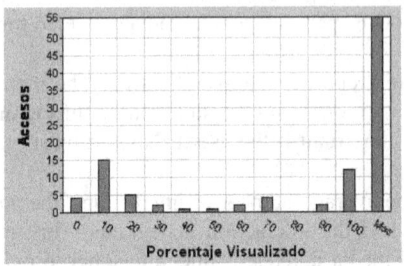

Fig. 2. Media visualized percent histogram

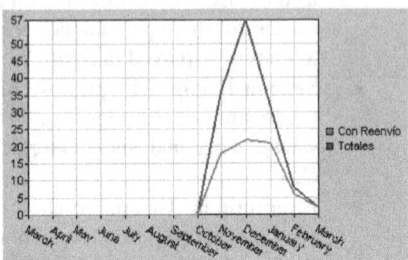

Fig. 3. Deliver quality

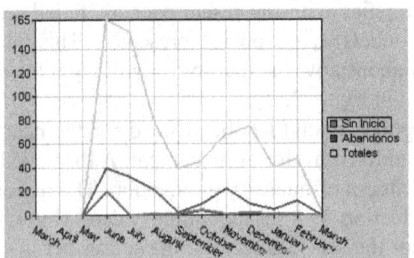

Fig. 4. Fast leaving and mistaken reproduction report

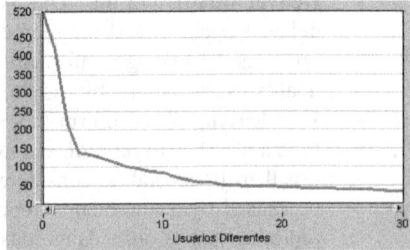

Fig. 5. Loyalty study

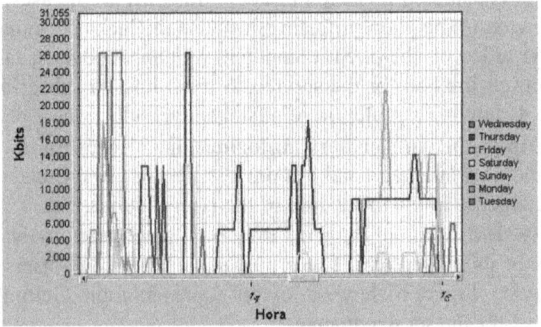

Fig. 6. Bandwidth consumed

7   Case of Study

To evaluate the behaviour and to check its possibilities, the analysis tool has been integrated in a real video streaming service. www.lne.es is the Internet news service of *La Nueva España* newspaper. This digital service has an important number of accesses and has reached the 8th position in the ranking of digital news sites in Spain.

In 2001, www.lne.es presented its video-on-demand service developed by the **Computer Science Department from the University of Oviedo**. The number of visits and the volume of information have risen since then. Nowadays, the service has a good reputation because of the level of its own production.

This multimedia service had always been monitored by a simple tool, which counted the number of visits. This tool did not offer the possibility of obtaining information such as: length of clients' reproductions, timetable of accesses, etc, only the evolution in the number of accesses was shown. The usage of the analysis tool has allowed to obtain new information and to improve the configuration of the service. Moreover, interesting information about the network bandwidth has been sent to the network operator, which provides the Internet link, to improve the quality of service.

7.1 Service Description

The multimedia section of www.lne.es has an architecture shaped by three servers. One of them supports the web pages used to access the videos, and the others are, the video streaming server and the analysis server. The section can be accessed from two links in the main page (one in the menu and one in a box in the left side), and one link in the rest of the pages. These links load the main page of the multimedia section where the videos are referenced. Two types of display are used to reproduce the videos; the first one visualizes the video using the real player program, and the second one displays the video by using the real player plug-in integrated in the web page.

The RealServer [13,14] is the technology used to stream the videos delivered on demand when a subscriber performs a request.

The analysis server stores all the modules of the analysis tool, including the database, the web server, and loaders and analysers.

7.2 Content Description

The multimedia service contents have been classified in 7 subsections by their subject, which are the following: *News, Music, Tourism, Conferences, Short films, Visits* and *Others*.

News subsection groups all kind of current information, such as: interviews, reports, and news. The length ranges go from 30 second, the shortest, to 20 minutes the longest.

Music subsection covers all kinds of information related to music, like video-clips (short length), and interviews to musicians and producers (around 20 minutes).

Tourism subsection has videos about nature, culture and tourism. Their length varies from 30 to 45 minutes and they are produced by *Productora de Programas del Principado*.

Conferences subsection presents records of "*Ciclo de Conferencias de Ciencia y Tecnología y Cultura de la Universidad de Oviedo*". Although they have a scientific subject they are considered for the general public. Their length goes from 1 to 2 hours, and they have an interactive index to move to different parts of the lecture.

Short film subsection contains movies whose length is shorter than 15 minutes.

Visits subsection includes excursions of several schools to *La Nueva España* headquarters and their length is under 2 minutes.

The last subsection is *Others* which groups videos whose subject cannot be included in the rest.

All the videos are available in 3 different qualities. The users can select them depending on the network connection bandwidth. These qualities are: modem, broadband and plus, and the differences among them are bandwidth required and size of screen. Modem quality consumes a bandwidth of 56 kbps and has a resolution of 160x120 pixels. Broadband quality has a screen size of 320x240 pixels and needs a bandwidth of 90 kbps. Finally, plus quality has a resolution of 320x240 pixels and requires an average bandwidth of 200 kbps.

Some of these parameters have been changed during the process of analysis to improve the quality of service. Moreover, the videos are coded with the **SureStream** technology of RealNetwork, which can adapt partially the required bandwidth to the available bandwidth.

Nowadays, the service has around 200 videos available in all the qualities.

7.3 Analysis Results

The four months that have been analysed with the tool, have provided quite interesting results and they have allowed to correct several parameters of the service. Some of them are the following:

- One of the most dangerous incidences appeared when the analysis started. The service presented an important number of mistaken reproductions. This condition is produced by the non-existence of a suitable plug-in on the client computer. Although the service reported to the users about the need of the plug-in, the problem persisted. A plug-in detector was installed and the number of mistaken reproductions decreased widely.
- The required bandwidth by plus and broadband qualities has decreased. Originally, plus quality consumed 450 kbps. Due to the high number of reproductions with transmission problems, the bandwidth was reduced to 400 kbps. However, this decrease was not enough, because the main number of subscribers came from *Telecable* and its best access connection provided a bandwidth of 256 kbps. Finally the required bandwidth was fixed to 200 kbps. Since then, the delivering problems have considerably been reduced.

  The broadband quality had originally a required bandwidth of 110 kbps. Two reductions were necessary to remove the delayed packets and resends. Finally, the bandwidth was fixed to 90kbps.
- When the analysis started, the service had an important number of fast leavings. This negative element appeared specially in long videos. To correct this situation shorter videos were produced since that moment. Nowadays, the number of fast leavings has decreased and the length of reproductions has increased.
- Originally, the service provided an additional quality, which combined the sound with the slides. It was called photo-show, but it never reached an interesting number of visits. So, it was taken out.

- The first section of the www.lne.es video-on-demand service was the *Conferences*. However, the number of visits was very low, and was decreasing daily. Moreover, the length of reproductions was so short that the service manager decided to stop the productions of videos for this section.
- Currently, two subjects have reached an important success. The general news and the game show news. The producers have boosted in making this sort of videos with a short length. The general number of the reproductions and their length has increased.
- The initial bandwidth in the server output was 1 Mbps. However, when the number of simultaneous reproductions was raised, an extension to 2 Mbps was required.

All these analyses have widely raised the number of visits and their quality. Today, the video-on-demand service of www.lne.es has reached a good popularity and its subscribers are increasing every day.

8   Conclusions

The analysis tool has achieved a great improvement in the video-on-demand service of www.lne.es. Its reports have provided very interesting knowledge to the manager who has reconfigured the service to obtain the best behaviour possible. To clarify the results and to make the suitable modifications in the service, a configuration methodology has been developed.

On the other hand the tool is providing interesting information to configure and validate a simulation model developed for a video-on-demand service.

9   Future Work

The tool behaviour has been checked successfully, however, new analyses must be added. For example, by making a deep studio of the client interaction.

This work is included in a project about analysis, modelling and configuration of streaming services, and its results are being used to develop a performance model for video-on-demand services and to build configuration methodologies. This model will be integrated in the network model, presented in [15,16], to simulate the network operator behaviour.

Acknowledgments

This research is financed by the network operator *Telecable* and *La Nueva España* inside the projects of NuevaMedia, Telemedia and ModelMedia.

References

1. C. Griwodz, M. Bär, Lars C. Wolf: Long-term Movie Popularity in Video-on-Demand System, ACM Multimedia, Seattle (USA), 1997.
2. D. Loguinov, H. Radha: Measurement Study of Low-bitrate Internet Video Streaming, ACM SIGCOMM Internet Measurement Workshop (IMV), November 2001.
3. Jussara M. Almeida, Jeffrey Krueger, Derek L. Eager, Mary K. Vernon: Analysis of Educational Media Server Workloads, NOSSDAV 2001, Port Jefferson, NY, June 2001.
4. M. Chesire, A. Wolman, G. Voelker, H. Lavy: Measurement and Analysis of a Streaming-Media Workload, USENIX Symposium on Internet Technologies and Systems, March 2001.
5. S. Jin, A. Bestavros: GISMO, A Generator of Internet Streaming Objects and Workloads, ACM SIGMETRICTS, November 2001.
6. Eric W. Wong, V. Lee, K. Ko, K Tang: Multimedia-on-Demand System, ICC2001 IEEE International Conference on Communications, Helsinki, July 2001.
7. http://www.analog.cx/
8. http://www.mrunix.net/webanalizer
9. http://www.sane.com
10. E. Veloso, V. Almeida, W Meira, A. Bestavros, S. Jin: A Hierarchical Characterization of a Live Streaming Media Workload, Internet Measurement Workshop, Marseille, November 2002.
11. J. R Arias, F. J. Suárez, D. F. García, X. G. Pañeda, V. G. García. "Evaluation of Video Server Capacity with Regard to Quality of the Service in Interactive News-On-Demand Systems". Protocols and Systems for Interactive Distributed Multimedia (PROMS2002). Coimbra, Portugal, November 2002.
12. J. R. Arias, F. J. Suárez, D. F. García, X. G. Pañeda, V. G. García. "A Set of Metrics for Evaluation of Interactive News-on-Demand Systems". ACM International Multimedia Conference. Juan les Pins, France. December 2002.
13. RealNetworks: Helix Universal Server Administration Guide, July 2002.
14. RealNetworks: RealServer 8 Administration Guide, October 2000.
15. M. García, X. G. Pañeda, D. F. García, V. G. García, J. R. Arias. "Modeling and Performance Evaluation of an HFC Network Operator". Protocols for Multimedia Systems (PROMS2000). Cracow, Polonia. October 2000.
16. M. García, X. G. Pañeda, D. F. García, V. G. García. "A Tool for Performance Prediction of an HFC Operator, Based on a Queuing Network Model Simulation". International Syposium on Performance Evaluation of Computer and Telecomunication Systems (SPECTS2001). Orlando, Florida (USA). July 2001.

Extending an Open MPEG-4 Video Streaming Platform to Exploit a Differentiated Services Network

Stavroula Zoi, Dimitrios Loukatos, Lambros Sarakis, Panagiotis Stathopoulos, and
Nikolas Mitrou

National Technical University of Athens, ECE Department,
9 Heroon Polytechneiou Str., 15773 Zographou, Athens, Greece
{vzoi,dlouka, ls6, pstath}@telecom.ntua.gr,
mitrou@softlab.ece.ntua.gr

Abstract. This paper describes extensions implemented on the MPEG4IP streaming platform, to exploit Differentiated Services. These extensions are based on concepts of proposed QoS frameworks and are implemented by exploiting platform communication capabilities. Within this context, a *Packet-marking layer component* is introduced performing packet Type of Service (ToS) marking. In the case of live streams, semantics are captured in real-time during encoding, and propagated to the transmission layer. In the case of pre-encoded streams, information about the semantics is included in the media file metadata and provided as hints to the streaming server. Furthermore, a *Video Quality Study* component enables the user to preview loss effects on a video stream before its transmission, by simulating packet losses during encoding. In this way new video quality metrics and packet marking algorithms can be investigated. The applicability of certain QoS policies on the extended platform is experimentally evaluated over a Differentiated Services testbed.

1 Introduction

MPEG-4 [1] is very promising for the delivery of mixed media services over a wide range of networks. However, experimental results with Quality of Service (QoS) are usually restricted to stream traces [2], and simulated networks [3], [4]. The bursty nature of MPEG encoded video streams makes them very susceptible to transient packet losses and quality degradation is not always captured by packet-level metrics. Several error resilience mechanisms have been defined for MPEG-4 video streams to prevent propagation of errors and loss of synchronization [5].

On the other hand, the Differentiated Services (DiffServ) framework [6] supports the differentiation of packets, not only belonging to different competitive streams, but also within the same stream, therefore defining several priority levels. This is achieved by marking the Type of Service (ToS) [7] byte of each packet header.

This paper describes extensions implemented over the open-source MPEG4IP platform, to exploit Differentiated Services. These extensions are based on concepts of proposed QoS frameworks and are implemented by exploiting communication

M.M. Freire, P. Lorenz, M.M.-O. Lee (Eds.): HSNMC 2003, LNCS 2720, pp. 385-394, 2003.

capabilities of the platform. Within this context, a *Packet-marking layer component* is introduced which applies a packet ToS marking policy to the stream, based on user-defined parameters. Towards defining those parameters and studying relevant quality metrics, a *Video Quality Study* component is under development enabling the user to preview loss effects on a video stream before it is transmitted to the network. This is achieved by producing artificial distortions to the stream during encoding.

In the case of live streams, semantics are captured in real time during encoding, and are propagated to the network transmission layer. In the case of pre-encoded streams, information about the semantics is included in the metadata of the media file and provided as hints to the streaming server. The applicability of certain QoS policies based on these extensions is experimentally evaluated over a laboratory-based Differentiated Services testbed.

The rest of the paper is organized as follows: Section 2 describes related work concerning QoS packet differentiation mechanisms, as well as proposed QoS application frameworks. Section 3 discusses compatibility with the concepts of those frameworks and presents the extensions implemented on the MPEG4IP platform. In Section 4, the applicability of a representative QoS policy on the extended MPEG4IP platform is evaluated through experiments. Finally, in Section 5 conclusions and further research based on the work conducted are presented.

2   Related Work

The concept of applying, to video streams, packet differentiation policies according to contribution to quality is not new [8], [9]. In [10], [11] priority-dropping mechanisms are examined for layered video streams. In MPEG-encoded video, *Intra (I)* frames are treated differently by the network than *Predictive (P)* or *Bidirectional (B)* frames [12].

In MPEG-4 encoding, high compression is achieved at the cost of low error resistance and therefore, error resilience mechanisms are necessary [5]. Several studies concerning the transmission of MPEG-4 video over the Internet and mobile networks have been conducted. For example, in [13] object-oriented MPEG-4 video coding is exploited to implement dynamic prioritization schemes by varying bit allocation to different video objects. In [14] a technique for altering MPEG-4 encoding parameters is presented to increase error robustness, based on the fact that frames with high motion degree are more sensitive to errors. In [15] a method for prioritizing data partitioned MPEG-4 video for transmission over mobile networks is examined over simulated GPRS data channels. Although the transmission of MPEG-4 video has been studied mainly in simulated environments, very little work has been realized in real MPEG-4 based application environments. This is mainly because existing end-to-end MPEG-4 streaming platforms (commercial or open-source) do not have QoS extensions. On the other hand, the problem of defining frameworks for QoS–aware multimedia applications has not been exhausted yet, although some studies have already appeared in the literature [16], [17].

3 Extending an Open-Source MPEG-4 Video Streaming Platform to Support QoS Mechanisms Based on Packet Differentiation

3.1 QoS Application Framework Concepts

The framework proposed in [16] is not directly applicable in our case as it relies upon a dynamic QoS monitoring network scheme, in order to guarantee synchronization requirements of SMIL presentations. In [17] the "QCompiler" programming framework is presented and experimentally evaluated for quality aware ubiquitous multimedia applications. Four layers are defined: (1) a *high-level application specification* layer allowing the user to specify quality requirements, (2) a *metadata compilation* layer which compiles the requirements of layer 1 to a quality specification, (3) a *binding* layer which prepares a quality specification to be executed in a specific environment and (4) a *run-time metadata execution* layer, which uses the bound quality specification to manage and control a quality aware multimedia application. A similar layering is adopted in this work.

What is important in the ***High-Level Application Specification*** layer is the mapping of stream subsets to different user quality levels, for example ***High***, ***Medium***, and ***Low***, as illustrated in Fig. 1. The definitions of these subsets are based on the mechanisms described in Section 2. They can be roughly categorized to frame-based and block/object-based, as illustrated in Fig. 2. In the block/object-based case different colors correspond to the assignment of different importance to entities within a video frame, thus defining several quality levels. However, more work is required on the association of such QoS levels with subjective quality metrics [18].

Fig. 1. Different user quality levels

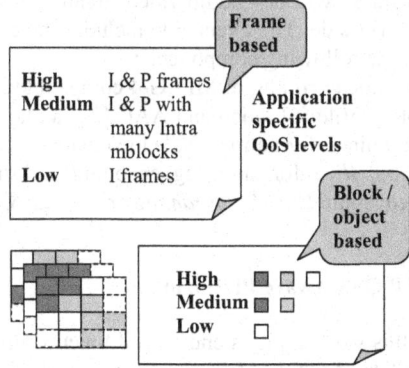

Fig. 2. Mapping of stream specific characteristics to quality levels

In the *Metadata Compilation* layer, high-level stream quality requirements are incorporated into lower-level metadata descriptions, produced during encoding. This is the case for pre-encoded streams. For live streams, these requirements are transferred from the encoding to the transmission layer, by mapping every quality level to an arithmetic value, for example. Every semantic entity (e.g. video frame, video object) is associated with one of these values, during encoding. The metadata descriptors related to quality, and the arithmetic values can be thought of as the quality specification, for pre-encoded and live streams correspondingly.

The *Binding* layer is responsible for preparing the quality specification to be executable in a specific environment (e.g. by mapping a network service interface to standard socket system calls). For DiffServ, packet differentiation and assignment to the different classes is achieved through marking of the ToS byte of the packer header, with a value corresponding to a Per Hop Behavior (PHB) [19].

In the *Run-time Metadata Execution* layer the metadata descriptions are parsed and different QoS levels are assigned to different network classes, e.g. through DiffServ compliant ToS marking performed by the streaming server. In live streams the streaming server uses directly the arithmetic descriptors assigned to each packet during packetization, to mark each of them with a ToS value (see Fig. 3).

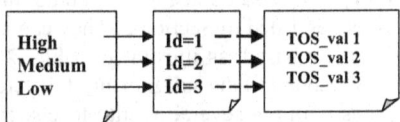

Fig. 3. Mapping of different quality levels to ToS values

3.2 The MPEG4IP Streaming Platform – Existing Features

The MPEG4IP project [20] is an open-source (C/C++ based) package providing a standards-based end-to-end system for encoding, decoding, and streaming, over the UDP/RTP protocol stack, MPEG-4 audio/video streams. It consists of two main parts: the *client* and the *server* side. The client side includes the content decoders, while the server side includes the following components:

✓ A toolkit for off-line encoding of MPEG-4 compatible streams (Divx [21] or ISO MPEG-4 simple profile [5] video and AAC [22] audio). In this package a utility for incorporating hint information inside the mp4 file metadata is also included.
✓ An application (*mp4live*) for capturing, encoding, and streaming A/V streams.
✓ The open-source Apple *Darwin Streaming Server (DSS)* [23].

3.3 The MPEG4IP QoS Aware Platform

The framework of this work exploits end-to-end functionalities of MPEG4IP, and the networking capabilities of C/C++. In order to include TOS marking the source code of the MPEG4IP-0.9.2 API was modified by using the *setsockopt()* function of the Socket networking API. DiffServ compliant packet marking is performed by setting the six bits of the Differentiated Service (DS) byte to the appropriate DS CodePoint value, corresponding to Assured Forwarding (AF) [24] classes AF11 (0X28), AF12 (0X30) and AF13 (0X38). In order to identify stream semantics exhaustive study of the encoding process has been performed. Two cases were examined:

Live video streams. The *mp4live* was enhanced by differently marking packets according to the semantics captured during encoding by a *Packet-marking layer component*, as illustrated in Fig. 4.

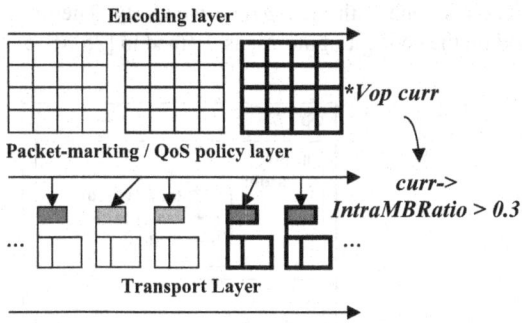

Fig. 4. The Packet-marking/QoS policy layer

This component is responsible for setting the packet's ToS byte. Pointer variable curr (*Vop curr) points to a basic structure (Vop), holding the fields of the currently encoded frame (*Video Object Plane (VOP)* in MPEG-4 terminology), and macroblock data produced during encoding. Variable curr was transferred from the *Encoding* to the *Packet-marking/QoS policy* layer. Through a suitable user interface, the packet-marking component can be instructed by the user as to which packet marking to apply. For the time being, user defined parameters are defined for frame-based policies, such as the assignment of priorities to different frame types, or macroblock related data (e.g. percentage of Intra-coded macroblocks - denoted as *IntraMBRatio* - in a P frame). For example, in Fig. 4 the marking algorithm of Fig. 5 is applied.

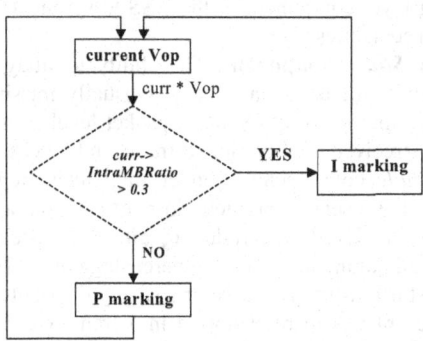

Fig. 5. The ToS marking algorithm

Other more complex algorithms are also applicable in the same way (e.g. those of Section 2), as long as the currently encoded VOP structure is accessible by the Packet-marking layer component.

Pre-encoded streams. The DSS is used to packetize and transmit the stream over the network. Because the server is unaware of the MPEG-4 payload, packetization is realized based on *metadata* descriptions, which describe media data *by reference*. In MPEG4IP this is done with the *mp4creator* utility. The metadata format for an .mp4 file is based on the concept of atoms, as defined in [25] (See Fig. 6).

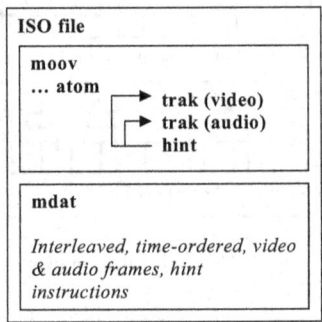

Fig. 6. The mp4 file structure

The *mdat* atom abstracts the structure holding the actual media data. The *moov* is an atom whose sub-atoms define the metadata for a presentation. Every media track has its own timeline, samples (e.g. frames) and properties. The mp4 file, also, describes how to synchronize different tracks. *Hint tracks* contain instructions for the streaming server on how to packetize media track data for transmission, e.g. in MPEG4IP based on RFC 3016 [26]. The *MP4 library* API of MPEG4IP was exploited for instructing the Packet-marking layer component of the DSS to set the TOS byte of each packet, according to stream semantics.

The *Video Quality Study* component. The ability to study media quality metrics, based on the semantics of a media stream is usually missing from proposed QoS frameworks. Current metrics (e.g. PSNR or packet level metrics) can't always relate packet losses with perceived quality, due to frame and other dependencies. Therefore, a *Video Quality Study* component is under implementation inside the MPEG4IP platform, enabling the user to preview loss effects on a stream before this is transmitted. This is achieved by producing artificial distortions during encoding, based on user-defined parameters, such as, percentage of I/P/B frames to be distorted, pattern of frame distortions (consecutive or sparsely distributed), percentage and type (Inter/Intra) of macroblocks to be distorted in a frame etc. Fig. 7 illustrates quality degradation of a live stream captured by a still camera. This was caused by distorting the bitstream of 15 consecutive I frames, which were then discarded at the decoder.

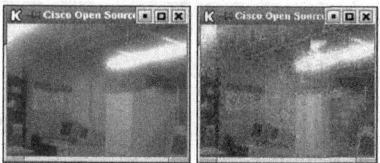

Fig. 7. Quality degradation after 15 consecutive I frame loss in a still camera period

Distortions (like above) may correspond to certain packet loss conditions (e.g. bursty losses, with several consecutive frames being discarded) therefore indicating different quality levels expected by a certain QoS policy, under realistic conditions.

4 Experimental Evaluation on a Diffserv Laboratory Testbed

4.1 Experiments Platform Topology

An extended version of the MPEG4IP-0.9.2 package, DSS v.3, a PC with competing traffic and a DiffServ router were exploited (Fig. 8). The platform was based on Linux PCs and a Linux router. The TG traffic generation utility produced competing traffic. Built in traffic control and DiffServ capabilities of Linux were exploited. The AF PHB was implemented at the router using Random Early Detection (RED).

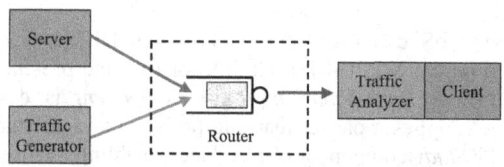

Fig. 8. The experimental platform

4.2 Experiment Scenarios and Results

A set of experiments based among others on the marking policy of Fig. 5 was conducted with the QoS-aware MPEG4IP platform. The following configuration for RED parameters was used: **limit 60KB min 8KB max 45KB burst 20 avpkt 1000 bandwidth 10Mbit probability 0.4**. The video stream was encoded with the MPEG4IP divx encoders at 256 kbps, and its traffic profile can be seen in Fig. 9.

The tg utility was exploited to produce competing (UDP) traffic of average rate 1.2 Mbps, exponentially distributed inter-packet intervals of average 0.003 sec, and packet length of 400 bytes. Packet losses observed are illustrated in Table 1.

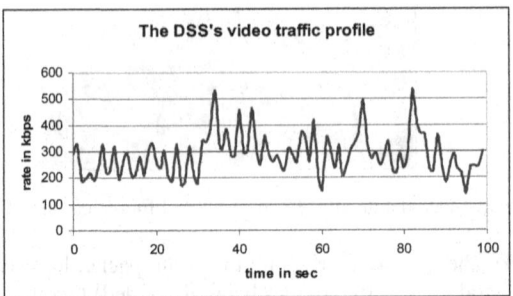

Fig. 9. The traffic profile of the video stream

Packet types	Packet losses	Total packets
I & P frames with IntraMBRatio> 0.3	0	433
P frames with IntraMBRatio <=0.3	63	7964
Tg packets	9404	64246
Total packets	9467	63275

Table 1. Losses are experienced in P frames with IntraMBRatio < 0.3.

5   Conclusions and Further Work

In this paper QoS extensions for exploiting a DiffServ network are studied and implemented on the MPEG4IP platform, for live and pre-encoded MPEG-4 encoded video streams. A *Packet-marking layer component* is described which captures semantics and applies a packet marking policy. Towards studying quality metrics, a *Video Quality Study* component is introduced enabling the user to preview loss effects on a video stream before transmission. In this way the user can contribute to the selection of a suitable QoS policy, according to the desired quality level. The applicability of an indicative QoS policy is experimentally evaluated over a laboratory-based DiffServ testbed. The contribution of this paper is on integrating into an end-to-end streaming platform QoS mechanisms, which have been studied mainly in simulated networks. Several implementation aspects have been addressed and experimental results have illustrated the applicability of those mechanisms on the extended platform.

Several directions for further work can be built on the work presented. More sophisticated packet-marking mechanisms will be explored, and the Video Quality Study Component will be expanded to provide also quantitative results, based on existing (e.g. PSNR, MOS) or other defined metrics. Furthermore, multi-stream application scenarios with synchronization requirements will be studied within such a QoS framework for quantitative guarantees [16]. Experimentation so far has been done for specific scenarios and more work is needed to generalize the results.

6 Acknowledgement

This work is partly funded by the IST ADAMANT project.

References

1. http://mpeg.telecomitalialab.com/
2. F.H.P. Fitzek, M. Reisslein, "MPEG-4 and H263 Video Traces for Network Performance Evaluation", IEEE Network, vol. 15, no. 6, pages 40-54, November/December 2001.
3. V. Marques, R. Cadime, A. de Sousa, A.M. Oliveira Duarte, "DMIF based QoS Management for MPEG-4 Multimedia Streaming: ATM and RSVP/IP Case Studies, ConfTele 2001".
4. P. Bocheck, Y. Nakajima and S. F. Chang, "Real-time Estimation of Subjective Utility Functions for MPEG-4 Video Objects", Proceedings of the Packet Video'99 (PV'99), New York, USA, April 26-27, 1999.
5. ISO/IEC 14496-2 , "Information technology – Coding of audio-visual objects", Part 2: Visual.
6. S. Blake, D. Black, M. Carlson, E. Davies, Z. Wang, W. Weiss, "An Architecture for Differentiated Services", RFC 2475, December 1998.
7. W. Richard Stevens, "UNIX Network Programming", Volume 1, second edition, ISBN 0-13-490012-X.
8. E. Masala, D. Quaglia, J.C. De Martin., - "Adaptive Picture Slicing for Distortion-Based Classification of Video Packets.", 2001 IEEE Workshop on Multimedia Signal Processing, Cannes, Francia, pp. 111-116.
9. Miska M. Hannuksela, Ye-Kui Wang, and Moncef Gabbouj, "Sub-picture: ROI coding and unequal error protection", IEEE 2002 International Conference on Image Processing (ICIP'2002), Sept. 2002, Rochester, New York, USA
10. Tao Tian, Adam Li, Jiangtao Wen, and John Villasenor. Priority Dropping in Network Transmission of Scalable Video. *IEEE International Conference on Image Processings*, Volume III, pp. 400-403, September 2000.
11. Jin-Gyeong Kim, JongWon Kim, and C.-C. Jay Kuo, "Internet video packet categorization with enhanced end-to-end QoS performance," in *Proc. SPIE Visual Communications and Image Processing `2002*, San Jose, CA, Jan. 2002.
12. W. Tan and A. Zakhor, "Packet classification schemes for streaming MPEG video over delay and loss differentiated networks," Proceedings of Packet Video Workshop, Kyongju, Korea, April 2001
13. Cellatoglu, S. Fabri, S. T. Worall, A. M. Kondoz, "Use of Prioritised Object-Oriented Video Coding for the Provision of Multiparty Video Communications in Error-Prone Environments", IEEE VTC-Fall, Amsterdam 1999, pp 401-405
14. S.T. Worall, A. H. Sadka, P. Sweeney, A.M. Kondoz, "Motion Adaptive Error Resilient Encoding for MPEG-4", IEEE ICASSP 2001, Salt Lake City, USA, May 2001, Vol. 3, pp. 1389-1392
15. S.T. Worrall, S. Fabri, A.H. Sadka, A.M. Kondoz, "Prioritisation of Data Partitioned MPEG-4 Video over Mobile Networks", ETT-European Transactions on Telecommunications, Vol. 12, No. 3, May/June 2001
16. C. Chang and S.W. Hsieh, "An Adaptive QoS Guarantee Framework for SMIL Multimedia Presentations with ATM ABR Service", IEEE Globecom 2002
17. D. Wichadakul, X. Gu, K. Nahrstedt, "A Programming Framework for Quality-Aware Ubiquitous Multimedia Applications", ACM Multimedia 2002
18. "Mean Opinion Score (MOS)", ITU-T P.800 Specification.

19. D. Black S. Brim B. Carpenter F. Le Faucheur, "Per Hop Behavior Identification Codes", RFC 3140, June 2001
20. http://mpeg4ip.sourceforge.net/
21. http://www.divx.com/
22. ISO/IEC 14496-3, "Information technology – Coding of audio-visual objects", Part 3: Audio
23. http://developer.apple.com/darwin/projects/streaming/
24. J. Heinanen, F. Baker, W. Weiss, J. Wroclawski, "Assured Forwarding PHB Group", RFC 2597, June 1999.
25. ISO/IEC 14496-6, "Information technology – Coding of audio-visual objects", Part 6: Systems
26. Y. Kikuchi, T. Nomura, S. Fukunaga, Y. Matsui, H. Kimata, "RTP Payload Format for MPEG-4 Audio/Visual Streams", RFC3016, November 2000.

Multiple Description Coding for Video Streaming over Wireless Networks

Manuela Pereira*, Marc Antonini, and Michel Barlaud

I3S laboratory of CNRS, University of Nice-Sophia Antipolis
Bâtiment Algorithme/Euclides, 2000 route des Lucioles
06903 Sophia Antipolis Cedex, France
{pereira, am, barlaud} @i3s.unice.fr

Abstract. We present a system for video streaming over Internet from
a server to a wireless client. We show that this system is well adapted
to the unpredictable and varying nature of Internet and is effective in
presence of channel failures caused by the mobile communication. The
proposed system uses a superposition of several Multiple Description
Coding (MDC) schemes, each with $N = 2$ descriptions, to reach rate
scalability and adaptability to varying channel conditions. Each MDC
($N = 2$ descriptions), that we will call base MDC has associated a bit
rate and a redundancy. In [1, 2] we show that the base MDC is well
suited for transmission over 3G channels and we present results using
UMTS simulator.

In the proposed method, multiple descriptions (MD) are generated by the
coder and downloaded in the server, leaving to the server the only task
to choose sending out the right description at the right time depending
of channel conditions (bandwidth and loss rate).

1 Introduction

The use of video streaming over Internet knew an enormous increase in the past
few years being the design of Internet video streaming a challenging task due to
the unpredictable and varying nature of network conditions. Furthermore, the
increasingly access of Internet from wireless, often mobile terminal, comes up
with additional problems. If in the former problem is considered that packets
arriving to client are uncorrupted in the case of wireless communications this
is not guaranteed. It is why effectiveness in presence of channel failures is so
important in wireless streaming.

Internet only offer best-effort service, so there is no guarantees on: bandwidth, delay jitter or loss rates. So, the video streaming system must be able to
adapt video rate to available bandwidth and must be robust to packet losses.
Conventional approaches for dealing with packet loss for static data, such as retransmission may not be possible in streaming context due to real time nature of
the content. Thus, additional mechanism are needed to provide streaming media
delivery over packet networks.

---

* Research partially supported by PRAXIS XXI grant SFRH/BD/1234/2000

M.M. Freire, P. Lorenz, M.M.-O. Lee (Eds.): HSNMC 2003, LNCS 2720, pp. 395–405, 2003.

In streaming video the client performs a demand to a server that transmits media packets over a network that serves fairly several clients. The server can implement intelligent transport mechanisms, by sending out the right packets at the right time, but the amount of computation that it can perform for each media stream is very limited due to the large number of stream to be served simultaneously. Then, the task to compress video signal is left to the encoder. Therefore this task as to be done without the a priori knowledge of the channel conditions (bandwidth and loss rates). This is why representations that allow rate scalability must be adapted to varying network throughput without requiring computation at the media server. Multiple redundant representations are an easy way to achieve this task and will be used in the present work.

1.1   Prior Work on Video Streaming

Almost all present approaches use Forward Error Correction (FEC) and/or Automatic Repeat reQuest (ARQ). For instance, in [3] they use a two-layer scalable video coder combined with unequal error protection. In [4] has been proposed a generalized MD ($N > 2$ descriptions) coding through the usage of FEC codes for streaming video. In [5] they use a hybrid FEC/ARQ approach known as incremental redundancy. In [6] is used a media layer representation for transmission over current heterogeneous networks. In [7] they use adaptive media playout to reduce the delay introduced by the client buffer. They consider retransmission of lost media packets. To minimize retransmission in [8] the authors use pre-stored representations of certain frames at the server such that the chosen representation only uses previous frames, as reference, received with very hight probability.

The approaches above use standard video coders (MPEG-2/4, H.263). In such schemes retransmission of lost media packets is essential for a video streaming application over error-prone channels. Continuous video playout at the receiver can only be guaranteed if all packets are available due to the interdependency of successive video packets introduced by motion compensated prediction. In [9] is used the three-dimensional (3-D) SPIHT with a new method of partitioning the wavelet coefficients into spatial-temporal tree blocks to achieve error resilience. However, they had to sacrifice the progressiveness of the first block of the bitstream to get error resilience. The method also have the problem that if a portion at the beginning part of the bitstream is lost they can not reconstruct anything from the bitstream. This is also a problem of the above layered approaches. Such kind of approach essentially prioritize data and thereby support intelligent discarding of the data. Therefore, layered approaches doesn't seem adequate for Internet where all packets are equally likely to be lost, so video can be completely lost if there is an error in the base layer.

An alternative to layered methods are the joint source and channel coding method, known as MDC. They have proven to be an effective way to provide error resilience with a relatively small reduction in compression ratio. In the MD problem (reduced to the simplest case of two descriptions), a source is described by two descriptions with side rates R_1 and R_2. These two descriptions individually lead to reconstructions with side distortions D_1 and D_2, respectively; the two descriptions together yield a reconstruction with central distortion $D_0 \leq D_1$ (and D_2). Each description or MD stream is independent from each other and is typically of roughly equal importance.

A number of MD video coding algorithms have recently been developed, which provide different tradeoffs in terms of compression performance and error resilience [10, 11, 12, 13, 1]. Some MDC schemes dedicated to streaming video coding and using path diversity have recently been developed. In [14] MD coding is used to code a media stream into multiple complementary descriptions, which are distributed across the edge servers in a Content Delivery Network (CDN). They exploits path diversity provided by the different network path that exist between a client and its nearby edge servers. Also in [15] is proposed MDC with path diversity. This coding scheme assumes that there are several parallel channels between the source and destination, and that each channel may be temporarily down or suffering from long burst errors.

The proposed method use MDC schemes, and even if it could easily be adapted to take advantage of path diversity we will present it for the case when only a path is considered.

1.2   Main Contributions of the Paper

We propose a MDC scheme with $N > 2$ descriptions, that presents rate scalability and robustness to packet losses. The proposed scheme is a superposition of several MDC schemes with $N = 2$ descriptions. The base MDC scheme ($N = 2$) is the one presented in [16, 17] for still image and extended in [18] for video. In [2] we show the effectiveness of this method under channel failures due to transmission over 3G channels. This method uses Discrete Wavelet Transform (DWT) (3D Scan-Based DWT for video case) and an efficient bit allocation technique to find an optimal trade-off between efficient compression and robustness from losses. It was shown in [16] that high compression efficiency is achieved even when comparing with SDC compression schemes in noiseless case. We propose to use this base MDC scheme to code the video signal at different bit rates to get rate scalability. In order to get robustness to packet losses we propose to adapt the amount of added redundancy according to underlying channel error characteristics, as it is done in the algorithm presented in [19] for BSC and Gaussian channels and extended in [2, 1] for 3G channels.

In this way we propose to generate different descriptions for different bit rates (adapted to variable bandwidth) and different redundancies (adapted to loss rate).

The paper is organized as follow. In section 2 we give a short presentation of the base MDC for $N = 2$ descriptions. For further details use references [16, 19]. In section 3 we explain how we use this base MDC to reach a general MDC $N > 2$ descriptions. Finally, results are presented in section 4. We conclude in section 5.

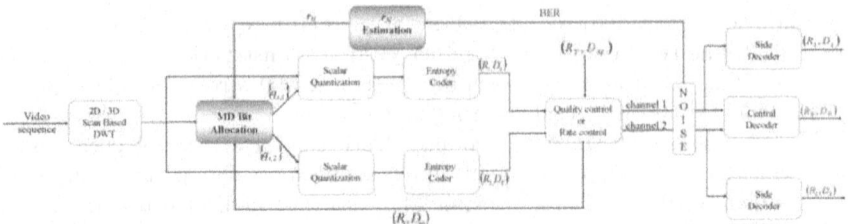

Fig. 1. Base MDC

2   Base MDC

This base MDC scheme includes a 3D Scan Based DWT coder that allows the development of a stripe based MDC. It focus on the special case in which there are two channels of equal capacity between a transmitter and a receiver. In such a scheme, a sequence of source symbols is given to an encoder to produce two independent bitstreams of equal importance. The amount of redundancy is dispatched on the different descriptions by taking into account the channel model and state. This base MDC is presented in fig. 1.

The aim in such scheme is to find, for a given redundancy between the descriptions, which combination of scalar quantizers across the various wavelet coefficients subbands will produce the minimum total central distortion D_0 while satisfying the side bit rates R_l, and side distortions constraints D_l. This allocation problem is a constrained problem which can be solved introducing the Lagrange operators. The Lagrangian functional for this constrained optimization problem, as given in [16] is the following:

$$J\left(\{q_{i,1}, q_{i,2}\}\right) = D_0 + \sum_{j=1}^{2} \lambda_j (R_j \le R_l) + \sum_{j=1}^{2} \mu_j (D_j \le D_l) \tag{1}$$

For a source with generalized Gaussian distribution [20], D_0 has been written in [21, 22] as (2).

$$D_0 = \sum_{i=1}^{\#SB} \Delta_i \sigma_{i,0}^2 D_{i,0} \left(\frac{q_{i,1}}{\sigma_{i,1}}, \frac{q_{i,2}}{\sigma_{i,2}}\right) \tag{2}$$

In (2) the Δ_i is an optional weight for frequency selection. The expected central distortion is estimated based on the channel state and the a priori channel model as (3).

$$D_{i,0}\left(\frac{q_{i,1}}{\sigma_{i,1}}, \frac{q_{i,2}}{\sigma_{i,2}}\right)\} = \frac{1}{\sigma_{i,0}^2} \frac{1}{1+r_N} \left[min\left(\sigma_{i,1}^2 D_{i,1}, \sigma_{i,2}^2 D_{i,2}\right)\right.$$
$$\left. +r_N \times max\left(\sigma_{i,1}^2 D_{i,1}, \sigma_{i,2}^2 D_{i,2}\right)\right] \tag{3}$$

The $\sigma_{i,j}^2 D_{i,j}(\frac{q_{i,j}}{\sigma_{i,j}})$ is the Mean Square Error for the ith subband in the case of a generalized Gaussian distribution. r_N is the weighting parameter associated to the redundant subbands, called redundancy parameter. The amount of redundancy, i.e., the importance of the redundant subbands, depends on the channel BER. Taking into account the Shannon theorem 10 of [23] it is proposed in [19] to compute the redundancy parameter as $r_N = \frac{H_y(x)}{max(H(x))}$ where $H(x)$ is the entropy of the input and $H_y(x)$ the conditional entropy or the equivocation. For this, we use $C = max(H(x) - H_y(x))$ where C is the channels capacity. For example, in the case of Rayleigh models an upper bound approximation for the normalized channel capacity was introduced by Lee's [24] as $\eta = \frac{C}{B} \approx log_2 e.e^{\frac{-1}{\gamma}}(-e + ln\gamma + \frac{1}{\gamma})$ bits/symbol, where γ is the signal to noise ratio (SNR). This model is considered to compute the r_N when adapting to the behavior of UMTS channels.

The resultant system for a two channels scheme ($j \in \{1,2\}$) that provides the optimal sets of quantization steps $\{q_{i,1}\}$, $\{q_{i,2}\}$ as given in [16] is the following:

$$
\begin{cases}
\dfrac{\partial D_{i,j}}{\partial R_{i,j}}\left(\dfrac{q_{i,j}}{\sigma_{i,j}}\right) = \dfrac{-\lambda_j a_i}{\Delta_i \sigma_{i,j}^2 (C_{i,j} + \mu_j E_j)} & \textbf{(a)} \\[4mm]
\sum_{i=1}^{\#SB} a_i R_{i,j}\left(\dfrac{q_{i,j}}{\sigma_{i,j}}\right) - R_l = 0 & \textbf{(b)}.
\end{cases}
\tag{4}
$$

The a_i is the quotient of the size of the subband divided by the size of the whole image (e.g., $a_i = \frac{1}{2^{2i}}$ in the dyadic case); $E_j = 2 \times (D_j - D_l)$ if $D_j > D_l$ or 0 otherwise; and $C_{i,j}$ is $\frac{1}{1+r_N}$ if $min(\sigma_{i,1}^2 D_{i,1}, \sigma_{i,2}^2 D_{i,2}) = \sigma_{i,j}^2 D_{i,j}$ or $\frac{r_N}{1+r_N}$ otherwise. Solution for the expression of $\frac{\partial D_{i,j}}{\partial R_{i,j}}\left(\frac{q_{i,j}}{\sigma_{i,j}}\right)$ can be found in [22].

3   Proposed MDC for Video Streaming

The proposed general MDC is a superposition of the base MDC presented in previous section. More precisely, we divide our signal into sub-signals or Group Of Pictures (GOP) representing the video at different time. For each GOP, the base MDC is performed for different bit rates and redundancies. In this way we generate several descriptions adapted to different channels conditions, as presented in table 1. We note that redundancy 1 gives maximal robustness and redundancy 0 gives maximal quality. Intermediate values of redundancies give a trade-off between quality and robustness. We can see more precisely in fig. 2 the relation between distortion and bit rate when the redundancy parameter was calculated for 10 % packet loss (this represents one line of the table 1). Fig. 3 shows the relation between distortion and packet loss for a bit rate fixed at 200Kbps (this represents one columns of the table 1).

These Multiple descriptions generated by the coder are downloaded to the server. This one only have to choose sending out the right description at the right time depending of channel conditions (bandwidth and loss rate).

Redundancy / Bit rate		100kbs	200kbs	...	X Mbs
1	Description 1	$D_{1,1,1}$	$D_{1,1,2}$	...	$D_{1,1,n}$
	Description 2	$D_{2,1,1}$	$D_{2,1,2}$	...	$D_{2,1,n}$
0.5	Description 1	$D_{1,2,1}$	$D_{1,2,2}$	...	$D_{1,2,n}$
	Description 2	$D_{2,2,1}$	$D_{2,2,2}$	...	$D_{2,2,n}$
...		...	...	...	...
0	Description 1	$D_{1,m,1}$	$D_{1,m,2}$	...	$D_{1,m,n}$
	Description 2	$D_{1,m,1}$	$D_{1,m,2}$	...	$D_{1,m,n}$

Table 1. Different pre-stored descriptions for an interval time of video (for a GOP).

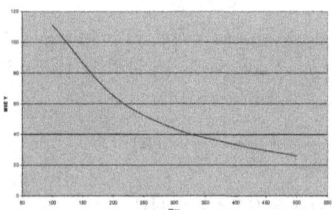

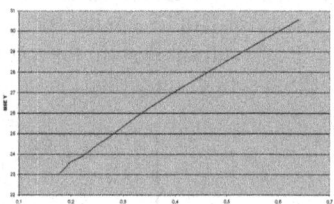

Fig. 2. MSE of Y component of QCIF Foreman video for bit rates from 100 to 500 Kbps. 10 % probability of packet loss.

Fig. 3. MSE of Y component of QCIF Foreman video compressed at 500 Kbs for different probabilities of packet loss (i.e. different r_N values). $r_N = 1$ means hight packet losses.

The server can choose the description with the bit rate that is more suitable for each client and which redundancy is most adapted to the present loss rate. Furthermore, the server can continue sending descriptions corresponding to the same GOP of video but with less redundancy (better quality) while there is time for it. With this scheme we avoid the added delay of methods using retransmission that have to wait for the packet delivery state. Then, the server will repeat the above process for the next GOP of the video. The server will always start a GOP with the redundancy most suited for the present channel condition and continues sending descriptions that will enhance the video quality.

The computation of the number of bits the server can send for each GOP can be done based on the last packet delays. Let us define δ as the interval of emission between two successive packets, rtt the average of the last packets delays and pbr the packet size (in bits). We need also to define t as the time at which the decoder is scheduled to extract the next GOP from its input buffer and decode it. So, it corresponds to the delivery deadline by which the descriptions corresponding to the next GOP must arrive at the client. In such a scenario, the number of bits that it is possible to send can be computed as $n \leq \frac{(t+\delta)(pbr)}{rtt+\delta}$. The server can use this n to decide if it is possible to send more descriptions with less redundancy, in order to improve playout quality, or if it starts sending descriptions for the next GOP.

4   Results

For spatial decomposition our coder uses 9-7 biorthogonal filter [20] and performs a three levels decomposition. For temporal decomposition it uses the lifting (2,2) filter and performs a two levels decomposition. The bit allocation procedure is followed by a simple scalar quantization and the encoding of each subband uses context-based arithmetic bit-plane coder [25] (see fig. 1). In order to provide synchronization and minimize the error propagation in the case of errors in the packets due to the mobile communication, each spatio-temporal subband is divided into blocks. Then, arithmetic coding is synchronized on each block. For error detection, we use the Smart Arithmetic Coding method presented in [1].

We use a $K = 2$ state Markov model to simulate the Internet channel, as suggested by [26], and we consider $T = 100$ ms as the interval between successive packets. For the mobile channel we use UMTS simulator [1] . UMTS channel presents three different models: indoor, pedestrian, and vehicular. They are defined in [27].

To make comparisons, we present the results obtained with the proposed MDC when subject to noise or not. We present also some results obtained when transmission of a singular description coder (SDC) with a similar codec. All channel simulations were performed 5 times for Internet simulations and 10 times in UMTS simulations. Note that mean PSNR values are computed by averaging decoded MSE values of each simulation and then converting the mean MSE to the corresponding PSNR values. Visual results of video presents always the frames 10, 20, 30, 40, 50, ... of the video. The Y component is the most sensitive to noise. We only present numeric results for this component.

Fig. 1 present the mean PSNR of different frames for Y when transmission over Internet. The packet loss is 10% unconditional loss probability for the probe packet and 18% of conditional probe loss probability in fig. 1 (a) and 5% for both in fig. 1 (b). We can see that when comparing with the SDC case we have a gain of 4 dB for the first case and more than 5 dB for the second one.

We show some visual results in fig. 5. Fig. 5 (a) for the SDC case and fig. 5 (b) for the proposed MDC. We can realize that with the proposed system we have a good quality. Furthermore, the results presented in this Internet simulations are the worst quality the client can get with the present system. This because we consider that the server only sends a group of descriptions. But we note that further descriptions the server sent to client will always enhance the playout quality. There is any dependency between descriptions as in the case of layered methods.

In the next results we show that the proposed method is well suited for transmission over 3G channels and in this way can even be used for wireless streaming.

---

[1] The authors wish to thank France Telecom R&D for providing an UMTS simulator.

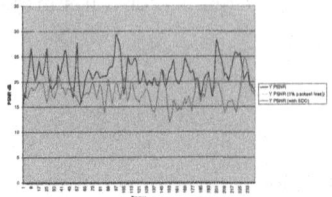
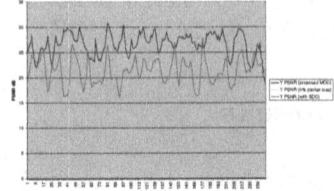

(a) Average Y-PSNR (0% packet
loss): 30.16 dB; Average Y-PSNR
(proposed MDC): 21.78 dB; Average
Y-PSNR (with SDC): 17.62 dB.

(b) Average Y-PSNR (0% packet
loss): 30.40 dB; Average Y-PSNR
(proposed MDC): 26.74 dB; Average
Y-PSNR (with SDC): 21.35 dB.

Fig. 4. QCIF Foreman video compressed at 200 Kbs. Internet channel. Left: with
10% unconditional loss probability for the probe packet and 18% of conditional
probe loss probability. Right: 5% packet loss. Without retransmission.

Fig. 7 present the mean PSNR of different frames for Y when transmission over
UMTS channel for the three different models respectively. The BER in this case
is 0.01. Finally we show some visual results in fig. 1 for the UMTS case. Fig. 1
(a) for the SDC case and fig. 1 (b) for the proposed MDC. One more time we
can realize that we have an attractive gain when comparing with the SDC case.

5   Conclusions

In this paper we propose a MDC system that avoids problems related with
layered approaches. The proposed scheme is a superposition of several MDC
schemes with $N = 2$ descriptions well adapted to variable bandwidth. The base
MDC scheme ($N = 2$) includes scan-based DWT and an efficient bit allocation procedure that dispatches source redundancy between the different channels (adapted to loss rate). The amount of redundancy is estimated based on
the channel state and the a priori channel model. In the proposed method all
descriptions that reach the decoder can be used to enhance the video quality.

The proposed system downloads in the server the different descriptions. The
server only have to chose the right description at the right time. Furthermore,
in the presented system the server continues sending less redundant descriptions
while it is possible, i.e., while real-time decoding remain possible. It does not
need to wait for information about packet delivery since every description that
reach the decoder enhance the video quality. In this way, we avoid delay problems
related with standard video coders that have to use retransmission. Our results
show that the proposed MDC system is efficient even for wireless streaming.

(a) Using SDC. Y-PSNR: 20.50 dB; U-PSNR: 38.94 dB; V-PSNR: 40.62 dB.

(b) Using the proposed MDC. Y-PSNR: 26.76 dB; U-PSNR: 38.82 dB; V-PSNR: 40.52 dB.

Fig. 5. Foreman video compressed at 200 Kbs and transmitted over an Internet simulator for 5 % packet loss.

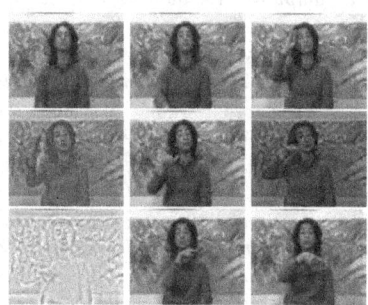

(a) Using the SDC.

(b) Using the proposed MDC.

Fig. 6. Silent video compressed at 200Kbits/s and transmitted over UMTS channel - Vehicular - at 0.001 ber.

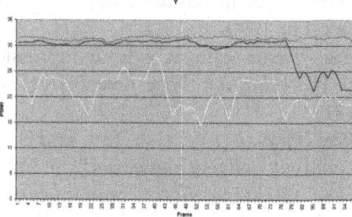

Fig. 7. Mean PSNR's of each frame for Y component for UMTS Pedestrian channel at 0.01 ber; Pink: no noise (PSNR = 31.47 dB); Blue: Proposed MDC (PSNR = 28.02 dB); Yellow: SDC case (PSNR = 20.00 dB).

References

[1] M. Pereira, M. Antonini, and M. Barlaud, "Multiple description image and video coding for wireless channels," *EURASIP Signal Processing: Image Communication, Special issue on Recent Advances in Wireless Video*, submited, 2003.

[2] ——, "Multiple description video coding for UMTS," in *Picture Coding Symposium*, Saint-Malo, France, April 2003.

[3] K. Stuhlmuller, M. Link, and B. Girod, "Scalable internet video steaming with unequal error protection," in *Packet Video Workshop*, NY, US, April 1999.

[4] R. Puri, K. Ramchandran, K. Lee, and V. Bharghavan, "Application of fec based multiple description coding to internet video streaming and multicast," in *Packet Video*, Sardinia, Italy, May 2000.

[5] J. Chakareski, P. Chou, and B. Aazhang, "Computing rate-distortion optimized policies for streaming media to wireless clients," in *Data Compression Conference*, Snowbird, UT, April 2002.

[6] Z. Miao and A. Ortega, "Optimal scheduling for streaming of scalable media," in *Asilomar Conf. on Signals, Systems and Computers*, Pacific Grove, CA, October-November 2000.

[7] M. Kalman, E. Steinbach, and B. Girod, "Adaptive media playout for low delay video streaming over error-prone channels," *IEEE Trans. on Circuits and Systems for Video Technology*, 2001.

[8] Y. Liang, , and B. Girod, "Low- latency streaming of pre-encoded video using channel-adaptive bitstream assembly," in *ICIP*. Rochester, NY, US: IEEE, September 2002.

[9] S. Cho and W. Pearlman, "Error resilience and recovery in streaming of embedded video," *Signal Processing, Special Issue on Image and Video Coding Beyond Standards*, vol. 82, pp. 1545–1558, November 2002.

[10] S. Wenger, G. Knorr, J. Ott, and F. Konssentini, "Error resilience support in h.263+," *IEEE Trans. on Circuits and systems for Video Technology*, pp. 867–877, November 1998.

[11] V. Vaishampayan and S. John, "Interframe balanced-multiple-description video compression," in *ICIP*, October 1999.

[12] A. Reibman, H. Jafarkhani, Y. Wang, M. Orchard, and R. Puri, "Multiple description video coding using motion-compensated prediction," in *ICIP*. Kobe, Japan: IEEE, October 1999.

[13] J. Apostolopoulos, "Error-sesilient video compression via multiple state streams," in *International Workshop on Very Low Bitrate Video Coding (VLVB*, October 1999, pp. 168–171.

[14] J. Apostolopoulos, T. Wong, W. tian Tan, and S. Wee, "On multiple description streaming with content delivery networks," in *IEEE Infocom*, June 2002.

[15] J. Apostolopoulos, "Reliable video communication over lossy packet networks using multiple state encoding and path diversity," in *VCIP*, January 2001.

[16] M. Pereira, M. Antonini, and M. Barlaud, "Channel adapted multiple description coding scheme using wavelet transform," in *ICIP*. Rochester, NY, US: IEEE, September 2002.

[17] ——, "Low complexity multiple description coding scheme using wavelet transform," in *EUSIPCO*, Toulouse, France, September 2002.

[18] ——, "Channel adapted multiple description coding scheme using wavelet transform," in *ICME*. Laussanne, Switzerland: IEEE, August 2002.

[19] ——, "Multiple description coding for noisy-varying channels," in *Proc. IEEE Data Compression Conf (DCC)*, Snowbird, US, March 2003.

[20] M. Antonini, M. Barlaud, P. Mathieu, and I. Daubechies, "Image coding using wavelet transform," *IEEE Trans. on Image Processing*, vol. 4, no. 8, pp. 1053–1060, August 1992.

[21] C. Parisot, M. Antonini, and M. Barlaud, "3D scan-based wavelet transform for video coding," in *MMSP*. IEEE, October 2001.

[22] ——, "3D scan-based wavelet transform and quality control for video coding," *EURASIP Special Issue Multimedia Signal Processing*, vol. 2003, no. 1, pp. 56–65, January 2003.

[23] C. Shannon, "A mathematical theory of communication," *The Bell System Technical Journal*, vol. 27, pp. 379–423, 623–656, July, October 1948.

[24] W. Lee, "Estimate of channel capacity in Rayleigh fading environnment," *IEEE Trans. on Vechicular Technology*, vol. 39, pp. 187–189, August 1990.

[25] C. Parisot, M. Antonini, and M. Barlaud, "Ebwic: A low complexity and efficient rate constrained wavelet image coder," in *ICIP*, Vancouver, Canada, September 2000.

[26] J. Bolot, "Characterizing end-to-end packet delay and loss in the Internet," *Journal of Hihh-Speed Networks*, 1993.

[27] *Selection procedures for the choice of radio transmission technologies of the UMTS*, Tr 101 112 v3.2.0 ed., ETSI (European Telecommunications Standards Institute, April 1998.

A Playout Time Oriented Retransmission Scheme for Multimedia Streaming Systems

Hiroaki Hagino[1], Yuichiro Miyazaki[1], Yuko Onoe[1], Yukio Atsumi[2],
Hirotaka Komaki[3], Masaaki Taniguchi[3], and Nagatsugu Yamanouchi[4]

[1] Network Laboratories, NTT DoCoMo, 3-5, Hikarinooka, Yokosuka,
Kanagawa, 239-8536, Japan
{hagino, miyazaki, yuko}@netlab.nttdocomo.co.jp
[2] School of Business Administration, Sensyu University, 2-1-1, Higashimita,
Tama, Kawasaki, Kanagawa, 214-8580, Japan
atsumi@isc.senshu-u.ac.jp
[3] IBM Japan, Ltd., 1623-14, Shimotsuruma, Yamato,
Kanagawa, 242-8502, Japan
{KOMAKI, TANIGUCHI}@jp.ibm.com
[4]Department of Information Science, Toho University, 2-2-1, Miyama,
Funabashi, Chiba, 274-8510, Japan
yamanouc@HyperResearch.com

Abstract. In this paper, we propose a *playout time oriented retransmission
scheme* for multimedia streaming. In the scheme, when the client detects a
packet loss, it transmits a retransmission request packet to the server. In multimedia streaming, a packet which does not arrive at the client until its playout
time is not played on the client. The server estimates time to play the packet
and time which the packet arrives at the client if it is retransmitted. If estimated
time to play the packet is later than the time when the packet arrives at the client, the server does not retransmit the packet. This reduces wasteful traffic
overhead generated by packets which is not played on the client if they are retransmitted. In this paper, we also discuss results of our experiments for comparing our scheme to the general NACK based retransmission scheme proposed
by IETF. The results show that our scheme drastically reduces traffic overhead
generated by retransmission and hardly degrades the number of successful retransmitted packets at all.

1 Introduction

Recent high-speed networks such as xDSL have made audio and video streaming
services feasible. In general, it is known that a QoS (Quality of Service) control approach is necessary for assuring the continuity of streaming contents playout[1].
Many papers have tackled QoS control, but packet losses remain inevitable because
the network condition between the server and the client changes dynamically and
drastically during playout.

Several proposals have described retransmission schemes for recovering lost
streaming packets. One of the most popular schemes, based on RTP (Real-Time

M.M. Freire, P. Lorenz, M.M.-O. Lee (Eds.): HSNMC 2003, LNCS 2720, pp. 406-415, 2003.
© Springer-Verlag Berlin Heidelberg 2003

Transport Protocol)[5], was proposed in [2-4]. In the scheme, when the client detects packet losses, it transmits a *retransmission request packet* to the server. The server then retransmits the lost packets to the client. The header of a streaming packet in the scheme has a field that holds the packet's priority. For streaming Mpeg movies, for example, I-picutres have higher priority than P-pictures and B-pictures. The server prioritizes packet delivery to favor I-picutres; one idea is that only I-picutres are retransmitted. This function reduces the traffic overhead generated by retransmission at the cost of a drop in content quality.

The scheme proposed in [2-4] does not, unfortunately, suit the streaming service. If a streaming packet does not arrive at the client until after its playout time, it is discarded by the client. This problem arises since the scheme places no importance on the playout time of each packet. Therefore, the scheme can generate wasteful traffic even if it does not retransmit packets with low priority.

This paper proposes a *playout time oriented retransmission scheme* for multimedia streaming. In our scheme, the server retransmits only those packets that have high priority and that are predicted to arrive at the client before their playout time. Our scheme is an extension of the scheme proposed in [3]. Our scheme also makes use of the priority field in a header of streaming packet. In our scheme, the retransmission request packet header holds the *playout time of buffer's top* field, which indicates the playout time of the top packet in the client's buffer. The server determines and stores the RTT (Round Trip Time) between the server and the client; it compares the stored RTT value to the difference between the playout time of the top packet in the client's buffer and the playout time of the lost packet reported in the retransmission request packet. Only if RTT is smaller does the server retransmit the packet to the client. If RTT is larger, the server does not retransmit the packet, because the packet would not arrive at the client until after its playout time.

We design and implement the multimedia streaming system with our proposing scheme. Experiments evaluate the impact of adding our scheme. The results of the experiments show that our retransmission scheme drastically reduces the number of retransmitted packets and hardly degrades the number of retransmission packets which arrive at the client until playout time of the packets.

The reminder of the paper is organized as follows. Section 2 describes our proposing scheme. Protocol design and implementation for our scheme are discussed in section 3. In section 4, we show and consider results of our experiments. Finally, we conclude this paper in section 5.

2 Playout Time Oriented Retransmission Scheme

2.1 Conventional Retransmission for Scheme Multimedia Streaming

In TCP, if the sender cannot receive an ACK packet from the receiver, the sender stops to transmit streaming packets. So, TCP is not suitable for real-time applications such as multimedia streaming. On the other hand, in UDP, the sender continues to transmit packets whether the packets which have been sent by the sender arrive at the receiver or not. So, multimedia streaming contents, in general, is transmitted not over

TCP but over UDP. RTP is most popular protocol for transmitting streaming packets over UDP. However, both UDP and RTP do not have a packet retransmission function. In multimedia streaming, if a lot of packets are lost, contents playout at the client may be stopped. Even if the number of lost packets is a few, video quality at the client is drastically degraded in some case. Because, some frames have only information of finite difference from previous or/and next frames in general video encoding techniques. For instance, in Mpeg encoded contents, frames called I-picutres have full image information of themselves, and then they can be displayed if other packets are lost. On the other hand, frames called P-picture only have information of finite difference from their previous packets. B-picture only has a information of finite difference from their previous and next packets. So, P-pictures and B-pictures cannot be displayed accurately if their previous or next packets are lost. If a few packets consisting of an I-picutre are lost, all P-pictures and B-pictures needing finite difference from the I-picutre cannot be displayed accurately. Namely, packets consisting of I-picutres are very important for multimedia streaming, and their lost may considerably degrade video quality.

To solve this problem, [2-4] have proposed an RTP expansion for selective packet retransmission. The retransmission control proposed in [2-4] is very simple one. If a lost packet is important, the server retransmits the packet. If not, the server does not retransmit it. However, the RTP retransmission function proposed in [2-4] has a crucial problem. In multimedia streaming system, as mentioned above, packets which do not arrive at the client until their playout time are discarded. So, traffic generated by the packets is wasteful. The wasteful traffic compresses network resource between the server and the client. In the worst case, more lost of packets is generated by packet retransmission. From this point of view, it is not enough for multimedia streaming system that the server retransmits only important packets.

2.2   Playout Time Oriented Retransmission Scheme

To reduce wasteful traffic generated by retransmitted packets, we propose the playout time oriented retransmission scheme. In our scheme, when packets are lost, the client performs as following.

1. The client checks identifiers of lost packets, such as sequence number.
2. The client checks playout time of packet which is buffered at the top of client buffer. In the following part of this paper, we call the playout time PBT (*Playout time of buffer's top*).
3. The client creates a *retransmission request packet (RRP)*. The packet has fields for identifiers of lost packets and PBT.
4. The client transmits the RRP to the server.

The server buffers packets transmitted by itself into a *retransmission buffer*. It is assumed that the server obtains RTT between the server and the client. When the server receives the retransmission request packet transmitted from the client, it performs as following.

1. **Buffer search phase**: The server searches packets which are requested in the RRP in the retransmission buffer. If a requested packet does not exist in the retransmission buffer, our retransmission control of the packet is finished.
2. **Importance decision phase**: The server checks importance of each requested packet. Our retransmission control of an unimportant packet is finished.
3. **Playout time decision phase**: The server estimates whether a retransmitted packet arrives at the client until its playout time based on RTT and PTP. If a requested packet is not estimated not to arrive at the client until its playout time, our retransmission control of the packet is finished. The detail of estimation is mentioned in the next subsection.
4. The server pushes the packets which fulfill the all above conditions into its transmission buffer.

As a result, our scheme can reduce traffic generated by wasteful retransmitted packets. In the next subsection, we discuss the detail of process in the playout time decision phase.

2.3 Detail of Playout Time Decision Phase

Concept of the playout time decision phase in our scheme is shown in Figure 1. The client which detects packet lost transmits a RRP to the server. Then, the server retransmits the packets to the client after the above mentioned three phases. In this subsection, we discuss the playout time decision phase. In the playout time decision phase, if the following equation is satisfied, a packet requested in the RRP is retransmitted.

$$t_1 > RTT + t_0 + d \qquad (1)$$

The parameters t_0 and t_1 indicate the time when the client detects packet lost and the playout time of the requested packet in the RRP, respectively. RTT is the RTT between the server and the client. It is thought that $RTT + t_0$ indicates the time when the packet requested in the RRP arrives at the client. If t_1 is larger than $RTT + t_0$, the server decides that the packet will arrive at the client until playout time, and then retransmits the packet to the client. If not, the server does not retransmit the packet. By the way, d indicates processing delay in the server and the client. This parameter must be determined based on performance of the server and the client.

3   Design and Implementation of Playout Time Oriented Re-transmission Scheme

3.1 Protocol Design

In this section, we design a protocol with playout time oriented retransmission scheme.

Our protocol is an expansion of RTP retransmission protocol proposed in [2-4]. In the protocol proposed in [2-4], the server can perform selective retransmission based on importance of each packet. We add selective retransmission function based on playout time of each packet to the protocol proposed in [2-4]. The added function needs parameters such as t_0, t_1, RTT, and d in the equation (1). RTT, RTT between the server and the client, can be calculated in RTP framework. The server calculates RTT between the server and the client by using SR (Sender Report) packet and RR (Receiver Report) packet. On the other hand, the server can obtain the playout time of the packet requested in RRP (t_1 in the equation (1)) because the server has the packet in own retransmission buffer at the playout time decision phase. Processing delay in the server and the client (d in the equation (1)) must be previously determined. However, the server cannot obtain the last parameter in the equation (1), t_0, in the protocol proposed in [3]. So, we add a field of t_0 to RRP in [3]. The other packets in [2-4] are not modified in our proposal. The format of retransmission request packet is shown in figure 1. We explain each fields of the packet format shown in figure 1 below.

Version (V): This field identifies the RTP version. The current version is 2.

Padding (P): If set, the padding bit indicates that the packet contains additional padding octets at the end which are not part of the control information but are included in the length field.

Feedback message type (FMT): This field identifies the type of the feed back message and is interpreted relative to the type. FMT=1.

Payload type (PT): This is the RTCP packet type which identifies the packet as being an RTCP feedback message. PT=RTPFB (Transport layer feed back message)=205.

Length: The length of this packet.

SSRC of packet sender: The synchronization source identifier for the originator of this packet.

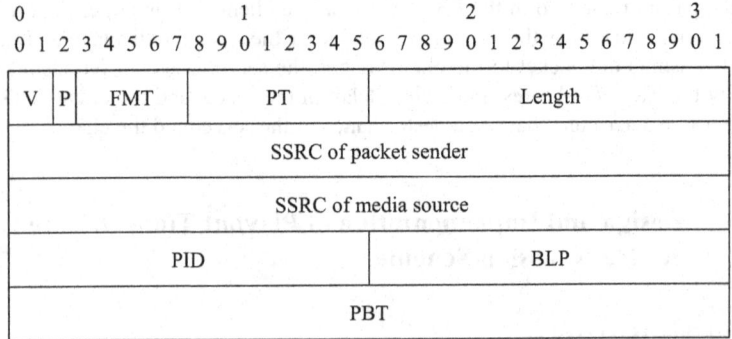

Fig. 1. The packet format of retransmission request packet in our protocol. PTP (Playout time of Top Packet) field is added to the retransmission request packet in [3]

SSRC of media source: The synchronization source identifier of the media source that this piece of feed back information is related to.

Packet ID (PID): The PID field is used to specify a lost packet. Typically, RTP sequence number is used for PID.

Bitmask of following lost packets (BLP): The BLP allows for reporting losses of any of the 16 RTP packets immediately following the RTP packet indicated by the PID.

Playout time of Buffer's Top (PBT): This field identifies the playout time of top packet of the client buffer.

The client can detect packet lost when it discovers jump of sequence number. For example, it is assumed that the client receives the 110th packet in the next of the 100th packet. It immediately creates a RRP in which PID is 101st and BLP indicates packet lost from the102nd packet to the 109th packet.

3.2 Implementation of Multimedia Streaming System with Proposed Scheme

We implement the multimedia streaming system with playout time oriented retransmission scheme. Our system targets 1 to 1 streaming services. The client accesses a web page provided by a streaming server, and chooses a contents. The server controls a session with the client by using RTSP. The server delivers Mpeg4 video data and G.723, MP3, or AAC audio data to the client. Our system is established by VisualC++6.0 on Windows2000.

4   Evaluation of Playout Time Oriented Retransmission Scheme

4.1   Environment of Our Experiments

We make use of our establishing *internet simulator* to configure network delay and packet loss rate freely. The simulator is settled between our server and our client. In our experiments, network delay changes from 50ms to 250ms, and average packet loss rate changes from 1% to 10%. The client starts to playout contents after 2 seconds buffering. Parameter d in the equation (1) is set 0 in our experiments. In this environment, we compare our proposed scheme to conventional one proposed in [2-4].

4.2   Results of Our Experiments

We have a lot of results of our experiments. However, because of space limitations, we show some of them in this paper.

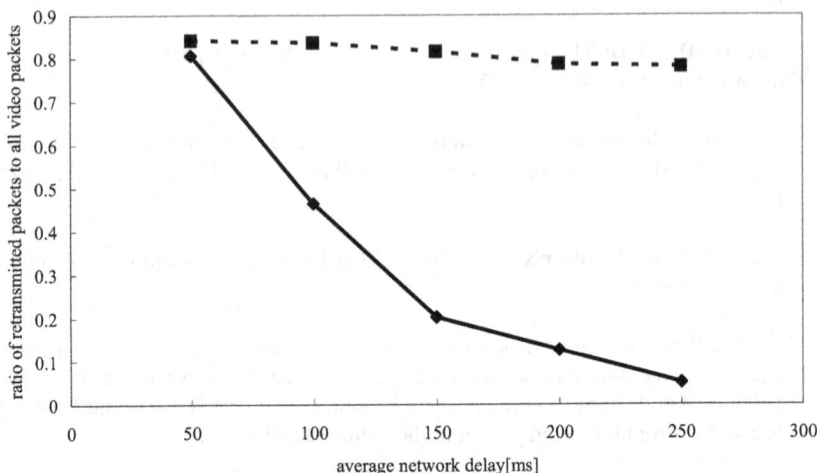

Fig. 2. Ratio of retransmitted packets to all video packets. The solid line shows experimental result of our proposed scheme, and the dotted line means the conventional scheme proposed in [2-4]. As network delay becomes longer, ratio of retransmitted packets to all video packets becomes lower in our proposed scheme

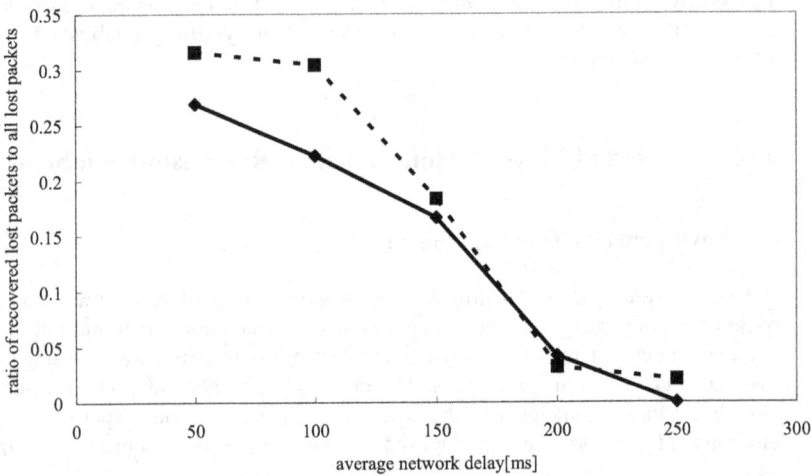

Fig. 3. Ratio of recovered lost packets to all lost packets. The solid line is experimental result of our proposed scheme, and the dotted line indicates the conventional scheme proposed in [2-4]. Ratio of recovered lost packets to all lost packets is much the same in both our scheme and the conventional one

Ratio of retransmitted packets to all video packets

On ratio of retransmitted packets to all video packets, we compare our proposed scheme to the conventional one proposed in [2-4]. The result with 1% average packet loss rate is shown in figure 2. In figure 2, the horizontal axis is network delay, and the vertical axis indicates ratio of retransmitted packets to all transmitted video packets. This figure shows that our scheme reduces the number of retransmitted packets as the network delay becomes longer, while ratio of retransmitted packets to all video packets hardly changes in this experiments in the conventional scheme. This is because packets requested in RRP is thought not to arrive at the client until their playout time in long delay environment. On the other hand, in short delay environment, ratio of retransmitted packets to all video packets is much the same in both our scheme and the conventional one.

Ratio of recovered lost packets to all lost packets

On ratio of recovered lost packets to all lost packets, we compare our proposed scheme to the conventional one proposed in [2-4]. The result with 1% average packet loss rate is shown in figure 3. In figure 3, the horizontal axis is network delay, and the vertical axis indicates ratio of recovering lost packets to all lost packets. This figure shows that ratio of recovering lost packets to all lost packets is much the same in both our scheme and the conventional scheme. From the figure2, it becomes apparent that ratio of retransmitted packets to all video packets hardly changes as the network delay changes. Therefore, it is thought that the conventional scheme retransmits a lot of wasteful packets in long delay environment.

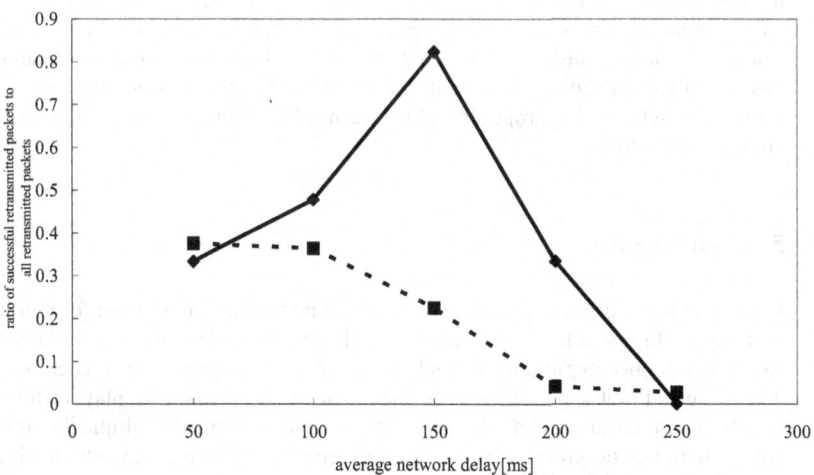

Fig. 4. Ratio of packets which arrive at the client until their playout time to all retransmitted packets. The solid line shows experimental result of our proposed scheme, and the dotted line is that of the conventional scheme. Our scheme has performance peak at 150ms network delay, while ratio of packets which arrive at the client until their playout time to all retransmitted packets of the conventional scheme performs monotone decreasing as network delay becomes longer

Ratio of successful retransmitted packets to all retransmitted packets

On ratio of successful retransmitted packets to all retransmitted packets, we compare our proposed scheme to the conventional scheme proposed in [2-4]. The result with 1% average packet loss rate is shown in figure 4. In figure 4, the horizontal axis is network delay, and the vertical axis indicates ratio of successful retransmitted packets to all retransmitted packets. The conventional scheme shows monotone decreasing as network delay becomes longer. On the other hand, when network delay is not over 150ms, ratio of successful retransmitted packets to all retransmitted packets of our scheme becomes higher as network delay becomes larger. When network delay is over 150ms, ratio of successful retransmitted packets to all retransmitted packets of our scheme becomes lower as network delay becomes larger, similarly to the conventional one. Based on figure 2 and 3, when network delay is below 150ms, the number of all retransmitted packets is a lot. So, ratio of successful retransmitted packets to all retransmitted packets is low. On the other hand, when network delay is over 150ms, the number of successful retransmitted packets is small. So, ratio of successful retransmitted packets to all retransmitted packets is low. From these reasons, in our experiments, our proposed scheme has the best performance at 150ms network delay. Network delay which gives our proposed scheme the best performance changes as the length of buffering time of client at the start of playout of contents changes. In our experiments, the client buffers contents for 2 seconds at the start of playout of contents. Because our proposed scheme decides whether the server retransmits packets or not based on comparing amount of buffering packets to network delay, if the length of buffering time becomes longer, network delay which gives our proposed scheme the best performance becomes larger. Namely, if characteristics of network are given, the length of the best buffering time is decided. By the way, in short network delay environment, our proposed scheme retransmits wasteful packets similarly to the conventional scheme. This fact shows that our proposed scheme performs in unexpected manner in short delay environment. Although we believe that we can improve our scheme by setting d appropriate value, we have to study essential solution to this problem in the future.

5 Conclusion

In this paper, we propose playout time oriented retransmission scheme for multimedia streamaing. In our scheme, the server decides whether it retransmits packets or not based on not only importance of each packet but also playout time of each packet. If it is evaluated that a packet does not arrive at the client until its playout time, the packet is not retransmitted. We also design and implement multimedia streaming system with our proposed scheme. From the results of our experiments in which we compare our scheme to the conventional scheme, we show advances of our scheme. Our scheme drastically reduces the number of retransmitted packets compared to the conventional scheme, while ratio of successful retransmitted packets to all retransmitted packets is much the same to the conventional one. In the future, we will study essential solution to poor ratio of successful retransmitted packets to all retransmitted packets in short delay environment.

References

1. Aurrecoechea, Z., Campbell, A. T., and Hauw, L.: A survey of QoS architectures Multimedia Systems, Vol. 6. (1998) 138–151
2. Miyazaki, A., Fukushima, H., Hata, K., Wiebke, T., Hakenberg, R., Burmeister, C., Takatori, N., Okumura, S., and Ohno, T.: RTP Payload Formats to Enable Multiple Selective Retransmissions, draft-ietf-avt-rtp-selret-05.txt, IETF (2002)
3. Ott, J., Wenger, S., Sato, N., Burmeister, C., and Rey, J.: Extended RTP Profile for RTCP-based Feedback (RTP/AVPF), draft-ietf-avt-rtcp-feedback-05.txt, IETF (2003)
4. Rey, J., Leon, D., Miyazaki, A., Varsa, V., and Hakenberg, R.: RTP Retransmission Payload Format, draft-ietf-avt-rtp-retransmission-07.txt, IETF (2003)
5. Schulzrinne, H., Casner, S., Frederick, R., and Jacobson, V.: RTP: A Transport Protocol for Real-Time Streaming Protocol, RFC1998, IETF (1996)
6. Schulzrinne, H., Rao, A., and Lanphier, R.: Real Time Streaming Protocol, RFC2326, IETF (1998)

On the Capacity Requirements of ASONs versus OTNs

Sophie De Maesschalck, Didier Colle, Danny Willems, Mario Pickavet, and
Piet Demeester

Dept. of Information Technology, Ghent University - IMEC,
Sint-Pietersnieuwstraat 41, B-9000 Gent, Belgium
{sdemaess, dcolle}@intec.rug.ac.be

Abstract. Automatic Switched Optical Networks (ASON) are currently a hot
topic in optical network research. This paper studies the capacity savings that
can be obtained with this networking paradigm, compared to the more classical
approach of a static Optical Transport Network (OTN) supporting semi-
permanent connections. The results shown in this paper confirm the cost-
efficiency that can be achieved with an ASON-based network due to the sharing of network resources network. The influence of traffic parameters as the Inter-Arrival Time (IAT) and the Holding Time (HT) of the switched connections
on this capacity saving are studied. Also the effect of the topology is investigated.

1 Introduction

The popularity of the Internet and its related services has been and will continue to be
one of the main reasons for the explosive growth of the traffic volume. Bandwidth-
hungry applications as the exchange of multimedia files (e.g. peer-to-peer applications) are very popular and more applications and services of that sort are expected to
be developed in the near future. Other emerging applications are e.g. the Storage Area
Networks (SAN), used for back-up and disaster recovery of mission-critical information, and the Optical Virtual Private Network (OVPN) services that connect several
office locations of a single company or connect a large company to its clients for
business-to-business transactions. Today's traffic is also more dynamic than ever.
Applications such as SAN ask for high-capacity bit pipes for a limited period of time.
The interconnection pattern of an Internet Service Provider (ISP), for instance, also
varies significantly over time. The typical diurnal transition in the traffic pattern between business peak hours and after-work hours is an example of this variation. The
large volume of (dynamic) traffic generated by these emerging applications together
with traditional voice and data traffic has to be transported over the backbone network., which today is typically based on optical technology [1]. The introduction of
the Wavelength Division Multiplexing (WDM) technique in the optical backbone
network has opened tremendous amounts of bandwidth. Up to 160 wavelength channels of 10 Gbps (with 40 Gbps channels just around the corner) can be transported
over a single optical fiber. For the moment, WDM is only deployed in static point-to-
point connections, to provide high-capacity bit pipes between the client layer equip-

M.M. Freire, P. Lorenz, M.M.-O. Lee (Eds.): HSNMC 2003, LNCS 2720, pp. 416-425, 2003.

ment, typically IP. Traffic is transported optically between the client layer equipment, where it is converted from the optical to the electrical domain, processed (e.g., switched) and converted back to the optical domain for further transmission. The electronics in the IP routers are however not able to keep up with the achievable bit rates in the optical domain, and they thus become the new bottleneck. By introducing Optical Cross-connects (OXCs) in the backbone network, it becomes possible to keep the traffic demand in the optical domain, by establishing lightpaths between the routers. At the network nodes, the transit traffic is no longer converted to the electrical IP domain, but stays in the optical domain until it has reached its destination. The backbone network is now a true Optical Transport Network (OTN). The reconfigurability of today's OXCs is however quite limited. When the switching pattern of an OXC has to be changed (e.g. because the traffic demand pattern has changed), an operator has to go out on the field to the OXC location and manually change the switching pattern. The lightpaths established in the optical backbone network are thus quasi-permanent. Another disadvantage is the fact that the wavelength channels used by the established lightpaths are continuously reserved, even when there is no actual traffic flowing through them. It has indeed been observed that the client usually doesn't use a permanent connection continuously, but is active only a certain fraction of the time. It is obvious that this leads to a very inefficient network use.

Automatic Switched Optical Networks (ASON) [1-4] are the answer to these problems. An ASON-based optical network can establish permanent connections, through the network management system (just as in OTNs), but also allows switched connections. These can be set up and torn down by a simple request of the client layer (typically an ISP), depending on the bandwidth requirements at that moment. The use of sophisticated technologies to control the switching of the optical signal from an ingoing to an outgoing port in the OXCs by means of an optical control plane, will allow very fast provisioning of the switched lightpaths. The evolution from a classical OTN to the advanced ASON will allow to only reserve the capacity of a wavelength when it will be used. The wavelengths are no longer reserved permanently, as is the case for OTN, where they are reserved even in the situation that there is no actual traffic flow. With ASON, its capacity will be released so it can be used by another lightpath, between other IP routers. The capacity in the network will thus be used more efficiently as the resources are shared over time, opening the door for important cost savings. Moreover, the capacity currently installed in the static OTN network may not have to be upgraded as quickly as originally predicted, due to the transition to ASON. In fact, the cost advantage that can be achieved with the ASON architecture compared to OTNs is caused by the difference in statistical multiplexing. OTN with its semi-permanently established connections is based on statistical end-to-end multiplexing, while the switched connections in an ASON are link-by-link statistically multiplexed.

In this paper, the capacity requirements of a traditional OTN are compared with those of an ASON, and this under various traffic assumptions. The potential savings in terms of capacity are quantified for some test networks. Section 2 elaborates on the generation of the traffic demand for an OTN and an ASON, and the dimensioning process for both types of networks. In Section 3 some results of different case studies are presented. The conclusion is formulated in Section 4.

2 Network Dimensioning for OTN and ASON

2.1 ASON Switched Connections Traffic Demand

As said before, today's traffic is highly dynamic. With ASON, the client layer has the possibility to ask for a lightpath at the time it needs it, and only for the duration it needs it. The traffic offered to an ASON is thus characterized by two parameters: the Inter-Arrival Time (IAT) and the Holding Time (HT). The IAT is the time between consecutive switched connection requests. The HT is the time between the set-up and tear-down of a switched connection. Both are illustrated in Fig. 1.

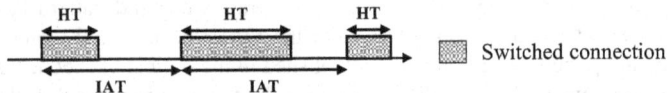

Fig. 1. Inter-Arrival Time and Holding Time

Some work has already been done in order to come up with realistic values for the IAT and the HT for typical ASON services. In [4-5] some estimations were given for ASON-based services that would typically be requested by the banking sector or an ISP. Also in [6-7] dynamic traffic models are shortly discussed. It is however apparent that there is no straightforward answer to the question of what is the most suited teletraffic model [8]. New applications and services emerge, different applications have different time characteristics, etc. In this paper we assume that both the IAT and the HT of the switched connections between a node pair are exponentially distributed:

$$HT(x) = a.e^{-a.x}, \ IAT(x) = b.e^{-b.x}. \tag{1}$$

The traffic model is thus loosely based on the Erlang traffic model. The mean values of these exponential distributions for the IAT and the HT are parameters that will be varied, in order to study their influence on the achievable capacity savings between ASON and OTN.

In order to make the problem somewhat easier to handle, we will divide the time in discrete time slots. At the beginning of such a time slot a switched connection can be set up or torn down. We also assume that more than one connection can be set up at the same time between a certain node pair. The traffic demand offered to the ASON can then be modeled as a succession of traffic matrices, with a new traffic matrix being drawn up at the beginning of each time slot. This is illustrated in Fig. 2 and Fig. 3. The exact duration of the time slots in minutes or hours is one of the design variables of the problem In this paper we assume that the complete duration on the simulation period equals half a day or a complete day. The results shown in this paper are for a simulation interval that consists of 100 time slots. We have experimented with simulation intervals that consisted of more and less time slots. With less time slots, the results were highly dependent on the number of time slots in the simulation interval, while dividing the simulation interval in more time slots did not significantly change the results, but augmented the simulation time.

2.2 OTN Permanent Connections Traffic Demand

In an OTN, no switched connections can be set up; all traffic has to be transported using permanent connections. The traffic pattern offered to the backbone network is thus not going to change, at least not over the limited time period we are studying in this paper (static traffic pattern). These permanent connections will, as the term implies, be established permanently in the network, but they will probably not convey actual traffic all the time. Part of the time they will be empty high-capacity bit pipes. In order to asses the performance of both OTN and ASON under more or less similar circumstances, the permanent connections should be able to transport the same amount of traffic as the switched connections under the same Grade of Service (GoS). This will be guaranteed if the permanent connection traffic demand matrix that is offered to the OTN is derived from the succession of the switched connections traffic demand matrices in the following way:

Let M_{ij}^P denote the capacity expressed in number of wavelengths of the permanent connection demand between node i and node j in the permanent connections traffic demand matrix, and let $M_{ij}^{S_k}$ denote the capacity expressed in number of wavelengths of the switched connection demand between node i and node j in the switched connections traffic demand matrix at the beginning of time interval k, then

$$M_{ij}^P = \underset{k}{Max}(M_{ij}^{S_k})\qquad(2)$$

The capacity of the permanent connection traffic demand between a node pair is thus the maximum over the capacity of the switched connections traffic demands between this node pair over all 100 considered time slots. This is illustrated in Fig. 2 for the traffic demand between a single node pair. In the ASON case, three switched connections with capacity 1 are requested at the beginning of a certain time slot and later torn down. In the OTN case however, to make sure that this traffic can indeed be supported, a permanent connection traffic demand with capacity 3 has to be supported. The practical implementation of this methodology is illustrated in Fig. 3.

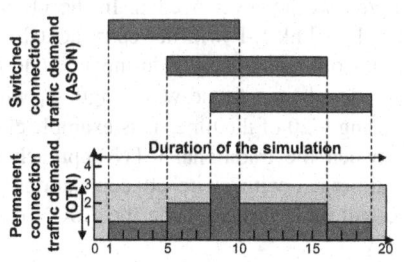
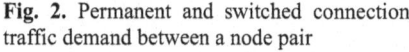
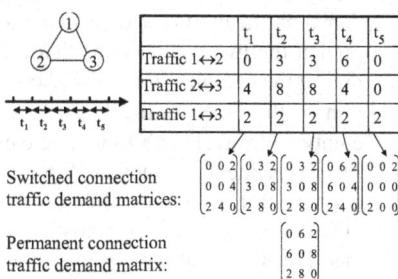

Fig. 2. Permanent and switched connection traffic demand between a node pair

Fig. 3. Example of the offered permanent and switched connection traffic demand

2.3 Network Dimensioning Model

The goal of this paper is to compare the dimensioning of an optical backbone network under permanent connection traffic (traditional OTN) with that under switched connection traffic (ASON), from the point of view of the capacity that needs to be installed in the network. The topology of the optical backbone network is fixed. All links are assumed to have more than enough fibers installed to accommodate the traffic demand. The connections will be routed along the shortest path. This enables us to determine the number of line-systems that has to be installed on each link in the network, and the size of the OXCs. The routing and dimensioning of the network under permanent connection traffic is simple and straightforward, as there is only a single traffic matrix. In the ASON case with its switched connections, the situation is however somewhat more complex. In the methodology we applied, for each single traffic matrix [$M_{ij}^{S_k}$] at the beginning of time slot k, the optical backbone network is dimensioned. As the routing is a simple shortest path routing, connections that exist for more than a single time interval will follow the same route for their whole duration. The capacity that is actually needed on the links in the network to guarantee that all switched connection traffic demands can be accommodated is the maximum on each link of the capacity installed to support the traffic demand over all time slots, thus:

$$Cap_{link\,ij} = \underset{k}{Max}(Cap_{link\,ij}^{k}) \tag{3}$$

where $Cap_{link\,ij}$ is the capacity that is needed on link i-j to accommodate all traffic, over all time slots, and $Cap_{link\,ij}^{k}$ is the capacity needed on link i-j to accommodate the traffic offered to the network during time slot k.

It is easy to see with the simple example of Fig. 4 that ASONs enable the sharing of network resources and thus allow capacity and cost savings. This figure depicts a very simple network with two traffic demands: one between nodes A and B and another between nodes C and D. Both traffic demands are routed along the link E-F. In the case of ASON only one wavelength is needed on this link to support both traffic demands. In the OTN case two wavelengths are however needed. In the OTN approach the two wavelengths that are needed on link E-F will not carry actual travel during the complete time period considered. Both will be empty during a certain fraction of the time: during 11/20 of the considered time frame wavelength λ_1 will be empty and wavelength λ_2 will be empty during 9/20 of the time. This example clearly illustrates the fundamental difference between the traditional OTN approach with permanent connections and the ASON approach with switched connections. The OTN case makes use of statistical end-to-end multiplexing while the ASON case is based on statistical link-by-link multiplexing.

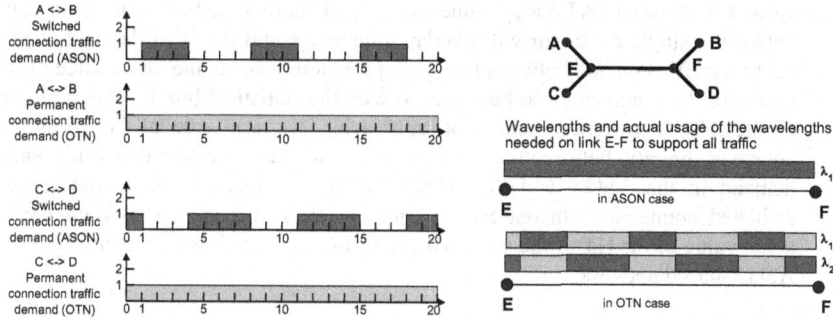

Fig. 4. Difference in statistical multiplexing between OTN and ASON

3 Case Studies

The above-explained methodology to dimension an OTN and an ASON, in order to compare their performance, has been applied to some case studies, discussed below.

3.1 Case Study 1

The results shown in this section are for a nord-Italian optical backbone network, with 16 OXCs connected by 36 links in a mesh topology. In this paper we will focus on the capacity requirements in the optical layer when the optical layer is an OTN or an ASON. With the introduction of a cost model for both cases, also the differences in cost could be studied, but this is a quite complicated task. The tarification and billing scheme for both network types will probably be different. One might assume that an operator would ask some kind of switched connection set-up fee, and then bill based on the duration of the switched connection. He would however want to make sure that a switched connection is not be more expensive than a permanent one, as clients would then have no reason to prefer a switched connection.

As said before, the traffic offered to switched networks like ASONs is characterized by its HT and IAT. Another parameter is the Maximum Capacity per Connection (MCC): the maximum number of wavelengths per connection. In Subsections 3.1.1 and 3.1.2, the MCC has been limited to 10 and the influence of the mean value of the HT and the IAT on the capacity needed in an ASON and an OTN is investigated.

3.1.1 Influence of the Holding Time

Fig. 5 shows the effect of a changing mean value of the HT on the ratio of the capacity needed to accommodate all traffic in the ASON case and that in the OTN case, when the mean value of the IAT remains constant (in the case of Fig. 5 the IAT is 5). In the left side of this figure we can see that as the mean value of the HT of the switched connections increases, the capacity that needs to be installed in the network increases, both for ASON and OTN. This was expected, as an increasing HT mean value for constant IAT mean value means that more switched connection demands between a single node pair will overlap on average and thus that the permanent connection traffic demand between that node pair increases. As the mean value of the HT increases, less gain can also be achieved with the statistical link-by-link multiplexing of the ASON switched connection approach. The right side of Fig. 5 shows the course of the ratio between the capacity needed to accommodate all traffic connection demand in the ASON and the OTN case. As the mean value of the HT of the switched connections increases, the capacity ratio also increases. With increasing mean value of the HT of the switched connections, it gets less interesting to deploy an ASON-based network.

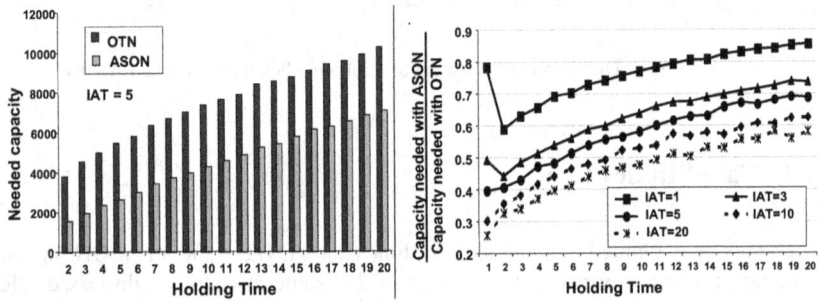

Fig. 5. Influence of the mean value of the HT on the capacity ratio between ASON and OTN

3.1.2 Influence of the Inter-Arrival Time

Fig. 5 already indicated that the capacity ratio between ASON and OTN decreases with increasing mean value of the IAT. This can also be observed in Fig. 6, which shows the required capacity in the OTN and the ASON case for a mean value of the HT of 5 and a increasing IAT (left side) and the influence of a changing mean value of the IAT on the capacity ratio (right side). As the mean value of the IAT increases for constant HT mean value, less switched connections overlap, and thus the permanent connection traffic demand will decrease. For a smaller mean value of the IAT, less gain can again be achieved with the statistical link-by-link multiplexing of ASONs.

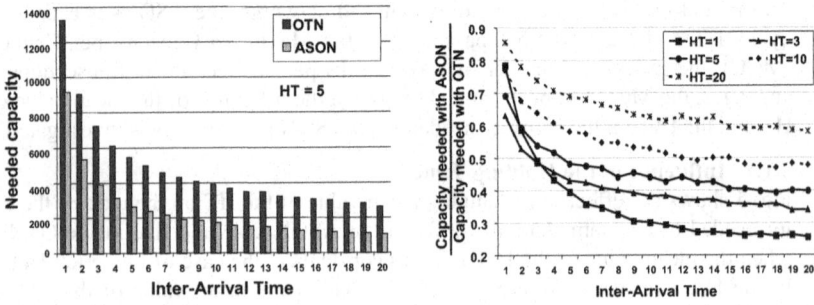

Fig. 6. Influence of the mean value of the IAT on the capacity ratio between ASON and OTN

The curves in Fig. 5 and Fig. 6 show however an, at first sight unexpected result for a mean value of the HT of 1 and a small IAT. The capacity ratio has a higher value than we would expect from the course of the lines in the graphs. This is however partially caused by the statistical model used in our simulations. If the mean value of the HT or IAT is 1, each connection will have a HT or IAT of exactly 1. This is a quite logical assumption, as a connection with a HT of 0 doesn't make much sense. At the beginning of a time slot, only a single new connection can be set up between a certain node pair, and this connection can only last for the duration of a single time slot. It is thus impossible to have a capacity requirement between two nodes higher than the MCC. In the OTN case, the maximal capacity required between two nodes is thus at most the MCC. The upper bound of the capacity that has to be installed on a link in an OTN can thus be obtained by multiplying the number of connections routed over that link with the MCC. At the same time, due to the low mean value of the IAT, many new connections will be requested and set up between a node pair in the switched case (ASON). This increases the chance that switched connections between various node pairs and with maximum capacity will overlap on a link in the ASON network. For low HT and low IAT, the capacity required in the ASON case will thus be quite high. The combination of these two effects, the quite low amount of required capacity in the OTN case and the relative high amount of capacity needed in the OTN case, causes the bending capacity ratio curve for small HT and small IAT.

At first sight, one might assume that for a HT and IAT of 1, the capacity ratio between ASON and OTN should be 1 (same amount of capacity is needed in both cases). This is however not the case and can easily be understood with an example similar to the one of Fig. 4. A single switched connection traffic demand can have a capacity between 1 and MCC. In Fig. 7, the MCC equals 2. The successive switched connections that are requested will thus have a capacity of 1 or 2 (see connection demand between nodes A and B and between nodes C and D in Fig. 7).

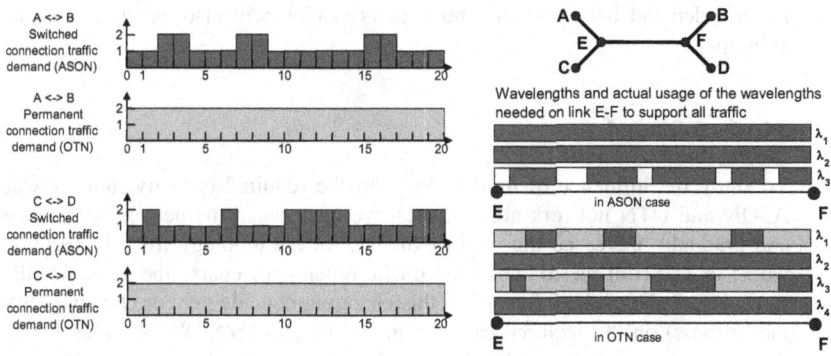

Fig. 7. Required capacity ratio between ASON and OTN when the HT and the IAT are 1

However, the chance that all switched connections that are routed along a certain link (E-F in the example) will have a capacity of equal to the MCC in the same time slot is less than 1. This chance decreases of course as more connections with a higher MCC are multiplexed on a single link. In Fig. 7, four wavelengths are needed on link E-F in the OTN case, but only three wavelengths have to be installed to support the switched connections of the ASON case. The required capacity ratio is here thus 0.75 (<1).

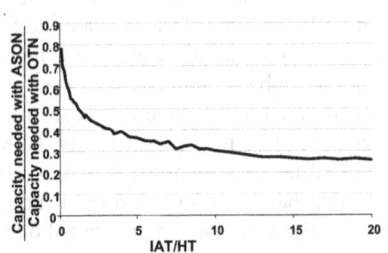

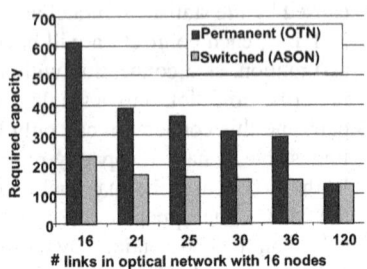

Fig. 8. Influence of the ratio IAT/HT on the required capacity ratio

Fig. 9. Influence of the node degree on the capacity ratio between ASON and OTN

Fig. 8 summarizes the required capacity ratio between ASON and OTN as a function of the ratio between the mean value of the IAT and the HT. It can be observed that the capacity ratio has its lowest value (most advantage with ASON compared to OTN) when the mean value of the IAT is much larger than that of the HT, or when the traffic offered to the network is quite low (what was of course expected). When the ratio IAT/HT equals 1, the required capacity ratio attains a value around 0.5. When the mean value of the HT and IAT are (almost) equal, small overlaps are possible between consecutive switched connection demands between a single node pair. This means that the upper bound of the permanent connection demand is twice the MCC. In the ASON case, however, due to the statistical link-by-link (instead of end-to-end) multiplexing these small overlaps will be easily handled by the switched connection demand between other node pairs (which will also experience such small overlaps).

3.2 Case Study 2

To study the influence of the topology on the required capacity ratio between the ASON and OTN network architectures, we have taken the network of Section 3.1, and gradually increased the number of links in the topology from 16 (original network) to 120 (full mesh). The total traffic remains of course the same for all situations. Fig. 9 shows the influence of this changing node degree (or changing degree of meshedness) on the required capacity in ASON and OTN. We see that in the OTN case, the required capacity decreases with increasing number of links. This could be expected, since we use a shortest path routing strategy. As the number of links in the network increases, the connections have to make, on average, a smaller detour from source to destination node than in the case of a sparser network. In the ASON case, the required capacity is less influenced by the number of links in the topology. It only decreases a bit for increasing number of links. The connections also make on average a smaller detour, but since with an increasing number of links in the network, the average number of connections routed per link also decreases, the gain of the link-by-link statistical multiplexing diminishes. The required capacity ratio between ASON and OTN increases thus with increasing number of links in the network topology (increasing degree of meshedness or node degree); in Fig. 9, from a ratio around 0.3 for 16 links to 1 for 120 links. For the case of a full mesh network, the required capacity with ASON and with OTN is of course the same. Since there is a direct link between each node pair, only the traffic between that node pair will be routed on this direct link. Both for ASON and OTN the capacity that needs to be installed on a link is thus the maximum over the connection traffic demand between the end nodes of the link.

4   Conclusions

From the presented study, it is clear that ASONs can be the answer to the ISP's wishes of flexible and cost-efficient solutions to transport the increasing amount of traffic. The capacity requirement that an ASON poses to the optical layer is lower than that of an OTN, as resources can be shared (statistical link-by-link multiplexing in ASONs versus end-to-end statistical multiplexing in OTNs). The exact capacity savings that can be achieved depend of course on (the ratio of) the mean value of IAT and HT of the switched connections offered to the ASON. The capacity saving decreases with increasing IAT and a constant mean value of the HT, and increases for a constant value of the IAT with increasing HT. Summarized, the lower the amount of offered traffic (small HT, large IAT) the larger the capacity-efficiency of an ASON compared to a traditional OTN. Also the topology of the network has an influence: the cost savings that can be obtained with ASON decrease with increasing average node degree, as the effect of the statistical link-by-link multiplexing diminishes.

References

1. Ramaswami, R.: Optical Fiber Communication: from transmission to networking. IEEE Com. Mag. 50th An. Comm. Issue (2002) 138-147.
2. ITU-T Rec. G.8080: Architecture for the automatic switched optical networks (ASON).
3. ITU-T Rec. G.807: Requirements for the Automatic Switched Transport Network (ASTN).
4. Proc. IST Lion/Optimist workshop on Intelligent High-Capacity Optical Networks. Oct. 2002, Turin, Italy.
5. Spadaro, S. et al.: Network Applications and Traffic Modelling for ASONs. Proc. ECOC (2002), Copenhagen, Denmark, Vol. 4, 10.2.3.
6. Hulsermann, R. et al.: Dynamic Routing algorithms in transparent optical Networks. Proc. ONDM (2003), Budapest, Hungary, 293-312.
7. Spaeth, J.: Dynamic routing and resource allocation in WDM transport networks", Comp. Netw. 5 (2000) 519-538.
8. Spadaro, S. et al.: Teletraffic Engineering Methods for ASONs. subm. to Opt. Netw. Mag.

Crosstalk Effects in Large Strictly Non-blocking Optical Switches Based on Directional Couplers

Luís Cancela and João Pires

[1] Dept. of Electrical and Computer Engineering and Instituto de Telecomunicações,
Instituto Superior Técnico, Portugal
lcancela@mail.telepac.pt, jpires@lx.it.pt

Abstract. Imperfect isolation of switching elements inside optical space switches gives rise to leakage signals that can result in homodyne crosstalk. One way to reduce the influence of this phenomenon is to guaranty that only one signal traverses a switching element at a time. Nevertheless, for large optical space switches, based on this concept, the homodyne crosstalk can still have some influence. An analysis of the impact of this phenomenon, in this kind of switches, is developed. The results are compared with the ones obtained in switches built with no crosstalk restrictions and show that there is a compromise between the switching element crosstalk and the network cost. The analysis uses a rigorous approach based on the Gaussian Quadrature Rules method and the switches considered in this paper belong to the family of strictly non-blocking Horizontal Expanded and Vertical Replicated Banyan network.

1 Introduction

Strictly non-blocking optical switches are one of the building blocks of Optical Cross-Connects (OXC), which are key devices in WDM (Wavelength Division Multiplexing) transport networks [1]. In these switches a connection can always be established between an idle input and an idle output regardless of the state of the switch. This behavior avoids the blocking states of blocking structures, or the need to tear down and rearrange connections in rearrangeable non-blocking structures, which are undesirable characteristics in the context of optical transport networks, due to the huge amount of information carried by these networks.

These switches can be implemented using space structures based on directional couplers acting as a 2x2 switching element and designed using Horizontal Expanded and Vertical Replicated (HEVR) Banyan networks [2]. These networks use two strategies to achieve the non-blocking condition. The first one is the vertical replication, in which a number of copies of a Banyan network is employed. The second one combines the vertical replication with horizontal expansion, in which the single planes to be replicated include more stages than in a basic Banyan network.

The crosstalk due to imperfect isolation of switching elements is a major limiting factor on the design of large HEVR Banyan optical switches. Homodyne crosstalk, appearing when the signal and the crosstalk have the same wavelength, is particularly damaging. One way to reduce this effect is to guaranty that only one signal crosses a switching element at a time [3]. In these switches the interfering signals are always of second order, so the impact of homodyne crosstalk is greatly reduced, when compared

M.M. Freire, P. Lorenz, M.M.-O. Lee (Eds.): HSNMC 2003, LNCS 2720, pp. 426-441, 2003.

with switches with no crosstalk restrictions. Nevertheless, the switches based on this concept continue to suffer from the influence of homodyne crosstalk, in particularly, when the dimension of the switch is large.

The main purpose of this paper is to compare the impact of homodyne crosstalk in a strictly non-blocking optical switch based on a HEVR Banyan network with and without crosstalk restrictions.

An accurate modeling of the impact of this kind of crosstalk on the system performance is required, as well as a detailed analysis of the scaling of component crosstalk with switch size. The evaluation of the impact of homodyne crosstalk on the performance of an optical signal routed by the switch uses a Gauss Quadrature Rules (GQR) method [4], since this technique allows the evaluation of the average bit error rate (BER) with any desired accuracy. This method is also compared with the saddle-point (SP) approximation, a methodology employed by some authors, [5,6], to deal with crosstalk problems. Also, in some situations, where the number of interfering terms is large the simplistic Gaussian approximation is used. The network cost, expressed in terms of the number of switching elements required by the switching matrix, is also considered in the analysis.

2 Horizontal Expanded and Vertical Replicated (HEVR) Banyan Networks

The Banyan network has been considered by some authors [7,8] for designing optical space switches based on directional couplers. This network, despite being a blocking network, offers the advantage of having a small number of couplers along any path between an input-output pair, thus reducing propagation losses and crosstalk. More exactly the Banyan network requires $\log_2 N$ stages (N is the number of inputs/outputs) with $N/2$ switching elements in each stage [2,7]. Another interesting feature comes from the fact that these networks can serve as a base for constructing many classes of switching networks [2], including strictly non-blocking networks.

As referred before, the strictly non-blocking HEVR Banyan network is derived from the basic Banyan network using two strategies. The first one is the vertical replication, in which a number of planes of a Banyan network (each plane can be viewed as a different copy of the network), known as the replication factor, is used. The second one, combines the vertical replication with horizontal expansion, in which the single planes to be replicated include more stages than in a basic Banyan network, allowing a smaller replication factor. The additional stages are added by means of the mirror imaging technique [2]. The maximum number of additional stages is $n-1$, where $n = \log_2 N$. In this situation a HEVR Banyan network is called a Cantor network, where each plane has 2^{n-1} possible paths for every connection, in contrast with the only one in the basic Banyan network.

In addition to the strictly non-blocking property the HEVR Banyan network can be also classified in terms of crosstalk restrictions [3]: 1) Type I switch – no crosstalk restrictions are imposed to the signal routed by the switch, *i.e.* two signals can traverse any switching element at the same time; 2) Type II switch – every switching element is used to route only one signal at a time.

Having in mind these two kinds of switches the replication factor K that guarantees a strictly non-blocking condition, with a number of additional stages m, is given by[3]

$$\text{Type I switch: } K \geq \begin{cases} \frac{3}{2}2^{\frac{n-m}{2}} + m - 1, & n+m \text{ even} \\ 2^{\frac{n-m+1}{2}} + m - 1, & n+m \text{ odd} \end{cases} \tag{1}$$

$$\text{Type II switch: } K \geq \begin{cases} 2^{\frac{n-m+2}{2}} + 2m - 1, & n+m \text{ even} \\ \frac{3}{2}2^{\frac{n-m+1}{2}} + 2m - 1, & n+m \text{ odd} \end{cases} \tag{2}$$

Table 1 shows the replication factor (calculated using (1) and (2)) in terms of the switch size N and the number of additional stages m. As expected, the replication factor decreases, when the number of stages increases and Type II switch is more demanding in terms of the replication factor for the same switch size.

Table 1. Replication factor and the number of additional stages for three switch sizes

m / N	1024		4096		16384	
	Type I	Type II	Type I	Type II	Type I	Type II
0	47	63	95	127	191	255
1	32	49	64	97	128	193
2	25	35	49	67	97	131
3	18	29	34	53	66	101
4	15	23	27	39	51	71
5	12	21	20	33	36	57
6	11	19	17	27	29	43
7	10	19	14	25	22	37
8	10	19	13	23	19	31
9	10	19	12	23	16	29
10	-	-	12	23	15	27
11	-	-	12	23	14	27
12	-	-	-	-	14	27
13	-	-	-	-	14	27

The number of switching elements required to built a switch is also an important characteristic, because is a measure of the cost of the network. For the network under consideration the number of switching elements is given by

$$C(n,m) = 2^{n+1} Y + (m+n)2^{n-1} K \tag{3}$$

where $Y = \sum_{i=0}^{\lceil \log_2 K \rceil - 1} 2^i$ is the number of switching elements in each splitter or combiner.

As an example, Figure 1 shows a 1024x1024 Type I switch, with $m = 0$ (there is no horizontal expansion). The first and the last stage of the network correspond to 1024 splitters 1x64 (only 47 outputs are used) and 1024 combiners 64x1 (only 47 inputs are used), respectively. Between these stages there are 47 copies (the replication factor is equal to 47 as concluded from Table 1) of the basic 1024x1024 Banyan network. Note that, for this network $Y = 63$ (there are 63 switching elements in each splitter or combiner), so that, the number of switching elements is equal to 369664.

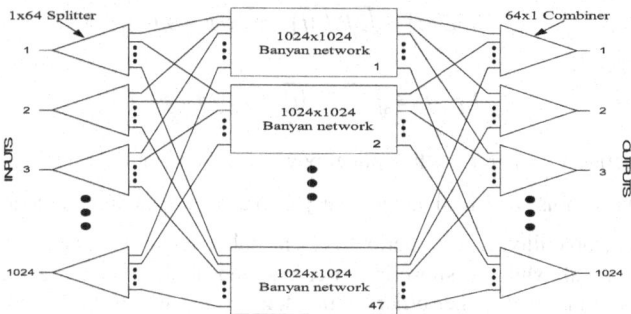

Fig. 1. 1024x1024 Type I switch with $m = 0$

3 Signal and Crosstalk Modeling

In order to model the signal and crosstalk propagation through the switch, it is assumed that each switching element is based on a 2x2 directional coupler, which is characterized by the crosstalk X_c. This crosstalk is due to undesirable coupling between the two waveguides of the coupler and gives rise to multiple leakage paths between any input and any output in a large optical switch. Assuming that the switching element crosstalk is small enough, so that only primary and secondary interfering electrical fields are relevant, the electrical field at the selected output for an NxN HEVR Banyan network can be given by

$$E(t) = \alpha E_s(t) + j\sqrt{X_c}\left(\sqrt{1-X_c}\right)^{M+2y-1}\sum_{k=1}^{M} E_{k,1}(t) + \tag{4}$$

$$\left(j\sqrt{X_c}\right)^2\left(\sqrt{1-X_c}\right)^{M+2y-2}\sum_{k=1}^{\binom{M}{2}+y} E_{k,2}(t)$$

with $\alpha = \left(\sqrt{1-X_c}\right)^{M+2y}$ (where $M = n+m$ and $y = \lceil \log_2 K \rceil$ is the number of stages in each splitter / combiner), $E_s(t)$ the electrical field entering the switch at the selected input corresponding to the desired signal, $E_{k,1}(t)$ and $E_{k,2}(t)$ the primary and secondary interfering electrical fields, respectively, arising from the N inputs of the switch. For the case of the 1024x1024 Type I switch with $m = 0$ (Figure 1) there are 10 primary interfering fields, which is equal to the number of stages of a 1024x1024 Banyan network and 51 secondary interfering fields. Equation (4) assumes that all the switch inputs are on and the polarisation for the signal and crosstalk terms is identical (*i.e.* worst case situation).

Using external modulation and assuming that the signals at all the switch inputs have the same wavelength, the electrical fields, $E_s(t)$ and $E_{k,x}(t)$ (with $x = 1,2$), can be given by

$$E_s(t) = \sqrt{2Pd_s(t)} \exp[j(\omega t + \phi_s(t))] \tag{5}$$

$$E_{k,x}(t) = \sqrt{2Pd_{k,x}(t)} \exp[j(\omega t + \phi_{k,x}(t))] \tag{6}$$

respectively, where P is the optical power, ω is the optical frequency, $\phi(t)$ is the laser phase noise and $d(t)$ is the binary data sequence taking on values of 1 and 0, with equal probability, in a bit period T_b. The subscript s, in (5) and (6), states for the desired signal, while the subscript k,x corresponds to the interfering terms.

Assuming that higher order beating terms (*i.e.* superior to second order) can be neglected, the current originated from the photodetection of the lightwave given by (4) can be approximated as

$$i(t) \approx I_s \alpha^2 \left[d_s(t) + 2\sqrt{d_s(t)} \varepsilon \sum_{k=1}^{M} \sin(\Delta\phi_{s,(k,1)}(t)) \sqrt{d_{k,1}(t)} - \right. \tag{7}$$

$$2\sqrt{d_s(t)} \varepsilon^2 \sum_{k=1}^{\binom{M}{2}+y} \cos(\Delta\phi_{s,(k,2)}(t)) \sqrt{d_{k,2}(t)} + \varepsilon^2 \sum_{k=1}^{M} d_{k,1}(t) -$$

$$\left. 2\varepsilon^2 \sum_{k=1}^{M-1} \sum_{n=k+1}^{M} \cos(\Delta\phi_{(n,1),(k,1)}(t)) \sqrt{d_{n,1}(t)d_{k,1}(t)} \right]$$

where

$$\varepsilon = \sqrt{X_c/(1-X_c)} \ . \tag{8}$$

In (7) $I_s = R_\lambda P$ is the average photocurrent with R_λ the photodiode responsivity, and $\Delta\phi$ is the laser phase noise difference between the different signals that are photodetected by the receiver. Since the different signals come from independent laser sources, $\Delta\phi$ can be treated as a uniformly distributed random process [9]. The first term inside the brackets, in (7), is the selected data signal, the second term is the primary data-crosstalk beating terms, the third term is the secondary data-crosstalk beating terms, the fourth term is the intensity crosstalk and finally the fifth term is the secondary crosstalk-crosstalk beating terms.

The photocurrent described by (7) is filtered by a baseband filter with impulse response $h_R(t)$, that is assumed to provide a 100% raised cosine equalization [10]. The decision variable after sampling the filtered signal at instant t_0 is given by

$$V = i(t_0) * h_R(t_0) + N_{th} = Z + N_{th} \ . \tag{9}$$

In (9) the asterisk denotes convolution, Z is a random variable that includes the influence of signal-crosstalk and crosstalk-crosstalk beat noise, and N_{th} is a filtered version of the receiver circuit noise. Here, it is assumed that the shot noise due to the signal can be neglected and the random variable N_{th} is Gaussian with zero mean and variance σ_{th}^2.

Assuming that $d(t)$ is modeled as a rectangular pulse, as well as a perfect extinction ratio, the random variable Z, when $d_s = 1$, can be written, using (7) and (9), as

$$Z_1 \approx A_S \left[1 + 2\varepsilon \sum_{k=1}^{q_1} \sin\left(\Delta\phi_{s,(k,1)}(t_0)\right) - 2\varepsilon^2 \sum_{k=1}^{q_2} \cos\left(\Delta\phi_{s,(k,2)}(t_0)\right) \right. \tag{10}$$
$$\left. + \varepsilon^2 q_1 - 2\varepsilon^2 \sum_{k=1}^{q_1-1} \sum_{n=k+1}^{q_1} \cos\left(\Delta\phi_{(n,1),(k,1)}(t_0)\right) \right] * h_R(t_0)$$

with q_1 and q_2 the number of primary and secondary interfering terms in the logical state one, respectively, and $A_s = \alpha^2 I_s$. When $d_s = 0$, Z can be written as,

$$Z_0 \approx A_S \left[\varepsilon^2 q_1 - 2\varepsilon^2 \sum_{k=1}^{q_1-1} \sum_{n=k+1}^{q_1} \cos\left(\Delta\phi_{(n,1),(k,1)}(t_0)\right) \right] * h_R(t_0) \ . \tag{11}$$

Having in mind the two types of switches described in section 2, some useful considerations must be done in order to simplify the analysis of homodyne crosstalk.

3.1 Crosstalk in Type I Switch

In Type I switch the selected signal is contaminated with all the noise terms presented in (7). However, the noise resulting from secondary beating terms, which includes the intensity crosstalk, is generally very small in comparison with the noise originated from primary data-crosstalk beating terms, so only these ones are considered. In this way, (7) can be further simplified reducing to,

$$i(t) \approx I_s \alpha^2 \left[d_s(t) + 2\sqrt{d_s(t)} \varepsilon \sum_{k=1}^{M} \sin\left(\Delta\phi_{s,(k,1)}(t)\right) \sqrt{d_k(t)} \right] \ . \tag{12}$$

In this situation, when $d_s = 1$ Z can be written as

$$Z_1 \approx A_S \left[1 + 2\varepsilon \int_0^{T_b} \sum_{k=1}^{q_1} \sin\left(\Delta\phi_{s,(k,1)}(\tau)\right) h_R(t_0 - \tau) d\tau \right] \ . \tag{13}$$

On the other hand, when $d_s = 0$, that variable reduces to $Z_0 = 0$.

3.2 Crosstalk in Type II Switch

As in Type II switch every switching element is only capable of routing one signal at a time, (7) can be simplified,

$$i(t) \approx I_s \alpha^2 \left[d_s(t) - 2\sqrt{d_s(t)} \varepsilon^2 \sum_{k=1}^{\left(\frac{M}{2}\right)+y} \cos\left(\Delta\phi_{s,(k,2)}(t)\right)\sqrt{d_{k,2}(t)} \right] . \qquad (14)$$

In this situation, when $d_s = 1$ Z can be written as

$$Z_1 \approx A_S \left[1 - 2\varepsilon^2 \int_0^{T_b} \sum_{k=1}^{q_2} \cos\left(\Delta\phi_{s,(k,2)}(\tau)\right) h_R(t_0 - \tau) d\tau \right] . \qquad (15)$$

On the other hand, when $d_s = 0$, that variable reduces to $Z_0 = 0$.

4 BER Evaluation Methods

A common procedure to evaluate the impact of crosstalk on transmission performance comprises the BER calculation by using the probability density function (PDF) of the decision variable. In the present case this procedure involves a number of difficulties. Actually, as can be concluded from (13) and (15) the random variable Z_1 depends on the beat noise components, that have a sinusoidal dependence on the uniformly distributed random process $\Delta\phi_{s,(k,x)}(t)$ (with $x = 1,2$), on the number of interfering terms that are on the logical state one, as well as on the baseband filtering effects. These problems make very difficult to calculate the PDF of Z_1 and as a consequence the PDF of the decision variable V.

An alternative methodology can be applied to describe the statistics of the decision variable. This methodology involves the use of the moment generating function (MGF).

In order to simplify the calculation of the MGF of the random variable Z_1 it is assumed that the baseband filter bandwidth is wider than the signal-crosstalk and crosstalk-crosstalk beat noise spectrum [9]. Under these assumptions that variable can be written as

$$Z_1 = A_S\left(1 + W_1\right) \qquad (16)$$

$$
\text{where} \quad W_1 = \begin{cases} 2\varepsilon \sum_{k=1}^{q_1} \sin\left[\Delta\phi_{s,(k,1)}(t_0)\right], \text{ for Type I switch} \\ -2\varepsilon^2 \sum_{k=1}^{q_2} \cos\left[\Delta\phi_{s,(k,2)}(t_0)\right], \text{ for Type II switch.} \end{cases} \tag{17}
$$

The variable W_1 is a result of a sum of statistically independent random variables. Therefore, its moment generating function, denoted by $M_{W_1}(s)$, is given by

$$
M_{W_1}(s) = \begin{cases} I_0\left(s2\varepsilon\right)^{q_1}, \text{ for Type I switch} \\ I_0\left(s2\varepsilon^2\right)^{q_2}, \text{ for Type II switch} \end{cases} \tag{18}
$$

where $I_0(.)$ represents the modified Bessel function of the first kind of order zero. By using (16) and (18) it can be shown that the MGF of Z_1 is given by

$$
M_{Z_1}(s) = \begin{cases} \exp(sA_s)I_0\left(s2\varepsilon A_s\right)^{q_1}, \text{ for Type I switch} \\ \exp(sA_s)I_0\left(s2\varepsilon^2 A_s\right)^{q_2}, \text{ for Type II switch.} \end{cases} \tag{19}
$$

The knowledge of the MGF of Z_1 is the starting point to calculate the BER using both the GQR method and the SP approximation, as will be shown in sections 4.1 and 4.2. In section 4.3 the Gaussian approximation is also explained.

4.1 Gauss Quadrature Rules Method

As seen before, the decision variable V depends on the random variables Z_1 and N_{th}. In this way, the average BER can be obtained by averaging the conditional BER for the number of interfering terms in the logical state one over all possible values of Z_1 giving

$$
\text{BER} = \begin{cases} \left(\dfrac{1}{2}\right)^{M+1} \sum_{q_1=0}^{M} \binom{M}{q_1} I_1 + \dfrac{1}{4}\,\text{erfc}\left[\dfrac{D}{\sqrt{2}\sigma_{th}}\right], \\ \qquad\qquad \text{for Type I switch} \\ \left(\dfrac{1}{2}\right)^{\left(\frac{M}{2}\right)+y+1} \sum_{q_2=0}^{\left(\frac{M}{2}\right)+y} \binom{\left(\frac{M}{2}\right)+y}{q_2} I_1 + \dfrac{1}{4}\,\text{erfc}\left[\dfrac{D}{\sqrt{2}\sigma_{th}}\right], \\ \qquad\qquad \text{for Type II switch} \end{cases} \tag{20}
$$

where
$$\mathrm{I}_1 = \left(\frac{1}{2}\right) \int_{-\infty}^{+\infty} \mathrm{erfc}\left[\frac{Z_1 - D}{\sqrt{2}\sigma_{th}}\right] p(Z_1) dZ_1 \tag{21}$$

In the above equations, I_1 denotes the conditional BER when the data signal is in the logical state one, $\mathrm{erfc}(x)$ is the complementary error function, $p(Z_1)$ is the PDF of Z_1, and D is the decision threshold level. The evaluation of (21) requires the numerical computation of an integral that depends on the PDF of Z_1, which is not known explicitly. To overcome such difficulty one can apply the GQR method [4]. This method is based on the calculation of the first $2N_Q + 1$ (N_Q is the number of terms used in the GQR method) moments of Z_1, and permits to write (21) in the following form [4]:

$$\mathrm{I}_1 \approx \left(\frac{1}{2}\right) \sum_{j=1}^{N_Q} w_{jq} \mathrm{erfc}\left[\frac{x_{jq} - D}{\sqrt{2}\sigma_{th}}\right] \tag{22}$$

where w_{jq} and x_{jq} are the weights and abscissas, respectively, of the integration method. It should be noted that the integral in (21) can be evaluated with any desired accuracy by using an appropriate number of moments. The $2N_Q + 1$ moments of Z_1 can be obtained using the following relation [4]:

$$< Z_1^p >= \frac{d^p M_{Z_1}(s)}{ds^p}\bigg|_{s=0} \tag{23}$$

where $< Z_1^p >$ represents the moment of order p of Z_1. However, when a large number of moments is required it is more practical to use a recursive procedure in alternative to (23) to evaluate the moments. This procedure is based on the knowledge of the cumulants of Z_1, and is described in References 11 and 12.

4.2 Saddlepoint Approximation

The saddlepoint approximation, which gives an approximated value for the BER, has been used by different authors to analyze the impact of crosstalk on optical networks [5,6].

To apply this method it is required the MGF of the random variable V. However, this MGF depends on the number of interfering terms in the logical state one, assumed as binomially distributed. In this way, a mean value for the MGF is required, which can be obtained by a statistically weighted average of the MGF for each value of q_1 or q_2. For $d_s = 1$ this value is given by

$$\left\{\begin{array}{l} \left(\dfrac{1}{2}\right)^M \displaystyle\sum_{q_1=0}^{M} \binom{M}{q_1} M_{Z_1}(s_1) M_{th}(s_1), \\[2mm] \text{for Type I switch} \\[2mm] \left(\dfrac{1}{2}\right)^{\binom{M}{2}+y} \displaystyle\sum_{q_2=0}^{\binom{M}{2}+y} \binom{\binom{M}{2}+y}{q_2} M_{Z_1}(s_1) M_{th}(s_1), \\[2mm] \text{for Type II switch} \end{array}\right.$$

(24)

$$M_{V_1}(s_1) =$$

where $M_{Z_1}(s_1)$ is given by (19) and $M_{th}(s_1)$ is the MGF of the random variable N_{th} [10]. For $d_s = 0$, the MGF of V reduces to $M_{V0}(s_0) = M_{th}(s_0)$, since it is assumed a perfect extinction ratio.

So, considering the SP approximation, the average BER can be written as [5]

$$\text{BER} \approx \frac{1}{2\sqrt{2\pi}} \left[\frac{\exp[\Phi_0(s_0)]}{\sqrt{\Phi_0''(s_0)}} + \frac{\exp[\Phi_1(s_1)]}{\sqrt{\Phi_1''(s_1)}} \right] \tag{25}$$

where $\Phi_i(s_i) = \ln[M_{V_i}(s_i)] - s_i D - \ln|s_i|$ and $\Phi_i''(s_i)$ is the second derivative of $\Phi_i(s_i)$, with $i = 0,1$. The computation of the parameters s_0 and s_1 follows from

$$\begin{array}{ll} \Phi_0'(s_0) = 0, & \text{with } s_0 > 0 \\ \Phi_1'(s_1) = 0, & \text{with } s_1 < 0. \end{array} \tag{26}$$

4.3 Gaussian Approximation

The Gaussian approximation due to its simplicity has been used extensively in crosstalk studies. Using this approximation Z_1 can be treated as Gaussian and (21) reduces to

$$I_1 \approx \frac{1}{2} \text{erfc} \left[\frac{A_S - D}{\sqrt{2(\sigma_{s,x}^2 + \sigma_{th}^2)}} \right] \tag{27}$$

where $\sigma_{s,x}^2$ denotes the beat noise power. In the case of homodyne crosstalk this noise power can be easily evaluated and is given by

$$\sigma_{s,x}^2 = \left\{\begin{array}{l} \left(A_s \alpha^2 2\varepsilon\right)^2 \dfrac{1}{2} q_1, \text{ for Type I switch} \\[2mm] \left(A_s \alpha^2 2\varepsilon^2\right)^2 \dfrac{1}{2} q_2, \text{ for Type II switch.} \end{array}\right. \tag{28}$$

5 Results and Discussion

The described methods can be applied to evaluate the impact of homodyne crosstalk on the performance of an optical signal routed through an optical space switch based on a strictly non-blocking HEVR Banyan network built with directional couplers. Since in Type II switch the number of interfering terms is large, *e.g.* for a 1024x1024 switch there are 51 interfering terms, the Gaussian approximation is used, in conformity with the Central limit Theorem (CLT), to evaluate the impact of homodyne crosstalk. For Type I switch the GQR method and the SP approximation are used, since the number of interfering terms is not enough to apply the CLT, *e.g.* for a 1024x1024 switch there are 10 interfering terms.

It is assumed that all the optical signals present at the input of the switch have a bit rate of 2.5 Gbit/s, and the GQR method uses $N_Q = 14$ to ensure an appropriate accuracy [4]. Furthermore, it is considered a fixed decision threshold set at midway between the "one" and "zero". The impact of homodyne crosstalk is evaluated in terms of the power penalty, which is computed by taking the ratio of the required optical power to achieve a BER of 10^{-9} with a crosstalk level of X_c, to that optical power to achieve the same BER with zero crosstalk.

Figure 2 shows the dependency of the power penalty on the switching element crosstalk for different switch sizes, for Type I and Type II switches. The switches considered have no horizontal expansion, which corresponds to the case where the number of switching elements along a path of a connection is minimal and so, the crosstalk impact is smaller.

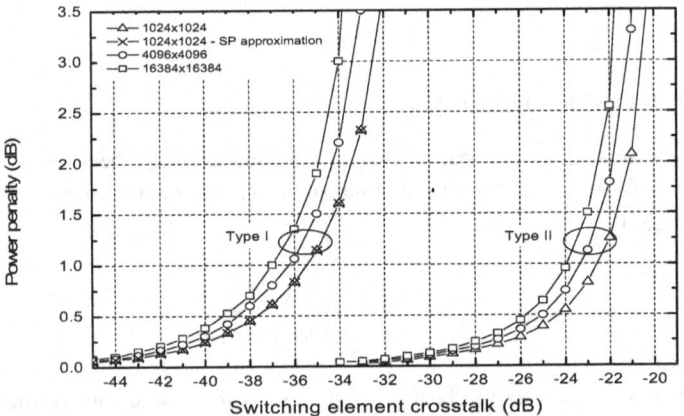

Fig. 2. Power penalty versus switching element crosstalk for different switch sizes, for Type I and II switches, with no horizontal expansion

As can be observed in Figure 2 the results obtained with the GQR method and the SP approximation are very close, so that, for clarity, the curves obtained with the SP approximation are not further included in subsequent figures. The results also show that a 1024x1024 Type I switch is feasible providing that the switching element crosstalk is kept below -35.5 dB, assuming a 1 dB power penalty. For the Type II switch the switching element crosstalk can be relaxed to -22.5 dB for the same power penalty.

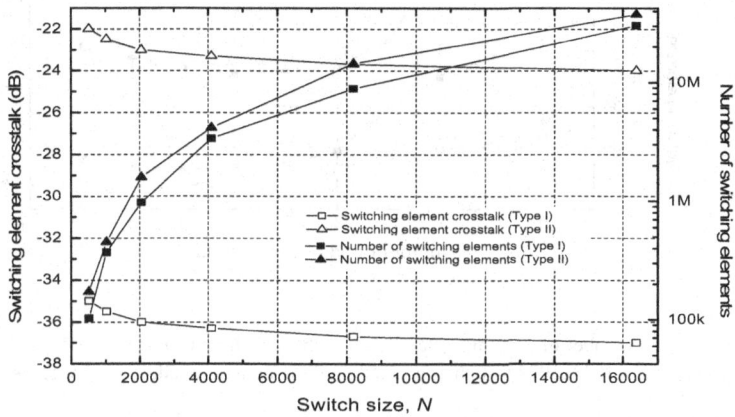

Fig. 3. The number of switching elements and the switching element crosstalk (@ 1 dB power penalty) for different switch sizes with no horizontal expansion

Figure 3 shows that there is a compromise between the switching element crosstalk that allows a 1 dB power penalty and the network cost (or the number of switching elements) for both types of switches, with no horizontal expansion. In particular, it can be observed that for a 4096x4096 Type I switch the required switching element crosstalk is -36.3 dB and the number of switching elements needed is 3375104. However, if Type II switch is used instead, the switching element crosstalk can be as high as -23.3 dB, and the number of switching elements increases to 4161536 (a 23% raise).

Figures 4 and 5 show the compromise between the switching element crosstalk (@ 1 dB power penalty) and the number of switching elements, as a function of the additional stages m, for both types of switches.

In particular, Figure 4 shows this compromise for a 1024x1024 switch. It can be observed from Table 1 that when this switch has one additional stage the minimum replication factor that guarantees a strictly non-blocking condition is 32 for Type I switch, which leads to approximately 243712 switching elements. In this situation a switching element crosstalk of -35.9 dB can be used in order to allow a 1 dB power penalty. The same situation for a Type II switch implies a replication factor of 49, which leads to 404992 switching elements and a switching element crosstalk of -23 dB. In Figure 4 it can be also noticed that the number of switching elements have a minimum for 6 and 7 additional stages for Type II and Type I switches, respectively.

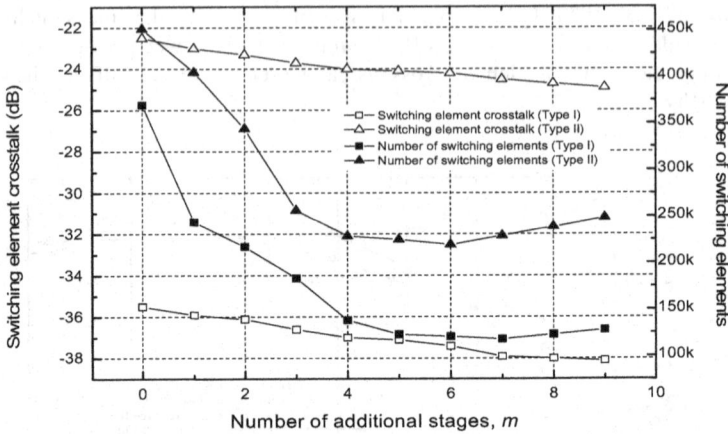

Fig. 4. The number of switching elements and the switching element crosstalk (@ 1 dB power penalty) for a 1024x1024 switch as a function of the number of additional stages m

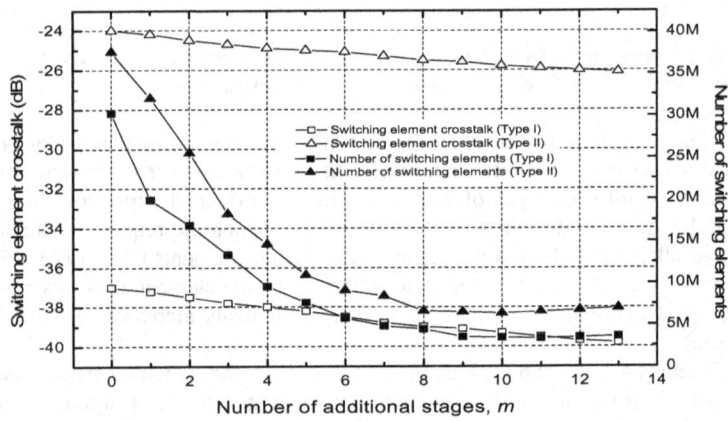

Fig. 5. Same as Figure 4 for a 16384x16384 switch

In the same way, Figure 5 shows that a 16384x16384 Type I switch with 13 additional stages needs 3588096 switching elements and a switching element crosstalk of -39.8 dB (@ 1 dB power penalty). However, if no horizontal expansion is used, the number of switching elements increases to 30261248 and the switching element crosstalk needed is -37 dB.

Figures 6 and 7 show the power penalty as a function of the switching element crosstalk with the number of additional stages m as a parameter, for two switch sizes.

From these figures it can be concluded that, for a particular switching element crosstalk, as the number of additional stages decreases the power penalty also decreases. This behavior can be explained by noticing that less stages in the path of a connection leads to less interfering terms, which will reduce the influence of homodyne crosstalk.

As can be seen, in Figure 6, for a 1024x1024 Type I switch with no horizontal expansion, the switching element crosstalk must be less than -35.5 dB in order to get a power penalty of 1 dB. When the number of additional stages increases to seven, the switching element crosstalk must be less than -38 dB for the same power penalty. For a 1024x1024 Type II switch the switching element crosstalk can as high as -22.5 dB for $m = 0$.

For a 16384x16384 Type I switch (see Figure 7) the switching element crosstalk must be less than -37 dB when no extra stages are used for a 1 dB power penalty. This is the most costly situation (requires a replication factor of 191), but the one for which the switching element crosstalk requirements are less restrictive. The cheapest structure corresponds to a network with 11 additional stages. As the counterpart, the required crosstalk becomes 2.5 dB lower than in the case with no extra stages. For a Type II switch with $m = 0$ and $m = 11$, the switching element crosstalk needed for a 1 dB power penalty is -24 dB and -26 dB, respectively.

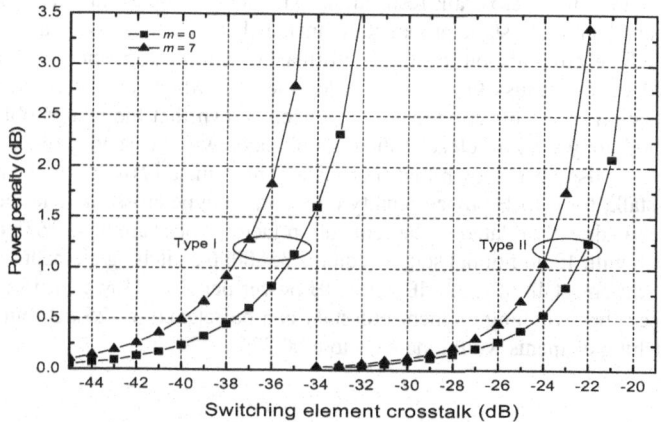

Fig. 6. Power penalty versus switching element crosstalk for a 1024x1024 switch, for both types of switches, as a function of the number of additional stages m

6 Conclusions

This paper has analyzed the limitations imposed by homodyne crosstalk on the design of optical space switches based on a strictly non-blocking HEVR Banyan network

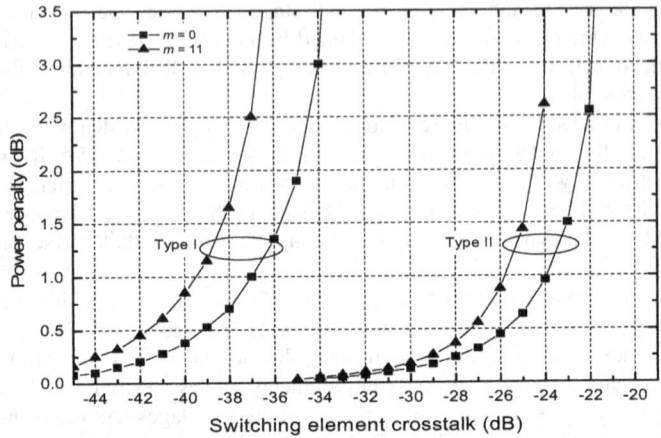

Fig. 7. Same as Figure 6 for a 16384x16384 switch

with and without crosstalk restrictions. The analysis takes into account the modeling of signal and crosstalk propagation inside the switch, as well as the influence of homodyne crosstalk on system performance. The performance evaluation has been based on the Gauss Quadrature Rules method, which allows an accurate and fast evaluation of the bit error rate. It has been shown that the results obtained with this methodology are very close to the ones obtained with the saddlepoint approximation.

It has also been shown that there is a compromise between the switching element crosstalk, for a 1 dB power penalty due to homodyne crosstalk, and the network cost, which is directly related to the replication factor. For example, a 16384x16384 Type I switch with 13 additional stages requires 3588096 switching elements and a switching element crosstalk of -39.8 dB (@ 1 dB power penalty). However, if a Type II switch is used the switching element crosstalk can be relaxed to -25 dB, but the number of switching elements would increase to 6987776.

References

1. O´Mahony, M., Simeonidou, D., Yu, A., Zhou, J.: The Design of a European Optical Network. J. Lightwave Technol. Vol. 13 nº5 (1995) 817-828
2. Pattavina, A.: Switching Theory. Wiley (1998)
3. Vaez, M., Lea, C.: Strictly Nonblocking Directional-Coupler-Based Switching Networks Under Crosstalk Constraint. IEEE Trans. Comm. Vol. 48 nº2 (2000) 316-323
4. O´Reilly, J., da Rocha, J. R. F.: Improved Error Probability Evaluation Methods for Direct Detection Optical Communications Systems. IEEE Trans. Information Theory. Vol. IT-33 nº6 (1987) 839-848
5. Monroy, I. T., Tangdiongga, E.: Performance Evaluation of Optical Cross-Connects by Saddlepoint Approximation. J. Lightwave Technol. Vol. 16 nº3 (1998) 317-323

6. Iannone, E., Sabella, R., Avattaneo, M., de Paolis, G.: Modeling of In-Band Crosstalk in WDM Optical Networks. J. Lightwave Technol. Vol. 17 n°7 (1999) 1135-1141
7. Okayama, H., Okabe, Y., Kamijoh, T., Sakamoto, N.: Optical Switch Array Using Banyan Network. IEICE Trans. Commun. Vol. E82-B n°2 (1999) 365-372
8. Murphy, E. *et al.*: 16x16 Strictly Non-blocking Guided-Wave Optical Switching System. J. Lightwave Technol. Vol. 14 n°3 (1996) 352-358
9. Gimlett, J., Cheung, N.: Effects of Phase-to-Intensity Noise Conversion by Multiple Reflections on Gigabit-per-Second DFB Laser Transmission Systems. J. Lightwave Technol. Vol. 7 n°6 (1989) 888-895
10. Einarsson, G.: Principles of Lightwave Communications. Wiley (1996)
11. Calvez, L., Genin, R.: Recursive Methods for Numerical Computation of the Coefficients of a Generalization of the Gram-Charlier Series. Proceedings of the IEEE. (1976) 1254-1255
12. Cramèr, H.: Mathematical Methods of Statistics. Princeton Univ. Press. New York (1946)

Multiplexers and Demultiplexers Based on Fibre Bragg Gratings and Optical Circulators for DWDM Systems

Rosa Romero[2,1], Orlando Frazão[1], Filip Floreani[4], Lin Zhang[4], Paulo V.S. Marques[3,1], and Henrique M. Salgado[3,1]

[1] INESC Porto - UOSE, Unidade de Optoelectrónica e Sistemas Electrónicos,
4169-007 Porto, Portugal
{rromero,ofrazao}@inescporto.pt, psmarque@fc.up.pt, h.salgado@ieee.org
[2] FEUP - DEEC, Faculdade de Engenharia da Universidade do Porto
4200-465 Porto, Portugal
[3] FCUP - Dep. de Física, Faculdade de Ciências da Universidade do Porto
4169-007 Porto, Portugal
[4] Photonics Research Group - Aston University,
Birmingham B4 7ET, U. K.
{floreanf,l.zhang}@aston.ac.uk

Abstract. Two different architectures of multiplexers/demultiplexers based on 4×1 and 1×4 configurations are discussed. These architectures are implemented using apodized fibre Bragg gratings as optical filters and optical circulators. The spectral characteristics of the devices for channel separations of 100 GHz and 50 GHz are analysed and their performance is evaluated. Optical switch and cross-connect configurations are also demonstrated.

1 Introduction

A multiplexer (MUX) is an optical filter that combines signals at different wavelengths arriving at its input ports into a single signal leaving the output port; a demultiplexer (DEMUX) performs the opposite function. These kinds of passive components are used in wavelength division multiplexing (WDM) networks to achieve more complex functions such as wavelength add/drop multiplexing and switching of optical signals. Moreover, MUX/DEMUX may be cascaded to realize wavelength selective optical cross-connects. Several MUX/DEMUX devices in fibres have already been presented in the literature, for instance, a four-port fibre-optic ring resonator using an optical fibre coupler [1], a non-linear optical loop mirror [2], a fused fibre splitter followed by strong fibre grating pass-band filters [3] and a combination of optical circulators and WDM couplers [4]. These references are examples of different configurations and passive components used until the present days. In this paper two configurations for MUX/DEMUX are presented. They use a combination of apodized fibre Bragg Gratings (AFBG) and optical circulators (OC). The use of AFBGs reduces the insertion losses, in

M.M. Freire, P. Lorenz, M.M.-O. Lee (Eds.): HSNMC 2003, LNCS 2720, pp. 442–451, 2003.

comparison with uniform fibre Bragg Gratings (FBG), and increases the number of channels for multiplexing and demultiplexing. These configurations are studied and their spectral characteristics compared. The application of these devices to achieve more complex network functions such as optical switching and optical cross-connects (OXC) are also discussed.

2   FBG Filters Fabrication

Optical filters for DWDM systems should have specific spectral characteristics in order to guarantee that all the information is completely transmitted to the receiver without interferences. The filters in this paper are based on AFBGs, because for an optimum operation they should have a narrow bandwidth without lateral sidelobes. There are several techniques to fabricate AFBGs: a phase mask with variable diffraction efficiency [5], automatic pure apodization [6], using electric arc discharges [7], UV-pulse interferometry [8] or, using uniform phase-masks, stretching the fibre during inscription [9], a recently developed polarization control method [10], uniformly moving the phase-mask while scanning with the beam along the fibre [11] and the predominant dithering phase-mask technique [12]. All AFBGs used in this paper were fabricated using the dithering phase-mask technique. Exposure to ultra-violet light was achieved through a frequency doubled laser argon-ion CW at 244 nm. The set-up for AFBGs fabrication is shown in Fig. 1. The spectral response of the apodized and non-apodized

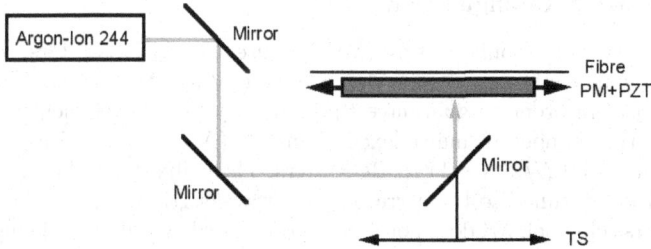

Fig. 1. Fabrication set-up for dithering phase-mask apodization technique.

fibre Bragg gratings is shown in Fig. 2. The non-apodized grating was written using a uniform diffractive phase mask illuminated with a KrF laser operating at 248 nm. The AFBG exhibits a suppression of the sidelobes of about 10 dB in comparison with the non-apodized FBG. This characteristic is very important to reduce the crosstalk between channels and achieve the required low bit-error rate, the principal property for good bit rate reception. Because of the length of the AFBG (35 mm) in comparison with 10 mm for the non-apodized FBG, the FWHM is smaller, 0.14 nm for the AFBG, in comparison with 0.20 nm for the FBG, which allows a system to increase the number of channels for data transmission.

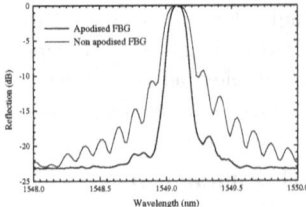

Fig. 2. Comparison between apodized and non-apodized FBG.

3 MUX/DEMUX DEVICES

Several configurations for multiplexing and demultiplexing have been presented in the literature. Here two different configurations are going to be presented using AFBGs filters and OCs. Insertion loss is compared between both architectures. The possibility of obtaining more complex structures relevant in WDM networks, such as cross-connects is also discussed. Both MUX and DEMUX operation is demonstrated with 4 input channels but they can be increased to a large number of channels (N), albeit at the expense of increasing the number of AFBGs and OCs.

3.1 MUX Configurations

The first MUX configuration (MUX I) uses six AFBGs filters, and three OCs for the multiplexing of four channels (Fig. 3-a). All AFBGs filters should be identical in order to guarantee the necessary filtering efficiency of channels. If N is the number of multiplexed channels, $(N-1)$ optical circulators will be required and $N/2(N-1)$ AFBGs filters. The suffix N (in AFBGN) means that the FBG is tuned to the corresponding wavelength λ_N. It can be observed that the first channel, λ_1, does not need an optical AFBG filter for being multiplexed. However the multiplexing of channel four, λ_4, (in general the last channel) needs an optical AFBG filter, tuned at λ_4, at each input port for being redirected to the output port. The other MUX configuration (MUX II) is shown in Fig. 3-b. It can be seen that a smaller number of AFBGs is needed while the number of OCs is the same. For N channels, the number of optical circulators and AFBGs filters are in this case $(N-1)$. Also the AFBG has fewer restrictions than in MUX I, which makes this architecture easier to fabricate.

In this MUX II each wavelength channel needs only an optical AFBG filter to be redirected to the output port. Moreover, the last channel, λ_4, is automatically redirected to the output port without requiring an additional AFBG. Experiments were carried out to obtain the spectral response of the devices at 100 GHz and 50 GHz channel separation. Fig. 4 and Fig. 5 show the output response for 100 GHz and 50 GHz, respectively, when a broadband optical source is applied to this combination of optical filters.

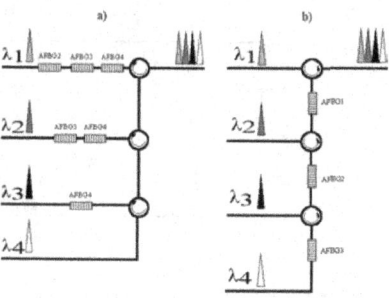

Fig. 3. a) MUX I and b) MUX II configurations.

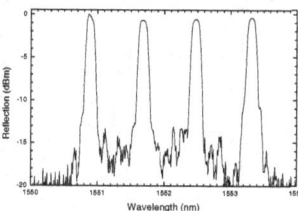

Fig. 4. Output of MUXs at 100 GHz.

It can be observed that sufficient channel discrimination is obtained at 50 GHz: the cross-talk isolation level is 14 dBm in comparison with 16 dBm for the 100 GHz case. This is a result of the apodization profile of the FBG.

3.2 DEMUX Configurations

Demultiplexers are more difficult to fabricate than multiplexers, because of the requirements in channel separation to reduce crosstalk. They must have better optical filtering properties than MUXs, in order to ensure good accuracy at the output, and avoid the mixing of information from two different channels. The architecture of demultiplexer I (DEMUX I) is shown in Fig. 6-a. It has the same number of gratings and OCs of MUX I. Operation of DEMUX I is symmetrical to MUX I and both configurations have the same insertion losses. Every wavelength, λ_N, requires a tuned AFBGN optical filter in all the output ports but none at its output port. On the other hand, channel one (λ_1) does not need any filter to be redirected to the desired output port.

The demultiplexer configuration II (DEMUX II), shown in Fig. 6-b, is more interesting than DEMUX I. It is basically a mirror image of MUX II. All the filters at the output ports are tuned to the desired wavelength except the last one. It needs three AFBGs and three OCs for four channels and the demultiplexing of N channels requires $N - 1$ AFBGs and OCs. The output of the

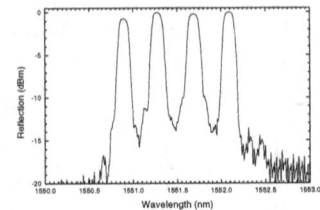

Fig. 5. Output of MUXs at 50 GHz.

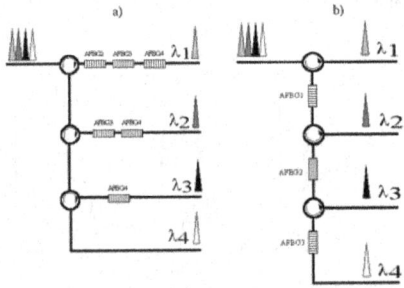

Fig. 6. a) DEMUX I and b) DEMUX II configurations.

four channels is shown in Fig. 7 and Fig. 8 for 100 GHz and 50 GHz channel separation, respectively. A third configuration demultiplexer III (DEMUX III) is presented in Fig. 9. This was obtained by adding two gratings FBGN and FBGN' at the output of each channel of the DEMUX II tuned on both sides of the corresponding AFBGN, which operate in transmission and eliminate the sidelobes, even more, and thus reduce crosstalk. Fig.10 shows the response of the DEMUX III with the two FBGs (with a FWHM of 0.2 nm) placed at the output port of each channel. When comparing Fig. 8 with Fig. 10, a clear suppression of the sidelobes, i.e., a reduction of crosstalk levels can be observed at the output port of DEMUX III.

3.3   Insertion Loss of MUX/DEMUX

Insertion loss has also been studied. This is determined essentially by the response of the OCs. Each circulator has an insertion loss of 0.4 dB between each port and if the AFBGs are considered to have 100 % reflectivity, the insertion loss, L, can be calculated as a function of the number of channels. Since the number of AFBGs filters and OCs for the MUX and the DEMUX is equal, the insertion losses are the same, although this value varies with the different architectures. Using N channels in configuration MUX/DEMUX I, the insertion loss is $L(dB) = 0.4 + (N - 1)0.8$, where N is the number of channels, and

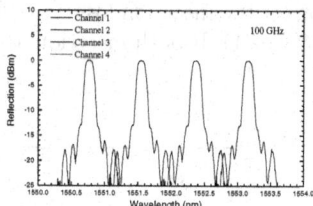

Fig. 7. DEMUX output at 100 GHz.

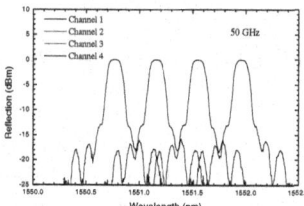

Fig. 8. DEMUX output at 50 GHz.

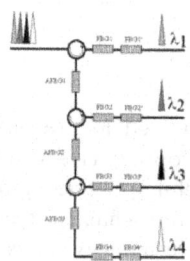

Fig. 9. DEMUX III.

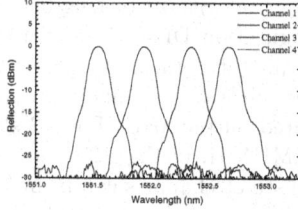

Fig. 10. Output of DEMUX III at 50 GHz.

0.4 is the insertion loss of each port of the circulator. On the other hand, the theoretical calculation for the insertion loss of configuration MUX/DEMUX II is given by $L(dB) = 0.4(N + 1)$. If both insertion losses are compared, see Fig. 11,

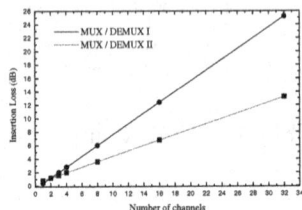

Fig. 11. Insertion loss versus number of channels for both architectures.

configuration II gives better results. Using four channels, MUX/DEMUX I has an insertion loss of 2.8 dB, whereas the insertion losses of MUX/DEMUX II is only 2 dB. As the number of channels increases, the performance of MUX/DEMUX I becomes significantly worse than for MUX/DEMUX II. In conclusion, configuration MUX/DEMUX II has lower insertion losses and, due to the fact that it uses fewer components, reduces fabrication costs.

4   Optical Switch

Optical networks have the need for wavelength sensitive nodes such as optical add-drop multiplexers, optical cross-connects and optical switches. An all-optical switch is a very useful optical component in optical networks. Although nowadays, the use of electromechanical technology is dominating the market, fibre Bragg grating based technology has advantages over this one as they allow all-optical operation. Fibre Bragg grating based all-optical switches permit all-optical wavelength channel control, that is, routing of the optical channels can be achieved without the need for optical to electrical and back to optical (O-E-O) conversion. Perspectives point to the need of all-optical switches in the near future in order to cope with increasing bandwidth and switching speed requirements. The configuration DEMUX II can also be operated as an optical switch by applying strain/temperature to the AFBGs. The tuning of the optical AFBGs filters changes the way a channel is routed through the optical switch sending it to the desired output port. Fig. 12 shows a possible optical switch architecture using DEMUX II. In Fig. 12 it can also be seen, that with a variation of $1200\,\mu\varepsilon$, four distinct channels can be switched to any output port. The corresponding temperature variation needed is also shown. In this case, a $120\,^{\circ}C$ temperature variation is required for the same number of channels. Three possible tuning solutions (the ones inside the dotted line rectangles) for the optical

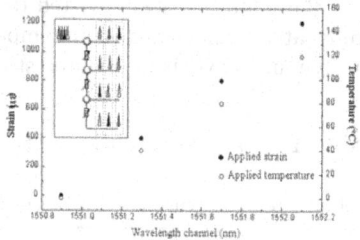

Fig. 12. Wavelength channel switch dependence with strain or temperature.

AFBGs filters are also shown. The number of combinations for N channels is $N!$. Notice that when the $N - 1$ AFBGs filters are tuned to the desired wavelength, the Nth wavelength will be automatically redirected to the last output port.

5   OXC Architectures

The passive optical components that have been presented in this work can be cascaded to achieve optical cross-connects. These OXCs can be classified into dynamic or static structures and, in general, they have the same number of input/output ports. In static OXCs, all the filter components are fixed, but in dynamic OXCs the filters can be tuned to the desired wavelength using temperature or PZT actuators. An example of a static wavelength 2×2 OXC is shown in Fig. 13-a. This kind of static architecture is highly limited in terms of its functionality for this reason the devices of most interest are dynamic ones (Fig. 13-b). With MUX II/DEMUX II configurations, which have the best per-

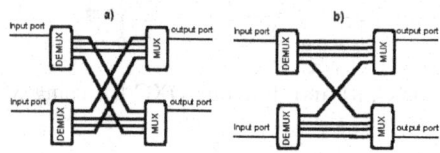

Fig. 13. Static a) and dynamic b) OXC architectures.

formance, two examples of static/dynamic OXC are shown in Fig. 14-a and Fig. 14-b, respectively. Both OXCs architectures have twelve OCs and ten AFBGs filters. Configuration II has been used because of its low insertion losses and reduced number of filters compared to configuration I. The highest insertion loss is 3.2 dB using four channels in input port 1 and 2. In the static OXC, all AFBGs are fixed. Table 1 shows the routing possibilities for each channel at the input port. For example, if λ_1 and λ_4 at input port 1 are routed to port 2, signals λ_1

and λ_4 at input port 2 are automatically routed to port 1, i.e., the wavelengths at input port 2 are treated symmetrically in comparison to the wavelengths at input port 1. The dynamic OXC is more interesting because it has three func-

Table 1. Example of routing of the static OXC

Input port 1	Output port 1	Output port 2
λ_1	0	1
λ_2	1	0
λ_3	1	0
λ_4	0	1

tionalities. The first functionality is the bar-state switching, where all the filters are tuned (ON) for each wavelength channel, which results in routing of the wavelength channels to the corresponding output port. Another functionality is cross-state switching, in which all the filters are detuned (OFF), see Fig. 14-b, i.e., the wavelength channels at each of the input ports are routed to the adjacent output ports. The last functionality is the simultaneous selective channel switching sending each desired channel to any given port.

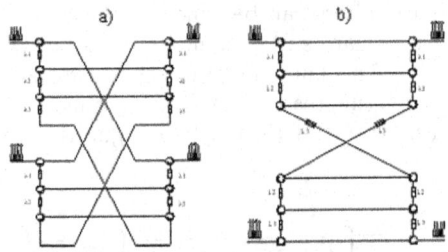

Fig. 14. Static OXC, a) and dynamic OXC b), using MUX/DEMUX II configurations.

6 Conclusion

Two configurations of MUX/DEMUX based on apodized FBGs and optical circulators, have been presented and compared in terms of their spectral characteristics. This work leads to conclude that MUX/DEMUX II has better performance in comparison with MUX/DEMUX I. It has lower insertion losses and it needs a smaller number of optical filter components. A filtering technique was applied in DEMUX II that reduced even further the crosstalk levels. It has been demonstrated that these devices have good characteristics for operation with channel spacing up to 50 GHz. An optical switch and a static/dynamic cross-connect were also shown as applications in DWDM systems.

References

[1] Davies, P. A. and Abd-El-Hamid, G.: 'Four-port fibre-optic ring resonator', *Electronics Letters*, 1988, **24**(11), pp. 662–663.

[2] Blow, K. J., Doran, N. J., and P., N. B.: 'Demostration of the nonlinear fibre loop mirror as an ultrafast all-optical demultiplexer', *Electronics Letters*, 1990, **30**(10), pp. 962–964.

[3] Mizrahi, V., Erdogan, T., DiGiovanni, D. J., Lemaire, P. J., MacDonald, W. M., Kosinski, S. G., Cabot, S., and Sipe, J. E.: 'Four channel fibre grating demultiplexer', *Electronics Letters*, 1994, **30**(10), pp. 780–781.

[4] Pan, J. J. and Shi, Y.: 'Dense wdm multiplexer and demultiplexer with 0.4 nm chanel spacing', *Electronics Letters*, 1998, **34**(1), pp. 74–75.

[5] Albert, J., Hill, K. O., Malo, B., Theriault, S., Bilodeau, F., Johnson, D. C., and Erickson, L. E.: 'Apodisation of the spectral response of fibre Bragg gratings using a phase mask with variable diffraction efficiency', *Electronics Letters*, 1995, **31**(3), pp. 222–223.

[6] Albert, J., Hill, K. O., Johnson, D. C., Bilodeau, F., and Rooks, M.: 'Moire phase masks for automatic pure apodisation of fibre Bragg gratings', *Electronics Letters*, 1996, **32**(24), pp. 2260–2261.

[7] Rego, G., Romero, R., Frazão, O., Marques, P. V. S., and Salgado, H. M.: 'Apodisation of uniform fibre bragg gratings using electric arc discharges', *IEEE Proc. WFOPC 2002 (Glasgow, Scotland)*, 2002, pp. 13–16.

[8] Cortes, P. Y., Ouellette, F., and LaRochelle, S.: 'Intrinsic apodisation of Bragg gratings written using UV-pulse interferometry', *Electronics Letters*, 1998, **34**(4), pp. 396–397.

[9] Kashyap, R., Swanton, A., and Armes, D. J.: 'Simple technique for apodising chirped an unchirped fibre Bragg gratings', *Electronics Letters*, 1996, **32**(13), pp. 1226–1228.

[10] Jensen, J. B., Plougman, N., Deyerl, H. J., Varming, P., Huebner, J., and Kristensen, M.: 'Polarization control method for ultraviolet writing of advanced bragg gratings', *Optics Letters*, 2002, **27**(12), pp. 1004–1005.

[11] Loh, W. H., Cole, M. J., Zervas, M. N. Barcelos, S., and Laming, R. I.: 'Complex grating structures with uniform phase masks based on the moving fibre-scaning beam technique', *Optics Letters*, 1995, **20**(20), pp. 2051–2053.

[12] Cole, M. J., Loh, W. H., Laming, R. I., Zervas, M. N., and Barcelos, S.: 'Moving fibre/phase mask-scanning beam technique for enhanced flexibility in producing fibre gratings with uniform phase mask', *Electronics Letters*, 1995, **31**(17), pp. 1488–1490.

Optical Performance Monitoring in High Speed Transparent DWDM Networks through Asynchronous Sampling

Paulo S. André [a,b], António L.J. Teixeira [a,c], Mário J.N. Lima [a,c],
Rogério N. Nogueira [a,b], José F. da Rocha [a,c], and João L. Pinto [a,b]

a) Instituto de Telecomunicações
b) Departamento de Física da Universidade de Aveiro
c) Departamento de Electrónica e Telecomunicações da Universidade de Aveiro
Campus Universitário de Santiago, 3810-193 Aveiro, Portugal,
Tel: +351 234377900, pandre@av.it.pt

Abstract. In this paper we will show the application of asynchronous histograms for monitoring very high data rate systems. We will describe the method and its results for simulated and experimental data. From the results we show the possibility of obtaining an amplitude description of the eye diagram from one completely closed eye observed by asynchronous, under-sampled amplitude histograms. A theoretical model for the histograms has been obtained and tested with experimental and simulated signal at 10 Gbit/s and 40 Gbit/s.

1 Introduction

The increasing use of dense wavelength division multiplexing (DWDM) as a way to increment nowadays systems capacity is leading DWDM technology to a point where it is being widely used in very different situations and configurations. With the advent brought by the versatility of this technique, the migration to all-optical transparent photonic networks is already on the way. Within these future networks, it is possible to observe many different signal formats and data rates, since all processing and routing functions are performed transparently and optically. Due to the advantages of this technique, the optical layer has grown its interest and is now considered in the networks hierarchy. However, protection is now one of the greatest difficulties in this kind of systems, due to the referred amount of formats and data rates that can flow within this technology.

This fact brings many difficulties to the implementation of channel BER monitoring techniques. The different bit rates, require a very broadband and precise clock recovery system, which is quite difficult to implement and if available, can be very expensive. On the other hand the different pulse formats require a very habile receiver and decoder with quite large margins to achieve synchronization and pulse shaping in order to obtain the widest decision time window.

Also, the network management, control and survivability in a multi-vendor, multi-operator and multi-costumer all-optical environment requires the ability to measure the optical data performance, detect degradation, failure and provisioning means of

M.M. Freire, P. Lorenz, M.M.-O. Lee (Eds.): HSNMC 2003, LNCS 2720, pp. 452-461, 2003.

failure location and isolation in order to constantly maintain the quality of service (QoS) [1]. Actually the current DWDM networks are managed, protected and monitored in the digital domain. This requires channel termination and decoding at an optical receiver. Several examples of this are currently implemented in the networks, for example, the detection of the parity bits related with payload or frame checking and error checking (however, those codes cannot supply channel performance data). An example is the BIP-8 (bit interleaved parity) mechanisms from synchronous digital hierarchy (SDH) / synchronous optical network (SONET) that allows error monitoring and the consequent use of the management capabilities of these standard transmission protocols for protection providing. This method, due to the need of the decoding at the rate of transmission, synchronization and processing is quite expensive and therefore limitative due to transparency loss. Transparency is beginning to be one of the network requirements, due to the surge of many widely used formats, such as: SDH / SONET, plesiochronous digital hierarchy (PDH), Gigabit Ethernet, asynchronous transfer mode (ATM), internet protocol (IP), etc. Thus, the ability to monitor the in-service signal quality independently of the signal format is essential. Therefore, the utilization of monitoring techniques also in the optical domain is an advantage that can simplify the task of maintaining the needed quality of service (QoS).

These facts lead the industry and the researchers to look for other ways of monitoring the system performance with less cost and complexity and that at the same time could give enough information for the needs in each situation. Optical performance monitoring (OPM) is an approach that allows characterization of some of the channel parameters without prior knowledge of the origin, transport history, format or contend of the data at arbitrary points of the network without decoding the data. Furthermore OPM should be unobtrusive, accurate, unambiguous, comprehensive and cheap [2].

One can divide the present methods into three main tiers of channel analysis: optical channel monitor (OCM); optical channel analyser (OCA) and optical channel drop (OCD).

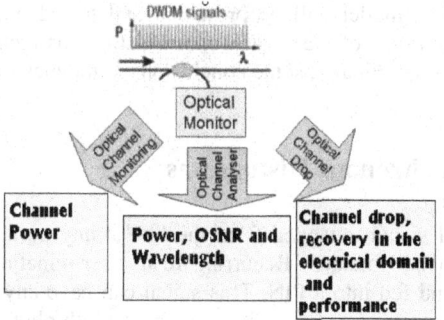

Fig. 1. Three tiers optical monitoring: OCM- Optical Carrier Monitoring, OCA- Optical Channel Analyser, OCD- Optical Channel Drop.

Optical amplifiers and other components in the light path can induce signal distortions and these are even worst when aging and environmental effects affect their optical

454 Paulo S. André et al.

profile, also when power varies sharply, due to add/drop of channels. OCM's were specially developed for these cases and to be aggregated with dynamic gain equalizers, however, they will also find use in applications such as fault isolation and channel routing supervision allowing the characterization of channel presence/absence. This technique provides the first tier of optical monitoring capability.

As predictable, the effect of gain equalizing, brings some system stability but does not improves necessarily the optical signal to noise ratio (OSNR), so, its is needed to have a tighter control over the DWDM wavelengths in order to accommodate higher spectral efficiency. Precise information of channel power, wavelength, OSNR, is needed for increased functionalities of the networks, such as precise tuning of wavelength and power adjust at the transmitter/intermediate node, by means of information travelling in an optical supervisor channel. These functionalities are performed by the OCA's, which are slightly more costly than the OCM's and therefore should be paced in a less massive way through the networks. However, since OSNR is not directly related with data quality [3], BER testing devices will always be needed for qualifying, troubleshooting, and turning up of networks. This is the reason for the existence of the third tier of monitoring capability, where getting a permanent BER test functionality in certain network elements is needed, complying in this way with service level agreements. Since this last method when performed in a synchronous way, is quite complex and expensive, cheaper alternatives are needed, which is the case of asynchronous monitoring, subject of this paper.

Several OPM approaches have been proposed, specially the used of asynchronous histograms [3, 4, 5]. However in these methods is necessary to remove cross-point data, defined at an arbitrary threshold value. By other end, the obtained average SNR differs from the real SNR by a constant value, which depend on the receiver parameters and on the threshold used to cut the cross-point data values.

The method presented in this paper does not require the cut of the cross-point data values, and the effective SNR value is obtained as well as the pulse rise time.

This paper will start by a brief description of the asynchronous histogram method and its theoretical model will be presented and tested with simulated results. Will be reported the usage of the asynchronous histograms method to access the quality of a 40 Gbit/s signal. Finally, some conclusions of the methodology will be outdrawn.

2   Asynchronous Histograms

The optical signal is tapped from the line at any point and a copy of the travelling signals can be obtained. Recurring to a discriminating filter, one channel can be extracted and fed into a PIN. This signal can have any shape and any bit rate. After detecting an optical signal with a high bandwidth photodiode (bandwidth higher than the bitrate), the electrical signal is asynchronously sampled. From this the amplitude histograms can be obtained from the asynchronous samples. The method of asynchronous histograms is obtained by sampling at a given rate (smaller than the rate of the signal) the channel in analysis. The samples are collected and an amplitude histogram is obtained from them.

a)   b)

Fig. 2. a) Synchronous eye diagram, b) asynchronous eye diagram with superimposed amplitude histogram.

Therefore without knowing the exact bit rate and performing clock recovery for synchronization, a signal like the one in eye diagram of figure 2 a) becomes something like the one in figure 2 b), where the samples can occur at any amplitude level and no eye opening is obtained for having a correct decision. Also, in figure 2 b), superimposed we present the amplitude histogram of the samples, which reinforces the idea of the absence of a clear decision point. The signal that is presented has a raised cosine shape and is driven at 2.5 Gbit/s. However, any other bit rate is suitable for the analysis.

As can be noticed in figure 2, if the samples are correctly triggered with the incoming signal, one can chose the decision timing, and thus evaluating the best decision time bye the eye opening. However, if sampling is not triggered and performed at a rate that is not correlated with the stream, the decision time is quite irrelevant and no eye can be obtained. However if one observes correctly the density of the amplitudes of the samples, one can notice that, in the optical "1" and "0", there is quite a high density of samples, when comparing to the remaining amplitudes. It can be understood that the rise time of the signal will play an important role in the density of the intermediate levels by contributing with nearly uniform distribution between the "1" and "0" levels. Superimposed to that distribution, are the two distributions that correspond to the two symbols, with their correspondent distortion effects (Noise from different sources, and other effects from the transmission).

The histogram's shape is dependent on the pulse format that is subject of this analysis. The inter-peaks amplitude is dependent on the shape rise time. These two parameters give us the possibility of extracting the pulse shape main parameters.

3   Asynchronous Histogram Model

In this section the model used to represent the asynchronous histogram will be present. A signal is defined as a temporal variation of the amplitude. The amplitude swing, between the logic symbols power levels ($A0$ to $A1$) is divided in infinitesimals bins intervals, Δ. The probability of a signal to fall in one of those amplitude slots is proportional to relative time passed from the moment it enters the lower/upper limit to the upper/lower limit, respectively. This time can be obtained by inverting the amplitude versus time function, of the basic pulse shape, if we consider no noise present.

In the absence of noise and if the sequence and the acquisition time are long enough, the probability of having each of the possible transitions for a binary system, a "1"→"1", a "0"→"0", a "1"→"0" or a "0"→"1" are equal to 1/4.

The time reminded in the bins correspondent to the $A0$ and $A1$ levels ($[A_0, A_0 + \Delta[$ and $[A_1 - \Delta, A_1]$, respectively), considering that the transitions functions are similar in the two edge, is:

$$P_{0,1}(a) = \frac{T - 2 \cdot t_{pi}}{2}.$$

(1)

where $f^1(.)$ is the inverse of the transition function T is the period and t_{pi} is the time the signal stay in the interval $[A_0 + \Delta, A_1 - \Delta[$. For the remaining bins, $[A_i, A_i + \Delta[$, the probability is:

$$P_i(a) = \frac{2}{T}\left(f^{-1}(a) - f^{-1}(a - \Delta)\right).$$

(2)

The transition function considered represents a raised-cosine pulse shape:

$$f(t) = \frac{A_0 + A_1}{2} + \frac{A_1 - A_0}{2} \cdot sen\left(\frac{\tau \cdot \pi \cdot t}{T} - \frac{\pi}{2}\right).$$

(3)

The τ parameter governs the raising time. However other transitions could be considered, such as linear transition, low pass filtered or gaussian filtered and are described by the expression (4), (5) and (6), respectively.

$$f(t) = A_0 + \frac{A_1 - A_0}{\tau \cdot T} \cdot t.$$

(4)

$$f(t) = A_0 + (A_1 - A_0) \cdot exp\left(-\frac{t \cdot ln(1/9)}{\tau \cdot T}\right).$$

(5)

$$f(t) = A_0 + \frac{(A_1 - A_0)}{2} \cdot erfc\left(\frac{2 \cdot (t - \tau \cdot T)}{\tau \cdot T}\right).$$

(6)

After generating the histograms without noise, the noise function can be added by convolving this histogram without noise with a histogram of the noise distribution. Considering that the variance of the noise is dependent on the detected intensity one should do, bin by bin, a calculation of the noise variance value and its convolution with the corresponding bin, and only after the sum of the individual convolution results.

Figure 3 show the noiseless eye diagram, used in the model to obtain the asynchronous histogram. The simulated diagram is superimposed to a real eye diagram. In this case a low pass filtered transition function was considered.

Fig. 3. Simulated noiseless eye diagram superimposed to a real eye diagram.

In order to test our model we have implemented a simulation setup in a commercial available photonic simulator. In the optical source the CW signal from a DFB laser is externally modulated at a 10 Gbit/s with a NRZ sequence, the used sampling rate was 320 GHz and a pulse rising time of 25 ps considered. After the optical source an EDFA with a variable noise figure was used to degrade the signal to noise ratio of the optical signal. Finally the signal is tapped and injected in a high bandwidth receiver and asynchronous sampled with a 1 GHz sampling rate, by other hand the signal is synchronous received and its performance accessed by the conventional way.

We must keep in mind that the only considered a signal degradation source was the noise, which is only possible for fully dispersion compensated low average power system.

In figure 4 a) and 5 a) we find the simulated synchronous eye diagram obtained with different values of the Q factor, 28.45 and 5.17, respectively, and its asynchronous histograms presented in figures 4 b) and 5 b).

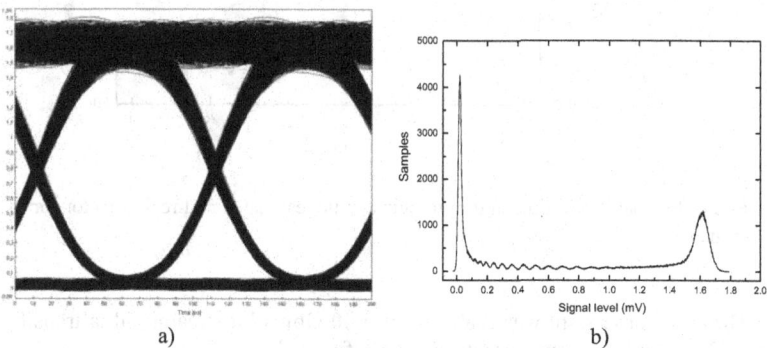

a)   b)

Fig. 4. a) Synchronous eye diagram obtained by numerical simulation for a 10 Gbit/s system. b) Asynchronous amplitude histogram obtained from the eye diagram . Q = 28.45.

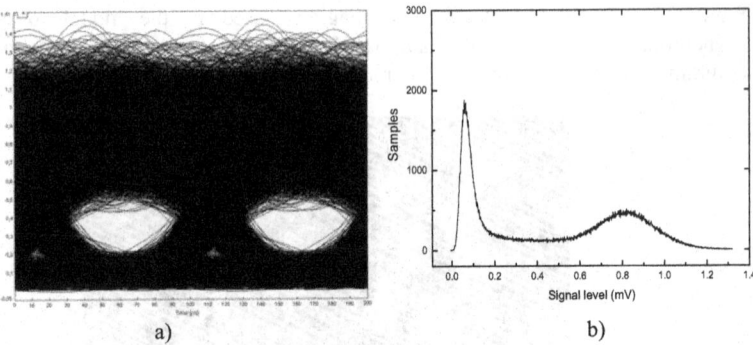

a)   b)

Fig. 5. a) Synchronous eye diagram obtained by numerical simulation for a 10 Gbit/s system. b) Asynchronous amplitude histogram obtained from the eye diagram . Q = 5.17.

The histogram model was adjusted to the asynchronous amplitude histograms in order to minimize the error between them, from the minimization process the Q factor and the 10 % → 90 % rising time were obtained. Figure 6 displays these two parameters obtained from simulated values of the Q factor, we can observe that the more accurate results were obtained for the low values of Q.

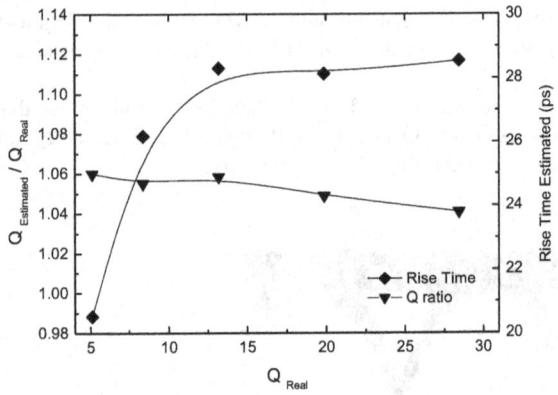

Fig. 6. Estimated rise time and ratio between the estimated and real Q factor for the 10 Gbit/s sequence.

The same procedure was realized for a 40 Gbit/s bit stream with a transition time of 6.125 ps and the results are displayed in figure 7.

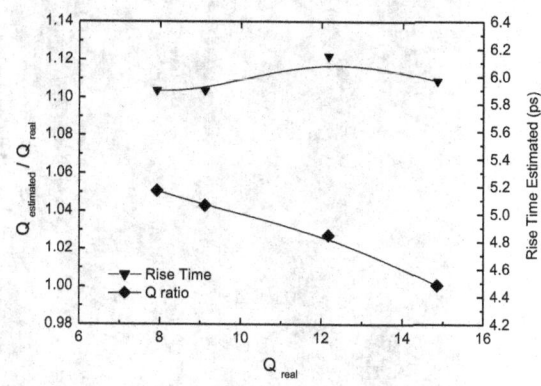

Fig. 7. Estimated rise time and ratio between the estimated and real Q factor for the 40 Gbit/s sequence.

4   Performance Assessment

The proposed model was tested for a 40 Gbit/s sequence with a 12.5 ps rise time experimental data. In figure 8 a) and b) are show the eye diagram and the bit sequence of the test bit stream

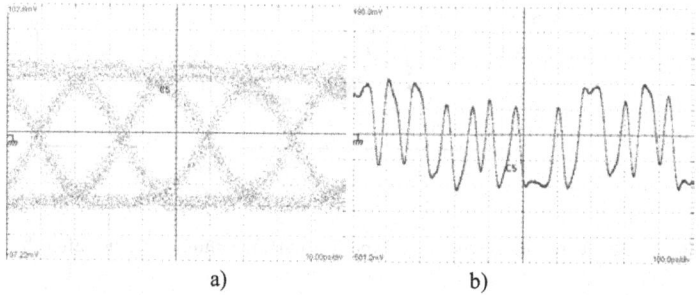

a)   b)

Fig. 8. 40 Gbit/s sequence: a) Eye diagram, b) bit sequence.

This high speed signal was asynchronous detected and the respective asynchronous eye diagram showed in figure 9, with the asynchronous histogram superimposed.

The asynchronous histogram model was adjusted to the experimental results. From the minimization process the following values for the Q factor and rise time, were obtained, respectively: 10.16 and 11.0 ps. The real Q value was 11.00 and the rise time was 12.0 ps. In the figure 10 are show the results generated after the minimization and the experimental values of the asynchronous histogram.

Fig. 9. 40 Gbit/s sequence asynchronous eye diagram and asynchronous histogram..

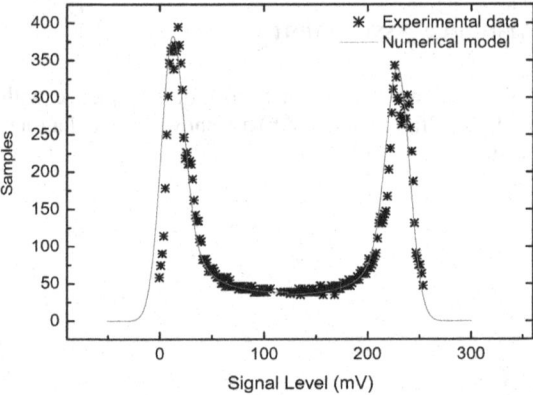

Fig. 10. Asynchronous histogram,. Experimental and simulated values after the minimization.

5   Conclusions

An asynchronous amplitude histograms method has been described, it allows very low data sampling, it is bitrate and shape transparent. A theoretical model for the histograms has been obtained and tested with experimental and simulated signal at 10 Gbit/s and 40 Gbit/s. The results are quite interesting giving the possibility, from an asynchronous collection of samples, to obtain important information of the signal.

Acknowledgements

The authors would like to acknowledge the FCT projects: WIDCOM (POSI/35574/99/CPS/2000) and WONET (POSI/2001/CPS/40009) and the SFRH/BD/7043/2001 scholarship.

References

[1] K. Mueller, N. Hanik, A. Gladisch, H.-M. Foisel, C. Caaspar, "Application of Amplitude Histograms for Quality of Service Measurements of Optical Channels and Fault Identification", in Conference proceedings of ECOC 99, 26-30, Nice, France, 26-30 Sept. 1999.

[2] Richard Habel, Kim Roberts, Alan Solheim, James Harley, "Optical Domain Performance Monitoring", in Conference proceedings of OFC 2000, WK3-1 174-175, Baltimore, USA, 7-10 March 2000.

[3] Seiji Norimatsu, MasanoriMaruoka, "Accurate Q factor Estimation of Optically Amplified Systems in the Presence of Waveform Distortions", Journal of Lightwave Technology, Vol. 21, n. 1, pp. 19-27, 2002.

[4] P. S. André, A. L. J. Teixeira, Teresa Almeida, M. Pousa, J. F. da Rocha and J. L. Pinto, *Optical signal quality monitor for transparent DWDM networks based on asynchronous sampled histograms*, Journal of Optical Networks, vol. 1, n.3, pp.118-128, Março 2002.

[5] P. S. André and J. L. Pinto, A. L. J. Teixeira, M. J. N. Lima and J. F. da Rocha, *Bit error rate assessment in DWDM transparent networks using optical performance monitor based in asynchronous sampling*, OFC 2002, ThGG96, pp. 749-750, Anaheim, EUA, Março 2002.

Performance Comparision between TCP-Reno and Freeze-Snoop TCP/SACK over cdma2000 Network Environments

Sang-Hee Lee[1], Hong-Gu Ahn[1], Jae-Sung Lim[1], Sung Kim[2], Sang-Yun Lee[2], and Myung-Sung Lee[2]

[1] The Graduate School of Information and Communication, Ajou University,
San 5, Wonchon-dong, Paldal-gu, Suwon 442-749, Korea
{dreami, piriboy, jaslim}@ajou.ac.kr
[2] Network RD center, SK Telecom,
9-1, Sunae-dong, Pundang-gu, Sungnam City, 463-784, Korea
{kims, sylee, mslee}@sktelecom.com

Abstract. In this paper, we present both an architecture with a wireless TCP server and a wireless TCP scheme called Freeze-Snoop TCP/SACK. Freeze-Snoop TCP/SACK is a modified TCP scheme for wireless network environments to improve performance of TCP under retransmission mode. When the WTCP server enters retransmission mode, it freezes retransmission timer of sender side not to drop the congestion window at sender side. It yields a significant performance improvement in wireless networks with lossy links. For performance evaluation, we calculate the throughput benefit by using freezing instead of slow start when timeout of sender side is happened by packet loss at wireless link. For simulations, we implemented cdma2000 network with the WTCP server using the NS-simulator.

1 Introduction

Third generation mobile devices and services will transform wireless communications into on-line, real time connectivity. 3G wireless technologies will allow an individual to have immediate access to location specific services that offer information on demand. Such multimedia services require reliable and fast packet transmission. Therefore, in wireless networks, the use of TCP is necessary to support various multimedia services. However, the standard TCP such as TCP-Reno is not a suitable mechanism for the wireless networks. In wired environments, the main reason of performance degradation was network congestion. On the contrary with wired case, the packet loss leads to performance degradation in wireless environments. Unstable link status due to fading and mobility of nodes results in packet losses.

Because the standard TCP was developed for wired networks, it performs the congestion control mechanisms when packet losses happen in wireless link. The congestion control algorithm assumes specifically that both losses and delays are

M.M. Freire, P. Lorenz, M.M.-O. Lee (Eds.): HSNMC 2003, LNCS 2720, pp. 462–470, 2003.

caused by network congestion. Accordingly, it leads to unnecessary congestion control, and thus it results in performance degradation in wireless environments. In this paper, we introduce a new server called WTCP server(Wireless TCP server) into cdma2000 networks and propose a modified snoop TCP mechanism which is based on a freeze scheme. For performance evaluation, we calculate the throughput benefit by using freezing instead of slow start when packet loss is happened on wireless link. For simulations, we implemented cdma2000 network with the WTCP server using the NS-simulator[1].

The rest of this paper is organized as follows. In the next section we review several modifications of TCP that have been proposed to improve TCP performance in wireless environments. In section 3, we present a system model and the proposed Freeze - Snoop TCP. Then we evaluate system performance by latency calculation and computer simulations in section 4. Finally, concluding remarks are given in section 5.

2   Related Wireless TCP Schemes

In this section, we discuss some protocols that have been proposed to improve performance of TCP over wireless networks[2-8]. There are some modifications from the basic TCP in order to perform more efficiently in high-latency and error-prone wireless networks with Internet services.

Indirect-TCP(I-TCP)[3], for example, is a method which splits a TCP connection between FH and MH into two separate connections and hides TCP from the wireless link by using a protocol optimized for wireless link. However, the Indirect-TCP cannot maintain end-to-end TCP semantics, and it must have a large buffer to keep all the packets which are transmitted from the sender.

An alternative for improving performance such as ELN(Explicit Loss Notification)[4] needs to modify TCP in FH(Fixed Host) and MH(Mobile Host). The ELN defines special option called ELN bit in TCP ACKs. When a packet is dropped on wireless networks, a cumulative acknowledgement due to the lost packet is marked to identify what the loss occurred in wireless link.

Snoop TCP[5, 6] also improves the poor performance of TCP over wireless link. It also uses a module which is introduced at the BS. FH and MH operate on the standard TCP. When FH sends a packet, the BS stores it in the Snoop buffer and forwards to the MH. The buffered packet is used for local retransmission when packet losses occur in wireless links. The Snoop module monitors an acknowledgement from the MH and retransmits the packet when duplicated ACKs arrive. This is the way that the BS hides packet losses from the FH by not propagating duplicated ACKs, thereby it prevents unnecessary invocations of the congestion control mechanisms at the FH.

Although the Snoop satisfies the end-to-end semantics and it does not modify the FH and MH, it needs some modification of the BS. Furthermore, it can make some problems in the cdma2000 system, which has the link layer recovery protocol called RLP(Radio Link Protocol)[7] and packet scheduling schemes implemented at link layer.

TCP westwood[8] is a new protocol to increase performance of TCP regardless of link environments. Its main idea is to continuously estimate, at the TCP sender, packet rate of the connection by monitoring ACK reception rate. The estimated connection rate is then used to compute congestion window and slow start threshold settings after a congestion episode. It certainly improves TCP performance, however it has to modify the TCP sender side.

The last enhancements to TCP for wireless channel that we review here are called M-TCP[9] and Freeze TCP[10,11]. These methods use the freeze approach and aim at preventing packet losses by disconnection of wireless links. In the M-TCP, an intermediate host, called SH(Superior Host), takes care of the disconnection. When the SH gets ACKs from an MH, it saves the ACK of the last byte, in order to prevent loss of outstanding packets. If the MH is disconnected from nowhere, then the SH stops getting the ACKs and assumes that the MH has been temporarily disconnected and sends the ACKs of the last byte that it saved previously. The Freeze-TCP does not require any intermediary and any change on the sender side. Instead of intermediate node, the receiver handles the task of identifying an imminent disconnection due to potential handoff, fading signal strength, or any other problems. Both of them use freezing function when the wireless link disconnection is expected.

3   Freeze-Snoop TCP/SACK

3.1   Network Architecture

The proposed network architecture is shown in Fig.1. It is based on cdma2000 wireless network and adopts WTCP server to support wireless TCP service. The BS is connected to a node called the PDSN(Packet Data Service Node), which performs CDMA specific functions such as soft handoffs, encryption, power control, etc. It also performs link layer retransmission using RLP. The PDSN terminates PPP with the MH and forwards PPP/IP packet to the BS[12].

The BS fragments the packet received from PDSN into a number of radio frames, and then performs transmission and local retransmission of these radio frames using RLP protocol. It also schedules the radio frames received from the PDSN on the wireless link using a scheduling algorithm. The MH receives the radio frames and if it discovers loss of radio frames, it requests local retransmission using the RLP protocol. However, the RLP may not recover wireless packet loss perfectly even through it performs retransmissions repeatedly. Therefore, proper TCP mechanisms for wireless networks are needed.

The proposed WTCP server is located behind the PDSN. We implemented the proposed Freeze-Snoop TCP/SACK module at WTCP server. A new packet arrives from the FH, and the WTCP server adds it to its buffer and passes the packet onto the MH. The WTCP server also monitors all ACKs sent from the MH. When a packet loss is detected, the WTCP server performs local retransmission of the loss packet to the MH. When local retransmission is happened, WTCP server sends ACK with zero-window.

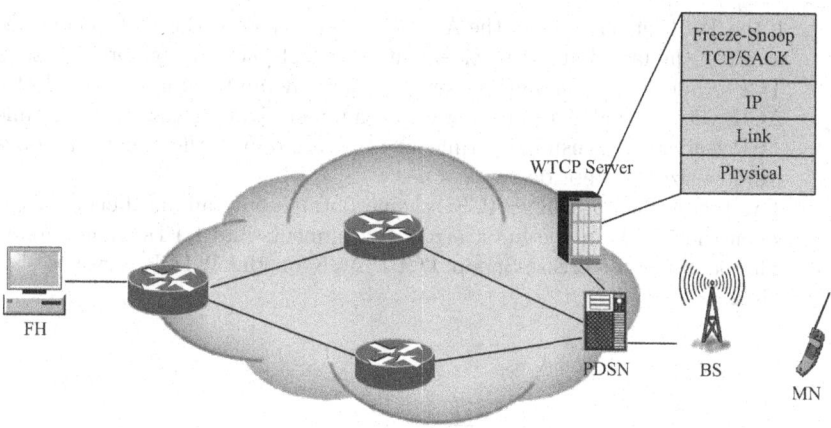

Fig. 1. System Model

The WTCP server can maintain the connections with several PDSNs and control packets for each PDSN. Hence, it has advantages with respect of cost and implementation. The proposed scheme does not need the modification of current BSs.

3.2   Operation Flow

When a sender does not receive any acknowledgement from a receiver until RTO (Retransmission Time-Out) expires, the sender retransmits loss packets and enters the slow start. The slow start mechanism reduces the window size to one. The window size is doubled at every round trip period until reaching ss_threshold (slow start threshold) and then increases linearly until a packet loss is experienced or maximum window size is reached.

If packet loss is happened in wireless link, a snoop agent locally retransmits the loss packet instead of sender. It prevents that sender becomes aware packet loss at wireless link. However, it sometimes causes the slow start at sender. Specially, the difference between delay of wireless link and wired link is remarkable and the packet loss is generated randomly. Finally, it degrades the system throughput significantly where high latency channels are involved.

The proposed TCP scheme can improve this throughput degradation using the freezing scheme. When local retransmission is originated, WTCP server sends an ACK, which is set the sequence number by the previous ACK number and the received window size to zero.

If the TCP sender receives the ACK with zero window, the TCP sender becomes aware of the fact that the receiver cannot accept packets anymore. Consequently TCP sender stops sending packets temporarily, and waits for arrival of a new ACK with available received window number. During this waiting time, the TCP sender's retransmission timeout timer is stopped; thereupon the congestion window size does not decrease.

The Freeze-Snoop TCP/SACK scheme obtains outstanding benefit, especially when the MH is in the burst error environments and RTTs change frequently. The operation of Freeze-Snoop TCP/SACK on the WTCP server is shown in Fig.2.

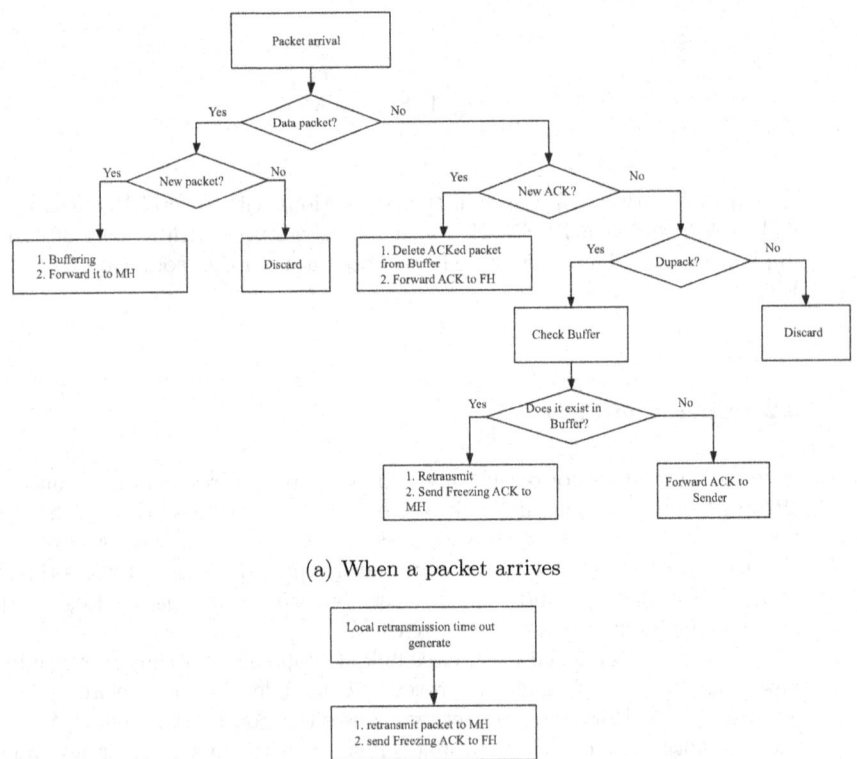

(a) When a packet arrives

(b) When local retransmission timeout occurs

Fig. 2. Operation of Freeze-Snoop TCP/SACK at WTCP Server

4   Performance Improvement of Freeze-Snoop TCP/SACK

4.1   Time Latency

The main advantage of proposed scheme is that when the WTCP server enters retransmission mode, it freezes all packet retransmit timers and does not drop the congestion window at sender side. The benefit of proposed scheme depends on the time latency.

If the freezing time is longer than the growing time of window from 1 to previous window, it cannot gain any benefit. Therefore, the benefit can represent the difference between freezing time and window growing-up time. In this paper, we define the freezing time as T_{Freeze} and the growing time of previous window size as T_W.

When W is the window size before timeout (is originated), the growing up time of window W in slow start is as following.

$$T_{W\_1} = n + (CWND - ss\_threshold) \cdot RTT$$
$$when\ log_2(ss\_threshold) = n \quad and \quad (ss\_threshold)\ mod\ 2^n = 0 \qquad (1)$$

At this time, if ss_threshold is not exponent value of 2, T_W becomes

$$T_{W\_2} = (\lfloor n \rfloor + 1) + (CWND - ss\_threshold) \cdot RTT.$$
$$when\ log_2(ss\_threshold) = n \quad and \quad (ss\_threshold)\ mod\ 2^n \neq 0 \qquad (2)$$

On the other hand, the number of local retransmission influences the freezing time. When local RTT and local RTO between WTCP server and MN are SRTT and SRTO respectively, T_{Freeze} becomes as following.

$$T_{Freeze} = \alpha \cdot SRTT + (\beta - \alpha) \cdot SRTO \qquad (3)$$

Here, α is the number of local retransmission by duplicated ACK, $\beta - \alpha$ is the number of local retransmission by retransmission timeout and β is the total number of local retransmission for recovery of a loss packet. Finally, we can obtain the benefit of freezing when

$$T_W - T_{Freeze} > 0. \qquad (4)$$

4.2   Computer Simulation

To evaluate performance of the proposed Freeze-Snoop TCP/SACK scheme over cdma2000 network, we carried out the computer simulations using the network simulator(ns-2). According to the measurement results at SK commercial network, we assume that mean wireless link delay is 500ms. We also assume that frame losses do not happen in reverse link, whereas frame error rate is from 0.1% to 5% in forward link. We consider only one connection between an FH and an MH. Table 1 represents simulation parameters.

Table 1. Simulation Parameters

Parameters	Value
TCP Version	- TCP Reno
	- Snoop with TCP Reno
	- Freeze-Snoop TCP/SACK
Application	FTP
TCP/IP Segment Size	1500 Bytes
Wired Link Speed	1.5 Mbps
Wired Link Delay	5/300 ms
Wireless Link Speed	144/384 Kbps
Wireless Link Delay	500 ms
Max cwnd size	50
Doppler frequency	FdT = 0.01, 1.0
RLP Version	2-3 RLP
Error Model	- Uniform for Random error
	- 2-state Markov model for Burst error
Simulator	NS-2.1b8a
Simulation Time	600(s)

Fig. 3(a) and 4(a) shows the transmission rate in random error environments. Freeze-Snoop TCP/SACK gets better performance than TCP-Reno and Snoop protocol. Especially, proposed scheme maintains high transmission rate even if FER becomes high, whereas the transmission rate of the TCP-Reno is decreased. Also, it maintains acceptable performance in the burst error environments(Fig. 3(b) and Fig. 4(b)).

The proposed scheme maintains a good throughput when frame error rate is increased. It is because Snoop and TCP/SACK can rapidly recover from packet loss at wireless link and ACK with zero window can prevent the decreasing of sender's window.

Snoop protocol makes benefits by means of reducing the number of congestion control, and it gets to use the channel bandwidth maximally. However, snoop protocol can raise sender's timeout when mobile host is under error environments.

In Fig. 3(b) to Fig. 4(b), TCP Reno and proposed scheme shows better performance when wired link delay is 5ms than 300ms. But, TCP-snoop shows better performance when wired link delay is 300ms. It is due to local retransmission at TCP-snoop.

When duplicated ACK is received from MH, snoop performs local retransmission without forwarding duplicated ACK to FH. If wired link is short between FH and WTCP agent, it may lead to timeout of sender. Short wired link also leads to TCP sender's timeout. When TCP-snoop timeout is happened at WTCP server, it may bring about TCP sender's timeout. During local retransmission, TCP sender's timer can be expired.

But, proposed scheme overcomes this problem by using freezing mechanism.

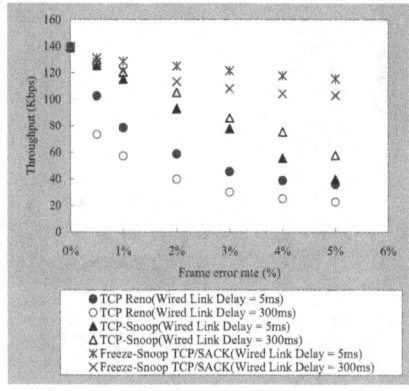

(a) Random error environments

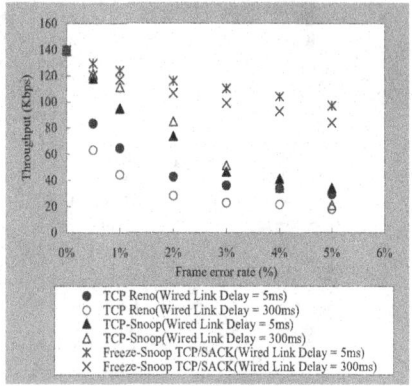

(b) Burst error environments

Fig. 3. Transmission rate(Wireless Link Speed = 144Kbps)

Freezing mechanism prevents the reducing of sender's window by sending ACK with zero window. As shown in section 4.1, the benefit of Freezing mechanism is related to freezing time. Through comparison Fig. 3(b) and Fig. 4(b), proposed scheme represents better performance when wireless link speed is faster. It means that the proposed scheme get more benefits when freezing time is short.

5   Conclusion

We have proposed a new TCP scheme called Freeze-Snoop TCP/SACK to improve the TCP performance over the wireless networks. The proposed scheme improves performance of TCP/SACK by using some mechanisms such as freezing and snoop. Also, it has implemented at WTCP server, which handled the packet loss at wireless link. WTCP server eliminates the need of modification at base station.

The simulation results carried out over cdma2000 network show that the proposed scheme makes better efficiency in both random and burst error environments.

Specially, it maintains a good throughput when frame error rate is increased. Because Snoop and TCP/SACK can rapidly recover from packet loss at wireless link and ACK with zero window can prevent the decreasing of sender's window, proposed scheme accomplishes an improvement of the system performance.

References

1. Bajaj, S., et al.: Virtual InterNetwork Test bed: Status and Research Agenda. Technical Report,University of Southern California (1998) 98–678
   http://www.isi.edu/nsnam/ns/

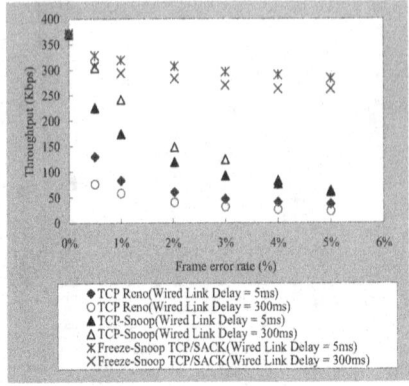
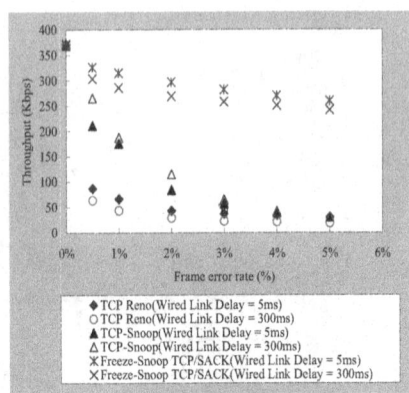

(a) Random error environments   (b) Burst error environments

Fig. 4. Transmission rate(Wireless Link Speed = 384Kbps)

2. Liu, J. : Transport Layer Protocol for Wireless Networks. Ph.D. thesis University of South Carolina (1999)
3. Badrinath, B.R., Bakre, A.: I-TCP: Indirect TCP for Mobile Hosts. Proc. 15th Intl Conference on Distributed Computing (1995) 136–143
4. Balakrishnan, H., Katz, R.H.: Explicit Loss Notification and Wireless Web Performance. Proc. IEEE Globecom Internet Mini-Conference (1998)
5. Balakrishna, H., Katz, R.H., et al.: Improving TCP/IP Performance over Wireless Networks. Proc. 1st ACM Intl Conf on Mobicom (1995)
6. Rendon, J., et al.: SNOOP TCP Performance over GPRS. Proc. IEEE VTS 53rd Vehicular Technology Conference Spring (2001) 2103–2107
7. TIA/EIA/IS-707: Data Services Option Standard for Wideband Spread Spectrum Digital Cellular System. TIA/EIA/IS-707 (1998)
8. Casetti, C., Gerla, M., Mascolo, S., Sansadidi, M.Y., Wang, R.: TCP Westwood: End-to-End Congestion Control for Wired/Wireless Networks. Wireless Networks Journal 8 (2002) 467–479
9. Brown, K., Singh, S.: M-TCP: TCP for Mobile Cellular Netowrks. ACM CCR, Vol. 27, No. 5 (1997)
10. Goff, T., Moronski, J., Phatak, D.S., Gupta, V.: Freeze-TCP: A True End-to-end TCP Enhancement Mechanism for Mobile Environments. Proc. IEEE INFOCOM (2000) 1537–1545
11. Costa, G.M., Sirisena, H.R.: Freeze TCP with Timestamps for Fast Packet Loss Recovery after Disconnections. Proc. SPECTS (2002)
12. Chan, M.C., Ramjee, R.: TCP/IP Performance over 3G Wireless Links with Rate and Delay Variation. Mobicom (2002)

RD-TCP: Reorder Detecting TCP

Arjuna Sathiaseelan and Tomasz Radzik

Department of Computer Science, King's College London,
Strand, London WC2R 2LS
{arjuna,radzik}@dcs.kcl.ac.uk

Abstract. Numerous studies have shown that packet reordering is common, especially in high speed networks where there is high degree of parallelism and different link speeds. Reordering of packets decreases the TCP performance of a network, mainly because it leads to overestimation of the congestion of the network. We consider wired networks with transmission that follows predominantly, but not necessarily exclusively, symmetric routing paths, and we analyze the performance of such networks when reordering of packets occurs. We propose an effective solution that could significantly improve the performance of the network when reordering of packets occurs. We report results of our simulation experiments which support this claim. Our solution is based on enabling the senders to distinguished between dropped packets and reordered packets.

1 Introduction

Research on the implications of packet reordering on TCP networks indicate that packet reordering is not a pathological network behavior. For example, packet reordering occurs naturally as a result of *local parallelism* [7]: a packet can traverse through multiple paths within a device. Local parallelism is imperative in today's Internet as it reduces equipment and trunk costs. Packet reordering occurs also due to multi-path routing. A network path that suffers from persistent packet reordering will have severe performance degradation.

TCP receivers generate cumulative acknowledgements which indicate the arrival of the last in-order data segment [8]. For example, assume that four segments A, B, C and D are transmitted through the network from a sender to a receiver. When segments A and B reach the receiver, it transmits back to the sender an *ack* (acknowledgement) for B which summarizes that both segments A and B have been received. Suppose segments C and D have been reordered in the network. At the time segment D arrives at the receiver, it sends the *ack* for the last in-order segment received which in our case is B. Only when segment C arrives, the *ack* for the last in-order segment (segment D) is transmitted.

TCP has two basic methods of finding out that a segment has been lost.

Retransmission timer

    If an acknowledgement for a data segment does not arrive at the sender at a certain amount of time, then the retransmission timer expires and the data segment is retransmitted [8].

M.M. Freire, P. Lorenz, M.M.-O. Lee (Eds.): HSNMC 2003, LNCS 2720, pp. 471–480, 2003.
© Springer-Verlag Berlin Heidelberg 2003

Fast Retransmit

When a TCP sender receives three *dupacks* (duplicate acknowledgements) for a data segment X, it assumes that the data segment Y which was immediately following X has been lost, so it resends segment Y without waiting for the retransmission timer to expire [3]. Fast Retransmit uses a parameter called *dupthresh* which is fixed at three *dupacks* to conclude whether the network has dropped a packet.

Reordering of packets during transmission through the network has several implications on the TCP performance. The following implications are pointed out in [9]:

1. When a network path reorders data segments, it may cause the TCP receiver to send more than three successive *dupacks*, and this triggers the Fast Retransmit procedure at the TCP sender for data segments that may not necessarily be lost. Unnecessary retransmission of data segments means that some of the bandwidth is wasted.
2. The TCP transport protocol assumes congestion in the network only when it assumes that a packet is dropped at the gateway. Thus when a TCP sender receives three successive *dupacks*, the TCP assumes that a packet has been lost and that this loss is an indication of network congestion, and reduces the congestion window to half its original size. If multiple retransmits occur for a single window, the congestion window decreases quickly to a very low value, and the rate of transmission drops significantly.
3. TCP ensures that the receiving application receives data in order. Persistent reordering of data segments is a serious burden on the TCP receiver since the receiver must buffer the out-of-order data until the missing data arrive to fill the gaps. Thus the data being buffered is withheld from the receiving application. This causes unnecessary load to the receiver and reduces the overall efficiency of the system.

We used a network simulator to get indication about the extent of the deterioration of the TCP performance when reordering of packets occurs, and the summary results from some of our simulations are shown in Table 1, columns 1–4 (we present the details of our simulations in Sections 4 and 5). For example, when the gateways were of the *Drop-tail* type and the queue sizes were 65, we observed that the TCP throughput decreased by 18% when reordering of packets occurred (Table 1, the first row).

We propose extending the TCP protocol to enable TCP senders to recognize whether a received *dupack* means that a packet has been dropped or reordered. The extended protocol is based on storing at the gateways information about dropped packets. Based on this information the sender is notified whether the packet has been dropped or reordered. We call this protocol RD-TCP (Reorder Detecting TCP).

RD-TCP should perform better than the standard TCP, if reordering of packets commonly occurs and if the senders receive confirmation, via the bits

Table 1. Normalized TCP throughput in an example network

type of gateways	queue size	standard TCP, no reordering	standard TCP, reordering	RD-TCP, reordering
Drop-tail	65	1.00	0.82	0.98
Drop-tail	20	1.00	0.87	1.03
RED	65	1.00	0.86	0.98
RED	20	1.00	0.88	0.98

set in *acks*, for the large proportion of dropped packets (it is not necessary that the senders receive confirmation for all dropped packets). Thus the performance of RD-TCP should be better than the performance of the standard TCP for networks, for which the following three conditions are true. Conditions 2 and 3 together insure that the senders are notified about most of the dropped packets.

1. Reordering of packets is common.
2. Large proportion of routing is symmetrical, that is, the acknowledgement packet is sent along the same path followed by the data packet.
3. Large proportion of gateways record information of dropped packets.

Paxson's study on the Internet [1] shows that approximately half of the measured routes are symmetrical, but for the local area networks this proportion should be considerably higher. The performance of RD-TCP which we observed in our simulations, are summarized in Table 1, column 5. Thus in our simulations RD-TCP performed significantly better than the standard TCP. In fact, it performed almost as well as if no reordering of packets occurred.

Section 2 presents the previous work related to our study. Section 3 presents the details of our proposed solution. In Sections 4, 5 and 6, we describe and discuss our simulations. We conclude this paper with a short discussion of the further research in Section 7 and a summary of our work in Section 8.

2   Related Work

Several methods to detect the needless retransmission due to the reordering of packets have been proposed:

- The Eifel algorithm uses the TCP time stamp option to distinguish an original transmission from an unnecessary retransmission [4].
- The DSACK option in TCP, allows the TCP receiver to report to the sender when duplicate segments arrive at the receiver's end. Using this information, the sender can determine when a retransmission is spurious [5].
- A method has been proposed by [6], for timing the *ack* of a segment that has been retransmitted. If the *ack* returns in less that $3/4 \times RTTmin$, the retransmission is likely to be spurious.

– [9] proposes various techniques for changing the way TCP senders decide to retransmit data segments by estimating the amount of reordering in the network path and increasing *dupthresh* by some value K, whenever a spurious fast retransmit occurs.

These methods show ways of improving the TCP performance when a packet has been retransmitted in the event of reordering. In our paper, we try to improve the performance by preventing the unnecessary retransmits that occur due to the reordering event by allowing the TCP sender to distinguish whether a *dupack* received for a packet is for a dropped packet or for a reordered packet and takes the appropriate action.

3   Our Proposed Solution

When the TCP sender sends data segments to the TCP receiver through intermediate gateways, these gateways drop the incoming data packets when their queues are full or reach a threshold value. Thus the TCP sender detects congestion only after a packet gets dropped in the intermediate gateway. When a packet gets reordered in the gateway or path, the TCP sender finds it impossible to distinguish whether the data packet has been dropped or reordered in the network. In this paper we try to solve this problem by proposing a solution to distinguish whether the packet has been lost or reordered in the gateways, by having a data structure that maintains the sequence number of the packet that gets dropped in the gateway. When an *ack* for some data packet P_k arrives at the gateway, the data structure is searched to check whether the sequence number of the packet P_{k+1} has been dropped by that particular gateway or not. If the packet has been dropped, then a *dropped* bit is set in the *ack*. When the sender receives an *ack*, it checks for the *dropped* bit and if it is set, then the sender knows that the packet has been dropped and retransmits the lost packet after receiving three *dupacks*. If the *dropped* bit is not set, then the TCP sender assumes that the packet has been reordered in the network and waits for 'k' more *dupacks* ('3+k' in total) instead of three *dupacks* to resend the data packet. We term our new version of TCP as RD-TCP (Reorder Detecting TCP).

Assume a network with source node A and destination node B with intermediate gateways R1 and R2. Node A sends data packets P_1, P_2, P_3 to node B through the gateways R1 and R2. If R1 drops packet P_2 due to congestion in the network, then node B will not receive P_2. On receipt of packet P_3, node B sends a *dupack* (each having sequence number P_1) through the gateways R2 and R1. Node A receives this *dupack* assuming the routing is purely symmetrical. Now in our proposed solution, when R1 drops packet P_2, the sequence number of packet P_2 is inserted into our data structure at R1, which in our case is a hashtable. Node B will not receive packet P_2. When node B receives packet P_3, it sends a *dupack* When gateway R2 receives an *ack* (having sequence number P_1), it checks whether the sequence number for packet P_2 (P_{1+1}) is available in its data structure. Since R2 does not have an entry, it does not set the *dropped* bit. When gateway R1 receives the *ack*, it checks for the sequence number for packet P_2, and finds that the sequence number is present in the data structure. Gateway R2 then sets the *dropped* bit in the *ack*, meaning that the packet has been dropped by the gateway. When the sender receives three *dupacks* with the *dropped* bit set, the sender retransmits the dropped packet.

Suppose the packet P_2 had been reordered in the gateway, the receiver B assuming the packet has been dropped, sends a *dupack* on receipt of packet P_3. When gateway R2 receives the *ack*, it checks for the sequence number entry in its hashtable and finds that there is no entry for it, and does not set the *dropped* bit. Similarly when gateway R1 receives the *ack*, it checks for the sequence number in its hashtable and finds that there is no entry for it, and does not set the *dropped* bit. When the sender node A receives a *dupack*, it checks for the *dropped* bit of each of these 2 *acks*, and when '3+k' *dupacks* with the *dropped* bit not set are received, the packet is resent and fast recovery is triggered. If the value of 'k' is not large enough, then the TCP will continue to send unnecessary retransmissions. If the value of 'k' is set too large, fast retransmit may not be triggered leading to retransmission timeout. The best value of 'k' depends on the impact of reordering and could be varied depending on the current network conditions as proposed in [9] i.e. if the TCP sender detects spurious retransmits even though it has incremented the value of 'k', then the sender can further increase the value of 'k' to reduce the number of unnecessary retransmissions that occur due to reordering.

3.1   Details of the Implementation

Data Structure Used   We use a hashtable to maintain the flow ids and the dropped packet numbers (PNO_i) for the respective flow ids (F_{id}). The flow id is the index and the packet numbers are the items in the list for a particular flow id.

Recording Information about Dropped Packets

– Initially, the hashtable is empty.
– When a packet $< F_{id}, PNO_i >$ gets dropped in the gateway, the corresponding flow id (F_{id}) is used as the index to check the hashtable to find out whether there is an entry for that particular flow. If an entry is present, then sequence number of the dropped packet (PNO_i) is inserted into the end of the list of the corresponding flow id. If an entry is not present, an entry is created, and the sequence number of the dropped packet is entered as the first entry in the list.

Processing the *ack* Packets   When an *ack* $< F_{id}, PNO_i >$ arrives at the gateway,

– If the *dropped* bit is already set (some other gateway has dropped the packet), then pass on the packet.

- If the *dropped* bit is not set, the corresponding flow id (F_{id}) is used as the index to check the hashtable. If no entry is present for that particular flow id, the *dropped* bit is not set.
- If entry is present, then the corresponding list is searched to check whether the sequence number (PNO_{i+1}) is present. If present then the *dropped* bit is set accordingly. If the entry was not present, the *dropped* bit is not set. During the searching process, if a sequence number less than the current sequence number that is used for searching is encountered, the lesser sequence number entry is deleted from the list. This means that the packet with the lesser sequence number has been retransmitted.
- When the list is empty, the flow id entry is removed from the hashtable.

Removing Inactive Lists There may be cases where possible residuals (packet sequence numbers) may be left in the list even though that particular flow has become inactive. To remove these unwanted residuals and the list for that particular flowid, we could have another hash table that maintains a timestamp of the last *ack* packet that has passed through the gateway for the flow whose entry is already present in the main hash table (When an entry is created in the main hash table for a particular flow, an entry is also created in this hashtable simultaneously). It uses the flow id (F_{id}) as the index of the hashtable. The timestamp entry for that particular flow is regularly updated with the timestamp of the last *ack* that has passed through the gateway. Regularly, say every 300 ms, the entire hashtable is scanned, and the difference of the timestamp entry in each index with the current time is calculated. If the difference is greater than a set threshold (say, 300ms), then it means that the flow is inactive currently and the entries of both the hashtables for that particular flow are removed.

3.2   Storage and Computational Costs

In our implementation we do not have to maintain the list of all the flows that pass through a particular gateway i.e. we do not maintain per-connection state for all the flows. Despite the large number of flows, a common observation found in many measurement studies is that a small percentage of flow accounts for a large percentage of the traffic. It is argued in [11] that 9% of the flows between AS pairs account for the 90% of the byte traffic between all AS pairs. It is shown in [2] that large flows could be tracked or monitored easily by using SRAM that copes up with the link speed. Our monitoring process records only flows whose packets have been dropped. To get some rough estimate of the amount of memory needed for our implementation, let us assume that there are $200,000$ concurrent flows passing through one gateway, 10% of them have information about one or more dropped packets recorded in this gateway, and a non-empty list of sequence numbers of dropped packets has on average 10 entries. Thus the hash table will have $20,000$ non-empty entries and the total length of the lists of sequence numbers of dropped packets will be $200,000$. We need 4 bytes for each flow id, 4 bytes for each packet sequence number, and another 4 bytes for each pointer. This means that the total memory required would be about 2.5 MB. This is only a rough estimate of the amount of extra memory needed, but we believe that it is realistic. Thus we expect that an extra 8MB SRAM would be highly sufficient to implement our solution.

The computational cost mostly depends on the average length of a list of sequence numbers of dropped packets. If a flow has not dropped any packets in the gateway, then the computation done would be to check whether an entry for that particular flow id is present or not. This takes constant time computation. If a flow has a non-empty list of sequence numbers of dropped packets, then this list has to be searched whenever an *ack* for that particular flow passes through the gateway. This computation takes $O(n)$ time, if the lists are implemented in the straightforward linear way, or $O(\log n)$ time, if the lists are implemented as suitable balanced trees (n denotes the current length of the list).

We believe that the improvement of the throughput offered by our solution justifies the extra memory and computational costs, but further investigations are needed to obtain a good estimate of the trade-off between the costs and benefits.

4   Simulation Environment

We use the network simulator ns-2 [10] to test our proposed solution. We created our own version of a reordering gateway and made minor changes to the TCP protocol. Assume nodes A and B are the sender nodes, nodes C and D are the destination nodes and R1, R2 are routers. Nodes A and B are each connected to router R1 via 10Mbps Ethernet having a delay of 1ms. The routers R1 and R2 are connected to each other via 5Mbps link with a delay of 10ms. Nodes C and D are each connected to router R2 via 10Mbps Ethernet having a delay of 1ms. Our simulations use 1500 byte segments. We have conducted experiments with both Drop-tail and RED gateways. The queue sizes used were 20 and 65 segments. In our experiments we have used FTP traffic flows between source node A and destination node C via routers R1, R2 and between source node B and destination node D. For Drop-tail queues, we have simulated an average of 6 reorder events per second and the pattern of reordering is consistent through out the experiments using Drop-tail queues. For RED queues, we have simulated an average of 4 reorder events per second and the pattern of reordering is consistent throughout the experiments using RED queues.

5   Impact of Reordering

In this section, we compare the throughput performance of the simulated network using TCP, with and without reordering events for both Drop-tail and RED gateways each having a queue size of 65 segments. The reason why we chose a queue size of 65 was to prevent packet drops so that we can easily verify the impact of reordering on a network where there is no packet drops. When reordering occurred in Drop-tail gateways, there was a 17.9% reduction in throughput performance when compared to the throughput performance of the network without any reordering events (refer Table 2 (first row, columns 2 and 3)). Similarly when reordering occurred in RED gateways, there was a 13.8% reduction in throughput performance when compared to the throughput performance of a network without any reordering events (refer Table 3 (first row, columns 2 and 3)). This shows that persistent reordering degrades the throughput performance of a network to a large extent.

6   Results

We performed various tests by varying the value of 'k'. When $k = 0$ (*dupthresh* $= 3$), the network behaves as an ordinary network with persistent reordering events using TCP. When $k = 1$, the performance of the network is similar to the network with $k = 0$. When $k > 1$, the throughput increases rapidly by reducing the number of unnecessary retransmits that occur due to reordering. We have summarized the results for $k = 2$ (*dupthresh* $= 5$) in Tables 2 and 3.

queue size	standard TCP, no reordering	standard TCP, reordering occurs	RD-TCP, reordering occurs
65	6144680	5042040 (-17.9%)	6007620 (-2.2%)
20	5787400	5042040 (-12.8%)	5867480 (+1.0%)

Table 2. Comparison of throughput performance of the network using Drop-tail gateways for different queue size.

We compared the throughput performance of the network with reordering events using TCP to the same network with reordering events using RD-TCP with a Drop-tail queue size of 65. Figure 1 shows the comparison of the throughput performance of RD-TCP and TCP using Drop-tail queues. The total number of bytes received at the end of the 10 minute simulation by the network with reordering using TCP was 5042040 bytes, whereas the total bytes received at the end of the 10 minute simulation by the network with reordering using RD-TCP was 6007620 bytes. Interestingly we achieved 19.1% increase in throughput performance when compared to the same network with persistent reordering using TCP. There was only a 2.2% reduction in throughput performance when compared to the throughput performance of the network without any reordering events using TCP (refer Table 2 (first row, columns 2 and 4)).

We compared the throughput performance of the network with reordering events using TCP to the same network with reordering using RD-TCP with a RED queue size of 65. The total number of bytes received by the two receivers at the end of the 10 minute simulation by the network with reordering using TCP was 5294600 bytes, whereas the total bytes received by the two receivers at the end of the 10 minute simulation by the network using reordering with RD-TCP

queue size	standard TCP, no reordering	standard TCP, reordering occurs	RD-TCP, reordering occurs
65	6144680	5294600 (-13.8%)	6016860 (-2.1%)
20	6016860	5308460 (-11.7%)	5898280 (-1.9%)

Table 3. Comparison of throughput performance of the network using RED gateways for different queue size.

was 6016860 bytes. Interestingly we achieved 13.64% increase in throughput performance when compared to the same network with persistent reordering using TCP. There was only a 2.1% reduction in throughput performance when compared to the throughput performance of the network without any reordering events using TCP (refer Table 3 (first row, columns 2 and 4)).

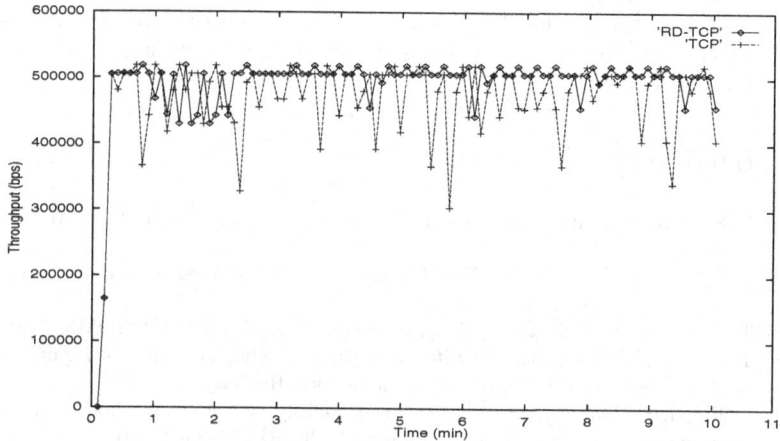

Fig. 1. Comparison of throughput performance of the network with reordering events using RD-TCP with k = 2 vs the same network with reordering events using TCP with a Drop-tail queue size of 65.

7 Further Work

- We have proposed a mechanism for enabling the senders to distinguish whether a packet has been lost or reordered in the network. We have initially simulated and tested our protocol on networks whose routing are symmetric. Further work has to be done to test the efficiency of our protocol for various levels of asymmetric routing.

- Our proposed solution should be compared with the other solutions that have been mentioned in the related work section. These methods show ways of improving the TCP performance when a packet has been retransmitted in the event of reordering.
- Further simulations and testing needs to be carried out to find the efficiency of the protocol when there is an incremental deployment i.e when there are some routers in a network which have not been upgraded to use our mechanism.

8 Conclusion

In this paper, we proposed a solution that prevents the unnecessary retransmits that occur due to reordering events in networks that follow symmetrical routing paths, by allowing the TCP sender to distinguish whether a packet has been lost or reordered in the network. This was done by maintaining information about dropped packets in the gateway and using this information to notify the sender, whether the packet has been dropped or reordered the gateway. We have also showed that our solution improves the throughput performance of the network to a large extent.

References

1. Paxson, V.: End-to-End Routing Behaviour in the Internet. ACM SIGCOMM (1996)
2. Estan, C., Varghese, G.: New Directions in Traffic Measurement and Accounting. ACM SIGCOMM (2002)
3. Jacobson, V.: Congestion Avoidance and Control. ACM SIGCOMM (1988)
4. Ludwig, R., Katz, R.: The Eifel Algorithm: Making TCP Robust Against Spurious Retransmissions. Computer Communication Review, 30(1)(2000)
5. Floyd, S., Mahdavi, J., Mathis, M., Podolsky, M.: An Extension to the Selective Acknowledgement (SACK) Option for TCP. RFC 2883 (2000)
6. Allman, M., Paxson, V.: On Estimating End-to-End Network Path Properties. ACM SIGCOMM (1999)
7. Bennett, J., Partridge, C., Shectman, N.: Packet Reordering is Not Pathological Network Behaviour. IEEE/ACM Transactions on Networking (1999)
8. Postel, J.: Transmission Control Protocol. RFC 793 (1981)
9. Blanton, E., Allman, M.: On Making TCP More Robust to Packet Reordering. ACM SIGCOMM (2002)
10. McCanne, S., Floyd, S.: Network Simulator. http://www.isi.edu/nsnam/ns/
11. Fang, W., Peterson, L.: Inter-as-traffic patterns and their implications. IEEE GLOBECOM (1999)
12. Allman, M., Balakrishnan, H., Floyd, S.: Enhancing TCP's Lost Recovery Using Limited Transmit. RFC 3042 (2001)
13. Cisco NetFlow: http://www.cisco.com/warp/public/732/Tech/netflow

Explicit Loss Notification to Improve TCP Performance over Wireless Networks

Gergö Buchholcz[1], Adam Gricser[1], Thomas Ziegler[2], Tien Van Do[1]

[1]Department of Telecommunications, Budapest University of Technology and Economics
Magyar tudósok körútja 2., Budapest, Hungary
buchholcz@hit.bme.hu, gricser@hit.bme.hu, do@hit.bme.hu
[2]Telecommunications Research Center Vienna (ftw.)
Tech Gate Vienna, Donau-City-Straße 1/3. Stock A-1220 Wien, Austria
ziegler@ftw.at

Abstract. In this paper we propose a novel TCP congestion control algorithm to overcome the weakness of the original TCP mechanism in wireless environments. The primary aim of the new algorithm is to cope with packet losses due to bit errors in the radio interface. Our solution is based on the idea of Explicit Loss Notification (ELN) to notify the sender about packet losses in the wireless channel. We also performed extensive simulations with different kind of traffic and error models to demonstrate the performance improvement of the proposed algorithm compared to the original TCP.

1 Introduction

TCP was developed with two aims in the early 80's. It provides a reliable data transfer protocol and it adapts to the network load situation in a fair way. The first goal can be achieved by TCP's ARQ mechanism [1], while the second goal is reached by the congestion avoidance mechanism. The performance of the previously standardized TCP types (Tahoe, Reno [2], New Reno [3]) can be considered adequate in wired environments, but the data transfer rate is strongly degraded due to the high bit error rate of the radio interface in wireless networks.

In this paper we introduce a new flow control algorithm which is based on the Explicit Loss Notification (ELN) approach. The main idea is that the receiver notifies the sender when a packet corruption is recognized on the wireless link. We show that significant performance improvements can be achieved without the modification of network nodes.

The rest of paper is organized as follows. In Section 2 we summarize the related work previously proposed to increase TCP efficiency over wireless links. Section 3 describes the details of our ELN proposal. Section 4 discusses our proposed algorithm. Section 5 specifies the simulation environment and presents the simulation results. Finally, Section 6 concludes this paper.

M.M. Freire, P. Lorenz, M.M.-O. Lee (Eds.): HSNMC 2003, LNCS 2720, pp. 481–492, 2003.

2   Related Works

Approaches to improve the performance of TCP over wireless links [4] can be classified as follows.
- **Split-Connection approach**: Normally, TCP connections established in a wireless environment include the wired part as well. Therefore, an obvious idea is to
  split the connection into two parts at the base station. In the wireless link, either
  TCP or a specialized protocol can be used. The split-connection approach suffers
  from a major disadvantage that every packet has to be stored and processed at the
  base station. Therefore, huge memory consumption and processing overhead
  should be maintained at the base station.
- **Link-layer protocols:** Proposals aims at the development of a more reliable link-
  layer protocol to hide the unreliable behavior of wireless channels from the TCP
  layer. The two main classes of techniques employed by theses protocols are: error
  correction (using techniques such as forward error correction --FEC), and retransmission of lost packets by automatic repeat request (ARQ). The main advantage of the link-layer based proposal is that it fits naturally into the layered hierarchy of the network protocol stack. Since it affects only separate links of the network, it can be applied on wide range of scenarios.
- **End-to-End proposals:** The main idea of these TCP improvement proposals is
  that additional information about the data flow available for the receiver may help
  the sender to improve the flow control mechanism. Some of the main techniques
  are Selective ACKnowledgements (SACK)[5], HeAder ChecKsum option
  (HACK)[6] and Explicit Loss Notification. The major advantage of end-to-end
  proposals is that only the communicating peers need to be modified, the rest of the
  network stays as is.
  - o Contrary to standard versions of TCP using cumulative acknowledgements,
    SACK [5] provides detailed information to the sender on packets that are re-
    ceived but out of order. SACK uses the option field in the TCP header for sig-
    naling. This technique potentially enables the sender to recover quickly from
    multiple packet losses within a single transmission window.
  - o The Header Checksum Option proposal is based on the idea that even damaged
    TCP packets may contain correct headers. Since the payload is much longer
    than the header, the probability for bit corruptions to occur only in the payload
    is high. Retrieving the correct header from a corrupted packet, the receiver is
    able to send negative acknowledgements back to the sender. This helps the
    source to improve the retransmission strategy [6].
  - o The Explicit Loss Notification proposal is built upon the idea that the MAC
    layer is able to detect packet losses and notify the TCP layer. Future duplicate
    acknowledgements corresponding to the lost packet will indicate that a non-
    congestion related loss occurred. Upon receiving duplicate acknowledgements,
    the sender may perform retransmissions without invoking the associated con-
    gestion–control procedures [4].
  - o TCP Westwood (TCPW) [10] exploits two basic concepts: the end-to-end es-
    timation of the available bandwidth, and the use of such an estimate to set the
    slow start threshold and the congestion window after a congestion episode.

That is, after three duplicate acknowledgements or after a timeout. In contrast to TCP-Reno, which simply halves the congestion window after three duplicate acknowledgements TCPW attempts to make a more "informed" decision. It selects a slow start threshold and a congestion window that is consistent with the effective connection rate at the time congestion experienced.

3 The ELN Proposal

This section describes the basic properties of the ELN algorithm proposal investigated in this paper [4]. The fundamental idea behind the Explicit Loss Notification proposal is that the MAC layer of the receiver node is able to detect the corrupted packets. The conventional MAC layer drops the packet immediately as it realizes bit corruption. In this case TCP considers the corrupted packet to be lost due to congestion after the timer expires, which follows the reduction of the sending rate of the data flow. It is obvious, that informing the TCP sender about the corrupted packet, hence giving it the ability to distinguish between packet losses due to congestion and packet losses due to wireless link errors, would increase the overall performance of the data flow. This performance improvement can be gained by avoiding unnecessary reductions of the TCP window.

In the proposal the MAC layer at the receiver propagates the loss information to the higher layers, thus the TCP receiver can send loss notifications to the TCP sender. Since the TCP data receiver may handle multiple connections simultaneously, it is not enough to know the fact of a packet loss but the packet exact address (IP address and port no.) is also important. Using information on the exact address the packet's sender can be informed about the loss. There are two main possibilities to gain the lost packet's identifiers. Forbidding simultaneous TCP connections is a restricted but feasible solution for low performance mobile hosts when they run web browsers. New HTTP [7] standards provide the ability of a persistent connection, thus only one TCP session may be enough at a time. If there is a demand for simultaneous TCP connections at the mobile host, the sender of the corrupted packet must be determined. The TCP sender is identified by the port number in the header of the TCP packet, thus this information has to be retrieved from the corrupted TCP packet. Accomplishing this task is possible using the Header Checksum Option [6]. Since in most TCP packets the payload is much longer than the header bit errors are likely to appear in the payload leaving the header intact. By adding a special option field to the TCP header containing a checksum for the header only, the validity of the TCP header can be verified [6]. With this mechanism, the TCP sender can be identified from an intact TCP header and the receiver can send loss notifications to the proper TCP peer entity.

The ELN proposal has two major properties that affect the applicability in wireless networks.

- First it is an end-to-end proposal: modifications are made only to protocol layers in the two communicating end nodes. This property makes the ELN technique scalable and easily applicable compared to proposals that need to modify inner network nodes as well.

- The second property is that only the last link of the connection (Base Station to Mobile Node) is monitored by the receiver's MAC layer in order to detect packet losses. Communicating TCP peers do not have additional information about neither the packet losses on possible inner wireless links of the network, nor about packets traveling in upload direction (Mobile Node to Fixed Host). As a consequence only the download direction can be optimized by this method. For these reasons the ELN proposal is best to apply in networks containing only wireless links between the mobile nodes and the base station. In mobile networks it is very common to have only one wireless link at the mobile node, and download direction is still dominant in most cases (e.g. Web browsing), thus applying the ELN proposal even with these restrictions may produce significant benefits.

4   Overview of the Mechanism

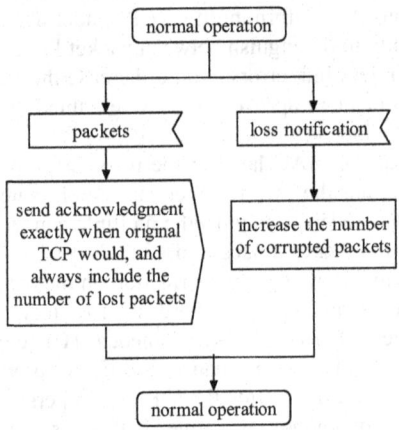

Fig. 1. The operation of the TCP-ELN receiver

In this section we explain the operation of the improved TCP entities. Without loss of generality we consider one TCP flow. The operation of the receiver TCP-ELN entity is illustrated in **Figure 1**. Assume that a notification is sent to the receiver TCP layer every time a packet corruption is detected by the MAC layer. The TCP-ELN receiver has now two events to handle: receiving a loss notification or receiving an intact TCP packet. In the first case the only task it performs is increasing the overall number of packets corrupted during the connection. Upon receiving an intact TCP packet, the TCP-ELN receiver behaves exactly as the original except for including the number of corrupted packets counted so far in every acknowledgement. We use the TCP options field in acknowledgements to carry this information. For the remainder of the paper this field will be referred to as the *corruption counter field*.

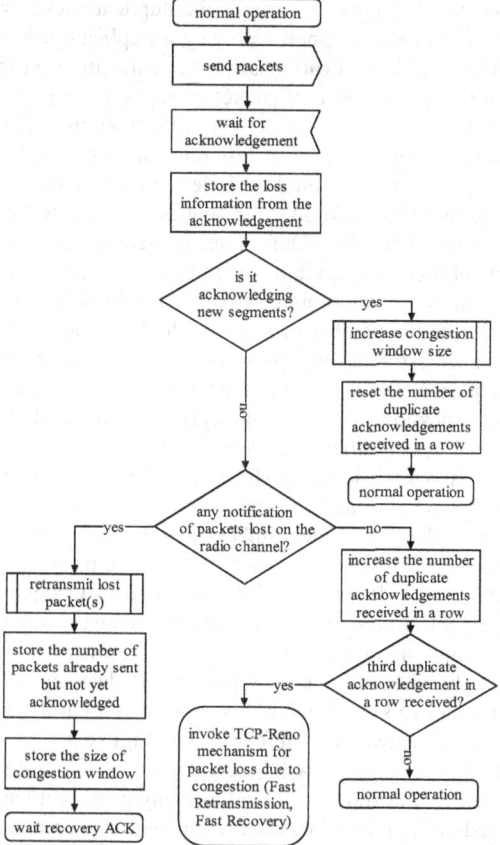

Fig. 2. The operation of the TCP-ELN sender

This additional information embedded in every TCP acknowledgement enables the TCP-ELN sender to distinguish between the causes of packet losses (see **Figure 2 and 3**). Packet losses are indicated either by a timeout or by three duplicate acknowledgements triggering fast retransmit, fast recovery. Because a timeout is a very strong indication for network congestion, the mechanisms invoked in this case remain unchanged.

Normally TCP sends out several new segments depending on the size of the congestion window and awaits acknowledgements. Whenever an acknowledgement arrives, the source checks whether it is acknowledging new segments or segments that have been previously acknowledged. In case of receiving an ACK acknowledging new segments, TCP operates as usual. It increases the window size by an increment depending on the state of the sender (Slow Start or Congestion Avoidance); resets the number of previously received duplicated acknowledgements (Fast Retransmit) and finally transmits new segments according to the new congestion window size. This part of the protocol remained unchanged as shown in the upper part of **Figure 2**.

The lower part of **Figure 2** presents the duplicate acknowledgement management of the TCP-ELN protocol. Upon receiving a duplicate acknowledgement the sender checks if there is any notification of packet corruption on the radio channel or not. The decision on the existence of packet corruption is based on comparing the values of the *corruption counter field* received in the acknowledgements. The increment of the *corruption counter field* since last retransmission due to corruption equals the number of packets corrupted on the wireless link since then. If the increment is larger than zero, the duplicate acknowledgement is assumed to be an indication of packet corruption on the radio link. Otherwise, if there is no increment, the duplicate acknowledgement is considered to be the indication of congestion or packet reordering.

If there is no notification about a packet corruption, the TCP sender proceeds as usual. It increases the number of received duplicate acknowledgements, and invokes Fast Retransmit-Fast Recovery procedures if the third duplicate acknowledgement arrives in sequence. Obviously, the sender checks the loss notifications for all subsequent duplicate acknowledgements it receives before invoking Fast Retransmit.

Otherwise, if loss notifications indicate that the packet was corrupted and lost on the wireless channel the sender performs a different procedure. It first retransmits the lost packet(s) (loss notifications may indicate the loss of several subsequent segments). Afterward it stores the number of packets already sent but not yet acknowledged and the size of congestion window for future purposes.

The TCP source will get several duplicate acknowledgements before the recovery acknowledgement arrives. While awaiting the recovery acknowledgement the source has no information about network congestion (duplicate acknowledgements can only indicate a single packet loss as they point to the last segment arrived in order at the receiver). In order to keep the data transmission rate at the same level the sender enters a new state as shown in the left branch of **Figure 3**.

Normally the TCP sender will receive as many duplicate acknowledgements preceding the recovery acknowledgement as many packets it has already sent but not yet acknowledged at the time of the fast retransmit. The reception of more duplicate acknowledgements is indicating that the retransmitted packet was lost either due to congestion or due to wireless link error. In order to avoid retransmitting the same packets again, the sender invokes the congestion resolving mechanisms [2] of the original TCP protocol when the number of received duplicate acknowledgements exceeds the expected amount. Every time a duplicate acknowledgement arrives and the limit is not exceeded the sender increases the window size by 1 segment. Increasing the window size enables the source to send new segments to the receiver while waiting for the recovery acknowledgement. Note that opening the window in this state does not increase the speed of data flow and is necessary to keep the speed constant, since no new segments are acknowledged by duplicate acknowledgements.

Upon receiving the recovery acknowledgement (the right hand side of Fig. 3) the sender has to investigate whether network congestion evolved while waiting for the recovery acknowledgement or not. As mentioned above, no congestion indication can be retrieved from the duplicate acknowledgements. The lack of proper information is

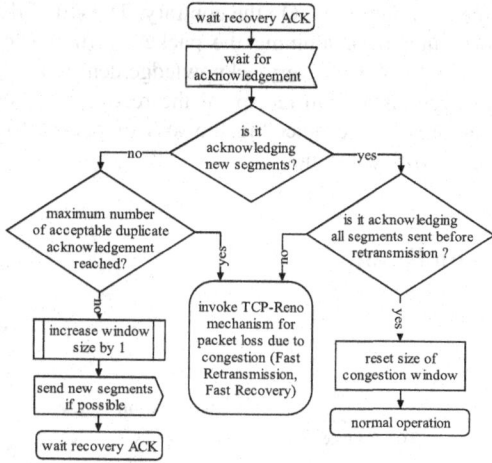

Fig. 3. Handling ACK at the TCP-ELN sender

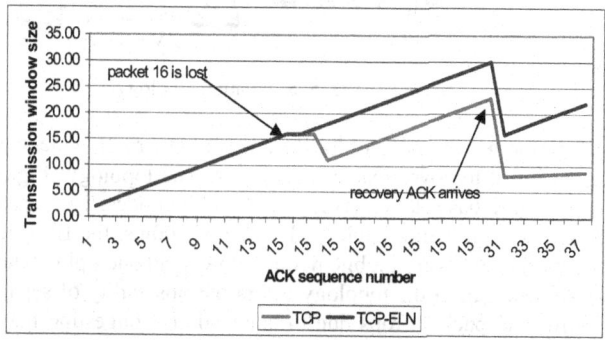

Fig. 4. Transmission window size in the presence of packet loss

resolved with a simple and conservative assumption. A partial recovery acknowledgement is considered to be a sign of congestion. In case of a partial acknowledgement the congestion resolving mechanisms of the original TCP are invoked (Fast Retransmit - Fast Recovery). Otherwise, if a full recovery acknowledgement arrives (i.e. all segments sent before the retransmission are acknowledged by this packet) the sender resets the congestion window to the size it had when the packet was lost before fast retransmit and resumes normal operation (**Figure 3, right hand side**). Setting the congestion window to the value before detection of the loss (and not halving it as original TCP Reno would do) is justified by the fact that the packet loss has been detected as a loss due to packet corruption.

The simple scenario of the new protocol's behavior compared to the original one is illustrated in **Figure 4.** When packet 16 is lost on the wireless channel due to bit corruption the original TCP Reno protocol goes through the recovery phases [2]. After the recovery TCP Reno halves the congestion window and unnecessarily de-

creases the speed of data flow. On the contrary, TCP-ELN detects that the loss is due
to packet corruption by examining the packet corruption counter, resends the lost
packet, and waits for the recovery acknowledgement without halving the congestion
window at fast retransmit. On receipt of the recovery ACK it resets the congestion
window to the size before detecting the loss of packet 16 keeping the amount of
packets in the network constant.

5   Simulation Results

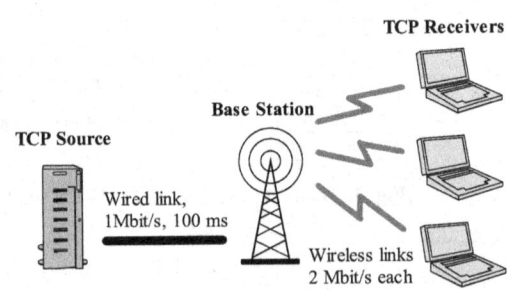

Fig. 5. Simulation topology

To measure the performance of TCP-ELN we have run a wide variety of simulations
that are designed to cover realistic scenarios. The topology (**Figure 5**) consists of 5
nodes: a server, a base station (BS), and 3 mobile nodes. The server node connects to
the BS with a 1 Mb/s link having a latency of 100ms, the BS offers a 2 Mb/s bandwidth connection to every mobile node in download and upload directions. Using this
bandwidth distribution the topology offers the possibility of separating packet drops
due to error and packet drops due to congestion. Congestion may occur only at the
link from the server to the BS, packet loss due to bit error can occur only at the radio
links.

For traffic simulation FTP and web traffic is generated. The bulk FTP traffic is
used to measure the steady state behavior of the protocol, while web traffic is used to
examine the dynamic behavior. In the first group of simulations one FTP session is
started at every mobile node. In the second group 5 web sessions are started at the
mobile nodes. We measure the ftp throughput and the response time of web traffic.
We use the SURGE model [8] to generate Web traffic which is based on real traffic
traces and has been proved to generate realistic workloads. Uniform and Markov
error models are two different approaches of modeling the lossy link behavior. Both
of them are used to simulate packet loss at the link level. The mean value of the uniform distribution is varied between 0 and 0.2. Integrating channel fading and radio
link parameters the Markov model takes the characteristics of wireless channels into
account.

Table 1. Parameters of the Markov model

Model number	User speed	Average error rate	Average error burst length
1	Pedestrian (1.5Km/h)	0.001	1.4913
2		0.01	4.0701
3		0.1	13.6708
4	intermediate	0.001	1.0083
5		0.01	1.0838
6		0.1	1.8629
7	High (100Km/h)	0.001	1.0024
8		0.01	1.012
9		0.1	1.1317

Using the Markov model we simulate radio links that a pedestrian and radio links that a high-speed user can experience with different packet drop probabilities (A more detailed description of Markov error model can be found in [9]).

The different speed parameters with the same average error rates result in different expected values of burst error length as shown in Table 5.1. Note that due to the behavior of the physical channel the correlation of packet errors (the average burst length) is decreasing as the speed increases.

Figure 6 shows the results of FTP traffic with uniform error model. The curves show that in error free transmission both protocols – the original and TCP-ELN – produce the same throughput. This is in accordance with the fact that TCP-ELN behaves exactly the same as the original protocol when there is no loss notification. In case of packet corruption TCP-ELN can achieve a 60-200% improvement in throughput for the examined error rates. The higher the error rates are the better the new protocol's relative performance improvement is (see the right side of **Figure 6**). While the original protocol closes the congestion window as often as a packet is lost the TCP-ELN tries to avoid unnecessary window reductions.

FTP throughput and the relative improvement with the Markov error model is shown in **Figure 7**.

As it can be seen in on the right side of **Figure 7** the relative improvement is between 110% and 140% for the high loss scenario (bulk 3,6,9). The improvement is between 60% and 120% for the medium loss scenario (bulk 2,5,8). Naturally, in the case of low loss (bulk 1, 4, 7) the relative throughput increase is somewhat lower.

Comparing the throughput and improvement values measured over uniform error with the ones produced over Markov error model, an interesting correlation can be recognized. Investigate the throughput values over an average error rate of 0.1 (10%). This error rate corresponds to the 3rd, 6th and 9th bulk in figure 6.3. Over the uniform model TCP-ELN produced a throughput of *8407 kBytes/s*. The values for the Markov models 3, 6 and 9 are *18433, 9965, 8685 kBytes/s* respectively. As the speed parameter of the Markov model increases the average length of an error burst decreases. Thus

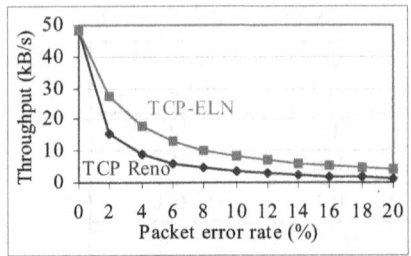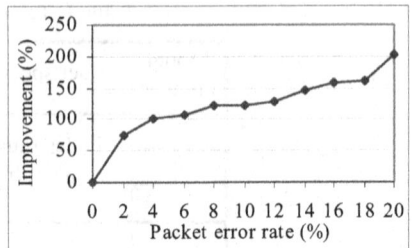

Fig. 6. The throughput and the relative improvement over FTP traffic with the uniform error model

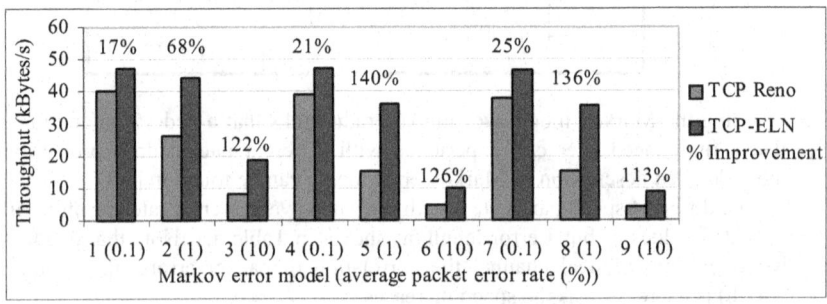

Fig. 7 The throughput and the relative improvement over FTP traffic with Markov error model

at higher speeds – as packet loss becomes sporadic – the Markov error model converges to the uniform error model. According to the results TCP-ELN is more effective when packet losses occur in bursts. Uniform, sporadic errors force the sender to reduce the size of congestion window more frequently than bursty errors with the same average error rate. In the third group of Markov models when the speed is the highest and the packet errors are barely correlated (distribution is close to uniform) the value of throughput is nearly the same as in the case of uniform distribution.

In the web traffic simulation 5 sessions are used per mobile node. Each session simulates web page downloads with random object sizes, user think times, inter-object sizes and number of objects per page according to the SURGE model. The average response time of these downloads can be seen in the corresponding figures. In **figure 8** the uniform error probability results are shown. **Figure 9** shows the web results with the Markov error model.

The average response times with the uniform error model are 10% to 60% better when using TCP-ELN. **Figure 8** shows that at higher error rates the improvement becomes larger.

In case of web traffic and the Markov error model (see **figure 9**) we observe slight improvements in case of low mean error rates (bulk 1,4,7), improvements between 15% and 30% in case of medium mean error rates, and 30% to 50% in case of high mean error rates.

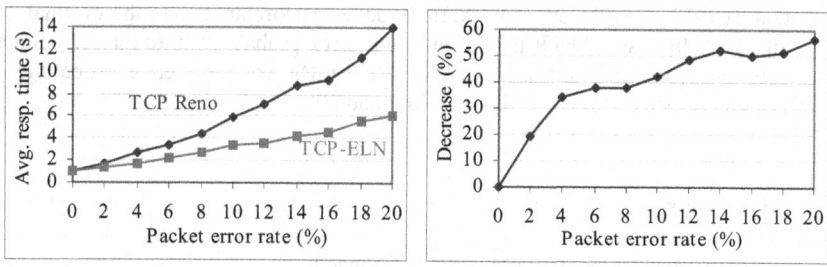

Fig. 8. The average response time and relative improvement of web traffic with the uniform error model

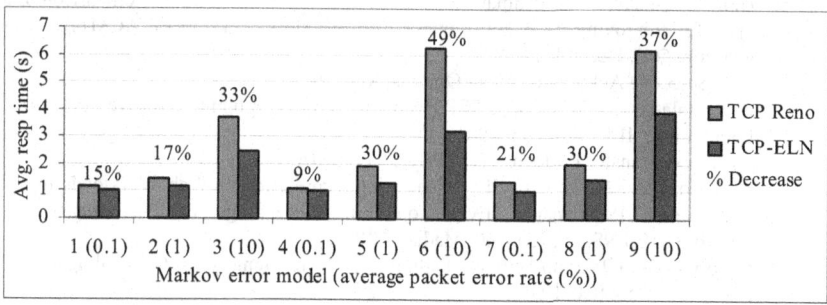

Fig. 9. The average response time and the relative improvement of web traffic with the Markov error model

6 Conclusions

In this paper we have proposed a new technique to improve TCP's low performance on wireless networks. The TCP-ELN protocol is based on the idea of the Explicit Loss Notification mechanism. TCP-ELN allows the TCP source to differentiate between packet losses due to wireless link error and packet losses due to congestion. Avoiding unnecessarily halving the congestion window when a packet is lost due to link error, the improved protocol guarantees higher performance than original TCP.

We have explained the algorithm in detail and clarified the circumstances under which TCP-ELN can be used. TCP-ELN has applicability restrictions in terms of the network topology, the data flow direction, and the number of simultaneous flows at a mobile host in case the Header Checksum Option is not used. However, in spite of these practical limitations the new protocol is able to increase TCP performance in most common scenarios.

Our simulation experiments have shown that TCP-ELN dramatically improves the performance of TCP over wireless links in a wide variety of environments. We have tested the protocol's performance over random and bursty erroneous links with two different types of traffic, static FTP bulk load and dynamic web traffic. Results prove that TCP-ELN produces a substantially better performance than the original TCP in all cases. In case of FTP traffic and high error probability throughput is improved between 110% and 200%. In case of Web traffic and high error probability mean response times are reduced between 30% and 60%.

References

1. W. Richard Stevens, TCP/IP Illustrated, Volume 1
2. TCP Slow Start, Congestion Avoidance, Fast Retransmit, and Fast Recovery Algorithms, Network Working Group, RFC 2001
3. The NewReno Modification to TCP's Fast Recovery Algorithm, RFC 2582
4. H. Balakrishnan, V. N. Padmanabhan, S. Seshan, and R. H. Katz, A Comparison of Mechanism for Improving TCP Performance over Wireless Links, IEEE/ACM Trans. on Networking, 5(6), December 1997.
5. TCP Selective Acknowledgment Options, RFC 2018
6. R. K. Balan et. al, TCP Hack: TCP Header Checksum Option to Improve Performance over Loosy Links, IEEE Infocom 2001
7. Hypertext Transfer Protocol - HTTP/1.1, RFC 2616
8. P. Barford and M. E. Crovella, "Generating Representative Web Workloads for Network and Server Performance Evaluation," in Proceedings of Performance '98/ACM SIGMETRICS '98, pp. 151-160, Madison WI.
9. Performance of TCP on Wireless Fading Links with Memory, A. Chockalingam, M. Zorzi, Ramesh R. Rao, ICC 1998
10. Andrea Zanella, Gregorio Procissi, Mario Gerla, M.Y. "Medy" Sanadidi : TCP Westwood: Analytic Model and Performance Evaluation, Globecom 2001

Comparing Performance of SRAMT-LE Vs. Other Layered Encoding Schemes Regarding TCP Friendliness

Christos Bouras and Apostolos Gkamas

Research Academic Computer Technology Institute, 61 Riga Feraiou Str, GR-26221 Patras, Greece
Computer Engineering and Informatics Dept., Univ. of Patras, GR-26500 Patras, Greece
{bouras, gkamas}@cti.gr

Abstract. In this paper we describe a hybrid sender and receiver-based adaptation scheme for multicast transmission of multimedia data using layered encoding, which we call SRAMT-LE (Sender-Receiver based Adaptation scheme for Multicast Transmission using Layered Encoding). The most prominent features of SRAMT-LE are its distributed (to sender and receivers) transmission rate estimation algorithm and its innovative RTT (Round Trip Time) estimation algorithm based on one-way delay measurements. SRAMT-LE is using both a TCP model and an AIMD (Additive Increase Multiplicative Decrease) algorithm in order to estimate a TCP friendly bandwidth share. We evaluate SRAMT-LE and compare it with a number of similar layered encoding schemes available to the literature (PLM, RLC, MLDA). Main conclusion of this evaluation was that SRAMT-LE has friendly behavior against the dominant traffic types of today's Internet and has a relative good behavior comparing with the other layered encoding schemes available to the literature.

1. Introduction

The multicast transmission of real time multimedia data is an important component of many current and future emerging Internet applications, like videoconference, distance learning and video distribution. The heterogeneous network environment that Internet provides to real time applications as well as the lack of sufficient QoS (Quality of Service) guarantees, many times forces applications to embody adaptation schemes in order to work efficiently. In addition, any application that transmits data over the Internet should have a friendly behavior towards the other flows that coexist in today's Internet and especially towards the TCP flows that comprise the majority of flows. We define as TCP friendly flow, a flow that consumes no more bandwidth than a TCP connection, which is traversing the same path with that flow ([12]).

The methods proposed for the multicast transmission of multimedia data over the Internet can be generally divided in three main categories, depending on the number of multicast streams used: (1) The sender uses a single multicast stream for all receivers ([1], [3], [16]). (2) Simulcast: The sender transmits versions of the same video, encoded in varying degrees of quality. This results to the creation of a small number of multicast streams with different transmission rates ([8], [6], [4]). (3) The sender uses layered encoded video, which is video that can be reconstructed from a

M.M. Freire, P. Lorenz, M.M.-O. Lee (Eds.): HSNMC 2003, LNCS 2720, pp. 493-502, 2003.

number of discrete data layers, the basic layer and more additional layers, and transmits each layer into different multicast stream ([10], [9], [14], [15]).

In this paper, we briefly present an adaptation scheme for multicast transmission of multimedia data over best effort networks, like the Internet, which provides the most satisfaction to the group of receivers, with the current network conditions. We call this adaptation scheme SRAMT-LE (Sender-Receiver based Adaptation scheme for Multicast Transmission using Layered Encoding) and it is a hybrid sender and receiver-based adaptation scheme. SRAMT-LE is trying to transmit TCP friendly multicast flows with the use of layered encoding video. SRAMT-LE creates n layers (the basic layer and n-1 additional layers) and transmits each layer in different multicast streams, each one within certain bandwidth limits. The basic layer provides the basic video quality and each additional layer improves the video quality. A receiver in order to be able to decode the video layers and present the video information must receive the layer k and also the layers 1-(k-1) and then we say that the receiver is in layer subscription level k. More information regarding SRAMT-LE and a detail evaluation of SRAMT-LE can be found in [5]. In this paper we give also a detail comparison of the SRAMT-LE with other layered encoding schemes available to the literature. Main target of this comparison is to compare the SRAMT-LE performance of the performance of other layered encoding schemes available to the literature against the following criteria: TCP friendliness, Stability, Scalability and Convergence time to stable state. The above parameters set outline well the behavior of a layered encoding congestion control scheme.

2.   Description of SRAMT-LE

With the use of SRAMT-LE, the sender transmits multimedia data to a group of m receivers with the use of multicast. Sender is using the layered encoding approach, and transmits the video information in n different layers (the basic layer and $n-1$ additional layers). The receivers join the appropriate number of layers, which better suit their requirements.

2.1   Sender Operation

The sender generates n different layer managers. Each layer manager is responsible for the transmission of a video layer. Each receiver manager corresponds to a unique receiver. In addition, the synchronization server is responsible for the management, synchronization and intercommunication between layer managers and receiver managers. We have added an application specific part (APP) to the RTCP receiver reports, which the receivers sent to the RTP/RTCP session of the basic layer, in order to include the receivers' estimation about the TCP friendly bandwidth share $r_{r\_tcp}^i$ in the path between the receiver and the sender, the packet loss rate estimation l_i in all layers, which this receiver is listening and the receiver layer subscription level (the maximum layer up to which the receiver is listening) k. Receiver managers store the last value of $r^i_{r\_tcp}$, l_i and k from the receiver, which represent, and these information is used for the adjustment of layers transmission rates.

When a receiver manager receives a RTCP receiver report from the receiver i (which represents) is using the packet loss rate l_i to estimate the transmission rate r^i_{AIMD} of the receiver i with the use of an AIMD (Additive Increase Multiplicative Decrease) algorithm (which has been presented in [2]). In addition, the receiver manager is using the analytical model of TCP presented in [12] in order to estimate a TCP friendly bandwidth share $r^i_{l\_tcp}$ in the path between the receiver and the sender: If the receiver experiences packet losses, a TCP friendly bandwidth share $r^i_{l\_tcp}$ (in bytes/sec) is estimated with the use of the equation (1) (where t^{r-i}_{RTT} is the sender estimation for RTT between that receiver and the sender), and l_i is the packet loss rate that the receiver i reports):

$$r^i_{l\_tcp} = \frac{P}{t^{r-i}_{RTT}\sqrt{\frac{2l_i}{3}} + 4t^{r-i}_{RTT}\min(1,3\sqrt{\frac{3l_i}{8}})l_i(1+32l_i^2)} \tag{1}$$

If the receiver does not experience packet losses, in order to estimate a TCP friendly bandwidth share $r^i_{l\_tcp}$, the $r^i_{l\_tcp}$ must not be increased more than a packet / RTT. For this reason receiver manager calculates the new value of $r^i_{l\_tcp}$ by adding (T_{rr}/t^{r-i}_{RTT}) packets (where T_{rr} is the time space between the current and the last receiver report of receiver i) to the previous value of $r^i_{l\_tcp}$ (the $r^i_{l\_tcp}$ is expressed in bytes/sec):

$$r^i_{l\_tcp} = r^i_{l\_tcp} + \frac{T_{rr}}{(t^{r-i}_{RTT})^2}P \tag{2}$$

Then the receiver manager selects as receiver's i preferred transmission rate r^i the minimum of the $r^i_{r\_tcp}$, r^i_{AIMD}, $r^i_{l\_tcp}$:

$$r^i = \min(r^i_{r\_tcp}, r^i_{AIMD}, r^i_{l\_tcp}) \tag{3}$$

Each time one receiver manager receives a receiver report in the basic layer session form the receiver, which represents, informs synchronization manager in order to adjust the layers' transmission rates. The adjustment of layers transmission rates has as target to produce TCP friendly cumulative transmission rate for any layer subscription level k. For this reason the synchronization manager polls the r^i values of the receivers that are listening only to basic layer (layer 1) and sets as transmission rate of layer 1 $r_{layer-1}$ the minimum value of r^i of the receivers that are listening only to basic layer. Then polls the r^i values of the receivers that are listening up layer 2 and sets as transmission rate of layer 2 $r_{layer-2}$ the minimum values of r^i minus the $r_{layer-1}$. This procedure repeats for all the layers:

$r_{layer-1} = \min(r^i)$ for all receiver i listening up to layer 1 (basic layer)

$r_{layer-2} = \min(r^i) - r_{layer-1}$ for all receiver i listening up to layer 2

$$\tag{4}$$

...

$$r_{layer-n} = \min(r^i) - r_{layer-n-1} \quad \text{for all receiver } i \text{ listening up to layer n}$$

In addition, the sender includes to all the RTP packets, which transmits, the transmission rate of all the layers. This information can be used from the receivers in order to change their subscription level and accommodate better their requirements.

2.2   Receiver Operation

Each receiver measures the following parameters of the path, which connects it with the sender: (1) Packet loss rate (l_i): The receiver calculates the packet loss rate during the reception of sender layers based on RTP packets sequence numbers. (2) RTT estimations (t_{RTT}^{e-i}): The receiver makes an estimation for the RTT between it and the sender based on one way delay measurements with the use of RTP packets timestamps. The receiver emulates the behavior of a TCP agent with the use of the analytical model of TCP presented in [12] and estimates a TCP friendly bandwidth share $r_{r\_tcp}^i$ every RTT time. If the receiver experiences packet losses is using the following equation in order to estimate a TCP friendly bandwidth share (in bytes/sec):

$$r_{r\_tcp}^i = \frac{P}{t_{RTT}^{e-i} \sqrt{\frac{2l_i}{3}} + 4t_{RTT}^{e-i} \min(1,3\sqrt{\frac{3l_i}{8}})l_i(1+32l_i^2)} \tag{5}$$

If the receiver does not experience packet losses, in order to estimate a TCP friendly bandwidth share $r_{r\_tcp}^i$, the $r_{r\_tcp}^i$ must not be increased more than a packet / RTT. For this reason receiver calculates the value of $r_{r\_tcp}^i$ with the following equation (in bytes/sec):

$$r_{r\_tcp}^i = r_{r\_tcp}^i + \frac{1}{t_{RTT}^{e-i}} P \tag{6}$$

Each time the receiver sends a receiver report to the sender, using the RTP/RTCP session of the basic layer, includes the average value of $r_{r\_tcp}^i$ since last receiver report. In addition the receiver has the capability to add or remove layers based on the information that gathers itself and the information that sender includes in to RTP packets. The receivers' layer subscription changes are synchronized at the end of a specific time period T_{epoch}, which we call epoch. The receiver change their layer subscription (add or remove layers) using the following procedure: At the end of each epoch, each receiver compares the value of the $r_{r\_tcp}^i$, with the cumulative transmission rates of the sender layers and change its layer subscription level up to layer k in order to satisfy the following constraint:

$$r_{r\_tcp}^i <= \sum_{j=1}^{k} r_{layer-j} \tag{7}$$

We declare as unsuccessful layer change the situation when a receiver joins (or leaves) a layer and after a sort time period (T_{change}) drop (or add) again this layer.

During our performance evaluation, we observe that the unsuccessful layer changes by the receivers cause instability to the operation of SRAMT-LE and must be avoided. In order to avoid unsuccessful layer changes by the receivers, when a receiver makes an unsuccessful layer change we avert the receiver to make the layer change, which was unsuccessful, for the next $2^k * T_{change}$ time (where k the number of continuant unsuccessful layer changes since the last successful layer change). Due to fact that T_{change} affects linearly the value $2^k * T_{change}$ and the k affects the value of $2^k * T_{change}$ exponentially, we set T_{change} to 5 seconds but other values of T_{change} can also be used.

2.3   SRAMT-LE Details

In this paragraph we present some details regarding the operation of SRAMT-LE (more detailed information can be found in [5]):

- *Packet Loss Rate Estimation:* In order to prevent a single spurious packet loss having an excessive effect on the packet loss estimation, receivers smooth the values of packet loss rate using the following filter, which computes the weighted average of the m most recent loss rate values $l_{i,j}^m$.

- *RTT Estimations:* When a receiver i receives a RTP packet from a sender layer, uses an algorithm based on one way measurements in order to estimate the Round Trip Time (RTT) between the sender and the receiver.

- *Extensions to RTP/RTCP:* RTP provides an extension mechanism to allow individual implementations that require additional information to be carried in the RTP data packet header. SRAMT-LE uses the extension mechanism of RTP in order to add to the additional fields in to RTP header and new application specific part (APP) to the RTCP reports.

- *Synchronization of stream changes:* Similar research has shown ([10]) that, if the receivers synchronize their layer changes, the synchronization problems can be minimized. For this reason the receivers' layer changes are synchronized in the end of each epoch.

- *Scalability issues:* In order to ensure that, when the group of the participants increases, the sender will collect feedback information representing all the receivers, we use the partial suppression method proposed in [11] to control the transmission of the RTCP reports.

3.   Comparing SRAMT-LE with Other Layered Encoding Schemes

In this section we compare the performance of SRAMT-LE mechanism with other mechanism founded to the literature regarding the following parameters: TCP friendliness, Stability, Scalability and Convergence time to stable state. The above parameters set outline well the behavior of a layered encoding congestion control scheme. We compare the SRAMT-LE with the following layered encoding schemes:

- *PLM* ([9]): PLM stands for "Packet pair receiver-driven Layered Multicast" and is based on a cumulative layered scheme and on the use of packet pair to infer the bandwidth available at the bottleneck to decide which are the appropriate layers to join. PLM assumes that the routers are multicast capable but does not make any assumption on the multicast routing protocol used. PLM is receiver driven, so all the burden of the congestion control mechanism is at the receivers side. The only assumption we make on the sender is the ability to send data via cumulative layers and to emit for each layer packets in pairs (two packets are sent back-to-back). PLM is highly scalable due to the receiver-driven cumulative layered scheme. PLM does not require either any signaling or feedback.
- *MLDA* ([14]): MLDA stands for "Multicast enhanced Loss-Delay based Adaptation algorithm". MLDA is a hybrid sender and receiver-based adaptation scheme that combines on the one hand various well known concepts for multicast congestion control such as receiver-based rate calculation, layered transmission and dynamic into a unified congestion control architecture. Scalability in MLDA is based on partial suppression method.
- *RLC* ([15]): RLC stands for "Receiver-driven, Layered Congestion control algorithm". RLC is designed to support one-to-many communication to potentially large sets of receivers with different bandwidth requirements. RLC uses a hierarchical, layered scheme for data transmission, where receivers can join to one or more multicast groups to receive data at a rate approximately matching their bandwidth to the source - this translates into different quality levels in the case of multimedia streams, or in faster transfer times for reliable data communication. Scalability in RLC comes from full decentralization of functionality: each receiver takes congestion control decisions autonomously.

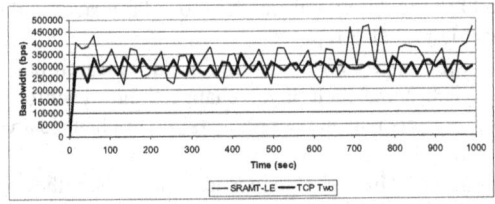

Fig. 1. Bandwidth distribution on C1-C3 bottleneck link

Figure 1 shows the bandwidth distribution to bottleneck link shared by SRAMT-LE and a TCP connection with the same RTT time. As this figure indicate that SRAMT-LE is in general fair towards to TCP connections and treats the heterogeneous group of the receivers with fairness. SRAMT-LE behaves as is expected, and shares the available bandwidth with the TCP connection with the same RTT delay. The behavior of SRAMT-LE ("seeking" for available bandwidth and reaction to congestion) leads some times to get more bandwidth share than TCP and some times to get less bandwidth share than TCP, but in long term both the SRAMT-LE and the TCP flows get the approximately the same bandwidth share of the bottleneck links.

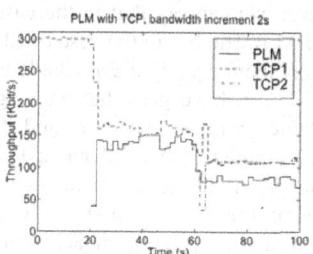

Fig. 2. PLM performance against TCP traffic

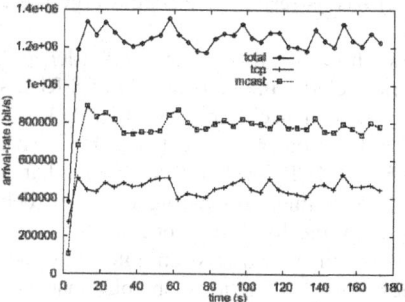

Fig. 3. RLC performance against TCP traffic

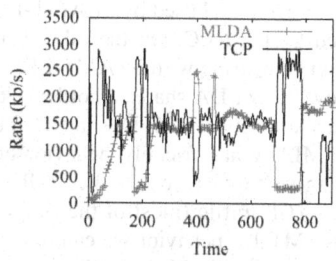

Fig. 4. MLDA performance against TCP traffic

Figure 2 shows how the PLM shares a bottleneck link initially with one TCP connections and later on with two TCP connections. The simulation scenario was the following: Initially the first TCP connections transmits data and at the 20th second starts the transmission of the PLM session and finally at the 60th second starts the transmission of the second TCP connection over the bottleneck link. As figure 2 shows, the PLM session adapts all most perfectly to the available bandwidth in presence of TCP flows. Comparing the PLM behavior with the SRAMT-LE behavior we can draw the following conclusions: PLM has more stable transmission rate and change its transmission rate in steps comparing with SRAMT-LE which can not keep its transmission rate stable and changed it continues during the entire experiment (figure 1). In long term, we can say that in the case of PLM, TCP traffic gets more bandwidth that the PLM traffic but in the case of SRAMT-LE, TCP and SRAMT-LE traffics are share almost them equally the available bandwidth. In order to summarize, both PLM and SRAMT-LE have good behavior against the TCP traffic with PLM offering a more stable transmission rate and SRAMT-LE offering more fair bandwidth sharing. In addition, the PLM has a fast convergence time to the stable state after the transmission of the TCP traffic to the bottleneck link. The main disadvantage of PLM is the fact that assumes that the routers of network testbed support some kind of a fair queuing mechanism that allocates each flow a fair bandwidth share. Only under this assumption, is it possible to use PLM for congestion control. The fact that the Internet router does not support fair queuing mechanisms at the moment (and it is not expected to support fair queuing mechanisms in large scale to the near future) has as result the difficult large scale deployment of PLM to the Internet.

Figure 3 shows how the RLC shares a bottleneck link with TCP traffic. The simulation scenario includes the transmission of 8 RLC sessions together with 8 TCP connections over a bottleneck link. As figure 3 shows, RLC is slightly more aggressive than TCP, but this was expected as RLC considers closely spaced losses as a single event, whereas TCP does not. On the other hand, TCP and RLC do not starve each other when competing. Comparing the RLC behavior with the SRAMT-LE behavior we can draw the following conclusions: Both RLC and SRAMT-LE have some fluctuation on their transmission rates but they keep relative stable their transmission rates. In addition, it is obvious that SRAMT-LE has more friendly behavior against TCP traffic than RLC has. In addition, both RLC and SRAMT-LE have similar convergence times to the stable state. In order to summarize, SRAMT-LE has better behavior against the TCP traffic comparing with RLC and this is because the TCP analytical model used by SRAMT-LE is more accurate than the TCP analytical model used by the RLC. On the other hand, the RLC has a much more simple implementation comparing with SRAMT-LE.

Figure 4 shows how the MLDA shares a bottleneck link with TCP traffic. Figure 4 shows the bandwidth share between MLDA and TCP traffic in the bottleneck link. As figure 4 shows, the MLDA has friendly behavior against TCP traffic most of the simulation time but in some cases either the TCP traffic starves MLDA traffic or MLDA traffic starves TCP traffic (most of the starve cases). Comparing the MLDA behavior with the SRAMT-LE behavior we can draw the following conclusions: The SRAMT-LE behavior is friendlier that MLDA behavior against TCP traffic mainly due to the fact the SRAMT-LE traffic does not starve TCP traffic as MLDA traffic does in some cases. In addition, MLDA has long convergence times to the stable state comparing with SRAMT-LE. Moreover, both MLDA and SRAMT-LE do not keep their transmission rates stable but they have fluctuation on their transmission rates. In order to summarize, both MLDA and SRAMT-LE have similar behavior but the MLDA has the drawback of big convergence time to the stable state and starving of TCP traffic in some cases.

Table 1 summarizes the comparison of SRAMT-LE against the others layered encoding schemes. As this table shows, SRAMT-LE has good performance against TCP traffic and in general terms has good performance comparing with the other layered encoding schemes. The main drawback of the SRAMT-LE mechanism is the fact that SRAMT-LE has fluctuation on its transmission rate and it is not keep its transmission rate stable. This has as result the TCP connections also to have fluctuation on their transmission rates as reaction to the continues changing network conditions due to the above mentions SRAMT-LE behavior.

Table 1. Comparison of SRAMT-LE with the other layered encoding schemes

Parameter / Mechanism	SRAMT- LE	PLM	RLC	MLDA
TCP friendliness	Very Good	Good	modest	Good
Stable transmission rate	No	Yes	Yes	No
Convergence time	Relative fast	Very fast	Relative fast	Modest
Stable operation	Yes	Yes	Yes	No
Limitations	No	fair queuing mechanism in routers	No	No
Scalability	Well - partial suppression method	Well - not require feedback for the client	Well - not require feedback for the client	Well partial suppression method

4.   Conclusion - Future Work

In this paper, we present the behavior investigation of the SRAMT-LE, a mechanism for multicast transmission of adaptive multimedia data in a heterogeneous group of receivers with the use of layered encoding. SRAMT-LE is using a hybrid sender and receiver-based adaptation scheme and uses both a TCP model and an AIMD algorithm to estimate a TCP friendly bandwidth share. We investigate the behavior of SRAMT-LE through a number of simulations. We compare also the behavior of SRAMT-LE with other layered encoding schemes available to the literature. Main conclusion of the evaluation was that SRAMT-LE has friendly behavior against the dominant traffic types (TCP traffic) of today's Internet and good behavior during congestion condition. In addition SRAMT-LE provides good performance comparing with other layered encoding schemes available to the literature.

Our future work includes the investigation of the fluctuations in SRAMT-LE transmission rate in order the SRAMT-LE to transmit more smooth transmission rates. In addition, we plan to investigate to dynamically adding more layers instead of the static number of layers that SRAMT-LE supports now. Moreover we plan to implement a prototype of SRAMT-LE and evaluate its operation over the real Internet and compare the results of the Internet evaluation with the simulation results, which are presented in this paper.

References

[1].   J.-C. Bolot, T. Turletti, I. Wakeman, "Scalable Feedback Control For Multicast Video Distribution In The Internet", In Proceedings of SIGCOMM 1994, London, England, August 1994, pp. 139-146.

[2].   Ch. Bouras, A. Gkamas, "Streaming Multimedia Data With Adaptive Qos Characteristics", Protocols for Multimedia Systems 2000, Cracow, Poland, October 22-25, 2000, pp 129-139.

[3].   C. Bouras, A. Gkamas, "A Mechanism For Multicast Multimedia Data With Adaptive Qos Characteristics", 6th International Conference on Protocols for Multimedia Systems-PROMS 2001, Enschede, The Netherlands, October 17-19 2001, pp. 74-88.

[4].   Ch. Bouras, A. Gkamas, An. Karaliotas, K. Stamos, "Architecture And Performance Evaluation For Redundant Multicast Transmission Supporting Adaptive Qos", 2001 International Conference on Software, Telecommunications and Computer Networks (SoftCOM 2001), Split, Dubrovnik (Croatia) Ancona, Bari (Italy), October 09-12, 2001.

[5].   C. Bouras, A. Gkamas, "SRAMT-LE: A Hybrid Sender And Receiver-Based Adaptation Scheme For TCP" Communication Networks and Distributed Systems Modelling and Simulation Conference (CNDS-03 Part of the 2003 Western MultiConference), Marriott Orlando Airport, Orlando, Florida, January 19 - 23 2003, pp. 71-76

[6].   S. Y. Cheung, M. Ammar, X. Li, "On the Use of Destination Set Grouping to Improve Fariness in Multicast Video Distribution", INFOCOM 96, San Fransisco, March 1996.

[7].   S. Floyd, V. Jacobson, "Random Early Detection Gateways for Congestion Avoidance", IEEE/ACM Transactions on Networking, vol. 1,4: pp. 397-413, 1993.

[8].   T. Jiang, E. W. Zegura, M. Ammar, "Inter-Receiver Fair Multicast Communication Over The Internet", In Proceedings of the 9th International Workshopon Network and Operating Systems Support for Digital Audio and Video (NOSSDAV), June 1999, pp. 103-114.

[9].   Legout and E. W. Biersack. "PLM: Fast convergence for cumulative layered multicast transmission schemes". In Proceedings of ACM SIGMETRICS'2000, Santa Clara, CA, USA, June 2000

[10].   S. McCanne, V. Jacobson, "Receiver-Driven Layered Multicast", 1996 ACM Sigcomm Conference, August 1996, pp. 117-130.

[11].   J. Nonnenmacher, Ernst W. Biersack, "Optimal Multicast Feedback", in Proceedings of the Conference on Computer Communications (IEEE Infocom), San Francisco, USA, Mar. 1998.

[12].   J. Pandhye, J. Kurose, D. Towsley, R. Koodli, "A Model Based TCP-Friendly Rate Control Protocol", Proc. International Workshop on Network and Operating System Support for Digital Audio and Video (NOSSDAV), Basking Ridge, NJ, June 1999.

[13].   H. Shculzrinne, S. Casner, R. Frederick, V. Jacobson, "RTP: A Transport Protocol for Real-Time Applications", RFC 1889, IETF, January 1996.

[14].   D. Sisalem, A. Wolisz, "MLDA: A TCP-Friendly Congestion Control Framework For Heterogeneous Multicast Environments", in Eighth International Workshop on Quality of Service (IWQoS 2000), Pittsburgh, PA, June 2000.

[15].   L. Vicisano, L. Rizzo, and J. Crowcroft, "TCP-like congestion control for layered multicast data transfer", in Proceedings of the Conference on Computer Communications (IEEE Infocom), San Francisco, USA, Mar. 1998.

[16].   J. Widmer, M. Handley, "Extending Equation-Based Congestion Control To Multicast Applications", in ACM SIGCOMM, August 2001.

Design and Development of a SIP-based Video Conferencing Application

Bengisu Tulu, Tarun Abhichandani, Samir Chatterjee*, and Haiqing Li

Network Convergence Laboratory
School of Information Science
Claremont Graduate University
Claremont, CA 91711, USA.
{bengisu.tulu, tarun.abhichandani, samir.chatterjee,
haiqing.li}@cgu.edu

Abstract. Media communication using SIP is providing us with capabilities to architect applications over ubiquitous platforms including the Internet. Although there are certain attempts to make media-enabled applications, there exists a need to deploy security and directory features that constitute middleware services. The software application, described in the paper, is part of a research initiative in Internet2 community to deploy middleware services on video conferencing application. The paper describes the architecture of a Java-based SIP Client and the results of interoperability tests between four SIP user agents. Efforts are being made to enable the application with secured middleware features.

1   Introduction

There is a growing trend to use multimedia communications over IP-based networks including the global Internet. A few organizations have successfully deployed Voice over IP (VoIP) while others are experimenting with technology and organizational issues including justifying a business case. While VoIP has a head start, video conferencing over IP–based networks is relatively new. Several organizations intend to use video conferencing for collaboration, remote work and virtual meetings. In particular the higher education community has plans to deploy video conferencing solutions over Internet2 [1].

For such applications to work, we need signaling protocols as well as media handling capabilities. SIP [2] and H.323 [3] have been used for VoIP with SIP gaining popularity as a flexible session oriented protocol approved by the IETF. However, in the video conferencing space, we could not find many academic or commercial applications[1] that use SIP. Most commercial video systems use H.323 protocol over ISDN lines. Only recently have we started to see the migration of these products to IP-based

---

* This material is based upon work supported by the National Science Foundation under Grant No. 022710. Any opinions, findings, and conclusions or recommendations expressed in this material are those of the author(s) and do not necessarily reflect the views of the National Science Foundation.

[1] MSN Messenger is a SIP client from Microsoft.

M.M. Freire, P. Lorenz, M.M.-O. Lee (Eds.): HSNMC 2003, LNCS 2720, pp. 503-512, 2003.

networks. Not only is there a need to develop and deploy SIP-based video conferencing applications, there are several requirements within the higher education community that must be met. These requirements include the ability to search directories for
finding SIP users, enterprise-level authentication, and having proper authorization
policies in place, which facilitates inter-campus video communications. Privacy and
confidentiality of users is also needed. Moreover proper accounting and billing is an
integral part to manage a converged network with voice and video applications.

In this paper, we present the design, architecture and implementation of a SIP-
based video conferencing application. We also discuss our experience of deploying
the client and providing service through our lab. We point out certain performance
features of the client and finally conclude with a discussion of future work.

2   Application Design and Architecture

Session Initiation Protocol (SIP) is the Internet Engineering Task Force (IETF) standard for IP Telephony. It is an application layer control protocol that can create, modify, and terminate multimedia sessions [2]. Different types of entities are defined in
SIP: user agents, proxy servers, redirect servers, and registrar servers. Figure 1 shows
a simple SIP call flow including these entities.

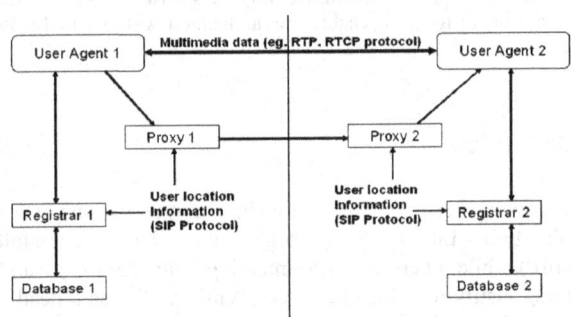

Fig. 1. A typical SIP configuration [Modified from 4].

Network Convergence Lab (NCL) at Claremont Graduate University (CGU) is
hosting two sip proxies: one commercial proxy from Dynamicsoft, and other open
source proxy from Vovida. Dynamicsoft proxy is used as the main proxy for the test
bed CGU offers to the Internet2 community. Vovida proxy is used for testing purposes. Both proxies run on the default port 5060 however, the registrar ports differ:
5070 for Vovida and 6060 for Dynamicsoft registrar.

Although there are open source SIP stacks such as Vovida and NIST, Dynamicsoft commercial stack was used to develop CGUsipClientv1.1. Dynamicsoft provides a comprehensive SIP stack including all the authentication mechanisms included in the latest RFC [2] which are not available in open source user agent SIP
stacks. Dynamicsoft stack also provides multiple levels of API that allows applica-

tions with various complexity levels. The architecture of the Dynamicsoft user agent SIP stack is provided in Figure 2 labelled as Dynamicsoft Architecture.

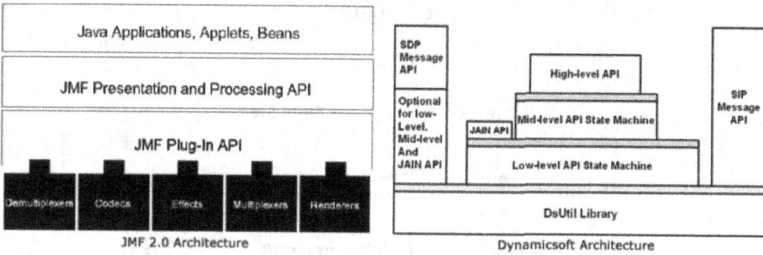

Fig. 2. JMF and Dynamicsoft Architecutures

Dynamicsoft proxy and registrar provides authentication for users. Authentication type, which could be basic or digest [5], is assigned to each user during the registration process. For each registration request, registrar challenges the users for authentication based on the authentication type. The user agent is responsible for requesting the necessary information from the user and sending it to the registrar for authentication. Proxy also challenges each user for all requests except ACK and BYE message. If a user agent is challenged, it would have to resubmit its request with credentials, the request and credentials will be verified by proxy against those in the location server [6]. Further, location server would verify against the database in which it stores the details of users.

Java Media Framework (JMF) 2.1.1 Sun libraries were used to develop a SIP based video conferencing application. JMF 1.0 API (the Java Media Player API) enabled programmers to develop Java programs that presented time-based media. JMF 2.0 API extended the framework to provide support for capturing and storing media data, controlling the type of processing that is performed during playback, and performing custom processing on media data streams [7]. JMF 2.0 architecture is provided in Figure 2 labelled as JMF 2.0 Architecture.

Among other alternatives to implement CGU client, JMF was selected since Java was decided to be used for client development. Further, JMF can be used in applets and in stand-alone applications developed in Java. JMF also offers an easy to use library and source code.

CGUsipClientv1.1 architecture is presented in Figure 3. There are two main Java packages – *cgusip.client* and *cgusip.utils* – that structure CGUsipClientv1.1. The *utils* package handles the existing instances of sip connections and calls. The client pack age has three main components: *gui*, *sip*, and *media*. The *gui* package handles all aspects of the client user interaction. The *sip* package handles the necessary interaction between the CGUsipClientv1.1 and the Dynamicsoft sip stack for creating and terminating sessions and initiating and receiving calls. The *media* package is in charge of making media connections using JMF and Dynamicsoft media libraries.

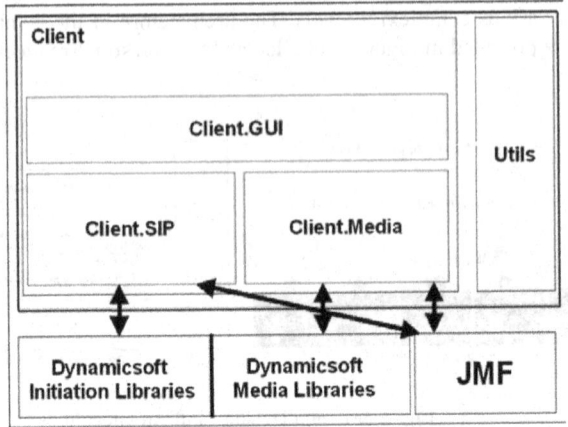

Fig. 3. CGUsipClientv1.1 Architecture

CGUsipClientv1.1 is capable of registering to a SIP proxy/registrar and making multiple calls (up to 5 lines are available) to any user capable of receiving SIP calls. In addition, the client provides connection to a private address book and the enterprise directory.

In order to download the installation files for CGUsipClientv1.1, each user needs to register through a website by providing minimum information about them: name, email address, and password for the sip client. During this registration process the following are created (1) a sip user account in the Oracle database, (2) an entry in the enterprise directory (ED) of the CGU NCL lab, (3) an entry linked to this ED user in the commObject , explained in section 3, (4) a private address book file in the web server. This enables users to reach their personal address books from any location. Figure 4 labelled as User Registration Process illustrates registration process.

CGUsipClientv1.1 also provides the callerID option for users. In the registration the user can upload a picture that will be used during the invite process to provide detailed information about the caller. Figure 4 labelled as Caller ID Process illustrates working of Caller ID feature.

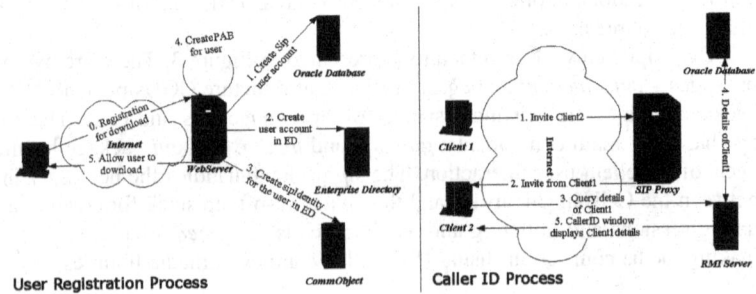

Fig. 4. User Registration and Caller ID Process Flows

Video formats that CGUsipClientv1.1 supports are h.263, h.261, and jpeg. H.263 is the default codec for video sessions and users are not allowed to change it. However, all three video formats are supported for incoming video. Future version of the client will allow users to change this parameter. The supported audio formats and their description are provided in Figure 5. The default audio codec is g.723 and this can be modified by the user

Codec	Appropriate Scenarios
g.723 GSM	Best suited for PC-to-telephone and PC-to-PC calls. Used when the speed is 56K or less
DVI ULAW	Best suited for PC-to-PC calls. Do not use if the speed is less than 56K

Fig. 5. Supported Audio Codes

CGUsipClientv1.1 runs on local port 8000 and users are not allowed to modify this parameter. In the next version, this parameter will be configurable by users. The audio port range is from 4000 to 5000. The video port for this client is on 65500. We haven't tested multiple video performances on the same machine. Therefore, users are not allowed to change this port and receive video connections from different sources. In case of multiple calls, the video and audio of the active call is projected. Figure 6 shows a snapshot of a call between two clients.

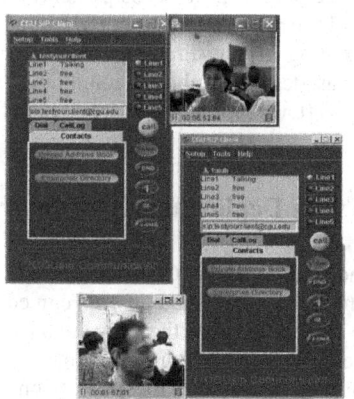

Fig. 6. . CGUsipClientv1.1 snapshots

SIP and H.323 standards, which are used for video conferencing, do not include any solution for NAT and Firewall issues. Although some RFCs [8,9], various internet drafts [10,11,12,13] and industry practices [14] are being proposed to solve this problem, these have not been materialized into a standard yet. Therefore, CGUsipClientv1.1 does not work behind NAT or firewall. New version may provide NAT/FW support.

3   Middleware

Middleware refers to a suite of systems that exist between an application and various network services. Network services include providing platform for (a) security for authorization, authentication and secured transmission of messages (b) directories for identification and searching. Middleware tries to bind network services with the application. Middleware, in CGUsipClientv1.1, development focuses on implementing security and directory services.

For directory services, we have implemented an architecture that is recommended as a draft [15] by ViDeNet group of Internet2 community. One of the purposes of the group is to define a structure for video and voice communications that could reside in an Lightweight Directory Access Protocol (LDAP) directory. The draft proposed by the group suggests objects that need to be inherited by enterprises, which plan to implement directory structure for voice or video communications. The draft proposes creation of certain classes to support communication architecture. It suggests creation of two classes; commURIObject and commObject and other protocol specific classes that enterprise would choose to support such as SIP, H.323 or VRVS. Every enterprise that needs to support this structure has to create a protocol specific object to hold attributes for communication and update enterprise directory to maintain association between a user and their communication attributes. To achieve this, ED needs to be updated to include an attribute called commURI from commURIObject. commURI is an LDAP Uniform Resource Locator (URL) that refers to protocol specific attributes.

At CGU we have implemented commObject structure on openLDAP, an open-source directory service platform. In CGUsipClientv1.1 interface, there is a clickable icon that displays an html page onto a browser listing white page entries in ED. ED displays all users existing in that directory. Each entry in ED has a link, which is commURI 'pointer' as described above. commURI 'pointer' navigates to another page that enumerates various attributes that are needed for communication.

4   Experience with Deployment over Internet2

Network Convergence Lab (NCL) at CGU has made the software available to participants of ViDeNet[2] through its web site http://ncl.cgu.edu/sipclient/index.php. Through the web site, visitors intending to use the software have to provide their details including their email address. This email address becomes their unique SIPURI for registration purposes. A SIP proxy normally supports only one domain. However, since CGU SIP proxy is used by various campuses for proof of concept, multiple domain support was necessary. Therefore, domain part of each email address is verified against the domain database of the proxy. If a domain does not exist, the domain database is updated. In addition, every registered member is required to have an entry in ED. Further, every registered user is provided with a SIP URI on which they can be contacted if conferencing session is desired by other SIP UA. This SIP URI is one of the communication attributes in commURI. Other significant communication attributes being proxy domain address and registrar domain address. Proxy and registrar domain ad-

---

[2] Information on ViDeNet can be found at www.vide.net.

dress for every registered member is server address of Dynamicsoft proxy hosted by CGU in its campus. Every member who has downloaded the software registers itself with proxy at CGU. The website mentioned above provides an interface to directory services; ED and commObject attributes.

4.1   Interoperability Issues

Before deploying on Internet2, CGUSipClientv1.1 had been successfully tested for point-to-point voice and video communication. There was a need to test the client with other clients and proxies after initial period of distribution.

NCL has two servers in its premises; a Linux-Based server hosting Vovida proxy and a Windows 2000 Advanced Server hosting Dynamicsoft (DS) proxy. For testing, a collaborative effort was arranged between Tim Poe at University of North Carolina, Chapel Hill, Tyler Johnson at University of North Carolina, Chapel Hill, and Chris Arnold at Radvision. Chris Arnold was using MSN Messenger and Siemens SIP client. Tyler Johnson was using MSN Messenger. Students at CGU were using CGUsipClientv1.1 application, Vovida's user agent and MSN Messenger. The results of interoperability test are provided in Figure 7.

CALLER	CALLEE	Registered to	Call Established	Audio Established	Video Established
cgu	cgu	DS,Vovida	√	√	√
cgu	vovida	Vovida	√	NT	NA
cgu	msn	DS,Vovida	√	√	X
cgu	siemens	DS, Vovida	X	X	X
cgu	mcu	X*	NT	NT	NT
msn	cgu	DS, Vovida	X	X	X
msn	msn	DS, Vovida,RTC	√	√	√
msn	siemens	Vovida	√	√	√
msn	siemens	DS	√	X	X
msn	vovida	Vovida	√	NT	NA
msn	mcu	RTC	√	√	√
siemens	cgu	DS, Vovida	X	X	X
siemens	msn	Vovida	√	√	√
siemens	msn	DS	√	X	X
siemens	siemens	NT	NT	NT	NT
siemens	vovida	NT	NT	NT	NT
siemens	mcu	RTC	√	√	√
vovida	cgu	Vovida	√	NT	NA
vovida	msn	Vovida	√	NT	NA
vovida	vovida	Vovida	√	NT	NA
vovida	siemens	NT	NT	NT	NT
vovida	mcu	X*	NT	NT	NT

NT   Not Tested
NA   Not Applicable since vovida client does not have video support
(*)   They were never able to register to the same proxy

Fig. 7. Interoperability between different clients

To summarize the testing, it was found that all user agents except Vovida were able to register with Dynamicsoft proxy. MSN Messenger proved to be efficient in terms of interoperability performance as long as clients registered to Microsoft RTC server. MSN Messenger and Siemens SIP user agent were not able to call CGUsip-Clientv1.1. Media communication remain untested with Vovida user agent. Video session could not be established between MSN Messenger and CGUsipClientv1.1 because MSN Messenger supports a proprietary video codec developed by Microsoft. Further, MSN Messenger, registered with Dynamicsoft, Microsoft RTC or Vovida, was not able to call CGUsipClientv1.1 because MSN Messenger does not provide for separate entries for Proxy and Registrar. Hence, a user cannot specify separate ports for Proxy and Registrar.

For conference testing Radvision MCU was used. Radvision MCU needs to register its services to a SIP proxy in order to provide conferencing services. During this registration it does not provide a SIP URI. It registers by three parameters, registrar, proxy, and domain. Once it registers its services, the users can call MCU by calling the assigned user name by the administrator. Due to this behavior, it cannot register to any proxy except Microsoft RTC server. As a result, any client who could not register to RTC was not able to join a conference call

4.2   Performance Evaluation

During the preliminary performance testing of the CGUsipClientv1.1, two systems were used for a point-to-point video conferencing call. The configuration of these systems is provided in Figure 8.

Four metrics were identified for performance testing: CPU load, video frames per second, audio and video bit rates. Recent testing with CGUSipClientv1.1 provided the following performance results shown in Figure 8. All the values represent received video and audio performance ranges during a "2 minute" call.

The performance provided in Figure 8 is achieved after the initiation phase is over. During the initiation phase the CPU load changes as shown in Figure 9.

	Configuration				Performance			
	CPU	Memory	O/S	Camera	CPU Load	Frames Per Second	Kbits Per Second (Audio)	Kbits Per Second (Video)
System 1	Pentium4 1.8GHz	256MB	Windows 2000	Intel CS330	40-50%	10-17	63/5.3	524 – 77.7
System 2	Pentium4 1.8GHz	256MB	Windows XP	Logitech Express	40-50%	12-25	63/5.3	655 - 120

Fig. 8. System configurations and their performances during the call or after the call is established

Action	CPU load
Client was started	80%
Registered to registrar	50%
Call initiated	30%
Caller ID information requested	45%
Audio connection established	60%
Video connection established	50% - 70%

Fig. 9. Call initiation performance

5   Conclusion

In this paper, we highlight the following contributions:

- Built an effective SIP-based video conferencing desktop client that runs on top of SUN's JMF and a commercial SIP stack from Dynamicsoft
- We believe this is the first directory-service enabled video client that facilitates easy searching.
- The client provides authentication using native mode SIP authentication that uses the Digest mechanism with MD5 hashing.
- To make the download and deployment efficient, we have implemented web services that include support for commObject creation, user accounts on a location server, and caller ID service.

Our future work will involve analyzing interoperability problems encountered in greater details. We are planning implementation of an enterprise-wide authentication mechanism and exploring single-sign-on with Kerberos and X.509 digital certificates. We also intend to explore various authentication and authorization policies for video services. Finally a big challenge is to develop federated identity management and authorization in which various domains work with each other to obtain attributes about users and make decisions to forward a call or not. Those would be reported in a future article.

Acknowledgment

We are indebted to several people who have helped shape our thinking that we have described in this paper. Everyone that makes Internet2 VidMid so special deserves our thanks. We thank Ken Klingenstein, Bob Morgan, Scott Canter and Michael Gettes for educating us with the federated administration concept. We also thank Egon Verharen, Tyler Johnson, Nadim El-Khoury, Tom Barton, Aditya Srinivasan, Doug Sicker, Jon Peterson and folks at RADVISION for several brain storming conference calls.

References

[1] R.S. Dixon, "Internet Videoconferencing: Coming to your Campus Soon!," *EDUCAUSE QUARTERLY*, no.4, Nov. 2000, pp.22-27.
[2] J. Rosenberg, H. Schulzrinne, G. Camarillo, A. Johnston, J. Peterson, R. Sparks, M. Handley, E. Schooler, "SIP: Session Initiation Protocol," *IETF RFC 3261*, June 2002.
[3] International Telecommunication Union, "Packet based multimedia communications systems," *Recommendation H.323*, Telecommunication Standardization Sector of ITU, Geneva, Switzerland, Feb. 1998.
[4] R. Radovic, I. Crkvenac; and S. Srbljic; "Formal definition of SIP end systems behavior," *International Conference on Trends in Communications EUROCON'2001*, vol: 2, pp. 293 - 296, 2001.
[5] S. Salsano, L. Veltri, D. Papalilo, "SIP Security Issues: The SIP Authentication Procedure and Its Processing Load", *IEEE Network*, vol. 16, no. 6, pp.38-44, Nov/Dec 2002.

[6] Dynamicsoft Proxy Server 5.2 Administrator's guide, 2001.
[7] "Java Media Framework API Guide" [online] Mountain View, California 94043-1100 U.S.A., Nov. 1999 [cited March 11, 200], available from World Wide Web: <http://java.sun.com/products/java-media/jmf/2.1.1/specdownload.html>.
[8] P. Srisuresh, J. Kuthan, J. Rosenberg, A. Molitor, A. Rayhan, "Middlebox Communication architecture and framework" RFC 3303, Internet Engineering Task Force, August 2002.
[9] R.P. Swale, P.A. Mart, P. Sijben, S. Brim, M. Shore "Middlebox Communications (MIDCOM) Protocol Requirements" RFC 3304, Internet Engineering Task Force, August 2002.
[10] J. Rosenberg, J. Weinberger, C. Huitema, R. Mahy "STUN – Simple Traversal of UDP Through Network Address Translators" Version 05, Internet Engineering Task Force Internet-Draft, work in progress, Expires June 2003.
[11] S. Sanjoy, P. Sollee, S. March "MIDCOM-unaware firewall/NAT Traversal" Version 01, Internet Engineering Task Force Internet-Draft, work in progress, Expires October 2002.
[12] J. Rosenberg, J. Weinberger, C. Huitema, R. Mahy, "Traversal Using Relay NAT (TURN)," Internet Engineering Task Force Internet-Draft, work in progress, Expires March 2002.
[13] J. Rosenberg, J. Weinberger, H. Schulzrinne, "An Extension to the Session Initiation Protocol (SIP) for Symmetric Response Routing," Internet Engineering Task Force Internet-Draft, work in progress, Expires March 2003.
[14] "Network Convergence: An Overview of the Ridgeway IP Freedom Solution" Ridgeway Systems and Software, Austin TX, [cited March 11, 200], available from World Wide Web: <http://www.wave3software.com/pdfs/ipfreedom/NetworkConvergence.pdf>.
[15] Thomas Barton, Nadim El-Khoury, Michael Gettes, Tyler Johnson, Sasha Ruditsky, Art Vandenberg, Egon Verharen: NSF Middleware Initiative Draft, work-in-progress, Expires November 2002; available from World Wide Web: <http://middleware.internet2.edu/video/draftdocs/draft-nmi-edit-vidmid_vc-commObject_White_Paper-1.0.html>.

Optimal On-Demand VoIP Quality in an H.323 Network*

Rafael Estepa, Antonio Estepa, Rafael Rivero, and Juan M. Vozmediano

Área de Ingeniería Telemática, Universidad de Sevilla
Camino de los Descubrimientos s/n, E-41092 Sevilla
Tel.: +34 95448 7384
{rafa, aestepa, rrivero, jvt}@trajano.us.es

Abstract. The perceived quality of a VoIP call depends both on terminal and network performance. A proper selection of the terminal working parameters, such as codec or packetization, may reduce the QoS requirements imposed on the network to grant the expected end-to-end quality. This paper introduces an application-level QoS management model to provide user-selected end-to-end call quality with optimal transport resource usage. The model adapts the QoS entities and interfaces defined by the ETSI TIPHON QoS Management Reference Architecture to H.323 networks, integrating call and QoS signalling. It is further enhanced by defining a resource optimization policy and a signalling procedure.
As a result, the IP Telephony Service Provider can fullfill the user's expectations at the best cost/performance tradeoff.

1 Introduction

The speech communication quality is a subjective concept: it depends on the voice transmission quality modified by the perception and expectations of the user. Due to this inherent subjectivity, and the variation among individuals, performing opinion tests is the preferred method to assess the quality of a communication system. The final outcome of such a test is a score ranging from 1 (bad) to 5 (excellent), known as Mean Opinion Score (MOS) [1].

The high cost and time required to perform these tests impelled the development of methods to predict the average user opinion from objective, measurable transmission parameters such as delay, echo and terminal features.

Among these methods, the E-Model [4], developed by the ETSI as a planning support tool for the traditional voice networks, seems to be flexible enough to be taylored to assess the QoS of VoIP services. The E-Model outcome is a quality score, named Transmission Rate factor (R), ranging from 0 to 100, which can be directly mapped to the MOS. This score is derived from an additive expression that takes into account several physical, measurable parameters. Whereas some of these parameters are out of the scope of QoS management, and may be

* The work leading to this article has been partly supported by CICYT and the EU under contract number 1FD97-1003-C03-03.

M.M. Freire, P. Lorenz, M.M.-O. Lee (Eds.): HSNMC 2003, LNCS 2720, pp. 513–521, 2003.

considered as fixed, some other can be tuned to enhance the quality of the call in a QoS-enabled [2,3] IP network.

Provision of a guaranteed quality IP transport service requires the allocation of transport resources. Service providers do need to minimize the amount of network resources spent in providing the desired QoS for voice calls.

In the TIPHON documents [6], ETSI describes a framework for enabling end-to-end QoS control. The *entities* of this framework are organized into two planes. The required end-to-end QoS levels are established within the so-called IP Telephony Application Plane between end users and service providers. Decissions determining QoS, specific to the application, will take place in this Plane (e.g. codec type, packetization, etc). The IP Transport Plane provides a QoS service to the Application Plane, controlling and accounting general non-application specific parameters affecting QoS to achieve the quality requirements requested by the application. This framework can be directly applied to H.323, the ITU-T VoIP standard [7].

This paper proposes a QoS Management Model where users request the desired call quality in terms of a MOS figure. A functional entity selects and informs the optimal working parameters for every involved element, both network elements and terminals. The optimization tool is the E-Model, and the neccesary communication among functional entities is carried out according to TIPHON and H.323.

The rest of the paper is organized as follows. Section 2 describes the proposed reference model. The signalling procedures between the different functional entities will be described in section 3, and section 4 addresses the optimization procedure. The reference model has been implemented in an experimental testbed described in section .

2 Reference Model

The proposed reference model focuses onto a scenario where terminals belong to a single H.323 zone. The H.323 zone can be identified with a TIPHON system with a single Service Domain and a single Transport Domain. For simplicity, signalling in a multiple-domain scenario is not considered, and it does not affect the main issues of resource optimization.

The model layout, which includes the identification of H.323 elements with TIPHON functional entities, is determined by the following design considerations:

- Call setp-up time shall not be increased. This means that QoS parameters will be carried by the existing call signalling flows, instead of adding new connections for QoS data exchange. This requires the QoS Policy Entity (QoSM,) which mediates requests for end-to-end QoS with every other entity, to be implemented in the H.323 Gatekeeper. The Gatekeeper is the only network element which acts as a master for both clients.
- Sensitive QoS information shall be held in a trusted place and exchanged only between trusted parties. Thus, the QoSM will be liable for computing and

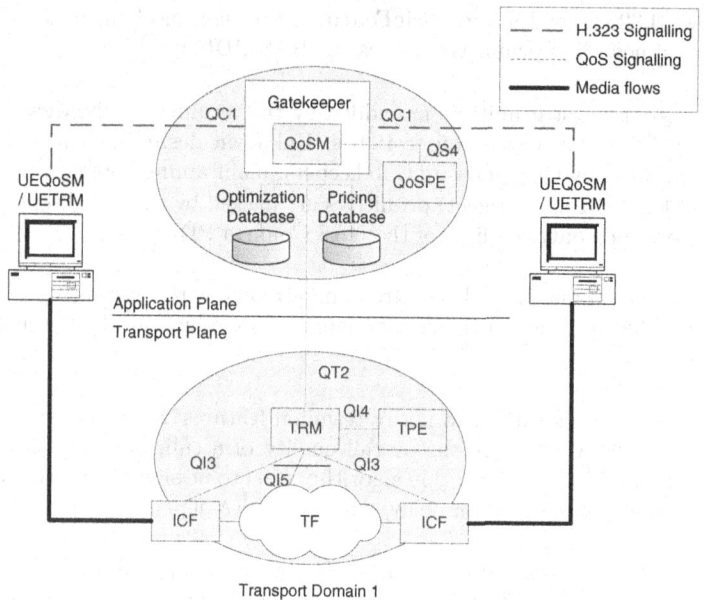

Fig. 1. Reference Model

signalling the optimal reservation scheme to the Transport Resource Manager Entity (TRM), which manages the resource reservation in the Transport Plane. Terminals will neither need nor be allowed to communicate with the TRM.

- Existing terminals shall not require any change to benefit from resource optimization. This means that no mandatory signalling procedures will be introduced, and that the information needed by the QoSM, such as the codecs used for a call, must be retrieved by routing the H.225 and H.245 [8,9] signalling.

The resulting reference model is depicted in Fig. 1, where design decisions show up as model constraints: relationship between QoSM and Gatekeeper is made explicit, cost and optimization data management is regarded to the QoSM, and both H.225 and H.245 signalling are routed through the Gatekeeper.

3   Signalling

The signalling procedures to exchange the QoS parameters between functional entities may follow TIPHON guidelines, except for the TIPHON QC1 interface, between the QoSM and the terminals.

To avoid increasing the call setup time, QC1 primitives will use previously existing terminal-Gatekeeper *Registration Admission and Status* (RAS) signalling flow. H.323 provides a **genericFeature** extension mechanism to ease the addition of new data primitives to existing RAS PDUs:

- QoS request primitives are added by the terminal to the **desiredFeatures** field of the RAS Request PDUs. Unknown desired features can be safely ignored by QoS-unaware Gatekeepers, maintaining compatibility.
- QoS confirm (or reject) primitives are packed by the Gatekeeper in the **supportedFeatures** field of the RAS Confirm PDUs.

The requirement of backward compatibility with existing H.323 clients and the addition of new features mandate the introduction of the following procedures:

- Profile registration, to notify terminal features. Several terminal characteristics may influence the overall quality of a call, but only those which are inputs of the optimization algorithm need to be signalled: terminal delay (excluding packetization delay, which is codec-dependent) and access network delay.

  Since this information is not negotiable nor supposed to change, this should be a registration-time request-only signalling procedure. Consequently, it primitives will be encapsulated in RAS-Request PDUs.

  For optimization-unaware terminals, this information must be made statically available to the QoSM, whether as default values or through a profile database.
- Quality request, to ask for a quality level in terms of MOS. This procedure will be confirmed and work on a per-call basis, as quality requirements may vary according to endpoint's local policies for each call.

  The requested MOS value will be transported in the Request message, and the granted value in the Response. The RAS *Admission Request* (ARQ) and *Confirmation* (ACF) PDUs are the most suitable vehicles for exchanging these primitives between terminals and QoSM.

  For optimization-unaware terminals, the expected quality level for a call may be given to the QoSM as a default value. Alternatively, the QoSM can learn it by asking the QoS Policy Entity (QoSPE), which determines the user's entitlement to QoS service classes.
- Mininal-cost codec and packetization configuration, from the terminal available capability set. For optimization-unaware terminals, learning the codec and packetization by the QoSM does not require QC1 signalling; it can be done through H.245 routing, thus guaranteeing backward compatibility.

  The QoSM answer to the terminal will be carried in the ACF, as the expected quality level is an essential parameter for the optimization process. This answer will carry the list of suitable codec types and configuration, sorted by resource usage. Along with each codec, the QoSM will specify the optimal number of frames per packets and the optimal size for the jitter-compensation buffer.

3.1   Overview of Signalling Procedure

The overall signalling procedure in the Service Domain is sketched in Fig. 2. The **genericFeature** extensibility mechanism defined for the H.225 RAS signalling will be used to convey QC1 messages; for the rest of interfaces, proper transport methods may be employed.

Table 1. Parameters of the QoS signalling primitives

Primitive	Parameter
QC1.QoSMreq	QoS Service Class (MOS value)
	List of H.245 capabilities
QS4.QoSPEreq	QoS Service Class
	Caller and Called IDs
QS4.QoSPEconf	QoS Service Class
	Caller and Called IDs
QC1.QoSMconf	QoS Service Class
	(Sorted) list of H.245 capabilities
QT2.TRMQreq	Transport QoS parameters (Delay, Jitter, Packet loss)
	Traffic Descriptor (Bit rate, MTU)
	Transport Addresses
	Packet Transport Protocol
QT2.TRMQconf	Transport QoS Parameters
	Transport Addresses
	Packet Transport Protocol

The QoS parameters interchanged across the Service Domain interfaces are summarized in Table 1. They comply to the definitions for third-party establishment of a QoS controlled bearer in the TIPHON specification, with the following exceptions:

- The QC1 interface has been taylored to seamless integrate with H.323 signalling. Information that can be extracted from RAS, H.225, or H.245 signalling, is excluded from QC1 messages, avoiding data duplication. Messages will contain only the expected quality and supported H.245 capabilities.
- As there is no way to know which codec or transport address will be used for media channels until QC1 admission is finished, resource reservation is delayed until a logical channel is opened.

There are no explicit procedures for QoS reservation tear-down. Since H.225 and H.245 are routed, the QoSM shall monitor logical channel activity and free reserved resources through the QT2 interface upon finishing the call or closing a logical channel.

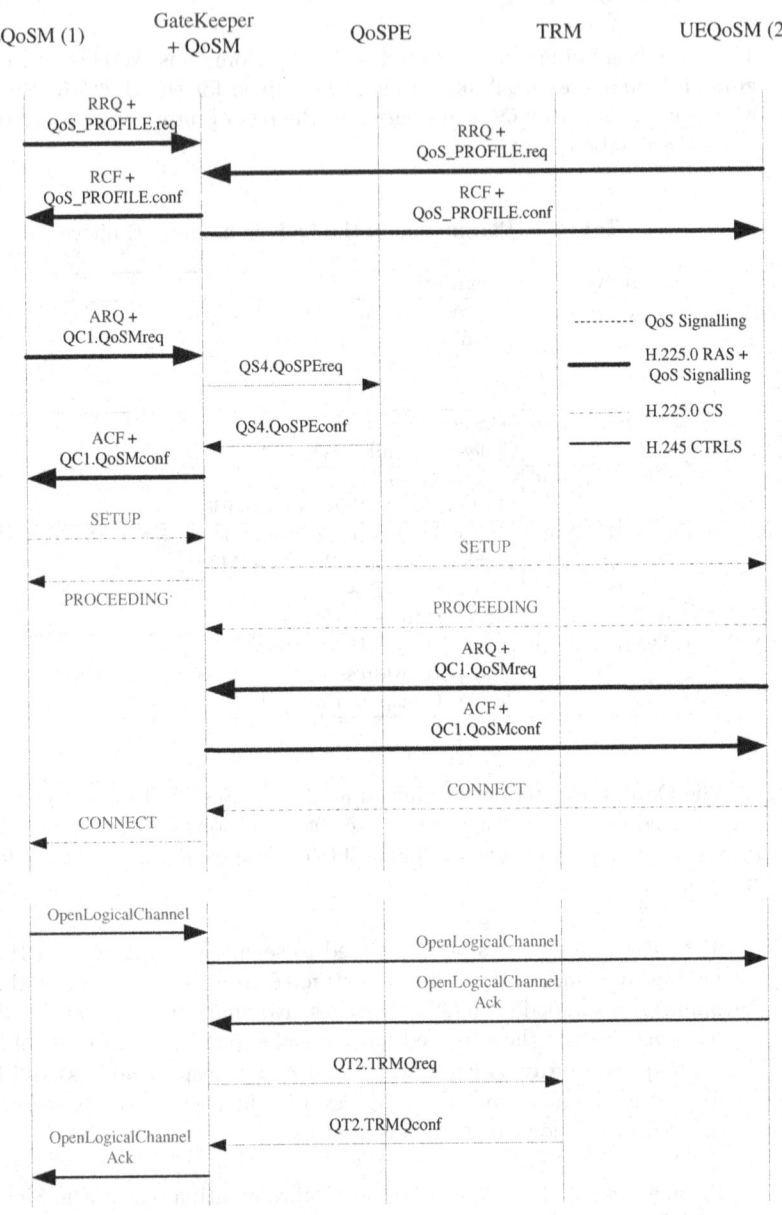

Fig. 2. Overview of signalling procedure in the Application Domain

4   Optimization

The QoSM is liable for requesting the TRM the transport-level QoS performance parameters (delay, delay variation and packet loss probability) corresponding to the service-level QoS parameters (codec, packetization and end-to-end expected quality). The proper valued are tied by the E-Model.

Although the mapping between encoding and bandwidth needs is quite simple, translating quality expectations to delay, jiter and packet loss is more complex. The optimization procedure find the resources both sufficient and necessary to achieve the targeted quality. This involves a two-step process:

- Finding suitable combinations of transport-level parameters which yield the desired quality.
- Sorting those combinations according to cost criteria, to choose the best candidate.

4.1   Finding Solutions

The E-Model inverse function can be used to find valid candidates in the combination of transport-level parameters. The *input* is the desired quality level (or R factor), and the *output* will be the space of possible parameter values.

Only the E-Model parameters related to encoding and transport parameters will be allowed to vary, whilst the others are mantained as fixed values. These parameters are the codec type, number of frames per packet, network end-to-end delay and packet loss probability.

Any combination of E-Model parameters, plus its associated R value, will be called an *optimization point*. The number of such points can be limited, since the parameters have a practical range of variation and can be considered as discrete (for instance, practical delay values for real-time communication may be limited from 1 to 500 ms, and only take integer values into consideration).

Therefore, and since there is no easy way to find the inverse E-Model function, the QoSM will store a precomputed table for real-time solution search. Each row will contain:

- Codec type, from those for which the E-Model parameters are known.
- Number of frames per packet, according to the codec type.
- Total network end to end delay, ranging from the packetization delay to 500 ms, in 5 ms steps.
- Packet loss probability. As the influence of packet loss in perceived quality for the codec type is tabulated for a few values, only those values will be stored.
- The corresponding R value.

Optimization points with unacceptably low R values will not to be stored. An actual implementation considering the voice codecs currently parametrized by E-Model gives a size of 10,000 rows, which can be easily managed. Network limitations and user profiles can be used to further discard unfeasible points at run-time.

4.2 Comparing Solutions

Once the suitable candidates have been found, they have to be sorted by resource consumption. Five factors affect this usage; the first three ones are mainly related to link capacity, whereas the other two relate to router queue size:

- Required bandwidth.
- Maximum delay.
- Maximum delay variation.
- Maximum packet loss probability.
- Maximum PDU size.

Cost information on each of these factors should be provided by the service provider. The cost of unaffordable values should be indicated as *infinity*. The cost of each feasible optimization point should be evaluated according to this pricing information. Required bandwidth, PDU size, and maximum packet loss probability are taken from the optimization point data. The cost of end-to-end delay, on the other hand, requires a further tuning.

The delay value stored in the optimization point stands for total network delay. This includes the maximum delay variation (as the jitter compensation buffer in the receiver will add up to this amount of delay), and excludes terminal and packetization delays. To compute the cost of delay, terminal and packetization should be sustracted from the optimization point delay. The remaining budget must be shared between network delay and delay variation, such that the total pricing is minimal.

The algorithm used to sort the capabilities declared by a terminal through the QC1 interface is just a double iteration of the optimization algorithm, both on codec and number of frames per packet. Only the best R figure for each codec type will be considered, updating the frames per packet parameter if necessary. descriptor.

5 Implementation Issues

The reference model has been fully implemented in an H.323 environment. The implementation was based on open source code from the OpenH323 project. Modifications in the C++ code of the OpenH323 clients were needed to support the MOS selection by the user and the QoS-aware signalling described in section 3.

The QoSM has been implemented and integrated into the OpenH323 Gatekeeper, running in a Pentium II at 650 MHz with a 256 kB of RAM. Its optimization module was designed to minimize the number of working points to be evaluated, yielding a look-up table of 8 MB and look-up times shorter than 20 ms to find the optimal configuration.

Finally, the performance of the system was tested with the aid of the Net-Nist network emulator. The signalling modifications were fully operational, and conversations with different user-selected MOS levels showed noticeable quality differences. A more precise test of the achieved MOS would requiere a previous validation and tunning of the E-Model for VoIP scenarios, which is work in progress [10].

6   Conclusion

The relationship between MOS and network and terminal parameters implies that the costs associated to a VoIP call, as they depend on transport resource usage, may be reduced by properly selecting the terminal settings.

A method to map quality expectations to network QoS requirements has been introduced, within the framework of a QoS management model for end to end call quality control. This model yields the best cost/performance tradeoff by minimizing resource usage for a given call.

The necessary adaptation of TIPHON QoS entities and interfaces can be easily accomplished without breaking backwards compatibility. This has been proved by an experimental implementation.

The application of the proposed model would enable providers to maximize the resource utilization, allowing for a reduction of charges and an increment in the number of customers without service degradation, and obtaining a competitive advantage over traditional network management strategies.

References

1. ITU-T Recommendation P.800. (1996-08) "Methods for subjective determination of transmission quality".
2. R. Braden, D. Clark, S. Shenker. "Integrated Services in the Internet architecture: an Overview". RFC 1633. See also the IETF "Integrated Services" Working Group, *http://www.ietf.org/html-charters/intserv-charter.html*
3. S. Blake, D Black, M. Carlson, E. Davis, Z. Wang, W. Weiss. "An architecture for differentiated services", RFC 2475.
4. ETSI ETR 250 (1996-07). "Speech communication quality from mouth to ear for 3,1 kHz handset telephony across networks"
5. ITU-T Recommendation G.107 (2000-05). "The E-Model, a computational model for transmission planning"
6. ETSI TS 101 329-3 v2.1.2 (2002-01). "Signalling and control of end to end Quality of Service (QoS)"
7. ITU-T Recommendation H.323 Draft v4 (2000-11). "Packet-based multimedia communications systems"
8. ITU-T Recommendation H.225.0 (2001-03). "Call signalling protocols and media stream packetization for packet-based multimedia communication systems"
9. ITU-T Recommendation H.245 (2000). "Control protocol for multimedia communication"
10. ITU-T Recommendation G.113, Appendix I. "Provisional planning values for the equipment impairment factor Ie"

VAD for VoIP Using Cepstrum

R. Venkatesha Prasad[#], H.S. Jamadagni[#], Abhijeet Sangwan[*], Chiranth M.C[*]

[#]CEDT, Indian Institute of Science, Bangalore, India,
[*]Department of E&C, PESIT, Bangalore, India.

Abstract. As telephony services are being supported on Internet the focus is now on multiplexing many speech streams by exploiting the speech characteristics. The multiplexing gain is an important factor when applications such as teleconference service are ported on to the Internet. Here we discuss Voice Activity Detection (VAD) for Voice over Internet Protocol (VoIP) based on Cepstrum. VAD aids in saving bandwidth of a voice session. Such a scheme would be implemented in the application layer thus VAD is independent of the lower layers. The standard codecs would inherently have the VAD algorithms to reduce the bandwidth. However they are costly and computationally complex. In this paper, we compare the quality of speech, level of compression and computational complexity of our method of Cepstrum based VAD with the standard GSM and ITU-T G.729 codecs. Bandwidth reduction is achieved by not transmitting the non-speech packets. Our algorithm adapts to the varying background noise.

1 Introduction

Traditional voice-based communication uses Public Switched Telephone Networks (PSTN) [3]. Such systems are expensive when the distance between the calling and called subscriber is large because of dedicated connection. The current trend is to provide this service on data networks [10]. Data networks work on the best effort delivery and resource sharing through statistical multiplexing. Therefore, the cost of services compared to circuit-switched networks is considerably less. However, these networks do not guarantee faithful voice transmission. Voice over packet or Voice over IP (VoIP) systems have to ensure that voice quality does not significantly deteriorate due to network conditions such as packet-loss and delays. Therefore, providing Toll Grade Voice Quality [5] through VoIP systems remains a challenge. In this paper we concentrate on the problem of reducing the required bandwidth for a voice connection on Internet using Voice Activity Detection (VAD), while maintaining the voice quality.

VAD algorithms find the beginning and end of talk spurts. VAD is used in non real-time systems like Voice Recognition systems, Compression and Speech coding [4,6,11]. VAD is also useful in VoIP, in which stringent detection of beginning and end of talk spurts is not needed.

In VoIP systems the voice data (or payload for packet) is transmitted along with a header on a network. The header size for Real Time Protocol (RTP, [9]) is 12 bytes.

M.M. Freire, P. Lorenz, M.M.-O. Lee (Eds.): HSNMC 2003, LNCS 2720, pp. 522-530, 2003.

The ratio of header to payload size is an important factor for selecting the payload size for a better throughput from the network. Smaller payload helps in a better real-time quality, but decreases the throughput. Normally, 10ms-40ms speech frames are used in VoIP systems. The requirements of VAD algorithms for VoIP applications are:

    a)   Low computational requirements (not more than one packet time)
    b)   Toll grade quality voice reproduction
    c)   Saving in bandwidth to be maximized

1.1 Speech Characteristics

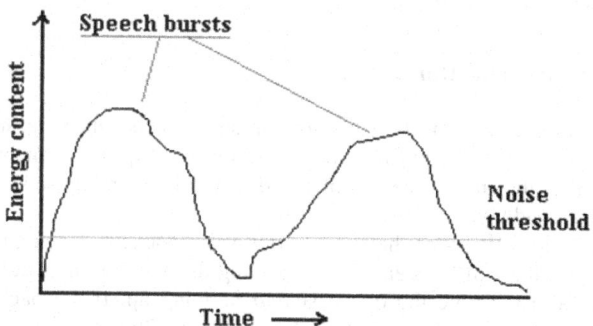

Fig. 1. A typical speech signal

Conversational speech is a sequence of contiguous segments of silence and speech (Fig.1) [20].   VAD algorithms take recourse to some form of speech pattern classification to differentiate between voice and silence periods. Thus, identifying and rejecting transmission of silence periods helps reduce Internet traffic.

1.2 Background Noise

The term 'silence segment' does not refer to a period of zero-energy, but of incomprehensible sound. VAD algorithms have to deal with silence periods having small audible content.

1.3 Desirable Aspects of VAD Algorithms Include:

- A Good Decision Rule: A physical property of speech that can be exploited to give consistent judgement in classifying segments of the signal into silence or otherwise.
- Adaptability to Changing Background Noise: Adapting to non-stationary background noise improves robustness, especially in wireless telephony where the user is mobile.

- Low Computational Complexity: Internet telephony is a real-time application. Therefore the complexity of VAD algorithm must be low to suit real-time applications.

2 Parameters for VAD Design

The differentiation of the voiced signal into speech and silence is done on the basis of speech characteristics. The signal is sliced into contiguous frames. A real-valued non-negative parameter is associated with each frame. If this parameter exceeds a certain threshold, the signal frame is classified as ACTIVE; else it is INACTIVE.

2.1 Choice of Frame Duration

ACTIVE Frames need to be embedded in suitable packets adhering to the network protocol being used for transmission. VoIP receivers queue up incoming packets in a packet-buffer that allows them to play audio even if incoming packets are delayed due to network conditions.

Consider a VoIP system having a buffer of 3-4 packets. Having packet duration of 10ms allows the VoIP system to start playing the audio at the receiver's end after 30 to 40ms from the time the queue started building up. If the packet duration were 50ms, there would be an initial delay of 150-200ms, which is unacceptable. Therefore, the packet duration must be chosen properly. Current VoIP systems use 20-40ms packet sizes.

For ease of DCT computation, frame duration of 8ms, corresponding to 64 samples is used ($64 = 26$), to avoid padding. An 8ms frame can cover 125Hz and above in cepstrum domain. A 40ms packet will have 5 frames.

2.2 Encoding Specifications

The specifications for encoding speech for VAD algorithms are that of Toll Grade Quality [5]:
- 8 kHz sampling frequency
- 256 levels of linear quantization (8 Bit PCM)
- Single channel (mono) recording.

The advantage of using linear PCM is, the voice data can be transformed to any other coding (such as G711, G723, G729) for compressing the voice data packet.

2.3 Adaptability to Background Noise

A fixed threshold would be 'deaf' to varying acoustic environments of the speaker. The scheme must have the wherewithal to adapt the threshold online and in real-time.

An arbitrary initial choice of the threshold is prone to deteriorated performance. For finding the initial threshold of non-speech frames, algorithm may be trained for a small period by a prerecorded speech sample that contains only background noise. Alternately, as users are not active as soon as the call is established, we may assume that the initial 200ms of the sample does not contain any speech. To adapt to the change in the background noise a simple adaptive technique for updating the threshold considering only non-speech frames has been used (as given in [8]).

3 Cepstral VAD

In this paper, we present a Cepstrum based VAD algorithm adopted from [7], wherein the analysis is done for enhancing the speech quality when it is under real car noise. Here the same technique is used for VoIP voice packets to detect the presence of speech. However, we calculated the Cepstral coefficients by using DCT (Discrete Cosine Transform) instead of the usual DFT spectrum that has been newly proposed in [13]. This is a new way of feature extraction and in addition it reduces the computation, as DCT is a real transform. Use of DCT Cepstrum (DCTC) [13] has the advantage of carrying the binary phase information along with the magnitude information when compared to DFT based Cepstrum. This often results in less error in the Cepstral coefficients. The phase of noise is arbitrary where as for speech it is deterministic.

3.1 Background

In a VoIP end terminal (user terminal), the speech is sampled at 8KHz sampling rate from the audio card with 8/16 bit linear quantization. These samples are packetized at 20ms-40ms intervals. The DCT - Cepstrum is computed as shown in Figure 2.

In each packet smaller frames are constructed as discussed, we take frames that contain 64 samples that corresponds to 8ms of speech. The Cepstrum coefficients are calculated for each frame as shown above. For i^{th} frame (with speech signal Xi[n]), Cepstral coefficients is computed as follows,

$$C_i[n] = \text{idct}(\log(\text{dct}(\text{hamming}(X_i[n])))) , \qquad (1)$$

where $n = 1$ to 64.

We take this 64 dimensional vector to calculate the distance from the origin. We take L2 Norm to find the distance. The basis of the algorithm is that the frames in which the speech is not present have very low values of the cepstral distance around the origin. The Cepstrum peak due to the voiced excitation is more compared to the noise frame (non-speech frame). The Cepstra coming from noise are known to have much lower variances than those for speech especially in the case of low 'quefrency'. We are using in our algorithm, all the coefficients without confining to first few. For want of finding the energy of speech packets, we are considering vocal tract and source information regarding the activity. We are not confining ourselves to modeling vocal tract here. With all the coefficients we are using full information of the signal provided by Cepstrum. While taking the difference in distance between speech frame and non-speech frame, the energy of the non-speech packet is subtracted. Hence, the higher value of difference cepstrum would imply a speech frame, and consequently a packet.

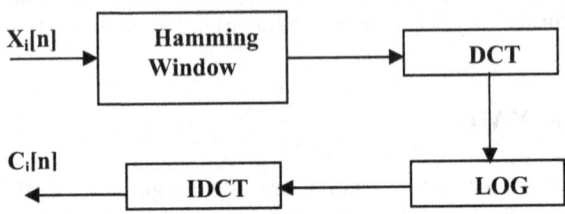

Fig. 2. Computation of Cepstrum Coefficients Ci[n] from the signal speech of one frame Xi[n]

3.2 Algorithm

In a VoIP call as soon as the call is established, the audio card will start recording the speech input. The user will see a message to imply that the call has been established. Usually the response time of the user before speaking into the microphone is at least 200ms. Thus the first 25 frames in our case have the recording of background noise. The Cepstral coefficients of the background noise is thus calculated and averaged.

Step 1 : Calculate the $C_i[n]$ for the ith cepstral coefficient, for $i = 1$ to 25, $n = 1$ to 64, i.e. for the first 25 frames, 64 cepstral coefficients, using Equation (1).

Step 2 : Compute $C_{th}[n]$

$$C_{th}[n] = \frac{1}{25} \sum_{i=1}^{25} (C_i[n]) ,$$

(2)

for $i = 1$ to 25, $n = 1$ to 64

Step 3: Compute the first approximation of the threshold of non-speech frames (first 25 frames) using,

$$d_{th} = \frac{1}{64} \sum_{i=1}^{64} (C_{th}[n])^2 .$$

(3)

Step 4: For all i frames, $i > 25$, compute $C_i[n]$,

$$d_i = \frac{1}{64} \sum_{i=1}^{64} \left(C_i[n] - C_{th}[n] \right)^2 .$$ (4)

Step 5 : The **decision rule** for detection of speech activity is

If $abs(d_i) > k.abs(d_{th})$, **then** frame is ACTIVE (5)

Else the frame is INACTIVE
where $k = 2$

Step 6: The threshold d_{th} is updated using the following equation only if a frame d_i is identified as a non-speech frame in *Step 5*. (Adaptive Threshold).

$$d_{th(new)} = p.d_{th(old)} + (1-p).d_i ,$$ (6)

where $p = 0.8$

In Step 1 and 2, we compute the threshold cepstral coefficients for the first 25 frames corresponding to 200ms. In Step 3 we compute the average of threshold cepstral coefficients. In Step 4, the relative distance between the current cepstral vector and the threshold is computed. The step 5 makes the decision whether the frame has speech or not. The value of 'k' in Step 5 is experimentally set to 2. A packet is resolved as having Speech if it carries at least one ACTIVE frame. For example, a packet carrying 40ms speech will have 5 frames (of 8ms each).

At step 6 the background noise is continually updated only upon detection of INACTIVE frames. The parameter 'p' updates the threshold and decides the rate of change of adaptation as well. Sangwan, et. al. [21] have discussed the selection of 'p' as well as second and third-order adaptability.

4   Results & Discussions

MATLAB was used to test the algorithm developed on various sample signals. The test templates used varied in loudness, speech continuity, background noise and accent. Both male and female voices have been used. The performance of the algorithms was studied on the basis of the following parameters:
1   Floating Point Operations (FLOPS) required: The total number of floating point operations is calculated for all algorithms to compare their relative complexity. This parameter is useful in comparing algorithms of their applicability for real-time implementation.
2   Percentage compression: The ratio of total INACTIVE frames detected to the total number of frames formed expressed as a percentage. A good VAD should have high percentage compression.

3   Subjective Speech Quality: The quality of the samples was rated on a scale of 1 (poorest) to 5 (best) where 4 represents toll grade quality. The input signal was taken to have speech quality 5. The speech samples after compression were played to independent jurors randomly for an unbiased decision.

4   Objective Assessment of Misdetection: The number of frames which have speech content, but were classified as INACTIVE and number of frames without speech content but classified as ACTIVE are counted. The ratio of this count to the total number of frames in the sample explored as a percentage is taken as the **%MISDETECTION**. This gives a quantitative measure of VAD performance. Though this number represents the quality of speech after applying a VAD technique, the quality of speech has to be assessed only by the subjective grading of the speech which is equivalent to MoS. This number gives an approximate assessment of the performance of the algorithm. To find an average values of misdetection a long speech file up to 3minutes are used.

An effective VAD algorithm should have high compression and a low number of FLOPS while maintaining an acceptable Speech Quality (and low misdetection)
It is necessary to note that the percentage compression also depends on the speech samples. If the speech signal were continuous, without any breaks, it would be unreasonable to expect high compression levels.

Table 1. The speech sample results [1]

Speech input	% of Compression	FLOPS (Max)	Subjective Quality	% Misdetection of packets
Sample 1	30	40000	4	16
Sample 2	17	40000	4	29
Sample 3	25	40000	4	25
Sample 4	29	40000	4	6
Sample 5	30	40000	4	30

The FLOPS are found using the MATLAB function. These results are compared with G.729B and GSM AMR VAD in Table 2.

Table 2. The VAD features of G.79B and GSM-FR

Speech input	% of Compression	FLOPS (Max)	MoS	% Misdetection of packets
G.729B	64 to 8kbps	3.9×10^6	4	13.4
GSM-AMR (VAD1)	64 to 12.2kbps	3.4×10^6	4	15

---

[1] Subjective Quality is based on majority decision of 7 listeners.
% of Compression is the saving in bandwidth.
% Misdetection is manually determined.

Table 2. shows an important aspect of our algorithm and the standard codecs. The numbers in the table 2 are compiled from many sources [15, 16, 17, 18,19]. Though the percentage misdetection is less in the standard codecs, the cost of computation is higher. MIPS to FLOPS conversion is taken as 1 MIPS = 3.2MFLOPS[14]. GSM VAD assumes stationary background noise. Therefore, it misses the low energy unvoiced speech [6].

5 Conclusions

We have presented an algorithm for VAD that can be implemented on a PC in real-time. The speech quality was observed to be of 'good' quality. The comparison with standard codecs shows a remarkable saving in the computation costs. Nonetheless, the saving in bandwidth is high for the standard algorithms. These standard algorithms are proprietary and implemented using DSPs. In VoIP systems, normally, the speech activity of a speaker is found to be around 40% [22]. Thus our algorithms would be saving at least 50% of the bandwidth at a lesser cost. With our algorithm the bandwidth reduces approximately to 32kbps where as in standard codecs it can be up to 8kbps. Thus the trade off is between the cost of the codecs and saving in bandwidth.

The advantage of these algorithms is in providing the teleconference applications wherein streams from a large number of participants have to be handled. There is a less possibility of codecs being available at all user terminals and thus forcing all the participants to use linear PCM. If VAD is applied to each stream at an intermediate server, computational capability of the servers cannot scale up for a large number of streams for coding the signals at a server.

Our VAD algorithm applied to PCM coded speech, which is a waveform coding, preserves the speech characteristics compared to parametric coding used in G.729 and GSM. This is an important aspect while mixing many streams in a conference. A word of caution is that the Cepstrum is noise sensitive and computationally expensive compared to energy-based algorithms [12].

References

1. Abhijeet Sangwan, Chiranth M.C, H.S.Jamadagni, Rahul Sah, R. Venkatesha Prasad, Vishal Gaurav, VAD Techniques for Real-Time Speech Transmission on the Internet, The Fifth International Conference on High-Speed Networks and Multimedia Communications HSNMC'02, July 3-5, 2002 - Jeju Island, S. KOREA.
2. A. Sangwan, Chiranth M. C, R. Shah, V. Gaurav, R. Venkatesha Prasad "Voice Activity Detection for VoIP- Time and Frequency domain Solutions", Tenth annual IEEE Symposium on Multimedia Communications and Signal Processing, Bangalore, Nov 2001, 20-24.
3. J.E. Flood, Telecommunications Switching - Traffic and Networks, Prentice Hall India
4. Jongseo Sohn, Nam Soo Kim and Wonyong Sung, "A statistical model-based voice activity detection", IEEE Signal Processing Letters, Vol. 6, no. 1, January 1999
5. Kamilo Feher, Wireless Digital Communications, Prentice Hall India, 2001

6.   Khaled El-Maleh and Peter Kabal, "Comparison of Voice Activity Detection Algorithms for Wireless Personal Communications Systems", IEEE Canadian Conference on Electrical and Computer engineering, May 1997, 470-473
7.   Petr Pollak, Pavel Sovka, and Jan Uhlir, "Cepstral Speech/Pause Detectors", proc. of IEEE Workshop on Nonlinear Signal and Image Processing, Neos Marmaras, Greece, June 1995, 388-391.
8.   Petr Pollak and Pavel Sovka, and Jan Uhlir, "Noise Suppression System for a Car", proc. of the Third European Conference on Speech, Communication and Technology - EUROSPEECH'93, Berlin, Sept 1993, 1073-1076
9.   RTP, Real Time Protocol, RFC 1889, http://www.ietf.org/rfc/rfc1889.txt
10. Stefan Pracht and Dennis Hardman, Agilent Technologies - "Voice Quality in Converging Telephony and IP Networks", Ciscoworld Magazine - White Paper 2001
11. Y.D.Cho, K.Al-Naimi and A.Kondoz, "Mixed Decision-Based Noise Adaption for Speech Enhancement", IEEE Electronics Letters Online No. 20010368, 6 Feb 2001.
12. R. Venkatesha Prasad, Abhijeet Sangwan, H.S. Jamadagni, Chiranth M.C, Rahul Sah, VishalGaurav Comparison of Voice Activity Detection Algorithms for VoIP, published at The Seventh IEEE Symposium on Computers and Communications, ISCC'2002, Taormina, Sicily, ITALY, July, 2002.
13. R. Muralishankar and A. G. Ramakrishnan, "DCT Based Pseudo Complex Cepstrum", ICASSP, Vol. 1, Orlando, Florida, May 2002, 521-524.
14. M.R. Swanson, T. Critchlo, R. Kessler, and L.B. Stoller. "The Design of the Schizophrenic Workstation System," In the Proceedings of the Third Usenix Mach Symposium, April 1993
15. Jerry D. Gibson (ed.), Multimedia Communications - Directions & Innovations, Academic Press, 2001
16. Thomas Enderes Swee Chern Khoo Clare A. Somerville Kostas Samaras   Mobile Networks and Applications Volume 7 , Issue 2 (April 2002) . 153-161
17. http://www.nuntius.com/solutions11.html (ITU-T recommended vocoders)
18. http://www.cisco.com/warp/public/788/voip/codec_complexity.html (G729)
19. Jianping Zhang, Wayne Ward and Bryan Pellom, "Phone Based Voice Activity Detection Using Online Bayesian Adaptation with Conjugate Normal Distributions," in ICASSP'2002, Orlando Florida, May 2002.
20. B. Gold and N. Morgan, Speech and Audio Signal Processing, John Wiley Publications.
21. Abhijeet Sangwan, H.S. Jamadagni, Chiranth M.C., Rahul Sah, R. Venkatesha Prasad, Vishal Gaurav, Second and Third Order Adaptable Threshold for VAD in VoIP, ICSP, Beijing, Aug 2002, 1693-1696.
22. Khaled El-Maleh and Peter Kabal, Natural quality background noise coding using residual substitution, EUROSPEECH, Budapest, Sep 1999, Vol. No 5, 2359-2362.

Development of a Voice over IP Applications for a Metropolitan Area Network

Alexandre Heck, Pascal Lorenz, and Hervé Bloch

University of Haute Alsace
34, rue du Grillenbreit
68008 Colmar - France
a.heck@uha.fr, lorenz@ieee.org

Abstract. This paper investigates the development between telephony IP service and IP network performances through some experimentation on a Metropolitan Area Network (MAN). We propose to develop Voice over IP (VoIP) tests to qualify end-to-end voice communications on the Metropolitan Area Network. We focus on how to qualify the Quality of Service (QoS) and how to manage the coexistence of Voice over IP applications with traditional data applications.

1. Introduction

The goal of our work is to verify how it would be possible to develop telephony IP service for a MAN network. We have studied several aspects enabling to verify the architecture of a network through different parameters, such as the encoding methods, delay of transmission, jitter, etc ...

The end-to-end delays are influenced by IP terminal buffering, H.323 packetization, and network transmission steps. The end-to-end audio/video quality depends on input and output devices, analogue/digital and digital/analogue circuit noise, coding distortion and bandwidth limitation in the IP network.

The QoS issues associated with the IP terminal are the choice of codecs in the terminal, the performance of the codec, the signal/call processing delays, the processing delays associated with the security issues and the performance of echo-canceling devices.

The operators use more and more VoIP because they can use the same equipment to transmit voice and data over Internet. The development of VoIP implies the integration of the PSTN (Public Switched Telephone Network) network. Therefore gateways should be used to interconnect SS7 protocol with IP protocol. The three majors protocols for VoIP and SS7 over IP are H.323, MGCP (Media Gateway Control Protocol) and SIP (Session Initiative Protocol) [1], [3], [5].

M.M. Freire, P. Lorenz, M.M.-O. Lee (Eds.): HSNMC 2003, LNCS 2720, pp. 531-538, 2003.

2. Experimentation Environment

QoS defined in CCITT Recommendation E.800 may be considered as the generic definition reproduced as below: *"The collective effect of service performance which determine the degree of satisfaction of a user of the service".*

We have developed our test network over the Colmar city Metropolitan Area Network. This network is composed by a central "level 2" COM 21 switch using an ATM network. The ATM network is used to separate the different community of users and to offer an adapted quality of service [10], [11], [12], [13], [16].

2.1 Network Architecture

The Colmar MAN is used essentially for the data transmission to connect end-users via cable-modems. A buffer is implemented on the COM 21 switch and a 2 Mbit buffer is offered to each cable-modem.

Our ATM network is based on the MPOA (Multi Protocol Over ATM) protocol, which allows the configuration of Virtual LANs associated to selected user groups.
Specific attention is given to performance and QoS (Quality of Service) measurements [17].

Some tests are performed with 128 and 384 kbit/s rates. We have done some video transmission tests with our platform. For video transmission, the QoS is unacceptable at 128 kbit/s: good video quality can only be obtained for still images, moving images have restricted quality as well in video and audio. Our plate-form provides acceptable quality for video transmission at 384 kbit/s.

The used architecture in the Metropolitan Area Network is described on the following figure.

The host configuration includes machines, graphic interfaces, audio/video codecs and the network access interfaces based on 10 Mbit/s, 100 Mbit/s, Fast Ethernet, Switched Ethernet and 155 Mbit/s ATM protocols.
Quality of Service evaluation is related to end-to-end multimedia applications with LAN-to-LAN interconnection.

Each endpoint of our architecture can be described as follow.

In our architecture, the used cable-modem is connected to a "COM 21" switch and takes into account USP and TCP flows: the TCP flows for data traffic and UDP flows for voice/video traffic.

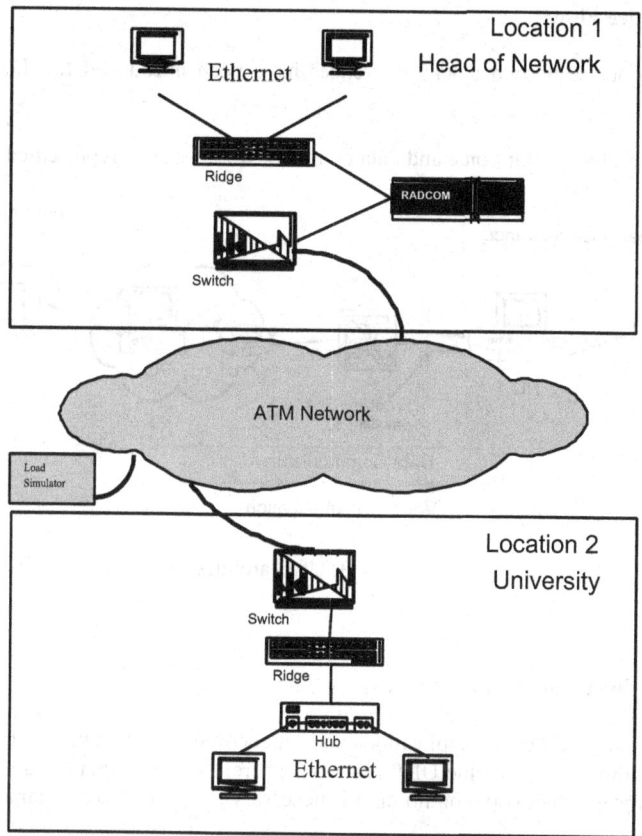

Fig 1. Colmar MAN architecture

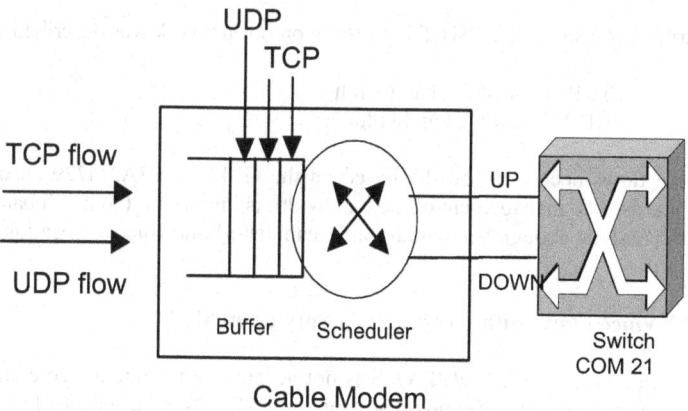

Fig 2. Description of the endpoint

2.2 Voice Flows

To do our tests, two clocks references have been introduced for the voice over IP traffic.

The architecture for voice and data communications can be represented as follows:

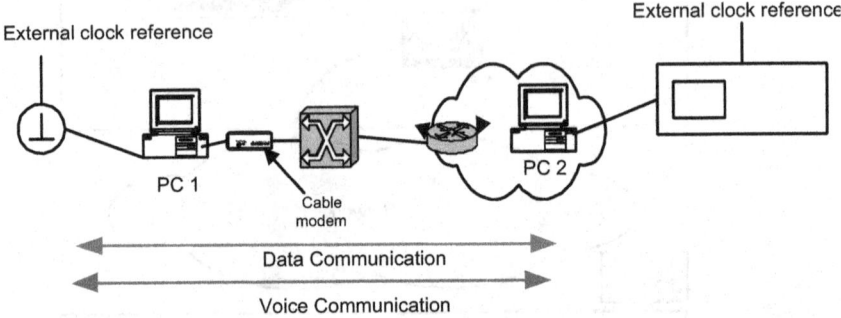

Fig. 3. Used architecture

2.2.1 Voice Flows Constraints

Voice over IP (VoIP) applications and videoconferencing applications are streaming applications based on the UDP protocol. Therefore voice streams cannot dynamically be adapted to network condition: it is necessary to apply QoS mechanisms [4].

Voice applications are sensible to jitter and to delay transmission, which produce some echo and distortion problems [2], [8], [9].

During our tests the UDP/TCP repartition on our network was described as follow:

    - TCP: 97 % of the bandwidth
    - UDP: 3% of the bandwidth.

Voice flows need a bandwidth based on the G711, G723A, G729 encoding Codecs standards. The management of the bandwidth is important: too much bandwidth is not useful and not enough bandwidth traffic can disturb the voice application.

2.2.2 Voice Flows without Quality of Service on MAN

A communication without IP QoS is not acceptable for interactive communications. Communication delay should be no more than 200 ms to be acceptable [14], [15].

This phenomena has two principal factors:

- ATM/UBR mode does not enable to separate each community of users; then a CBR mode has been used for the VoIP transmissions to ensure that there is no influence between the different communities. Therefore, a CBR class was used with a traffic shaping mode.

- more the buffer size increases, more the jitter will grow. Our links are based on a 256 kbps downstream and a 128 kbps upstream.

The CBR upstream voice traffic measured during our tests is represented as follows:

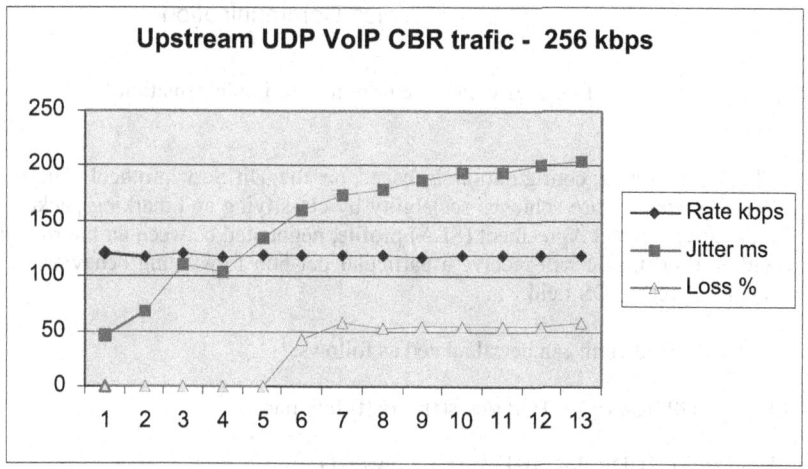

Fig. 4. CBR upstream voice traffic

For the G711 standard (which gives the better audio clarity), a 150 ms average delay has been measured. To measure the jitter, an EVA test equipment was used [6], [7].

3. QoS Implementation

To ensure a minimal use of the modem buffer (for the upstream traffic which is limited to 128 kbps and which is not configurable), we have implemented a router enabling to do traffic management.

The architecture used in our implementation can be represented as follows:

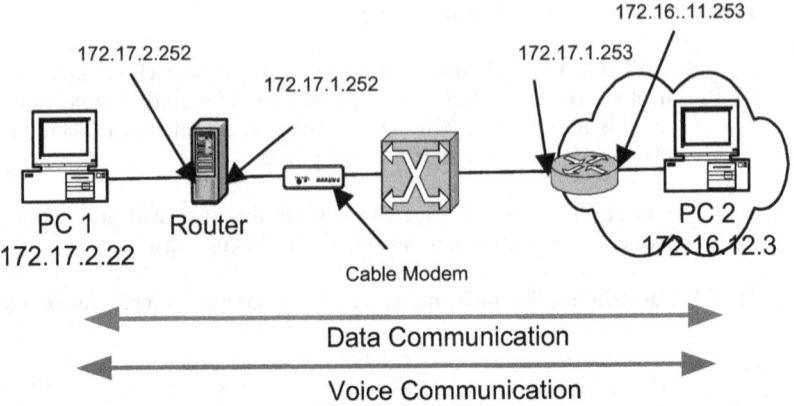

Fig. 5. Architecture used for our implementation

The Linux router configuration is based on the DiffServ protocol. Differentiated Services architecture achieves scalability by classifying and marking packets. Based on a Service Level Agreement (SLA) profile, negotiated between an Internet provider and an user, traffic will receive a particular per-hop forwarding behavior on routers that interpret the DS field.

The used bandwidth can be calculated as follows:

Bw = UDP flows (t) + TCP flows(t) + Bs(t)/link rate

With Bs(t) = UDP flows(t-1) + TCP flows(t-1)

Bw=Used Bandwidth
Bs=Buffer used for the transmission

The buffer modem has been implemented on a EF (Expedited Forwarding) class with the following repartition: 80 % of traffic (102 kbps) for voice flows and 10 % of traffic for data application.
If there is no voice traffic, then the entire available channels are used for the data traffic. A 10 % (which corresponds to term Bs/link rate =0) provision of the traffic must be respected to avoid any buffer saturation.
This method gives good results but it is difficult to implement this later for each particular user: it is only applicable if there is few users.

Three Codecs have been tested with the G771, G723A and G729 protocols. For the G711 Codec transmission, we can observe that for a delay of 150 ms, the quality is equal to 4,4; which corresponds to 98 % of users satisfied by the voice quality.

Our simulation results can be represented as follows:

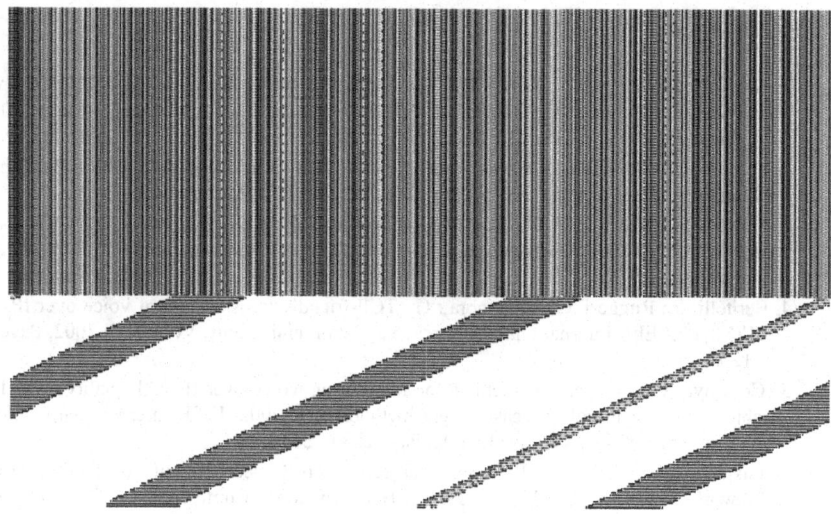

Fig. 6. Results of the simulation

With the G723 Codec, an encoding and decoding time of 2x30 ms give poor results for voice. The G711 Codec gives the best adapted encoding method. The G729 Codec gives medium quality of voice and lay out the problem of clients that have not implemented it.

4. Conclusion

Deploying Voice over IP solutions over a MAN need some tests and simulations to be sure to have good results.
We have developed some applications for performance measurements applied to VoIP systems. Two types of services for our MAN network have been studied:
- a first one based only on data and
- a second one based on voice and data.

The different simulations tests have shown that our solution offer real QoS services for the users.
Some methods for the simulations and for the tests are experimented: performance aspects have been carefully analyzed in various environments. The end-to-end Quality of Service aspects have been approached, but need further studies.
We will develop our application for platforms based on MPLS and we will study the QoS through the development of VPN (Virtual Private Networks).

References

1. Sze, H.P.; Liew, S.C.; Lee, J.Y.B.; Yip, D.C.S.: A multiplexing scheme for H.323 voice-over-IP applications, IEEE Journal on Selected Areas in Communications, Volume 20 Issue 7 , Sept. 2002 , Page 1360 –1368

2. Lee, D.J.Y.: Tunnelling wireless voice with software defined vocoder, IEEE 55th Vehicular Technology Conference, VTC Spring 2002, Volume 4, 2002, Page 1623 -1625

3. Lingfen S.; Ifeachor, E.C.: Perceived speech quality prediction for voice over IP-based networks, ICC 2002. IEEE International Conference on Communications, Volume 4 , 2002 , Page 2573 –2577.

4. Beritelli, F.; Ruggeri, G.; Schembra,: G., TCP-friendly transmission of voice over IP, 2002. ICC 2002. IEEE International Conference on Communications, Volume 2, 2002, Page 1204 –1208.

5. Conway, A.E.: A passive method for monitoring voice-over-IP call quality with ITU-T objective speech quality measurement methods, ICC 2002. IEEE International Conference on Communications, Volume 4, 2002, Page 2583 –2586.

6. Lakaniemi, A.; Rosti, J.; Raisanen: Subjective VoIP speech quality evaluation based on network measurements, ICC 2001. IEEE International Conference on Communications, Volume 3, 2001 , Page 748 –752.

7. Li Zheng; Liren Zhang; Dong Xu: Characteristics of network delay and delay jitter and its effect on voice over IP (VoIP), ICC 2001. IEEE International Conference on Communications, Volume 1, 2001, Page: 122 –126.

8. Kampichler, W.; Goeschka, K.M.: Plain end-to-end measurement for local area network voice transmission feasibility, Ninth International Symposium on Analysis and Simulation of Computer and Telecommunication Systems, 2001, Page 235 –240

9. Das, A.; Fu Xiaowen: Convergence in technology and regulation-the IP telephony case, ICMIT 2000, Proceedings of the 2000 IEEE International Conference on Management of Innovation and Technology, Volume 1, 2000, Page 168 -173

10. Tajima, K.; Hashmani, M.; Yoshida, M.: A resource management architecture over differentiated services domains for guarantee of bandwidth, delay and jitter , EUROCOMM'2000, Information Systems for Enhanced Public Safety and Security. IEEE/AFCEA, 2000, Page 242 –249

11. Griffeth, N.; Hao, R.; Lee, D.; Sinha, R.K.: Interoperability testing of VoIP systems, Global Telecommunications Conference, GLOBECOM '00, Volume 3, 2000, Page 1565 -1570

12. Hua Zou; Hongman Wang; Wenxin Mao; Bai Wang; Focant, S.; Handekyn, K.; Chantrain, D.; Marly, N.: Prototyping SIP-based VoIP services in Java, ICCT 2000. International Conference on Communication Technology Proceedings, Volume 2, 2000, Page 1395 -1399

13. Lorenz, P.: Quality of service and new architectures for future telecommunications networks, MILCOM 2000. 21st Century Military Communications Conference, Volume 2, 2000 , Page 695 -698

14. Raisanen, V.I.; Rosti, J.: Application-level IP measurements for multimedia, Eighth International Workshop on Quality of Service, 2000, Page 170 –172

15. Mishra, P.P.; Saran, H.: Capacity management and routing policies for voice over IP traffic, IEEE Network, Volume 14, Issue 2, March-April 2000, Page 20 –27

16. Gun Seo; Woo-Chang Hwang; Youngok Rhee: An implementation of VoIP cable modem, TENCON'99, Volume 2, 1999, Page 1532 -1535

17. Kroth, N.; Mark, L.; Tiemann, J: A framework for testing IP QoS over ATM networks: implementation and practical experiences, ICATM '99. 2nd International Conference on ATM, 1999, Page 212 –219

Traffic Model Characterization of an HFC Network

Manuel Garcia[1], Daniel F. Garcia[1], Victor G. Garcia[1], and Ricardo Bonis[2]

[1] University of Oviedo, Campus de Viesques, 33204 Gijon, Spain
[2] TeleCable, s.a., Scientific Park, 33206 Gijon, Spain.

Abstract. This paper describes the traffic model developed to represent the traffic observed on the telecommunication network of a cable operator providing data services. The operator network is based on a hybrid fiber coax (HFC) network using ATM technology. The traffic model is based on the measurements taken on the upstream channels of the network and represents the behavior of the subscribers by simulation.

The proposed traffic model has two characteristics which distinguish it from other traffic models. Firstly, it considers aggregated traffic, so no distinction between types of traffic is needed. Secondly, the parameters of the traffic model are directly related to the network configuration.

1 Introduction

In all performance studies of telecommunication systems, it is necessary to establish a traffic model. The traffic model collects the characteristics of the real traffic and is used to evaluate the performance of the systems which manage this traffic. The final results of the performance study will depend directly on the accuracy of the traffic model used.

Traffic models have been developed in parallel to the evolution of telecommunication systems. This evolution can be broken into two different stages. In the first stage, referred to as traditional traffic models, traffic models were associated mainly to Poisson or Markov processes. The second stage began in the early 90's when the studies done by [1], showed that modern telecommunication systems exhibit the statistical property of self-similarity. Subsequent studies show that self-similarity is an inherent property of the traffic in modern telecommunication systems. Thus, in the late 90's research into traffic models which consider the property of self-similarity began, using different approaches to reproduce traffic self-similarity. Some of the most important traffic models developed are: the $PT \otimes \lambda$ model, [2], the *M/Pareto* model, [3], and the *N-Burst* model, [4].

All these models have two common characteristics: firstly, they consider homogeneous traffic, that is, traffic produced by only one kind of source or application, and secondly, the traffic model parameters are obtained from real traffic analysis, but these parameters have no relationship with the characteristics of the telecommunication system evaluated. This situation results in simplified traffic models, difficult to apply to real telecommunication systems because the

M.M. Freire, P. Lorenz, M.M.-O. Lee (Eds.): HSNMC 2003, LNCS 2720, pp. 539–549, 2003.
© Springer-Verlag Berlin Heidelberg 2003

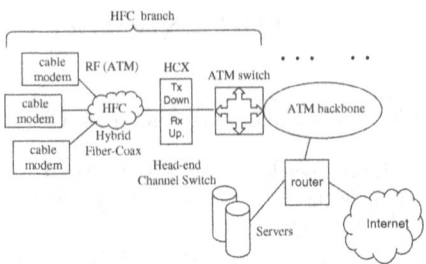

Fig. 1. Architecture of the HFC system

real traffic is aggregated, and there is no clear correspondence between system characteristics and traffic model parameters.

This paper presents the traffic model developed to represent the traffic on an HFC cable network using ATM technology for data transmission. This traffic model overcomes these limitations considering the aggregated traffic on the HFC network, and the traffic model parameters are directly related with the HFC network characteristics. The parameters of this traffic model are related to the number of subscribers assigned by the cable operator to each channel, and the time of day. Thus, the traffic model provides traffic evolution in time.

The proposed traffic model is based on a broad analysis of the traffic measurements on all the channels of the HFC network over two different periods of time, [5]. The analysis carried out establishes relationships between the statistical values of the traffic and the number of subscribers on the channel. Considering these relationships and the HFC network characteristics, the traffic model is built using a simulation program able to reproduce the traffic observed on the channels.

The paper is organized as follows. Section 2 briefly describes the HFC network on which the traffic model is based. Section 3 outlines the most relevant aspects found in the analysis of the traffic measurements. The development of the traffic model is commented in Section 4. The results obtained with the traffic model are presented and compared with the real measurements in Section 5. Finally, the conclusions and future research are presented in Section 6.

2   System Description

This paper focuses on the traffic registered on an HFC network. This technology combines fiber optic and coax cables to transmit signals. The traffic model developed is based on the traffic measurements belonging to the HFC network operator TeleCable, s.a., one of the most important cable operators in Spain. A scheme of the whole HFC network can be seen in Fig. 1. This HFC operator provides data services in an area that includes three cities. The cable network is organized as a group of parallel HFC branches, communicated by an ATM backbone. In each HFC branch the signal is distributed using fiber cables organized in a tree hierarchy until the final optical nodes are reached. The information servers and the access to Internet are located in one of the cities.

In the subscribers' homes, data services are accessed through a cable modem, connected to a home PC. This cable modem transforms the Ethernet packets into ATM cells, and it negotiates access to the HFC network, so determining the maximum speed at which it can transmit. In the data transmission based on HFC networks there are two channels with very different characteristics: the downstream channel, used to send data to the subscribers, and the upstream channel, used by the subscribers to return data requests. The downstream channel is shared by all the subscribers and has a greater bandwidth, 30 Mbps. On the other side, there are 6 upstream channels in each HFC network, and each subscriber is assigned to one of them; the bandwidth of these channels is 1.9 Mbps. The last elements in the HFC branch are the head-end channel switch (HCX) and the ATM switch. The HCX element manages all the traffic belonging to the HFC branch and the ATM switch connects the HFC branch to the rest of the network.

Finally, the data service conditions of the cable operator are: an unlimited 24 hour "flat rate", maximum bandwidth limits of 128Kb/64Kb (downstream/upstream) and a "best effort" quality of service, that is, all the subscribers share the channel.

3   Traffic Analysis

This section presents the most important results of the analysis of the traffic measurements of the HFC network, to be used in the traffic model development. A more complete presentation of the analysis can be found in [5]. These traffic measurements were taken on all the channels, and represent traffic evolution over time, registered as a percentage of the channel bandwidth used.

The first useful result obtained from the analysis was the establishment of a close linear relationship between the mean traffic values registered on all the channels and the number of subscribers assigned to each of them. Figure 2 shows the graphs obtained for the downstream and upstream traffic for the last set of measurements. The points obtained are adjusted using a simple linear regression model. The same kind of relationship was found for the peak values of the traffic against the number of subscribers assigned to the channel, as can be seen in Fig. 3. In each graph the regression line obtained and its equation are shown. Furthermore, two lines mark the limits of the confidence interval for the predictions with a 95% level of confidence.

The main conclusions obtained from the analysis are that there are linear relationships between traffic properties and one of the most important system parameters: the number of assigned subscribers to each channel. These relationships are maintained for the two groups of measurements, but with different coefficients in the relationships due to the effect of the temporal evolution of

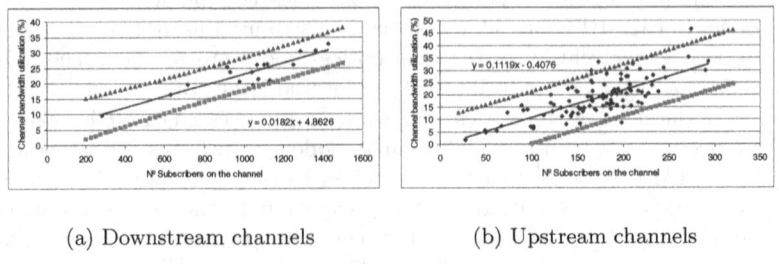

(a) Downstream channels   (b) Upstream channels

Fig. 2. Relationship between mean traffic and subscribers, 2002 measurements

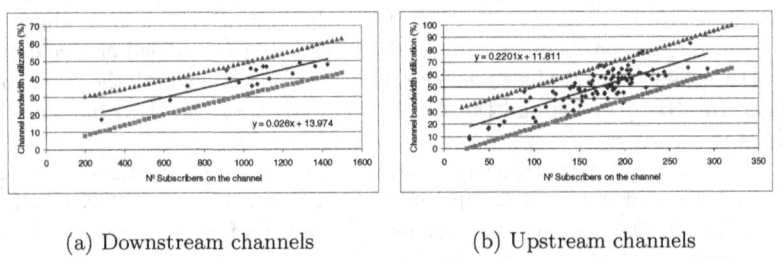

(a) Downstream channels   (b) Upstream channels

Fig. 3. Relationship between peak traffic and subscribers, 2002 measurements

the traffic. Other relevant results from the analysis, were the linear relationships between peak traffic and mean traffic values, and the fact that traffic on the HFC network channels exhibit the property of the self-similarity.

The results of the relationships obtained support the following assumptions: the subscribers on each channel connect to the network in a similar way (it is not possible to know the number of connected subscribers on each channel with the measurements available), and that all the connected users use the network in a similar way. These aspects and the traffic characteristics identified in the analysis are considered in the development of the traffic model.

4   Traffic Model Development

The objective of the traffic model is to represent how the subscribers use the HFC network. The traffic model will consider only the traffic on the upstream channels, because the subscribers send their requests through these channels. The traffic on the downstream channels is influenced by the upstream traffic, and can be represented as the upstream traffic modified by a factor which depends on the size of the information requested by the subscribers.

In order to reproduce the real traffic values on the upstream channels the traffic model must consider three elements: the upstream channel characteristics, the media access control (MAC) protocol, and the user profile (the way in which subscribers demand service from the HFC network). In the following subsections the influence of each element on the development of the model is described.

4.1   Upstream Channel

Each upstream channel is represented as a shared media with a transmission payload of 1.5525 Mb/sec. This is so because, with few exceptions, the HFC operator does not apply quality of service differences. As a result, all subscribers receive the best effort quality of service, that is, all of them compete for the channel.

4.2   Cable Modem and MAC Protocol

Communication on the upstream channels of the cable operator uses a proprietary protocol. This protocol corresponds to a Time Division Multiple Access (TDMA) protocol. Access to the channel is organized in frames which are repeated continuously: in this protocol a frame is sent across the upstream channel every 102.4 milliseconds. The frame is composed of 512 ATM cells, of which only 414 are devoted to data transmission. The rest are used for communication requests, opportunities to join the channel, synchronization, conflict resolution and control.

Of the 414 useful ATM cells, each cable modem can use a maximum of 63 cells in each frame. However, the cable operator can control the total number of available cells in each frame depending on the bandwidth assigned to the subscriber. Although subscriber contracts with different bandwidths are possible, on the dates when the measurements were taken all the subscribers had the same bandwidth: 128Kb/64Kb, that is 128Kb for the downstream channel and 64Kb for the upstream channel. This bandwidth in the upstream channel corresponds to a maximum value of 16 ATM cells per frame for each subscriber. This value is reduced as the number of subscribers using the network increases because of the effect of the best effort quality of service.

The way in which the information is sent produces a burst effect on the channel, which results in the traffic self-similarity observed in the analysis. Each cable modem works as an ON/OFF process. During the assigned time in the frame it can send up to 16 ATM cells, the ON period. Then it must wait until the next frame for a new transmission, this waiting time is the OFF period. This happens for all cable modems, so in each frame there are sequences of used cells followed by groups of unassigned or unused cells. This pattern is similar for each frame, and is modified as the number of subscribers on the channel changes.

4.3   User Profile

This is the most relevant element in the development of the traffic model, because the diversity of subscribers' behavior is represented with a reduced set of parameters. Two factors must be considered: when and how the subscribers use the network.

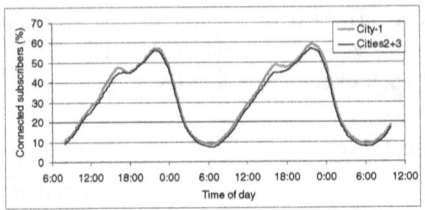

Fig. 4. Evolution of connected subscribers to the network

When Subscribers Connect to the HFC Network. The access to the network is controlled by a Dynamic Host Configuration Protocol (DHCP) server, which assigns an IP address to each subscriber. This element registers the number of IP addresses assigned in each logical sub-network managed by the cable operator; it also can distinguish between IP addresses belonging to one of the cities and the group of the other two cities.

Figure 4 represents the percentage of the total connected subscribers in time for the cities where the cable operator provides services. Both lines show approximately the same evolution, in spite of the difference in the total number of subscribers. This pattern has been observed in all the sub-networks managed by the cable operator. Thus, it is possible assume that the number of connected subscribers on all the upstream channels follows a similar pattern. Based on these measurements and using the Fourier analysis, a compact expression to model the cyclic evolution of connected subscribers is obtained as follows.

First, the number of connected subscribers in each sample period is expressed as a percentage of the total number of subscribers. Then the direct Fourier transform is applied to the values obtained. Finally, to obtain a compact expression, the inverse Fourier transform is used, but truncated to 90% of the spectral power to reduce the number of necessary coefficients. This percentage represents a tradeoff between the number of coefficients used and the errors committed.

Using the expression obtained from the inverse Fourier transform, the percentage of connected subscribers for each sample period is calculated; then, multiplying the number of subscribers assigned to each upstream channel by the percentage obtained, gives the number of connected subscribers. However, the definitive number of connected subscribers is obtained from a normal distribution with a mean the value obtained in the previous step, and a standard deviation of a 5% of the mean value. This result is obtained from the analysis of the variations of the global connected subscribers over time.

How Subscribers Use the HFC Network. The second step in the development of the user profile is to determine how the subscribers demand services across the network. In this point, the following assumption is made: the traffic on the upstream channels can be divided into two types, *interactive* traffic, which depends on the number of connected subscribers, and *non-interactive* traffic, which represents constant traffic over time, independently of the number of connected subscribers. This assumption can be confirmed in two ways.

The first way is from the analysis of the traffic measurements taken in the Internet access router, and separated by services. There are many services identified, three of which are the most representative. The first is the peer-to-peer (P2P) application known as *Edonkey*. This application, which represents 53.35% of the global upstream traffic, exhibits a constant pattern, independent of the number of connected subscribers. On the other hand, the P2P application *Morpheus* and the HTTP protocol, which contribute to the global upstream traffic with 14.26% and 12.32% respectively, both show a cyclical pattern and are therefore dependent on the number of connected subscribers.

The second way to confirm the existence of two types of traffic is to compare the daily evolution of traffic and subscribers. Firstly, the aggregated upstream traffic is calculated for both groups of cities. Secondly the evolution of connected subscribers in both groups of cities, available from the DHCP server, is considered. Dividing upstream traffic by connected subscribers, a new time series which represents the traffic per subscriber is obtained. This new time series has a surprising form: during the periods of high traffic and high number of connected subscribers it remains almost constant, while in the periods of low activity it exhibits a peak. This behaviour confirms that during the period of human activity the interactive traffic dominates, while in the period of low activity non-interactive traffic is more significant.

The next step will determine the percentage of traffic belonging to each type. The different percentages are calculated considering that during the period of human inactivity, traffic is exclusively non-interactive. Thus, on each upstream channel the percentage of non-interactive traffic is obtained by averaging the traffic values at early morning hours. Later, all the values obtained were related to the peak to mean traffic rate, and the points adjusted by a potential model.

The calculation process followed to obtain the traffic model parameters, from the number of subscribers assigned to each upstream channel both for the interactive and non-interactive traffic, is:

1. The mean traffic on each upstream channel is obtained from the relationship shown in Fig. 2(b):

$$Mean = 0.1119 \times Subs - 0.4076 \tag{1}$$

2. The peak traffic on each upstream channel is obtained from the relationship shown in Fig. 3(b):

$$Peak = 0.2201 \times Subs - 11.811 \tag{2}$$

3. The peak to mean rate is obtained by dividing the values obtained from (2) and (1). From this value, the percentage of non-interactive traffic is calculated from a potential model:

$$Nint = 44.579 \times \left(\frac{Peak}{Mean} \right)^{-3.312} \tag{3}$$

4. The percentage of non-interactive traffic will be generated by a source, at which the size of the request and the time between requests will determine the non-interactive traffic.

5. In order to calculate the interactive traffic, the percentage of interactive traffic per subscriber is obtained. Firstly, the value of interactive traffic is obtained as the difference between the mean traffic, calculated with (1), and the non-interactive traffic, (3). Secondly, the mean number of effective connected subscribers on the channel is calculated. Effective connected subscribers are the number of connected subscribers minus the non-interactive subscribers, that is, the interactive subscribers. These values are obtained considering the subscribers' evolution function and the number of subscribers assigned to the channel:

$$Int = \frac{Mean - Nint}{(\overline{perc} - perc_{min}) \times Subs} \tag{4}$$

6. The interactive traffic will be generated by an infinite server sending requests from the active subscribers. As in the case of the non-interactive traffic, the size and the inter-request time are determined to obtain the required traffic volume.

4.4 Traffic Model Implementation

The traffic model has been implemented using QNAP2[3], a modeling language based on the queuing network paradigm. This language permits the system model resolution by queuing network methods or by discrete event simulation. The traffic model developed represents the behaviour of each upstream channel using a combination of queuing elements and algorithmic language. The model reproduces the evolution of subscribers in time, their requests and the MAC protocol.

The simulation model is organized in two blocks: on one side the subscribers' requests and on the other side the upstream channel and its MAC protocol. The subscribers' requests are represented using two queue elements: a source element for the non-interactive traffic, because its behavior is constant and has little variation of the number of subscribers using the channel; and an infinite server for interactive traffic, where the number of elements sending requests change according to the subscriber evolution function. The upstream channel is represented by two stations, one of them represents the behavior of the physical channel and the other supports the characteristics of the MAC protocol.

5   Results

In this section, the results obtained with the HFC traffic model are presented and validated showing the traffic model results to be statistically equivalent to the real traffic. Thus, using this traffic model it is possible to predict the

---

[3] QNAP2 was developed by INRIA and is a trademark of SIMULOG.

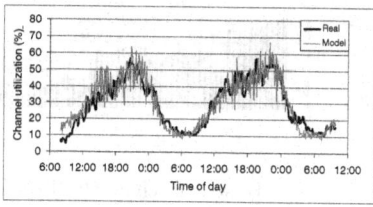
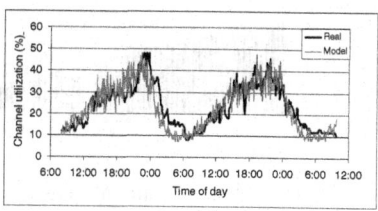

(a) Upstream channel GI01CC02-
UP7

(b) Upstream channel GI02CC01-
UP8

Fig. 5. Examples of traffic comparisons

traffic evolution on the upstream channels and the level of channel utilization. Results have been obtained for 54 upstream channels using the implemented traffic model, these results have been validated by three methods: comparison of traffic profiles, comparison using confidence intervals, and comparison of some statistical properties.

Figure 5 shows two examples of the comparison of traffic profiles. In the majority of cases the results obtained with the traffic model for each upstream channel are very close to the real traffic. In a few cases the adjustment is not perfect, due to an underestimation of the non-interactive traffic.

The technique of validation by comparison of confidence intervals is described in [6], and is based on calculating the confidence interval for the difference series ($\xi = Real - Model$). If the calculated confidence interval includes zero, both series are statistically equivalent. Applying this method for all the upstream channels the confidence interval obtained for the traffic model is $[-11.33, 13.55]$.

Finally, the statistical properties to compare are the autocorrelation function and the coefficient of self-similarity. The autocorrelation function is an important statistical property, because the form of the autocorrelation graph provides information about traffic characteristics. The autocorrelation graphs obtained range from perfect adjustment to a slight difference in the lower half of the graph for the worst cases, Fig. 6 represents the autocorrelation graphs obtained for the best and worst cases.

The statistical property of self-similarity, closed linked to the autocorrelation function, is also compared. This property is measured by a coefficient called the *Hurst* coefficient. In this HFC network the values of the *Hurst* coefficient were determined in [5]. The comparison of the *Hurst* coefficients for real traffic and the simulated traffic show very similar values. The difference between values is lower than 10% except in two cases, and the mean difference is 2.77%.

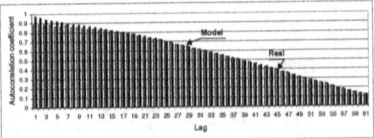 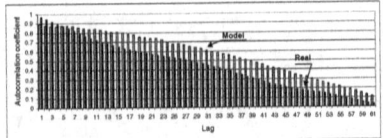

(a) Upstream channel GI01CC01-UP7

(b) Upstream channel GI07CC02-UP5

Fig. 6. Comparison of the autocorrelation graphs, the best and worst adjustment

6 Conclusions

This paper describes the development of a traffic model based on traffic measurements taken on the channels of a real HFC network. An analysis of these measurements shows that relationships between traffic properties and the number of subscribers assigned to each channel can be established, and that these relationships are consistent in time. Using these relationships and the information provided by the DHCP server, a procedure to obtain the traffic model parameters is established. The traffic model is represented by a simulation program which reproduces traffic evolution. A comparison of the real and the simulated traffic concludes that the traffic model developed is a valid approximation to the real traffic registered on the upstream channels of the HFC network.

The main characteristics of the traffic model are: the traffic model considers the aggregated traffic on the HFC network, so no distinction between traffic protocols is necessary, and the traffic model parameters are obtained from the characteristics of each HFC upstream channel, so a direct relationship between the system and the traffic is established.

Currently, this work is being continued with the development of a simulation model of the whole HFC network. Using this model it will be possible to predict the channel utilization of all the network channels as well as in the ATM backbone and Internet access channels. Long term objectives are to obtain an analytical expression for the traffic model with the number of assigned subscribers instead of a simulation program, and to improve the traffic model using a richer group of measurements.

References

1. W. Leland, M. Taqqu, W. Willinger, D. Wilson. On the self-similar nature of Ethernet traffic (Extended version). IEEE/ACM Trans. on Networking. Vol 2, n° 1, pp 1-15. February 1994.
2. P. Fiorini. Modeling Telecommunication Systems with Self-Similar Data Traffic. PhD Thesis, Dept. Computer Science and Eng., University of Connecticut. 1997

3. R.G. Addie, M. Zukerman, T.D. Neame. Broadband traffic modeling: simple solutions to hard problems. IEEE Comunications Magazine, Vol. 36, n° 8, pp 88-95. August, 1998.
4. L. Lipsky, H.-P. Schwefel, M. Greiner, M. Jobmann. Comparison of The Analytic N-Burst Model with Other Approximations to Self-similar Telecommunications Traffic. Technical Report, TUM and BRC. November, 2000.
5. M. Garcia, X.G. Pañeda, D.F. Garcia, V.G. Garcia, R. Bonis. Traffic Analysis of Data Transmission on Hybrid Fiber Coax Network. Proceedings of the IASTED International Conference on Communication Systems an Networks, CSN 2002, pp 172-177. Malaga, Spain. September, 2002.
6. A.M. Law And W.D. Kelton. Simulation modeling & analysis, 2nd Edition. McGraw-Hill International, 1991.

Modeling Self-similar Traffic through Markov Modulated Poisson Processes over Multiple Time Scales

António Nogueira[1], Paulo Salvador[1], Rui Valadas[1], and António Pacheco[2]

[1] University of Aveiro / Institute of Telecommunications Aveiro
Campus de Santiago, 3810-193 Aveiro, Portugal
{nogueira, salvador}@av.it.pt, rv@det.ua.pt
[2] Instituto Superior Técnico - UTL / Department of Mathematics and CEMAT
Av. Rovisco Pais, 1049-001 Lisboa, Portugal
apacheco@math.ist.utl.pt

Abstract. In recent years several studies have reported peculiar types of traffic behavior, such as long-range dependence and self-similarity, which can have significant impact on network performance. In this paper we propose a novel traffic model and parameter fitting procedure, based on Markov Modulated Poisson Processes (MMPPs), which is able to capture variability over many time scales, a characteristic of self-similar traffic. The fitting procedure matches the complete distribution at each time scale, and not only some of its moments as it is the case in related proposals. Our results show that the proposed traffic model and parameter fitting procedure closely matches the main characteristics of measured traces over the time scales present in data.

keywords: Traffic modeling, self-similar, time scale, Markov Modulated Poisson Process.

1 Introduction

An efficient design and control of data networks needs to take into account the main characteristics of the supported traffic. Due to the growing diversity of services and applications, there is a strong requirement to make frequent measurements of packet flows and to describe them through appropriate traffic models. Since the work by Leland *et al.* [1] several studies have shown that network traffic may exhibit properties of self-similarity and/or long-range dependence (LRD) [1, 2, 3, 4], which have significant impact on network performance. Self-similar traffic shows identical statistical characteristics over a wide range of time scales. In general, self-similarity implies long-range dependence, and vice-versa.

Several works have addressed the impact of LRD on network performance. References [4, 5, 6, 7] study the case of a single queue and conclude that the buffer occupancy is not affected by autocovariance lags that are beyond the so-called critical time scale (CTS) or correlation horizon (CH), which depends on system parameters such as the buffer capacity. Similar conclusions are observed for the case of tandem queues in [8]. Thus, matching the LRD is only required within the time scales specific to the system under study. One of the consequences of this result is that more traditional

M.M. Freire, P. Lorenz, M.M.-O. Lee (Eds.): HSNMC 2003, LNCS 2720, pp. 550–560, 2003.

traffic models, such as Markov Modulated Poisson Processes (MMPPs), can still be used to model traffic exhibiting LRD. The use of MMPPs also benefits from the existence of several tools for calculating the queuing behavior and the effective bandwidth.

In this paper we propose a novel traffic model and parameter fitting procedure, which captures self-similar behavior over a range of time scales. The traffic model is a superposition of discrete-time MMPPs (dMMPPs), where each dMMPP represents a specific time scale. The parameter fitting procedure matches, at each time scale, a dMMPP to the empirical probability function characteristic of that time scale. The number of states of each dMMPP is not fixed a priori; it is determined as part of the fitting procedure. The accuracy of the fitting procedure is evaluated by applying it to measured traffic traces that exhibit self-similar behavior: the well-known pOct Bellcore trace and a trace of aggregated IP WAN traffic. We compare the probability function at each time scale, and the queuing behavior (as assessed by the loss probability and average waiting time), corresponding to the measured and to synthetic traces generated from the inferred models. Our results show that the proposed fitting method is very effective in matching the probability function at the various time scales and leads to an accurate prediction of the queuing behavior.

Fitting procedures for MMPPs with an arbitrary number of states mainly concentrate on matching first- and/or second-order statistics, without addressing directly the issue of modeling on multiple time scales [9, 10, 11, 12, 13]. Yoshihara *et al.* [14] developed a fitting method for self-similar traffic based on the superposition of 2-MMPPs, that matches the variance at each time scale. In this way, the resulting MMPP reproduces the variance-scale curve characteristic of self-similar processes. Our contribution is to develop a procedure that matches the complete distribution at each time scale (and not only the variance) in order to reproduce accurately self-similar behavior.

The paper is organized as follows. Section 2 gives the required background on MMPPs and self-similarity and presents the various steps of the parameter fitting procedure. Section 3 briefly describes the data traces used in the numerical evaluation and in section 4 we discuss the results. Finally, section 5 presents the main conclusions.

2   Inference Procedure

Our inference procedure is closely related to the notion of distributional self-similarity. Consider the continuous-time process $Y(t)$ representing the traffic volume (e.g. in bytes) from time 0 up to time t and let $X(t) = Y(t) - Y(t-1)$ be the corresponding increment process (e.g. in bytes/second). Consider also the sequence

$$X^{(m)}(k) = \frac{1}{m} \sum_{i=1}^{m} X((k-1)m+i), k = 1, 2, \dots \qquad (1)$$

obtained by averaging $X(t)$ over non-overlapping blocks of length m. $Y(t)$ is exactly self-similar when it is equivalent, in the sense of finite-dimensional distributions, to $a^{-H}Y(at)$, for all $t > 0$ and $a > 0$, where H ($0 < H < 1$) is the Hurst parameter.

Clearly, the process $Y(t)$ can not be stationary. However, if $Y(t)$ has stationary increments then again $X(k) = X^{(1)}(k)$ is equivalent, in the sense of finite-dimensional distributions, to $m^{1-H} X^{(m)}(k)$. This illustrates that a traffic model developed for fitting self-similar behavior must preferably enable the matching of the distribution on several time scales. Note also that, in general, self-similarity implies LRD, and vice-versa. An excellent overview of self-similarity and LRD can be found in [15].

The inference procedure estimates one dMMPP for each time scale that matches a probability mass function (PMF) characteristic of that time scale. The resulting dMMPP is obtained from the superposition of all dMMPPs inferred for each time scale. An (homogeneous) Markov chain $(Y, J) = \{(Y_k, J_k), k = 0, 1, \ldots\}$ with state space $I\!N_0 \times S$ is a dMMPP if and only if Y has non-decreasing sample paths and

$$P(Y_{k+1} = m, J_{k+1} = j | Y_k = n, J_k = i) = p_{ij}\, e^{-\lambda_i} \lambda_i^{m-n}/(m - n)! \qquad (2)$$

for $k = 0, 1, \ldots, m, n \in I\!N_0$ with $n \leq m$, and $i, j \in S$, where $\lambda_i, i \in S$ are nonnegative real constants and $\mathbf{P} = (p_{ij})$ is a stochastic matrix. In this case we say that (Y, J) is a dMMPP with set of modulating states S and parameter (matrices) $\mathbf{P}$ and $\mathbf{\Lambda}$, and write $(Y, J) \sim \text{dMMPP}_S(\mathbf{P}, \mathbf{\Lambda})$, where $\mathbf{\Lambda} = (\lambda_{ij}) = (\lambda_i \delta_{ij})$. The matrix $\mathbf{P}$ is the transition probability matrix of the modulating Markov chain J, whereas $\mathbf{\Lambda}$ is the matrix of Poisson arrival rates. If S has cardinality r, we say that (Y, J) is a dMMPP of order r (r-dMMPP). When, in particular, $S = \{1, 2, \ldots, r\}$ for some $r \in I\!N$, then we write simply that $(Y, J) \sim \text{dMMPP}_r(\mathbf{P}, \mathbf{\Lambda})$.

The superposition of independent dMMPPs is still an dMMPP. More precisely, if $(Y^{(l)}, J^{(l)}) \sim \text{dMMPP}_{r_l}(\mathbf{P}^{(l)}, \mathbf{\Lambda}^{(l)})$, $l = 1, 2, \ldots, L$, are independent, then their superposition $(Y, J) = (\sum_{l=1}^{L} Y^{(l)}, (J^{(1)}, J^{(2)}, \ldots, J^{(L)}))$ is a dMMPP$_S(\mathbf{P}, \mathbf{\Lambda})$ where $S = \{1, 2, \ldots, r_1\} \times \ldots \times \{1, 2, \ldots, r_L\}$,

$$\mathbf{P} = \mathbf{P}^{(1)} \otimes \mathbf{P}^{(2)} \otimes \ldots \otimes \mathbf{P}^{(L)} \qquad \text{and} \qquad \mathbf{\Lambda} = \mathbf{\Lambda}^{(1)} \oplus \mathbf{\Lambda}^{(2)} \oplus \ldots \oplus \mathbf{\Lambda}^{(L)} \qquad (3)$$

with $\oplus$ and $\otimes$ denoting the Kronecker sum and product, respectively. In our approach L, the number of considered time scales, is fixed a priori and the dimensions of the dMMPPs, $r_1, r_2, \ldots, r_L$, are computed as part of the fitting procedure.

The flowchart of the inference method is represented in figure 1 where, basically, four steps can be identified: (i) compute the data vectors (corresponding to the average number of arrivals per time interval) at each time scale; (ii) calculate the empirical PMF at the largest time scale and infer its dMMPP; (iii) for all other time scales (going from the largest to the smallest one), calculate the empirical PMF, deconvolve it from the empirical PMF of the previous time scale and infer a dMMPP that matches the resulting PMF; and (iv) calculate the final dMMPP through superposition of the dMMPPs inferred for each time scale. We will now describe these steps in detail.

2.1 Aggregation Process

Having defined the sampling interval, Δt, the number of time scales, L, and the level of aggregation, a, the aggregation process starts by computing the data vector corresponding to the average number of arrivals in the smallest time scale (where the interval length equals the sampling interval), $N^{(1)}(k)$. Then, it calculates the data vectors of remaining time scales, $N^{(l)}(k)$, $l = 2, ...L$, corresponding to the average number of arrivals in intervals of length $\Delta t a^{(l-1)}$. This is given by

$$N^{(l)}(k) = \left\lceil \frac{1}{a} \sum_{i=0}^{a-1} N^{(l-1)}(k+i) \right\rceil, \quad \frac{k-1}{a} \in I\!N_0 \tag{4}$$

and $N^{(l)}(k) = N^{(l)}(k-1)$, for $\frac{k-1}{a} \notin I\!N_0$, where $\lceil x \rceil$ is the ceiling function. Note that the block length of equation (1) is related with a and l by $m = a^{l-1}$. The empirical distribution of $N^{(l)}(k)$ will be denoted by $\hat{p}^{(l)}(x)$.

2.2   Calculation of the Empirical PMFs

This step infers the PMFs that, at each time scale, must be fitted to a dMMPP. For the largest time scale, this PMF is simply the empirical one. For all other time scales l, $l = 1, 2, ..., L-1$, the associated dMMPP will model only the traffic components due to that scale. For time scale l, these traffic components can be obtained through deconvolution of the empirical PMFs of this time scale and of previous time scale, i.e., $\hat{f}_p^{(l)}(x) = [\hat{p}^{(l)} \otimes^{-1} \hat{p}^{(l+1)}](x)$. However, this may result in negative arrival rates for the dMMPP$^{(l)}$, which will occur whenever $\min\left\{x : \hat{p}^{(l+1)}(x) > 0\right\} < \min\left\{x : \hat{p}^{(l)}(x) > 0\right\}$. To correct this, the dMMPP$^{(l)}$ will be fitted to

$$\hat{f}^{(l)}(x) = \hat{f}_p^{(l)}(x + e^{(l)}) \tag{5}$$

where $e^{(l)} = \min\left(0, \min\left\{x : \hat{f}_p^{(l)}(x) > 0\right\}\right)$, which assures $\hat{f}^{(l)}(x) = 0$, $x < 0$. These additional factors are removed in the final step of the inference procedure.

2.3   Approximation of the Empirical PMFs by a Weighted Sum of Poisson Distributions and Inference of the dMMPP Parameters

Before inferring the dMMPP$^{(l)}$ parameters, $l = 1, 2, ..., L$, function $\hat{f}^{(l)}$ is approximated by a weighted sum of Poisson probability functions, using an algorithm that progressively subtracts a Poisson probability function from $\hat{f}^{(l)}$. The most important steps of this algorithm are depicted in the flowchart of figure 2 and will be explained in the next paragraphs.

Let the ith Poisson probability function, with mean $\varphi_i^{(l)}$, be represented by $g_{\varphi_i^{(l)}}(x)$ and define $h_{(i)}^{(l)}(x)$ as the difference between $\hat{f}^{(l)}(x)$ and the weighted sum of Poisson probability functions at the ith iteration. Initially, we set $h_{(1)}^{(l)}(x) = \hat{f}^{(l)}(x)$ and, in each step, we first detect the maximum of $h_{(i)}^{(l)}(x)$. The corresponding x-value, $\varphi_i = [h_{(i)}^{(l)}]^{-1}\left(\max h_{(i)}^{(l)}(x)\right)$, will be considered the ith Poisson rate of the dMMPP$^{(l)}$. We then calculate the weights of each Poisson probability function, $w_i^{(l)} = \left[w_{1i}^{(l)}, w_{2i}^{(l)}, ..., w_{ii}^{(l)}\right]$, through the following set of linear equations:

$$\hat{f}^{(l)}(\varphi_m^{(l)}) = \sum_{j=1}^{i} w_{ji}^{(l)} g_{\varphi_j^{(l)}}(\varphi_m^{(l)}) \qquad (6)$$

for $m = 1, ..., i$ and $l = 1, ..., L$. This assures that the fitting between $\hat{f}^{(l)}(x)$ and the weighted sum of Poisson probability functions is exact at $\varphi_m^{(l)}$ points, for $m = 1, 2, ..., i$. The final step in each iteration is the calculation of the new difference function

$$h_{(i)}^{(l)}(x) = \hat{f}^{(l)}(x) - \sum_{j=1}^{i} w_{ji}^{(l)} g_{\varphi_j^{(l)}}(x). \qquad (7)$$

The algorithm stops when the maximum of $h_{(i)}^{(l)}(x)$ is lower than a pre-defined percentage of the maximum of $\hat{f}^{(l)}(x)$ and r_l, the number of states of the dMMPP, is made equal to i.

Note that the number of states of each dMMPP depends on the level of accuracy employed in the approximation of the empirical PMF by the weighted sum of Poisson probability functions.

After r_l has been determined, the parameters $p_{ij}^{(l)}$ and $\lambda_j^{(l)}$, $j = 1, 2, ..., r_l$, of the r_l − dMMPP, are set equal to

$$\pi_j^{(l)} = w_{jr_l}^{(l)} \qquad \text{and} \qquad \lambda_j^{(l)} = \varphi_j^{(l)}. \qquad (8)$$

The next step is to associate, for each time scale l, one of the dMMPP$^{(l)}$ states with each time slot of the arriving process. The state that is assigned to a time interval is calculated randomly according to the probability vector $\theta^{(l)}(k) = \{\theta_1^{(l)}(k), ..., \theta_{r_l}^{(l)}(k)\}$, with

$$\theta_i^{(l)}(k) = g_{\lambda_i^{(l)}}(N^l(k)) \Big/ \sum_{j=1}^{r_l} g_{\lambda_j^{(l)}}(N^l(k)), \qquad (9)$$

where $i = 1, ..., r_l$, $l = 1, ..., L$ and $g_\lambda(y)$ represents a Poisson probability distribution function with mean λ. The elements of this vector represent the probability that the state j had originated the number of arrivals $N^{(l)}(k)$ at time slot k from time scale l.

After this step, we infer the dMPPP$^{(l)}$ transition probabilities, $p_{ij}^{(l)}$, $i, j = 1, ..., r_l$, by counting the number of transitions between each pair of states. If $n_{ij}^{(l)}$ represents the number of transitions from state i to state j, corresponding to the dMPPP$^{(l)}$, then

$$p_{ij}^{(l)} = n_{ij}^{(l)} \Big/ \sum_{m=1}^{r_l} n_{mj}^{(l)}, j = 1, ..., r_l \qquad (10)$$

The transition probability and the Poisson arrival rate matrices of the dMPPP$^{(l)}$ are then given by $\mathbf{P}^{(l)} = (p_{ij}^{(l)})$ and $\mathbf{\Lambda}^{(l)} = (\lambda_i^{(l)}\delta_{ij})$, for $l = 1, ..., L$.

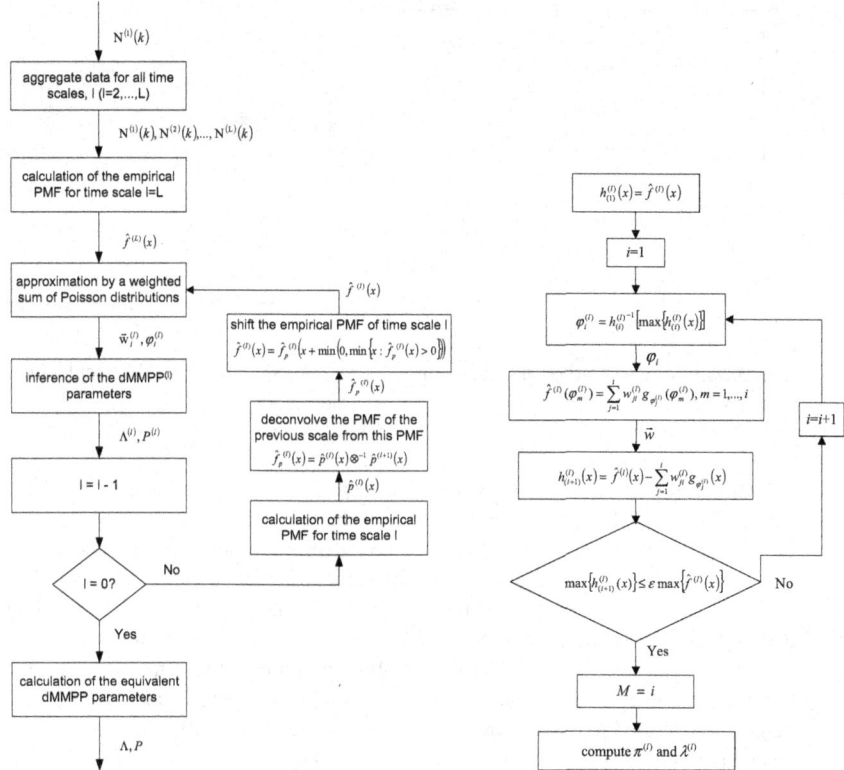

Fig. 1. Flow diagram of the inference procedure.

Fig. 2. Algorithm for calculating the number of states and the Poisson arrival rates of the dMMPP$^{(l)}$.

2.4 Final dMMPP Model Construction

The final dMMPP process is constructed using equation (3), where the matrices $\mathbf{\Lambda}^{(l)}$ and $\mathbf{P}^{(l)}$, $l = 1, ..., L$, were calculated in the last subsection. However, the additional factors introduced in sub-section 2.2 must be removed. Thus, $\mathbf{\Lambda} = \mathbf{\Lambda} - \sum_{l=1}^{L-1} e^{(l)} \cdot \mathbf{I}$ where $\mathbf{I}$ is the identity matrix.

3 Overview of the Traffic Traces

We consider two traffic traces to evaluate the fitting procedure: (i) the well-known and publicly available pOct LAN trace from Bellcore [1] and (ii) a trace corresponding to the downstream Internet access traffic of approximately 65 simultaneous users, measured at the access link of a Portuguese ISP (to an ADSL network). The traffic analyzer was a 1.2 GHz AMD Athlon PC, with 1.5 Gbytes of RAM and running

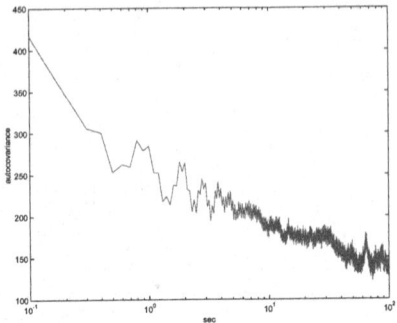
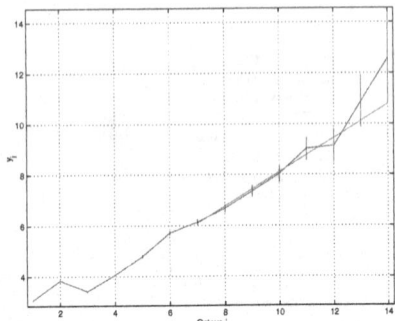

Fig. 3. Autocovariance of packet counts, trace pOct.

Fig. 4. Second order Logscale Diagram, trace pOct.

WinDump; we recorded the arrival instant and the IP header of each packet. The main characteristics of the selected traces are described in Table 1.

We assess the self-similar (LRD) behavior through the semi-parametric estimator developed in [16]. Here, one looks for alignment in the so-called Logscale Diagram (LD), which is a log-log plot of the variance estimates of discrete wavelet transform coefficients, against scale, complete with confidence intervals about these estimates at each scale. Traffic is said to be LRD if, within the limits of the confidence intervals, the log of the variance estimates fall on a straight line, in a range of scales from some initial value j_1 up to the largest one present in data and the slope of the straight line, which is an estimate of the scaling exponent α, lies in $(0, 1)$.

Both traces exhibit self-similar (LRD) behavior. For example, taking the case of trace pOct, the analysis of its autocovariance function (Figure 3) lead us to suspect that it exhibits LRD, due to the slow decay for large time lags. This is confirmed by the scaling analysis, since the y_j values in the Logscale Diagram are aligned between a medium octave (7) and octave 14, the highest one present in data (Figure 4). A similar analysis was made for the other trace, also revealing the same self-similar (LRD) behavior.

4   Numerical Results

We assess the suitability of the proposed dMMPP fitting procedure using several criteria: (i) comparing the Hurst parameters of the original and synthesized (from the inferred dMMPP) data traces; (ii) comparing the probability functions of the average

Trace name	Capture period	Trace size (pkts)	Mean rate (byte/s)	Mean pkt size (bytes)
October	Bellcore trace	1 million	322790	568
ISP	10.26pm to 10.49pm, October 18th 2002	1 million	583470	797

Table 1. Main characteristics of measured traces.

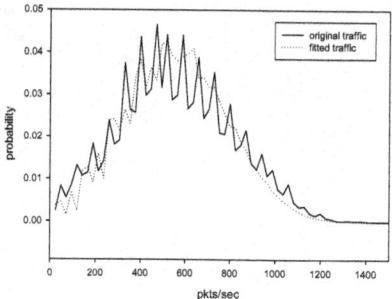
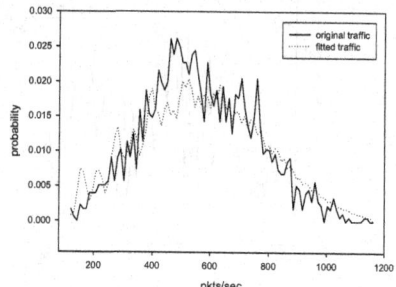

Fig. 5. Probability mass function at the smallest time scale, trace pOct.

Fig. 6. Probability mass function at the intermediate time scale, trace pOct.

number of arrivals in different time scales, obtained for the original and synthesized traces and (iii) comparing the queuing behavior, in terms of packet loss ratio (PLR), of the original and synthesized traces, using trace-driven simulation. All simulations were carried out using a fixed packet length equal to the mean packet length of the trace. For all traces, the sampling interval of the counting process was chosen to be 0.1s and three different time scales were considered: 0.1s, 1s and 10s. For each trace, the estimation procedure took less than 1 minute, using a MATLAB implementation running in the PC described above, which shows that the procedure is computationally very efficient.

In order to verify that the proposed fitting approach captures the self-similar behavior, we compare in Table 2 the Hurst parameters estimated for the original and fitted traffic, for each selected data trace. Table 2 also includes the range of time scales where the y_j follow a straight line, inside brackets near to the corresponding Hurst parameter value. There is a very good agreement between the Hurst parameter values of the original and fitted traffic, so LRD behavior is indeed well captured by our model.

The next evaluation criteria is based on the comparison between the probability functions of the original and fitted traces, for different time scales. Starting with trace pOct, it can be seen in Figures 5, 6 and 7 that there is a good agreement between the probability functions of the original and fitted traces, for all time scales. Recall that the fitting procedure explicitly aimed at matching the probability function at the various time scales; these results confirm that the procedure is effective in performing this task. Due to space limitations, for the case of the ISP trace we only show the comparison between the probability functions at the smallest time scale in Figure 8. However, a good agreement also exists at the three times scales.

Considering now the queuing behavior, we compare the PLR obtained, through trace-driven simulation, with the original and fitted traces. Two different sets of utilization ratios were used in the simulations: for trace pOct, we used $\rho = 0.6$ and $\rho = 0.7$ and, for trace ISP, the selected values were $\rho = 0.8$ and $\rho = 0.9$. This is due to the lower burstiness of the ISP traffic, which leads to lower packet losses for the same link utilization. From figures 9 and 10, it can be seen that the PLR is very well approximated by the fitted dMMPPs for both utilization ratios. Nevertheless, as

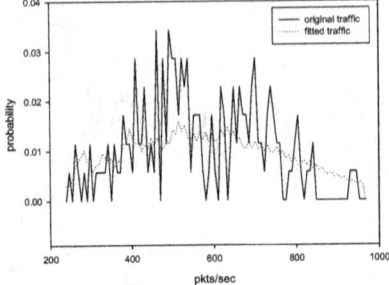

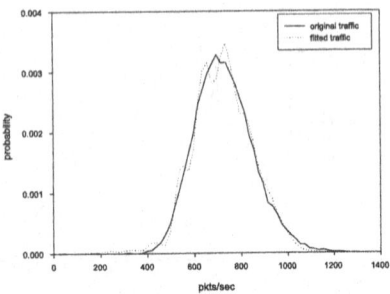

Fig. 7. Probability mass function at the largest time scale, trace pOct.

Fig. 8. Probability mass function at the smallest time scale, trace ISP.

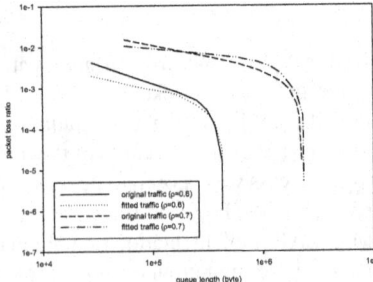

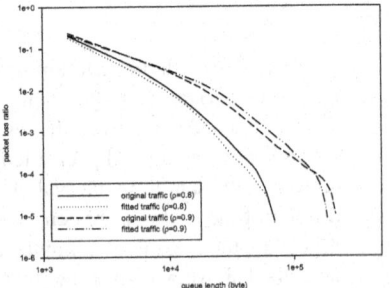

Fig. 9. Packet loss ratio, trace pOct.

Fig. 10. Packet loss ratio, trace ISP.

the utilization ratio increases the deviation slightly increases, because the sensitivity of the metrics variation to a slight difference in the buffer size is higher.

As a final remark, we can say that the proposed fitting approach provides a close match of the Hurst parameters and probability mass functions at each time scale, and this agreement reveals itself sufficient to drive a good queuing performance in terms of packet loss ratio. The computational complexity of the fitting method is also very small.

Trace	original	fitted
October	0.941 (6,12)	0.962 (6,12)
ISP	0.745 (6,13)	0.784 (4,13)

Table 2. Comparison between Hurst parameter values

5 Conclusions

In this paper we have proposed a novel traffic model and parameter fitting procedure, based on Markov Modulated Poisson Processes (MMPPs), which is able to capture self-similarity over a range of time scales. The fitting procedure matches the complete distribution at each time scale, and not only some of its moments as it is the case in related proposals. We evaluated the procedure by comparing the probability function at each time scale, and the queuing behavior (as assessed by the loss probability), corresponding to measured traffic traces and to traces synthesized according to the proposed model. Two traffic traces were considered, all exhibiting self-similar behavior: the well-known pOct Bellcore trace and a trace of aggregated IP WAN traffic. Our results show that the proposed traffic model and parameter fitting procedure closely matches the main characteristics of the measured traces over the time scales present in data.

Acknowledgements: This research was supported in part by Fundação para a Ciência e a Tecnologia, the project POSI/42069/CPS/2001, and the grant BD/19781/99.

References

[1] W. Leland, M. Taqqu, W. Willinger, and D. Wilson, "On the self-similar nature of Ethernet traffic (extended version)," *IEEE/ACM Transactions on Networking*, vol. 2, no. 1, pp. 1–15, Feb 1994.

[2] J. Beran, R. Sherman, M. Taqqu, and W. Willinger, "Long-range dependence in variable-bit rate video traffic," *IEEE Transactions on Communications*, vol. 43, no. 2/3/4, pp. 1566–1579, 1995.

[3] M. Crovella and A. Bestavros, "Self-similarity in World Wide Web traffic: Evidence and possible causes," *IEEE/ACM Transactions on Networking*, vol. 5, no. 6, pp. 835–846, Dec 1997.

[4] B. Ryu and A. Elwalid, "The importance of long-range dependence of VBR video traffic in ATM traffic engineering: Myths and realities," *ACM Computer Communication Review*, vol. 26, pp. 3–14, Oct 1996.

[5] D.P.Heyman and T.V.Lakshman, "What are the implications of long range dependence for vbr video traffic egineering?," *IEEE/ACM Transactions on Networking*, vol. 4, no. 3, pp. 301–317, June 1996.

[6] A. Neidhardt and J. Wang, "The concept of relevant time scales and its application to queuing analysis of self-similar traffic," in *Proceedings of SIGMET-RICS'1998/PERFORMANCE'1998*, 1998, pp. 222–232.

[7] M. Grossglauser and J. C. Bolot, "On the relevance of long-range dependence in network traffic," *IEEE/ACM Transactions on Networking*, vol. 7, no. 5, pp. 629–640, Oct 1999.

[8] A. Nogueira and R. Valadas, "Analyzing the relevant time scales in a network of queues," in *SPIE's International Symposium ITCOM 2001*, August 2001.

[9] P. Skelly, M. Schwartz, and S. Dixit, "A histogram-based model for video traffic behaviour in an ATM multiplexer," *IEEE/ACM Transactions on Networking*, pp. 446–458, Aug 1993.

[10] S. Li and C. Hwang, "On the convergence of traffic measurement and queuing analysis: A statistical-match and queuing (SMAQ) tool," *IEEE/ACM Transactions on Networking*, pp. 95–110, Fev 1997.

[11] A. Andersen and B. Nielsen, "A Markovian approach for modeling packet traffic with long-range dependence," *IEEE Journal on Selected Areas in Communications*, vol. 16, no. 5, pp. 719–732, Jun 1998.

[12] P. Salvador and R. Valadas, "A fitting procedure for Markov modulated Poisson processes with an adaptive number of states," in *Proceedings of the 9th IFIP Working Conference on Performance Modelling and Evaluation of ATM & IP Networks*, June 2001.

[13] P. Salvador, A. Pacheco, and R. Valadas, "Multiscale fitting procedure using Markov modulated Poisson processes," *Telecommunications Systems*, vol. 23, no. 1-2, pp. 123–148, June 2003.

[14] T. Yoshihara, S. Kasahara, and Y. Takahashi, "Practical time-scale fitting of self-similar traffic with Markov-modulated Poisson process," *Telecommunication Systems*, vol. 17, no. 1-2, pp. 185–211, 2001.

[15] K. Park and W. Willinger, "Self-similar network traffic: an overview," in *Self-Similar Network Traffic and Performance Evaluation*, K. Park and W. Willinger, Eds. Wiley-Interscience, 2000.

[16] D. Veitch and P. Abry, "A wavelet based joint estimator for the parameters of LRD," *IEEE Transactions on Information Theory*, vol. 45, no. 3, Apr 1999.

Evaluation of Steady-State Probability of Pareto/M/1/K Experiencing Tail-Raising Effect[⋆]

Younsuk Koh[1] and Kiseon Kim[2]

Kwangju Institute of Science and Technology (KJIST), 1 Oryong-dong, Buk-gu,
Gwangju 500-712 Republic of Korea
{ysko, kskim}@kjist.ac.kr

Abstract. To resolve the problem of evaluating for the steady-state probability of Pareto/M/1/K showing the tail-raising effect, we propose an empirical model of the steady-state probability and justified by evaluating the mean queue length and delay by simulations.

1 Introduction

The Internet traffic data are well known to possess extreme variability and bursty structure in a wide range of time scales differently from the Poisson process, which property is characterized by self-similar process. Queueing behaviors of self-similar traffic differ from those of Markovian traffic, since the self-similar traffic holds large variation.

Since the interarrival time of self-similar traffic is characterized as heavy-tailedness and Pareto distribution is a simple heavy-tailed distribution, Pareto traffic model is widely used in Internet traffic modelling.

Until now, queueing behaviors on Pareto traffic model are known less than than those of Markovian traffic. Queueing behaviors of Pareto queue with infinite buffer size is known by authors of [1]. The authors proposed the transform approximation method for calculating the geometric parameter of GI/M/1, and applied the results of GI/M/1 to the analysis of Pareto/M/1. On the queueing behaviors of Pareto queue with the finite buffer size, only the packet loss probability is known by [2] and [3]. The authors of [2] derived the asymptotic loss probability of GI/M/1/K and the authors of [3] extended the results of [2] for applying the results to Pareto/M/1/K with a moderate buffer size. By the result of [3], the loss probability of Pareto/M/1/K decays more slowly than that of M/M/1/K as buffer size increases. Pareto/M/1/K and M/M/1/K are one of representatives of self-similar and Markovian queue model, respectively.

Until now, there is no way to predict the mean queue length of Pareto/M/1/K analytically. This is a goal of this paper. For predicting the mean queue length, the steady-state probability should be known. The mean queue length is very

---

[⋆] This work was supported in part by the Korea Science and Engineering Foundation (KOSEF) through the Ultrafast Fiber-Optic Networks Research Center at Kwangju Institute of Science and Technology (KJIST), Gwangju, 500-712, Korea.

M.M. Freire, P. Lorenz, M.M.-O. Lee (Eds.): HSNMC 2003, LNCS 2720, pp. 561–570, 2003.
© Springer-Verlag Berlin Heidelberg 2003

important to estimate the queueing delay. Since the steady-state probability for Pareto/M/1/K exposes a tail-raising characteristic at buffer edge, it is difficult to predict the steady-state probability. Also the steady-state probability of self-similar queue with a finite buffer size is different from a simple truncation and normalization of that for an infinite buffer queueing system [4]. The steady-state probability of M/M/1/K can be derived by normalization [5].

The mean queue length of M/M/1/K with a moderate buffer size can apply the result of the infinite queue, since the loss probability of M/M/1/K decreases rapidly as the buffer size increases, and the mean queue length of M/M/1/K used a moderate buffer size is close to that of M/M/1. However, since the loss probability of Pareto/M/1/K is decayed slowly, mean queue length of Pareto/M/1/K with a moderate buffer size differ from that of Pareto/M/1. This is the reason why we try to predict the steady-state probability of Pareto/M/1/K (Refer to fig. 4.). Thus we propose a model for a steady-state probability of Pareto/M/1/K, considering the tail-raising effect, and calculate the mean queue length and delay.

In the next section, we introduce a Pareto queue model and the known facts on Pareto/M/1 and Pareto/M/1/K. In section 2, we propose the function approximation method for calculating the geometric parameter instead of transform approximation method [1]. In section 3, we propose a model for a steady-state probability of Pareto/M/1/K, and the steady-state probability, mean queue length and delay are compared with the results of simulation. Finally, in section 4, we summarize the conclusions.

2   Known Facts on Pareto Queue Model

2.1   Pareto Queue Model

Fig. 1 illustrates the queue model for the experiments. The system is a single FIFO queue, Pareto distributed interarrival time with the average, λ, the exponential distributed service time with the average, μ, and buffer size, K. The queue type of this system is Pareto/M/1 if the buffer size is infinite or Pareto/M/1/K, if the buffer size is finite. Utilization (ρ) is defined as the ratio of the average arrival rate (λ) of input traffic to the average service rate (μ) of output link.

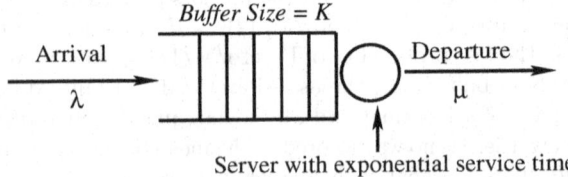

Fig. 1. Queue model.

Pareto distributions are characterized by two parameters: α and β. Parameter α is called shape parameter that determines heavy-tailed characteristics, and β is called cutoff or the location parameter that determines the average of interarrival time. The probability density function, $f(x)$, and cumulative distribution function, $F(x)$, of Pareto distribution are non-zero for positive x, and given respectively as follows:

$$f(x) = \frac{\alpha\beta^\alpha}{(\beta+x)^{\alpha+1}}, \tag{1}$$

$$F(x) = 1 - \frac{\beta^\alpha}{(\beta+x)^\alpha}. \tag{2}$$

According to α, the first or second moments of Pareto distribution are finite or infinite. The distribution can be classified three ranges as the range of α, $0 < \alpha \leq 1$, $1 < \alpha \leq 2$ and $2 < \alpha$. In $0 < \alpha \leq 1$, both of mean and variance are infinite and the arrival process is self-similar, and the utilization is zero. For $1 < \alpha \leq 2$, mean is given by $\frac{\beta}{\alpha-1}$, and variance is infinite and the arrival process is self-similar. In $\alpha > 2$, the mean and variance are given by $\frac{\beta}{\alpha-1}$ and $\frac{\alpha\beta^2}{(\alpha-1)^2(\alpha-2)}$, respectively. The arrival process is non-self-similar and also queueing behavior is similar to Poisson queue behavior. The heavy-tailed characteristics of Pareto distribution cause the self-similarity which means burst within burst. The degree of self-similarity (H) is represented by α as follows [6] :

$$H \sim \begin{cases} \frac{1+\alpha}{2}, & 0 < \alpha \leq 1 \\ \frac{3-\alpha}{2}, & 1 < \alpha \leq 2 \\ \frac{1}{2}, & \alpha > 2 \end{cases}. \tag{3}$$

In this paper, we consider only the range of $1 < \alpha < 2$.

2.2   Known Facts on Pareto Queue

The queueing behaviors of Pareto/M/1 go after those of GI/M/1, since GI/M/1 deals with a general distribution that includes Pareto distribution. The steady-state probability of the number of packets in the system is given by

$$\pi_k = \begin{cases} 1-\rho, & k = 0 \\ \rho(1-\sigma)\sigma^{k-1}, & k \geq 1 \end{cases}. \tag{4}$$

The mean number of packets in the queueing system including the packet being served is calculated by $L = \sum_{k=1}^{K} k\pi_k$ and given by

$$L = \frac{\rho}{1-\sigma}, \tag{5}$$

By the Little's theorem, delay called the mean response time is given by $T = \frac{L}{\lambda}$, and represented as

$$T = \frac{1}{\mu} \cdot \frac{1}{1-\sigma}. \tag{6}$$

The parameter σ is called as geometric parameter and the value of parameter is equal to utilization ρ in M/M/1 [5], but is greater than utilization and less than 1 in Pareto/M/1 [1,3]. This signifies that the tail of the infinite queue of Pareto/M/1 is thicker than that of M/M/1. Also mean queue length and delay of Pareto/M/1 are greater and longer than those of M/M/1, respectively [1].

When the queue has the finite buffer, the loss probability of Pareto/M/1/K is greater than those of M/M/1/K. The loss probability of M/M/1/K is known as

$$P_{loss}^{(K)} = \left(\frac{1-\rho}{1-\rho^{K+1}} \right) \rho^K. \tag{7}$$

By the result of [3], the loss probability of Pareto/M/1/K is given by

$$P_{loss}^{(K)} = \left(\frac{1-\sigma}{1-\sigma^{K+1}} \right)^a \sigma^K, \tag{8}$$

where parameter a is calculated by

$$a = \lim_{K \to \infty} \frac{\log(1 + \mu A'(\mu - \mu\sigma))}{\log(\frac{1-\sigma}{1-\sigma^{K+1}})}. \tag{9}$$

The Laplace-Stieltjes transform $A(s)$ of the Pareto interarrival density is expressed as a power series of the incomplete gamma function in [6]. Since the value of $A(s)$ is convergent, the power series can be approximated as

$$A^*(s) = \alpha \Gamma(-\alpha) \left[(\beta s)^\alpha e^{\beta s} - \sum_{n=0}^{N} \frac{(\beta s)^n}{\Gamma(n-\alpha+1)} \right], \quad for \quad 1 < \alpha < 2. \tag{10}$$

Convergence can be certified with the ratio test [7]. We name this approximation as function approximation method.

By combining the definition of ρ and the relation of $\sigma = A(\mu - \mu\sigma)$, the geometric parameter is expressed as follows:

$$\sigma = \alpha \Gamma(-\alpha) \left[\gamma^\alpha e^\gamma - \sum_{n=0}^{N} \frac{\gamma^n}{\Gamma(n-\alpha+1)} \right], \tag{11}$$

where $\gamma = \frac{(1-\sigma)(\alpha-1)}{\rho}$ and $0 < \rho < 1$. This equation is independent of μ, but dependent of utilization (ρ). By using root finding technique and the fact of $0 < \sigma < 1$, the geometric parameter is estimated simply. As ρ is closed to 0, or α is closed to 2, γ becomes great.

For calculating the accurate geometric parameter to apply GI/M/1 results to Pareto/M/1 analysis, the value of N should is determined. If $\alpha \Gamma(-\alpha) \frac{\gamma^n}{\Gamma(n-\alpha+1)}$ is equal to or less than 10^{-8}, we approve that the value of eq. (11) gets to the real value. The results of function approximation method is the exactly same to those of transform approximation with 10^6 approximation points. However, the required CPU times for calculating the geometric parameters when α is fixed and $\rho = 0.1, 0.2, 0.3\ 0.4, 0.5, 0.6, 0.7, 0.8,$ and 0.9 are about 950 sec by transform approximation but 0.08 sec by function approximation method, measured by Perl program [8]. In eq. (9), $A'(s)$ is obtained by the differentiation of eq. (10) easily.

3   A Model for the Steady-State Probability of Pareto/M/1/K

3.1   Tail-Raising Effect

The tailing effect means that $\bar{\pi}_k$ is greater than $\bar{\pi}_{k-1}$ as the state k increases [4]. The authors of [4] have observed a very sharp increase in the edge of finite buffer with a high Hurst parameter H by the trace based simulation of the measured self-similar traffic. The steady-state probabilities of the infinite queue and M/M/1/K decrease at the ratio of σ and ρ, respectively as k increases. Eq. (4) and the following equation make sure of the above fact. The steady-state probability of M/M/1/K is given by

$$\bar{\pi}_k = \frac{(1-\rho)\rho^k}{1-\rho^{K+1}}. \tag{12}$$

This equation is the result that the steady-state probability of M/M/1 is normalized by the complement of the overflow probability at buffer size K, $1 - \rho^{K+1}$. Note that the probability that packets are stored over buffer size K in an infinite system at arrival instant is defined as overflow probability.

Since the steady-state probability of Pareto/M/1/K shows the tail-rating effect at the edge of the queue, it cannot be represented by normalization like M/M/1/K. This is a reason for requiring a model for estimating the tail-raising effect. It is obvious that the steady-state probability of Pareto/M/1/K is close to that of Pareto/M/1 as the buffer size increases as the loss probability is zero.

3.2   A Model for the Steady-State Probability of Pareto/M/1/K

In the above subsection, we explain that the steady-state of the input traffic model without tail-raising effect like M/M/1/K can be calculated by normalization. But the steady-state probability of Pareto/M/1/K should be calculate by the different method. If the loss probability is not negligible, the steady-state probability of Pareto/M/1/K displays tail-raising. So we model the steady-state probability of Pareto/M/1/K as the sum of a portion to go to the probability of infinite queue as the buffer size increases and a portion to display the tail-raising.

The empty probabilities of the infinite and finite queue are $1 - \rho$ and $1 - (1 - P_{loss})\rho$, respectively. We already know the loss probability of Pareto queue and $(1 - P_{loss})\rho$ means the offered load $\bar{\rho}$ to the system. Since the empty probability of the finite queue decreases as the ratio of $\frac{1-\bar{\rho}}{1-\rho}$, we consider the other steady-state probability may decrease as the same ratio. This is the way to get the portion to go to the steady-state probability of the infinite queue. Note that $\bar{\rho} = \rho$ if $P_{loss} = 0$.

The other potion portrays the tailing-raising effect. Since the potion of tailing effect means probability, the value at each state k and the sum of each state are less than 1. And as the state k goes to the buffer edge K, the value increases. That is, the model of tail-raising effect increases monotonically near to buffer edge as the state k goes to the buffer edge K, and the value and the sum of each value are less than 1. The function of $(\frac{a}{K+b-k})^n$ increases monotonically as the state k increases, and if we choose to be $a < b$, the value of function at each k keeps less than 1 and the sum of the function from $k = 1$ to $k = K$ fits to the difference of $\bar{\rho}$ and the sum of the potion to go to the infinite steady-state probability. Note that the sum of the steady-state probability from $k = 1$ to $k = K$ is equal to $\bar{\rho}$. Although n may determine the tail-rasing rate near to the buffer edge, the parameter is set to 1. The value is not optimized.

Thus we model the steady-state probability of Pareto/M/1/K as follows :

$$\bar{\pi}_k = \frac{1-\bar{\rho}}{1-\rho}\rho(1-\sigma)\sigma^{k-1} + \frac{b}{K-k+a}, \qquad 1 \leq k \leq K. \tag{13}$$

As the state k goes to K, the term of $\frac{b}{K-k+a}$ increases and the value increases and is positive in the given range if a and b are positive. And if b is greater than a, $\frac{b}{K-k+a}$ is less than 1. The parameters a and b should be chosen to be $\sum_{k=1}^{K}\bar{\pi}_k = \bar{\rho}$. Therefore, eq. (13) satisfies fully the conditions for the steady-state probability for the Pareto/M/1/K.

At the edge of the buffer, the steady-state probability $\bar{\pi}_K$ must be greater than $\frac{1-\bar{\rho}}{(1-\rho)}\rho(1-\sigma)\sigma^{k-1}$, which can be considered as the lower bound of the steady-state probability. Let the steady-state probability of the finite queue at packet arrival instant $\bar{r}_k$. The probability $(\bar{r}_K)$ that the queue is full when a packet arrive at the queue is the loss probability. And the probability $\bar{\pi}_k$ has the relation of $\bar{\pi}_k = \bar{\rho}\bar{r}_{k-1}$ by the basic queueing theory. Since $\bar{r}_k$ is tail-raising or decreasing at the ratio of σ which is greater than $\bar{\rho}$, we can know intuitively that $\bar{\pi}_K = \bar{\rho}\bar{r}_{K-1} < \bar{r}_K = P_{loss}$. That is, the loss probability is an upper bound of $\bar{\pi}_K$. By experiments, we know that the real $\bar{\pi}_K$ is equal to the arithmetic mean of the upper and lower bound. Applying the estimated $\hat{\pi}_K$, the parameter b is given as follows :

$$b = a\left(\hat{\pi}_K - \frac{1-\bar{\rho}}{1-\rho}\rho(1-\sigma)\sigma^{K-1}\right). \tag{14}$$

By this equation, we can abbreviate a parameter and the parameter a can be calculated from the basic concept that $\sum_{k=1}^{k=K}\bar{\pi}_k = \bar{\rho}$.

In case of M/M/1/K, the offered load is equal to $\frac{1-\rho^K}{1-\rho^{K+1}}\rho$, and $\sigma = \rho$. The summation of the first term of eq. (13) from $k = 1$ to $k = K$ is equal to $\bar{\rho}$. Accordingly. the first term of eq. (13) is exactly same to that of M/M/1/K. This fact signifies that the second term of eq. (13) is equal to zero. That is, b is equal to zero, and tail-raising is not occurred in M/M/1/K. In Pareto/M/1/K, as the buffer size K increases, the empty probability at steady state and tail effect goes to $1 - \rho$ and zero, respectively.

Fig. 2 shows the comparison with the estimation and simulation in the steady-state buffer size. Fig. 1 show the steady-state probabilities when α is 1.2, 1.4, 1.6, 1.8 or 2.0, the buffer size K is 50, 100, 150 or 200 *packets* and utilization (ρ) is equal to 0.8.

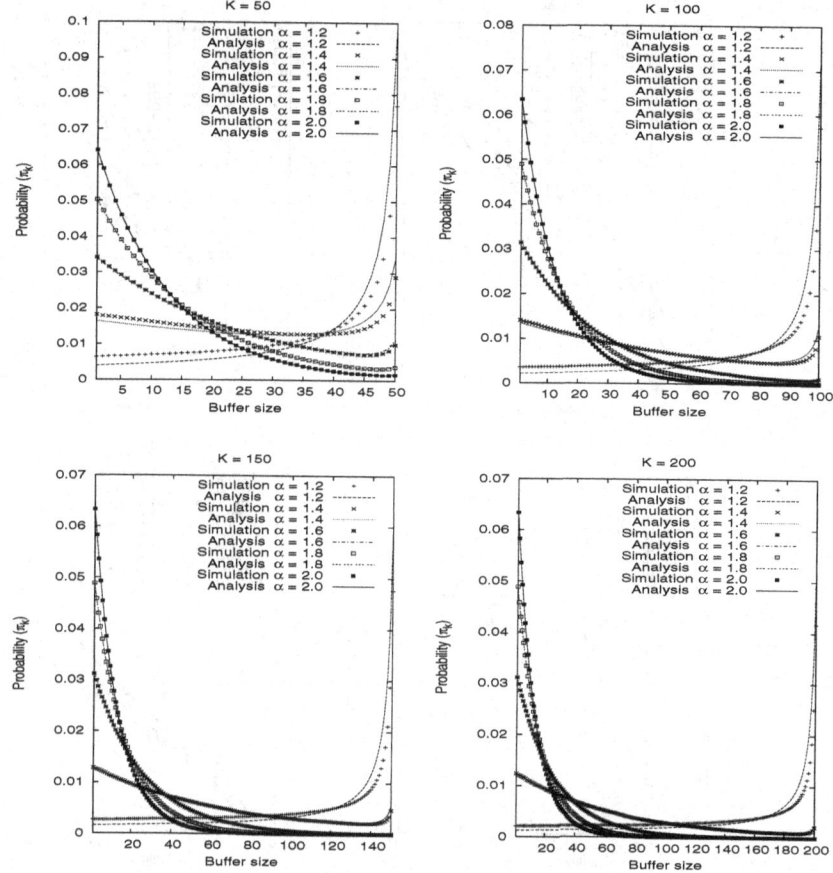

Fig. 2. Steady-state probabilities when α is 1.2, 1.4, 1.6, 1.8 or 2.0, the buffer size K is 50, 100, 150 or 200 *packets* and utilization is qual to 0.8

3.3   Mean Queue Length and Delay

The occupancy of a queue with the finite buffer is represented as mean queue length calculated from steady-state probability. Mean queue length is calculated by the product of the steady-state probability and the state as $\bar{L} = \sum_{k=1}^{K} k\bar{\pi}_k$. Mean queue length of Pareto/M/1/K is represented as

$$\bar{L} = \sum_{k=1}^{K} k \left(\frac{1-\bar{\rho}}{1-\rho}\rho(1-\sigma)\sigma^{k-1} + \frac{b}{K-k+a} \right), \quad 1 \leq k \leq K. \quad (15)$$

Fig. 3 shows a comparison of mean queue length between simulation and analysis using eq. (15).

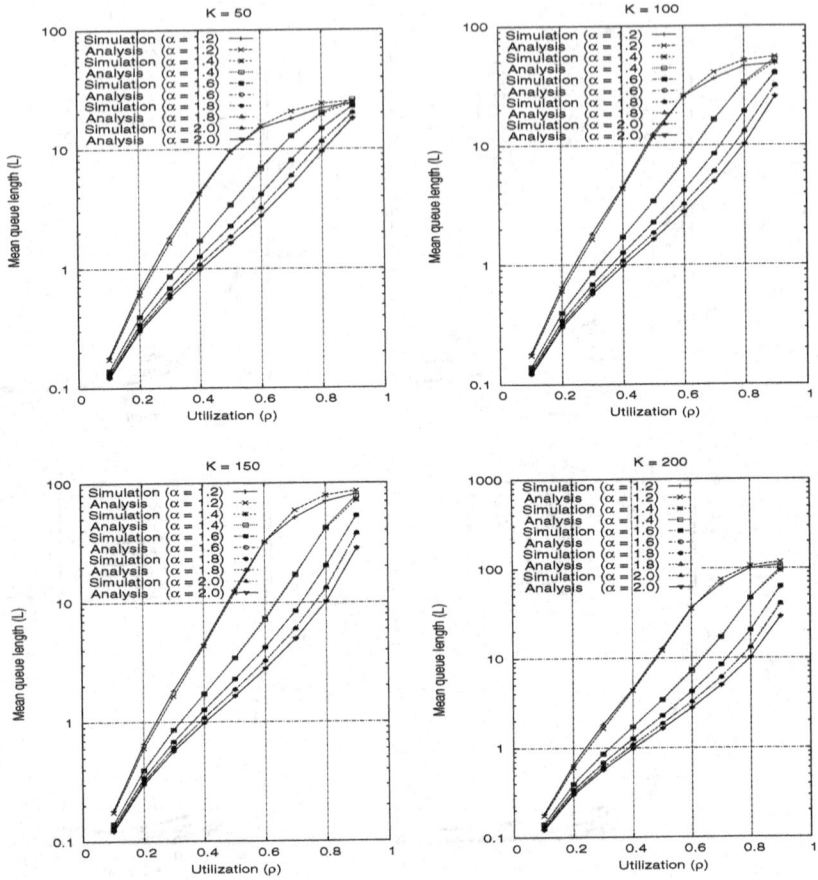

Fig. 3. Mean queue length when α is 1.2, 1.4, 1.6, 1.8 or 2.0, and the buffer size K is 50, 100, 150 or 200 *packets*

Mean queue length for M/M/1 and M/M/1/K are given by

$$L = \frac{\rho}{1 - \rho},$$

(16)

and

$$\bar{L} = \frac{\rho}{1 - \rho} - \frac{K + 1}{1 - \rho^{K+1}} \cdot \rho^{K+1}.$$

(17)

Fig. 4 shows the difference between mean queue length of Pareto/M/1/K with $\alpha = 1.2$ and M/M/1/K when the buffer sizes are 50 and 200 *packets*. The upper figures show that mean queue length for Paret/M/1 and Patero/M/1/K. When the shape parameter and buffer size are 1.2 and 50 *packets*, respectively, the mean queue length of Pareto/M/1/K differs from that of Pareto/M/1 over

$\rho = 0.5$. Although the buffer size increases as four times, mean queue length of Pareto/M/1/K differs significantly from that of Pareto/M/1 over $\rho = 0.6$ as before. However, mean queue length of M/M/1/K is the exactly same to that of M/M/1 in the range of $0 < \rho < 0.9$ when the buffer size is 50 *packets*, and if the buffer size increases as four times, mean queue length of M/M/1/K are the same to that of M/M/1 in the range of $0 < \rho < 1$. This means that the loss probability of M/M/1/K with $K = 200$ is actually near to zero, and the buffer size of 200 *packets* can be considered as the infinite buffer size. However, the loss probability of Pareto/M/1/K cannot be neglected. Thus in delay analysis of M/M/1/K with a moderate buffer size, that of M/M/1 can be applied, but in the delay analysis of Pareto/M/1/K, that of Pareto/M/1 cannot applied. This is the reason why we study the mean queue length of Pareto/M/1/K. The delay is calculated by Little's theorem that the mean queue length is equal to the arrival rate of packets to the system times delay like the infinite queue.

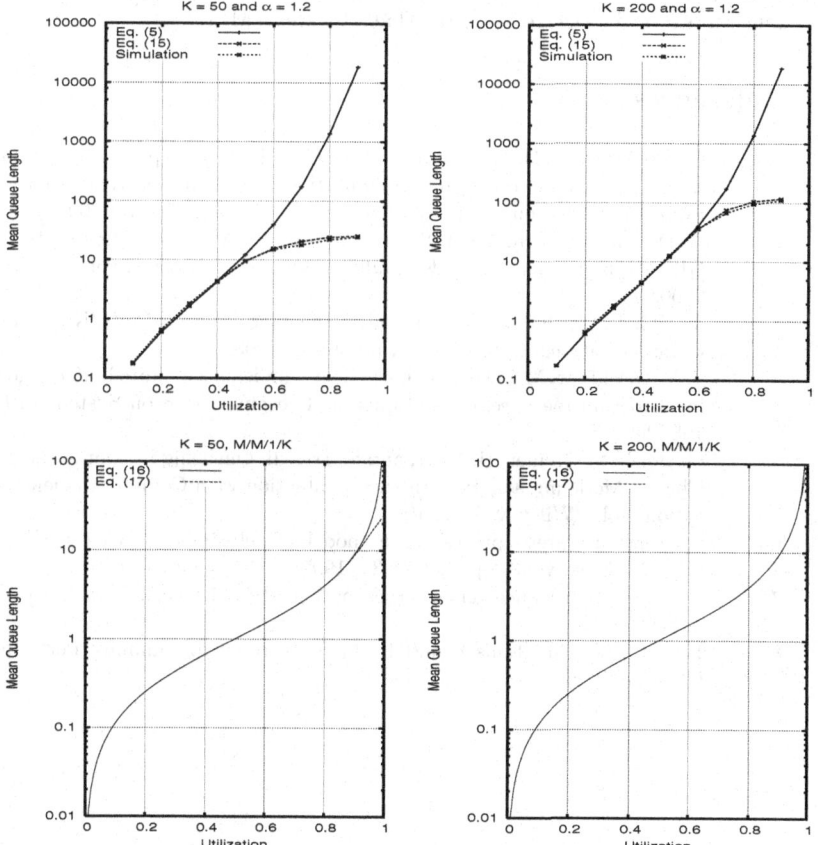

Fig. 4. Mean queue length Pareto/M/1/K of $\alpha = 1.2$, 1.4, 1.6, 1.8 and 2.0, and M/M/1/K when the buffer size K is or 200 *packets*

4   Conclusion

In this paper, we have analyzed the the steady-state probability, mean queue length and delay of Pareto/M/1/K, extending the results of Pareto/M/1. For applying the GI/M/1, we propose a method for estimating the geometric parameter called function approximation method. And since there is no way to analyze the mean queue length of Pareto/M/1/K, we approach as a model for estimating the steady-state probability. Since the Pareto traffic causes the buffer edge effects, we propose a model for estimating tail-raising effect and predict the the steady-state probability of the finite queue.

The model is verified by M/M/1/K. The results calculated by the model is sufficient to predict the steady-state probability of Paret/M/1/K queue. Using the model, we compare the mean queue length between the Pareto/M/1/K and M/M/1/K. By increasing the buffer size, the mean queue length of M/M/1/K converges to that of M/M/1 easily, but that of Pareto/M/1/K system requires much more buffer size to converge that of Pareto/M/1.

References

1.   C. M. Harris, P. H. Brill, and M. J. Fischer: Internet-type queues with heavy-tailed interarrival times and computational methods for their analysis. INFORMS Journal on Computing, vol. 12, no. 4, pp. 261-271, 2000.
2.   B. D. Choi, B. Kim, and I. S Wee: Asymptotic behavior of loss probability in GI/M/1/K queue as K tends to infinity, Queueing Systems, vol.36 pp.437-442, 2000.
3.   Y. Koh and K. Kim: Loss probability behavior of Pareto/M/1/K queue, IEEE Communications Letters, vol. 7, pp. 39-41, 2003.
4.   S. Y. Devadhar, M Gerla and J. Yu: The significance of finite buffer edge effects in histogram measurements of queues, Telecommunication Systems, PP. 177-193, 2001
5.   G. Bolch, S. Greiner, H. Meer, and S. Trivedi: Queueing Networks and Markov Chains: Modeling and Performance Evaluation with Computer Science Application, John Wiley & Sons, 1998.
6.   J. Gordon: Pareto process as a model of self-similar packet traffic, IEEE GLOBECOM, vol.3, pp. 2232-2235, 1995.
7.   E. Kreyszig: Advanced engineering mathematics (4th ed.), John Wiley & Sons, 1976.
8.   L. Wall, T. Christiansen and R. L. Schwartz: Programming Perl, 2nd ed., O'Reilly, 1996.

A Comparative Study on Simulation Models for Self-similar Traffic

Rita Girão-Silva and José Craveirinha

Department of Electrical and Computer Engineering, FCTUC / INESC-Coimbra
Pólo II, Pinhal de Marrocos, P-3030-290 Coimbra, Portugal
Tel.: +351.239.796252; Fax: +351.239.796247;
{rita,jcrav}@deec.uc.pt

Summary. The explosive growth in Internet traffic has stressed the importance of the study of stochastic models enabling to represent the self-similar nature of this type of traffic. This paper presents a comparison of some models and algorithms that may be used to simulate self-similar traffic, namely the $M/G/\infty$ process, the aggregation of ON/OFF reward renewal processes, Fractional Autoregressive Integrated Moving Averages (F-ARIMA) and Fractional Gaussian Noise (FGN). The comparison is based on the complexity of the implemented algorithms, the processing times, the accuracy of the estimation of the Hurst parameter H and possible limitations and advantages of the underlying models. A discussion of possible correction techniques for the estimation of H using the variance-time plot is also presented.

1 Introduction

The explosive growth in Internet data traffic has made the study of the nature and statistical characteristics of this type of traffic increasingly important. Since the seminal work of [1], many measurement based studies have shown that this traffic, unlike Markovian type traffic, has a property of self-similarity[1] expressed by similar or identical key statistical features (namely concerning the correlational structure) in all time scales. In the case of exactly 2nd-order self-similarity the correlation function has the form $\rho(k) = 0.5\left((k+1)^{2H} - 2\,k^{2H} + (k-1)^{2H}\right)$ with Hurst parameter[2] $H : 0.5 < H < 1$. This property is analogous to the one of fractal objects which have the same structural properties in different space scales. Various models were developed enabling to represent the essential features of self-similar traffic. A possible application of such models is in the context of simulation models for system QoS analysis or network performance evaluation.

The paper is organised as follows. In sect. 2 a brief description of some self-similar models (the $M/G/\infty$ process, the aggregation of ON/OFF reward

---

[1] There are different definitions of self-similarity in the literature not necessarily equivalent. Here we follow the definitions and the nomenclature presented in [2].
[2] The Hurst parameter H gives an indication of the degree of self-similarity of a certain process.

M.M. Freire, P. Lorenz, M.M.-O. Lee (Eds.): HSNMC 2003, LNCS 2720, pp. 571–580, 2003.

renewal processes, F-ARIMA and FGN) and the corresponding implementation algorithms, are presented. Sect. 3 reviews two methods for estimation of the Hurst parameter from the process sample paths in the various models: the variance-time plot and the Whittle estimator. Concerning the first method, the problem of the parameter underestimation is discussed together with possible correction techniques. Sect. 4 presents the analysis of the traffic simulation results obtained with the different algorithms, focusing on the comparison between the theoretical values and the estimates of the variance and correlation function, and the problematic of the accuracy of the estimation techniques for H. In the conclusions, a comparison between the implemented methods is presented concerning computational efficiency, applicability, accuracy of the H estimation techniques and the possible limitations and advantages of the methods.

2   Implemented Traffic Generators

There are various simulation algorithms enabling to generate computationally traces of different self-similar type traffic models. For each of the models and their algorithms a few simulations runs were performed. Random number generators with different seeds were used in different replications of the simulation runs. Due to space limitations, the review of the models and a formal description of the implemented algorithms are not presented here and can be seen in [3].

2.1   M/G/∞ Process

A discrete-event simulation model was implemented to generate asymptotically self-similar traffic through sequences of observations of the busy server process of the M/G/∞ queue [4]. The connection inter-arrival times are negative-exponential with mean 1 and the service times are heavy tailed, with a Pareto distribution[3] where $a = 1$ and $\beta_P \in]1; 2[$ thereby guaranteeing the busy server counting process is asymptotically 2nd-order self-similar[4] with $H = (3 - \beta_P)/2$ $(0.5 < H < 1)$. As we are considering a discrete time process, the counting instants are spaced by one unit. For the simulation runs a total of 5000 arrivals have been considered. The total number of expected observations was 5000. Five replications were made for each of the values of the shape parameter $\beta_P = 1.3; 1.5; 1.7$.

---

[3] A random variable τ with Pareto distribution with shape parameter β_P and location parameter a has $P\{\tau \leq x\} = 1 - (a/x)^{\beta_P}$, with $\beta_P \geq 0$, $x \geq a$.

[4] A process $X = \{X_t, t \in \mathbb{N}\}$ is asymptotically 2nd-order self-similar with Hurst parameter H if $\rho^{(m)}(k) \rightarrow \rho(k) = 0.5 \left((k+1)^{2H} - 2 k^{2H} + (k-1)^{2H}\right)$, as $m \rightarrow \infty$ and $k \geq 1$ (i.e. the correlation structure of the process is maintained asymptotically under large scale time aggregation) where $\rho(k)$ is the autocorrelation function of X and $\rho^{(m)}(k)$ is the autocorrelation function of the aggregated process $X^{(m)} = \{X_i^{(m)}, i \in \mathbb{N}\}$ obtained by averaging m values of X over non-overlapping blocks of size m: $X_i^{(m)} = \frac{1}{m} \sum_{t=m(i-1)+1}^{mi} X_t$. X is asymptotically self-similar if $X_t \overset{d}{=} m^{1-H} X_t^{(m)}$, as $m \rightarrow \infty$, where the equality is in the sense of any finite dimensional distribution.

2.2   Aggregation of Renewal Reward Processes

A self-similar process can be constructed by the aggregation of many renewal reward processes with infinite variance inter-renewal times [1,5]. Consider M traffic sources. For each of them, a renewal reward process can be defined and interpreted as the amount of information sent by the source into the net. The rewards are assumed to take the values 0 or 1 when the source is OFF (in an idle state) or ON (sending information) respectively. At the instant $t = 0$, the sources have an equal probability of being in the ON or OFF state. We assume the ON and OFF intervals alternate and their duration is heavy tailed. At the instant t the process of interest is the aggregation of the traffic produced by the M sources, which is asymptotically self-similar with Hurst parameter H. For the simulation runs a total of $M = 50000$ sources have been considered and 5000 observations were made (one at each integer instant of time). The Pareto distribution to obtain the heavy tailed inter-renewal times has a location parameter of 1 and a variable shape parameter $1 < \beta_P < 2$, so $H = (3 - \beta_P)/2$. Five replications were made for each of the values of $\beta_P = 1.3; 1.5; 1.7$.

2.3   Fractional ARIMA (0,d,0)

While the previous models try to reflect directly or asymptotically key stochastic properties of the traffic sources namely the heavy tailedness of the connection durations or associated file sizes, other type of models are based on specific statistical properties of certain time series. This is the case of the F-ARIMA(0,d,0) process, which is considered to generate asymptotically 2nd-order self-similar traffic [6]: if $0 < d < 0.5$, then the process has a self-similar behaviour, with Hurst parameter $H = d+0.5$. Two different algorithms to generate a F-ARIMA (0,d,0) process were implemented: one was proposed by Hosking [7,8], the other by Davies and Harte [6,9]. In the simulation runs of both models, a total of 5000 observations were made. For the Hosking method, five replications were performed with different values of d: $d = 0.1; 0.2; 0.3; 0.4$. For the Davies and Harte method, five replications were performed with different values of d: $d = 0.1; 0.2; 0.3$. For $d > 0.34$ the simulation run couldn't be performed because some conditions to run the algorithm were not satisfied (see [3]).

2.4   Fractional Gaussian Noise

Two different algorithms to generate a FGN process were implemented. One was proposed by Paxson [10] and the other by Davies and Harte [6,9] (it is the same method as the one mentioned for the F-ARIMA(0,d,0), based on the autocovariance function, which is different for the two processes). In the simulation runs of the model using the method by Paxson, a total of 4096 observations were made (the number of observations must be a power of 2); using the method by Davies and Harte, a total of 5000 observations were made. For both models, five replications were performed, with different values of H: $H = 0.6; 0.7; 0.8; 0.9$.

3   Estimation of the Hurst Parameter

3.1   Variance-Time Plot

Let $X = \{X_t, t \in \mathbb{N}_0\}$ be the process of interest. If the variance V_m of the aggregated process $X^{(m)}$ is known $(V_m = Var[X^{(m)}] = \sigma_X^2 m^{2(H-1)})$ the Hurst parameter has to verify $H = 1 + 0.5 \log_m (V_m/\sigma_X^2)$, $\forall m \in \mathbb{N}$ [2]. That is, a variance-time plot can be obtained by plotting $\log (V_m/\sigma_X^2)$ against $\log(m)$. The corresponding slope is used to calculate an estimate $\hat{H} = 1 + 0.5 \cdot$ slope. To estimate the value of H from a sample of n observations of X, a calculation of an estimate of V_m was made, for $1 < m \le \lfloor n/M_{min} \rfloor$, taking the minimum number of different values of $X^{(m)}$ used to calculate a variance as $M_{min} = 5$. For each value of m an estimate $\hat{H}_m$ of the Hurst parameter was calculated. Afterwards the average value of the sequence $\{\hat{H}_m\}$ was calculated, giving a final estimate $\hat{H}$ of the Hurst parameter of the process of interest.

Correction Factor For higher values of H the variance-time plot values tend to be lower than expected [10], because the variance-time plot is based on an asymptotic relationship which demands a larger sample path of X_t. Another problem that arises is a bias towards the underestimation of H [6,10] when this technique is used. Therefore there may be significant inaccuracy in the estimate of H caused by the estimation technique and not by the failure of a process to display the expected self-similar characteristics.

Let $\hat{V}_m$ be a biased estimate of V_m. The bias depends on the correlation function of the aggregated process, $\rho_{X^{(m)}}$, because $E[\hat{V}_m] = \sigma_{X^{(m)}}^2 \left(1 - \frac{\delta_M(\rho)}{M-1}\right)$ where M is the number of values of $X^{(m)}$ and $\delta_M(\rho) = 2 \sum_{k=1}^{M-1} \left(1 - \frac{k}{M}\right) \rho_{X^{(m)}}(k)$ (see [6]). To compensate for the bias $\epsilon(m) = \sigma_{X^{(m)}}^2 \frac{\delta_M(\rho)}{M-1}$, a corrected estimate $\hat{V}_m' = \hat{V}_m + \epsilon(m)$ is considered so that $E[\hat{V}_m'] = E[\hat{V}_m] + \epsilon(m) = \sigma_{X^{(m)}}^2$. In the bias $\epsilon(m)$ the value $\sigma_{X^{(m)}}^2$ can be substituted either by $\hat{V}_m'$ or by $\hat{V}_m$.

Making the first mentioned substitution, $\hat{V}_m' = \hat{V}_m + \hat{V}_m' \cdot \frac{\delta_M(\rho)}{M-1} \Leftrightarrow \hat{V}_m' = \frac{\hat{V}_m}{1 - \frac{\delta_M(\rho)}{M-1}}$. The estimated Hurst parameter for the aggregation factor m is $\hat{H}_m' = \hat{H}_m - \frac{1}{2} \log_m \left(1 - \frac{2}{M-1} \sum_{k=1}^{M-1} \left(1 - \frac{k}{M}\right) \hat{\rho}_{X^{(m)}}(k)\right)$ and the average value of the sequence $\{\hat{H}_2', \cdots, \hat{H}_{\lfloor \frac{n}{5} \rfloor}'\}$ is calculated, giving a final estimate $\hat{H}'$ of the Hurst parameter of the process of interest.

Making the second mentioned substitution, $\hat{V}_m'' = \hat{V}_m + \hat{V}_m \cdot \frac{\delta_M(\rho)}{M-1} \Leftrightarrow \hat{V}_m'' = \hat{V}_m \cdot \left(1 + \frac{\delta_M(\rho)}{M-1}\right)$. The estimated Hurst parameter for the aggregation factor m is $\hat{H}_m'' = \hat{H}_m + \frac{1}{2} \log_m \left(1 + \frac{2}{M-1} \sum_{k=1}^{M-1} \left(1 - \frac{k}{M}\right) \hat{\rho}_{X^{(m)}}(k)\right)$ and the average value of the sequence $\{\hat{H}_2'', \cdots, \hat{H}_{\lfloor \frac{n}{5} \rfloor}''\}$ is calculated, giving a final estimate $\hat{H}''$ of the Hurst parameter of the process of interest.

According to [6] since the actual autocorrelation function $\rho_{X^{(m)}}$ is not known, but rather an estimate of it $(\hat{\rho}_{X^{(m)}})$ can be calculated, these corrections don't always minimize the problem of the underestimation of H. Although $\rho_{X^{(m)}}$ has to be positive $\forall m$, in some cases the value of $\hat{\rho}_{X^{(m)}}$ is negative which leads to an even stronger underestimation. Here we also propose to consider a technique such that in a situation where it is known that a specific synthetic trace is self-similar, the calculation of the correction terms $\hat{H}'_m - \hat{H}_m$ or $\hat{H}''_m - \hat{H}_m$ is made and if a term is negative then it is neglected for the purpose of further calculations.

3.2   Whittle Estimator

The Whittle estimate is a maximum likelihood estimate [10,11]. Let $f(\lambda, H, 1)$ be the power spectrum of a self-similar process $\{X_t, t \in \mathbb{N}_0\}$ with Hurst parameter H and adequate normalization so as to have variance 1, and $I(\lambda)$ be the periodogram of a sample with n observations of the process. The Whittle estimate of H is the value $\hat{H}_W$ which minimizes $\tilde{g}(\hat{H}_W) = \sum_{i=1}^{n'} \frac{I(\lambda_i)}{f(\lambda_i, \hat{H}_W, 1)}$ (with $n' = \lfloor (n-1)/2 \rfloor$ and Fourier frequencies $\lambda_i = 2\pi i/n$). This technique was applied to the F-ARIMA(0,d,0) and the FGN processes. The power spectrum of the F-ARIMA(0,d,0) process is (see [6]) $\frac{1}{2\pi} f(\lambda, H, 1) = \frac{1}{2\pi} \left(2 \left| \sin \frac{\lambda}{2} \right| \right)^{1-2H}$. As for the FGN process (see [6,10]) $f(\lambda, H) = A(\lambda, H) \cdot (|\lambda|^{-2H-1} + B(\lambda, H))$ with $A(\lambda, H)$ and $B(\lambda, H))$ given in [10]. This function isn't used directly in the envisaged calculations [6]: it has to be divided by $\theta = \exp\left(\frac{2}{n} \sum_{i=1}^{n'} \ln\left(\tilde{f}'(\lambda_i, H) \right) \right)$.

4   Analysis of Results

To compare the behaviour of a process in different time scales, four plots were obtained, corresponding to successively smaller time scales. As an example consider the plot of a self-similar process (sect. 2.2) in Fig. 1. A similar variation can be identified in the considered time scales, due to the "fractal" property of the self-similar processes. Even at the biggest time scale the behaviour of the simulated processes doesn't show a pattern similar to white noise, as would happen in a non-self-similar model. The bursts in all the scales are a visual display of self-similarity.

4.1   Comparison of $\hat{V}_m$ and $\hat{\rho}_X$ with the Theoretical Values

As an example of the comparison of $\hat{V}_m$ with the theoretical value, consider Fig. 2: 2a is the plot of $\hat{V}_m$ and $\sigma_X^2 \cdot m^{2(\hat{H}-1)}$ for a self-similar process as described in 2.2 and 2b is the plot of both functions for a self-similar process of the FGN type, as described in [10]. Analysing Fig. 2a it's noticeable that both the theoretical and the estimated values are quite close. Their variation is quite similar and the estimate function oscillates around the theoretical function. The analysis of Fig. 2b also shows a similar variation of both functions but the estimated values don't oscillate around the theoretical values for lower m. In this case the estimate $\hat{H}$ is far from the true value of the Hurst parameter which can account for the discrepancy between the two functions. If the estimate $\hat{H}$ was higher (i.e.

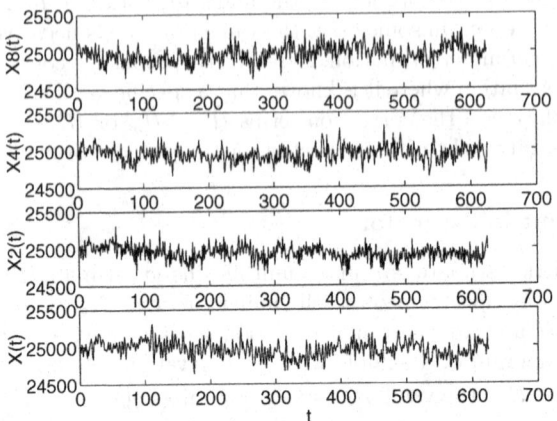

Fig.1. Self-similar process obtained by the aggregation of the traffic produced by ON/OFF sources, with $\hat{H} = 0.841$ and $H = 0.85$; $Xi = \{Xi_k = X_{ik-(i-1)}, 1 \leq k \leq (n/8)\}, i = 1; 2; 4; 8$

closer to H) then $\sigma_X^2 \cdot m^{2(\hat{H}-1)}$ would also be higher and would be closer to the estimated function.

To compare $\hat{\rho}_X(k)$ with $\rho_X(k)|_{\hat{H}} = 0.5 \left((k+1)^{2\hat{H}} - 2 k^{2\hat{H}} + (k-1)^{2\hat{H}} \right)$, where k is the time lag, these two functions were plotted for all the processes. As an example consider Fig. 3. Analysing this figure it's noticeable that both the theoretical and the estimated values are quite close, and the estimate function oscillates around the theoretical function. For small lags the autocorrelation function and its estimate are positive as expected: the higher the number of users in the system is at a given instant of time, the higher the number of users will be in the system at the next instant of time (because the service times are heavy tailed). The estimated autocorrelation function presents some statistical "noise"; as noted in [8] the estimate of the autocorrelation function becomes very imprecise for lags k_{High}, such that the amount of observations spaced by k_{High} is small.

4.2   Calculation of an Estimate of the Hurst Parameter

The quantitative self-similarity test used in this work was the calculation of an estimate of H by the variance-time plot method (possibly with the inclusion of correction factors) and the Whittle estimation method. A statistical analysis of the results was made: for a specific model the estimates of H in all the replications were considered and average values and 95% confidence intervals were obtained for each set of replications made for each value of the theoretical H. The results for some of the studied models are displayed in Figs. 4-5. For the M/G/∞ and the self-similar (sect. 2.2) traffic models (Fig. 4) the theoretical H is contained

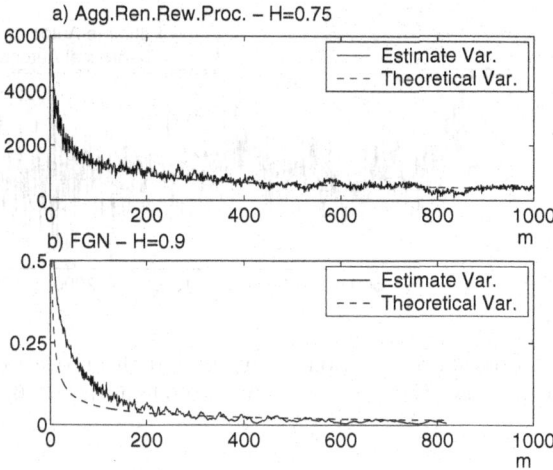

Fig. 2. Variance (estimate and theoretical) of the aggregated process $X^{(m)}$ resulting from: a) a self-similar process obtained by the aggregation of the traffic produced by ON/OFF sources, with $\hat{H} = 0.762$ and $H = 0.75$; b) a self-similar process FGN [10], with $\hat{H} = 0.687$ and $H = 0.9$

in the confidence interval, but the estimated values tend to be lower than the theoretical H because most of the confidence interval is to the left of the theoretical H. This is especially noticeable when the theoretical H is higher because the underestimation is stronger. With the corrections, this problem is reduced and the confidence intervals are slightly "shifted" to the right (so, the average values of the estimates tend to be closer to the theoretical H). Considering the estimates of H based on the variance-time plot for the F-ARIMA(0,d,0) process [7] and the FGN process [9] (Fig. 5), the theoretical H is not always contained in the confidence interval. There is a general bias towards the underestimation, especially when H is high. Again the introduced corrections (in particular $\hat{H}'$ and $\hat{H}''$, both without negative terms) tend to diminish this problem, reducing the underestimation error. For the other two processes, the F-ARIMA(0,d,0) process [9] and the FGN process [10], the theoretical H is not contained in the confidence interval in most cases in spite of the slight improvements obtained with the $\hat{H}$ corrections. However if the Whittle estimate is considered it's noticeable that these four models actually behave very well with respect to the H estimate. The confidence intervals for $\hat{H}_W$ always include the theoretical H. Generally speaking the Whittle estimator is very accurate and gives a good indication of the quality of the models. Although the calculations of estimates of H based on the variance don't guarantee good accuracy, the results of the Whittle estimate indicate that the traces obtained from these models have good statistical properties and correctly display self-similar characteristics in accordance with the values used as input to the simulation runs. A more detailed analysis is in [3].

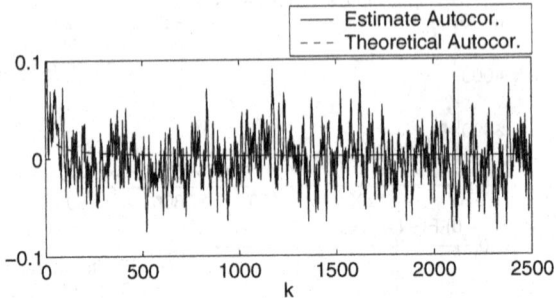

Fig.3. Autocorrelation function (estimate and theoretical) of an asymptotical self-similar process (M/G/∞), with $\hat{H} = 0.669$ and $H = 0.65$

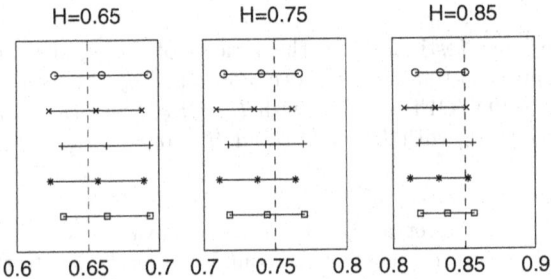

Fig.4. Mean value and confidence intervals of the estimated value of H, for a self-similar process obtained by the aggregation of the traffic produced by ON/OFF sources - ∘ $\hat{H}$; × $\hat{H}''$; + $\hat{H}''$ without negative terms; * $\hat{H}'$; □ $\hat{H}'$ without negative terms

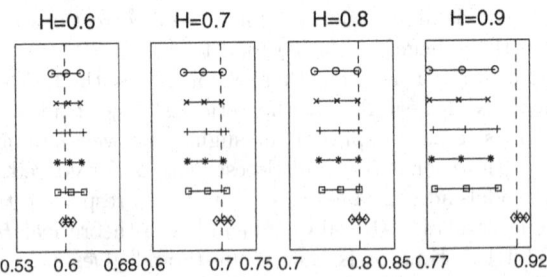

Fig.5. Mean value and confidence intervals of the estimated value of H, for a self-similar process FGN [9] - ∘ $\hat{H}$; × $\hat{H}''$; + $\hat{H}''$ without negative terms; * $\hat{H}'$; □ $\hat{H}'$ without negative terms; ◇ $\hat{H}_W$

5 Conclusions

Several important traffic simulation models displaying self-similar characteristics were studied and implemented. The comparison of the variance and the correlation function estimates $\hat{V}_m$ and $\hat{\rho}_X$ (obtained from the simulation) with the theoretical values shows functions with similar variations. The plots of the variance estimate display a known phenomenon: the underestimation of the variance (with further implications in the calculation of an estimate of H). As for the estimation of the autocorrelation function it's noticeable that it's not accurate. A quantitative test was also performed: the calculation of an estimate of H. For all the models a calculation based on the variance-time plot was made with the inclusion of correction factors; for the F-ARIMA and FGN models, a calculation based on the Whittle estimation technique was also made. A generic comparative analysis of the implemented models is displayed in Table 1.

Generally speaking, the models are quite robust because they can be used to generate synthetic traces of self-similar processes for all the input values of H in the range $1/2 < H < 1$. The exception is the Davies and Harte method for the generation of an F-ARIMA(0,d,0) process which can't be used when $H > 0.84$. The obtained simulation times[5] were quite variable mostly in the range from miliseconds to tens of seconds, reflecting the complexity and the computational cost of each iteration of the corresponding algorithms. The exception is the model obtained by the aggregation of renewal reward processes: this method took almost 20 h to fulfil a replication of the simulation, because very long arrays have to be manipulated causing, on average, a high processing cost per simulated observation. The complexity of the algorithms is also relevant in the context of computational efficiency. The least complex algorithm is the one used to generate a $M/G/\infty$ process since it has a linear complexity. The others have a quadratic complexity except the FGN model [10], with a complexity of $O(n \cdot \log n)$.

The Whittle estimation technique gives very good results for $\hat{H}_W$, that is very tight confidence intervals that always include the theoretical value H. This justifies the interest in the F-ARIMA and FGN models. However, the same conclusion couldn't have been obtained if only the estimation based on the variance-time plot had been used: this estimation technique typically presents an underestimation that accounts for the poor quality of the results in $\hat{H}$ in the F-ARIMA and FGN models where the improvements obtained by the studied correction techniques are in most cases insufficient to obtain confidence intervals containing the theoretical value of H. We also proposed the consideration of a variant of the correction techniques suggested in the literature [6] which enabled to obtain somehow better variance-based estimates of H especially for the $M/G/\infty$ and aggregation of renewal reward processes models. With the variance-time technique and in spite of the underestimation (which is always present) the results were quite good. Although the confidence intervals are not centered around the theoretical H (they're slightly "shifted" to the left of this value due to the under-

---

[5] The simulation code was written in C language and all the simulation runs were performed at a computer with a PentiumIII-1.2GHz processor.

Table1. General characteristics of the implemented models: number of replications for each simulation run (#R); number of observations in each replication (#Obs); simulation time for each replication; complexity of each algorithm; semi-lenghts of the 95% confidence interval for the estimates of H, based on the variance-time function (V) and the Whittle estimator (W)

Processes	#R	#Obs	Time	Complexity	Precision of 95% conf. int.
M/G/∞	5	5000	1.25s	$O(n)$	V:$(2-5) \cdot 10^{-2}$
Agg.Ren.Rew.Proc.	5	5000	20h	$O(n^2)$	V:$(2-3) \cdot 10^{-2}$
F-ARIMA(0,d,0)-[7]	5	5000	4.15s	$O(n^2)$	V:$(2-4) \cdot 10^{-2}$;W:$(3-10) \cdot 10^{-3}$
F-ARIMA(0,d,0)-[9]	5	5000	144.22s	$O(n^2)$	V:$(2-3) \cdot 10^{-2}$;W:$(1-2) \cdot 10^{-2}$
FGN-[10]	5	4096	0.04s	$O(n \cdot \log n)$	V:$(2-7) \cdot 10^{-2}$;W:$(6-20) \cdot 10^{-3}$
FGN-[9]	5	5000	139.94s	$O(n^2)$	V:$(2-5) \cdot 10^{-2}$;W:$(7-13) \cdot 10^{-3}$

estimation problem) they always include the theoretical value which means that the models are also adequate and can be reliably used to generate synthetic traces of self-similar traffic. To obtain more tight confidence intervals more replications for each set of input values and/or longer replications would be necessary.

References

1. W. E. Leland, M. S. Taqqu, W. Willinger, and D. V. Wilson. On the self-similar nature of Ethernet traffic (extended version). *IEEE/ACM Transactions on Networking*, 2(1):1–15, February 1994.
2. K. Park and W. Willinger. *Self-Similar Network Traffic and Performance Evaluation*, chapter 1 - Self-Similar Network Traffic: An Overview, pages 1–38. Wiley-Interscience, 2000.
3. R. Girão-Silva and J. Craveirinha. Report on a comparative study of simulation models for self-similar traffic. Research Report 3/2003 (ISSN 1645-26-31), INESC-Coimbra (www.inescc.pt), March 2003.
4. V. Paxson and S. Floyd. Wide area traffic: The failure of Poisson modeling. *IEEE/ACM Transactions on Networking*, 3(3):226–244, June 1995.
5. M. S. Taqqu and J. B. Levy. Dependence in probability and statistics: A survey of recent results. volume 11 of *Progress in Probability and Statistics*, pages 73–89, Boston, 1986. Birkhauser.
6. J. Beran. *Statistics for Long-Memory Processes*. Number 61 in Monographs on Statistics and Applied Probability. Chapman & Hall, 1st edition, 1998.
7. J. R. M. Hosking. Modeling persistence in hydrological time series using fractional differencing. *Water Resources Research*, 20(12):1898–1908, 1984.
8. M. W. Garrett and W. Willinger. Analysis, modeling and generation of self-similar VBR video traffic. In *Proceedings of SIGCOMM'94*, pages 269–280, 1994.
9. R. B. Davies and D. S. Harte. Tests for Hurst effect. *Biometrika*, 74:95–102, 1987.
10. V. Paxson. Fast, approximate synthesis of Fractional Gaussian Noise for generating self-similar network traffic. *Computer Communication Review*, 27(5):5–18, October 1997.
11. J. Beran. Statistical methods for data with long-range dependence. *Statistical Science*, 7(4):404–427, 1992.

Author Index

Lecture Notes in Computer Science

For information about Vols. 1–2646
please contact your bookseller or Springer-Verlag

Vol. 2687: J. Mira, J.R. Álvarez (Eds.), Artificial Neural Nets Problem Solving Methods. Proceedings, Part II. 2003. XXVII, 820 pages. 2003.

Vol. 2688: J. Kittler, M.S. Nixon (Eds.), Audio- and Video-Based Biometric Person Authentication. Proceedings, 2003. XVII, 978 pages. 2003.

Vol. 2689: K.D. Ashley, D.G. Bridge (Eds.), Case-Based Reasoning Research and Development. Proceedings, 2003. XV, 734 pages. 2003. (Subseries LNAI).

Vol. 2691: V. Mařík, J. Müller, M. Pěchouček (Eds.), Multi-Agent Systems and Applications III. Proceedings, 2003. XIV, 660 pages. 2003. (Subseries LNAI).

Vol. 2692: P. Nixon, S. Terzis (Eds.), Trust Management. Proceedings, 2003. X, 349 pages. 2003.

Vol. 2693: A. Cechich, M. Piattini, A. Vallecillo (Eds.), Component-Based Software Quality. X, 403 pages. 2003.

Vol. 2694: R. Cousot (Ed.), Static Analysis. Proceedings, 2003. XIV, 505 pages. 2003.

Vol. 2695: L.D. Griffin, M. Lillholm (Eds.), Scale Space Methods in Computer Vision. Proceedings, 2003. XII, 816 pages. 2003.

Vol. 2697: T. Warnow, B. Zhu (Eds.), Computing and Combinatorics. Proceedings, 2003. XIII, 560 pages. 2003.

Vol. 2698: W. Burakowski, B. Koch, A. Bęben (Eds.), Architectures for Quality of Service in the Internet. Proceedings, 2003. XI, 305 pages. 2003.

Vol. 2701: M. Hofmann (Ed.), Typed Lambda Calculi and Applications. Proceedings, 2003. VIII, 317 pages. 2003.

Vol. 2702: P. Brusilovsky, A. Corbett, F. de Rosis (Eds.), User Modeling 2003. Proceedings, 2003. XIV, 436 pages. 2003. (Subseries LNAI).

Vol. 2704: S.-T. Huang, T. Herman (Eds.), Self-Stabilizing Systems. Proceedings, 2003. X, 215 pages. 2003.

Vol. 2706: R. Nieuwenhuis (Ed.), Rewriting Techniques and Applications. Proceedings, 2003. XI, 515 pages. 2003.

Vol. 2707: K. Jeffay, I. Stoica, K. Wehrle (Eds.), Quality of Service – IWQoS 2003. Proceedings, 2003. XI, 517 pages. 2003.

Vol. 2709: T. Windeatt, F. Roli (Eds.), Multiple Classifier Systems. Proceedings, 2003. X, 406 pages. 2003.

Vol. 2710: Z. Ésik, Z, Fülöp (Eds.), Developments in Language Theory. Proceedings, 2003. XI, 437 pages. 2003.

Vol. 2711: T.D. Nielsen, N.L. Zhang (Eds.), Symbolic and Quantitative Approaches to Reasoning with Uncertainty. Proceedings, 2003. XII, 608 pages. 2003. (Subseries LNAI).

Vol. 2712: A. James, B. Lings, M. Younas (Eds.), New Horizons in Information Management. Proceedings, 2003. XII, 281 pages. 2003.

Vol. 2713: C.-W. Chung, C.-K. Kim, W. Kim, T.-W. Ling, K.-H. Song (Eds.), Web and Communication Technologies and Internet-Related Social Issues – HSI 2003. Proceedings, 2003. XXII, 773 pages. 2003.

Vol. 2714: O. Kaynak, E. Alpaydin, E. Oja, L. Xu (Eds.), Artificial Neural Networks and Neural Information Processing – ICANN/ICONIP 2003. Proceedings, 2003. XXII, 1188 pages. 2003.

Vol. 2715: T. Bilgiç, B. De Baets, O. Kaynak (Eds.), Fuzzy Sets and Systems – IFSA 2003. Proceedings, 2003. XV, 735 pages. 2003. (Subseries LNAI).

Vol. 2716: M.J. Voss (Ed.), OpenMP Shared Memory Parallel Programming. Proceedings, 2003. VIII, 271 pages. 2003.

Vol. 2718: P. W. H. Chung, C. Hinde, M. Ali (Eds.), Developments in Applied Artificial Intelligence. Proceedings, 2003. XIV, 817 pages. 2003. (Subseries LNAI).

Vol. 2719: J.C.M. Baeten, J.K. Lenstra, J. Parrow, G.J. Woeginger (Eds.), Automata, Languages and Programming. Proceedings, 2003. XVIII, 1199 pages. 2003.

Vol. 2720: M. Marques Freire, P. Lorenz, M.M.-O. Lee (Eds.), High-Speed Networks and Multimedia Communications. Proceedings, 2003. XIII, 582 pages. 2003.

Vol. 2721: N.J. Mamede, J. Baptista, I. Trancoso, M. das Graças Volpe Nunes (Eds.), Computational Processing of the Portuguese Language. Proceedings, 2003. XIV, 268 pages. 2003. (Subseries LNAI).

Vol. 2722: J.M. Cueva Lovelle, B.M. González Rodríguez, L. Joyanes Aguilar, J.E. Labra Gayo, M. del Puerto Paule Ruiz (Eds.), Web Engineering. Proceedings, 2003. XIX, 554 pages. 2003.

Vol. 2723: E. Cantú-Paz, J.A. Foster, K. Deb, L.D. Davis, R. Roy, U.-M. O'Reilly, H.-G. Beyer, R. Standish, G. Kendall, S. Wilson, M. Harman, J. Wegener, D. Dasgupta, M.A. Potter, A.C. Schultz, K.A. Dowsland, N. Jonoska, J. Miller (Eds.), Genetic and Evolutionary Computation – GECCO 2003. Proceedings, Part I. 2003. XLVII, 1252 pages. 2003.

Vol. 2724: E. Cantú-Paz, J.A. Foster, K. Deb, L.D. Davis, R. Roy, U.-M. O'Reilly, H.-G. Beyer, R. Standish, G. Kendall, S. Wilson, M. Harman, J. Wegener, D. Dasgupta, M.A. Potter, A.C. Schultz, K.A. Dowsland, N. Jonoska, J. Miller (Eds.), Genetic and Evolutionary Computation – GECCO 2003. Proceedings, Part II. 2003. XLVII, 1274 pages. 2003.

Vol. 2725: W.A. Hunt, Jr., F. Somenzi (Eds.), Computer Aided Verification. Proceedings, 2003. XII, 462 pages. 2003.

Vol. 2726: E. Hancock, M. Vento (Eds.), Graph Based Representations in Pattern Recognition. Proceedings, 2003. VIII, 271 pages. 2003.

Vol. 2727: R. Safavi-Naini, J. Seberry (Eds.), Information Security and Privacy. Proceedings, 2003. XII, 534 pages. 2003.

Vol. 2731: C.S. Calude, M.J. Dinneen, V. Vajnovszki (Eds.), Discrete Mathematics and Theoretical Computer Science. Proceedings, 2003. VIII, 301 pages. 2003.

Vol. 2733: A. Butz, A. Krüger, P. Olivier (Eds.), Smart Graphics. Proceedings, 2003. XI, 261 pages. 2003.

Vol. 2734: P. Perner, A. Rosenfeld (Eds.), Machine Learning and Data Mining in Pattern Recognition. Proceedings, 2003. XII, 440 pages. 2003. (Subseries LNAI).

Vol. 2743: L. Cardelli (Ed.), ECOOP 2003 – Object-Oriented Programming. Proceedings, 2003. X, 501 pages. 2003.

Vol. 2745: M. Guo, L.T. Yang (Eds.), Parallel and Distributed Processing and Applications. Proceedings, 2003. XII, 450 pages. 2003.

Vol. 2749: J. Bigun, T. Gustavsson (Eds.), Image Analysis. Proceedings, 2003. XXII, 1174 pages. 2003.

Vol. 2750: T. Hadzilacos, Y. Manolopoulos, J.F. Roddick, Y. Theodoridis (Eds.), Advances in Spatial and Temporal Databases. Proceedings, 2003. XIII, 525 pages. 2003.